The United States and the
End of British Colonial Rule
in Africa, 1941–1968

The United States and the End of British Colonial Rule in Africa, 1941–1968

JAMES P. HUBBARD

McFarland & Company, Inc., Publishers
Jefferson, North Carolina, and London

LIBRARY OF CONGRESS CATALOGUING-IN-PUBLICATION DATA

Hubbard, James P. (James Patrick), 1945–
The United States and the end of British colonial rule
in Africa, 1941–1968 / James P. Hubbard.
p.   cm.
Includes bibliographical references and index.

ISBN 978-0-7864-5952-0
softcover : 50# alkaline paper ∞

1. Great Britain — Colonies — Africa — History — 20th century.
2. United States — Foreign relations — Great Britain.
3. Great Britain — Foreign relations — United States.
4. United States — Foreign relations — 1945–1989.
5. Great Britain — Foreign relations — 1945–1964.
I. Title.
DT32.5.H83   2011   325'.341096 — dc22   2010042887

British Library cataloguing data are available

Front cover image © 2010 Shutterstock

Manufactured in the United States of America

*McFarland & Company, Inc., Publishers
Box 611, Jefferson, North Carolina 28640
www.mcfarlandpub.com*

For Rosemary

Table of Contents

vii

Preface

In 1945, Britain possessed a vast African empire. British colonies stretched from Gambia on Africa's western edge to Swaziland perched between South Africa and Mozambique in the far southeast. Together, Britain's African colonies encompassed almost 7.5 million square kilometers, about ten times larger than Britain and about 80 percent the size of the United States. The Sudan alone included 2.5 million square kilometers. In 1960, an estimated 95 million people lived in what were or had been Britain's African colonies. In the same year, 179 million people lived in the United States and 45 million in Britain. In 1960, Nigeria was thought to include 37 million people. More than 11 million lived in Sudan and more than 10 million in Tanganyika and Zanzibar combined.

On November 11, 1965, Ian Smith, prime minister of Southern Rhodesia, declared his country independent of Great Britain. Southern Rhodesia's declaration of independence marked the effective end of Britain's African empire. Southern Rhodesia's independence left only three small African territories, Bechuanaland, Swaziland, and Basutoland, still under British control. Together, the three territories included fewer than 2 million people and about 650,000 square kilometers. By September 1968, even these three would be independent.

Between 1945 and 1965, the United States was the sole global power. After the Second World War, the United States possessed the world's largest and most productive economy. It was a net creditor to the rest of the world. The United States also had vast military resources, including nuclear weapons. In military terms, the United States was rivaled only by Russia among the nations of the world. Moreover, the United States claimed a global role for itself. Perhaps by the end of the Second World War and certainly by 1950, the U.S. claimed an interest in every part of the world, including Africa. After 1950, events everywhere were a United States concern, even in Africa, a part of the world the United States had cared little about before 1939.

The coincidence of Britain's relinquishment of its African empire and the United States' world dominance suggests several questions. The basic question is, in fact, whether the relationship between the end of British control and United States power was more than coincidence. Did the United States cause, or help to cause, the end of Britain's African empire? Most observers concede that the state of the world played a part in Britain's decisions about Africa; some concede the United States had a role. The first goal of this study is to probe into this question. Starting with conversations between Franklin Roosevelt and Winston Churchill in 1941, it looks at interactions between the governments of the United States and Britain about colonial territories, and about African territories in particular, in search of evidence that the United States contributed to the demise of Britain's African empire.

1

A second set of questions relates to official U.S. attitudes and policies regarding colonial Africa. Until the Second World War, the United States government paid little or no attention to Africa. Beginning with wartime planning for a world organization, however, the U.S. found itself dealing first with issues related to colonial territories generally and later with issues related to colonial Africa. Many of these issues arose within the context of the United Nations, the world organization the United States had helped to create. To deal with such issues and to promote U.S. interests in Africa, the U.S. created and expanded organizations within the Department of State and stationed increasing numbers of U.S. officials in consulates around Africa. This study considers the policies the U.S. created to deal with colonial territories and with colonial Africa. In particular, it considers the extent to which the United States was opposed to colonial territories and favored independence. It looks at the steps the U.S. took to implement its policies and considers whether they were effective. This study looks for answers both among presidential policies and within the State Department itself, particularly in the interaction among the department's various parts and the interaction between the department in Washington and its staff in the field.

Another set of questions relates to the British decisions by which African colonies gained their independence. Even before the Second World War, British officials concerned with Africa sensed that new policies were needed. The arrangements that Britain had used since before the First World War to control large swaths of Africa seemed increasingly ill-suited to changing circumstances. This study looks at the new policies British leaders and officials devised. It considers British goals and methods, and relates them to broader concerns about Britain's place in a postwar world dominated by the United States. As it does with U.S. policies and actions, the study takes into account the views and actions of British elected leaders, civil servants at home, and officials in the field.

This study originated with a desire to understand U.S. actions regarding Africa. At first glance, portrayals of the United States in the twenty years after the Second World War seem problematic. It is depicted as a nation that is both the upholder of the postwar world order and a proponent of political change in Africa; Britain's special ally and, at the same time, a friend of African nationalists. This study sets out to resolve these apparent contradictions and to create a coherent picture of the United States' relationship to British colonial Africa. It also sheds light on the relationship between Britain and the United States between 1945 and 1965 and on how Britain's African colonies became independent.

This study focuses on Britain and the United States, in particular on policymakers in London and Washington. Nevertheless, it assumes that the principal impetus for political change in Africa originated in Africa itself. It assumes that African colonies became independent largely because of demographic, economic, and social changes within Africa. A focus on London and Washington does not imply that British or United States actions accounted solely, or even largely, for the rise of independent states in Africa. This study seeks to understand the roles Britain and the United States played in the political transformation of Africa and to understand how Britain and the United States reacted to changes in Africa.

What follows is an exercise in world history, a consideration of broad changes across the globe. It draws upon prior studies in African history (where I had my original training), British imperial history, and the history of U.S. politics and foreign policy, but adopts a different perspective from those fields. By adopting something of a mid–Atlantic perspective and considering thoughts and actions in Washington, London, and various colonial capitals, it attempts to paint a richer picture of political changes in British Africa in the two decades after the Second World War.

For U.S. policy and actions, the principal source was the State Department files housed in the National Archives in College Park, Maryland, especially the State Department Central Files. For British matters, the sources included the documents published in the series *British Documents at the End of Empire,* and the extensive secondary literature about the end of Britain's empire.

The study refers to Britain's African colonies by the names used at the time: Gambia, Sierra Leone, the Gold Coast (the current Ghana), Nigeria, the Sudan, Kenya, Uganda, Zanzibar, Tanganyika (which combined with Zanzibar to form the independent Tanzania), Northern Rhodesia (Zambia), Nyasaland (Malawi), Southern Rhodesia (Zimbabwe), Bechuanaland (Botswana), Swaziland, and Basutoland (Lesotho).

What follows would not have been possible without access to the Georgetown University, George Washington University, and University of Virginia libraries or to the National Archives at College Park, Maryland. I am grateful for this access. I am particularly grateful for the generous assistance provided by the archives staff in College Park.

1

The United States and Colonies, 1941–1945: Roosevelt Seizes the High Moral Ground

Before 1941, the United States remained a regional power, content to dominate the Western Hemisphere. Similarly, the United States had little reason and few occasions to articulate a policy towards other countries' colonies before the beginning of World War II. In 1941, however, Britain's bid for an alliance with the United States against Germany created an opportunity for Franklin Roosevelt to extend the United States' reach. Since Britain controlled an extensive overseas empire, the prospect of cooperation with Britain also prompted Roosevelt to articulate a U.S. position on colonial possessions. During the following four years, U.S. officials labored both to dominate the Anglo-American alliance and to convert Roosevelt's views on colonies into coherent policies.

Roosevelt and Colonies

Capturing Franklin Roosevelt's thinking is a challenge. Roosevelt was a complex, secretive, and devious person. He was adept at leaving visitors with the impression that he agreed with them. He was fond of releasing trial balloons and shifted his thinking in the face of changing circumstances. Henry Stimson, Roosevelt's secretary of war, observed that he "hops about in his discussions from suggestion to suggestion and it is very much like chasing a vagrant beam of sunshine around a vacant room." While Roosevelt may have maintained strategic consistency, even he admitted to tactical improvisation. To reporters, Roosevelt likened his administration to a football team with himself as captain. He told them that the captain might know the general strategy and what the next play would be. Even he would not know what the play after that would be until the team had run another play.[1]

With few exceptions, Roosevelt's pronouncements on colonialism and colonies were just talk. The Allies took little action regarding colonies during the war. They agreed that colonial issues had to wait until a victory over the Axis powers. Roosevelt's death in April 1945 came before the United States faced any real choices about colonial empires — whether, for example, to return colonies to their former masters, as in the case of Indochina and the Dutch East Indies, or how the international community would treat colonies in the postwar settlement. We do not know how Roosevelt would have acted regarding the colonies had he served out his fourth term.

Attempting to piece together Roosevelt's thinking during World War II about the European colonies and their future in the postwar world is worth the effort, however, even if the result falls short of being conclusive. Roosevelt discussed colonies and colonial issues in public and in private. He thought that dealing with the European empires would be one of the United States's major postwar challenges. More than most other American presidents, Roosevelt conducted his own foreign policy. During Roosevelt's tenure, the United States took a distinctive stance regarding colonies, a standard retained by Roosevelt's successors through Lyndon Johnson. Roosevelt's ideas played a significant role in shaping the U.S. proposals for a postwar international organization and that organization's approach to colonial territories. Roosevelt's wartime administration also marks the beginning of serious U.S. attempts to work out an official approach to the European colonies, including the British colonies in Africa.

Franklin Roosevelt described his fundamental reaction to British Africa at a press conference in February 1944. Recounting his stopover in Gambia at the time of the Casablanca conference, Roosevelt told of glum-looking natives going to work in rags. He was told, he said, that the prevailing wages were less than fifty cents a day plus a half-cup of rice. He noted the prevalence of dirt and disease, leading to a life expectancy of only twenty-six years. He concluded that the British took better care of their livestock. "It's just plain exploitation of these people."[2]

Roosevelt told his son, Elliott, that colonialism in Africa represented missed opportunities. Roosevelt said, "Imperialists don't realize what they can do, what they can create. They've robbed this continent of billions and all because they were too short sighted to understand that their billions were pennies, compared to the possibilities. Possibilities that must include a better life for the people who inhabit the land."[3]

Colonies posed real dangers, Roosevelt thought. Exploiting the resources of colonial countries without putting anything back into them, like education, health services, or decent standards of living, was storing up trouble that would lead to war. The millions of people in colonial countries ruled by a handful of whites could only be resentful. Millions of potential enemies were dangerous in Roosevelt's view. Unless positive steps were taken to change the colonial relationships, the colonial powers would find themselves pushed out. Roosevelt even blamed American casualties in the Pacific theater on the "short-sighted greed of the French and the British and the Dutch."[4]

After the war with Germany and Japan, Roosevelt suggested, a new approach to colonies would be needed. The United States would have to work hard to avoid being maneuvered by the colonial powers into supporting their ambitions. It should not take direct responsibility for any colonies. The British West Indies was a British headache that the U.S. did not want. In the postwar world, the colonial powers might be responsible for their colonies, but only as trustees on behalf of the international community. They would be responsible for reporting each year to an international organization about the progress of their stewardship of the colonies, improvement in literacy, declines in the mortality rate, and the like. Roosevelt suggested that several countries might act jointly as trustees.[5]

The international organization would be the responsibility of the great powers, the United States, Great Britain, the Soviet Union, and China. Roosevelt seems to have wanted to balance a sense that the great powers had to be responsible for stability and order around the world with recognition that the sensibilities of smaller nations had to be respected. An international organization might appeal to smaller nations, even if the great powers retained a controlling position. When Roosevelt was asked in October 1943 whether the United States should retain sovereignty over airbases it had built in foreign countries, he replied: "How would we like it if they said that to us?" Roosevelt's prewar Good Neighbor policy toward the Caribbean and South America evidenced the same aversion to a heavy-handed approach to weaker nations.[6]

In addition to receiving reports from trustee nations, the international organization would dispatch commissions to inspect the colonies and report on their findings. Roosevelt thought that what he referred to as pitiless publicity could right of lot of wrongs. In the same press conference in which Roosevelt described his repulsion at conditions in the Gambia, he told reporters that an inspection committee could find out where the British were not "coming up to scratch" and tell the whole world about it. On another occasion, Roosevelt reportedly told Churchill that he did not care who had the sovereignty over dependent areas so long as they were subject to international inspection.[7]

Independence would be the ultimate goal for most colonies. Roosevelt expressed impatience for schemes that would lead only to self-government or dominion status within the British commonwealth. Nevertheless, colonies would undergo a period of tutoring before becoming independent. Roosevelt thought that U.S. actions in the Philippines provided the colonial powers with the right model for preparing colonies for self-determination. For colonies like India, the tutorial period would be short. Colonies like Indochina needed more development and training. To Maxim Litvinov, the Soviet ambassador to the United States, Roosevelt suggested that Indochina and the Dutch East Indies might need twenty years to prepare for independence. Roosevelt's views on African colonies are not clear, but it seems that Roosevelt viewed them as needing considerable time before they could be independent. When he criticized British performance in the Gambia, he admitted that the colony was not ready for independence. Roosevelt recognized that granting some colonies independence would stimulate similar aspirations in others. "If one colony gets its freedom, the others will get ideas," he told his son.[8]

In Roosevelt's mind, the U.S. emergence after the war as one of the globe's great powers, if not the great power, was compatible with the simultaneous emergence of a host of newly independent states. Roosevelt saw the United States as one of the world's policemen, perhaps in concert with Great Britain, or with Great Britain, Russia and China. The world they would police would comprise independent states, some carved out of the European empires. The world's states would trade freely with each other and investments would flow freely around the world.

Colonies in the Atlantic Charter

Early in the U.S. wartime collaboration with Great Britain, Roosevelt staked out a distinctive public position on the future of the colonies. Once Winston Churchill replaced Neville Chamberlain as British prime minister in May 1940, he reversed a key Chamberlain policy and began to woo Roosevelt and seek American aid in the war against Germany. Churchill's courtship of Roosevelt led to their first meeting, off the coast of Newfoundland in August 1941. The press release issued after their meeting, styled by the U.S. government, the Atlantic Charter, contained language that the United States could claim called for the eventual end of the British colonies.

The British government had not anticipated a joint declaration. Churchill was surprised when Roosevelt broached the idea early in their meeting. According to Under Secretary of State Sumner Welles, who had close ties to Roosevelt, the president decided, before the conference, that a public statement would keep alive principles of international law and principles of moral and human decency. Roosevelt wanted to seize the moral high ground and avoid accusations, of, among other things, that Great Britain was luring the United States into protecting British imperial interests. A statement of basic principles might also deter Great Britain from concluding secret agreements with its allies. To ease British anxieties, Roosevelt suggested that the British prepare the first draft. With a draft in hand, the president, the prime minister, and their advisers set about writing a version they could accept. What emerged was a statement of eight principles on which, the press release stated, the United States and Great Britain "base their hopes for a better future for the world."[9]

The third principle dealt with the future of the colonies. "Third, they respect the right of all peoples to choose the form of government under which they will live; and they wish to see sovereign rights and self-government restored to those who have been forcibly deprived of them." Sir Alexander Cadogan, the permanent undersecretary in the British Foreign Office, drafted the original version with considerable input from Churchill. Welles deleted Cadogan's proposed wording about defending freedom of speech and thought. Since the Axis powers had abrogated these freedoms in the countries they conquered, Welles feared that American opponents of United States intervention would seize upon this as tantamount to a declaration of war. Roosevelt himself proposed the words about restoring self-government to which Churchill added the phrase "sovereign rights."

According to Elliott Roosevelt's account, Roosevelt made his distaste for colonies plain to Churchill during the Newfoundland meeting. He told Churchill that a stable peace must involve development of backward countries. The allies could not fight against fascist slavery without freeing people around the world from a backward colonial policy. According to the younger Roosevelt, the president added that colonialism had to be eliminated after the war. The United States would not underwrite colonialism or oppose independence movements like the one in India. According to Elliott Roosevelt, Churchill acknowledged that Britain was dependent upon American aid and the ultimate fate of the British colonies was in American hands. "You know that we know that without America, the empire will not stand," Churchill allegedly said.[10]

Once the United States entered World War II, the Atlantic Charter became a principal statement of its war aims. When the United States, Great Britain, the Soviet Union, and twenty-three other nations formalized their alliance against the Axis powers on January 1, 1942, they proclaimed that they subscribed to the common program of purposes and principles embodied in the Atlantic Charter. Propaganda issued by the Office of War Information referred repeatedly to the Atlantic Charter and its principles.

Throughout the war, Roosevelt maintained that the Atlantic Charter applied to the entire world, not simply the countries that bordered the Atlantic and, thus, to British colonies. He told reporters as much in a press conference on January 2, 1942, a day after the Allies issued their declaration. Roosevelt's fireside chat the following month contained a passage about the charter: "We of the United Nations are agreed on certain broad principles in the kind of peace we seek. The Atlantic Charter applies not only to the parts of the world that border the Atlantic but to the whole world; disarmament of aggressors, self-determination of nations and peoples, and the four freedoms — freedom of speech, freedom of religion, freedom from want and freedom from fear."[11]

Wendell Willkie's world tour later in 1942, as Roosevelt's personal emissary, provided another opportunity to highlight high-level American views on the ultimate fate of colonies. The Republican challenger to Roosevelt in the 1940 election, Willkie wanted to make the trip to demonstrate that Americans were united behind the war effort and to find out how the Allies could win the war quickly. Roosevelt assigned Willkie several tasks. Roosevelt and Willkie also arranged that Willkie would go as Roosevelt's special emissary, rather than an ambassador at large, so that Willkie would have official standing while retaining his freedom to speak his mind.[12]

On the subject of colonies, Willkie made full use of his license to speak freely. In October 1942, towards the end of the trip, Willkie visited Chaing Kai Shek's Nationalist Chinese government in Chunking. At the end of his stay, Willkie made a speech in which he said that the colonial days were past and that the war must mean an end to the empire of nations over other nations. The Allied coalition had to help colonial peoples become free and independent nations. It must set up firm timetables under which colonial peoples could develop their own governments. The Allies should issue guarantees that developing countries would not slip back into colonial status. Willkie was adamant that the issue of colonies could not wait until the end of the war. If change were delayed, it might be too little and too late.[13]

Back in the United States, Willkie repeated the same thoughts in a radio address to the American public and, later, in a book entitled *One World*. On the radio, Willkie said colonial people knew what freedom meant. They knew it meant the orderly but scheduled abolition of the colonial system. According to Willkie, the rule of one people by another people was not freedom and not what the Allies were fighting to preserve.[14]

The day after Willkie's radio address, reporters quizzed Roosevelt. The president said he did not see anything controversial in the speech. That the Atlantic Charter applied throughout the world was, according to Roosevelt, "old stuff." He and Secretary of State Hull had said so, on the record, several times. The press could quote Roosevelt to that effect.[15]

Willkie's speech received so much publicity that Churchill felt compelled to reply. After the British Eighth Army defeated the German and Italian forces commanded by Rommel at Alamein in North Africa in October 1942, spirits in London rose. Buoyed by the success at Alamein, Churchill gave a speech at Mansion House in London on November 10. He asserted that the British had not entered the war for profit or expansion. He went on to say, "Let me, however, make this clear, in case there should be any mistake about it in any quarter. We mean to hold our own. I have not become the King's First Minister in order to preside over the liquidation of the British empire."[16]

Roosevelt used press conferences to make the point that the Atlantic Charter was a statement of principles intended for implementation over the long term. After the February 1942 fireside chat in which Roosevelt mentioned the Atlantic Charter, reporters asked him whether he was referring to a recent statement by Chaing Kai Shek about Britain and India. Roosevelt replied that the charter applied to dozens of situations. Off the record, he added that the Allies needed to win the war before working out the details of governments and boundaries.[17]

In a December 1944 press conference, Roosevelt expounded on the Atlantic Charter's character at greater length. He told reporters that the charter was an objective and resembled other pronouncements made in centuries past. They had not yet been attained, but were sound, nonetheless. The charter was like Wilson's Fourteen Points, Roosevelt said, a step towards a better life for the population of the world. World conditions were better than they had been, but humankind had a long way to go. Conditions would continue to improve as long as people worked for it.[18]

Churchill's Interpretation of the Atlantic Charter

Roosevelt's interpretation of the Atlantic Charter was important because his counterpart at the Newfoundland meeting, Churchill, took a different view. In a speech to the House of Commons on September 9, 1941, Churchill described the principal features of the Atlantic ·Charter. About the third principle, regarding self-determination, Churchill said that questions had been asked. He said that it would be unwise for one party to an agreement, without consulting with the other party, to put special or strained interpretations on specific passages. Therefore he was speaking "in an exclusive sense." Churchill went on to say, "At the Atlantic meeting we had in mind, primarily, the restoration of the sovereignty, self-government and national life of the states and nations now under Nazi yoke, and the principles governing any alterations in the territorial boundaries which may have to be made. So that is quite a separate problem from the progressive evolution of self-governing institutions in the regions and peoples which owe allegiance to the British Crown."[19]

It is not obvious how Churchill reached his interpretation of the Atlantic Charter's self-determination provision. It is possible that Churchill and his staff were thinking in terms of Europe and did not grasp that this part of the charter could apply to the entire world, including the British empire. Perhaps Churchill thought that adding the phrase "sovereign rights" clarified that the declaration did not apply to the British colonies. Since colonies had not recently possessed their own sovereignty, a commitment to "restore" sovereignty could not apply to them. Or, perhaps, Roosevelt provided verbal reassurance that convinced Churchill that the principle applied only to Europe.

Regardless of how Churchill arrived at his view of the self-determination provision, he realized that his understandings with Roosevelt would not allow him to repudiate it. Therefore, in addition to noting that the self-determination principle applied primarily to the countries conquered by the Axis powers, Churchill asserted that the British had dealt with the issue of self-determination for their colonies. He said that Britain had made pledges to India and Burma regarding equal membership in the British commonwealth, subject "to the fulfillment of obligations arising from our long connection with India and our responsibilities to its many creeds, races, and interests." On the subject of self-government, Churchill claimed: "We have made declarations on these matters which are complete in themselves, free from ambiguity and related to the conditions and circumstances of the territories and peoples affected. They will be found to be entirely in harmony with the high conception of freedom and justice which inspired the joint declaration."[20]

Before making the speech in the House of Commons, Churchill shared a copy with John Winant, the U.S. ambassador to Great Britain. Winant thought Churchill's characterization of the self-determination wording ran counter to the general public's interpretation and would elicit little support in Britain or the United States. Winant thought it would intensify charges of imperialism and make Britain appear to have a do-nothing policy regarding India and Burma. He tried to persuade Churchill to change the speech. Churchill refused, stating that the cabinet had approved the wording and that it was a matter of internal British politics. Winant attributed Churchill's position to the influence of Leopold

Amery, the Indian secretary, and to a perceived need to take a firm position with Indian and Burmese nationalists.[21]

A year later Churchill had reason to share his view of the Atlantic Charter with Roosevelt himself. Churchill learned that the U.S. Office of War Information was preparing a statement on the charter's first anniversary. Churchill wrote to Roosevelt asking to see any proposed statement before its release. He reminded Roosevelt that they had, together, considered each line of the charter. Churchill wrote, "I should not be able, without mature consideration, to give it a wider interpretation than was agreed between us at the time. Its proposed application to Asia and Africa requires much thought."[22]

Roosevelt sidestepped the issue. The Office of War Information had prepared a statement. The draft statement included a paragraph stating the charter applied to the entire world and ending with the sentence: "It is a promise to all men that they will have the right to work out their own destinies under such form of government as they may choose, free from fear and want, free from tyranny and oppression." The paragraph did not, however, appear in the final version that Roosevelt forwarded to Churchill. Roosevelt did not share a draft with Churchill before releasing the statement. In transmitting the final version to Churchill, however, he noted that it contained nothing that might raise questions or controversy.[23]

On other occasions, Roosevelt made clear his disagreement with Churchill about the future of colonies. At a White House dinner in 1942, he remarked that Churchill did not understand that Americans were viscerally opposed to imperialism. To Churchill himself, Roosevelt said that Britain's four hundred years of acquisitive instinct was outmoded. History had changed and Churchill needed to adjust. On the way back from the Yalta conference, reporters asked Roosevelt about Churchill's characterization of the Atlantic Charter as a guide, not a rule, and reminded him of Churchill's assertion that he had not become prime minister to preside over the demise of the empire. Roosevelt's retort was that "dear old Winston" would never learn on that point. He had made his specialty on that point.[24]

Developing Policies Based on the Atlantic Charter

After the United States entered World War II, the State Department advertised the Atlantic Charter principles, especially the notion of self-determination. On Memorial Day 1942, Sumner Welles gave an address in which he announced that the age of imperialism was over. An Allied victory must bring the liberation of all peoples. The principles of the Atlantic Charter, Welles announced, must be guaranteed to the entire world. Secretary of State Hull thought Welles's speech premature. Hull apparently had not approved it in advance. Later in the year, Hull gave his own speech, intended as a corrective to Welles's enthusiasm. Hull stressed that peoples seeking independence had to demonstrate by their acts that they were worthy of it and ready for it. Hull argued that colonial powers had the responsibility to prepare dependent peoples for independence, as the United States had done in the case of Cuba and the Philippines. He said the United States stood on the side of freedom and independence.[25]

Despite Welles's enthusiasm, he was not the Roosevelt administration's most outspoken critic of the European empires. Vice President Henry Wallace favored immediate independence for colonial areas. In June 1942, he gave a speech laying out a program of international development and social reform, a New Deal for the entire world. Hull thought

Wallace unrealistic and worried that his public position would create impossibly high expectations.[26]

Wallace's views unsettled Churchill and the British. Wallace wrote a pamphlet entitled "Our Job in the Pacific," outlining his goals for the postwar world. Among other things, it advocated self-determination for colonial territories, including India. The British secret services obtained a copy of Wallace's manuscript before publication. When a copy reached Churchill's hands, it produced "cataclysms of wrath." The British ambassador to Washington, Lord Halifax, lodged a protest about Wallace's views with Hull.[27]

Public sentiment in the United States agreed in large part with Wallace's views. In a 1942 poll, 56 percent of Americans agreed that the British could be described as oppressors because of the unfair advantage they had taken of their colonial possessions. After British defeats in Asia and the fall of Singapore, important voices in the United States press were critical of the British and their empire. Columnist Walter Lippman wrote of the Western nations "putting away the white man's burden and purging themselves of an obsolete and obviously unworkable white man's imperialism." In an open letter to the people of England, the editors of *Life* magazine announced that the United States was not fighting to hold the British empire together. U.S. officials who came into contact with British colonial personnel in the field often came away suspicious. Another of Roosevelt's personal emissaries, Patrick Hurley, thought both Russia and Britain paid lip service to democracy but were secretly rebuilding old empires. When Willkie dined with senior British officials in Cairo, he encountered "Rudyard Kipling, untainted even with the liberalism of Cecil Rhodes."[28]

Roosevelt's administration contained both Anglophiles and Anglophobes. Nevertheless, the key senior figures shared more measured views of Anglo-American relations. Usually considered pro–British, Stimson thought the British a magnificent people. They had, nevertheless, lost their initiative. The Americans would have to win through their own efforts. Confronted with Anglo-American friction in the Pacific theater, Hull counseled patience. The United States could not alienate Britain in the Pacific and expect cooperation in the European campaign. Harry Hopkins conceded that the American people disliked British colonial policy and that the British were likely to take unfair advantage of the United States in trade matters. Yet he was certain that Britain and the United States would be on the same side in a future war. Dwight Eisenhower, Allied supreme commander in Europe, assured a friend that he was aware that the British saw every military problem from an imperial viewpoint. Eisenhower admonished, "One of the constant sources of dangers to us in this war is the temptation to regard as our first enemy the partner that must work with us in defeating the real enemy."[29]

Early in 1942, State Department staff began drafting a statement elaborating the Atlantic Charter principles, the self-determination principle in particular. Staff work on postwar problems had begun in the State Department as early as December 1939. The elaboration of the Atlantic Charter was intended to remove any confusion caused by Churchill's statement that it applied only to countries conquered by the Axis powers. In final form, as the Declaration on National Independence, the statement extended the Atlantic Charter principles to all nations. It called upon colonial powers to prepare dependent peoples for independence, through education and progressive steps toward self-government. The statement called for timetables for granting independence. It envisioned that the colonial powers would cooperate with each other through regional commissions. Like Hull's speech, the statement mentioned the responsibility of dependent peoples to do what was necessary to maintain efficient and stable government. In March 1943, Hull sent the draft declaration to Roosevelt, who approved it. The State Department provided a copy to the Foreign Office, in hopes of arriving at a joint declaration.[30]

The British drafted their own declaration on colonial policy and gave it to Hull in February 1943. The British declaration was intended to counteract criticism of British colonial policy by Willkie and others. The British declaration emphasized the responsibilities of the colonial powers and offered the prospect of regional commissions through which the colonial powers could cooperate in developing their colonies and leading them to responsibility for their own affairs. The most optimistic British officials believed that the United States and Britain shared considerable common ground on colonial matters and a carefully worded declaration could both leave the future of British colonies in British hands and satisfy the American broad commitment to self-determination.[31]

The draft U.S. declaration punctured hopes for an easy agreement. Some officials in London clung to the thought that, beneath the rhetoric, United States aims resembled British aims. Nevertheless, the official British response provided to Ambassador Winant in May 1943 raised fundamental objections to the United States declaration. The British doubted that a single declaration could apply to both colonies and the countries conquered by the Axis powers. The U.S. emphasis on independence was not acceptable. The British also objected to definite timetables for granting independence to colonial areas and were uneasy with what they saw as U.S. proposals for international administration of the colonial territories formerly held by enemy powers.[32]

Independence was a major sticking point. British officials realized that stressing independence as the future for colonies was consistent with the U.S. interpretation of the Atlantic Charter. Doing so, however, highlighted the disagreement between Roosevelt and Churchill about the charter. British officials assumed that independence meant severing all ties between the colonial power and its colonies. To the extent that British officials contemplated political changes in the colonies, they assumed that political change would not go that far. They assumed that political change would cease with the colonies exercising self-government, but with the British government in London maintaining a measure of control. During the war, British officials did not agree about the extent of future colonial self-government or about the nature of continuing British control. In many cases, they did not have clear notions of either. Nevertheless, they were confident that self-government was preferable to independence as the ultimate goal.

Fixing timetables, even for self-government, was taboo to British officials. It was impossible to predict when political change might take place, they thought. The process must be one of trial and effort. Many colonies were many generations away from being ready for self-government. Predicting when colonies that included more than one race could be welded into a community capable of governing itself was impossible.

Over the next year, the notion of a joint declaration drifted into a diplomatic limbo. Ambassador Winant failed to forward the British response to Washington. Officials in Washington assumed that the British were ignoring the proposed declaration. Hull pressed Foreign Secretary Anthony Eden about the declaration during the Quebec conference in August 1943. Only after several inquiries did Eden respond that he did not care for the United States draft and that independence was a particularly troubling point. Eden described that British empire as containing units with varying degrees of self-government, from a dominion, like Canada, through various types of colonies. Some colonies were never likely to achieve their own governments and, Eden said, independence could never properly describe what the British meant by self-government. At the same conference, Roosevelt gave a copy of the draft declaration to Churchill, who ignored it. At the subsequent Moscow conference, Hull provided a copy to Molotov, the Russian foreign minister. Eden said that he was not prepared to discuss colonial issues and added that Great Britain differed with the United States on this subject.[33]

The sentiments that populated the American version of the joint declaration became part of U.S. planning for a postwar international organization. In April 1944, Isaiah Bowman, president of Johns Hopkins University and a State Department adviser, visited London to meet with British officials as part of a group headed by Under Secretary of State Edward Stettinius. The topic of a joint declaration arose. The conversation did not proceed far, partly because Bowman had never seen the British reply to the United States draft. Bowman was persuaded, however, that a joint declaration constructed around general principles was unlikely and probably not helpful. When Bowman returned to Washington, he shared his conclusions with State Department officials. They continued to see merit in the joint declaration's overall message and were inclined to use it to describe the responsibilities of colonial powers as overseen by an international organization.[34]

Trade, Aid and Finance

Another principle laid out in the Atlantic Charter posed a threat to the British colonies as well. The fourth principle read: "They will endeavor, with due respect for their existing obligations, to further the enjoyment by all States, great or small, victor or vanquished, of access, on equal terms, to the trade and to the raw materials of the world which are needed for their economic prosperity."

United States Secretary of State Cordell Hull, in this case supported by Under Secretary Welles, believed that limitations on trade, like the trade preferences negotiated among Great Britain and its dominions in the Ottawa Agreements of 1932, had led to both the worldwide depression of the 1930s and to the unfolding war in Europe. Hull once termed the Ottawa agreements "the greatest injury in a commercial way that has been inflicted on this country since I had been in public life." With the onset of hostilities, Britain redoubled the financial and trade barriers around the British empire. It limited imports from non-sterling countries; pooled sterling balances in London rather than making them available to the dominions and colonies; and ensured that sterling that was released to trading partners could not be converted to other currencies.[35]

Pursuit of multilateral trade was the centerpiece of Hull's tenure as secretary of state. He spent much of the later 1930s negotiating a series of bilateral trade agreements, including one with Great Britain in 1938. Hull's views were consistent with long-time U.S. free trade and open door policies, favoring equal access to markets and raw materials. Roosevelt supported Hull, but his thinking on trade issues was not nearly as crisp or single-minded as that of his secretary of state.

Before the United States became involved in World War II, the British empire posed economic and financial issues, rather than political ones, for the U.S., particularly for the Department of State and the Department of the Treasury. Support for political independence and self-determination was a traditional value of U.S. foreign policy. Woodrow Wilson had included it in his Fourteen Points. Yet no one in official Washington in the late 1930s was seeking to free British colonies from imperial rule. Hull's State Department was, on the other hand, promoting multilateral trade, and Robert Morgenthau's Treasury Department was intent on establishing United States predominance in international finance, especially at the expense of the British.

In 1940, when Churchill approached the United States government for financial assistance in order to resist the Axis powers, Hull saw an opportunity to pry open the British empire and curtail trade preferences. In the first half of 1941, British and American negotiators were busy in Washington negotiating what became the Lend-Lease agreement. Early on, the State Department resolved that the price for U.S. financial aid should be a British commitment to forsake trade restrictions. Other U.S. officials were less than enthusiastic about this approach. Morgenthau and his treasury subordinates preferred to focus on British gold and dollar reserves. For Harry Hopkins and others, the first priority was aiding Britain. Nevertheless, the State Department secured draft language in the Lend-Lease agreement's critical provision, Article VII, which would have committed Britain to ending its trade preferences. John Maynard Keynes, the chief British negotiator, balked at the proposed language. When Roosevelt and his party left Washington for the Newfoundland conference, the issue remained unresolved.[36]

According to Elliott Roosevelt, the president's exchange with Churchill about colonies at the Newfoundland conference followed a similar exchange about trade restrictions. According to the younger Roosevelt, the president told Churchill that one of the preconditions for continued peace after the war would be the greatest possible freedom of trade. Roosevelt went on to blame the alleged backwardness of British colonies on British trade policy. Churchill's reply was that the trade that had made England great would continue under conditions prescribed by England's ministers. Roosevelt's retort was that he and Churchill would have to disagree on the issue.[37]

On the way to the Atlantic Charter conference, Welles and Roosevelt discussed at length how to open up international trade. Presented with a bland British draft regarding economic matters, Welles proposed extensive changes, most intended to produce the commitment to multilateral trade that State Department officials were seeking in the Lend-Lease negotiations. Roosevelt condensed Welles's proposed language into the phrase "without discrimination." Churchill demurred, contending that he could not agree to such language without consulting the leaders of the dominions. Churchill insisted on inserting the phrase "with due respect to existing obligations," which would preserve the Ottawa agreements and similar preferences. Welles resisted, but Roosevelt acquiesced, assuring Welles that the final language was more than he thought Churchill would concede.[38]

While the United States government struggled to translate the Atlantic Charter principles into postwar policies for an international organization and for the European colonies, it moved crisply to establish a postwar structure for international finance and trade. Officials in the Treasury and State Departments believed that new arrangements for international trade and finance were needed to avoid the economic and political crises of the 1930s. In most cases, they had clear notions of how international finance and trade should function after the war. They intended to put the United States in a dominant position and reduce Great Britain, its chief economic rival, to an inferior position. By the time of Roosevelt's death, the United States had not achieved all its goals for international trade and finance, but had made progress toward them.[39]

Early in the war, officials in both London and Washington began developing plans for reforming international finance after the war. Harry Dexter White in the Treasury Department and John Maynard Keynes, advisor to the Foreign Office, each led their government's effort to devise means to prevent future collapses of international trade comparable to the collapse of the 1930s. In 1943, the two men headed their country's delegations in negotiations over international finance. In the end, Keynes acceded to the essentials of White's plan. Keynes recognized that the United States was now the world's leading economic power and Britain was desperate for financial aid. Keynes recognized that White had built U.S. control of what would become the World Bank and the International Monetary Fund into the fabric of his proposal. In international finance, Britain could now hope only to function as the Americans' junior partner. White and Keynes went on to orchestrate their governments' acceptance of White's scheme and its acceptance by the Allies at the Bretton Woods conference in summer 1944.[40]

Lend-Lease

Anglo-American negotiations over Article VII of the Lend-Lease agreement continued into 1942. After the United States entered the war, Churchill wanted to postpone discussion of trade and financial issues until after an Allied victory. Roosevelt and his officials were concerned, however, that a failure to conclude a master Lend-Lease agreement with Britain would irritate the Congress, where skepticism about aid to Britain festered. Roosevelt and the State Department were concerned that the United States and Britain agree on trade concessions as Britain's consideration for Lend-Lease aid. Otherwise, the Congress would insist that Britain repay the United States for the aid and recreate the war debt issue that bedeviled Anglo-American relations after World War I. Faced with Churchill's stubborn resistance, Roosevelt offered concessions. Article VII would not commit Britain to doing away with imperial preference. It would commit Britain only to including imperial preference in future trade policy discussions. In those discussions, reductions in preferences would be linked to reductions in tariffs. With this understanding, Britain and the United States signed a master Lend-Lease agreement in February 1942.[41]

Despite the inconclusive end to the initial negotiations over Article VII, the United States used the Lend-Lease agreement during the war to solidify its financial position at the expense of the British. U.S. Treasury officials feared that Britain would use Lend-Lease aid not only to fight the war but also to accumulate financial reserves that it could use for postwar reconstruction. Therefore, with the reluctant cooperation of the State Department, Treasury managed the flow of Lend-Lease aid so that Britain's financial reserves remained between $600 million and $1 billion. Limiting British reserves ensured, among other things, that Britain would have to turn to the United States after the war for help in reconstruction. A country in need of financial assistance might be a country willing to negotiate trade concessions.[42]

Anglo-American trade negotiations in 1945 failed to produce an agreement. With multilateral trade as the object, the United States offered tariff reductions in exchange for elimination of imperial preferences. Great Britain countered that the two were not equivalent. Without an agreement, the United States returned to its trade policy of the later 1930s, bilateral trade agreements combined with most favored nation clauses. The United States would negotiate bilateral trade agreements with other countries, offering each trade partner equal treatment with the other American trade partners. Less committed to multilateral trade than Roosevelt's officials, Congress voted to renew the Reciprocal Trade Agreements

Act of 1934, the original cornerstone of Cordell Hull's trade policies. Roosevelt concluded that this satisfied the U.S. commitment to reduce tariffs. The State Department's Dean Acheson thought it was the most the administration could extract from the Congress. The British, Keynes in particular, viewed Hull's bilateral agreements much less favorably. Keynes referred to them, in an earlier negotiation, as the "clutch of the dead, or at least moribund, hand."[43]

In September 1944, at a meeting in Quebec, Roosevelt and Churchill revisited the issue of Lend-Lease aid. Churchill wanted an American commitment to substantial U.S. aid in the period between the defeat of Germany and the defeat of Japan. At the time, the best estimates were that this phase of the war would last eighteen to twenty-four months. Churchill wanted both war fighting aid and aid for reconstruction. Treasury Secretary Morgenthau, who accompanied Roosevelt to the meeting, had convinced Roosevelt to support a plan to eliminate German industrial capacity after the war. Churchill was not keen on the Morgenthau plan, thinking it draconian. Roosevelt was not keen on massive aid to Britain, particularly for reconstruction. The upshot of the meeting was that Churchill accepted the Morgenthau plan and Roosevelt accepted that the United States needed to provide substantial aid to Britain. Roosevelt did not put his commitment in writing.[44]

Neither aspect of the meeting fared well once Roosevelt returned to Washington. The Morgenthau plan seemed harsh to many in official Washington. State Department officials involved in trade issues were upset that Roosevelt had not extracted any trade concessions from Churchill in exchange for considering more aid. Hull later said that the Quebec meeting angered him as much as anything that happened while he was secretary of state. He resigned shortly after the meeting. Leaders and officials in Washington were not convinced that Britain was in dire need of more help. Under Secretary of State Stettinius dismissed the claim by British officials that Britain would not be able to repay postwar loans even with the resources of the empire at its disposal. In subsequent discussions with the British, U.S. officials reduced the proposed aid by about a billion dollars, to $5.5 billion. Aid for converting the British economy from a wartime to a peacetime orientation was still on the table, but the United States had not committed to any such aid.[45]

Congressional hostility to aid caused American officials to drag their feet. Churchill liked to think that Lend-Lease was a vehicle for the United States and the United Kingdom to pool their resources to fight the war. The Roosevelt administration sometimes talked as if that were the case, but usually acted as if the United States were aiding Great Britain and would expect some consideration in return. The consideration would not, however, involve repaying all the aid. Congress took a much less generous view. The Senate Committee to Investigate the National Defense Program, headed by the Democratic senator from Missouri, Harry S Truman, reported in November 1944 that Lend-Lease was not intended to shift Allied war costs to the United States. If the U.S. allies could not repay in dollars after the war, they might transfer international assets to the United States, the committee wrote. In March 1945, Acheson, representing the State Department, and Leo Crowley, director of the Lend-Lease program, appeared before a House committee. The committee was concerned about reports that Britain's financial reserves were increasing, presumably because of U.S. aid. The two administration officials promised the committee that Lend-Lease aid would not be used for postwar reconstruction. The Senate defeated a measure barring the use of Lend-Lease aid for postwar reconstruction only because Truman, now vice president, cast the tie-breaking vote.[46]

International Organization and Trusteeship

The eighth and last section of the Atlantic Charter dealt with disarmament. It included the phrase "pending the establishment of a wider and permanent system of general security." The words were all that remained of Churchill's attempt to get Roosevelt to commit to an international organization.

The initial British draft of the charter referred to an "effective international organization" that would provide security to all states. Welles retained the language in his revision, but Roosevelt removed it, substituting wording about disarming aggressors. When Churchill questioned Roosevelt about the absence of any reference to an international organization, Roosevelt replied that he feared suspicions and opposition at home. Roosevelt expressed skepticism about an international organization until after a transition period during which Great Britain and the United States would police the world. In order to satisfy League of Nations supporters within the British government, Churchill had the wording about a security system inserted later in the conference. Roosevelt accepted the change, explaining to Welles that he was not opposed to an assembly where the smaller nations could participate, but only after a transition period during which the United States and Great Britain held police powers.[47]

About the time State Department staff began drafting a general declaration on independence, other State Department officials embarked on designing an international organization to replace the League of Nations after the war. State Department officials set out to refine the mandates system administered by the League of Nations. Roosevelt was unenthusiastic about a postwar international organization, but the State Department, under Hull, believed that a better version of the League of Nations would be needed once the war was won. Roosevelt was content to have the State Department ponder postwar problems while he focused on winning the war. In general, Roosevelt did not think much of Hull or the State Department.

After World War I, the victorious Allies divided the former German colonies among themselves. Each recipient nation assumed a "mandate" to act as the "trustee" for the colony on behalf of the league. In Africa, Tanganyika and portions of Togoland and the Cameroons became the responsibility of Great Britain. The league attempted to oversee the trustee nations, but its efforts were ineffective. Britain administered Tanganyika in the same fashion as it did its other African possessions.

The State Department's initial proposals attempted to strengthen the mandates system. Freeing dependent peoples from foreign rule became an explicit goal. The initial draft allowed for the possibility that some dependent peoples might choose self-government and some form of association with the colonial power, rather than independence. The draft assigned trustee nations responsibility for educating colonial peoples for self-government and for achieving social and economic justice. Trustee nations would be responsible to a regional executive comprised of representatives of the colonial powers. The trustee nations would be responsible for submitting reports. The international executive would also have the right to inspect the dependent territories. Colonial peoples, for their part, would have the right to petition the international executive.[48]

Another State Department group determined that membership in the international organization should be restricted to states. The committee considered the possibility that entities not generally accepted as sovereign states such as dominions or colonies might be members. It dismissed the notion, however, because nation-states would continue to be vital parts of the postwar world. An international organization founded on any other basis would founder, they thought. The international organization was to be made of independent states.[49]

The most ticklish issue for State Department staff was determining the territories to which the trusteeship system would apply. Apparently at the urging of Welles, the staff's initial draft applied the system to all colonial territories, except those in the Western Hemisphere. Welles saw the Western Hemisphere as the responsibility of the United States. Hull thought Welles had gone too far. When Hull forwarded the staff proposals to Roosevelt in November 1942, he laid out three options. The trusteeship system could apply to all colonial territories. It could apply to the former mandates and territories formerly controlled by the Axis powers and, sometime later, to other colonial territories. Trusteeship could also apply only to the former mandates and former enemy territories with the colonial powers committing to observe certain principles. Hull recommended the last option. Roosevelt agreed. Hull disbanded the group headed by Welles and convened another committee under his own direction.[50]

Over the next year, State Department formulated plans for a postwar international organization. Sentiment remained, in the person of Welles until his departure in 1943, for including all colonial territories under a trusteeship scheme. An outline for a draft charter produced in summer 1943 looked more like Hull's ideas, however. It applied trusteeship only to territories placed under the authority of the international organization by treaty or other agreement. It provided that all member states were to apply to their dependent territories the same standards of administration established for trust areas. It omitted, however, any reference to preparing dependent peoples for self-government. Preparation for self-government was, perhaps, implied in the international organization's authority to modify or terminate trusteeship agreements.[51]

Roosevelt approved the draft outline in February 1944. He had reconciled his preference for the great powers acting as the world's policemen with plans for a postwar international organization. In approving the plans, Roosevelt reiterated that the international organization be empowered to investigate the status of colonies and other dependent areas. The State Department proceeded to assemble more detailed plans. The proposals were intended as the United States contribution to meetings with its principal allies at Dumbarton Oaks in Washington, D.C., beginning in August 1944. The detailed draft mentioned the duty of administering powers to foster the political development of dependent peoples and prepare them for self-government. It talked about granting independence or autonomous association with other states or groups of states. Following Hull's line, it mentioned the duty of dependent peoples to prepare themselves for self-government or independence and to demonstrate the capacity for maintaining stable government and safeguarding civil rights. The State Department's draft applied the trusteeship system only to former mandates and former enemy territories. Administering powers could also request that their dependent territories be included in the trusteeship scheme. A trusteeship council replaced the regional commissions as the body responsible for overseeing the trust territories. Here, Hull's notions prevailed over those espoused by Welles and Roosevelt. Membership on the trusteeship council would be split evenly between administering powers and non-administering powers. The council was empowered to conduct investigations of trust areas, to receive petitions from their inhabitants, and to receive reports from the administering authorities.[52]

The Dumbarton Oaks meetings did not deal with the trusteeship issue. While the State Department was focusing on a trusteeship system, the War Department realized that a broad commitment to trusteeship could undermine American postwar control of the Pacific islands held by the Japanese. Secretary of War Henry Stimson agitated against State's plans, arguing that discussion of trusteeship and territorial settlements at Dumbarton Oaks could prolong the war. Premature discussion of territorial settlements might discourage Russia from entering the war against Japan on the side of the Allies, Stimson argued. The State Department backed down and removed trusteeship from the Dumbarton Oaks agenda.

Trusteeship at Yalta

The issue of trusteeship arose again at the Yalta conference in February 1945. Edward Stettinius replaced Hull as secretary of state in November 1944. At Yalta, he proposed to Eden and Vyacheslav Molotov, the Russian foreign minister, that the five governments who were to be permanent members of the Security Council meet to discuss the trusteeship question before the proposed conference to establish the United Nations. The Dumbarton Oaks meetings had disposed of many other issues related to the proposed international organization. Eden and Molotov agreed to meet. When Stettinius reported the agreement in a meeting involving Roosevelt, Stalin, and Churchill, Churchill exploded. He said, "I absolutely disagree. I will not have one scrap of British territory flung into that area. After we have done our best to fight this war and have done no crime to anyone I will have no suggestion that the British Empire is to be put into the dock and examined by everyone to see if it is up to their standard. No one will induce me as long as I am prime minister to let any representative of Great Britain go to a conference where they would be placed in the dock and asked to justify our right to live in a world we have tried to save."[53]

Stettinius and Roosevelt assured Churchill that the proposal had nothing to do with the British empire. As possible targets for trusteeship, Stettinius mentioned the Pacific islands held as League of Nations mandates held by Japan. He referred to the possibility of colonial powers offering to place territories under trusteeships. Later, the Americans presented Churchill with a written statement, based on the proposals originally prepared for the Dumbarton Oaks meetings. It said that trusteeship would apply to former enemy territories and territories voluntarily placed under trusteeship, the two categories Stettinius had already mentioned, plus territories formerly held as mandates under the League of Nations. Stettinius and Roosevelt assured Churchill that placing specific territories in trust would be the subject of future agreements. Specific territories would not be discussed at either the proposed meeting of the five great powers or the conference for establishing the United Nations. Since Britain held several League of Nations mandates, notably Tanganyika, the written statement extended trusteeship's potential reach to British possessions. British officials harbored hopes that they could remove Tanganyika and their other mandates even from the limited supervision of the League of Nations. Nevertheless, Churchill accepted the United States statement.[54]

Commentators see real significance in the exchange at Yalta. Critics of Roosevelt and U.S. policies toward dependent peoples see in the Yalta discussions a failure to extend the concept of trusteeship to all colonial areas and a retreat from the principles of the Atlantic Charter.[55] Churchill's critics see in his performance at Yalta a failure to block international interference in the British mandates and to smother the notion of trusteeship.[56]

The agreement at Yalta for the five members of the proposed Security Council to discuss trusteeship before the United Nations organizing conference was a compromise. If the decision to limit the extent of trusteeship was an American retreat, the retreat started before the Yalta conference, when the State Department under Hull began converting the Atlantic Charter principles into policies. It is unlikely that most U.S. officials, including Roosevelt, saw the Yalta discussion as a retreat. They saw it as a pragmatic attempt to achieve the possible, to move forward on trusteeship without offending their British allies. To Roosevelt, the Atlantic Charter represented a lofty objective that might not be achieved in the short term. He believed one could adhere to the Atlantic Charter principles and pursue limited improvements in the meantime.

Perhaps Churchill dropped the ball at Yalta. Perhaps he did not grasp the significance of the United States written statement about trusteeship. Churchill knew that the U.S. was committed to changes in the colonial empires. What changes, and when they might occur, were not clear. Churchill realized the U.S. thought that changes were coming. He also realized that Britain had become the junior partner in the Anglo-American alliance and that the alliance had grown to include Russia, China, and others. In the conferences up to and including Yalta, Roosevelt discussed trusteeship and related matters with the other major allies, particularly Russia, before raising them with Churchill. With Roosevelt and Stalin in the room at Yalta, Churchill was outnumbered on colonial issues. After having stated the hard line British position, it is not surprising that Churchill accepted Stettinius's reassurances.

After the Yalta conference a committee comprised of representatives of the Departments of State, Interior, Navy, and War took up the State Department's proposals for trusteeship. The Department of the Interior was involved because it was responsible for United States possessions, Puerto Rico, for example. The bulk of the State Department's proposals caused no problems. Disagreement centered on the War Department's plans for the Pacific Islands. Even before the Yalta conference, Secretary of War Stimson urged that discussion of trusteeship be delayed indefinitely lest it interfere with the United States unfettered control of the islands captured from the Japanese. State Department officials argued that the U.S. had agreed to discuss trusteeship with its allies and could not enter the upcoming United Nations conference without formulating a proposal. The State Department obtained Roosevelt's approval of its overall approach combined with a commitment to meet with the three departments to reach a final decision. There the issue rested when Roosevelt died on April 12, 1945.[57]

Britain and a Postwar International Organization

The British government did not begin serious planning for a postwar international organization until mid–1943. Churchill's preferred future had the globe divided into regions with one of the great powers predominant in each and he resisted planning for anything else. Eden was skeptical of an international organization. His goal was to forge an Anglo-American alliance, which he saw as the best guarantor of peace and of British interests. Eden concluded that an international organization was the best means to draw the United States into an alliance and to avoid its withdrawal into its prewar isolationism. Eden thought that the British would have to accept whatever the United States proposed unless they had their own plans for an international organization. Churchill realized that the United States would not accept a regional arrangement. He acquiesced to the Foreign Office's recommendation that Britain begin planning for a postwar international organization.[58]

Churchill had a hard time taking an international organization seriously. In August 1944, Churchill and his cabinet met to discuss instructions for the British delegates to the Dumbarton Oaks conference. After twenty-five minutes of less-than-serious discussion, Churchill ended the conversation by saying, "There now, in twenty-five minutes, we've settled the future of the world. Who can say that we aren't efficient?"[59]

The British included trusteeship in their plans for an international organization with great reluctance. The Colonial Office opposed an international organization that played any role regarding dependent territories. The Colonial Office wanted to dismantle the mandates administered by the League of Nations. The office received support from an unexpected source. Ernest Bevin, Labour Party leader and minister of labor, advocated allowing mandatory powers to petition for terminating a mandate and assuming full sovereignty over a dependent area. During the war, the Colonial Office devoted time and energy to devising alternative schemes for control and development of the colonies. The Foreign Office was also concerned that trusteeship posed risks to continued British control of the colonies. It thought that the United States would insist on some form of trusteeship. To secure an American alliance and American financial aid, however, the Foreign Office was willing to allow an international organization a role regarding dependent territories. Colonial Secretary Oliver Stanley accepted that continued resistance to trusteeship was foolish. It would only serve to put the issue in the hands of all the delegations to the San Francisco conference. Stanley concluded that opening discussion in this "motley assembly" would be hazardous in the extreme. The final British position heading to San Francisco was that Britain would accept the concept of trusteeship. An international organization might be empowered to collect reports about colonial territories, but not to conduct investigations or receive petitions. Britain would not accept any erosion of its right to administer and exercise sovereignty over its colonies. Under no circumstances would Britain voluntarily place its colonies in trusteeship.[60]

Churchill's interchange with Roosevelt and Stettinius at Yalta regarding trusteeship represented one step in Britain's movement towards the U.S. position, but not the last step. After Yalta, Churchill asserted that Britain was not committed to continuation of the mandate system and that whatever was agreed at Yalta did not foreclose different agreements in the future. The cabinet committee responsible for postwar planning contemplated rejection of the Yalta agreement that colonial powers could voluntarily place their territories in trusts. The fear was that the United States would press Britain to do so.[61]

U.S. Policy on Africa

While State Department officials were designing the postwar world for colonial territories, they paid little attention to Britain's African colonies. The State Department officials planning for a postwar international organization assumed that the European colonial powers would retain control of their African colonies after the war. The colonial powers would, nevertheless, have to pledge adherence to certain principles, similar to those in the Atlantic Charter. In the view of Sumner Welles and others, however, Africa's lack of political and economic development meant that most African colonies would move slowly towards independence. Welles observed that political progress would be slow because "negroes are in the lowest rank of human beings."[62]

The only official public statement about Africa's future was Henry Villard's article

"American Relations with Africa" in the *Department of State Bulletin* in August 1943. Villard was as close to an African expert as the department had and senior British officials viewed him favorably. The following year, he became head of a newly organized African Division within State. In his article, Villard expressed the hope that equality of opportunity in trade would be found after the war in all African colonies. He noted that African conditions affected the security of the Western Hemisphere, therefore the United States was concerned about sore spots and frictions in colonial areas. The U.S. had no interest in controlling territory in Africa. That did not mean, however, that Americans would listen to "extremists who advocate the instant liberation of all dependencies from external control." Chaos and confusion would result from casting inexperienced people adrift on uncertain political seas, Villard wrote. The Anglo-Saxon democracies agreed that self-government was the correct goal. Nevertheless, economic progress must precede political independence, and very few Africans had expressed a desire for self-government.[63]

The Office of Strategic Services (OSS), the U.S. wartime civilian intelligence agency, gave nationalist groups, that is, anti–British, pro-independence groups, more credit. Although the nationalists' numbers were small, they had the potential to mobilize the masses against the British, their common oppressor, OSS predicted. Nationalist feelings were deeply rooted in British West Africa in particular, and their influence was likely to grow. The war, possible links with labor unions, the growing number of educated Africans, and shifts in world opinion were all likely to strengthen nationalist groups. Nationalist sentiments were strong enough that colonial officials felt compelled to make concessions whenever possible. OSS questioned Britain's ability to deal effectively with the nationalists. It doubted Parliament's and the Colonial Office's ability to carry out a program of economic development. It thought that self-government could well remain only a well-intentioned promise.[64]

U.S. Involvement in India

While British colonies were largely a theoretical concern for the Roosevelt administration, it did become involved in the political future of one British possession, India. By the beginning of the war, India had a large, militant pro-independence movement that threatened to withhold its support for the British war effort. Roosevelt's view was that the British should make a clear, firm commitment to grant India a measure of self-government, if only to secure Indian cooperation against the Japanese armies. Roosevelt shared his views with Churchill on several occasions. After Churchill rejected them, Roosevelt employed third parties to prod Churchill on the subject. In 1942 and 1943, Roosevelt dispatched two personal representatives to India: Louis Johnson, a West Virginia politician and former assistant secretary of war, and then William Phillips, a career diplomat.

The Johnson and Phillips missions followed similar trajectories. Both inserted themselves into exchanges between the Indian Congress, the principal nationalist organization, and senior British officials. Johnson became an active player in negotiations between Congress and Sir Stafford Cripps, dispatched by the British government to seek an accommodation with the Indian nationalists. Neither Johnson nor Phillips could bridge the differences between the British and the Indians. Both emissaries blamed British officials, especially Lord Linlithgow, the viceroy. Johnson thought that the Churchill government intended the Cripps mission to fail and that Linlithgow had cooperated in assuring its failure. Neither emissary secured meaningful support from Washington. Career civil servants in the State

Department favored a larger U.S. role in moving India towards independence, but Welles, Hull, and, most importantly, Roosevelt were anxious not to alienate their principal ally. Suggestions that the United States broker discussions between Congress and the British, for example, fell on deaf ears. Roosevelt told Secretary of Interior Harold Ickes, who favored a more aggressive U.S. stance on Indian independence, that he would be playing with fire if the British told him to mind his own business. Both Johnson and Phillips took pains to communicate to the Indian public that the United States favored self-determination after the war. When one of Phillips's letters, critical of the British, leaked to the American press, the British protested. The Roosevelt administration ignored their complaints.[65]

American opinion had some impact on the British in India. Churchill and his cabinet developed a plan for a Defense of India Council, to include Indian as well as British officials, in part to assuage U.S. concerns. Many in India believed that the Cripps mission was intended to deflect American criticisms of British policy. Nonetheless, Churchill was determined not to yield to the nationalists. Roosevelt was unwilling to go beyond offering advice in private and announcing in public the country's long-term commitment to self-determination.[66]

The United States and the Philippines

At the beginning of World War II, the United States and Roosevelt knew something about moving a colony to independence. In 1934, Congress passed and Roosevelt signed the Tydings-McDuffie Act, which granted the Philippines independence in ten years. Roosevelt and other U.S. officials were fond of pointing to the Philippines as a model for Britain and the other colonial powers to follow in divesting themselves of colonial possessions.

The United States gained possession of the Philippines as a result of the Spanish-American War of 1898. In 1896, Filipino nationalists, eventually led by Emilio Aguinaldo, rebelled against their Spanish rulers, but met defeat. Aguinaldo then found refuge in Hong Kong. After the U.S. Navy destroyed the Spanish fleet in Manila Bay in 1898, American officials helped Aguinaldo return from exile. The nature of any understanding between Aguinaldo and U.S. officials remains controversial. Aguinaldo claimed that the United States promised independence for the Philippines. U.S. forces and Filipino nationalist forces waged parallel campaigns against Spanish troops. Once the Spanish were defeated and Manila was in U.S. hands, fighting broke out between the United States Army and Aguinaldo's forces. After considerable indecision and vacillation, the McKinley administration in Washington decided to annex the Philippines. The U.S. forces suppressed the Filipino nationalist forces in three years of brutal fighting.

The Schurman commission, dispatched by President McKinley to investigate conditions in the Philippines, recommended limited self-government. The commission told McKinley that the United States could not withdraw from the Philippines. The Filipinos were not prepared for independence and could not maintain it. The United States should allow the Philippines limited autonomy under United States rule, provide civil liberties, and promote efficient administration. The commission urged that the United States manage Philippine finances to benefit Filipinos, and that the islands become financially self-sufficient.

To implement the Schurman recommendations, Congress passed the Cooper Act in 1902. The act provided for a bicameral legislature for the Philippines, an elected lower house with a Filipino majority and an upper house appointed by the American president, subject to congressional approval. An American governor, appointed by the president, would retain veto power over legislative acts. The Philippines would have two resident commissioners who could speak in the United States House of Representatives, but not vote. The governor would appoint one representative and the Philippine assembly the other.

A year earlier, the Supreme Court clarified the constitutional relationship of the Philippines and the United States. In the so-called Insular cases, the court ruled that certain fundamental rights such as those guaranteed in the Bill of Rights applied to the Philippines and Puerto Rico. The rest of the constitution did not apply unless the Congress passed legislation to that effect.

The United States reoriented the Philippine economy towards itself. The U.S. purchased from the Vatican the Catholic Church's extensive land holdings in the Philippines and distributed them in ways that benefited the wealthiest and best educated Filipinos. The Payne-Aldrich Act (1909) and the Underwood-Simmons Act (1913) established virtually free trade between the Philippines and the United States. Subsequently, more land was devoted to export crops, particularly sugar and tobacco, and less to food. The share of Philippines exports that went to the United States grew, from 32 percent of total exports in 1908 to 73 percent in 1926. Imports from the United States came to dominate the Philippine market. In 1908, imports from the United States accounted for 17 percent of total imports, rising to 60 percent in 1926.

The initial American political strategy within the Philippines was an alliance with some of the wealthiest and best-educated Filipinos. William Howard Taft, a member of a second Philippine commission established by McKinley and later the first civilian U.S. governor, settled on what he called a policy of attraction. He helped educated and wealthy Filipinos organize a political party, the Federalista Party, in 1901. The party's platform called for Philippine statehood within the United States after a period of development and education. Taft ensured that nearly all government posts open to Filipinos went to Federalista Party members. He banned all advocacy of independence and all parties other than the Federalista Party.

Independence remained a powerful lure, however. In 1905, the Federalista Party dissolved itself and reorganized as the Progesista Party, now advocating independence from the United States. In 1906, the governor lifted the ban on political parties in preparation for the first elections for the Philippine lower house scheduled for the following year. Although suffrage was limited to landowners, taxpayers, and the literate, roughly 3 percent of the population, the Progesista Party's embrace of independence was not sufficient to overcome its obvious connections to the United States. A new pro-independence party, the Nacionalista Party, organized by two lawyers, Manuel Quezon and Sergio Osmena, swept the field, winning fifty-eight of the eighty seats in the lower house. The Nacionalista Party remained the dominant Filipino party until after World War II.

Conquest and control of the Philippines were policies identified with the Republican Party. The Democrats took different positions. In 1910, after the Democrats gained control of the House of Representatives, a Democratic congressman, William Jones of Virginia, introduced legislation that would have granted the Philippines immediate autonomy and complete independence in 1921. The United States would retain control of naval stations and other facilities. Nevertheless, the full House never considered the legislation. Accepting the Democratic nomination for president for the 1912 election, Woodrow Wilson contended that the United States did not own the Philippines. It was merely holding the islands in trust for its inhabitants. Wilson hinted in other speeches that he contemplated early independence for the Philippines.

In 1916, the political aims of the Nacionalista Party and the Democratic Party converged to move the Philippines closer to independence. Quezon, who was one of the Philippine resident commissioners in Washington, and the Nacionalista Party felt threatened by the rise of a new pro-independence party linked to Aguinaldo. Although most Nacionalista leaders were content with continued U.S. rule in the short term, they could not afford to be seen as less than vigorous in their quest for independence. Quezon's favored alternative was a twenty-year timetable for independence. Congressional Democrats preferred more immediate action. President Wilson met with Quezon and agreed to support legislation that would grant the Philippines independence at an unspecified date. Although Senator James Clarke, a Democrat from Arkansas, introduced legislation calling for independence within four years, the Congress passed and Wilson signed legislation, the Jones Act, which committed the United States to granting independence at an unspecified future date when the Philippines had a stable government. *The New York Times* published reports that all significant Filipino political parties opposed the Clarke proposal. Wilson submitted legislation calling for independence for the Philippines, but only in 1920, after the Democrats had lost that year's election and he was about to leave office.[67]

The Jones Act combined with the actions of Wilson's appointee as governor, Francis Harrison, to shift political power to Filipinos. Under the Jones Act, most seats in both the upper and lower houses of the Philippines became elective. The Jones Act allowed the Philippine assembly to override the governor's veto, although the U.S. president could reverse the assembly's action. Harrison rarely used his veto power and conceded expanded powers to the assembly. Harrison reduced the number of Americans in Philippine government positions from three thousand at his arrival in 1913 to six hundred at his departure eight years later. He also increased the number of Filipinos in government positions to over thirteen thousand.[68]

Independence for the Philippines

By 1930, four factors had combined to put Philippine independence back on the U.S. political agenda. Mainstream Republicans remained opposed to independence, while Democrats retained their traditional pro–independence position. After ten years of solid Republican rule, however, the 1930 congressional elections put the Democrats in control of the House and a coalition of Democrats and progressive Republicans in effective control of the Senate. The onset of the Great Depression motivated the American Federation of Labor and other groups to press for limits on immigration from the Philippines. One goal was substituting white farm workers for Mexicans and Filipinos on California farms. Farm groups, particularly sugar producers and American investors in Cuban sugar, sought to limit competition from Filipino agricultural products. In a time of increasing international tension in Asia, the Philippines also appeared vulnerable, a possession of limited value that the United States could not easily defend. To many Americans, the Philippines were not worth the risk of U.S. involvement in another war.[69]

Secretary of State Henry Stimson, a former governor of the Philippines, led the Hoover administration's opposition to independence. Stimson argued that the Filipino people were unprepared for independence. Either anarchy or oligarchy would follow independence. A small class of Filipinos would rule the rest. An independent Philippines would be unable to protect herself from her larger Asian neighbors and a United States withdrawal would create a vacuum and promote further unrest in Asia. A Philippines controlled by the United States could, on the other hand, serve to promote U.S. trade with Asia, which had grown significantly during the 1920s, Stimson argued.[70]

The Hoover administration lacked the votes to block an independence measure. In 1932, Congress passed the Hare-Hawes-Cutting Act, which granted the Philippines independence after ten years in exchange for retention of certain U.S. military and naval bases. The act limited Filipino migration to the United States and curtailed Filipino access to U.S. markets. Hoover vetoed the bill, but the Congress overrode his veto.

The measure needed the approval of the Philippines Assembly. Some Filipino leaders thought that Hare-Hawes-Cutting was the best the Philippines could do, although the Congress had passed it for what were, it seemed to many Filipinos, the wrong reasons. Quezon took a harder line. He opposed the limitations of immigration, the closing of United States markets, and the continued U.S. military presence. At his urging, the Philippine assembly rejected the measure.

The Philippines Assembly's vote put the issue into the lap of the incoming Roosevelt administration. Candidate Roosevelt supported independence for the Philippines, but when Quezon attempted to negotiate with Roosevelt, he found the president non-committal. Roosevelt warned Quezon that the labor and producer groups favoring independence were strong and that the Philippines might get its independence immediately if he continued to press for more favorable trade and immigration provisions. Roosevelt was content to have Quezon negotiate the best deal he could get from Congress. Later, in a meeting with congressional leaders about Philippines legislation, Roosevelt allegedly said, "Let's get rid of the Philippines — that's the most important thing. Let's be frank about it."[71]

The bill that finally gained the approval of Congress and the Philippines Assembly, the Tydings-McDuffie Act, was broadly similar to Hare-Hawes-Cutting. It did not, however, mention military bases and specified that the United States and the Philippines would negotiate the fate of the U.S. naval bases in the Philippines. Tydings-McDuffie created a unicameral Philippines assembly and an elected president with extensive veto powers. A United States high commissioner would help manage the transition to independence. The bill extended voting rights to men and women over twenty-one years, but property and language restrictions limited the electorate to roughly 14 percent of the Philippine population.[72]

When Roosevelt submitted Tydings-McDuffie to Congress, his accompanying statement said that he was confident that any imperfections or inequalities in the bill could be corrected after proper hearings and in fairness to both peoples. In 1937, Roosevelt and Quezon took advantage one of the bill's provisions to appoint a joint United States-Philippines commission to study trade relations between the two countries. After extensive hearings, the commission recommended phasing in full tariffs over a fifteen-year period to allow the Philippine economy to adjust gradually. The economic groups that had sought independence in the first place were still strong, however, and the State Department opposed trade preferences for the Philippines. Congress eventually passed a watered-down version of the commission's recommendations, which Quezon thought inadequate.

By April 1945, the United States was clearly the senior partner in the Anglo-American alliance. U.S. wealth prevailed over Britain's war-induced poverty. Nevertheless, the policies towards colonial territories drafted by the State Department did not call for the immediate end of the British empire. In the Atlantic Charter, Roosevelt had positioned the United States in opposition to colonies and in favor of eventual self-government. Despite the dramatic language of the Atlantic Charter, however, Roosevelt's State Department produced proposals that tolerated colonial possessions. They contemplated continuation of British colonial rule for some time, particularly in Africa. Roosevelt put his anti-colonial ideas into action by meddling in Anglo-Indian affairs, but stopped short of an open break with the British. U.S. treatment of its colony in the Philippines suggested that the United States, and Roosevelt, favored political independence for colonies, but anticipated continued military and economic dominance over newly independent states by their former occupiers.

Churchill, Britain, and Empire, 1941–1945: Hands Off the British Empire

Winston Churchill was a fervent supporter of the British empire and of an American alliance. During World War II, Churchill and his government worried about how Britain's alliance with the United States would affect its colonial empire. Neither Churchill nor his ministers had a credible strategy for reconciling the Anglo-American alliance with preservation of Britain's colonies, but they cherished hopes that they could do so. Confronted with the Americans' professed support for colonial independence, the Churchill government felt compelled to compete. It issued its own pronouncements heralding political change in the colonies, although it was far from sure how political change should proceed.

During the war, significant developments also took place in the Colonial Office's thinking and in colonial practice in Africa. Within the Colonial Office, civil servants considered political changes in the African colonies. In the colonies, reform-minded governors set about strengthening British rule by co-opting educated Africans into government institutions.

Churchill's American Alliance

An Anglo-American alliance was central to Churchill's strategic thinking. Churchill believed Britain could not defeat Germany and Italy without the U.S. assistance. Russian assistance might be necessary, but a Russian alliance would be safe for Britain only if the United States was on its side. A partnership with the United States after the war might also allow Britain to survive as a world power as well as help maintain world peace. Courting the United States and Roosevelt, therefore, became one of Churchill's highest priorities once he replaced Chamberlain as prime minister. For Churchill, it was a blessing that Japan attacked the United States and brought it into the war. He wrote to Eden, his foreign secretary: "Greater good fortune has rarely happened to the British empire than this event which ... may lead, through the merciless crushing of Japan, to a new relationship of immense benefit to the English-speaking countries and to the whole world."[1]

Churchill was aware that Great Britain and the United States were rivals of long standing, particularly in trade and finance. He realized that Anglo-American relations since the end of World War I had often been frosty, even tense. He knew that many Americans resented and feared Great Britain and that anti–British sentiments played well with many U.S. voters. He also knew that the United States was apt to claim a larger place in the world for itself after the war, even at the expense of Great Britain. Regardless, Churchill made cooperation with the United States the keystone of his wartime administration. He put aside all the obvious reasons to mistrust the United States and concentrated on winning the war alongside the U.S.

How Churchill expected to reconcile his alliance with the United States, an open critic of European empires and a country intent on extending its power, with his intent to preserve the British empire is not clear. It is not clear, in fact, that Churchill had a long-term strategy for reconciling the two. During the war, Churchill relied on bluster. In speeches, such as the speech to the House of Commons after the Atlantic Charter conference and the speech at Mansion House in November 1942, and in various meetings with Roosevelt and other U.S. officials, Churchill denounced in vivid language any suggestion that Britain should change its approach to its empire. To his colleagues in government, Churchill's approach was the same. To Oliver Stanley, colonial secretary, about to depart for a visit to Washington in December 1944, Churchill wrote: "There must be no question of our being hustled or seduced into declaration affecting British sovereignty in any of the Dominions or Colonies. Pray remember my declaration against liquidating the British empire ... 'Hands off the British empire' is our maxim and it must not be weakened or smirched to please sob-stuff merchants at home or foreigners of any hue."[2]

Among the ministers and officials in Churchill's government were some less willing than Churchill to rely on the United States. Leopold Amery, secretary of state for India and a staunch supporter of imperial preference, was outspoken. He believed that defeating Hitler was only a means to preserving the empire. Replacing Hitler with Stalin, Chaing Kai Shek, or even an American president would be no consolation if, in the process, Britain lost its power and influence, Amery observed. Amery feared U.S. economic aims and policies. He said that he would prefer Hitler's "New Order" to Cordell Hull's "Free Trade." Lord Linlithgow, viceroy in India, doubted that compromising with the United States would buy off the ill feeling, misunderstanding, and prejudice found there. Sir R.J. Campbell, in the Washington embassy, thought that U.S. involvement in the colonies would be a combination of Henry Wallace uplift and the National Association of Manufacturers export drive and would harm areas that would be forced to run before they could walk.[3]

Other members of Churchill's coalition government, notably from the Labour Party, were more inclined towards change in the colonies, especially social and economic development. Before Churchill told the Commons that the Atlantic Charter did not apply to the British empire, Clement Attlee, Labour Party leader and lord privy seal, told an audience of West African students in London that the charter applied to peoples throughout the world. Arthur Creech Jones was a Labour Party spokesperson on colonial issues and parliamentary private secretary to Ernest Bevin, minister of labor in the Churchill government. He was suspicious of U.S. involvement in the colonies and advocated as much economic and social development as possible before self-government.[4]

Churchill's embrace of the United States and his pronouncements about preserving the empire made Foreign Secretary Eden and officials in the Foreign Office uneasy. Seeing the potential contradictions, they searched for ways to maintain an alliance with the United States without sacrificing British options. At times, this looked like shady dealing. In the economic and trade negotiations with the United States, the Foreign Office favored agreeing to whatever the U.S. wanted with the expectation, Keynes thought, that Britain would not have to honor its pledges. In 1945, a senior Foreign Office official, Richard Law, described the Atlantic Charter as a "dodge to get the United States a little further into the war." At other times, the Foreign Office argued for generous readings of American pronouncements. Sir Alexander Cadogan argued that when U.S. officials used the term "independence," they meant much the same thing as when British officials referred to "self-government." Eden saw in Roosevelt's warnings during his 1945 State of the Union address on the dangers of perfectionism in the context of the Atlantic Charter a sign that the U.S. president could be realistic on the subject of colonies.[5]

Eden and the Foreign Office found American statements on colonies irritating because they made cooperation between Britain and the United States more difficult. After Roosevelt lectured Eden that the British should give up Hong Kong as a gesture of goodwill, Eden commented to Harry Hopkins that he had never heard Roosevelt propose any such gestures by the United States. Foreign Office officials thought they could work with the Roosevelt administration and with the State Department. What worried them more was the Congress and American public opinion. During the Lend-Lease negotiations, Richard Law warned Churchill: "We are dealing now with the American government, who are our friends. They have made us an offer. Perhaps it is not a very fair offer. But it is difficult to conceive of a better offer, or one that imposes a lesser burden on us.... If we reject this offer; we are going to have to deal direct with Congress as we had to in 1923. Congress contains many of our enemies — we have enemies in the United States."[6]

Beginning in December 1942, Law headed a committee composed of senior officials from the Foreign Office, the Colonial Office, and other departments. The committee was to study American public opinion about the British empire. It was to recommend ways to encourage positive views of the empire in the United States and to secure recognition that the empire was a suitable partner for the United States in world affairs. Officials worried about attacks on the British empire in the American press and about indications that Americans thought that the British empire's day had passed. The goal was to steer "this great unwieldy barge, the United States of America, into the right harbor," to use the power of the United States to preserve the commonwealth and the empire. The committee concluded that American public opinion was more likely to favor a withdrawal from world affairs rather than an American imperialism that would displace British control of its colonies. Since British officials saw U.S. "isolationism" after World War I as a disaster and were counting on continued American support once the Axis powers were defeated, the committee thought it was preferable to encourage U.S. involvement in world affairs than to try to shut it out.[7]

Colonial Policy

Despite diverse views on the U.S. involvement with the colonies in the Churchill government, officials agreed on basic points. Continued British control of the colonies was critical. Only Britain could protect and develop the colonies properly. Britain must resist U.S. notions of joint trusteeship. Expanded international oversight of either trust territories or other dependent territories was equally unpalatable. Furthermore, "independence" was not the right way to describe the desired end state for colonies. It did not do justice to British notions of the empire and commonwealth as an association of self-governing states. It would lead to a multiplication of small national sovereignties, many incapable of standing on their own. Definite timetables for political progress were foolish. Who could predict when colonies would be ready for more autonomy? Colonies came in all shapes and sizes. A single approach to their political, economic, and social development was impracticable. It would be many generations before many colonies would be ready for self-government. During 1942 and 1943, a cabinet committee composed of Eden, Attlee, Stanley, and Cranborne considered the U.S. proposal for a declaration on national independence and settled on these very points.[8]

The first three colonial secretaries in Churchill's government, Lord Lloyd (May 1940–February 1941), Lord Moyne (February 1941–February 1942), and Viscount Cranborne (February 1942–November 22, 1942), the future Lord Salisbury, served for brief periods. Lloyd, who died in office, and Moyne served as the government's leader in the House of Lords. All three were die-hard Conservatives and minor figures within the government. Discomfort with the prospect of change characterized their ideas. Lord Moyne thought that terms like "democracy" and "self-governing institutions" should be used cautiously in relation to colonies. The goal, he thought, was to mold the institutions of each colony to suit its conditions and to fit within an imperial framework. Lord Cranborne thought that most African colonies would not be ready for complete independence for centuries. He wondered whether Britain ought to announce that it sought permanent control of the colonies rather than proclaiming self-government as the goal. If colonial subjects thought that the British intended to leave, they would always be impatient to move on to the next stage of political development. Cranborne thought that colonial peoples would cooperate in training and development programs if they thought the British were not prepared to leave.[9]

Oliver Stanley, colonial secretary from November 1942 until the end of the Churchill government in 1945, was a more influential figure, but nearly as conservative. He was wary of U.S. involvement. In 1943, he told an Oxford audience that the first principle was that administration of the colonies must remain in British hands. He was, he said, more interested in what Britain thought of the empire than what the United States thought. Irritated at what he saw as Foreign Office pandering to the United States, Stanley once wrote that he supposed the Foreign Office would be horrified at the thought of a colonial policy designed to benefit the colonies rather than appease the United States.[10]

Besides concerns about U.S. views of the colonies, politicians and civil servants in the wartime Churchill government shared a sense that Britain's colonies needed reform. The old ways were no longer acceptable. Some thought that Britain had no colonial policy at all, no clear idea of how it might deal with the inhabitants of its overseas possessions after the war. Britain needed something better to justify continued control and to persuade the United States that the British empire had a place in the postwar world. In 1940, those in charge of British propaganda called for a statement of postwar aims that would "sustain the spiritual motives of our own people, appeal to our supporters abroad (especially America), and counter the German conception of the new order." Change was in the air. No one could take for granted that the empire of the 1950s would look like the empire of the 1930s. A few believed that, after the war, Africans were unlikely to accept readily the political, social, and economic conditions common in the 1920s and 1930s. More Africans were obtaining European educations. They would want a larger role in the colonies' futures.[11]

A government needed to make a pronouncement. With the Atlantic Charter, the United States had planted its flag on the moral high ground. Britain needed something comparable, a public statement that would justify and explain continued British control of the colonies.

Churchill intended his speech to the House of Commons in the wake of the Atlantic

Charter to be such a statement, but it fell short. With the support of the War Cabinet, Churchill claimed that Britain did not need the Atlantic Charter for its colonies. It had already dealt with the issue of political change in India and Burma and, for the other colonies, had made complete, unambiguous declarations related to each colony's declarations. Even some long-time supporters of empire thought Churchill had struck the wrong note. Lord Lugard, a former governor of Nigeria, called the speech "unfortunate." More telling to those within in the government, the Colonial Office was hard pressed to produce such declarations. Once the office managed to compile a list of policy declarations by previous colonial secretaries, it was obvious Britain could not use them to bolster its position. Harold Macmillan, then a junior minister in the Colonial Office, wrote: "I do not think the PM can have realized the true nakedness of the land when he made the statement of September 9, 1941—the declarations are not complete in themselves, nor are they free from ambiguity. They are scrappy, obscure, and jejune—the PM must have written the declaration on his own."[12]

In a speech to the Commons in June 1942, Macmillan raised a new banner, "partnership." Macmillan argued that the future lay with larger organizations, not with small countries. Links between the colonies and Britain needed to be permanent. The links needed to be partnerships, which would produce understanding and friendship. Individual colonies might have particular needs and conditions and might exercise different levels of local responsibility, but the empire as a whole must deal with the most important issues, such as trade, finance, defense, and transportation. Some British officials thought "partnership" preferable to "trusteeship," an old term that described a paternalistic relationship. For a time, there might be junior and senior partners, but partners could also become equals.[13]

After the Anglo-American exchanges about a joint declaration on national independence failed to produce anything acceptable, Colonial Secretary Stanley decided to issue his own statement. After consulting with Eden and Churchill, Stanley told the Commons in July 1943 that Britain had already announced that the purpose of its colonial administration was to guide colonial peoples to self-government. Britain had pledged to build up social and economic institutions in the colonies and develop their natural resources. Like Churchill, Stanley portrayed these assertions as old news. Stanley said there was no need for him to make such proclamations, since Britain had done so. Doing so would be just one more speech and "it is deeds that count." He went on to discuss the need for social and economic development. He also argued against international oversight of colonies and in favor of colonial development through regional commissions.[14]

In using the term "self-government," Stanley was deliberately vague and ambiguous. "Self-government" could mean local self-government—control of a province, a region or a town by the inhabitants. Self-government could refer to a situation where the inhabitants of a colony controlled most, but not all, aspects of government. Finance, defense, and foreign affairs might remain the preserve of the colonial power. "Self-government" could also be synonymous with "independence." U.S. officials often used the term in this way. Before Stanley's speech, a senior Colonial Office civil servant pointed out that taking advantage of the term's ambiguity would be dishonest and unwise. Another wrote that making a distinction between self-government and independence would arouse suspicions in the United States. Stanley favored dominion status, meaning independence within the commonwealth, for only the larger colonies, but he saw no need to be clear and precise.[15]

None of the British statements created a counterweight to the notion of self-determination embodied in the Atlantic Charter. Public reaction in the United States and Britain was meager and lukewarm to the various British statements. Even knowledgeable insiders thought them insufficient. After Stanley's July 1943 speech, Lord Hailey, a long-time official in India and senior advisor to the Colonial Office during the war, urged Stanley to make a more detailed statement, committing Britain to granting responsible self-government to its African colonies. Before the war, Hailey had toured Africa and compiled a compendium of information about colonial rule, published as "An African Survey." Hailey thought that Africans would not cooperate with Britain without such a statement. Stanley disagreed.[16]

Contemplating Political Change in Africa

Interest in a different approach to the colonies, particularly African colonies, began to develop before the war. Malcolm MacDonald, colonial secretary from May 1938 until the fall of the Chamberlain government in May 1940, was a key figure. MacDonald was the son of former Prime Minister Ramsay MacDonald and sat in the coalition governments of the 1930s as a member of the breakaway National Labour Party. MacDonald had served as colonial secretary briefly before. He came into office in 1938 believing that attitudes among his civil servants and among colonial governors were out of date. Once the war began, he concluded that it would produce increased demands by Africans for political change. He thought that the government needed to be prepared with carefully thought-out plans.[17]

MacDonald believed that the ultimate aim of Britain's policy in its African colonies was self-government within the commonwealth. At an Oxford summer school for colonial officials in 1938, MacDonald explained that the spread of freedom in British possessions might be slow. Ultimately even the most backward colonies would become self-supporting and self-reliant members of the commonwealth, however. Each colony might follow a different path and the process might take generations, even centuries, but the long-term aim was the same.[18]

In October 1939, MacDonald convened a meeting of senior civil servants and advisers at the Carlton House hotel in London to discuss how Britain should develop institutions for self-government in its African colonies. The Carlton House meeting began an internal debate that was to consume considerable Colonial Office time and effort during and after the war. In the background was the question of what self-government meant, what powers a self-governing colony would possess. More to the fore were several inter-related questions: Should a self-governing colony have political institutions on the Westminster model, that is, institutions resembling Britain's own? This question included considerations of who had the right to vote. How should a colony move from its current institutions to self-governing institutions? What place, if any, would the political structures created for colonial rule have in the progression to self-government? What role would educated Africans have, both in a self-governing colony and in the movement towards self-government?[19]

During the war years, this was a discussion of theory, not of immediate action or planning. Nearly everyone involved assumed that self-government for African colonies was a distant prospect. It would not happen for decades, generations, or centuries. Because the changes involved would be evolutionary, the big decisions were still many years away. Nevertheless, Britain needed to begin considering how to proceed. Mistakes made at the beginning of the process could come back to haunt the government.

Political change was one of many topics the Colonial Office thought needed a new look. In 1941, Lord Hailey chaired a committee of four senior Colonial Office officials charged with considering postwar reconstruction in the colonies. Their agenda contained fifty items. Only two were overtly political: one on "constitutional advance" and another on "ultimate constitutional objectives."[20]

Establishing Westminster-style governments in African colonies provoked considerable skepticism, particularly among long-time colonial officials. At the Carlton House meeting, both Lord Lugard and Lord Hailey voiced doubts. Imagining a full-blown alternative to the Westminster model was difficult, however. Modifications, like indirect elections, had a certain appeal. Allowing Africans to elect members of a provincial or regional council and having the regional council elect members of a central legislature seemed a likely way to build on existing institutions, to control or limit popular movements, and to give a larger role to cooperative, reliable Africans.[21]

Not everyone agreed. Some thought that British ideas and institutions would prevail. The political institutions the British had created to rule the colonies might educate Africans in the workings of government, but the political institutions of a self-governing colony were likely to look like Britain's institutions. Trying to preserve African colonies as something like museum exhibits would be a mistake, some observed.[22]

To rule African colonies, the British relied on a small staff of British political officials — a governor and a small staff at headquarters with subordinate officials in the provinces, often styled "residents," and, below them, in districts, "district officers," or "district commissioners." District officers supervised local units, usually termed "native authorities" or "native administrations." Heading a native administration was an African official, loosely categorized as a "chief." Some native administrations featured a council to govern along with the chief or to advise the chief. Before World War I, the British, notably Sir Frederick Lugard (later Lord Lugard) in Nigeria, realized that Africans who would have had some claim to political power before the British conquest were more likely to be successful heads of native administrations. They would be more likely to command respect and obedience from the local population than someone whose only claim to power was a willingness to collaborate with the British. Therefore, the British set about preserving or recreating remnants of pre-conquest governments in the form of native administrations. The result was akin to a house constructed of recycled materials. The design was British, but bits and pieces of African institutions, some times large bits and pieces, were recognizable.

Native administrations represented basic government. They were responsible for maintaining law and order, adjudicating disputes, and collecting taxes. Some larger, wealthier, native administrations added other functions, like education or agricultural training. More often, such activities were the preserve of British government staff or non-governmental groups, like the Christian missions. Native administrations were authoritarian. Early in British rule, the government's principal strategy was to support the chiefs as they tried to maintain law and order. The British were more likely to dismiss a chief for failing to maintain order than they were for abusing other Africans or for stealing government funds. British officials at times attempted to rein in the most autocratic chiefs, perhaps by establishing a council of advisers. The native administrations of the early 1940s were far from democratic or popular institutions, however.

To someone in London thinking about launching long-term political change in Africa, the native administrations had a certain appeal. They worked. They maintained law and order. They collected taxes. The chiefs and other native administration officials seemed reliable collaborators. They held their positions because they were willing to cooperate with

British officials. Native administrations also seemed African, presumably familiar and accept-able to local people. It was tempting to consider native administrations as the starting point for constructing the political institutions of a self-governing colony and as a means to train Africans in government.

There were doubters. To some, "African" meant backward and inferior. British insti-tutions were surely the wave of the future. Even the conservative Lord Moyne doubted that native administrations could provide meaningful political advance. In mid–twentieth century Britain, public opinion increasingly held that government should be responsible for much more than maintaining law and order and collecting taxes. Governments built schools. They provided health and other public services. They encouraged economic growth. Native administrations hardly seemed capable of taking on new functions. They were like vintage cars: elaborate and dignified structures with little capacity for acceleration and strong ten-dencies to steer to the right, one official wrote. Native administrations were subordinate units in the colonial hierarchy and associated, in the minds of Africans, with the maintenance of British rule, some argued. Africans seeking political change would resist being steered towards them. They would seek a role in a colony's central government.[23]

Typically, a British colony had a rudimentary bicameral legislature consisting of two advisory councils, a legislative council, the lower house, and an executive council, the upper house. Both councils usually had an "official" majority; that is, British government officials filled a majority of the seats. The executive council included the heads of the principal gov-ernment departments and the governor's senior advisers. After 1925, the Gold Coast's exec-utive council included eight members, the governor, and seven senior British officials. The unofficial members of both councils were European representatives of business interests; Africans, appointed or elected on a limited franchise; and, in East and Central Africa, Euro-peans elected by their fellow settlers. The Gold Coast legislative council had thirty members: the governor as president, fifteen official members, and fourteen unofficial members. The unofficial members included nine Africans, six selected by a joint provincial council com-posed of African chiefs; three elected by voters in three towns, Accra, Cape Coast, and Sekondi. The governor normally retained extensive powers, including the power to veto legislation.

The principal alternative to promoting a different political role for the native admin-istrations was to enlarge African participation in the councils. The most common notion was to appoint more Africans to one or both. Hailey had a more complex idea. He thought that governors should appoint Africans as heads of government departments and have them serve in the executive council. He saw this not as a step towards representative government, but as a means to train selected Africans in the responsibilities of government. Otherwise, he thought they would develop into a permanent opposition.[24]

Educated Africans

A key tactic of British colonial rule in Africa before World War II was to minimize the role and influence of educated Africans. By 1900, Lugard and others concluded that unrest in India and Egypt was the work of the local people who had some European education. To avoid the same problems in the African colonies, the British sought other Africans as their principal collaborators, chiefs and other native administration officials. By the First World War, a few educated Africans sat in legislative and executive councils, particularly in West Africa. The British did not increase their number and British colonial governments in Africa were unenthusiastic about growth in the number of schools and pupils.

The British could exclude educated Africans from prominent political roles. Limiting the spread of education and the increase in educated Africans proved more difficult. The Christian missions were responsible for most schools in British colonial Africa. Colonial governments often sought to control them and limit their growth, but the missions had enough political influence in Britain to stymie most such efforts. Africans' acceptance of European education was mixed. Enough Africans embraced it and the opportunities for paid employment it offered that school enrollments in many areas grew rapidly. The colonial governments invested in schools as well, both schools it operated and schools run by the missions.

Government support of education reflected the view that improving Africans' lot was part of the colonial mission. It also reflected a contradiction embedded in the colonial situation. Government officials realized that limiting the number of educated Africans who gained paid employment in offices, schools, and the like would curtail their influence. It would undercut Africans' incentives to attend school or send their children to school. Nevertheless, the colonial governments could not function without educated Africans. Colonial governments paid Europeans far more than they paid Africans. They did not have the revenue needed to fill all, even most, government positions with Europeans. By 1939, the colonial governments were the biggest employers of educated Africans, as clerks, teachers, medical assistants, inspectors, and so on.

"Educated Africans" was a fuzzy concept. African lawyers, businessmen, and newspaper editors, especially in the coastal towns of West Africa, Freetown, Accra and Lagos were prime examples. Africans who had studied at universities in Britain or the United States, or Africans who had gained government employment on the strength of educational credentials certainly fell into the same category. Young Africans, usually men, with as little as a year or two of schooling and only limited English skills might also be included. The notion of "educated Africans" overlapped with another British bugaboo, the "detribalized" Africans, Africans who had moved from the countryside to towns and cities to work or to seek work. The British worried about such Africans partly because they had moved away from the control of the native administrations.

In British thinking about the African colonies' political future, chiefs and educated Africans were separate categories. Early in British rule, such was the case. Very few of the first men the British chose as chiefs had any European education. By 1939, the two categories overlapped. The British discovered that, all things being equal, an educated chief or native administration official, someone literate in English, was preferable to someone without any education. Inserting an educated African or two into a native administration council also offered real advantages to the British. In addition, chiefs often had the money to send their children and relatives to school as well the political influence to secure them places. In certain cases, the British also made a point of educating the sons and relatives of chiefs.

Educated Africans were at the heart of the problem for the wartime Colonial Office. To some, they were just a problem. Lord Cranborne referred to the "half-baked, semi-Europeanized intelligentsia in colonial territories." To others, they offered a problem and an opportunity. Educated Africans were likely to agitate for political power and a larger role in colonial government. Educated Africans had the skills and motivation the colonial governments needed if they were to become more capable, if they were to move beyond keeping the peace and collecting taxes. Co-opting educated Africans might divert the political pressure they might exert as well as strengthen the colonial apparatus.

Planning Political Change

In the course of the discussion of possible political change, the Colonial Office staff produced a paper laying out a five-stage process to self-government. At the first stage, the British would establish regional councils to which native administrations would send representatives. In the second and third stages, the councils would take on more responsibilities. Legislative councils and town councils would become more representative. At the fourth stage, unofficial representatives would form majorities of the legislative council. At the fifth, the colony would achieve some form of self-government. The process would be lengthy, consuming many years or generations. It would not apply to all colonies. It was absurd, an official wrote, to think that all existing colonial units were equally fit for self-government.[25]

Neither the Colonial Office paper nor any of the papers generated during the war constituted a new colonial policy, in the sense of a description of goals, methods, and proposed actions approved by the colonial secretary or the cabinet. It is not clear that the civil servants in the Colonial Office and their advisers reached a consensus. Nevertheless, the willingness to contemplate the possibility of significant change, of alternatives to the native administrations, and of a larger role for educated Africans represented an important intellectual shift from the conventional wisdom prevailing in official circles through the end of the 1930s. Official thinking had reached a watershed.

While the Colonial Office was not sure where history was taking it and the colonies or what it should do about it, official thinking displayed consistent elements. British responses to change would be political. The British should seek alliances with one group of Africans or another. The native administrations had allowed the British to rule the colonies before the war with a minimum of soldiers and policemen. A political arrangement would allow Britain to retain some degree of control after the war without military force or wholesale repression. What some critics termed "constitution-mongering" would be the favored tool. Britain would forge political alliances by tinkering with the makeup and responsibilities of advisory and representative bodies, and with the electoral franchise. The government in London, especially the Colonial Office, would play a larger role in shaping change in the colonies. The initiative would no longer remain with colonial governors. Methods would no longer be reactive and ad hoc.

Seizing the initiative was probably more important to the Colonial Office's civil servants than to its political leadership. In 1943 Stanley, in a meeting with Sir Arthur Richards, the new governor of Nigeria, raised the possibility of a government white paper setting out British policy for West Africa. Richards thought it a good idea. The paper could lay out general policy. He and other governors could fill in the blanks. Stanley's response was that the process should work the other way around. Richards and Sir Alan Burns, the governor of the Gold Coast, should agree on some ideas and propose them to the Colonial Office. The office could produce a white paper based on whichever ideas it favored.[26]

Changes in the Colonies: West Africa

Despite the Colonial Office's notion that it should take the initiative, the significant moves towards more prominent political roles for Africans in the early war years originated with reform-minded colonial governors. Governors in Britain's African colonies usually served for about five years. Frequently, an incoming governor came equipped with his own notions for reforming the colony's administration and determined to make his own mark. During the war, both Sir Alan Burns, governor of the Gold Coast, and Sir Bernard Bourdillon, governor of Nigeria, proposed appointing Africans to their colony's executive councils. Having served in West Africa and the West Indies, Burns arrived in the Gold Coast armed with several proposals, including appointing Africans as assistant district commissioners, positions heretofore reserved for Britons. Bourdillon had other ideas. He favored more economic development. He wanted to create regional councils with legislative and financial powers in each of Nigeria's three regions and to add Africans from the northern region to the legislative council. Burns's overall strategy was to offer concessions before agitation emerged. He thought that by keeping ahead of popular clamor, the British could convince "moderate and reasonable" Africans to support British rule. Neither governor thought that self-government was on the horizon. In proposing changes to the executive council, their aim was to reach out to articulate, educated Africans and add them to the chiefs as close collaborators with British officials. Burns intended to appoint a senior chief and another, presumably educated, African to the executive council.[27]

In opposing Burns's and Bourdillon's proposals, Cranborne raised three arguments that were to reappear over the next two decades. He thought that the governors were going too fast and that offering concessions before they were demanded would lead to more demands and sooner. He also thought that the governors had the process backward. Adding Africans to the central government should come at the end, not at the beginning. Hailey echoed this view. Cranborne pointed out, moreover, that changes in one colony would lead to changes in neighboring colonies. In West Africa, Africans in Nigeria, Sierra Leone, and Gambia would want whatever concessions Africans in the Gold Coast secured. Cranborne wanted the governors of all four territories consulted regarding the decision even if it meant delay or, perhaps especially if it meant delay. Since Cranborne doubted that all four territories were equally ready for political change, he thought change should not proceed in any of them.[28]

Cranborne initially rejected Burns's and Bourdillon's proposals, but the governors persisted. When the governors of Sierra Leone and Gambia indicated that they were not opposed to appointing Africans to executive councils, Cranborne proved unwilling to disagree with all his West African governors. Although some civil servants shared Cranborne's concern that one concession would lead inexorably to others, he acquiesced to Burns's and Bourdillon's recommendations.[29]

When Sir Arthur Richards, Bourdillon's successor as governor of Nigeria, proposed a new constitution for the colony in 1943, the nature of the debate changed. It was no longer a reforming governor squaring off with a reluctant colonial secretary. It was also clearer that colonial reforms need not produce greater political control by Africans or lead to self-government, even in the changed atmosphere of the war years.

Richards's focus was strengthening the British administration in Nigeria. He wanted a proposal that would be seen as an advance and that would lay the groundwork for further orderly advance. He proposed that the new constitution remain in place for at least nine years. He wanted to draw the colony's three regions most closely together, by creating comparable political institutions and procedures in all three. He wanted to encourage further development of the native administrations and enlarge the role of chiefs. He proposed that native administrations select representatives to regional houses of assembly. The regional houses would select representatives to the legislative council. No representatives of Nigeria's northern provinces currently sat in the legislative council. Richards opposed creating an unofficial majority in the legislative council. In fact, he proposed eliminating the council's four elected members, three elected from Lagos and one from Calabar. Gold Coast nationalists were already demanding an unofficial majority in their legislative council and Nigerian nationalists would, presumably, follow suit.[30]

Stanley, now colonial secretary, and some of his civil servants thought Richards was courting trouble. Educated Nigerians would think Richards's scheme reactionary, wrote Andrew Cohen, a senior Colonial Office official. While educated Nigerians were few in number, theirs was the only Nigerian opinion that was vocal. They could influence opinion in Britain and elsewhere and their opposition could threaten the success of Richards's scheme. Cohen thought Richards needed to reduce the role of British officials. He also doubted that Britain could postpone further political change in Nigeria for nine years. Stanley had raised the issue of an unofficial majority in the legislative council with Bourdillon. The colonial secretary insisted that Richards amend his plans to include an unofficial majority and to retain direct election of four legislative council members.[31]

In the Gold Coast, Burns was also writing a new constitution. He advocated an unofficial majority in the legislative council, but not a directly elected, unofficial majority. Gold Coast leaders were agitating for an elected majority along with appointment of legislative council members to the executive council. Burns was working towards a stronger relationship with senior chiefs. He did not intend to allow Gold Coast political leaders, notably J.B. Danquah, to dominate the legislative council. His recommendation was to grant an unofficial majority, which educated Africans would welcome. He intended to ensure that the majority was composed of members appointed by the governor or elected by councils dominated by chiefs and native administration officials.

In Sierra Leone, two Africans gained places on the executive council in 1943: one a chief, one a Creole, a descendant of freed slaves. Creoles predominated in Sierra Leone's principal town, Freetown, and were more likely to have adopted European culture, including formal education, than Africans in the rest of the territory. Sierra Leone consisted of the Colony, centered on Freetown, and the Protectorate, the bulk of the countryside. Just as in Nigeria and the Gold Coast, the changes in the executive council were not the only changes proposed by the British officials. A few Africans may have gained a larger political role. Nevertheless, the British were most concerned about shoring up their rule and tightly controlling a long-term evolution toward self-government.

Before the war, the British administration in Sierra Leone was concerned about a political movement, the West African Youth League, headed by I.T.A. Wallace-Johnson. Similar organizations emerged in Nigeria and the Gold Coast. Wallace-Johnson was a Creole, with labor union experience and links to like-minded Africans elsewhere in West Africa and Britain. The Sierra Leone administration was worried that the Youth League would gain support from both Creoles in Freetown and other Africans in the Protectorate, particularly workers in Sierra Leone's mines. British fears were realized when four candidates supported by the Youth League were elected to the Freetown city council. In June 1939, the Sierra Leone government enacted four ordinances seemingly intended to curb the Youth League; one allowed the preventive detention of British subjects. At the outset of World War II in September 1939, the British arrested Wallace-Johnson and detained him until 1944.

The British tinkered with electoral arrangements in Sierra Leone to allow change while maintaining control. Before the war, Governor Jardine flirted with the notion of eliminating elections to the Freetown city council, but the Colonial Office warned him off. Hailey and Stanley visited Sierra Leone during the war. They concluded that the British should curb Creole influence and slow the pace of political change until Africans in the Protectorate could play a larger role. The government proposed creation of advisory councils in twelve districts in the Protectorate, composed of chiefs and representatives of native administrations. The advisory councils would select members of a Protectorate assembly. The assembly would elect twelve members of the legislative council. The legislative council would have an elected majority, but one the British thought they could control. The British proposed to reconstitute the Freetown city council as well. At first, Africans welcomed the reforms, but suspicions grew within the Freetown community about British intentions to control the council. So few Freetown residents registered to vote that the British could not reasonably hold elections.

The British attempted to address some of the Youth League's grievances. Working conditions in the mines were high on the list. In the summer of 1939, the Sierra Leone legislative council enacted legislation that legalized trade unions and established procedures for arbitration of labor disputes. A newly appointed government labor secretary began to work with the eight unions that Wallace-Johnson had started.

East and Central Africa

Similar changes took place in other colonies' advisory councils before the end of the war. Africans entered the legislative councils in Kenya, Uganda, and Tanganyika. The two appointed in Tanganyika were chiefs. In Northern Rhodesia, an unofficial majority on the legislative council emerged, albeit of Europeans. Three of the five appointed Europeans were to represent African interests until Africans the British considered suitable were available.

In East and Central Africa, two issues complicated political calculations. The first was federation, the notion of combining several colonies into a single entity — Uganda, Kenya, and Tanganyika into an East African federation, and Southern Rhodesia, Northern Rhodesia and Nyasaland into a Central African federation. The second was the role, present and future, of European settlers, present in significant numbers in Kenya and Southern Rhodesia and in much smaller numbers in Tanganyika, Northern Rhodesia and Nyasaland. Southern Rhodesia's Europeans had gained effective internal self-government in the 1920s. Their counterparts elsewhere, especially in Kenya, sought similar arrangements. European settlers, especially in Central Africa, saw federation as a means to expand and consolidate their role. British officials flirted with notions of federation for other reasons — to achieve economies of scale or to create an economically viable unit. Africans opposed expanded powers for settlers and resisted federation proposals, for the same reasons that European settlers favored them. The British government had made several pronouncements that the aim of British rule was to protect African interests. As a result, British officials often found themselves at odds with settlers. At the same time, British officials perceived settlers as useful collaborators, whether to maintain British rule or to carry out economic development.

Sudan

Oversight of the Sudan government was the responsibility of the Foreign Office, not the Colonial Office. Nevertheless, political changes in the Sudan during the war paralleled those in other British colonies. The British administration moved to co-opt educated Sudanese while maintaining existing ties with other Sudanese. The British aim was to reinforce their rule and to start, carefully and slowly, to move towards self-government.

The Sudan was an anomalous creation. In 1898, Britain defeated the forces of Ahmed al-Mahdi and re-conquered the Sudan on behalf of Egypt, a province of the Ottoman Empire but subject to British control. In 1922, Britain declared Egypt independent. The British high commissioner in Cairo retained considerable powers and British troops remained. After the 1898 conquest, the British announced that the Sudan was a condominium, ruled jointly by Britain and Egypt. Britain's unilateral declaration of Egyptian independence did nothing to clarify the Sudan's status. Nor did negotiations between Egyptian and British officials throughout the 1920s. Despite the concept of joint rule, British officials in the Sudan saw themselves as protecting the Sudanese from the Egyptians. In 1924, the British used the assassination of Sudan's governor-general, Sir Lee Stack, by an Egyptian nationalist, and mutinies by Sudanese troops as justification to expel all Egyptian officials and troops from the Sudan. At the beginning of World War II, the Sudan looked like other British colonies. A small British staff presided over an array of political units akin to native administrations. On paper, the Sudan's governor-general reported through the British high commissioner in Cairo to the Foreign Office. In fact, he retained considerable discretion. In international law, the question of Sudanese sovereignty remained unsettled. Did it belong to Egypt, Britain, or to the Sudanese?

In the Sudan, British rule depended on political collaboration with several groups. The Sudan had its equivalent of "chiefs," African political leaders in the countryside, referred to in the Northern Sudan as the "shaykhs." In the towns, particularly Khartoum, the capital, educated Sudanese served in government posts. Soon after the re-conquest, the British courted 'Ali al-Mirghani, Sudanese leader of an Islamic brotherhood (in Arabic, *turuq*), the khatmiyya, and opponent of Ahmed al-Mahdi and his followers. During the World War I, the British turned for support against the Ottoman Turks to 'Ali al-Mirghani's chief rival, 'Abd al-Rahman, the posthumous son of Ahmed al-Mahdi, who retained the allegiance of his father's followers.

Between the wars, British attitudes towards their collaborators shifted more than once. The 1924 mutinies and their aftermath motivated the British to downplay the role of educated Sudanese in favor of the shaykhs. 'Abd al-Rahman's open support for the British government raised his stock with the administration, although some British officials feared that 'Abd al-Rahman's ill-concealed ambitions to rule the Sudan made him less than the ideal ally. In 1936, Britain signed a treaty with Egypt, intended largely to reinforce British control of the Suez canal in anticipation of a conflict in Europe. The treaty lifted some restrictions of Egyptian involvement in the Sudan. In addition, it announced, for the first time, that Britain administered the Sudan for the welfare of the Sudanese. Despite the treaty, the British sought to limit Egyptian access to Sudanese government posts by indicating that the first choice would always be a properly qualified Sudanese. The British also sought to associate educated Sudanese more closely with their administration. The British began to see themselves competing with Egypt for the loyalty of the educated Sudanese. They imagined that the educated Sudanese could be a counterweight to other groups, particularly 'Abd al-Rahman and his followers. In 1938, the government encouraged a sizeable group of educated Sudanese, most graduates of Gordon College in Khartoum, to organize themselves, as the Graduates Congress.

At first, the Congress remained within the cooperative role the government imagined for it. Shortly after its foundation, it informed the government that it intended to carry out charitable work and to communicate its members' views to the government. It did not intend to embarrass the government or pursue activities counter to government policy. Later the Congress petitioned for higher pay for educated Sudanese, but did so in moderate language. The government refused to discuss the issue. Eventually, the government acknowledged the Congress's criticisms. In 1940, after 'Ali Mahir, the Egyptian prime minister, visited the Sudan and attended a government-sanctioned tea party hosted by the Congress, the Congress sent him a memorandum without consulting the government. The government was displeased and threatened to dissolve the organization.[32]

In 1942, the Graduates Congress demanded Sudanese independence and precipitated a break with the government. The Congress sent the government a memorandum asking that, after the war, Egypt and Britain grant the Sudan the right of self-determination and the right to determine its relationship with Egypt. The Congress claimed to speak for all Sudanese. It referred to Sudanese support for the British war effort and to the pronouncements of British politicians and agreements reached by leaders of democratic nations. Sir Douglas Newbold, chief secretary in the Sudan government, effectively its chief operating officer, rejected the memorandum. The government announced that the Congress had forfeited its cooperation and recognition. Despite Newbold's subsequent attempts to repair the breach, many Congress members were offended.[33]

Despite rejecting the Congress's pleas for self-determination, Newbold favored reform. He attributed the Congress's petition to the announcement of the Atlantic Charter and the visits by Sir Stafford Cripps to the Sudan on his way to and from India. He saw some Congress actions as ill-advised agitation, a sandstorm that was fogging the basic issue. He urged that the government work to secure the cooperation of educated Sudanese, particularly by opening more government posts to Sudanese. Unless the government could rehabilitate the Congress into a respectable movement that the government could guide, the government would face a choice of either suppression or appeasement. Appeasement would lead to blackmail and premature concessions. Suppression would create frustration, friction, and violence and would probably drive educated Sudanese into the arms of the Egyptians. The Sudan government, Newbold thought, had an opportunity to act. It needed to do so quickly since the wider world was moving rapidly towards new political ideas. After the war, the government would have to compete with Egyptian blandishments.[34]

Newbold's notions found support in London and Cairo. Detaching the Sudan from Egypt figured prominently in the Foreign Office's thinking. Self-government was thought at least a generation away, but officials recognized the need to forge working relationships with both educated Sudanese and "tribal" leaders. Sir Miles Lampson (later Lord Killearn), British ambassador in Cairo, agreed. A Sudanese nationalist movement could help Britain counter Egyptian claims to the Sudan. The British needed to heed Sudanese aspirations. They should not frustrate the Sudanese to the point that they sought Egyptian help. Lampson thought that the British had erred in other colonies by losing patience with nationalist movements. Instead of working to maintain day-to-day control, they had grown frustrated with inept and undisciplined politicians and allowed nationalist movements to slip from their control. They then faced the unpleasant choice between concessions and repression.[35]

Sir Hubert Huddleston, governor-general of the Sudan, conceded that the Graduates Congress memorandum was evidence of genuine nationalist feeling in the Sudan. He was wary of change, and of educated Sudanese, however. He thought the Congress's actions reflected the views of younger extremists rather than saner, more balanced members. He thought the Congress unrepresentative of Sudanese popular opinion, even of educated Sudanese opinion. When the Foreign Office suggested a declaration that the future of the Sudan was as an independent state, Huddleston argued that educated Sudanese might like the idea, but other responsible elements would not. A declaration might be consistent with positions taken by government ministers in the House of Commons, but it was going too far for the Sudan.[36]

In 1943, the Sudan government established the Advisory Council for the Northern Sudan, responsible for providing advice to the Sudan government. Provincial councils composed of shaykhs and native administration officials chose the council's members. Most were native administration officials. The British hoped the council could displace the Graduates Congress as the focus for Sudanese political activity. Nevertheless, divisions among the Sudanese complicated matters. The British tried to associate both 'Ali al-Mirghani and 'Abd al-Rahman with the council, but 'Ali al-Mirghani and his followers eventually boycotted the council. Sudanese saw it as a preserve of 'Abd al-Rahman and his adherents.

Similar fractures appeared within the Graduates Congress. Sudanese impatient with government efforts and led by Isma'il al-Azhari, secretary of the Graduates Congress, organized a faction called Ashiqqa ("full brothers"). They won control of the Congress, displacing more moderate members, many of whom were associated with 'Abd al-Rahman. 'Ali al-Mirghani and the khatmiyya lent their support to the Ashiqqa, largely to ensure that 'Abd al-Rahman did not dominate the Congress the way he did the advisory council. 'Abd al-Rahman upped the stakes in 1945 by founding the Sudan's first political party, the Umma ("community" or "nation") party.

The Sudan government's political strategy failed before the end of the war. The British aimed to tie both native administration officials and educated Sudanese to the government and shield them from Egyptian pressure. Nevertheless, groups were organized into two opposing blocs, one led by 'Abd-ah-Rahman and the other composed of the Ashiqqa, led by al-Azhari, and of 'Ali al-Mirgani's khatmiyya. 'Abd al-Rahman had so closely associated himself with the government that his opponents began to look to Egypt for support and to offer union with Egypt as the Sudan's future.

In 1945, leadership of the Sudan government became less flexible. Newbold died in office in March 1945. Huddleston's choice to replace him as chief secretary was Sir James Robertson, an experienced administrator noted for a direct approach. Robertson's views appeared to resemble those of many of his fellow officials. He thought the Sudanese lacked the skills and education to stand on their own. The political parties and the Sudanese press produced pathetic nonsense, he thought. It was up to the British to set them straight.

By 1945, Britain could claim that it was on the side of the angels, committed to bringing its colonies to self-government. British leaders, however, surrounded the concept of self-government with enough mental reservations that Britain was committed, in fact, to no particular set of actions. Civil servants had thought about how Britain might manage political change within the colonies, but they had reached no definite conclusions. Political and economic change seemed certain, but their precise nature was undetermined.

Political changes had already taken place in the African colonies. In West Africa, colonial governors had drawn educated Africans into the colonial governments. The governors' goal was to strengthen British rule by securing the cooperation of prominent educated Africans. In the Sudan, British efforts to court educated Africans had already encountered difficulties. Sudanese leaders remained divided and some were looking outside the Sudan for assistance against the British.

3

The Truman Administration, 1945–1952: Global Power and Colonies

The seven and a half years of Harry Truman's administration saw a transformation in the United States relationship with the rest of the world. With the Allies' victory over Japan, the United States stood as the world's richest and most powerful nation. Alone among the major powers, its domestic industry and infrastructure remained intact. Its economy was booming. It was the globe's principal creditor, owed vast sums by the other victorious allies. In August 1945, the United States possessed armed forces unparalleled in American history in size and strength. In 1945, the United States fielded ninety-four divisions—sixty-nine in Europe, and twenty-five in Asia and the Pacific. By dropping atomic bombs on Hiroshima and Nagasaki, the United States demonstrated that it had and would use new weapons of awesome destructiveness. These facts alone meant that American interactions with the rest of the world after World War II would differ from those of the prewar era, when the U.S. was one of several regional powers.

From a position of strength, the Truman administration reworked fundamental United States foreign policy. Like the Roosevelt administration, it discarded the longstanding notion that U.S. interests lay principally in the Western Hemisphere. Within two or three years, it also discarded Roosevelt's idea that the United States should police the world in cooperation with the other great powers. The Truman administration conceived of the United States as the leader and predominant power in a worldwide coalition that confronted Russia, the second most powerful nation, and its allies. A key U.S. goal was to prevent the expansion of Russian influence and control anywhere around the globe. For the first time in American history, the United States acknowledged important interests in Europe and forged formal alliances with Great Britain, France, and the lesser Western European nations. For the first time, the United States also staked a claim to interests throughout the rest of the globe. By the end of the Truman administration, it had backed up that claim with actions in several regions outside Europe, particularly the countries surrounding the eastern Mediterranean, Iran, and East Asia. The U.S. announced its new role in statements such as Truman's 1947 speech to Congress, in which he proclaimed the so-called Truman doctrine. The Truman administration wrote more detailed, secret descriptions of its global role, such as the paper known as National Security Council (NSC)—68.[1]

The U.S. route from the Western Hemisphere power of 1938 to the global power of 1952 was neither simple nor straight. Harry Truman and his administration struggled to devise a foreign policy and to sort out the foreign policy legacies of the Roosevelt administration, especially regarding Russia. One participant recalled the "quality of bewilderment and moral untidiness" that characterized U.S. diplomacy at the time. He saw the confrontation between the United States and Russia as "the result of the cumulative, mutually reinforcing series of mistakes and misunderstandings — an elaborate counterpoint in which our government and that of the Soviet Union seemed almost to be working hand-in-hand to simplify the ideological map at the expense of minor political forces, intermediate groups, and nuances of opinion."[2] Other aspects of the Truman administration's formulation of foreign policy were also untidy. The Truman administration sought and gained bipartisan support for its foreign policy, not least because it frequently lacked Democratic majorities in Congress. Nevertheless, some congressional Republicans contested the new approach to foreign policy. A sizeable group of Republicans led by Senator Robert A. Taft opposed a global role for the United States. Taft and his supporters saw virtue in tending to interests in the Western Hemisphere and vice in extending the United States reach to Europe and the rest of the world. They opposed key elements of the Truman administration's program: an enlarged military, foreign aid, low tariffs, and multi-lateral trade policies.

Regarding U.S. policy towards Great Britain and its African colonies, the Truman administration was also a period of transformation. The marked changes in the relative power and wealth of the United States and Great Britain after World War II made changes in U.S. policy highly likely. The assumption of a global role made them inevitable. In the case of Britain's African colonies, it was not so much a case of changing policies, but of developing policies. While the United States did not follow up its claim to worldwide interests in every instance, asserting a global role made it far more likely that the U.S. government would have to consider its relationship to Britain's African possessions.

Truman and Colonies

Whatever Harry Truman's strengths, he was not Franklin Roosevelt. Where Roosevelt kept a finger in many pies, Truman delegated. Whereas Roosevelt conducted much of his foreign policy from the White House, Truman told a constituent in 1943: "Diplomacy has always been too much for me." Like Roosevelt, Truman criticized the State Department's career officials, but he relied on the Department of State far more than Roosevelt did. Roosevelt's foreign policy notions were complex, dynamic, and often cloudy. Truman's views were straightforward and direct. He was apt to assume the worst about nations that resisted American policies. Roosevelt held vivid views of Britain, both distrust of its aims and recognition that its survival was critical to United States interests. Truman seemed indifferent to Britain. Roosevelt forged a unique working relationship with Churchill. Truman thought Churchill too clever and given to "hooey" and "soft soap." According to Truman, Churchill's successor as prime minister, Clement Attlee, talked like the "much overrated" Anthony Eden. Ernest Bevin, Attlee's foreign secretary, was an "English John L. Lewis."[3]

Roosevelt evinced concern for people around the world, including in Asia and in Africa. Truman's attitudes were prosaic and parochial. Truman included in his memoirs the standard, official U.S. position on colonialism. He was, Truman wrote, always opposed to colonialism. Colonialism was anathema to Americans. The Philippines were proof of the country's commitment to self-determination. If there was an issue about granting nations their independence, it was not one of principle, but of method and procedure. Truman's reaction to the choice of a rising Democratic politician, Chester Bowles, to become U.S. ambassador to India, suggests, however, that Truman viewed the rest of the world with a jaundiced eye. Truman was appalled at Bowles choice. He said: "I thought India was pretty jammed with poor people and cows wandering the streets, witch doctors and people sitting on hot coals and bathing in the Ganges and so on. But I did not realize that anyone thought it was important."[4]

Dean Acheson

Four secretaries of state served under Truman: Edward R. Stettinius, (April-June 1945); James F. Byrnes (July 1945–January 1947); George C. Marshall (January 1947–January 1949); and Dean G. Acheson (January 1949–January 1952). Stettinius's brief tenure focused on establishment of the United Nations. Byrnes and Marshall were involved in negotiations with Russia and with America's European allies. They spent long periods away from Washington. The U.S. relationship with Great Britain was among their concerns, but neither appears to have held distinctive views about the future of Britain's empire. Acheson served as under secretary of state, the department's number two position, under Byrnes and Marshall from 1945 to 1947, and acted as secretary while they were overseas. Acheson also served as secretary throughout Truman's second term, 1949 to 1952. Acheson had a close working relationship with Truman, beginning with his service as under secretary of state.

Acheson had warmer feelings for Britain and British officials than Truman. As a successful Wall Street lawyer in the 1930s, Acheson gained a reputation as pro–British. At the State Department, Acheson viewed favorably Britain's long-time contributions to world order and stability. He assumed that the United States and Great Britain would continue to cooperate to foster stability and order in the aftermath of the Second World War. Acheson had a high regard for Foreign Secretary Bevin and established a strong working relationship with him. Acheson also worked closely with Sir Oliver Franks, British ambassador to the United States from 1948 to 1952. At Acheson's instigation, Acheson and Franks held regular off-the-record meetings, at Acheson's or Franks's home. They discussed issues, attempted to anticipate problems, and drafted official messages to be exchanged between their departments.[5]

Congressional Republicans attacked Acheson as pro–British. Acheson's stylish dress and his New England, Episcopalian, Ivy League background fit the image. Acheson was apt to favor British interests more than Truman, his boss. Nevertheless, Acheson was a tough-minded advocate for what he perceived as U.S. interests. He favored cooperation with London because he thought it promoted U.S. aims. As assistant secretary of state in the Roosevelt administration, Acheson was a dogged negotiator with John Maynard Keynes and British officials over the terms of the Lend Lease program. Once Acheson saw that Britain could not hold its own in areas where its influence had been dominant, like the eastern Mediterranean, he was quick to claim a larger role for the United States.[6]

If Acheson favored Britain, the Truman administration included key officials skeptical of the British and their long-term prospects. Secretary of the Treasury John Snyder thought the United States should distance itself from Britain's financial troubles. Secretary of Defense Louis Johnson opined that Britain was finished and that there was no point in the U.S. trying to bolster it. The United States should write Britain off and cooperate with the parts of the British empire and commonwealth that were useful. Will Clayton, assistant secretary for economic affairs in the State Department, saw the British hanging on, hoping that the United States would help preserve the empire. Clayton thought the United States ought to tell the British that it could not save the empire and did not intend to try. The British should work with the U.S. to save Europe.[7]

Britain and the United States interacted on many issues during the Truman administration. Characterizing their overall relationship in the period is not simple and perhaps not even possible. It appears that the two countries drifted apart immediately after the war. Closer dealings did not develop again until George Marshall became secretary of state. Acheson pursued cooperation with the British, but within limits. For a 1949 foreign ministers meeting, the British produced a Foreign Office paper describing a "special relationship" between the two countries. Acheson was, he later reported, horrified to discover that a paper existed "which spelled out this common law marriage in a way which I thought would utterly destroy us if it were ever known, either to our allies or anybody in the United States." Acheson managed to remove the paper from the meeting's agenda.[8]

Acheson had little interest in the world outside the United States and Europe. He focused his attention on Europe and European affairs. While secretary of state, he made only one trip to South America. Only reluctantly did Acheson find himself immersed in Asian issues, in Japan, China, and Korea. Acheson's initial stance was that western Asia and Africa were of any interest only because the America's principal Western European allies had possessions and interests there. Acheson left them in the care of lesser State Department officials until the last two years of his tenure as secretary, when he took a personal interest in Egypt and Iran. When George McGhee became assistant secretary of state for the Near East, South Asia, and Africa in 1949, he was instructed that he should consider himself the secretary of state for those areas. Acheson occasionally made demeaning comments about non–European peoples. Dean Rusk, a State Department colleague, observed that Acheson "did not give a damn about the little red, yellow, black people" in various parts of the world. Another State Department veteran heard Acheson say things about Indochinese "that he wouldn't want to repeat." Acheson told a Congressional committee in executive session that aspirations for independence outside Europe would end in chaos. Non-European peoples were largely illiterate and lacked the simplest ideas of social organization. They did not know how to make schools, public health systems, or even roads. Acheson belittled criticisms of colonialism from what he characterized as the "hallelujah" section. Acheson claimed critics of colonialism favored the right of everybody to do what he wanted in his part of the world. Favoring liberty everywhere was an emotional and shallow view that overlooked the vital role of political and military power, he claimed.[9]

Department of State

By the end of the Truman administration, the State Department had been transformed. From about 1,100 domestic employees in 1940, it had grown to nearly nine thousand by 1950. Staff in the key policy-making offices, the Office of the Secretary and the geographical and political offices, grew from about 130 in 1938 to nearly four hundred in 1948. The number of career diplomats grew from 737 in 1936 to 1,217 in 1950. Secretary Marshall and Under Secretary Acheson took steps to organize and manage the department's decision making, in particular by creating an Executive Secretariat in 1947. In 1949, a sweeping reorganization created several new bureaus within the department, notably the Bureau of Near Eastern,

South Asian and African Affairs and, to handle U.S. dealings with the United Nations, the Bureau of International Organization Affairs.[10]

To State Department professionals, Anglo-American cooperation in the latter stages of the Truman administration was different from similar cooperation in the early years of the Second World War. Instead of the alliance of two great powers evident in Roosevelt and Churchill's early dealings, the Anglo-American relationship now featured a senior and a junior partner. A 1950 State Department paper argued that a working relationship between Britain and the United States had to start with a British recognition that global power and responsibility had shifted to the United States. United States objectives and policies merited great weight. The United States needed to recognize British influence and experience in world affairs and the importance of Britain and its empire to U.S. security. U.S. officials had to understand how difficult it was for their British counterparts to accept that the United States now held a position of world dominance.[11]

The department's resources devoted to African affairs grew along with the rest, but remained relatively small and isolated. The Division of African Affairs in Washington gained new personnel. By 1952, the United States maintained consulates or consulates-general in six of Britain's fifteen African colonies: Accra (Gold Coast), Lagos (Nigeria), Dar-es-Salaam (Tanganyika), Salisbury (Southern Rhodesia), Mombassa, and Nairobi (Kenya). Assistant Secretary McGhee set out to improve training for State's Africa-based staff, bringing some back to the United States for a year of graduate training. He also organized meetings of the Africa-based staff and consulted panels of African experts. According to McGhee, his staff felt estranged from the rest of the department. They tended to favor the interests of colonial peoples over those of the colonial powers, most of which were U.S. allies. As a result, conflicts between McGhee's bureau and the Bureau of European Affairs occasionally developed. Some thought that the department's African posts remained a dumping ground for senior Foreign Service officers who were unlikely to gain the highest Foreign Service rank before they retired.[12]

Attitudes towards Britain and her colonies varied among the senior State department officials. British diplomats in Washington considered Loy Henderson, director of Near Eastern and African affairs between 1945 and 1948, an improvement over his predecessor, Wallace Murray. They thought Murray was difficult and openly hostile. Murray advocated firmer United States pressure on Britain to move India towards independence. Henderson was friendly and helpful, "a very loyal friend" to the British. Henderson was uncomfortable with anti-colonialism and tried to adopt a "realistic and pragmatic" approach to Britain's problems. The British were much less fond of McGhee, even if he had attended Oxford on a Rhodes scholarship. McGhee was enthusiastic and self-assured. British officials characterized him as the sort of American who thought that, with dollars and a wrench, one could change the world.[13]

The End of Lend Lease

As the war neared its conclusion, British officials recognized that substantial financial aid from the United States was critical. Without U.S. dollars, the British government faced the prospect of crushing austerity at home and the loss of colonies abroad. The first actions of the Truman administration regarding financial aid to Britain were far from encouraging, however. At Roosevelt's death, the issue of postwar Lend Lease aid remained unresolved.

Churchill thought he had secured Roosevelt's agreement regarding such aid at the 1944 Quebec conference, but Congress was opposed. Key members of the executive branch were at odds. The official directly responsible, Leo Crowley, head of the Foreign Economic Administration (FEA), favored cutting off aid to Britain and to Russia. In April 1945, Crowley curtailed shipments intended for Britain. After the German surrender on May 8, Truman ordered further reductions. In late May, when Churchill sent a telegram asking for continued aid, Truman took Crowley's advice over that of Acheson and Clayton. He limited munitions shipments to whatever the Joint Chiefs of Staff would approve. On July 5, the White House issued a directive that the executive branch should follow the letter and spirit of the Lend Lease legislation. The United States would provide only aid for the fight against Japan. The Joint Chiefs took this as license to halt all shipments to British troops in Europe. When Clayton and other officials protested, Truman agreed to allow shipments to British troops assisting in the redeployment of United States troops to the Pacific theatre. Once Japan surrendered, those shipments ended. On August 17, Truman approved a memorandum prepared by Crowley and the FEA that stated that the administration intended to adhere to Congress's intent regarding Lend Lease. All aid was to cease, therefore. All materials on their way to foreign governments or received by foreign governments but not consumed were to be returned to the United States unless an agreement regarding reimbursement was reached.[14]

Truman's decision hit British leaders hard. In Parliament, Churchill called it a rough and harsh decision. Attlee later wrote that the British were in no position to bargain. They had exhausted their resources and seen the United States take over export trade that Britain had dominated. Cutting off Lend Lease was a body blow, Attlee thought. In the House of Commons, Attlee noted that while Lend Lease had allowed Britain to fight the war, its cancellation left Britain far worse off than those who had been providing assistance.[15]

Truman later characterized the decision to cut off Lend Lease as a mistake, a product of his inexperience. The Truman administration was going through growing pains in the spring and summer of 1945, as the war came to an abrupt and surprising end. Truman was inexperienced and uninformed about much of what had gone on in the Roosevelt White House. The conflicting sources of advice that Roosevelt tolerated were competing for Truman's ear and he had yet to decide whom to trust. Nevertheless, Truman's mistake, if that is what it was, had to do with the timing and manner with which the United States ended Lend Lease, not that it ended aid to its allies. Congress had mandated a halt to Lend Lease. The contrary voices within the Truman administration were arguing for a more graceful transition, not provision of massive aid to Britain. Even Roosevelt, before his death, had been reluctant to follow through on the understanding reached with Churchill at Quebec.[16]

United States Loan to Britain

John Maynard Keynes summed up the situation for the Attlee cabinet. Ministers should assume that, with the cessation of Lend Lease, Britain was virtually bankrupt. Facing a "financial Dunkirk," Britain would have to withdraw from its overseas responsibilities and accept the role of a second-class power, like the newly liberated France. At home, austerity more severe than that in wartime would be needed. The Labour government would have to postpone its social programs and it would be at least five years before Britain could cure the situation. Keynes warned the cabinet that no acceptable financial agreement with the

United States was in sight. The U.S. would demand British acceptance of its commercial and financial program, in particular, dismantling the sterling area and discarding trade preferences within the British empire. Getting the U.S. Congress to ratify any acceptable agreement would be difficult.[17]

Keynes was not as clear about the agreement Britain could expect to reach with the United States. He estimated that Britain needed $5 billion. He thought that the United States would make available between $3 and $5 billion. He advised ministers against borrowing from the U.S. and seems to have thought that a U.S. grant to Britain was possible. He warned ministers that the United States would expect Britain to change its financial and commercial foreign policies to fit U.S. preferences. Despite glimmers of optimism, Keynes warned that Britain would have to accept whatever terms the United States offered. Yet Keynes seems to have believed that the U.S. would not demand such changes as the price for financial aid.[18]

Fundamental change was what the United States expected. Clayton and Fred Vinson, Truman's new secretary of the treasury, believed that Britain's financial problems were a major obstacle to achieving open markets and multilateral trade. Unless Britain regained financial health, it would be unable to adopt the U.S. program. They recommended U.S. aid to Britain, but they remained focused on achieving American dominance and on implementing U.S.–preferred financial and commercial policies. They recommended a loan to Britain, not a grant. They recommended that the loan be contingent on certain British actions: eliminating empire trade preferences, dismantling the dollar pool administered by the London government on behalf of the dominions and colonies, and writing down the sterling balances belonging to the dominions and colonies but controlled by the British government. Clayton described the U.S. position as loading "the negotiations with all the conditions the traffic would bear."[19]

The negotiations in Washington between a British delegation headed by Keynes and a U.S. delegation headed by Vinson and Clayton were heated and prolonged. As Keynes had predicted to the cabinet, the British had to accept the U.S. terms. Hugh Dalton, the chancellor of the exchequer, described the process: "We retreated slowly and with bad grace and with increasing irritation from a free gift to an interest free loan and from this again to a loan bearing interest; from a larger to a smaller total of aid; and from the prospect of loose strings, some of which would be only general declarations of intention, to the most unwilling acceptance of strings so tight that they might strangle our trade and indeed our whole economic life."[20]

The result was a U.S. loan to Great Britain of $4.4 billion, $3.75 billion in new money and the rest from funds originally appropriated for Lend Lease. The British were to repay the loan over fifty years, starting after a six-year grace period, with 2 percent interest. The agreement was a settlement of Lend Lease. The British got to keep all Lend Lease supplies and installations in their territory. The British agreed to free up the sterling balances gradually, accept the Bretton Woods agreements, and make sterling fully convertible one year after congressional approval of the loan.

The loan to Britain had its critics within the U.S. government. Within the Truman administration, Clayton had a reputation as a hard-nosed negotiator and a fervent advocate of multi-lateral trade. Acheson worried that the loan was insufficient and took less pleasure in imposing the American will on Britain than other Truman officials. Secretary of War Stimson and Secretary of the Navy James Forrestal, usually considered tough-minded, shared similar misgivings. Stimson characterized the final agreement as "somewhat cold-blooded."

Congress was reluctant to be even as generous as Clayton. Congressional deliberations consumed six months. Final approval owed a great deal to fears that the United States needed British support against Russia.[21]

Events over the next several years demonstrated that U.S. negotiators had over-reached. The United States was stronger financially than they had calculated and its western European allies, particularly Britain, were weaker. The U.S. had also underestimated the costs and difficulties involved in repairing war damage across Europe. The terms of the British loan required Britain to make sterling fully convertible a year after Congressional approval. When Britain did so in summer 1947, the results were disastrous. The outflow of capital from London threatened to wipe out British financial reserves and undermine the value of the pound. The British government found itself seeking U.S. permission to re-impose exchange controls. In 1949, the scenario was repeated. The value of Britain's imports exceeded the value of its exports to a degree that threatened its financial reserves. The British had to seek American assistance in devaluing the pound sterling. Recognizing that all the economies of Western Europe were at risk in 1947, the United States implemented the Marshall Plan, a program of financial assistance far larger than anything contemplated at the end of the war.

Besides helping Britain weather the financial crises of 1947 and 1949, the United States deferred the critical financial and commercial changes it had demanded of Britain. As a step towards new trade policies, the terms of the British loan required Britain to participate in an international trade conference. The 1946 Geneva conference revealed considerable agreement among the twenty-three participating nations. It produced the General Agreement on Tariffs and Trade, a framework for continuing efforts to reduce trade barriers, among other things. Nevertheless, at Geneva and at subsequent trade negotiations, the United States settled for agreements in principle with Britain without meaningful, immediate implementation. Trade barriers within the empire were reduced somewhat, but remained in place. The sterling area with its exchange controls persisted. Contrary to terms of the British loan, Britain imposed restrictions on U.S. exports to its colonies. Britain's practice of bulk purchases from its colonies of agricultural commodities, a violation of multilateral trade principles, went unchallenged.

United States negotiators were hindered by clear indications that support for multilateral trade was far from universal within the U.S. government, particularly in Congress. British negotiators could point to the U.S. agreement with the newly independent Philippines, with its preferential tariffs and import quotas, or to a proposed Latin American trade charter that allowed bilateral commodity agreements. In the midst of the Geneva talks, the Congress passed legislation raising the U.S. tariff on wool imports. Clayton had to return to Washington to urge Truman to veto it. By 1948, reconstruction efforts had restored much of Western Europe's productive capability. European nations needed to increase their exports to the United States in order to earn dollars. Nevertheless, when the Reciprocal Trade Agreements Act, the principal United States vehicle for mutual reduction of trade barriers, came before Congress for renewal, the Republican majority voted only a one-year renewal, instead of the requested three-year term, and added several damaging amendments.[22]

Atomic Weapons

In the postwar world, atomic weapons were perceived, particularly in the United States, as defining global power. A nation that could produce and deploy atomic weapons could claim superiority over other nations. The interactions of Britain and the United States regarding atomic weapons followed the same trajectory as their dealings in international trade and finance. Wartime collaboration was followed by a disorderly transition period from which the U.S. emerged holding the upper hand.

Churchill and Roosevelt negotiated three agreements regarding atomic weapons: the Quebec Agreement of August 1943, the Declaration of Trust of June 1944, and the Hyde Park Memoire of September 1944. The Quebec agreement gave the U.S. president sole authority to determine Britain's rights for postwar industrial application of atomic energy. Nevertheless, the main thrust of the agreements was cooperative development and control of atomic weapons. Churchill described them to his colleagues as based on "indefinite collaboration in the postwar period subject to termination by joint agreement." Churchill confessed some apprehension about the agreements, but argued that they were the best terms the British were likely to get. Britain's ties to the United States had to be permanent, Churchill wrote, and he professed no fear the U.S. would maltreat Britain.[23]

Despite the agreements, the U.S. played the larger role in atomic matters during the war. The Manhattan Project, which developed and built the first atomic bombs, was an American undertaking, financially and operationally. The Pacific theatre was a U.S. responsibility. The British perceived the decision to use the bomb against Japan as a United States decision, a responsibility of the U.S. president.

Truman was inclined to have the U.S. follow its own course on atomic matters. He told reporters in the fall of 1945 that only the United States had the capacity and resources to build the bomb. If other countries wanted to catch up, they would have to do it on their own.[24]

In November 1945, Truman negotiated a series of agreements with Attlee and MacKenzie King, the Canadian prime minister, that appeared to commit the United States to continued cooperation in atomic matters with no stated exceptions or limitations. Within six months, appearances proved deceiving. When the British attempted to activate the agreements, to obtain the engineering and technical information needed to build a nuclear plant, Truman refused to hand over the information. Truman claimed that the United States was bound to provide only basic scientific research. In an April 1946 telegram, he told Attlee that he would not have signed the agreement had he known that it obligated the U.S. to help Britain build an atomic energy plant. Given that the U.S. government was publicly advocating international control of atomic energy, Truman asserted that popular opinion in the United States would not allow him to assist the British.[25]

If Truman closed the door to cooperation, Congress locked it. Members of Congress professed concerns about the executive branch's failures to keep them fully informed about atomic matters and about the administration's apparent willingness to share atomic information with foreign countries. Senator Arthur Vandenburg, a Republican spokesman on foreign policy, told Truman that Britain was far more dependent on the United States than the United States was on Britain. The U.S. was always bailing Britain out and was now proposing to share its latest and most prized possession, Vandenburg contended. Senate Democrats, led by Senator Brien McMahon of Connecticut, drafted legislation that asserted civilian, not military, control of atomic energy and imposed strict limits on information about atomic matters that the United States would share with other countries. The Senate passed the McMahon Act in June 1946. The House strengthened it and sent it to Truman for his signature. Content to have further reason to deny Britain atomic information, Truman signed the bill. Cooperation with Britain became more difficult politically when in May 1947 Acheson shared with Congress the full extent of Roosevelt's commitments to Churchill regarding atomic weapons.[26]

British officials considered atomic cooperation with the United States critically important. They were not easily deterred. Shortly after arriving in Washington as Britain's ambassador, Oliver Franks saw relations with the United States about atomic matters as bound up with the larger issue of U.S. willingness to treat Britain on more or less equal terms as a first-class power. Attlee protested Truman's decision to withhold engineering and operational information. After passage of the McMahon Act, the British repeatedly attempted to salvage some sort of collaborative arrangement with the U.S. regarding atomic matters. For a time, the United States and Britain had an agreement regarding the disposition of uranium ore. Unwilling to accept second-class status, the Attlee government resolved to develop its own atomic weapons.

The Truman Doctrine

In March 1947, Truman addressed a joint session of Congress to request U.S. aid to Greece and Turkey. Truman laid out for the Congress and the general public important strands of his new foreign policy, the so-called Truman Doctrine. Truman claimed for the United States global responsibilities. He justified the new responsibilities in terms of protecting other nations from armed minorities and outside pressure. He spoke in terms of promoting freedom and majority rule while opposing terror, oppression, and tyrannical minorities. He acknowledged, but did not emphasize, that the United States, in assuming new responsibilities, was taking on Great Britain's former role.

The immediate occasion for Truman's speech was the British government's notification to the U.S. that it would no longer be able to provide economic and other aid to Greece and Turkey. Towards the end of the war, British troops occupied Greece. The British supported conservative Greek politicians against leftist forces in what degenerated into a civil war. Yugoslavia and other Russian allies provided aid to the left-wing groups. Russia asserted that it should share with Turkey control of the Dardanelles, the straits between the Mediterranean and the Black Sea. Great Britain and the United States provided Turkey with aid during and after the war in order to assure Turkish neutrality. On February 21, 1947, the Attlee government sent the Truman administration notes indicating that British aid would end in six weeks.

The British notes made a splash in Washington. State Department officials were already considering U.S. aid to Greece, but the arrival of the British notes sparked a crisis. Acheson, as under secretary, saw them as an opportunity to assert State Department leadership. The State Department set to work developing proposals and selling them to Secretary of State Marshall, Truman, and congressional representatives. The British notes signaled, to some U.S. officials, a historic shift in world politics. The British note came on the heels of announcements that Britain would cede India its independence and that it would abandon its mandate in Palestine. Moreover, the British economy virtually halted during the difficult winter of 1946–47. One State Department official characterized the notes as "an irrevocable admission of impotence." Another reported that Secretary Marshall thought that the world had arrived at a point in its history unparalleled since ancient times. Heretofore optimistic about British capabilities, Acheson told a reporter that the British were finished. According to Acheson, the problem was that the United States was not ready to take their place.[27]

In requesting aid to Greece and Turkey, Truman described a world facing two alternatives. Left on their own, nations could choose majority rule and freedom. Faced with armed minorities or with outside pressure, nations might accept totalitarian regimes, characterized by the tyranny of the minority, by terror, oppression, and suppression of personal freedoms. According to Truman, Greece and Turkey might be the problem of the moment, but the challenge to free nations existed around the globe.

Although Truman did not mention Russia in his speech and referred to communists only once, his speech was considered anti–Russian and anti-communist. The administration had gained congressional support only by emphasizing the anti–Russian and anti-communist intent of its proposals. When Marshall blandly described the State Department's recommendations to key members of Congress, the response was luke-warm. Only when Acheson chimed in with a vivid portrayal of the dangers of Russian and communist advances from the eastern Mediterranean into Asia, Europe, and even Africa did the senators and congressmen respond. Vandenburg told Acheson that if the administration would make that argument to the Congress and the county, he would support it.[28]

The United States needed to act, Truman told the Congress. Greece and Turkey needed help now. U.S. foreign policy sought to ensure that nations could choose their way of life, free of coercion. The United States had defeated Japan and Germany with this in mind. The U.S. had helped establish the United Nations, but the United Nations was not in a position to help. America had to act on its own to make sure that the objectives of the United Nations were realized. Truman made it clear that U.S. responsibilities extended beyond Greece and Turkey to all free nations.

Truman acknowledged that the U.S. faced a challenge in the eastern Mediterranean because Great Britain could no longer provide aid. Otherwise, he did not refer to Britain or its changed circumstances. Acheson and others in the Truman administration saw a basic shift in great power politics, favoring the United States at Britain's expense. They chose not to present the Truman Doctrine in those terms, however. In public statements, Acheson denied that the U.S. was setting out to rescue the British or to displace them. Administration spokesmen were instructed to avoid mentioning the British. In supporting the administration, Vandenburg argued that British actions in Greece were a continuation of a long tradition. U.S. aid, on the other hand, was something new and positive.[29]

The Truman Doctrine was more important in Washington than elsewhere. The Greek and Turkish governments benefited from the American proclamation of support, but aid did not arrive for some time. British officials did not perceive their notes as marking a major shift in their policies. Eliminating aid to Greece and Turkey was a tactical retreat. Some British officials even saw the episode as benefiting Britain, by drawing the United States more definitely into the eastern Mediterranean, where it might support British interests. In the United States, on the other hand, Truman and his officials found a formula in the Truman Doctrine speech that could secure bipartisan political support for a wider U.S. role around the world. Striking anti–Russia and anti-communist notes allowed the Truman administration to overcome Republican and popular opposition to U.S. involvement in great power politics outside the Western Hemisphere.[30]

Truman Administration and Colonies

Given the American postwar global role, the Truman administration found itself confronting the fate of European colonies around the world. As the war ended, its first actions favored restoration of the colonial empires. Truman arranged for Hong Kong to be surrendered to British, rather than Chinese, forces. The United States withdrew its troops from Indochina, making way for British and French forces.

Truman was continuing, not changing, his predecessor's policies. In wartime meetings, Roosevelt had raised the notion of removing Indochina from French control and converting it into a United Nations trust territory. As the war approached its conclusion, however, Roosevelt changed his mind. He concluded that the local peoples were not ready for self-government and that colonialism was preferable to anarchy. Attempting to change Indochina's status would also upset his British and French allies.[31]

The Truman administration proved willing to welcome newly independent states without pushing the colonial powers to grant independence. The Truman administration was quietly supportive of British decisions to concede independence to India, Pakistan, Burma, and Ceylon. It was willing to have the former Italian colony of Libya gain its independence and for Italian Somaliland to embark on a ten-year timetable to independence. When the long and tortured dealings of the Netherlands with its Southeast Asian colony seemed headed for more conflict, the United States intervened. In 1949, the Truman administration threatened to withhold aid funds from the Netherlands if it did not grant independence to Indonesia. Indochina was the principal exception to the Truman administration's tolerance of nationalist movements. The Truman administration viewed the Viet Minh's communist ideology as a threat to U.S. interests and supported French efforts to suppress the nationalist movement.

Independence for the Philippines

The Truman administration faced a decision regarding the future of America's principal colony, the Philippines. The Tydings-McDuffie Act of 1934 provided for Philippine independence in ten years. In the wake of the Japanese attack on Pearl Harbor in December 1941 and as Japanese armies were overrunning the Philippines, the Philippine government under President Quezon requested immediate independence so that it could negotiate with Japan. Roosevelt refused, repeating the promises incorporated in the Tydings-McDuffie Act. The United States evacuated Quezon and his government to Australia, but many prominent Filipino politicians cooperated with the Japanese. During the war, the future of the Philippines remained a live issue. Secretary of War Stimson, a former governor of the Philippines and, as Hoover's secretary of state, an opponent of Philippine independence, remained skeptical about independence, pointing to the need for U.S. bases in the Philippines. Trade relations between the United States and the Philippines, postwar rehabilitation of the Philippine economy, and the fate of Filipino collaborators with the Japanese figured in the discussions. In 1943, the Congress enacted Joint Resolution 93, introduced by Senator Millard Tydings, a Democrat from Maryland, which authorized the president to grant the Philippines independence following its liberation from the Japanese and the restoration of constitutional government. The resolution authorized the U.S. retention of more military facilities in the Philippines than did Tydings-McDuffie. Roosevelt seemed poised to use the authority sooner rather than later when he died, leaving the issue to Truman.

The debate continued in the first months of the Truman administration. U.S. business interests favored delaying independence for five or ten years. Paul McNutt, whom Truman re-appointed as U.S. high commissioner in the Philippines, opposed independence. Stimson counseled patience, arguing that the United States was more likely to negotiate favorable relations with the Philippines before granting the colony its independence, rather than after. The OSS pointed out that the colonial powers would seize upon any deviation from the provisions of Tydings-McDuffie as an excuse to retain their colonies in eastern Asia. Truman does not appear to have had strong views on the Philippines before he became president. His memoirs report that his goal was to make the Philippines as independent as Cuba.[32]

Trade relations were a sticking point. Before the war, the Roosevelt administration and the Congress agreed that preferential trade relations between the United States and the Philippines would be phased out gradually after independence. In 1945, Jasper Bell, a Democratic congressman from Missouri and chairman of the House Insular Affairs Committee, introduced legislation purportedly aimed at postwar rehabilitation of the Philippines that would make trade preferences permanent. Bell's argument was that trade preferences and other provisions favoring U.S. businesses would prompt American private sector to invest in the Philippines and restore its economy. The State Department and others in the Truman administration were opposed to permanent trade preferences because they ran counter to the U.S. commitment to multilateral trade. Granting the Philippines preferences would undermine the U.S. efforts to push Britain and others to eliminate preferences. Moreover, only 3 percent of prewar U.S. exports went to the Philippines, while 40 percent went to countries within the British empire.[33]

A compromise measure emerged by the end of 1945. The Philippines would have its independence. Congress accepted the State Department's alternative trade proposal: a period, ultimately eight years, of trade preferences followed by a longer period, twenty years in the final version, of gradually declining preferences. The bill retained Bell's proposals for allowing American companies to own mines, forests, and other resources in the Philippines, despite the prohibition included in the 1936 Philippines constitution. The value of the Filipino peso would be tied to that of the United States dollar and the U.S. president would have to approve any changes in the peso's value. The United States would grant the Philippines $620 million for rehabilitation, only about half of what the Philippine government wanted. Only $100 million would be available until the Philippines accepted the proposed trade arrangements.

Truman signed the legislation, but advertised his misgivings. He observed that he had reservations about some provisions and urged reconsideration later. He asserted that preferential trade relations were not administration policy. He characterized the bill as a rehabilitation measure intended to have private enterprise revive the Philippine economy. On that basis, he was willing to approve it.[34]

The Philippine government accepted the U.S. proposals, but not easily. Both major Filipino political parties, the Nationalista and the Liberal parties, publicly favored independence, although many leaders were thought to harbor reservations. In the 1946 Philippine elections, the Liberal Party headed by Manual Roxas won, with Roxas elected president. Roxas was a protégé of General Douglas MacArthur and had an eventful wartime career. He accompanied the Quezon government into exile in Australia, but returned to the Philippines to lead resistance against the Japanese. Captured by the Japanese, he served in the Philippine government that cooperated with Japan. Arrested by U.S. forces as a collaborator, he was cleared by MacArthur. Faced with a Philippine legislature unlikely to approve the U.S. proposals, Roxas managed to have enough hostile members ousted, ostensibly for vote fraud, to ensure passage. He arranged that the vote to amend the constitution to allow foreign ownership of natural resources take place the night before independence. Under the pre-independence constitution, only a simple majority vote was necessary, while the new Philippine constitution mandated a two-thirds vote.

On July 4, 1946, the Philippines gained its independence, but remained within the orbit of the United States. McNutt and Roxas later negotiated an agreement on military bases, granting the United States ninety-nine-year leases on at least sixteen sites. The Philippine economy was also tightly tied to the U.S. economy. One U.S. analyst commented in 1946 that the Philippines was still dependent on the United States militarily, economically, and politically. Its independence was largely a matter of "face."[35]

U.S. Policies Towards Colonies

Outside the United Nations, the Truman administration paid little attention to colonial issues and stuck to well-worn paths when it did address them. Soon after Truman took office, Stettinius provided him with a compendium of U.S. foreign policies. The compendium identified two objectives for dependent peoples: promoting educational, physical, social, and economic growth and training for ultimate independent sovereignty. In an October 1945 speech, Truman proclaimed that the United States believed that all peoples prepared for self-government should be permitted to choose their form of government, without outside interference. Truman said that this policy applied around the world, in Europe, Asia, and Africa as well as the Western Hemisphere. Secretary of State Byrnes dismissed the suggestion of an international conference on colonial educational and social issues. He said that the colonial powers would think the United States was encouraging political agitation if it proposed a conference. It would be more difficult for the United States to work with the colonial powers and to complete establishment of the trusteeship system.[36]

The newly expanded State Department began to produce analyses that touched on Britain's African colonies. A December 1946 report saw considerable agreement between the United States and Britain regarding colonial policy, asserting that both saw self-government as the long-term goal. The report stated that Britain had given Africans a larger political role in Nigeria and the Gold Coast and was taking steps to safeguard the "millions of untutored blacks in the hinterland." Britain had much to do before the inhabitants of any of the West African colonies could control their government, the report added. A 1947 report noted that nationalist movements were active in some territories, but most colonial peoples were politically inactive or favored the British connection.[37]

Trade and commercial issues received as much attention as political issues. Stettinius's policy compendium stated that the U.S. had acquiesced when the colonial powers imposed trade and commercial restrictions in Africa during the war. With the end of hostilities, it expected that "open door" policies would resume. The 1946 report stated that the only problems the United States encountered in Britain's West African colonies had to do with the tight economic controls imposed by Britain. The report went on to list specific concerns about petroleum sales in the colonies and restrictions on West African exports of cocoa, tin, lumber, and goatskins.[38]

Through 1949, high level, public statements of U.S. policy regarding colonies, including Britain and its African colonies, were brief and infrequent. If they broke any new ground, it was to omit Cordell Hull's caveats about dependent territories needing to accept the responsibilities of independence. In 1948, Secretary of State Marshall told the United Nations General Assembly that the U.S. was mindful of the obligations included in the United

Nations charter for the development of the non–self-governing territories. The United States believed that these territories should receive all possible assistance so that they could achieve independence or free association with other states. The following year, Secretary of State Acheson stated in a speech that the U.S. supported the aspirations of non–self-governing peoples to achieve self-government or independence at the earliest practicable date.[39]

Internal State Department documents put less emphasis on independence. A 1948 policy statement regarding Anglo-American relations noted that U.S. policy towards the British empire was "subject to our general policy of favoring eventual self-determination of peoples." The emphasis was on the need for British friendship and cooperation. The stated U.S. policy for the British empire was that it maintain its integrity. Britain should retain control of its outlying possessions and any British retrenchment should be orderly. Territory over which Britain relinquished control should not fall into less friendly hands.[40]

Disagreements Within the State Department

The potential contradiction inherent in seeking British cooperation and supporting independence sparked disagreements within the State Department which followed functional lines. Staff responsible for assembling majority support within United Nations bodies for U.S. positions were less likely to support British positions than the officials who handled Anglo-American relations. The State Department organization responsible for Africa was not a fervent promoter of independence. The responsible assistant secretary, George McGhee, believed that most territories in Africa were a long way from independence. Progress toward self-government needed to be geared to political, economic, and social progress, he thought. Premature independence would do African peoples a disservice. The disagreements also reflected ideological differences. Oliver Franks, British ambassador to the United States, discerned three groups among State Department officials. A few consistently supported British positions on colonial questions. Others wanted to support Britain on strategic or other grounds, but doubted that British policies were viable. A third group empathized with dependent peoples.[41]

A prominent promoter of closer ties to Britain and less support for independence was George Kennan. In the late 1940s, Kennan headed the Policy Planning Staff, a small, highly placed office created by Marshall to generate policy ideas. Kennan had a low opinion of non–European peoples. He thought them impulsive, fanatical, ignorant, lazy, unhappy, and prone to mental disorders and other biological deficiencies. After Indian Prime Minister Nehru visited Washington, Kennan warned Acheson that leaders such as Nehru often tended to be neurotic products of exotic backgrounds and tentative Western educational experiences, racially and socially embittered against the West. Kennan thought that the U.S. needed to rethink its policy toward dependent territories and reach an understanding with the British. A Policy Planning Staff paper advocated that the Western European countries address their economic weakness by collaborating in the economic development of Africa. The paper saw the British commitment to self-government for its colonies as an obstacle to their development as a source of raw materials and foodstuffs for Europe. When other members of the Policy Planning Staff pointed out that self-government was U.S. policy, Kennan's first reply was that there was no prospect of self-government for many African areas. Pressed further, he professed to see no conflict between the sort of economic development envisioned and support for self-government when African colonies were ready for it.[42]

Similar recommendations came from a State Department official in the field. In early 1950, Perry Jester, the consul general in Dakar, argued for a clarification of U.S. policy towards Africa. Public statements in favor of self-determination by U.S. officials convinced the colonial powers that the United States intended to liquidate their empires, Jester contended. Self-determination might make sense for India or Indonesia, but Africans were too primitive for independence in the near future. African states granted independence prematurely would become Russian pawns. The United States needed to reassure the colonial powers that it was not pushing for premature independence. It needed to work with them to foster development in Africa, while remaining silent on the question of independence.[43]

The disagreements within the State Department at times leaked out and complicated dealing with British representatives. In the midst of preparations for talks with the British in July 1950, a State Department staffer urged that senior State Department officials be made aware of the bureaus' inability to agree on the U.S. position. The staffer also warned against exposing differences to public view. In dealing with the Foreign Office, the staffer admonished, State Department officials ought to avoid identifying themselves as representing one State Department organization or another. They should present themselves as representing the State Department.[44]

Writing a Policy Paper on Colonialism

Senior State Department officials thought a paper laying out U.S. policies toward dependent areas would resolve the disagreements within the department and provide a sounder basis for dealing with United Nations issues. As early as July 1948, Philip Jessup, acting chief of the United States mission at the U.N., proposed a colonial policy paper to Dean Rusk, director of the State Department's Office of United Nations Affairs. Rusk adopted the notion and circulated a memorandum throughout the department arguing for a long-range policy regarding emergent nations. The Rusk memorandum led to series of draft papers produced over the course of 1949. During 1950, a State Department committee produced more draft papers. In 1952, another State Department group took up the task, beginning its work with the last draft produced by the 1950 committee.[45]

In proposing a meeting to begin the 1950 effort, John Hickerson, assistant secretary of state for United Nations affairs, laid out the State Department's goals for a policy paper. Hickerson thought the department needed to reassure itself that its policy toward colonial areas was right and reasonable in light of its wider implications and long-range importance. A paper might also lead to an improved attitude on the part of the colonial powers regarding U.N. activities in the colonial field. It might help the United States explain its position to the non-colonial powers and convince them that intelligent restraint was needed if the United Nations was to solve colonial problems. Hickerson imagined that agreement on detailed principles, approved at a high level, could eliminate handling colonial issues on an ad hoc basis and resolve conflicting attitudes among State Department officials.[46]

In trying to write a policy paper on colonial issues, the State Department followed procedures common to large organizations. The committees drew representatives from across the department. The 1952 Working Group on Colonial Problems included representatives of nine organizations within the department, including the Bureau of United Nations Affairs and the four "geographic" or regional bureaus responsible for dealing with individual countries. The committees met periodically to discuss and draft policies. They circulated successive drafts within the department and sought to incorporate the comments and suggestions they received into future drafts.[47]

The draft papers reiterated familiar positions. The United States should favor development towards self-government for all colonial peoples and towards independence where conditions were suitable. The United States should promote political and economic stability in colonial areas in order to prevent their domination by unfriendly movements or powers through aggression or subversion. The United States should seek to align dependent peoples with the U.S. Mutual understanding and cooperation with the colonial powers should be a U.S. objective, as well acceptance by the colonial powers of basic American objectives. The United States should seek to prevent Russia from earning a reputation as the champion of colonial peoples and to discourage dependent peoples from aligning themselves with Russia and its allies.[48]

Rather than identifying solutions, the papers, more often than not, restated the problems. The U.S. sought the cooperation not only of the colonial powers but of the non-colonial powers as well. The U.S. favored development towards self-government, but it had to be concerned about its own security. U.S. security concerns sometimes dictated slowing down progress toward self-government and independence. The United States wanted the cooperation of the colonial powers, but did not want to be identified with them, certainly not with the most conservative. It was in the immediate best interests of the U.S. to support the colonial powers, but it was in her long-term interests to convince colonial peoples that the U.S. had pursued, and would continue to pursue, policies that were in the colonial peoples' interests.

In terms of the independence versus self-government debate, the papers would have put the U.S. close to the British position of self-government in association with a colonial power. The papers were explicit that self-government was the goal for all dependent peoples. Independence was the goal only for territories where conditions were suitable. Echoing Hull's emphasis on the inhabitants' capacity for independence and their willingness to accept the responsibilities that went with independence, the papers argued that the capacities of a territory's inhabitants should dictate the pace at which a territory moved towards self-government. They also argued that such capacities should not determine whether a territory became independent or attained only self-government. They maintained that self-government demanded as much from inhabitants as did independence. The conditions that determined whether a territory was suited for self-government or independence had to do with the territory's size, its economic resources, its defensibility as a unit, and the status desired by the inhabitants. "Balkanization," the creation of many small states with precarious economies and unable to defend themselves was to be avoided. Such states would be at the mercy of communist pressures and infiltration. The papers went on to state that varying degrees of self-government were possible up to full independence. Federations of dependent territories would avoid the dangers posed by independence. The papers listed various types of association between a colonial power and its dependent territories that might fulfill the requirement of the United Nations Charter's Chapter Eleven, that territories be developed in the best interests of their inhabitants. The alternatives included trusteeship, voluntary union with the colonial power, and joint membership in a common political union.

Maintaining what the papers termed "United States security and general international security" was a critical goal. A 1949 draft argued that the progress of dependent areas was dependent on American security. It was appropriate that movement towards self-government be slowed in order to safeguard the U.S. Putting U.S. security first did not resolve basic dilemmas. The 1950 paper pointed out that while the immediate, obvious effects of a given policy, for example supporting a friendly administration in a "little known territory in Central Africa," might serve U.S. security interests, the longer term impact on the attitudes of local people and of the many anti-colonial states around the world might not. The same paper concluded that supporting the colonial powers in most instances best served the security interests of the United States. It also suggested accelerated political, economic, and social development in the colonies. The paper mentioned British East Africa, where nationalist movements were "still in an embryonic state," as an area where the U.S. could safely support colonial rule. The paper conceded that nationalist forces could challenge colonial administration to the point that it could not survive even through expending considerable resources, in Indonesia for example. The U.S. should accept the situation and encourage a peaceful transfer of power.

The State Department authors held out hope for the American ability to persuade the colonial powers of the wisdom of U.S. policies. The 1949 paper proposed that the United States explain to the colonial powers that it would consult with them on colonial issues. The U.S. should argue that dependent territories would turn to Russia if the U.S. became overly identified with them. It was essential that America develop a counter attraction to Russian proposals, even if it meant taking positions that displeased the colonial powers. The colonial powers would be better off if the U.S. maintained a position independent of them. The 1950 draft imagined that the United States could convince the colonial powers that it had a carefully considered, long-term colonial policy. Its positions on specific issues were not ad hoc decisions, dictated only by immediate considerations.

The State Department's efforts to contrive an improved, comprehensive policy toward colonial areas failed. None of the draft papers achieved approval at the assistant secretary level, that is, at the level of the heads of the geographic bureaus, much less approval by the secretary of state. Hickerson reported that the 1950 draft served as a general guide for U.S. positions in the United Nations. Hickerson added, however, that it was difficult to apply the paper's general principles to specific situations. The 1950 draft served as a background paper for Anglo-American talks on colonial issues. Benjamin Gerig, another senior State Department official, wrote that the 1952 group had identified the problems and compiled the relevant documentation. It facilitated review of papers regarding specific United Nations issues. Yet its authors believed that they had not completed their basic task, recommending a clear general policy on colonial questions.[49]

The policy-making exercise did not end arguments within the State Department regarding colonial policy. In mid–1952, Ridgway Knight of the Office of Western European Affairs circulated a paper that purported to support continuation of past policies. Knight characterized them as assisting both colonial powers and colonial peoples to move together towards self-government. Staff in the Bureau of United Nations Affairs interpreted the paper as a bid to shift U.S. support towards the colonial powers. They responded that favoring the NATO allies at the expense of dependent peoples would alienate newly independent states and threaten U.S. security. Whereas Knight's paper imagined that independence would not come to Africa for many years, the Bureau of United Nations Affairs argued that the trend was for early rather than late independence. The colonial powers needed to accelerate training and development. It would be a mistake for the United States to encourage any other policy.[50]

A Policy for Colonial Africa

In the wake of the State Department reorganization of 1949 and the appointment of George McGhee as assistant secretary for Near Eastern, South Asian and African affairs, the State Department officials responsible for Africa began their own efforts to construct a U.S. policy for Africa. McGhee convened a meeting of outside experts to discuss policy concerns. He organized a gathering of the State Department officials stationed in Africa south of the Sahara. The Bureau of Near Eastern, South Asian, and African Affairs produced its own policy documents. In May 1950, McGhee gave a speech that he later characterized as laying out the country's first comprehensive statement of its aims for Africa.

The group of eleven experts on Africa that met at the State Department in February 1950[51] acknowledged the issues facing policymakers, in particular the conflict between cooperation with the colonial powers and support for eventual self-government or independence. In making recommendations, the experts straddled some fences. They recommended that the United States should favor the interests of African peoples over those of the colonial powers. Yet the U.S. should not take independent positions regarding the timing for self-government or independence. The panel emphasized the U.S. interest in political and economic stability in Africa, in orderly political, social, and economic development, and in continued association of African territories with the U.S. and its allies. To dispel misunderstandings about U.S. policies, the panel recommended consultations with the colonial powers.[52]

The U.S. consular officials who gathered in Lourenco Marques, Mozambique, in February and March 1950 reached similar conclusions. Political and economic stability were key goals. America needed to protect its strategic interests and induce dependent peoples to remain aligned with the United States and its allies. The United States needed close ties with both the colonial powers and independent African states. The consular officials favored closer political cooperation with the colonial powers. Worried that a U.S. initiative might be misunderstood, they recommended that the United States wait for an invitation from the colonial powers. In the meantime, the U.S. should take steps to promote greater economic cooperation between itself and the colonial powers in Africa.[53]

The policy papers prepared by the Bureau of Near Eastern, South Asian, and African Affairs later in 1950 added two significant notes. They put more emphasis on U.S. commercial and economic interests in Africa, on the need for access to raw materials and on nondiscriminatory treatment of American businesses. They also stressed the importance of reassuring the colonial powers that the U.S. was not working to prompt premature independence for African colonies. They noted that the positions adopted by U.S. officials in the United Nations had upset representatives of the colonial powers and recommended consultations with the colonial powers to mollify their feelings.[54]

When McGhee addressed the Foreign Policy Association of Oklahoma City in May 1950, he stuck to the same script. He outlined four U.S. objectives for Africa: progressive development of African peoples toward self-government or independence; development of mutually advantageous economic relations between the colonial powers and their African colonies; preservation of the rights to equal economic treatment for all businesses in Africa; and creation of an environment in which Africans would want to be associated with the U.S. and its allies. McGhee said that Africa was experiencing a grace period, without crises or threat of communist intrusion. The United States needed to take advantage of the opportunity to work with the colonial powers to promote orderly development.[55]

As bland as the McGhee speech was, it upset French and Belgian officials. They complained that while they welcomed U.S. economic aid, they did not need the American views on political development. The State Department felt compelled to explain that McGhee had been misunderstood. The U.S. was committed to assisting the French promote orderly development.[56]

The Truman administration solidified U.S. dominance over Great Britain. It abruptly cut off Lend Lease regardless of the impact on Britain. To rescue Britain from financial ruin, it lent Britain $3 billion but imposed important conditions intended to reshape international trade and finance to suit the United States. Despite wartime pledges of cooperation, the Truman administration cut Britain off from significant technical expertise about atomic weapons.

The Truman administration did not use its power over Britain to effect wholesale changes in Britain's African colonies. The Truman administration did not know, in fact, what to do about Britain's African colonies. It was quietly supportive when Britain gave India and other Asian colonies their independence. It granted the Philippines, the principal colony of the U.S., its independence, although with important strings attached. In high-level pronouncements, the United States maintained Roosevelt's anti-colonial and pro-independence position. Nevertheless, the State Department had a better sense of the problems colonial areas posed than of U.S. solutions. Support for colonial self-government seemed, in particular, to conflict with the U.S. alliance with Britain and other European powers. State Department efforts to devise a colonial policy or an African policy consumed time and effort, but produced little.

4

Great Britain, the United States and Colonial Issues in the United Nations, 1946–1952: In the Middle of the Road

The Roosevelt administration's commitment to a postwar international organization responsible in some fashion for colonial territories forced the Truman administration to grapple with colonial issues. The Truman administration first had to participate in fleshing out the international organization, including its authority regarding colonial territories. Since the United Nations quickly took up colonial issues, the Truman administration also had to decide how to deal with them. Truman's State Department settled on a middle of the road policy; it attempted to remain on friendly terms with both colonial and anti-colonial factions within the United States. Not surprisingly, this approach often put the United States at odds with its British allies.

Writing the United Nations Charter

The negotiations leading to the establishment of the United Nations were the Truman administration's first significant interaction with Britain over its colonies. Since the San Francisco meeting began roughly two weeks after Truman's ascent to the presidency, Truman played almost no role and the U.N. negotiations fell into a kind of interregnum. Truman was president, but the decisions and personnel were part of the Roosevelt administration. The U.S. position was in the hands of its delegation to the San Francisco talks. The delegation included senior administration figures, key members of Congress, and veterans of the State Department's wartime policy debates regarding colonial matters. The delegation was bipartisan, including important Republicans such as Senator Arthur Vandenburg, Harold Stassen, and John Foster Dulles.

On the long train ride from Washington to San Francisco, the delegation resolved the most heated disagreement within the administration, the fate of the former Japanese possessions in the Pacific. It decided to push for a two-tiered trusteeship system, with powers administering so-called "strategic" trusteeship areas, like the islands formerly held by Japan, accorded more leeway. In San Francisco, discussions of colonial issues took place on two parallel tracks. Since the Big Five, the United States, Britain, France, Russia, and China, had agreed to meet and develop joint positions before the United Nations negotiations proper but had failed to do so regarding colonial issues, they met separately as the main negotiations progressed. Working with drafts produced by Britain and others, the United States, in the person of Harold Stassen, took the lead in developing the U.N.'s initial approach to the world's colonies. In general, the outcome reflected agreements among the Big Five.[1]

The United Nations Charter developed in San Francisco included three chapters related to colonies. Chapter Eleven was a declaration on what were termed, "non–self-governing territories." It described the responsibilities of U.N. members responsible for territories whose peoples had not attained full self-government. Chapter Twelve described the workings of an international trusteeship system. In accord with the American position, it distinguished between strategic trust territories and other trust territories. Chapter Twelve laid out the responsibilities of powers administering trust territories and described what territories might become trust territories. Chapter Thirteen provided for a Trusteeship Council operating under the authority of the U.N. General Assembly and responsible for overseeing administration of trust territories.

The goal for colonial territories, whether independence or self-government, was a central issue at San Francisco, just as it had been in the wartime exchanges between Britain and the United States. The British remained convinced that self-government differed significantly from independence. "Self-government" in this sense would allow Britain to keep its colonies within its control. Britain resisted attempts by Russia, China, and other, smaller nations to make independence the goal for all non–self-governing territories. The U.S. delegation was divided and unsure, mirroring the wartime discussions within the State Department. Some members argued that abandoning independence as the goal would cost the United States the support of smaller nations and of colonial peoples. The majority of the delegation, led by Stassen, argued that agreement with the British and among the Big Five was the more important, more immediate goal. Fearing that British resistance could endanger any agreement on colonial issues or that U.S. insistence would alienate the British, the U.S. delegation developed a compromise and pushed it through. Self-government would replace independence in Chapter Eleven as the goal for non–self-governing territories, while independence would remain in Chapter Twelve as the goal for trust territories. Chapter Eleven was also watered down to suit the British by adding the provision that movement towards self-government would be dependent on the circumstances of each territory and the state of development of its people. The U.S. delegation was sufficiently sensitive about the compromise that it later issued an explanatory statement. The delegation argued that independence was one form of self-government. The statement said that setting self-government as the goal did not preclude dependent peoples from attaining independence if they so desired and were willing to assume the associated responsibilities. It did not preclude their choosing a form of self-government other than independence, the statement also asserted.[2]

Another provision of Chapter Eleven attracted less notice. Building upon an Australian proposal, the United States promoted a requirement that countries administering non–self-governing territories submit to the Secretary General, for information purposes, reports on economic, social, and educational conditions in the territories. The final wording of what became Article 73e of the United Nations Charter made the reporting requirement subject to whatever limits security and constitutional considerations might require. Some within the U.S. delegation wanted to widen the Australian proposal to encompass political information, but fears that Congress and the United States military would object blocked expansion of the reporting requirement.

The trusteeship system described in Chapters Twelve and Thirteen incorporated many features favoring the administering powers. The Trusteeship Council was to include national representatives, divided equally between administering and non-administering powers. The Permanent Mandates Commission of the League of Nations, in contrast, consisted of ostensibly independent experts, with citizens of administering powers in the minority. As agreed at the Yalta conference, trust territories would include only former enemy territories, former League of Nations mandates, and territories voluntarily placed in trust. Territories would be placed in trust only after the United Nations and the administering power had agreed upon a detailed trusteeship agreement. The agreements negotiated allowed the administering powers to treat trust territories much as they did their other colonies.

The trusteeship system opened avenues by which the Trusteeship Council, and the United Nations, might become more involved with the trust territories. Administering powers were to provide annual reports to the Trusteeship Council regarding conditions in the trust territories. The Trusteeship Council could receive written petitions from colonial subjects. The Trusteeship Council could dispatch, with the agreement of the administering power, visiting missions to trust territories.

The U.S. delegation could take credit for providing these points of access. The original draft was British, but U.S. delegates insisted on allowing visiting missions. The British decided that they could not risk alienating the United States by seeking to shield trust territories from outside scrutiny. The most important compromise accepted by the United States was foregoing the right of inspection, something Roosevelt thought important.[3]

Prominent in both Chapters Eleven and Twelve were descriptions of the administering powers' responsibilities. Besides setting self-government as the long-term goal, Chapter Eleven directed administering powers to treat the interests of a territory's inhabitants as paramount and to provide for their economic and social advancement. Chapter Twelve included similar language plus language about respect for human rights. At the U.S. insistence and consistent with the its public commitment to multilateral trade, Chapter Twelve incorporated a paragraph requiring equal social, economic, and commercial treatment of U.N. members and their nationals within trust territories.

Negotiations over the U.N. Charter consumed two months and involved representatives of fifty nations. In the colonial arena, the focus was on the details, reporting requirements and the like. Stettinius, for whom the United Nations negotiations were his last major responsibility as secretary of state, thought the statements of high principles would prove more important. He believed that the high principles combined with world opinion would ultimately force the colonial powers to grant their possessions independence.[4]

The Charter in Operation

As early as February 1946, members of the United Nations sought a wider role for the U.N. in colonial affairs. On February 9, 1946, the General Assembly passed a resolution that proclaimed U.N. concern about the problems and political aspirations of the peoples of non–self-governing territories. The resolution asked the secretary general to include in his annual report a summary of the information provided by administering powers pursuant to Article 73e.[5]

This seemingly innocuous resolution led to contentious disputes between the colonial powers and other United Nations members. The colonial powers wanted to limit the exercise to the preparation of a summary by the secretary general's staff in the secretariat. U.N. members opposed to colonialism wanted the Trusteeship Council to review the information. The anti-colonial members also sought to create a permanent committee to review the information. The colonial powers objected that the charter did not provide for any such committee. When the General Assembly established temporary committees for the 1947, 1948, and 1949 sessions, the colonial powers sought to limit their recommendations to procedural matters and to bar them from substantive recommendations about non–self-governing territories. An Egyptian representative argued for a larger role for the Special Committee on Information and asserted that the committee represented the principle of accountability. A British delegate expressed deep concern, arguing that the policies implemented in non–self-governing territories fell within the domestic jurisdiction of the administering power. In 1949, the General Assembly gave the committee a three-year term, despite opposition from the colonial powers. The administering powers originally identified to the secretary general seventy-four territories that fell within the terms of Chapter Eleven and Article 73e. Subsequently the administering powers did not provide information about all the territories. In some cases, the colonial powers submitted information in one year, but declined to do so in succeeding years. In 1949, the Indian representative proposed that the U.N. ask the administering powers to provide information regarding their basis for halting the submission of information. The colonial powers objected that doing so would give the General Assembly an opportunity to decide which territories were self-governing and which were not. The colonial powers argued that only they were empowered to determine the constitutional position of their dependent territories.[6]

By 1949, other colonial issues had arisen and the colonial powers again found themselves on the defensive. Under what circumstances could a country administering a trust territory join it with other territories in an administrative union? Could the administering powers be required to submit plans for moving their dependent territories to self-government or independence? How should the Trusteeship Council go about reviewing information submitted by the administering powers about dependent territories? What petitions from inhabitants of dependent territories could the Trusteeship Council accept? Were Britain and France properly administering the Cameroons and Togoland, their trust territories in West Africa? Should all dependent territories be placed in trusteeship? The anti-colonial nations poked and prodded. The administering powers resisted.[7]

Competing for World Opinion

Prominent members of the U.S. delegation perceived that the United Nations was a political arena. In their view, the United States had to compete for the support of other nations. The fate of dependent territories was among the issues about which U.S. had to compete. The U.N. could not create the Trusteeship Council until it negotiated trusteeship agreements with the colonial powers. In January 1946, when the Trusteeship Council was not yet in place, John Foster Dulles, a member of the U.S. delegation to the General Assembly, worried that the United Nations needed to reassure world opinion that it was not neglecting dependent territories. In November of the same year, Dulles returned to the same theme, focusing on the U.S. role. He expressed agreement with the State Department's overall point of view regarding anticipated Russian opposition to the trusteeship agreements. Nevertheless, he warned against pushing trusteeship agreements through the assembly against Russian opposition. He warned that Russia could use the opportunity to lump the United States together with the colonial powers. Dulles saw the immediate propaganda issue as paramount. He argued that the U.S. had to demonstrate that it, and not Russia, was the defender of dependent peoples. Once the trusteeship agreements were in place, Dulles thought the Trusteeship Council would accomplish little. The administering powers could then do what they wanted in their dependent territories.[8]

In fact, the Russian delegates introduced resolutions seemingly designed to embarrass and pressure the colonial powers. In 1948, the Russian delegation proposed that the administering powers submit political information along with other information specified in Article 73e. The Russians argued that the lack of political independence was the chief reason for the low level of social and economic development in the dependent territories. The proposal authorized the Special Committee on Information to examine communications from inhabitants of dependent territories and to send representatives to the dependent territories twice a year to examine local conditions. The administering powers argued that the proposal went beyond anything contemplated by the framers of the United Nations Charter. The assembly did not adopt the proposal largely because it did not gain the support of the principal anti-colonial powers, India and the Philippines for example. Anti-colonial nations stated that they agreed in principle with the Russian proposal, but were willing to settle for a compromise measure hammered out in the Special Committee on Information. India criticized the administering powers for adopting a narrow, legalistic interpretation of the charter, but the anti-colonial nations accepted that no resolution could be implemented without the cooperation of the administering powers.[9]

Russian mischief-making was only a small part of the situation in the United Nations during the Truman administration. The numbers in the United Nations, outside the Security Council, worked against the colonial powers. The United Nations began with fifty members. Through 1952, nine new members joined, raising the total to fifty-nine. Russia and its closest allies numbered only four (Russia, Ukraine, Belarus, and Poland). The principal colonial powers also numbered only four (Great Britain, France, Belgium and Netherlands) or five, if the United States were included. The British Dominions could add another four (Canada, Australia, New Zealand, and South Africa) to a colonial coalition. The other thirty-seven original members possessed no colonies. Most had been colonies themselves and, like the United States, professed a traditional opposition to colonialism. Three of the most outspoken members on colonial issues, Egypt, India, and the Philippines, had recently gained their independence. India was particularly active, submitting anti-colonial proposals in most sessions. The nine members added by 1952 shifted the balance further against the colonial powers. Four had just won their independence (Israel, Indonesia, Burma and Pakistan). None of the other five (Afghanistan, Iceland, Sweden, Thailand, and Yemen) administered dependent territories.

British Resistance

In United Nations disputes over colonial issues, British representatives took a hard line. They resisted proposals they perceived as going beyond the letter of the U.N. Charter to expand United Nations involvement in dependent territories. British delegates argued against an Egyptian resolution urging administering powers to eliminate discrimination in education in dependent territories. The British position was that colonial policies fell within the domestic jurisdiction of the administering powers and were, therefore, outside the U.N. purview. Britain argued that Article 73e made providing information contingent on security and constitutional considerations and that only the administering powers could decide whether they needed to provide the information. Britain also took the position that the only responsibility the administering powers owed the United Nations regarding non self-governing territories, as opposed to trust territories, was providing the information specified in Article 73e. In addition, Britain sought to hold the U.N. to the letter of Chapters Twelve and Thirteen regarding the trust territories. During the 1948 General Assembly session, Britain voted against or abstained on seven of the eight resolutions regarding the trust territories. In three votes, Britain stood alone in opposition. On others, one or other of the colonial powers took the British side.[10]

Opposition to U.N. interference had the enthusiastic support of Arthur Creech Jones, colonial secretary during most of the Attlee administration. When India proposed that the administering powers convert some or all of their dependent territories into trust territories, Creech Jones addressed the General Assembly in opposition. He said that international public opinion could be an important safeguard for colonial territories, but only when it was informed, objective, and unprejudiced. The trusteeship system, he asserted, fell short of this standard. Public opinion in the colonies opposed United Nations intervention and it was a retrograde and humiliating step. Conditions in the British colonies surpassed those in some independent states, Creech Jones added.[11]

Jones listed for the Attlee cabinet these and other reasons for opposing the Indian resolution. Besides offending colonial peoples, creating more trust territories was unwise because the Trusteeship Council lacked the necessary confidence and experience. The matter fell within the discretion of the colonial powers. The measure was unnecessary because British administration of its dependent territories was comparable to that in its trust territories, the colonial secretary asserted. The measure would also retard British efforts to move its territories towards self-government. Moving towards self-government was a vital part of British colonial policy. Moreover, Britain had treaty obligations to various peoples within its dependent territories and could not transfer them to the United Nations.[12]

The ignorant and prejudiced nature of U.N. discussions of colonial affairs was a recurring theme for Creech Jones. To a group of colonial officers, he cited ignorance, ideological propaganda, sentimentalism, lack of realism, prejudice, and a natural dislike of colonialism as causes for attacks on British positions. To the Cabinet he argued that ignorance and prejudice had combined to produce in the Trusteeship Council's report to the General Assembly "a series of superficial, largely platitudinous and for the most part impractical recommendations." He characterized the Trusteeship Council itself as "a forum for largely ignorant and often malicious criticism of the administering authorities serving ends of political propaganda rather than the interests of the inhabitants of the trust territories."[13]

The greatest danger, according to Jones, was that the United Nations would intervene at critical stages of British negotiations with local nationalist leaders. Jones anticipated that, as Britain shifted political responsibility to local peoples, local leaders would push for faster progress toward self-government, regardless of a colony's readiness or the real interests of its inhabitants. If the U.N. were to interject itself into a colony's affairs, he warned, it would likely support the demands of local leaders. Britain would then be hard-pressed to control the rate of political advance.[14]

In 1949, Creech Jones professed to believe that Britain's tough stance on colonial issues had reduced pressure from other United Nations members. He accepted that the U.S. role was crucial. He argued that when the United States and Britain agreed on a position in the U.N. and were determined to defend it, they could block any hostile resolution. Jones also thought that the tension between the United States and Russia created an opportunity for Britain. The U.S. was too preoccupied with the Russians to spend much time on the British colonies. Britain needed to secure as much support for its colonial policies as possible while the U.S. was busy elsewhere. Jones also thought that the United States had moved closer to British positions on colonial issues. Britain needed to continue to foster cooperation with the U.S. on colonial issues. At worst, Britain needed to discourage the United States from favoring compromise positions on what the British considered matters of principle.[15]

Looking for Compromises

U.S. delegates to the United Nations opposed some British positions on colonial issues. When the Britain's draft trusteeship proposal for Tanganyika conceded no meaningful oversight role to the U.N., U.S. representatives objected. They pointed out that if trusteeship were to have a truly international character, it could not be an international sanction for a semi-colonial status. The Trusteeship Council had to have a role larger than making recommendations that the administering power might or might not accept. When the British argued that the Special Committee on Information should consider only procedural issues, the United States disagreed. It asserted that the committee was meant to provide an overall and balanced view of the dependent territories, something the specialized agencies of the U.N. could not provide.[16]

At other times, the United States fought off anti-colonial resolutions. When India proposed a permanent committee to collect and review information about the dependent territories, the U.S. argued successfully that a two-thirds vote of the General Assembly was needed for approval. The U.S. then assembled sufficient votes to defeat the proposal. United States delegates also took the position that a permanent committee went beyond the terms of the charter. In 1949, when India proposed that a territory had to be eligible for United Nations membership to be considered self-governing, the U.S. joined with Britain in opposing it within the General Assembly.

As Creech Jones sensed, compromise was the characteristic U.S. stance on colonial issues. In response to India's resolution for a permanent committee on information, the United States proposed a temporary committee with a one-year term. By 1949, when pressure for a permanent committee increased, the U.S. engineered a committee with a three-year life span. In addition, in 1949, the colonial and anti-colonial powers clashed over the criteria for determining whether an area was self-governing. The colonial powers saw a proposed study as undermining their authority. The U.S. response was to support the proposed study, but it also argued that the study and the administering powers' submission of information did not diminish the administering powers' authority to determine a dependent territory's constitutional status.[17]

Seeking a middle position was the U.S. approach. A 1947 draft position paper prepared by Benjamin Gerig, the senior State Department official responsible for the affairs of dependent areas, laid out three options regarding the General Assembly's treatment of information provided by the administering powers under Article 73e. Gerig imagined that the General Assembly could make only three types of recommendations: procedural recommendations; recommendations about broad functional areas, like education, without reference to specific territories; or recommendations about both functional areas and specific territories. In Gerig's view, confining the General Assembly to procedural recommendations would protect the colonial powers from criticism, but would make them, and the United States, appear defensive about conditions in their colonies. It would also increase the risk that other nations would perceive the U.S. as another imperialistic power. Focusing on functional recommendations would probably gain the support of the colonial powers and, since it seemed fair and appropriate, many non-colonial members as well. It would allow the U.S. to seize the initiative and pre-empt the most aggressive anti-colonial critics. Widening the recommendations to include specific territories would, however, cast the U.S. in the role of the protagonist of dependent peoples. If it led to criticism of U.S. policies in its dependent territories, it would generate domestic opposition to reporting under Article 73e. It might also prompt colonial powers to alter the constitutional status of their colonies in order to avoid any reporting. France had already threatened to do so, Gerig reported. Finally, Gerig asserted that the General Assembly lacked sufficient information to make useful recommendations about specific areas.

Gerig recommended his second option, recommendations about functional areas only. He proposed that the United States make clear that it was not seeking to avoid discussion of its own dependent territories. Another State Department working paper proposed what it termed a constructive approach to non–self-governing territories, an approach consistent with the traditional policy of promoting self-government or independence for peoples desirous and capable of maintaining it. The paper advocated avoiding association with either the more conservative colonial powers or with those intent on the immediate liquidation of colonial empires.[18]

The disputes within the United Nations about colonial issues were problematic to U.S. officials. Arguments between the colonial powers and other U.N. members complicated the U.S. efforts to assemble the broadest possible anti–Russian coalition. While approving the approach adopted by Gerig and other State Department officials, Dulles spoke of the difficulty involved in having to choose between the Western European colonial powers and dependent peoples. Francis Sayre, the head of the U.S. delegation, felt compelled, on one occasion, to lecture the Filipino and other delegations that resolutions framed in ways intended to irritate the colonial powers were the last way to promote the welfare of dependent peoples. Sayre warned that by creating splits between colonial and non-colonial powers, such resolutions played into Russian hands. Sayre admonished that the anti-colonial nations should not allow themselves to be used in this way.

In the debates over colonialism, smaller nations, not the United States, held the initiative. Acheson, in particular, expressed disdain for heated debates in which delegations from small countries without colonies were "swept away by emotional arguments." Rather than leading a coalition, the U.S. found itself reacting to anti-colonial proposals, struggling to kill the worst ones and find acceptable substitutes. Year by year, the compromises the United States could broker moved further and further in the direction the anti-colonial nations sought. Along the way, the members of the U.S. delegation were not always of one mind. Eleanor Roosevelt, a member in 1947, thought the Indian proposal for a committee to oversee dependent areas other than the trust territories was probably a good thing, even if it went beyond the terms of the charter. Sayre reminded her that the United States was intent on improving the lot of dependent peoples, but within the framework of the charter.[19]

Allies at Odds

British officials were nervous about U.S. positions on colonial issues. In 1948, John Fletcher-Cooke, British delegate to the U.N., reported to London that Gerig had said that the United States would follow a new line on colonial policy. The U.S. wanted, according to Fletcher-Cooke's report, to steal the Russians' thunder even if it meant upsetting the British. When the U.S. embassy in London reported to Washington that the Colonial and Foreign Offices took Fletcher-Cooke's report seriously, Dean Rusk telegrammed Gerig, telling him to cool Fletcher-Cooke off and assure him that the United States was not contemplating a different policy.[20]

In January 1949, the British formally voiced their concerns about U.S. policies regarding colonial issues in the United Nations. In an aide-mémoire to the State Department, the British Embassy in Washington warned against attempting to outbid the Russians for the support of dependent peoples. The Russians could raise the stakes indefinitely, to the point of undermining the colonial powers, the British message said. Instead, the United States should join with the United Kingdom in exposing Russian colonialism and in opposing Russian proposals in the Trusteeship Council.[21]

The State Department politely rejected the British proposal. Demonstrating the insincerity of immoderate Russian proposals was easy, the department replied. Russian proposals that seemed reasonable and progressive posed greater challenges. The United States, given what the State Department characterized as its traditionally liberal policy toward non–self-governing territories, would consider such proposals on their merits. It would seek to block Russia from appearing to be the champion for dependent peoples. The best way for the colonial powers to counter Russian initiatives was to consider favorably constructive proposals offered by other nations that would strengthen the trusteeship system and improve conditions in the trust territories. The colonial powers needed to pursue sound policies and make proposals of their own.[22]

Throughout 1949, the United States and Britain pursued their own approaches to colonial issues in the United Nations, despite concerns raised by officials. Seeking to steer a reasonable and moderate course and to maintain good relations with both colonial and non-colonial powers, the U.S. positioned itself with the majority on nearly all General Assembly votes dealing with colonial issues. Britain focused on drawing lines in the sand, resisting what it considered unreasonable proposals. Britain was willing to stand alone in opposition. At the end of the year, Fletcher-Cooke reported that on the seventeen General Assembly resolutions dealing with colonial issues, the United States and Great Britain voted together twice. On ten occasions, the U.S. voted for a resolution that Britain voted against. On two occasions, the U.S. initiated proposals that Britain opposed. A particular cause of disagreement was the Special Committee on Information. The U.S. joined with the majority in supporting its continuation, while Britain and other colonial powers threatened to boycott it. U.S. officials described the colonial powers' role as reluctantly passive, slightly haughty, sometimes irritated, and hardly ever openly and constructively helpful. British officials in New York and Washington continued to complain that the United States was playing the Russians' game.[23]

United States–Great Britain Talks

By the end of 1949, senior officials in both governments decided that formal talks were needed to address their differences. In December, Sir Oliver Franks, British ambassador in Washington, advised the Foreign Office that urgent action was required so that Britain and the U.S. could reach a meeting of the minds about colonial issues. Franks argued that Britain and the United States agreed on fundamental principles. Misunderstandings had arisen regarding U.N. issues, he thought. They needed to be dispelled. A week later, the State Department told its London embassy to inform the Foreign Office that the United States wanted a full exchange of views regarding colonial issues, with Britain and the other principal colonial powers. The embassy was to ask the Foreign Office not to reach conclusions or make a public announcement on colonial issues until after talks took place.[24]

Before the talks, British officials convinced themselves that a more constructive approach was needed in the United Nations. Franks proposed that Britain seek ways to accept with good grace resolutions that contained objectionable provisions, rather than opposing them. Rather than abstaining, Britain should seek to vote for resolutions while forcefully stating any reservations. When Franks lobbied Colonial Office officials, they reiterated their position that Britain must continue to oppose any suggestion that it was accountable to the United Nations for its administration of colonial territories or that it owed information on political and constitutional matters to the United Nations. Nevertheless, the paper the Colonial Office prepared for the Anglo-American talks took up Franks's suggestion that Britain try not to be negative regarding colonial issues in the United Nations. The Colonial Office thought that doing so would help gain U.S. support.[25]

The talks took place in London in May 1950, as part of the preparations for a meeting of the British, French, and United States foreign ministers. British and U.S. representatives pronounced them a success. The U.S. described its notions about colonial issues, drawing from conclusions reached at a conference of State Department officials in Lourenco Marques and the papers prepared in the State Department. The U.S. representatives described these notions as tentative. They also expressed a wish to work with the British to align the two countries' policies. British representatives voiced agreement on all major points. Both sides agreed that further, more detailed talks, particularly about Africa, were needed.[26]

The proclamations of success were overstated and premature. The meetings glossed over potential disagreements and postponed discussion of then-current disagreements. A U.S. representative acknowledged that the United States and Britain agreed on the long-term objectives for African colonies, namely some form of self-government and increased economic development. They could readily disagree, however, on the speed with which the colonies moved towards the objectives. Britain and the United States could also disagree about methods in the United Nations, where, the representative acknowledged, both countries were subject to pressure. Set aside for future discussion was the nature of the colonial powers' accountability to the United Nations, about which the U.S. and Britain had taken divergent positions.[27]

The discussions about colonial issues were a minor and, from a United States perspective, behind-the-scenes portion of the ministerial meetings. When a French representative suggested that a group discussing colonial issues prepare a public statement for the ministers, the British and U.S. representatives demurred. The U.S. representative pointed out that the United States wanted the talks to test its ideas about colonial matters against the experience of the British and French. The U.S. had not considered the possibility of a public statement and its position differed significantly from that of Britain and France, who held colonies in Africa. The group prepared a paper summarizing its discussions and noting widespread agreement. The foreign ministers did not discuss it, however.[28]

Britain and the United States held further talks in Washington in July 1950, the first in what became annual meetings to discuss tactics in the United Nations. Both sides went away pleased. The British described their new, more positive approach to colonial issues in the United Nations. John Hickerson, the lead United States negotiator, described the U.S. delegation as more than delighted. He expressed the hope that the United States could support Britain more frequently without abandoning its anti-colonial tradition. Both nations agreed that they should vote together on colonial issues in the United Nations whenever possible. They agreed that they would try to persuade non-colonial powers to soften their positions before the next U.N. session.[29]

In the short term, the Anglo-American understanding was effective from a British perspective. The British felt less isolated and beleaguered in the United Nations. During the 1950 General Assembly session, Britain voted for twelve of the eighteen resolutions on colonial issues, abstained on three, and voted against three. British and U.S. lobbying of the non-colonial powers seems to have had an effect. British officials thought that the non-colonial powers were no more understanding of the colonial powers' situation or approving of colonial rule. Rather, the British admitted, they were temporarily persuaded that attacking the colonial powers served only to increase the risk of communist infiltration into dependent areas.[30]

In the following United Nations sessions, Britain and the U.S. agreed on several colonial issues, but were hardly in lockstep. They agreed that the U.N. could discuss the factors by which one might evaluate whether a territory was self-governing, but that only the administering power could determine whether the territory was self-governing. They opposed establishing timetables for moving territories toward self-government. Britain voted against the resolution while the United States was content to abstain. Britain insisted that administering powers could rely on constitutional and security considerations to withhold information about dependent territories. The U.S. tried to persuade the British to drop that argument. The U.S. argued that the U.N. could not mandate submission of information, but urged administering powers to submit the information voluntarily. The U.S. thought submitting information could do no real harm and would appease the critics of colonialism. Britain and the other administering powers continued to resent and resist the Special Committee on Information. The U.S. warned that the Special Committee, where the colonial powers held half the seats, was preferable to the General Assembly, where the administering powers were outnumbered fifty-one to eight.[31]

By the end of 1951, officials in both Britain and United States concluded that the potential for meaningful, long-term cooperation in the United Nations was more limited than it first seemed. In London, Sir John Martin, a senior Colonial Office official, expressed satisfaction with the improvement in Anglo-American dealings regarding colonial issues in the U.N. Yet he warned that the United States looked at colonial issues with a different perspective. The causes of disagreements between Britain and the U.S. were deep-seated and unlikely to be resolved quickly, Martin thought. Disagreements on tactics were inevitable. Britain could take some comfort in knowing that at least U.S. officials understood British positions. A Foreign Office official observed that talks before a U.N. session were unlikely to anticipate all the issues that would arise. When Britain and the United States were reacting to the press of U.N. business, coordinating their positions was difficult. The Foreign Office perceived a fundamental conflict between the Colonial Office's preference for keeping the

United Nations out of the colonies and the U.S. interest in minimizing conflicts among its allies or potential allies within the United Nations. As long as the non-colonial countries pressed for a larger U.N. role in colonial affairs, U.S. support for British positions would be at risk.[32]

In Washington, a State Department official reported that Britain and the U.S. had come away from the 1950 talks with different understandings. The United States thought it had persuaded Britain to be more flexible. The British thought they had persuaded the United States to support British positions. Britain remained inflexible on key issues, however, and it was miffed that the U.S. support was not forthcoming. The appearance of happy agreement was misleading, he wrote. Agreement on general principles during relaxed, friendly talks in London or Washington was easy. Nevertheless, serious difficulties were bound to surface, particularly when specific issues arose in what the official called the relatively psychopathic atmosphere of the General Assembly. State Department staff complained that the colonial powers, including Britain, resisted proposals they could readily adopt, such as flying the U.N. flag in trust territories, and felt compelled to respond to every criticism. Some in the State Department thought that on key issues the positions of the colonial powers were frozen. In this view, the British saw a real danger that compromises on colonial issues could accumulate to the point that the United Nations gained substantial power over colonies.[33]

Disagreements in the State Department

When Britain and the U.S. failed to agree, conflicts within the State Department arose. In 1952, the colonial powers resisted proposals from non-colonial nations to include representatives of colonial subjects in Trusteeship Council delegations. The United States sought a compromise and thought it had British support. When the British withdrew their agreement and stated that they would not accept any instruction or advice about their delegation, the State Department struggled to draft new instructions for the U.S. delegation. In the end, the European bureau stood alone within the department. It opposed any instructions that were not acceptable to the colonial powers.[34]

State Department staff considered various approaches to resolving their differences, as well as the differences between Britain and the United States. One paper suggested that the U.S. should favor self-government for dependent territories, but oppose independence on the ground that more small states would make the world less secure. The same paper floated the idea that the U.S. work harder to keep contentious topics away from the United Nations. A senior State Department official, Philip Jessup, suggested to Acheson that talks about colonial issues might be more successful if the colonial powers initiated them. If the U.S. suggested talks, the colonial powers thought the United States was preaching at them and they became defensive. Jessup and Acheson wondered whether they could plant the idea with Sir Oliver Franks or a senior Foreign Office official who could then promote it with Sir Anthony Eden.[35]

1952 Meetings

By the September 1952 talks in preparation for the General Assembly session, Anglo-American relations regarding colonial issues in the United Nations had reverted to the conditions of 1949. The United States welcomed Britain's plans to adopt a positive approach in the upcoming session and agreed with several British positions on specific issues. Nevertheless, the two countries' approaches to the U.N. as it dealt with colonies were different. Britain took a hard line, seeking to block expansion of U.N. activity. The United States viewed nationalism, the desire of peoples to control their own countries, as irresistible in the long term. It was, therefore, unwilling to risk offending non-colonial countries by appearing to resist it.[36]

Consistent with the U.S. aim to maintain the broadest possible coalition in the United Nations, U.S. representatives at the 1952 talks stressed areas where Britain and the U.S. agreed. The U.S. joined with Britain in opposing firm timetables for moving dependent territories to self-government or independence and agreed that U.S. discussions of political conditions in specific dependent territories were undesirable and that the United Nations should not dispatch visiting missions to trust territories or hold plebiscites without the permission of the administering power.[37]

The British were not appeased. Sir Gladwyn Jebb, leading the British delegation, said that the goal was to halt discussions of political conditions. He wanted the United States to take a public position that such discussions were harmful and should end. The British argued that firm limits to U.N. activity must be set. Jebb returned to the argument that buying off the non-colonial nations through concessions on colonial issues was a mistake. The British representatives warned that the British delegation would have to consider withdrawing from the proceedings if a U.N. body attempted to discuss the political affairs of Britain's colonies.[38]

For the United States, John Hickerson replied that blocking discussions of political topics would be difficult, if not impossible. The U.S. aim was assemble a broad coalition. It could not afford to offend the non-colonial nations or be associated too closely with the colonial powers. It was trying to operate as a middleman, brokering compromises between the colonial and non-colonial powers. If the U.S. spoke out against holding political discussions, it would have to take an affirmative approach. The U.S. agreed that political discussions often served no purpose. It was planning to work behind the scenes to head them off or postpone them, but it was unlikely to join with the British to try to block them. The British should take a similarly positive approach. If Britain had consistently submitted the information about its dependent territories that the United Nations requested, a harmless request in the U.S. view, the non-colonial nations would be criticizing British behavior.[39]

British officials thought the U.S. position confused. Sir Christopher Steel responded to Hickerson that the United States could hardly act as a middleman when it was responsible for maintaining law and order throughout the world. Reporting to London, Franks described the U.S. unwillingness to be identified with Britain on colonial issues. He added that U.S. representatives continued to believe that the question of America's own dependent territories was "in some mystical way" irrelevant. A junior member of the Churchill government observed that the attitudes of the Guatemalans and the Egyptians were more consistent and understandable than those of the United States.[40]

From the British perspective, the annual talks qualified as only better than nothing. Franks bemoaned U.S. unwillingness to commit to supporting Britain on what it considered critical issues. A Foreign Office official thought the talks had only negative value, that is, "if they didn't take place, the Americans might act even more stupidly than they at present do."[41]

The hard line adopted by the British in the 1952 talks reflected an explicit decision by the Churchill government. The Colonial Office's position was that Britain should be willing to threaten to withdraw, and actually withdraw, from U.N. proceedings when they intruded into colonial issues. The Foreign Office dismissed walking out as both ineffectual and unworthy of a major power. Forced to resolve the disagreement, the Churchill cabinet accepted walking out as the tactic of last resort, but delegated responsibility for the decision to the head of the British United Nations delegation, Selwyn Lloyd, who considered walking out as inadvisable.[42]

During 1952, the political discussion of immediate importance in the U.N. concerned Tunisia and Morocco. Supported by the other colonial powers, France sought to keep the political situation in its two North African protectorates off the General Assembly agenda. Britain supported the French position because it feared that allowing the General Assembly to discuss Tunisia and Morocco would set a precedent that would apply to British possessions. Behind the scenes, Acheson pushed the French to institute reforms in North Africa in order to stifle nationalist agitation. Acheson sought to avoid a public break with France by not supporting proposals to put Tunisia and Morocco on the General Assembly agenda. Late in 1952, shortly before the end of the Truman administration, Acheson decided, nonetheless, that he could no longer resist pressure from non-colonial countries and the U.S. public. He had the U.S. delegation vote with a majority of the General Assembly to add Tunisia and Morocco to the agenda, much to French consternation.[43]

Britain and the United States found themselves out of step on colonial issues in the United Nations in the last months of the Truman administration. British representatives caught the U.S. delegation by surprise when they raised the possibility of walking out of the Special Committee on Information if its tenure were renewed for more than three years. Philip Jessup, head of the U.S. delegation, responded that the United States would have sought a compromise if it had been aware earlier of British views. In the end, the British decided not to threaten a withdrawal. When the U.N. Commission on Human Rights included the right of self-determination in a proposed Convention on Human Rights, Britain and the United States disagreed, arguing that self-determination was a principle, not a right. The two countries could not agree on tactics, however. The U.S. sought to soften the convention's wording through a series of amendments. The British preferred a vote on the original wording. The British argued that having a sizeable group of countries vote against the original version was better than having a small group vote against a watered-down version. The United States went ahead with its amendments, without British support. Individual members of the British delegation conceded that the U.S. amendments addressed Britain's concerns, but reported that the Foreign Office in London was committed to a hard line.[44]

Truman-Churchill Talks

The 1952 talks on colonial issues mirrored an earlier meeting between Truman and Churchill. Shortly after regaining office in October 1951, Churchill sought a meeting with Truman. U.S. officials anticipated that the prime minister was seeking to revive an Anglo-American partnership. Their recommendation was that the U.S. reassure the British prime minister that Anglo-American cooperation was important and warn him that if the cooperation became too obvious, it would damage relations with other United States allies. They noted the disadvantage to the United States of being too closely associated with the colonial powers. At the meeting, Churchill proposed an arrangement in which Britain would support U.S. interests in East and Southeast Asia while the U.S. bolstered British positions around the eastern Mediterranean. Truman and Acheson declined the offer, responding that the two areas were different. Communist movements in East and Southeast Asia threatened Western interests. On the other hand, the U.S. and Britain could come to terms with the nationalist forces in places like Egypt. While maintaining a friendly tone, Truman communicated clearly that he thought that the U.S. now held the upper hand. Acheson thought that Churchill was living in the past and that his proposed policies would prove disastrous. He told Churchill that Anglo-American agreement on mistaken policies was akin to a couple locked in an embrace as their rowboat was about to go over Niagara Falls. Churchill was amused, but not persuaded.[45]

"The middle ground" was where the U.S. preferred to be in colonial debates. Seeking to maintain the largest possible anti–Russian coalition in the United Nations, the U.S. tried to please both the colonial and anti-colonial powers. The U.S. tried to head off the strongest anti-colonial resolutions and water down others. It counseled anti-colonial countries that they should not let Russia lead them astray and warned Britain that it should soften its opposition to U.N. involvement in colonial territories.

Since Britain was firmly within the colonial caucus in the United Nations, it and the U.S. frequently found themselves at odds. Officials of both nations regretted the disagreements. Nevertheless, despite annual meetings to discuss colonial issues, the United States and Britain were at least as far apart on colonial issues in the United Nations in 1952 as they had been in 1948 or 1949. British officials realized that they could not look to the U.S. for overt and consistent support for their colonial policies.

Colonial Reform in London, 1946–1952: Fresh Ideas

Postwar British governments, Labour and Conservative, faced daunting problems. In particular, they found themselves virtually bankrupt but responsible for a vast overseas empire. Reconciling imperial responsibilities with straitened circumstances proved a long and difficult process. On the African continent, Britain was already committed to guiding its colonies to self-government, without specifying what that meant. The postwar governments, nonetheless, faced important and difficult issues regarding African self-government. Prominent among them were the nature of self-government, the process for guiding colonies to self-government, and the timing for doing so.

Postwar Britain

The Great Britain that the Truman administration dealt with was different from that which entered the Second World War and fought the war alongside the United States. Three months after Truman succeeded Roosevelt, a new government took office in Britain. In May 1945, the coalition government headed by Winston Churchill disbanded in preparation for a general election. In the election, the Labour Party won a landslide victory over Churchill's Conservative Party. The Labour Party leader, Clement Attlee, became prime minister, and Ernest Bevin, a long-time labor union official, became his foreign secretary. Attlee and the Labour Party remained in power until October 1951, when they lost a general election to the Conservative Party. Churchill headed a Conservative administration in Britain for the last fifteen months of the Truman administration. Bevin served as foreign secretary until March 1951, when illness forced his transfer to the post of lord privy seal. Herbert Morrison, another long-time Labour Party stalwart, then took Bevin's place. Anthony Eden served as Churchill's foreign secretary.

In 1945, Britain was nearly bankrupt. It had managed to fight the Axis powers successfully around the globe bolstered by $36 billion in U.S. aid. To fight the war, Britain had liquidated most of its dollar and gold reserves as well as its overseas investments. Whereas Britain began the war owed £3 billion, it ended the war owing £2 billion, largely due to the United States and to parts of the British empire and commonwealth.[1]

Britain's immediate financial prospects were grim. It needed to import much of its food and raw materials. It also needed to import materials and other products with which to rebuild its homes, industry, and infrastructure. The most likely source of manufactured imports was the United States, the only other major industrial economy still intact. The U.S. would expect payment in dollars or hard currency that Britain did not have. Britain's export trade had sunk to roughly one-third its prewar level. Experts thought that Britain would have to expand its exports by 50 to 75 percent to restore its prewar standard of living, not to mention the social programs the Labour government was committed to. Furthermore, many of Britain's traditional customers, the dominions and Latin America, had accumulated British debts. Selling to them would only reduce the debts, not generate new hard currency reserves. Other potential customers in Central and Eastern Europe lacked the money to pay for British goods. That Britain could produce goods for export gave it an advantage over most other European nations, but the advantage promised to be short-lived. Once other European economies revived and began to compete for exports, British industrialists and their bankers realized that Britain's aging and inefficient industries would put it at a disadvantage.[2]

Britain's financial straits were a part of a strategic dilemma that confronted the Attlee government. Britain was nearly broke. Nevertheless in early 1947 its overseas possessions were at their greatest territorial extent. Its army was as large as that of the United States. The financial and trade arrangements organized around the pound sterling remained intact. Britain could not match the power and wealth of the United States or Russia, but its resources exceeded those of any other nation, even those of the other European colonial powers. Britain had critical interests in Europe. It had fought two major wars in Europe within fifty years. Yet it held substantial interests elsewhere. It had long seen itself as being apart from Europe.

Successive British governments over the second half of the twentieth century struggled with this dilemma. Since the dilemma was profound, government policy twisted and turned as administrations explored alternative approaches. Since the dilemma was fundamental, the struggle touched most major aspects of government policy — foreign affairs, the military, foreign trade and finance, the domestic economy, and domestic policies. The fate of the British African colonies and Britain's relationship with the United States were two aspects of a far larger phenomenon.

Britain's postwar alliances signaled a nation struggling to find its place. The Attlee government initially imagined Britain standing somewhat aloof from Europe, allied with the dominions, Canada, South Africa, Australia, and New Zealand, and with the United States. The Attlee government attempted, but failed, to negotiate closer defense arrangements with the dominions. It did, however, enter into a formal alliance with France, in the 1947 Treaty of Dunkirk. As tension in Europe between Russia and the U.S. plus their respective allies increased, Britain also found itself joining with France and the Benelux countries in the Brussels Pact, and it joined with the United States and various European nations in the North Atlantic Treaty Organization. Despite the closer defense links with Western Europe, the Attlee government resisted U.S. pressure to pursue closer economic and financial ties to the continent.

Military expenditures were a challenge and a burden for the Attlee government. At the end of the First World War, the sluggish pace with which Britain released men from their military duties proved controversial. Nevertheless, the need to re-occupy and maintain order in Britain's overseas possessions drove the Attlee government to demobilize more slowly than the Truman administration did. In 1946, more than 18 percent of British men aged eighteen to forty-four remained in the armed forces, compared to 10 percent in the United States. British governments had avoided conscription. Yet the Attlee government left the wartime draft in place. Successive chancellors of the exchequer warned that military expenditures threatened British financial reserves and put in jeopardy the Attlee government's domestic program. In fact, the £300 million Britain spent to maintain troops in Germany and elsewhere overseas accounted for the government's entire budget deficit in 1946. Britain spent more than eighteen percent of its national income on defense in 1946 while the United States spent less than 11 percent. The Attlee government at first attempted to cut defense spending. Nevertheless, convinced that its alliance with the United States required a substantial commitment to the conflict in Korea, the Attlee government proposed to nearly double annual expenditures on defense in the three-year period after 1950–51.[3]

Attlee's Government and Empire

Clement Attlee harbored skepticism about overseas holdings. He opposed Britain accepting responsibility for any of Italy's former colonies in North Africa and Somalia. He thought that Britain had enough awkward colonial problems to deal with. He observed that the advent of air warfare and atomic weapons called into question the strategic rationale for many British colonies. Attlee thought that Britain would be hard pressed to defend itself and its colonies without an effective United Nations. Britain ought to concentrate on strengthening collective security rather than on control of bits of foreign real estate.[4]

The Labour Party had been critical of Britain's colonial policies without advocating independence, and other key members of the Attlee administration shared the prime minister's doubts. The chancellor of the exchequer, Hugh Dalton, was especially skeptical about retaining colonies. He thought that it would be a waste of British men and money to oppose Indian and Burmese nationalists. Britain should let these colonies become independent even if their inhabitants were incompetent to govern themselves. As chancellor, Dalton argued that Britain could not afford the military forces required to keep the colonies. In 1950 Dalton confided in his diary that, when Attlee offered him the post of colonial secretary, he had a "horrid vision of pullulating, poverty stricken, diseased nigger communities for whom one can do nothing in the short run, and who, the more one tries to help them, are querulous and ungrateful."[5]

Attlee's foreign secretary, Ernest Bevin, saw holding on to the empire as vital to Britain's future. In Bevin's view, the empire was a test of Britain's mettle. If Britain did not try to hold on to its possessions, it would lose the trust of potential allies and of the United States. In order to bargain successfully with the U.S., Britain had to stand firm in its colonies. Even after the Attlee government had granted independence to important colonies, Bevin was convinced that the remainder, especially the African colonies, could contribute substantially to British wealth and power.[6]

Attlee shared Bevin's concern that Britain remain a credible ally for the United States. For this and other reasons, Attlee supported Bevin in the end. Since the two together maintained a firm grip on the Labour government's foreign policies, the Attlee government set out to retain as much of the empire as possible. If forced to concede independence, it would preserve as strong links as possible between Britain and its former colonies. The Attlee government did not succeed in all cases. It was forced to let slip some colonies, indeed the largest colonies, but that was not for want of effort. The Attlee government conceded independence to India, Pakistan, Burma, and Ceylon, but only after prolonged and tortured attempts to reach understandings with local nationalists. Britain relinquished its mandate in Palestine and turned the problem over to the United Nations. It had spent several years searching for a solution acceptable to local peoples and the world community, including the United States. The Attlee government put a positive face on these developments, but it was making a virtue out of necessity. Britain lacked the resources, if not always the will, to resist nationalists' calls for independence. Elsewhere, in Africa, Southeast Asia (Malaya, Singapore and Hong Kong), Western Asia (Aden and the Trucial States), the eastern Mediterranean (Cyprus), the Pacific, and the Caribbean, the Attlee government clung to its colonies.

Greeks and Romans

The United States was central to the Attlee government's attempts to reconcile Britain's new weakness with its global presence. Yet relations with the U.S. posed their own challenges for Britain. The U.S. had been Britain's principal commercial and financial rival before the war, but her staunchest ally during the war. Without U.S. aid, Britain would have faced the unenviable choice of a negotiated peace with Germany or the sacrifice of its overseas possessions in order to concentrate its forces to defeat Germany in Europe. Despite nagging concerns about U.S. goals and methods, most British officials and politicians concluded that an alliance with the United States was critical to preserving British interests after the war. How to persuade the U.S. to support British aims was not clear, but most British leaders thought that wooing the United States was unavoidable.

While British officials recognized that the U.S. was capable of pursuing its own interests at Britain's expense, their principal concern was that after the war the U.S. would revert to its prewar foreign policy and retreat to the Western Hemisphere. Well into the Truman administration, British leaders worried that U.S. public opinion would sway the Congress and the administration against the traditional nemesis, foreign entanglements. British officials resented U.S. interventions into regions where the British had earlier been dominant. Yet they often rationalized that a U.S. presence offered the hope of support for British interests.

During the Second World War, Harold Macmillan quipped that the British were the Greeks, and the Americans, the Romans. The notion that British cleverness and hard-won experience of the world equipped Britons to influence the powerful but inexperienced and dimmer Americans had a long life in British official circles. Sometimes, officials believed that the U.S. would recognize British wisdom and experience and seek British advice. Other times British officials acted as if they could outwit their U.S. counterparts and lever United States resources to promote British interests.[7]

Officials in London spent more time and effort working on and worrying about their policies towards the United States than their counterparts in Washington did creating policies toward Britain. Britain and the U.S. had a firm alliance throughout the Truman years. The two countries recognized many mutual interests. The relationship was far from equal, however. The United States was critical to Britain's future. A break with the U.S. could be fatal. On the other hand, the U.S. imagined itself as the leader of a worldwide coalition, of which Britain was only one, albeit an important, member.[8]

An alliance with the United States put greater strain on Britain's limited resources. Britain's diminished resources dictated close ties to the U.S. Nevertheless, many British officials feared that the United States would not link itself with a demonstrably weak Britain.

To curry U.S. favor, British leaders were apt to spend beyond Britain's means. Britain maintained larger armed forces and more sophisticated, expensive weapons than its economic resources could readily support.

Bevin hoped that British dependence on the United States would be temporary. Bevin was blunt and combative. He had a solid working arrangement with Acheson, but his relations with Truman, Byrnes, and Marshall were strained. Bevin resented Truman's unwillingness or inability to work with Britain to resolve Palestine's future. Bevin saw Britain caught between an expansive United States and an expansive Russia. He feared that Britain and the other Western European nations would find themselves weak and isolated, but with far-reaching responsibilities in Asia and Africa. Bevin welcomed U.S. aid and support as a way to escape this trap. He was eager to demonstrate that the United States could rely on Britain and needed British cooperation to protect its interests. Nevertheless, he looked forward to the day, a decade or two in the future, when British dependence on the United States would become Anglo-American interdependence.[9]

Churchill and the Conservatives

When the Conservatives under Churchill took office in October 1951, Britain's financial situation remained precarious. R.A. Butler, the chancellor of the exchequer, warned his cabinet colleagues that Britain's balance of payments was in worse shape than in 1947 or 1949. In May 1952, Butler urged a review of Britain's overseas commitments. He wanted the government to review its overseas military arrangements, foreign policy, economic obligations to the commonwealth and the colonies, and obligations to foreign creditors. Butler thought that Britain could not continue to rely heavily on U.S. aid. The Marshall Plan was ending and the U.S. government had signaled its intention to concentrate on military, rather than economic, aid. Butler believed that economic aid disguised Britain's economic condition and inhibited vital reforms. He argued that Britain would have to put its economic house in order before it could expect economic cooperation and assistance from the United States. Later the same year Butler told the cabinet that Britain was trying to do too much. The defense program the Conservatives inherited from Attlee's government was beyond Britain's means.[10]

Harold Macmillan, minister of housing and local government in Churchill's cabinet, took issue with Butler. He contended that Butler underestimated the U.S. willingness to tolerate discriminatory tariffs imposed by Britain and the other members of the sterling area, particularly if such tariffs led to sterling's convertibility. The United States wanted a strong Britain and would overlook slow progress toward multilateral trade, Macmillan argued. Macmillan turned Butler's logic on its head. Butler's argument was that overseas commitments, including the colonies, required Britain to maintain substantial military forces. Military expenditures competed with essential and popular domestic programs and endangered Britain's long-term economic health. Macmillan's response was that world confidence in sterling depended on Britain's prestige as a great power, on its ability to impose its will on countries like Iran. Maintaining Britain's status required substantial armed forces. Without them, Britain's power, influence, and economic condition would continue to decline.[11] Anthony Eden wanted to retain Britain's overseas commitments, but recognized that Britain had to operate within an orbit around the United States. Eden accepted that Britain could not afford its current levels of defense and domestic spending. He warned, however, that the Russians were ready to fill any vacuum created by a British withdrawal. He doubted that reduced spending on the colonies was likely or that it would yield meaningful benefits. Eden, like Macmillan, contended that Britain's future, economic and otherwise, depended on maintenance of its prestige as a great power. Eden's solution was to shift the financial burdens of empire to others, especially the United States, while retaining as much political control as possible for Britain. Eden saw the need to involve the U.S. in defense arrangements in Southeast Asia and around the eastern Mediterranean. Eden acknowledged that the United States was wary of new foreign commitments. The United States did not want to prop up a declining British empire. Nonetheless, Eden claimed that if Britain could demonstrate that it was making the maximum possible effort, it might be able to shift the real burdens from British to American shoulders.[12]

Colonial Reform in London

For the Colonial Office and its civil servants, the Attlee governments were a period of vigorous activity, particularly up to 1948. The office expanded and reorganized. Its staff produced papers that laid out a different approach to the colonies, an approach thought better suited to the changed circumstances of the postwar world. The approach drew upon experiences in the colonies and on earlier staff work in London, but represented a revised approach to the African colonies.

Central to the Colonial Office's new vigor was Andrew Cohen, head of the office's new Africa division. After graduating from Trinity College, Cambridge, Cohen joined the Home Civil Service in 1932 and transferred to the Colonial Office the following year. Known for both energy and strong views, he rose to the level of assistant secretary by 1943. In 1947, he became the first assistant under secretary for African affairs. U.S. officials saw Cohen as the most influential civil servant in the Colonial Office, based on his quick thinking and ability to get things done. In their view, he dominated the political thinking of the Colonial Office during the Attlee administration.[13]

Cohen and others in the Colonial Office returned to arguments raised during the war. Britain needed a new approach to its colonies. The Colonial Office, rather than the colonial governors and other British officials in the field, needed to take the initiative. The colonies had changed and were continuing to change. If Britain had ever had a considered, comprehensive colonial policy, it was decades out of date. Waiting for a colonial governor to design and implement a reform and then pushing it on other colonies was no longer a viable strategy. The Colonial Office needed to think ahead and anticipate change. If it was not practical to produce firm plans with deadlines, it should be possible to develop templates that colonial governors could refer to as circumstances evolved.[14]

The Colonial Office in the Attlee years came to believe that significant change, especially political change, was inevitable in the African colonies in the near future. The office identified various factors leading to change. British defeats at the hands of the Japanese demonstrated that Europeans were not invincible. The African soldiers who served in the British forces during the war had seen the world and they would expect more when they returned home. Nationalist movements across Asia were clamoring for a larger political role for local peoples, even for independence. By 1948, the nationalists had won independence in the largest parts of the British Empire. In Africa, the British government had committed itself to economic and social development. Public opinion in Britain and international opinion favored raising standards of living and providing social services. Economic and social change would generate pressure for political changes. The expansion of formal education, from primary schools through university, would produce more Africans motivated to push for a larger political voice. Furthermore, the growth of trade between African colonies and the rest of the world would make political change more likely. Britain's colonies were likely to be subject to international agreements and international scrutiny. The British had set important precedents by granting colonial peoples more political power in Asia, Nigeria, and the Gold Coast. Local peoples would expect further advances. Finally, the Colonial Office was convinced that Britain lacked the means to impose its rule indefinitely in Africa. Colonies could not be retained against their will, Creech Jones told the cabinet in 1949.[15]

The Colonial Office thought that Britain needed to carry out a program of colonial reform. The long-term goal was to guide the colonies to responsible self-government within the commonwealth, while ensuring that the colonial peoples enjoyed a fair standard of living and were free from oppression. Britain needed to move forward with economic and social development efforts. For development efforts to succeed, Britain needed to create local governments in the African colonies that were effective in providing government services and representative of the local population. It needed to "Africanize" the colonial civil service, that is, replace British officials with properly educated and trained Africans. The London government needed to allow the colonies more autonomy. The Colonial Office needed to move away from managing the colonies and towards providing general guidance. Colonial governments with greater freedom of action would be better able to respond to local interests and secure local support. To satisfy demands for political change, Britain should implement steps that would put Africans in charge of a colony's central government.[16]

The Colonial Office's reform notions marked a break from the prewar focus on native administrations. By conceding Africans a potential role in central government, the Colonial Office increased the chances that British officials and politically engaged Africans would concentrate their attention on central government, rather than the native administrations. The stress on economic and social development meant that the typical native administration, competent to collect taxes and maintain law and order, was no longer acceptable. Local governments in the new regime needed to provide a range of public services. If colonial government was to gain the support and loyalty of local peoples, the native administration as a thinly disguised autocracy was unacceptable. Local governments could not remain the preserve of the chief or of a chief and a few council members. They needed to incorporate popular representatives and represent the local community in regional or national assemblies. Some native administrations provided public services. Native administrations in the Northern Provinces of Nigeria operated elementary schools. Some operated agriculture and forestry departments. In Northern Nigeria, British officials inserted educated Africans into some native administration councils. Nevertheless, the vast majority of native administrations across British Africa were far from the effective, representative local governments the Colonial Office imagined.[17]

Political Reforms

Among the proposals developed by the Colonial Office were changes in central government, divided into four stages. The office conceived of the program as a broad framework for political development over the next two or three decades. In the first stage, a colony's executive council would become its government and members of the executive council would take responsibility for specific government departments. The governor would retain final authority, but would delegate executive responsibility to executive council members. In the second stage, additional unofficial members, that is, members other than civil servants, would join the executive council. The new members would be responsible to a legislature. In the third stage, the executive council members responsible for government departments would become ministers. The governor would no longer have full responsibility for policy, but would rely on the advice of the ministers. The ministers would be responsible to a legislature through democratic elections. In the final stage, the colony would achieve full internal self-government. At this stage, ministers would be responsible for all government departments. As the executive council gained greater authority, the colonial secretary would reduce his control over the colony. In the end, he would retain only the authority to disallow legislation in exceptional circumstances.[18]

The Colonial Office thought the first stage should occur soon and the second stage not long afterward. Because the third stage required that ministers be accountable to the local population, it required colony-wide elections. The Colonial Office was not sure whether these should be direct or indirect elections. Whatever the form of elections, the Colonial Office anticipated that such elections, and the third stage, were far in the future.[19]

Key to the Colonial Office's plan was using the legislative council as the means to co-opt African political leaders. The Colonial Office anticipated that Britain would concede self-government to nationalist movements in each colony. Educated African politicians would lead the nationalist movements. British officials were apt to view such Africans as overly ambitious, unscrupulous, and self-interested. In the worst case, they would win the support of their uneducated countrymen and extract concessions from the British sooner rather later. In the best case, the British would bring the less extreme politicians into the central government and gain their support. By doing so, the British would buy time during which the colonial government could carry out economic and social development and build up units of local government.

Self-Government

The Colonial Office's reform proposals can be understood as an attempt to control the inevitable transition to self-government by corralling educated Africans, the anticipated agents of change. Africanizing the colonial civil service would co-opt more educated Africans by placing them in key administrative positions within the government. Offering changes in central government would allow the British to retain the initiative. Instead of responding to pressure, they would stay one step ahead of the nationalists. Economic and social development, more roads, clinics, schools, and the like, would minimize popular grievances and deprive African nationalist politicians of opportunities for winning popular support. The middle and late 1940s saw strikes and unrest across British Africa, caused by price inflation and other effects of the war. Popular unrest was on British minds. Turning the native administrations into representative local governments would give the uneducated masses in the countryside a voice in the political process. It would be the means to offset the influence of the educated minority, concentrated in the cities and towns and focused on the central government. Delaying direct elections to a national legislature would inhibit a small, unrepresentative minority at the center from dominating the political process.[20]

Before the war, the conventional wisdom in London was that the African colonies would achieve self-government in the distant future. In 1947, the Colonial Office's guess that the Gold Coast would gain internal self-government in about a generation represented a significant shortening of the timescale. The office reasoned that self-government would come first in the Gold Coast because the nationalist movement there seemed the most advanced. The office thought political advance would be slower elsewhere. In Central and East Africa, the absence of politically active Africans and the presence of European settlers eager for greater control over local affairs complicated the situation. Yet the Colonial Office did not imagine that the march toward self-government would be rapid. Questioned in 1950 by U.S. officials about the speed of political change in West Africa, Andrew Cohen explained that immediate steps were necessary to create a political system that would continue smoothly in the "comparatively long period" leading to self-government.[21]

For the Colonial Office, the aim was self-government, not independence. The precise difference between the two was unclear. The usual formulation, self-government within the commonwealth, implied continued ties between Britain and its former colony. The nature of those ties was usually unstated, but British officials hoped they would be stronger rather than weaker. "Responsible self-government," a term that the Labour government started to employ, implied a status like that of India or Pakistan. Terms like "internal self-government" or "self-government in domestic affairs," implied that Britain might retain control of functions like foreign relations, finance, and the military.

Some colonies might not gain self-government, at least by themselves. More than one Colonial Office study during the Attlee years argued that some colonies were too small, too poor, or too immature politically to achieve self-government. For the smallest and poorest, government in association with Britain would be necessary. Zanzibar and the Gambia might fall into this category. Other colonies could manage self-government only if combined with neighboring colonies.[22]

The Colonial Office flirted with a companion notion, that Britain should not grant self-government until a colony met specific criteria. In one version, West African colonies should not be self-governing until territorial unity was a reality. Sufficient trained Africans had to be available to administer the colony and political leaders had to be representative of the people. East African colonies should not be self-governing until the African community could play its "full part" with the European and Asian communities. Another version emphasized social and economic factors. Effective self-government required a healthy and vigorous people, equipped with education, technical knowledge and skills. They must be able to produce as much as possible for their own needs. They had to have something to sell to the outside world to pay for what they could not produce themselves. They must be able to govern themselves with reasonable honesty and efficiency.[23]

Creech Jones and the Colonial Governors

In February 1947, Creech Jones sent a dispatch to the governors of all African colonies. The first third of the dispatch described the reform proposals under consideration at the Colonial Office, including those dealing with native administrations. The final two-thirds dealt with the workings of the colonial governments, the responsibilities of district commissioners and the like. In the dispatch, Jones announced that he wanted to share his thinking regarding colonial reform with the governors. He said that he was unsure whether the Colonial Office should issue detailed guidance. In any case, he planned to wait until after discussions with colonial officers at a summer school in Cambridge in August 1947 and formal consultations with the African governors.[24]

Despite the limited nature of the office's reform notions and the tentative manner in which Creech Jones presented them to the governors, Sir Philip Mitchell, governor of Kenya, attacked the idea that Africans should soon play a larger political role. According to Mitchell, Africans were in a very primitive moral, cultural, and social state, even if some had made progress in material matters. Since, in Mitchell's view, there was no African nation, history, culture, or technical and economic development, the future of Africa was not synthetic nationalism, but incorporation into Western European civilization and economics. Mitchell thought that the future of Africa was as a continent rather than a collection of "Bulgarias" or "Liberias." Africans would share in future development to the extent that their natural abilities allowed. Mitchell added that the absence of past African achievement suggested that African participation would be limited. Mitchell asserted that the activities of African politicians with few exceptions were inspired by self-interest and accompanied by a marked lack of concern for truth, honesty, justice or good government. Mitchell insisted that the responsible position was to resist proposals for increasing Africans' role in government. Appointing Africans to legislative councils could produce a class of politicians committed only to sterile and unconstructive opposition.[25]

Mitchell included two historical analogies in his diatribe. He likened conditions in India, which was approaching independence and where he anticipated a collapse of law and order, to Europe at the end of the Roman Empire. He conceded that disorder in India was probably inevitable, but bemoaned that some applauded developments there as admirable. He worried that the same thinking was affecting officials concerned with Africa. Mitchell also argued that some believed that the British empire had reached the state of the Spanish empire at the beginning of the nineteenth century. As in the Spanish possessions, demagogues were concocting local nationalisms that would enable them to exploit and oppress the general population. Mitchell also turned his fire on those in Britain who supported nationalist movements in Africa. Their behavior gave the impression that Britain had lost the will to retain authority and that all it took to frighten the British government were current catchphrases or violent words and a little rioting.[26]

When the governors met with Creech Jones and Colonial Office staff in November 1947, other governors added their dissents. Governors of East and Central African colonies generally supported Mitchell's views. Sir John Hall, governor of Uganda, argued that a lack of character barred Africans from positions of executive responsibility. Within Uganda, there was a complete lack of unity and common purpose, he claimed. Lord Milverton (formerly Sir Arthur Richards), governor of Nigeria, reminded his East and Central African colleagues that the goal in West Africa was to create African states. Nevertheless, he objected to including Africans in executive councils. Supported by Sir Hubert Stevenson, governor of Sierra Leone, Milverton pushed for larger roles for committees of legislative council members, including Africans. He thought the inclusion of unofficial Africans in government should start at the bottom, not at the top.[27]

Cohen attempted to minimize the disagreement. He pointed out that Milverton's comments coincided with the Colonial Office proposals except regarding the introduction of Africans into executive councils. Cohen pointed out that the staff papers presupposed that it would be a long time before any African colony was ready for self-government. Interim policies were the issue of the moment. The proper basis for evaluating the proposal regarding executive councils was administrative efficiency and acceptance by local opinion, and not preparation for self-government.[28]

Labour's Program

In 1949, the Colonial Office produced a summary of the government's colonial policies for Labour Members of Parliament. It provided a picture of modest change in the political sphere. Of roughly four and a half pages, a page and a half discussed political and constitutional matters. The rest dealt with economic and social development under several headings. The constitutional section reiterated that self-government was the principal goal, along with decent standards of living and freedom from oppression. It added that the problems to be overcome in reaching the goal were numerous and complex. The summary stated that some colonies might achieve responsible self-government, but others might do so only in combination with others. Still others might achieve only control of their domestic affairs. A long paragraph on local government policy reported that units of local government were being developed to prepare Africans for participation in central government, among other things. The colonies, the summary stated, were evolving away from the old native administrations to forms of local government. Younger, more educated Africans would play a larger role. Local governments would be more representative. The summary did not mention an altered relationship between the Colonial Office and the colonies or a program of preferred steps towards self-government.[29]

The Labour colonial secretaries' penchant for describing their policies as evolutionary reduced further the impression of dramatic change in policy. In Parliament, the government said that it was following the lead given by Oliver Stanley in 1943 when he declared colonial self-government as the government's aim. Creech Jones observed that one could just as well argue that Stanley had been converted to Labour's long-time liberal, humane position on colonial policy. Addressing the Royal Empire Society in 1951, James Griffiths, Creech Jones' successor, offered a long-term view. He described constitutional changes in the Gold Coast as, not an isolated act of policy, but the logical consequence of a century of development.[30]

Attlee's colonial secretaries opposed blueprints or timetables for self-government and stated a preference for political responses to the circumstances of each colony. Creech Jones disavowed prearranged plans in his February 1947 dispatch. In 1948, he argued that dealing with nationalist movements did not involve uniformity of policy or externally imposed measures. Rather, it involved maintaining friendly relations with African peoples. According to Creech Jones, colonial governors, not the Colonial Office, should play the major role. In a 1949 communication to the cabinet, he argued that timetables had to be vague. Political development depended on each colony's social and political viability, not on extraneous considerations. In 1951, Griffiths repeated the notion that political progress in the colonies could not follow a timetable, but had to proceed with the political growth of the people.[31]

Despite the Colonial Office staff's fascination with a new relationship between the office and the colonies and with thinking ahead about political change, Attlee's government stuck with the traditional approach. The initiative remained with the colonial governors. It was up to them to manage the politics of their colonies. Staying one step ahead of nationalists remained the office's preference, but putting that maxim into practice was the governors' responsibility. The Colonial Office's biggest tools remained appointing new governors, which occurred every four or five years, or removing a governor, which occurred rarely.

The Attlee government's approach to colonial reform was in line with mainstream Labour thinking. Labour Party policy statements about colonial matters in 1942 and 1943 were modest and cautious. The emphases were on trusteeship and on economic and social development. The political change contemplated was a break with the reliance on native administrations. Colonial Office officials were pleased that Labour's views coincided with their own. The major Labour pressure group on colonial policy was the Fabian Colonial Bureau. Creech Jones was its chairperson before becoming colonial secretary. The bureau and its supporters thought it important to improve conditions in the colonies before granting self-government. Political power ought to pass to progressive, not reactionary, forces. Rita Hinden, the bureau's moving force, reported that hearing Kwame Nkrumah say that Africans wanted absolute independence left her cool. She thought social justice was more important than immediate independence. Partly in reaction to European events of 1939 and 1940, the bureau considered small, homogenous states vulnerable. It favored consolidating colonies into larger units and promoting partnership between Britain and its former colonies. Some within the Labour Party thought that Creech Jones was a captive of the Colonial Office staff and incapable of pursuing a vigorous policy. Some, notably Fenner Brockway, campaigned openly for fixing target dates for independence. The dissident voices were, however, marginal through the end of the Attlee governments.[32]

Mixed Reviews

Two State Department officials attended the 1947 Cambridge summer school. They were not favorably impressed. They detected defeatism among the participants, a sense that, unless the British regained their sense of mission, British rule would soon end. They thought the British overly sensitive to international criticism. In the wake of labor unrest in Kenya and Uganda and faced with nationalist agitation led by Nnamdi Azikiwe in Nigeria and Jomo Kenyatta in Kenya, the British were close to panic, or so the United States observers thought. The British were pushing reforms too rapidly. The State Department officials thought the British had created their own problem. They had educated a small clique of dissident politicians whose influence outweighed their numbers. Ignorant and politically unsophisticated natives were apt to fall under the spell of self-seeking and subversive politicians. The local government reforms the British were implementing had started a race for control of a self-governing state. The educated minority had a head start and the ignorant majority was slowly learning democratic techniques.[33]

The State Department official who attended the 1948 conference of African representatives came away with a more positive appreciation. He thought that the British were wise to explain their reform ideas, but not self-government, to the African members of legislative councils. Doing so might dispel the notions that Britain was imposing reforms from above and exploiting the colonies for its own benefit. The African participants might go home in a more constructive and enlightened frame of mind.[34]

Churchill's Government and Colonial Reform

When the Conservatives replaced Labour in October 1951, Cohen moved to tie the new government to existing policies. He persuaded Oliver Lyttelton, the new colonial secretary, to tell the House of Commons that the Churchill administration would follow the same policies as the wartime coalition and the Attlee government regarding self-government and social and economic development. After clearing the statement with Churchill, Lyttelton told the Commons that certain aspects of colonial policy were above party politics. Lyttelton announced that he would follow the fundamental policies embraced earlier by leaders of both parties. He would promote self-government as well as the health and welfare of colonial peoples. He acknowledged that the parties might disagree on the details, but he hoped that all could agree on the basic goals.[35]

Lyttelton's statement was consistent with earlier pronouncements in what it said and what it did not say. The reference to self-government was intentionally vague. The Colonial Office continued to see some advantage in leaving the proposed goal for political change undefined. Pairing self-government with development left open the possibility of insisting on a certain level of development as a precondition for political change.

The Conservatives' commitment to self-government was less than enthusiastic. Churchill retained a visceral support for empire. He resented the loss of India and viewed with disdain the Dutch withdrawal from Indonesia. Soon after taking office, Eden commented that he knew little of West Africa, but that well-informed people thought that the Britain had been moving at a "pretty dangerous political gallop there lately." Lord Ismay, the commonwealth relations secretary, observed that the average African in Northern Rhodesia had the mental caliber of a British child of ten and that Britain had to provide better food and education before granting full political emancipation. Nevertheless, Churchill and Eden were willing to delegate responsibility for most colonial issues to Lyttelton. Churchill took an interest only when military force was involved or when a new governor needed to be named.[36]

Lyttelton's basic attitude was resigned pragmatism. In his view, African colonies needed much more social and economic development before they would be ready for self-government. Self-government held a unique appeal, nevertheless. Nationalist leaders could not afford to be perceived by their followers as less than committed in their pursuit of constitutional change, he thought. In a world where other territories were gaining their independence and where communications were fast and effective, the pressure for political advance was irresistible. Britain could no long use military force to resist the pressure. Lyttelton concluded that the best Britain could do was offer piecemeal changes in order to retain support for a while longer. In the end, it would have to hand over power.[37]

Civil servants in the Colonial and Foreign Offices expressed similar views in the early 1950s. In June 1952, the Foreign Office produced a paper titled "The Problem of Nationalism." The paper accepted the possibility that Britain might use military force to retain control of a colony, but argued that sovereign independence for British possessions was both inevitable and desirable. Britain's principal aim should be to influence the speed of political change in the colonies.[38] The Colonial Office agreed that using force was possible, but argued that "by and large, it is inconceivable in the circumstances of the world today that we could use force actually to retain a large colony under British administration against the wishes of a majority of its people." Still enamored of the idea of self-government as something less than independence, the Colonial Office quarreled that independence was a dangerous illusion even for Britain. It proposed that Britain convince nationalists that continued links to Britain were preferable to independence.[39] The same Foreign Office paper argued that Britain had to take the United States and its opinions into account when dealing with nationalism. World opinion as expressed at the United Nations and British public opinion would be factors as well. U.S. cooperation was critical. With it, Britain could deal with the most dangerous manifestations of nationalism. Without it, Britain could achieve little. Britain needed to educate the U.S. government and public about British colonial policies. The Foreign Office acknowledged that involving the United States posed risks. Introducing U.S. influence was likely to reduce British influence and threaten British interests.[40]

Between 1946 and 1952, the British government reinforced its commitment to guiding its African colonies to self-government. Attlee's Labour government concluded that political changes in the African colonies were inevitable. Civil servants thought deeply about ways and means of managing political changes, but, in the end, the Attlee government reverted to a traditional approach, relying on colonial governors to engage with African nationalists and co-opt them into colonial governments. Churchill's second government was less than enthusiastic about the prospect of political change, but could not bring itself to disowning what had become a bipartisan policy.

6

Colonial Reform in West Africa, 1946–1952: A Good Beginning

When Colonial Office civil servants were considering colonial reform, the Gold Coast and Nigeria were in the forefront of their thinking. The two West African colonies seemed the most likely sites for political changes. Both featured relatively large numbers of educated Africans and active nationalist groups. As civil servants were contemplating new constitutional arrangements, nationalist groups in the Gold Coast and Nigeria were, in fact, agitating for a larger say in their territories' affairs. In both colonies, governors tried to use political changes to strengthen British control by bringing African nationalists into the colonial governments. Nationalists took up the governors' offers, but quickly demanded still larger roles in the colonial governments and an eventual transition to at least self-government.

Gold Coast

The Accra riots of 1948 marked the beginning of the end of Britain's control of the Gold Coast. In January 1948, Africans in the Gold Coast organized a boycott of imported goods, protesting the persistence of increased prices since the end of the Second World War. In late February, the Gold Coast government announced steps to address inflation and the Africans agreed to halt the boycott. A group of African ex-servicemen, veterans of the British army during World War II, sought permission to parade through Accra to highlight their own grievances about pensions and job opportunities. The government approved the parade route for February 28, the day the boycott was to end. When the veterans attempted to diverge from the approved route and march on the governor's house, police under British command opened fire. Two Africans were killed and four or five wounded. As word of the shooting spread, riots broke out in Accra and other towns. Shops, particularly those owned by Europeans and Lebanese, were attacked and Europeans stoned.

The government reacted energetically to the outbreak of violence. It deployed what police and troops it had[1] and contemplated bringing in additional troops from Gibraltar.[2] In an attempt to isolate the riots' organizers, the Gold Coast government on March 11 arrested six leaders of the colony's principal political party, the United Gold Coast Convention (UGCC), including J.B. Danquah, its president, and Kwame Nkrumah, its newly

94

appointed general secretary. It detained them in remote locations in the colony's Northern Territories. The government in London decided to dispatch a commission comprised of three Britons and chaired by Aiken Watson, a barrister, to investigate the causes for the riots and recommend remedial steps.

The Gold Coast government in Accra drew ominous conclusions from the riots. Rather than random violence, it saw the hand of the UGCC. It contended that the UGCC had engineered the violence and had used the ex-servicemen as both tools and cover for violent action. It claimed that the UGCC's ends were revolutionary, although the party claimed it was interested in attaining self-government for the Gold Coast by constitutional means. The government reported that the UGCC and the local African-owned newspapers portrayed the situation as out of control and the party as the only organization capable of restoring order. Behind the UGCC, the Accra government saw communist indoctrination and links to communist organizations overseas.[3]

Before the riots, the Gold Coast government had been concerned about the UGCC, its leadership, and possible communist links. The government saw the UGCC as the work of discredited politicians or politicians out of office, intent on displacing the African traditional leaders whom the British had incorporated into its administration. The UGCC focused its appeal on young men, particularly those with some Western education, in Accra and other coastal towns. The government worried about Africans who had been educated in Britain or the United States. British officials thought that nationalist agitation in Nigeria or elsewhere in the British empire was most likely to affect them.

The government perceived Danquah as smart and energetic, but unstable. It nevertheless saw him as a possible counterweight to Nkrumah. Nkrumah left the Gold Coast in the mid–1930s in search of an education in the United States (at Lincoln and Pennsylvania universities) and spent the war years in London consorting with various anti-colonial groups. In 1947, the UGCC leadership hired him as the organization's paid general secretary and he returned to the Gold Coast shortly before the riots. The Gold Coast government knew that Nkrumah had been associated with organizations in London that some officials considered communist. The government expected Nkrumah to seek support from these groups for the UGCC and to establish contact with communist groups in French West Africa.[4]

The Accra government's analysis of the UGCC's role in the riots was mistaken. The UGCC had no real ties to the ex-servicemen's group. Although Nkrumah was aware of the planned march, he and the UGCC leaders played no part in organizing or leading it. On the first day of the riots, Nkrumah and Danquah were not in Accra, but at a UGCC rally in Saltpond, seventy miles away. According to Nkrumah, they were as surprised by the violence as was the government. Nevertheless, the UGCC leaders attempted to profit from the riots. Returning to Accra, they met with local UGCC leaders to discuss how to turn the situation to their advantage. Danquah and Nkrumah each sent a telegram to the colonial secretary. They asked that the British government send a special commissioner to the Gold Coast authorized to hand over power to an interim government of chiefs and the people, and to call a constituent assembly.[5]

London's initial reaction to the riots was more restrained than Accra's. Creech Jones agreed with the governor, Sir Gerald Creasy, that the danger of communist activities existed and the public needed help to appreciate it. Nonetheless, Jones warned Creasy that the government did not want to alienate "responsible and educated elements" in Britain or Africa. They might see an emphasis on communism as an attempt to obscure other more legitimate causes for discontent or the desire for more rapid constitutional advance.[6]

Watson Commission

After holding hearings in the Gold Coast, the Watson commission released its report in June 1948. The commission concluded that the riots had a broad range of inter-related causes, political, economic, and social. The high cost of imported goods, the government's clumsy efforts to stem the spread of disease in the colony's cocoa trees, the slow development of education, a shortage of housing, the halting efforts to hire Africans in government posts, and the large number of disappointed ex-servicemen all fed distrust and discontent. In the political sphere, the government's public relations efforts were failures, the commission said. The government had not realized the influence of the chiefs was waning and relied too heavily on them. The government also gave them an overly large role in the legislative council established by the 1946 constitution. The commission concluded that the 1946 constitution left educated Africans frustrated. They considered it window dressing intended to block their quest for political power. The Watson commission thought that the creation of an elected African majority in the legislative council but without real political power was dangerous. It stimulated discontent without creating an outlet for reasonable political ambitions.[7]

The commission recommended that the Gold Coast government's reforms be as broad as the riots' causes. The government had to confront political, economic, and social problems. In the political sphere, the commission concluded that "a substantial measure of constitutional reform" was necessary to meet Africans' legitimate aspirations. Constitutional reform should include an assembly of forty-five elected members. The government should also establish local authorities with an elected element, regional assemblies with executive powers, and a board of nine ministers including five African members of the assembly nominated by the governor and approved by the assembly. The aim should be to give every African of ability an opportunity to help govern the country in order to gain political experience as well as experience political power.[8]

The Watson commission's embrace of educated Africans' political ambitions was less than passionate, however. The commission thought the government needed greater legal powers to deal with speeches designed to arouse disorder and violence. The commission opined that an atmosphere of stability could be maintained only if a revised Gold Coast constitution remained in place for at least ten years. Only after this probationary period would the constitution be reviewed and perhaps revised. The commission was certain that a small, literate minority, once given political power, would exploit the illiterate majority. Britain needed to remain in the Gold Coast until the literate minority had advanced beyond selfish exploitation, the bulk of the population was literate enough and experienced enough to protect itself from exploitation, and all areas of the colony had undergone the appropriate cultural, political, and economic development.[9]

The Watson commission thought little of Nkrumah. The commission believed that while in Britain, Nkrumah had communist affiliations and had become "imbued with a communist ideology." The commission reported Nkrumah's links in London with the West African National Secretariat, whose aim, the commission believed, was a "Union of West African Soviet Socialist Republics." The commission alleged that, as general secretary of the UGCC, Nkrumah occupied "the role held by all party secretaries in totalitarian institutions, the real position of power." The commission concluded that Nkrumah had proposed a program for the UGCC "which is all too familiar to those who have studied the technique of countries who have fallen victims of communist enslavement." According to the commission, the UGCC leadership, regardless of their protestations that they had not read Nkrumah's program, were eager to seize political power and for the time being were indifferent to the means adopted to attain it.[10]

The government in London accepted the Watson commission report, but with a few grumbles. Creech Jones reported to Atlee the commission's conclusions that the UGCC had not promoted the riots, but had attempted to exploit them, and that no evidence of communist instigation existed, although Nkrumah had communist contacts. Jones conceded that constitutional reform in the Gold Coast was consistent with British policy, although not as much reform as the commission recommended. Nevertheless, both Creech Jones and Andrew Cohen resented the commission's criticism of the 1946 Gold Coast constitution. They saw the constitution as a necessary step in the Gold Coast's evolution. Cohen detected a bias against the chiefs in the commission findings. He thought that they were still the recognized leaders of the people in most of the Gold Coast.[11] Cohen was also irritated that the commission recommended constitutional reforms that the Colonial Office had already chosen. It now looked as if the Colonial Office was making concessions only because of the commission's prodding. At the same time Cohen worried that despite official denials, the Accra riots had forced political reforms beyond what was advisable. Africans in the Gold Coast and Nigeria might conclude that serious disorders led to constitutional concessions.[12]

The British government thought the Accra riots offered three lessons. First, conditions in the Gold Coast could produce violent disturbances and destroy lives and property. Economic and social measures were, therefore, needed. Second, the chiefs and the local government institutions the British had created before 1948 had both failed to prevent the riots and to control them once they started. Nevertheless, the third and most important lesson was that unless the British were to expand their police and military presence at considerable cost, they needed to recruit Africans to participate in government and enable it to maintain law and order. The open questions were what Africans would these be and what enticements would they require to cooperate with the British.

Coussey Committee

In December 1948, the governor of the Gold Coast began implementation of the Watson Report recommendations. He appointed a committee of forty Africans, headed by (later Sir) Henley Coussey, an African judge, to devise a new Gold Coast constitution. Danquah, president of the UGCC, was included on the committee, but Nkrumah was not.

Before the committee submitted its recommendations in August 1949, African politics in the Gold Coast changed dramatically. Splits surfaced between the UGCC leadership and Nkrumah, and between the Africans, often older, better educated and more prosperous, who were more willing to work with the government and those, usually younger, less educated, and poorer, who favored more rapid advance to self-government. In June 1949, Nkrumah announced to a gathering of sixty thousand in Accra the formation of a new political party, the Convention Peoples' Party (CPP), committed to "full self-government now."

Senior officials in the Gold Coast government were alarmed. In their view, Nkrumah was still intent on establishing a Union of African Soviet Socialist Republics. Despite professed interest in nationalism, he was intent on disruption, they thought. At the center of his movement was a "small body of zealots, partly composed of fanatical anti-imperialists and nationalists and partly of gangsters." Officials claimed that Nkrumah planned to use a general strike and boycott to stop the government from maintaining essential services. Most in the Gold Coast wanted self-government but, officials thought, on a slower timetable than Nkrumah and his followers. Worrying to the British, the politicians who favored a more evolutionary approach lacked organization and a common platform much less imaginative and constructive plans with which to capture public opinion. British officials believed that the more moderate African leaders had not adjusted their thinking to accommodate the 1946 constitution.[13]

The Colonial Office was more sanguine. One official was amused that the Gold Coast government now portrayed the UGCC as the voice of responsible opinion. Officials took heart from the split between the UGCC leadership and Nkrumah. Their interpretation was that "Africans of substance" recognized that mob rule and race hatred, which they identified with Nkrumah and his followers, were incompatible with self-government. Moderate Africans, frightened of Nkrumah, would cooperate with the Gold Coast government to implement whatever the Coussey committee recommended. Once these Africans had gained some political power and were part of the government, the "emotional nonsense talked about self government" would disappear. Moderate Africans would be too busy with their governmental responsibilities and with their feud with Nkrumah and company.[14]

The Colonial Office wanted less alarm and more action in Accra. Officials in London were not convinced that Nkrumah's aims differed from those of the Gold Coast population. They were convinced that reform, especially the political proposals expected from the Coussey committee, would undercut Nkrumah and strengthen moderate Africans. Nevertheless, they thought the Gold Coast government lacked imaginative and constructive ideas with which to capture public opinion. London officials thought that the government in Accra needed to seize the initiative from Nkrumah and stay one step ahead of events. If the government did not give African moderates an alternative to Nkrumah's "self-government now," the Coussey committee might succumb to pressure and recommend steps the British could not accept. Even if the Coussey proposals were acceptable to the government, the Convention People's Party might grow strong enough to inspire widespread resistance to them. Non-cooperation, strikes, and boycotts were apt to degenerate into violence.[15]

Gold Coast officials pointed the finger back at London. The government was gaining more support, Accra officials asserted. To the extent that problems remained, the fault lay with London's failure to supply the men and material needed to redeem postwar promises of material progress. The Watson commission's response had undermined confidence in the government and demonstrated that violence paid political dividends. Creation of the Coussey committee made the Gold Coast government look like a caretaker waiting for the next round of constitutional change.[16]

When the Coussey committee made its recommendations in October 1949, London was predisposed to accept them. The committee proposed an enlarged legislative assembly of eighty-four members, although with seats filled through indirect elections. Executive power would be in the hands of the governor and an executive council composed of eight members of the legislature and three government officials ex-officio, the minister of defense and external affairs, the minister of finance, and the minister of justice. Certain powers would be "reserved" to the governor. He would have sole authority for internal security, the military, and foreign relations. The UGCC members of the committee objected to the governor's reserved powers. Some committee members also preferred a bicameral legislature. Even before the Coussey committee report was published, Colonial Office officials recommended that an executive council be empowered to initiate business. Officials hoped to "fasten executive responsibility onto the Africans as firmly as we can."[17] With the Coussey recommendations in hand, London insisted that the executive council remain responsible to the governor and declined to establish an elected leader of the legislature. Otherwise, the British accepted the committee's proposals.

In recommending approval to the cabinet, Creech Jones argued that constitutional concessions would rally moderate African opinion behind the British. Creech Jones described to the cabinet the agitation in the Gold Coast for immediate self-government and the split between what he termed the "extremists" and those of moderate opinion. Moderates, he wrote, recognized that full responsible government was not possible yet but still favored constitutional advance. If the British approved the bulk of the Coussey proposals, which Jones termed a "victory for moderate opinion," the governor would then have moderate opinion behind him, even if the extremists were not satisfied.[18]

At least one official in London raised a note of caution. Sir Norman Brook, secretary to the cabinet, observed that the Coussey proposals had clear weaknesses, but conceded that these were inherent in any scheme of limited self-government. He thought that the British had already committed themselves to constitutional changes. He reported that the Colonial Office thought the proposals had sufficient support within the Gold Coast. Brook added, however, that no constitution could both satisfy nationalist aspirations and retain ultimate British power. He noted that "extreme elements of political opinion" in the Gold Coast would press for more concessions.[19]

While considering the Coussey recommendations, the cabinet took up an issue that would emerge repeatedly in the future. Some cabinet members suggested that the British ought to commit themselves to reviewing the new constitution within a specified number of years, since it did not grant full self-government. Setting a timetable would blunt some of the criticism directed at the British at the United Nations and other international forums. Nevertheless, the cabinet rejected the suggestion. The majority view was that timetables unsettled local populations. Instead of applying themselves to making the most of the constitution in place, they pressed for additional constitutional changes.[20]

Positive Action

The Convention People's Party and the groups associated with it opposed the Coussey proposals. In November, the CPP organized a Ghana People's Representative Assembly with attendees from fifty organizations, but not the UGCC. The assembly rejected the Coussey recommendations and called for immediate self-government. In mid–December, Nkrumah, acting on behalf of the CPP, wrote to the governor that if a constituent assembly were not elected to consider the Coussey Report and draw up a new constitution, the CPP would begin a campaign of "Positive Action." According to Nkrumah, "Positive Action" included all legitimate and constitutional means, beginning with political agitation, newspaper, and educational campaigns and ending, if necessary, with strikes, boycotts and non-cooperation. In early January, after the Gold Coast Trades Union Congress declared a strike in support of workers in the government meteorological office, Nkrumah and the CPP called for a general strike as part of a campaign of Positive Action.

The Gold Coast government responded with what resources it had. During December, a senior official met with Nkrumah and other CPP leaders. He tried to persuade them that the Coussey recommendations established a constitutional means for them to gain power.

They only had to nominate and support candidates in the upcoming elections. He warned that political strikes were illegal and would lead to violence and disorder in the Gold Coast. After these and subsequent negotiations failed and the general strike materialized, a new governor, Sir Charles Arden-Clarke, declared a state of emergency and deployed police and troops. He had Nkrumah and other CPP leaders arrested and charged with various offenses. Nkrumah and several others were convicted and sentenced to prison terms ranging from six months to five years.[21]

Despite the unrest, Arden-Clarke maintained that the Colonial Office's strategy of a working relationship between the Gold Coast government and "moderate opinion" was still feasible. Although Arden-Clarke had come up through the ranks in the Colonial Service, he was appointed governor most likely because he was attuned to the latest thinking in the Colonial Office. He demonstrated a willingness not shared by many of his colleagues to work with aspiring African politicians. Arden-Clarke was not inclined to work with Nkrumah initially, however. In a letter home during the general strike, Arden-Clarke referred to "our local Hitler and his putsch." Writing to the Colonial Office, Arden-Clarke asserted that the CPP had disintegrated now that its leaders were in jail. He proposed to rally moderate opinion behind the Coussey proposals and encourage the creation of a strong moderate party capable of dealing with dissident elements. He proposed to argue that the responsibilities involved in the Coussey recommendations were as much as Africans could bear at present and that the British government would make no further concessions. Arden-Clarke admitted, nonetheless, that what he termed responsible opinion was only semi-articulate and unorganized and did not have a program to compete with calls for self-government now.[22]

A meaningful alternative to the CPP did not emerge. The remaining UGCC leaders and many chiefs agreed to cooperate, but it became clear that the CPP remained the Gold Coast's predominant political party. In late 1950, with elections under the new Gold Coast constitution only months ahead, Cohen reviewed for Arden-Clarke's benefit the options for dealing with the imprisoned Nkrumah. Cohen argued it was a matter, not of principle, but of political expediency. Would keeping Nkrumah in jail interfere with the functioning of the new executive council? Would releasing him later rather than sooner look like yielding to African pressure? Would it be better for Nkrumah to be inside the government or outside? How would releasing Nkrumah before the election affect the results? Should Nkrumah be released immediately after the election if, as anticipated, the CPP won a substantial number of seats?[23]

CPP Victory

The British thought that the electoral arrangements favored Nkrumah's opponents. Nevertheless, the CPP won nearly all the available seats — thirty-four of the thirty-eight seats popularly elected. Arden-Clarke had Nkrumah released from prison and invited him to form a government under the new constitution. Arden-Clarke argued that he had little choice. Nkrumah and his party had wide popular support and no other party was a serious rival to the CPP. If the British refused to work with Nkrumah, the new constitution would be stillborn and no one in the Gold Coast would trust the British government. The Gold Coast would plunge into "disorders, violence, and bloodshed," Arden-Clarke argued. Nkrumah justified working with the British in similar terms. According to Nkrumah, the CPP accepted office because remaining in opposition would have meant pursuing a negative course of action. Taking office would prevent "the stooges and reactionaries" from taking advantage. Once in office, the CPP could continue to work for self-government.[24]

Over the next two years, Arden-Clarke solidified a working relationship between himself and the British officials in the Gold Coast on the one hand, and Nkrumah and senior CPP leaders on the other. As early as March 1951, Arden-Clarke informed London that he saw real promise in Nkrumah. According to the governor, Nkrumah was a skillful politician. He could become a real statesman if he had the strength to resist the bad counsels of the "scallywags" around him. Nkrumah and the current CPP leaders were the best available option, willing to be reasonable and moderate, the party most likely to preserve law and order. According to Arden-Clarke, Nkrumah was vulnerable to attacks from the extreme CPP elements, including some backbenchers in the Legislative Assembly. It did not help that Danquah, the one-time moderate in British eyes, continued to embarrass the CPP government by calling for more rapid progress toward self-government. If Nkrumah could not appease the wilder elements in his own party, Arden-Clarke, thought, his government would fail and be replaced by one at least as aggressive in its pursuit of self-government. To undercut Nkrumah's opponents, real and potential, Arden-Clarke embarked on a program of concessions — releasing the other CPP leaders imprisoned with Nkrumah, releasing ex-servicemen imprisoned after the Accra riots, and, in 1952, allowing Nkrumah to be entitled "prime minister" and requiring the Gold Coast governor to consult the prime minister before appointing ministers.[25]

Cohen agreed with Arden-Clarke's strategy. According to Cohen, the aim of British policy was a smooth and gradual advance to responsible government. Maintaining a good relationship with African leaders like Nkrumah would ensure that newly independent African countries would remain within the commonwealth. Cohen argued that the better the relationship with Nkrumah and his like, the more likely Africans were to accept a slower pace toward full self-government. Cohen thought the Gold Coast (and, in this period, Nigeria) needed a considerable period of stability in order to develop "administrative and political efficiency." If Africans and African leaders trusted British intentions, they might be persuaded to allow a longer transitional period before additional steps towards responsible government.[26]

Cohen favored supporting Nkrumah, even if it meant faster progress toward responsible government. Cohen recognized that both Nkrumah's followers and his political opponents might push him to demand faster progress toward self-government. Should Nkrumah make such demands, the British ought to concede, Cohen argued. The alternative was pushing the Gold Coast government into the hands of extremists.[27]

Concessions to Nkrumah

Although Oliver Lyttelton, the colonial secretary in the Conservative government that came to power in October 1951, was less enthusiastic than Arden-Clarke or Cohen, he eventually gave way. Arden-Clarke explained to Lyttelton that keeping the Nkrumah-led CPP government in power for another year or two would foster responsible, moderate government. The price to be paid was further, minor constitutional change, allowing the elected head of the legislative assembly to be entitled "prime minister" and requiring the governor to consult with the prime minister before appointing ministers. Arden-Clarke thought he had persuaded Nkrumah that future constitutional changes could occur no faster than at yearly intervals. Nkrumah, Arden-Clarke said, believed that Lyttelton's Labour predecessor, James Griffiths, had promised further constitutional change. Lyttelton replied that he did not favor such rapid change, but saw no practical alternative. He felt bound to honor Griffiths's promise. He would present the changes to the cabinet and to the House of Commons as representing Arden-Clarke's considered advice, and not the result of pressure from Gold Coast leaders.[28]

Lyttelton and Arden-Clarke's discussion of constitutional changes in the Gold Coast sheds light on other facets of British official thinking in the early 1950s. Arden-Clarke raised what might be termed the "demonstration effect." Africans in the Gold Coast would evaluate British concessions in comparison with events in Libya and the Sudan, which were, in some minds, less ready for responsible government than the Gold Coast. Sir Thomas Lloyd, the senior civil servant in the Colonial Office, opined that the proposed concessions were the minimum acceptable in the Gold Coast, and a small price to pay for keeping the Gold Coast on the path of constitutional development. Arden-Clarke raised the specter of a more extreme Gold Coast government with stronger public support. If the British failed to make concessions to Nkrumah, they would soon face, Arden-Clarke believed, a united Gold Coast demand for more far-reaching changes. Finally, Arden-Clarke played his trump card. Faced with a demand for immediate self-government, Britain's only alternative would be to use armed force.[29]

When Lyttelton himself met with Nkrumah and the CPP ministers in July 1952, he tried to shore up the British position. After listening to ministers contend that the Gold Coast wanted immediate self-government and dominion status within the commonwealth, Lyttelton argued that the Gold Coast had a large measure of internal self-government. He added that achieving dominion status required the agreement of all members of the commonwealth, not just Britain. Lyttelton warned the Gold Coast ministers that they should be careful what they asked for. The Gold Coast needed British assistance, but Britain would not stay in the Gold Coast, Lyttelton said, unless the conditions were such that it could do a good job. The senior civil servant who recorded the meeting did not assume that Lyttelton was bluffing about an abrupt British withdrawal from the Gold Coast.[30]

Lyttelton's words had little effect. Nkrumah portrayed himself to Lyttelton as more conservative than many of his CPP colleagues and convinced of the need for a slower pace toward self-government. In September 1952, Nkrumah approached Arden-Clarke about more constitutional change — replacing the three ex-officio members of the executive council with elected ministers and convening a constituent assembly. Arden-Clarke's immediate response was that he was not authorized to discuss further changes. In relaying the news to London, Arden-Clarke attributed Nkrumah's behavior to two factors. He was inordinately concerned about opposition and was apt to follow advice from his supporters, regardless of his own views. Arden-Clarke also observed that Danquah favored a constituent assembly and CPP leaders feared being outbid for public support.[31]

By 1952, the alliance between Nkrumah and Arden-Clarke and between the CPP and British officials was so tight as to worry a Colonial Office official. W.G. Gorell Barnes fretted that the danger was no longer anti–British agitation, but British complicity in CPP exploitation of the general population. Gorell Barnes thought that CPP officials' past involvement in communist organizations reinforced the tendency of Africans to exploit their fellows. If the British ruled out the possibility of reinstating colonial rule, they could face the harsh choice of pulling out of the Gold Coast or continuing to support a dictatorial government.[32]

Doubts and Misgivings

During the Truman administration, the United States was a bystander to events in the Gold Coast. At high levels, the U.S. viewed favorably British efforts to manage political change in the Gold Coast. At lower levels and in the Gold Coast, attitudes were less positive. Compounding the basic grumpiness was the fact that State Department officials obtained much of their information from lower level British officials in London and in the Gold Coast who were often gloomy about political events in the colony. U.S. officials were fixated on possible links between African leaders and communism and some were apt to believe the worst.

In the six months before the Accra riots, E. Talbot Smith, the consul in Accra, provided Washington with a series of less-than-glowing reports about the Gold Coast. You could not, he reported, judge the "advance of the Gold Coast African" by the few that had some education or the handful who had received university educations in Britain. Regardless of what officials in London might believe, none of the long-serving British officials the consul met in the Gold Coast thought that the Africans in the Gold Coast could govern themselves in anything less than thirty years. The Africans were slow, backward, and hopeless, the consulate reported. Most officials would not even hazard a guess about when self-government might come. The UGCC had gotten off to a slow start, largely because of opposition from the chiefs. Without better leadership, the UGCC was unlikely to amount to much.[33]

One of the American officials who attended the 1947 British colonial conference at Cambridge echoed Smith's views. Joseph Palmer reported that Colonial Office officials at the conference made much of the fact that the Gold Coast would be the first African colony to achieve full self-government. They thought the Gold Coast would reach that stage in a generation. Nevertheless, when Palmer pressed them about what they meant by a generation, the reply was "probably thirty years." Palmer added that the officials at the conference who were stationed in African colonies thought that even this estimate was far too optimistic.[34]

Smith thought that Nkrumah, given his background, would try to make the UGCC a more radical organization and would seek to link it to nationalist organizations in London and Nigeria. The consul reported that local British officials thought that Nkrumah was a communist, but that they could offer no documentation.[35]

Initial reports to Washington from the London embassy reflected both British alarm at the Accra riots and initial confusion about their origins. Based on conversations with Colonial Office officials, the reports from London indicated that the Gold Coast government's failure to find jobs for veterans and to control retail prices for imported goods were partly to blame. The reports from London stressed the role of the UGCC. They contended that the riots were part of a plot to seize power in the Gold Coast, foiled only by the government's prompt deployment of troops. The UGCC was not a communist organization, the reports conceded, but some leaders were happy to accept support from communist organizations. Danquah was not a communist, but other UGCC leaders were influenced by Marxist ideas. Danquah seemed to have the upper hand within the UGCC and was trying to exploit Nkrumah's oratorical abilities. Nkrumah was a card-carrying communist, intent on overthrowing the British, the embassy contended.[36]

In subsequent conversations with U.S. representatives, senior Colonial Office officials played down any communist involvement in the Accra riots. Creech Jones advised that Danquah was not a communist. He could cause serious trouble, however. He was capable of seeming reasonable in private conversations with British officials, and adopting a different character in talks with other Africans. Nevertheless, Cohen discounted a communist conspiracy in the Gold Coast.[37]

Smith relayed the views of lower-level British officials in the Gold Coast. Experienced officials were surprised that violence had occurred in the Gold Coast, considered a peaceful colony, rather than Nigeria, where anti–British agitators held forth. The government put too much faith in the chiefs, who had made no effort to control the looting mobs, they thought. The British overlooked the Africans who made their livings in Accra and similar towns. They were "no longer under the thumb of the chief" and read the local newspapers with their "never ending agitation" against the British. The chiefs were willing to work with the British to prepare the Gold Coast for eventual self-government, Smith contended. The African intellectuals wanted independence immediately and were allowing themselves to be led by communists. The consul added his own view. While sympathetic to independence for the Gold Coast, he did not believe it would be possible for many years.[38]

Smith thought the Watson Report weak. The report was about what one might expect from the Labour government, according to Smith. The UGCC had flouted the government and mobs had caused £2 million damage. Both had gotten away with it. The government had arrested six UGCC leaders but failed to explain its reasons for doing so to the Watson commission. Nationalists in Nigeria would get the message.[39]

A 1950 CIA report was cautiously optimistic about the situation in the Gold Coast and British West Africa. The report posited that the area touched on U.S. interests in three ways: as a source of strategic metals (columbite and manganese), as a source of dollar income for an economically challenged Britain, and as a potential source of wartime bases and manpower. Violence had occurred and would reoccur, but nationalist movements were weak, the CIA concluded. British efforts at reform would avert a crisis in the short term. The British were engaged in "an orderly retreat" and, in the end, the British West African colonies would achieve something comparable to dominion status. Managing the transition to self-government would be the principal British challenge.[40]

In June 1951, Nkrumah came to the United States to give the commencement address at his alma mater, Lincoln University. During the trip, he met unofficially with George McGhee, the assistant secretary of state for Near Eastern, South Asian, and African affairs. The briefing materials prepared for McGhee capture the State Department's negative but uncertain thinking about the African leader. Nkrumah was described as the leader of the Convention People's Party, an "extremist" party that recently won an overwhelming majority in popular elections. The original version of the briefing memorandum said that Nkrumah appeared at one time to have been closely identified with communist organizations. The original version stated that although Nkrumah said his ultimate goal was full self-government for the Gold Coast, his political opponents claimed that communists dominated the CPP and that Nkrumah planned to turn the Gold Coast into a totalitarian country. A revised version of the memorandum played down Nkrumah's communist associations. It said that Nkrumah "was alleged to have been identified with communist organizations, but was never conclusively proven." The British, the new version added, did not believe that Nkrumah was a communist or that he would follow the communist line. Intense nationalism on the part of Africans, the revised version explained, had been frequently misinterpreted as communism.[41]

McGhee told Nkrumah that the British reforms in the Gold Coast might have prompted misgivings in some quarters, but they did not in the U.S. government. The traditional U.S. policy was to support orderly movements toward self-government. The United

States government appreciated the efficient manner in which the British and Africans had carried out the first stages of their bold experiment, as well as the moderation and responsibility demonstrated by African leaders. McGhee added that the United States was sure that the experiment would succeed, although the Gold Coast faced real obstacles in uniting a diverse population.[42]

After the CPP and Nkrumah took office, State Department reports to Washington resembled the official British analysis. Nkrumah faced challenges in controlling his followers and fending off his political opponents, they said. Nevertheless, the CPP was Britain's best hope for a responsible and cooperative partner in the Gold Coast. Britain would continue to make concessions to shore up the CPP's position. At the same time, State Department officials clung to fears that Nkrumah might be dangerous. In early 1952, William E. Cole, the consul in Accra, anticipated a confrontation between Arden-Clarke and Gold Coast leaders. He observed that if Nkrumah were waiting to change his tactics in order to strike a blow against imperialism, as his past flirtation with communism might suggest, the stage was set for another round of strikes and public disturbances.[43]

Nigeria

Nigerian agitation for self-government coalesced into a significant organization in 1944. On August 26, Dr. Nnamdi Azikiwe founded the National Council of Nigeria and the Cameroons (NCNC) with himself as secretary. Azikiwe had been educated in the United States and had operated a newspaper in the Gold Coast. When he returned to Nigeria in the late 1930s, he founded a newspaper, the *West African Pilot* (the first of several papers he would own and operate), in Lagos and immersed himself in Lagos and Nigerian politics. Since 1923, Lagos had elected three members of the Nigerian legislative council. Calabar elected one member. While Lagos was in Nigeria's Western Region and educated Yoruba dominated its politics, Azikiwe, although born in the Northern Region, was an Igbo with roots in Nigeria's Eastern Region. A political party, the Nigerian Youth Movement, emerged in Lagos in 1936. Its history was characterized by factional fights, with one of the factions led by Azikiwe. The NCNC was Azikiwe's attempt to create a political organization he could dominate and that would operate throughout Nigeria. The NCNC was less a political party than an umbrella for various Nigerian organizations — trade unions, smaller political parties, and organizations referred to as "tribal unions"— created to represent the interests of one of Nigeria's many ethnic groups. In January 1945, the NCNC held its first convention. It declared its aim as "internal self-government for Nigeria."

The NCNC's first opportunity to make its mark came in the summer of 1945. The Second World War had seen growth in the number and membership of trade unions in Nigeria as well as significant price increases without comparable pay increases for Nigerian workers. In June, ports, telecommunications, and railway workers went on strike, shutting down essential services across the country. Azikiwe supported the strikers through his newspapers. In July, the government banned his papers. Shortly thereafter, Azikiwe went into hiding. He claimed that his followers had uncovered a government plot to assassinate him. The strike ended when a commission of inquiry recommended an increase in cost of living allowances. Azikiwe and the NCNC had attracted public attention and earned some credit for a successful strike.

Richards Constitution

In 1945, the British government in Nigeria provided the NCNC with another target. The Colonial Office and the Nigerian government had been discussing a new constitution for Nigeria for several years. In March 1945, Sir Arthur Richards, the governor of Nigeria, abruptly announced a new constitution. The new constitution established regional assemblies in the Eastern, Western, and Northern Regions, each with unofficial members in the majority. The constitution expanded the legislative council to forty-four members, sixteen government officials and twenty-eight unofficial members. The number of unofficial members overstated the role potential opponents of British rule were likely to play under the new constitution, however. The governor would nominate five unofficial members of each regional assembly. The other members would be elected indirectly with the native administrations controlling the process. Each regional assembly would also name five unofficial members of the legislative council. The governor would name another nine unofficial members. Only the remaining four members of the legislative council would be popularly elected. As in the 1922 constitution, Lagos would elect three members and Calabar one.

The Richards constitution was an attempt to reform and consolidate long-standing elements of British rule in Nigeria. For the first time the legislative council would include members from all parts of Nigeria. Heretofore, the Northern Region had played no part in the council. Both the new regional assemblies and the expanded legislative council would serve to draw more Nigerians into government above the native administration level. Presumably, these Nigerians would be willing to cooperate with the British. Richards wanted to eliminate the elected seats, but the Colonial Office rejected the proposal. The native administrations represented a working relationship between African chiefs and their closest supporters on the one hand and British officials on the other hand. By linking the native administrations to the regional assemblies and the regional assemblies to the legislative council, the Richards constitution attempted to broaden this working relationship to include the regions and Nigeria itself.

The NCNC and other Nigerian politicians objected to the Richards constitution. Richards allowed little or no opportunity for Nigerians to review and comment on his proposals. Sir Bernard Bourdillon, Richards's predecessor, had promised that Nigerians would be involved in discussions of any new constitution. Moreover, the new constitution did not expand suffrage. It also appeared to give larger roles to chiefs and other Nigerians who might be expected to cooperate with the British. Critics claimed that the unofficial majorities in the regional assemblies and the legislative council were shams. They pointed out that the regional assemblies and the legislative council possessed limited powers and the governor retained considerable "reserved" powers.

From early 1945 through 1948, the NCNC campaigned against the Richards constitution. For much of 1946, a group of NCNC leaders headed by Azikiwe toured Nigeria, agitating against the constitution and other aspects of British rule. It raised funds to, among other things, pay for a delegation to London. Prominent among the NCNC's complaints were four ordinances proposed by Richards along with the constitution and adopted by the Nigerian government in 1945. The ordinances dealt with mining and land rights and with the appointment and deposition of chiefs. Azikiwe and the NCNC portrayed the land and mining ordinances as British attempts to lay claim to Nigerian assets. The chiefs' ordinance was proof, they claimed, that the chiefs were British puppets.

Azikiwe and his supporters were less than popular with senior British officials. Azikiwe, officials told London, was unscrupulous and untruthful. He would say whatever would advance his cause. He was no more to be trusted than Hitler had been. The NCNC did not have as much public support as it claimed. It had a following among the have-nots, the educated, semi-educated, and unemployed whose achievements had fallen short of their expectations, officials claimed. The NCNC was motivated, senior officials contended, by selfishness and a lust for power. It was willing to sacrifice the interest of the majority of Nigerians for the sake of its financial and political advancement. The NCNC had little support among responsible and intelligent Nigerians. Sadly, such Nigerians were unwilling to oppose it and Azikiwe, colonial officials complained.[44]

When it became known that the NCNC planned to send a delegation to London, Richards pressed the Colonial Office to take counter measures. The press and the public needed to be told that the NCNC intended to disrupt British rule and to achieve their own selfish ends, Richards wrote. The Colonial Office should contact the editors of *The Times* and *The Economist* to make sure that the British public was not misled and British colonial policy discredited.[45]

When the NCNC delegation reached London and met with Creech Jones, it submitted a memorandum calling for eventual Nigerian independence. The NCNC proposed Anglo-Nigerian joint rule for ten years, followed by a Nigerian interim government for five years and then by the grant of independence. Creech Jones was unmoved. He told the delegation that the Richards constitution would be modified and amended in light of experience. There was no question of setting it aside and substituting something different, particularly something that was not suited to Nigerian conditions. Jones advised the delegation to return to Nigeria and make the constitution work.

The NCNC delegation returned home determined to do anything but make the constitution work. In this, they did not carry the bulk of Nigerians with them, not even all the Nigerians involved in the government or politics or all those who opposed British rule. The NCNC, in its campaigns of the late 1940s, strove to become a pan–Nigerian political organization, if not the dominant pan–Nigerian political organization. The NCNC national tour during 1946 was the first serious attempt to involve all parts of the country in agitation against the British. The NCNC delegation to London included Nigerians of all sorts. Nevertheless, the NCNC under Azikiwe's leadership could not overcome the many fissures in the Nigerian body politic. Animosities and personal rivalries dating from pre–World War II politics in Lagos continued to have their effect. Moreover, Azikiwe was ambitious and combative, not an easy person to work with. Nigeria also encompassed many ethnic groups. Competition between the Yoruba, the most numerous ethnic group in the Western Region, and the Igbo, the most numerous group in the Eastern Region, was only the most obvious case of friction between Nigerian ethnic groups.

As the British officials had detected, support for the NCNC and similar political organizations was most common among Nigerians who had moved from the countryside to towns, who had at least some education of a European type, and who were employed in something other than farming. The economic and social changes that were behind the emergence of this population had spread very unevenly across Nigeria. In particular, education of a European type was far more widespread in the Eastern and Western Regions than it was in Nigeria's Northern Region. Various factors accounted for these social and economic differences. In the case of education, schools patterned after European models had started in southern Nigerian before those in the North. Christian missions were active in the South while government policy inhibited their growth in the North. Much of the North's population was

Muslim and not interested in schools operated by missionaries. The government was slow and stingy in developing its own schools. As of the late 1940s, potential recruits for the NCNC and other aspiring political parties were distributed unevenly across the landscape and among ethnic groups.

As soon as the NCNC delegation returned to Nigeria, disputes broke out. An immediate cause was the failure to account properly for the funds raised to send the delegation to London. Nigerian newspapers, tied to one political faction or another, traded accusations about the money. More fundamental was a disagreement about participating in the government created by the Richards constitution. Azikiwe and two others elected to the legislative council from Lagos decided to boycott legislative council sessions. The remnants of the Nigerian Youth Movement and others, notably Obafemi Awolowo, a rising figure from the Western Provinces, decided to put aside their misgivings and participate. These disagreements took on ethnic and regional flavors, with Igbo from the Eastern Provinces supporting Azikiwe and Yoruba from the Western Provinces opposing him. Early in 1948, Azikiwe and his followers decided to abandon their boycott and use the legislative council as a platform to harass the British. At the 1948 NCNC convention, Azikiwe took a more militant position than he had before, seeming to say that he now favored direct action, rather than constitutional steps, as the way to achieve independence. The British interpreted Azikiwe's more strident approach as an attempt to buttress his leadership position. They thought he sought to outmaneuver younger elements calling for more direct action. Nonetheless, Azikiwe's speech failed to persuade the bulk of the NCNC leadership and it widened the breach between him and those willing to work within the Richards constitution. The Convention adopted a document it characterized as a "Freedom Charter" but, after the Convention, the NCNC became less active.[46]

Zikist Movement

The NCNC's inactivity stemmed in part from the decision of its most militant members to go their own way. In 1945, a group of young Nigerians formed the Zikist Movement, committed to defending Azikiwe from attacks in the wake of the general strike. Through 1948, the Zikist Movement functioned as the NCNC's youth wing and attracted some of its most energetic members. Impatient with the lack of progress towards independence, the movement's leaders attacked the British and less militant Nigerians in a series of public speeches and statements during fall 1948. In December 1948, the movement issued a call for civil disobedience. The government responded by arresting the Zikist leaders and charging them with sedition. After trials lasting from November 1948 to March 1949, six Zikist Movement leaders were sentenced to prison terms and three were fined.

Zikist leaders harbored the notion that engineering Azikiwe's arrest would unify Nigerian nationalists and spark a renewed campaign for independence. Azikiwe was ambivalent towards the Zikists, however. Azikiwe was capable of making provocative speeches. His newspapers featured strident criticism of British rule, criticism that upset many British officials. Nevertheless, he was reluctant to ally himself with the Zikists. In 1948 and 1949, he urged the NCNC leadership to postpone a decision regarding a program of direct action. Hostile British officials attributed the reluctance to an unwillingness to take risks, in particular, the risk of going to jail. Other officials, more favorably disposed toward Azikiwe, perceived an adroit politician, adept at gauging public opinion and careful to maintain a neutral position until the last possible moment. They concluded that Azikiwe thought that the Zikists' push for direct action was premature. He saw that even the arrest and imprisonment of Zikist leaders had not stirred a public outcry.[47]

Azikiwe eventually disassociated himself from the Zikists. At the NCNC Convention in April 1949, Azikiwe spoke against them and behind the scenes urged that the NCNC postpone direct action at least until the next year when it could make better preparations. Some delegates attacked Azikiwe. When they asked Azikiwe why he was not in prison, he replied that he would sacrifice everything for Nigeria, but not simply to please irresponsible and undisciplined followers. After the Convention, Azikiwe continued to criticize the Zikists in his newspapers.[48]

Macpherson Reforms

Azikiwe was also responding to overtures from the British. Sir John Macpherson, who replaced Sir Arthur Richards as governor in February 1948, acknowledged that Azikiwe was a force to be reckoned with. Macpherson was unsure whether the British could co-opt him. Macpherson told Creech Jones that he was determined not to push Azikiwe toward violent action. If the NCNC were to embark upon direct action, it would be because Azikiwe had decided to do so, not because the British had driven him to it. When the Nigerian attorney general announced that he was about to order a search of the premises of the *West African Pilot*, Azikiwe's flagship paper, Macpherson tried to dissuade him, warning of the adverse political consequences. Senior British officials met with Azikiwe, urging him not to ally with the Zikists. After Azikiwe's rivals blocked his inclusion in the Nigerian delegation to the Colonial Office's 1949 conference in London, the British had him appointed to a commission studying the Africanization of the Nigerian civil service.[49]

Another reason for the lull in Nigerian politics beginning in 1948 was that Macpherson launched a broad reform program, one that resembled the Colonial Office's notions of colonial reform. In 1948, Macpherson announced plans to expand higher education, to reform the native administrations, to introduce more Nigerians into the civil service, and to replace the Richards constitution. Changes in the native administrations were most extensive and immediate in the Eastern Region. The pre-colonial political structures there had not included anything like chiefs and the chiefs appointed by the British wielded little influence. In the East, political structures resembling British local governments replaced the native administrations by 1950. The Nigerianization commission developed a policy that mandated that no non–Nigerian would be appointed to a government post if a qualified Nigerian were available. The government agreed to create Public Service Boards, responsible for hiring decisions, with Nigerian majorities. It would also fund over three hundred scholarships to train Nigerians for government posts.

The centerpiece of Macpherson's constitutional proposal was an extensive process of consultation. Over two years, meetings took place at divisional, provincial, and regional levels throughout Nigeria to discuss a new constitution. The culmination was a conference at Ibadan in October 1949. Fifty of the fifty-three participants were Nigerians. In less than two weeks, the Ibadan conference agreed on a draft constitution. The draft was forwarded to the colonial secretary in London. Griffiths gave his general approval and referred the constitution back to the Nigerian legislative council to resolve several outstanding issues. Once the legislative council dealt with them, the constitution went into effect in late 1951.

The recommendations that Macpherson forwarded to London included a provision that the constitution be reviewed from time to time within a period of five years. This sounded enough like a timetable for further constitutional changes to set off alarm bells in the Colonial Office. Officials preferred either no provision for reviewing the constitution or one barring a review for at least five years. Griffiths told Macpherson that he opposed timetables and preferred no mention of future reviews. Griffiths thought that raising the possibility of further changes undermined whatever political arrangements were in place. He urged Macpherson to allow the new constitution to operate for a reasonable period before considering any changes.[50]

The consultation process diverted considerable political energy from the issue of independence and into consideration of internal Nigerian issues, especially the relationship between the central government and subordinate political units. The Macpherson constitution called for a strong central government, but delegated considerable powers to three Regions, East, West, and North. Each region had a regional assembly. The Ibadan conference generated a minority report advocating that, instead of three regions, Nigeria include a large number of states, each focused on an ethnic group. Whether or not Lagos, which had long existed as a separate political unit, would be subsumed into the Western Provinces was also an issue. The original draft constitution gave the North, which was thought to include at least half Nigeria's population, thirty seats in the central legislature and the other regions twenty-two each. After Northern protests, the final version conceded half the seats to the North. The North wanted government revenues distributed to the regions based on population. The final version, however, distribution based on need, rather than population or derivation.

The Macpherson constitution gave larger roles to Nigerians than the Richards constitution. It fell short of the sort of parliamentary, democratic system found in Britain, however. The minority report from the Ibadan conference called for universal adult suffrage. Yet elections for the regional assembly and the central legislature in the Northern Region were indirect. The regional assemblies selected the region's representatives to the central council of state and several members of each regional assembly were appointed by British officials to represent special interests. The central council of ministers included six official members and twelve unofficial members, three from each region. The members from one region could, therefore, combine with the official members to block any action. The members of the council of ministers were characterized as ministers, but functioned as spokesmen for individual ministries, not as the responsible executives. The council of ministers was collectively responsible for its decisions, much like a British cabinet, even though the unofficial members did not necessarily belong to the same political party and were elected by the three regional assemblies. No provision was made for prime ministers at the central or regional levels.

In November 1949, police shot twenty-one striking coal miners at Enugu, in the Eastern Region. Riots fomented by Zikist leaders followed in four eastern towns and the police shot several rioters. Nigerian newspapers raised an outcry. The NCNC and its rivals in the Nigerian Youth Movement joined in a National Emergency Committee. Nevertheless, Nigerian politics remained on a constitutional path. Nigerian political leaders focused on competing within the framework of the Macpherson constitution. When an alleged member of the Zikist Movement tried to assassinate a senior British official in February 1950, the British rounded up the Zikist leaders. In April 1950, the government banned the organization. Azikiwe and other politicians voiced concern, but took no meaningful actions. The National Emergency Committee soon fell apart. As elections to the regional and central legislatures approached, the NCNC reorganized itself as a political party with individual members. It claimed a national role and favored a stronger central government. New parties also emerged. In the Western Region, the Action Group was the principal new party. In the Northern Region, native administration officials and educated Northerners, many of whom had close ties to the native administrations, formed the Northern Peoples Congress. Both new parties focused on winning the regional elections.

Through the end of 1951, British officials in Nigeria and London were optimistic about maintaining the upper hand in Nigeria. The Nigerian press continued to attack British rule and unrest remained a real possibility. Nevertheless, Macpherson believed that the British had retained the initiative by beginning consultations when they did. They were not reacting to public pressure. He told Creech Jones that the government had demonstrated that it was willing to move forward with a progressive and constructive policy in cooperation with the people. It had, therefore, gained public support. The most militant nationalists, the Zikists, were isolated. Because of personal, regional, and ideological differences, the major nationalist groups were unlikely to combine for very long in opposition to the British, Macpherson believed. The NCNC and the Nigerian Youth Movement had not cooperated for long. In the elections for the new regional and central legislatures, a different party won in each region: the NCNC in the East, the Action Group in the West, and the Northern Peoples Congress in the North. It might be ten years before Nigeria had a strong national leader and party like Nkrumah and the CPP, the British thought. They thought that the bulk of the population in the countryside, and particularly in the Northern Region, remained opposed to rapid change and were unlikely to support the nationalists.[51]

In January 1952, Macpherson learned that Lyttelton was prepared to have Nkrumah named prime minister. His immediate reaction was that all the good work of the previous three years was now at risk. In 1948, Macpherson complained when he thought that release of the Watson Report in the Gold Coast would increase the pressure for constitutional changes in Nigeria. Macpherson resolved the issue by accelerating his announcement of a new constitution. In early 1952, with the new constitution about to come into effect, Macpherson worried that he had few options. He told London that he had taken the risk of creating a constitution for Nigeria that exceeded its true capacity. He had overridden the objections of his British subordinates and Nigerians because he thought it critical to stay ahead of the pressure of events. He thought that, given even six months, he could make the new constitution work. Once the Action Group and the NCNC learned of the planned changes in the Gold Coast, however, Macpherson feared that they would either combine to demand similar changes in Nigeria or compete with each other in pressing for constitutional changes. In either case, the Northerners would take fright and resist more changes.[52]

The first significant challenge to the Macpherson constitution appeared in the middle of 1952. The Action Group and the NCNC both claimed to be the vanguard of Nigerian nationalism. Competition between the two parties was fierce. When Azikiwe was elected to the Western regional assembly, the Action Group, with a majority in the assembly, made sure that Azikiwe was not selected to represent the West in the central legislature. The NCNC had perhaps the better claim to be the leading force in Nigerian nationalism. It had a longer record of accomplishment and attempted to compete throughout Nigeria. The Action Group focused its attention on the Western Region, on the other hand. The British considered it the less militant party. Nevertheless, the Action Group was eager to compete on equal terms with the NCNC. In the middle of 1952, it submitted a memorandum to Macpherson cataloguing a host of complaints about the constitution. It demanded that the council of ministers be granted true ministerial responsibility.

More Worries

State Department reports from Nigeria during the Truman administration had a negative tone. Various consuls stationed in Lagos told Washington that the vast majority of Nigerians were uninterested in nationalist politics. The more intelligent Nigerian leaders realized that the country was far from ready for self-government. Leading nationalist figures were unscrupulous and greedy and the NCNC had much less support than it claimed. Few intelligent Nigerians outside the Eastern region supported Azikiwe, the reports claimed. At the same time, most Nigerians were unwilling to risk the wrath of Azikiwe's newspapers by openly opposing him. Nigeria was still several generations away from self-government; Nigerian politicians and political parties lacked the knowledge and skills needed to govern. When the Action Group formulated ambitious development plans for the Western Region, the consul concluded that Awolowo and his Action Group colleagues were ignorant of both the extent of Nigeria's financial resources and the proper means of financing government programs.[53]

Reports from Lagos to Washington highlighted the regional tensions within Nigeria. In 1947, Consul General Winthrop Greene opined that a political movement led by Igbos could not gain uncontested support in the West or North. Another 1947 report recounted conversations with Northern political leaders. It described leading Northerners' doubts that a unified Nigeria would ever be possible and the preference of Northern native administration officials for continued British rule. Amidst development of the Macpherson constitution, Consul General Willard Stanton reported that Northerners thought that Southern politicians had acquired only the veneer of civilization and were unfit to lead the country.[54]

Azikiwe got positive reviews from State Department officials. Despite Azikiwe's militancy and apparent tolerance for subversive practices, he was, according to one report, the most intelligent nationalist leader. With his personal appeal and rare intelligence for a West African, he could be a great value to Nigeria. Azikiwe was adamant about a timetable for self-government, but otherwise open to compromises. For some British officials, Azikiwe's newspaper empire was an occasion for criticism. A State Department report found Azikiwe's commitment to what it termed bourgeois capitalism reassuring. Somewhat harshly, Vice Consul Robert Ross faulted Azikiwe's attempt to assemble a national party without insisting on ideological discipline. If Azikiwe had been more selective in recruiting followers, Ross thought, maintaining discipline with the NCNC would be easier.[55]

More glowing were reports about Abubakar Tafewa Balewa. Tafewa Balewa was a former schoolteacher from the North who was involved in establishment of the Northern Peoples Congress. He represented the North in the legislative council under the Richards constitution and in the central legislature under the Macpherson constitution. Greene reported that Balewa's was the finest speech in the March 1947 legislative council session, remarkable for its clarity of diction and the effectiveness of its phrasing. A subsequent report characterized Tafewa Balewa as representing the most progressive element in the North and as possessing exceptional intelligence and public spirit.[56]

State Department officials were alert to signs of communist activity in Nigeria, but found little. They worried about the possibility that the Zikists would move towards communism. They passed along to Washington British assessments that Nduka Eze, the founder of the Nigerian Federation of Labor, was a communist. They reported his arrest and trial with some satisfaction. Nonetheless, they dismissed as baseless the notion that communists were behind the general strikes in Nigeria or the Gold Coast. Nigerians had too little contact with the outside world to grasp the concept of communism, they claimed. According to a 1951 report, Nigerian politicians were too opportunistic to become communist pawns. Most of them were thoroughgoing capitalists in the sense that they were out to make as much money as possible without regard to the means employed or the impact on their less-educated countrymen.[57]

The first reports of newly arrived consuls were often the most negative. When Winthrop Greene arrived in 1946, he concluded that the nationalist leaders were unscrupulous and greedy for power. The bulk of the population, he thought, did not care about what went on in Lagos or in the government. Their interests were personal and focused on their district and chief. A.W. Childs, in his first report, observed that all phases of life in West Africa were primitive in the extreme. Nigeria was several generations from self-government. The millions of illiterate Nigerians were satisfied with their carefree traditional existence and sufficiently ignorant to be unconcerned about nationalist politics.[58]

The State Department officials in Lagos cultivated sources throughout the Nigerian government, including police and intelligence officials. The junior British officials they met were pessimistic about Nigeria's future as well as skeptical about U.S. officials–grasp of Nigerian realities. Cooperation with such officials was often difficult. Senior British officials were more likely to flatter the U.S. officials and to develop working relationships. Governor Richards praised Greene for sitting through the legislative council sessions. Richards said he admired Greene's willingness to endure the hot meeting room without prospect of the three guineas per day paid to members. Macpherson arranged to meet with Consul C. Porter Kuykendall once a week. A senior British official told Vice Consul Ross that he thought the United States was the big brother in the family and Britain needed to conduct its affairs so as to retain U.S. support. The United States was Nigeria's most important friend. Nigeria could survive if Britain fell, but not if the United States collapsed as a world power.[59]

Reports from the Lagos consulate were positive about British attempts at reform. In 1946, Vice Consul Robert Johnson thought that the Richards constitution was a workable compromise and a logical step on the road to self-government. In 1952, Ross reported that Nigeria would fall apart without Macpherson and the senior British officials. Many Nigerian leaders realized that the British were indispensable, Ross reported, but were unwilling to admit it publicly. Macpherson was willing to risk public attacks by resisting unreasonable nationalist demands if it meant keeping Nigeria together.[60]

U.S. officials in Lagos reported approvingly Macpherson's efforts to write a new constitution without conceding real political power to the nationalist parties. They noted that the governor retained considerable powers under the new constitution. They anticipated that British efforts in the countryside would produce sufficient conservative candidates with no real ties to the political parties so that no party would predominate in the regional assemblies. Even if one party prevailed in a region, the regions were unlikely to cooperate, leaving the governor free to move his program forward. Macpherson and his immediate subordinates would be able to keep the Nigerian ship of state on an even keel for some time.[61]

At the same time, U.S. officials fretted about the United States becoming overly identified with the British in Nigeria. They reported that Nigerians had a positive attitude toward the United States but were unhappy that the U.S. seemed to support the British. Racial problems in the United States and the U.S. unwillingness to support Nigerian nationalism raised doubts about the U.S. commitment to its proclaimed ideals. U.S. statements about Russian imperialism did little good when Nigerians were most concerned about U.S. attitudes toward Africans and African-Americans.[62]

Colonial reform proceeded in the Gold Coast and Nigeria more or less as British officials intended. Constitutional changes led to more Africans participating in the colonial government. Some of the government's harsher critics now were focused on electoral politics and on legislative activity. Widening African participation in the colonial government seemed to reduce the risk of civil unrest. British governors in both colonies believed that concessions offered to African nationalists had allowed the British to stay a step ahead. Nevertheless, in both colonies, there were signs that Britain's grasp of the initiative was fragile. The British could readily find themselves offering further concessions whether they liked it or not.

7

Colonial Reform in East and Central Africa, 1946–1952: Rural Revolt and Federation

Britain's goal for East and Central Africa was the same as for West Africa, responsible government within the commonwealth, Andrew Cohen explained to U.S. officials in May 1950. The Colonial Office imagined a future in which the three communities in East and Central Africa — African, Indian, and European — would participate in government on an equal basis. Nevertheless, the Colonial Office had a clearer notion of the problems it faced in East and Central Africa than it had of solutions. The immediate problem was to narrow the gap between Africans, the vast majority of the population, and the two immigrant communities. Improving the Africans' political, economic, and social situation would take time, however. In the meantime, the immigrant communities would want faster political change. In particular, Britain could expect constant pressure from the European settlers for greater political power. The British feared the European settlers might turn to the Union of South Africa for support if they did not get what they wanted. The electoral victory in 1948 of the Nationalist Party and its policy of apartheid made British officials leery of South Africa. As of 1950, the Colonial Office considered that the Indian and European communities had accepted some political change, in the form of increased African participation in government, usually the appointment of educated Africans to the legislative council. Further political change, especially the granting of additional political power to legislative councils, must not outpace African development, however, lest it put Africans at a permanent disadvantage. A legislative council with an unofficial majority of Europeans and Asians might not welcome a larger African presence. The British also realized that although the African majority now seemed vulnerable, its numbers would give it strength in the future. As African participation in government increased, the Europeans and Indians would demand formal safeguards for their role in government. Now the British needed to safeguard Africans. In the future, it would need to safeguard the European and Indian minorities.[1]

East Africa

Given the uncertain nature of Colonial Office thinking about East Africa's future and the differences among the East African colonies, the Labour government struggled to devise a meaningful public statement about its policies. In November 1950, Griffiths proposed a public statement to address the anxiety and unrest he perceived in East Africa. He thought

115

that the South African government's implementation of apartheid, the willingness of European settlers to turn to South Africa for encouragement, and recent political changes in West Africa had generated anxiety. Griffiths wanted a statement of general principles, since he thought that the British had to deal with each colony's problems separately. His cabinet colleagues were skeptical that a general statement would do any good. The final statement talked about self-government, a partnership among the races, the need to safeguard the rights of all communities, and the need to consult with all about future policy. It downplayed the role of the London government by pointing out that the only real protection for East Africa's several communities was good relations among them.[2]

Labour had clearer ideas about the need to link Kenya, Tanganyika, and Uganda more closely. The three colonies shared a common customs and tariff system and the three governors met regularly to coordinate common activities. Wartime exigencies in particular had prompted increased inter-territorial cooperation. Labour thought that East Africa's future was as a single economic, if not political, unit. The Attlee government looked for more formal mechanisms to coordinate activities and to link the legislative councils in each colony with the coordinating body. In December 1945, the Colonial Office issued proposals for an East African High Commission, to consist of the three governors supported by an executive organization and a central legislature empowered to legislate regarding common activities. In the central legislature, the three communities would have equal representation: European and Indian members elected by the legislative councils, African and other members representing African interests appointed by the high commission.

Satisfying all three communities in all three colonies proved impossible. The Indian communities were favorably disposed. Equal representation with Europeans and Africans represented a breakthrough for them. The principal African political party in Kenya, the Kenya African Union, favored the proposals, but wanted the members appointed to represent African interests to be Africans. When the Kenya African Union solicited African opinion in Tanganyika and Uganda, however, it encountered fears that Kenya's Europeans would dominate a federation and that a federation would undermine understandings negotiated earlier with the British. Still, the strongest opposition came from Kenya's European community. They complained that the London government had not consulted them before issuing its proposals. They saw Kenya outnumbered in the high commission and the central legislature. They argued that, instead, a community's representation should be proportionate to its contribution to the colonies. European representation should be equal to that of the other two communities combined.

In order to establish the high commission, Creech Jones and the Labour government yielded to the Kenya Europeans. In 1947, it published new proposals with revised arrangements for representation in the central legislature. Without withdrawing the recommendation for equal representation for each community, the new proposals made a European majority among the unofficial members highly likely. The Kenya Europeans recognized a victory and embraced the proposals. Indian and African leaders were opposed. The official majorities in the three legislative councils approved the proposals and they went into effect in January 1948.

Kenya

The Kenya Europeans accepted the revised proposals for an East African High Commission because Sir Philip Mitchell, Kenya's governor, tied them to creation of an unofficial majority in the legislative council. Mitchell promised settler representatives that the legislative council would include fifteen government officials and twenty-two unofficial members after the high commission's creation. Although Mitchell added two African members to the council, raising the total to four, Europeans held eleven seats, equal to all other communities combined.

An unofficial majority was only a partial victory for the European community. In the new council, government officials could still combine with African or Indian members to create a majority. Earlier generations of European politicians had resisted such arrangements. The Kenya Electors Union, the most outspoken European political group, advocated self-government for Kenya under European control. It wanted the London government to avow publicly that European settlement in Kenya would be permanent and that maintenance of British leadership was the paramount consideration. All the Electors Union would concede to African interests was that they would play an increasing role in the colony based on their merit and ability.

While the Kenya government was placating the European community, it was attempting to co-opt educated Africans by bringing them into the government, in much the same way that West African colonial governments were. Besides increasing the number of African representatives to four, Mitchell made sure that all were Africans. Earlier, European missionaries charged with protecting African interests had served in the council. Mitchell also began reforms in local government, establishing elected councils in many localities. When Jomo Kenyatta, perhaps the best-known educated African in Kenya, returned from sixteen years in London, the Kenya government found him a place on a government board responsible for land policies. In 1951, when unrest prompted Griffiths to visit Kenya and meet with political leaders from all communities, his principal proposal for immediate action was to add two more Africans to the legislative council and to appoint an African to the executive council. Griffiths also promised a constitutional conference after the elections then scheduled for 1952. Nevertheless, Griffiths was careful to enlarge the legislative council so that Europeans continued to hold half the unofficial seats.

African Politics in Kenya

In the Kenya African Union (KAU), the Kenya government appeared to have an African political party with which it could deal, not unlike the Gold Coast's CPP or Nigeria's NCNC. The Kenya African Union originated in 1944, the creation of educated Africans, mostly schoolteachers or minor civil servants. Like several other early African political organizations, its origin owed something to patronage from senior British officials and, for a time, it enjoyed British support. It advocated self-government for Kenya under African leadership. To achieve its goals, it pursued constitutional methods: presenting petitions to the Kenya government, advising African members of the legislative council, and backing candidates in elections to local councils. Like the CPP and NCNC, the Kenya African Union cast itself as a national organization and attempted to attract members from all Kenya's ethnic groups.

Kenyan conditions in the postwar years were different from those in Nigeria or the Gold Coast, however. The Kenya government and the Kenya African Union operated in a different environment than their West African analogues. The most obvious difference was the presence of a sizeable European community that owned broad tracts of land, was well entrenched in the government, and was intent on ruling Kenya. Before the Second World War, Kenya had also witnessed heated disputes between Christian missionaries and the Kenya government on the one hand, and large segments of Kenya's Kikuyu-speaking population on the other. Furthermore, in the postwar years, conditions in Kenya's rural and urban areas, particularly those inhabited by Kikuyu, were such that appointing a few Africans to central government positions was unlikely to satisfy popular feeling.

During the 1920s and 1930s, two major disputes roiled Kenya. In the 1920s, Christian missionaries, particularly those from the Church of Scotland, sought to end the practice of clitoridectomy. The Kikuyu and others resisted. In 1925, the government confirmed the division of land within Kenya, restricting large portions of the best land for European ownership, the so-called "white highlands," and dividing the remainder into reserves for each of Kenya's ethnic groups. Kikuyu leaders protested. They induced the government to restudy the issue, but had their claims rejected.

The disputes motivated Kenya's Africans, particularly the Kikuyu, to create institutions similar to those established by the Europeans but under African control. Confronted with the missionaries' disapproval of clitoridectomy, Kikuyu Christians started their own churches. Educated Kikuyu, many of them Christians, also established their own schools and a teacher training college. Kenya Africans formed several political groups during the inter-war years. The Kenya Central Association (KCA) led the opposition to the missionaries and campaigned for return of lands given over to European owners. Kenyatta was a prominent member of the KCA. He edited its newspaper and went to London in 1931 to put its case before the London government. The Kenya government was sufficiently concerned about the KCA's influence that it took advantage of alleged meetings between KCA representatives and Italian officials at the beginning of World War II to ban the organization. KCA responded by going underground and operating as a clandestine organization.

Unrest Among the Kikuyu

In the postwar years, central and western Kenya, especially the Kikuyu reserves, were fertile ground for an organization hostile to British rule. The land allocated to Kikuyu could not produce sufficient food to feed the existing population. By the late 1940s, intensive cultivation reduced the land's capacity further. To compound the pressure on the land, many Kikuyu who had migrated westward to the Rift Valley and lived as squatters on European-owned farms were driven off the farms and back to the reserves after the war. Moreover, British policies and practices allowed some Kikuyu to amass large farms within the reserves and others to become landless. Tension between rich and poor farmers became intense. The prewar disputes also created cleavages between the chiefs appointed by the British, many of whom were rich farmers, and the Kikuyu willing to resist the missionaries and the Kenya government. Moreover, Kikuyu chiefs could not call upon the historic loyalties that some of their West African counterparts could. The machinery for administering the reserves owed much to British ideas and efforts and chiefs among the Kikuyu were something of a British innovation. Furthermore, British efforts to conserve the soil and promote improved agricultural techniques after the war drew them further into Kikuyu life and provoked more resistance. Finally, many young Kikuyu men left the reserves for Nairobi, only to find difficult conditions there. In a total population estimated at around 120,000 in 1950, British officials thought ten thousand Africans were unemployed in Nairobi. In 1948, estimates were that twenty-two thousand people in Nairobi's African areas lacked proper housing. Four thousand were without homes of any sort.

Africans clashed with the Kenya government in the late 1940s and early 1950s. In 1947, violent resistance to British-imposed conservation measures broke out in the Kikuyu reserves. The initial burst of resistance subsided, but, through 1952, the reserves witnessed a steady increase in attacks on chiefs and others seen as supporting the British. In 1947, African members of the legislative council demanded abolition of the kipande, a document that African males were required to carry with them when outside the reserves. The government first proposed to extend the requirement to all Kenyans. When the Europeans objected, the government backed down. The government then proposed to exempt anyone who could sign his name and produce two photographs of himself, in effect exempting virtually all Europeans. African leaders concluded that the government was acting in bad faith. In 1950, Africans interpreted a proposed charter for Nairobi as a threat to African lands and organized protest meetings. Two African town councilors who supported the new charter were assassinated and the government arrested two leaders of Nairobi's unrecognized African labor unions. The African response was a general strike in Nairobi.

Opponents of British rule among Kenya's Africans attempted to attract new supporters and to organize them. Labor unions emerged in Nairobi. KCA leaders and others created new organizations in rural areas and in Nairobi. To bind the members together, KCA leaders used elaborate oaths and oathing ceremonies adapted from earlier Kikuyu practices. Central to the organizing efforts were young Kikuyu, many of whom had served in the British army during the war and become involved in politics or crime in Nairobi after demobilization. Poor farmers and the landless were also ready recruits. The new organizations had passive support from a great many Kikuyu and other Africans in central and western Kenya.

The rising tide of violence put the Kenya African Union and Kenyatta, who became its president in 1947, in awkward positions. At the local level, many links existed between the KCA and the KAU. Kenyatta was involved in both organizations. The independent teacher training college he headed was located at Githunguri in an area known for its militant opposition to British rule. Kenyatta had also promoted oathing as an organizational tool before the government banned the practice. Kenyatta was aware of the organizing that was going on in the reserves, but probably remained deliberately ignorant of the details because he was subject to police surveillance. The KAU shared many of the militants' goals. It advocated a larger voice for the Kenya's Africans and eventual self-government. Nonetheless, the KAU saw itself as a constitutional means of expressing African grievances. A significant portion of the KAU leadership opposed violent action and the organizations that promoted it. Kenyatta considered a resort to direct action premature and preferred a constitutional strategy. He believed that the young militants underestimated the weight of the likely British response. As the violence increased, other KAU leaders called upon Kenyatta to speak out against it, a cry taken up by European newspapers and politicians. When Kenyatta gave a speech disavowing the organizations behind the violence, his critics claimed to hear in his metaphorical language the opposite message.

British officials and European politicians in Kenya saw no differences between the militants in the reserves and the educated politicians in the KAU. After the Kenya government implemented elected local councils in the reserves, British officials sought to thwart KAU participation and preserve the chiefs' influence. As the violence increased, British officials became convinced that Kenyatta and the KAU were responsible. They came to see Kenyatta as an evil genius at the heart of a conspiracy that stretched from the KAU into the Kikuyu reserves. When moderate KAU leaders wanted to hold meetings in the reserves to denounce the violence, British officials refused to cooperate.

The British responded to the ferment among the Kikuyu with repression. The Kenya government outlawed oathing and banned what it termed the "Mau Mau" society. It claimed the society was instrumental in the unrest. It raided homes and meetings and put on trial KAU leaders as well as militants. When Griffiths visited Kenya in 1951 and attempted to intervene in the conflict, the KAU, led by Kenyatta, offered a proposal intended to secure Africans a larger political role and demonstrate the effectiveness of constitutional methods. The KAU proposed adding twelve elected African members to the legislative council and produced a petition asking for redress of the Kikuyu land grievances. Faced with opposition from the European and Asian communities and from the Kenya government, Griffiths agreed to two additional appointed African members. He ignored the land issue, however.

When the initial round of repression failed to halt the violence, the British raised the stakes, declaring a state of emergency in October 1952. They arrested Kenyatta and 145 other African leaders. British officials in the reserves had come to believe that a state of emergency was necessary. They thought that Kenya's existing laws would not allow sufficiently drastic steps to restore law and order. Leaders of the European community agreed. During the summer of 1952, the legislative council witnessed heated debates on the issue and the Kenya newspapers carried stories about Mau Mau violence. Mitchell downplayed the situation, perhaps unwilling to admit serious problems on the eve of his retirement. Moreover, a state of emergency required the Colonial Office's approval. Officials in London were not easily convinced that extraordinary steps were necessary. Mitchell left Kenya in June 1952. His successor, Sir Evelyn Baring, did not arrive until the end of September. In the interval, the situation worsened.

After a tour of the troubled areas, Baring concluded the current methods were insufficient. He told Lyttelton that the Kikuyu chiefs and their supporters would lose confidence in the government if Kenyatta and his associates were not arrested. In the meantime, the chiefs risked assassination. Baring warned that the unrest would spread from the Kikuyu reserves across Kenya and the European community would then retaliate. Baring secured London's agreement, enthusiastic in the case of Churchill, less so in the case of the Colonial Office and the British military. He secured additional troops from the eastern Mediterranean, Uganda, and Tanganyika, declared an emergency, and moved against the African leaders.[3]

Skepticism

U.S. officials stationed in Kenya during the Truman administration painted a negative picture. They recognized that Africans were unhappy with their lot and had good reasons for being unhappy, but were critical of the African population and of its leaders. They saw the Indian community helping Africans to foment unrest and the European community unwisely resisting change. As unrest emerged, U.S. officials doubted the Kenya government's ability to deal with it or to address the underlying problems.

In August 1946, U.S. consul Joseph Touchette reported his observations on Kenya's Africans based on a conversation with an African soldier. Touchette reported that Africans in East Africa were beginning to resent British rule. They wanted a greater say in their government, more education, and an improved standard of living. Similar observations appeared in subsequent State Department reports. Consul Edmund Dorsz told Washington in late 1952 that the economic conditions in Kenya bred unrest among Africans. Price inflation was making the division between rich Europeans and poor Africans all the greater. The 1950 State Department conference in Lourenco Marques reported that Africans in East Africa wanted education because they thought it led to financial success. Education and promises made during the war had promoted greater interest in self-government.[4]

Recognizing that the Africans had real grievances did not stop State Department officials from holding low opinions of Africans and their leaders. Africans wanted an improved standard of living, but without having to work too hard for it, reported Touchette. A 1952 report from the Nairobi consulate referred to the state of "savagery, ignorance, and barbarism" in which most Africans in East Africa remained. Most Africans lacked enough knowledge of history to recognize the falsehoods uttered by lazy and unscrupulous leaders like Kenyatta, reports to Washington contended. The troubles in Kenya, U.S. officials in London and Nairobi reported, demonstrated the failings of Kenya's educated Africans. They had failed to stand up to the militants and had allowed demagogues to exploit real and fancied grievances.[5]

The Indian and European communities came in for their share of criticism as well. U.S. officials thought that Kenya's Indian community was helping educated Africans stir up opposition to the British. One official passed along a French report that the troubles in Kenya were the work of the "Hindu communist party" which was sending agents to Southeast Asia as well as East Africa. The European community failed to understand Africans' desires and ambitions, U.S. officials reported. Europeans' reactionary attitudes, the products of fear, would promote misunderstandings and lead to what they feared the most. Europeans were making no effort to educate Africans about their basic goodwill and integrity.[6]

As the situation worsened in 1951 and 1952, the U.S. consuls in Nairobi were skeptical about the Kenya government's ability to cope. They wondered whether the government had waited too long to act and whether they had sufficient troops and police to restore order. They reported that the police knew little about the organizations causing the violence. After the arrest of Kenyatta and the other leaders, Dorsz thought that the Kenya government was taking a risk. If the arrests did not halt the troubles, international opinion might conclude that the government had used the unrest as an excuse to imprison its most effective African opponents. Dorsz thought that the unrest stemmed from fundamental economic, social, and political problems. He doubted whether the Kenya government and the European community, should they be able to stifle the unrest, would be willing to take the steps needed to resolve the underlying problems.[7]

In the United Nations and within the United States, U.S. officials were willing to support the British efforts to deal with Kenyan unrest. In September 1952, the Foreign Office asked the State Department to help avoid a U.N. hearing on the Kenya situation. The Colonial Office's Sir John Martin told Assistant Secretary of State John Hickerson that allowing a Kenyan African to address the General Assembly would not be helpful. Hickerson promised to do what he could to avoid any such speech. In September 1952, U.S. immigration agents interviewed R. Mugo Getheru, a Kenyan studying at Lincoln University. They quizzed him about his political beliefs and his views about Kenyatta and the situation in Kenya. In November, Getheru received a notice requiring him to leave the country within thirty days. The Department of Justice, it was claimed, had confidential information that Getheru was deportable under the Internal Security Act. A public outcry prompted the Immigration and Naturalization Service to postpone the deportation until April 1953.[8]

Tanganyika: Twining's Reforms

By 1950, the legislative council in Tanganyika retained an official majority. Of the fourteen unofficial members, only four were Africans. Twice between 1945 and 1948, the unofficial members declined the government's offers to create an unofficial majority. A United Nations visiting mission in 1948 noted Tanganyika's meager political progress. When the Colonial Office dispatched a new governor, Sir Edward Twining, to the colony in 1949, one of his tasks was produce political reform before another U.N. visiting mission arrived in 1951.

Twining produced proposals that addressed local and central government. At the local level, Twining suggested converting native administrations into something more like democratic local governments, with elected councils. He proposed multi-racial provincial councils, with African members selected by native administrations, and Asian and European members elected directly. Each provincial council would elect one African and one non–African member of the legislative council, where an official majority would remain.

Twining presented his proposals to the unofficial members of the legislative council. Nevertheless, after eighteen months of hearings and debate, the unofficial members recommended more limited changes. The unofficial members proposed that each community, European, Asian, and African, have equal representation in the legislative council. Although the unofficial members conceded that members should be elected in the future, they proposed that the governor appoint all members, based on lists submitted by each community. The unofficial members recommended that each voter have three votes, casting one for a representative of each community, but believed that the government needed to study electoral methods further before moving forward.

The recommendations of the unofficial members gained the assent of most of the principal players, although the assent may have been unenthusiastic. Twining forwarded the recommendations to the Colonial Office. Although the recommendations were more limited than his own ideas, Twining was comfortable with gradual change. He believed that Africans needed extensive experience in local government before dramatic changes at the center were appropriate. The Colonial Office welcomed the concept of parity among the three communities, but worried about the speed of change. While registering disapproval of rapid change and a fixed timetable, Griffiths prodded Twining to wait no longer than five years to hold elections. The Tanganyika African Association, the closest approximation in Tanganyika to an African political party, accepted the recommendations as an interim measure. Aware that Europeans held half the unofficial seats in Kenya's legislative council, some Europeans remained opposed, but the European politicians who sat in the Tanganyika council approved the proposals.[9]

In general, the Tanganyika government took a leisurely approach to change. The government's economic development plans were less ambitious than the Colonial Office wanted. The Colonial Office imagined movement towards secondary education and the establishment of industries. The Tanganyika government focused on primary education, land rehabilitation, and infrastructure development. Replacing Europeans in government positions with Africans remained a low priority across East Africa. When Makerere University College in Uganda arranged to prepare African students for a University of London pass degree, the East African governments announced that only an honors degree would qualify an African for the administrative service. The Tanganyika government, for its part, sent few Africans to universities abroad and did not encourage them to study for an honors degree.

Signs of organized African opposition to British rule were rare in Tanganyika. The Tanganyika African Association underwent a revival in the early 1950s. In 1951, its leaders met with senior Colonial Office officials seeking to clarify how long Britain planned to wait before considering self-government for Tanganyika. The same year, the Tanganyika African Association submitted to the U.N. visiting mission a paper attacking parity among the races within the legislative council and demanding complete freedom for Tanganyika. Nevertheless, Tanganyika had few educated Africans. Unlike in Kenya, European settlement posed only minor issues and conditions in most rural areas were quiet.

Vulnerable to Visiting Missions

U.S. officials in Tanganyika thought its status as a United Nations trust territory might disrupt Tanganyika's placidity. They noted that officials and settlers in East Africa opposed the trust arrangement and preferred incorporating Tanganyika into a British East Africa. In response, Africans in Tanganyika feared that Kenyan settlers would succeed in undoing the trust arrangement. Nicholas Feld, the consul in Dar es Salaam, reported that British officials and European settlers were sensitive to criticism. They were suspicious of the 1948 United Nations visiting mission even before it issued its report. Feld thought that visiting missions were the only way the world would get a true picture of conditions in Tanganyika. The prospect of future missions might push the British to administer the territory in accord with U.N. principles. After the visiting mission criticized the slow pace of change in Tanganyika and the Tanganyika government took exception, Feld was more pessimistic. If the Tanganyika government would not accept criticism from an authoritative source like the Trusteeship Council, it would persist in its leisurely pace and fail to meet the territory's needs.[10]

At the United Nations, U.S. officials trod softly on Tanganyika issues without being in lockstep with the British. During consideration of a 1948 report, the State Department instructed the U.S. delegates that they should suggest that members of the Tanganyika legislative council be elected. The delegation should inform the British delegation in advance of the positions it proposed to take, however, and it should report to the State Department if the British raised any seemingly valid objections. When a committee of the Trusteeship Council recommended in 1952 that the British return some land in Tanganyika taken from Africans and given to European settlers, the United States supported Britain in opposing the recommendation. It worked to defeat a General Assembly resolution recommending the land's return. The State Department's analysis of the 1951 report noted that parity among racial groups in the legislative council would be inequitable and might cause friction and dissension. The analysis also recommended that U.S. accept the visiting mission's position that an official majority remain in the legislative council. As long as unofficials remained a minority within the legislative council, the division of unofficial seats was not an urgent issue.[11]

Uganda

During the Truman administration, the United States did not maintain a consulate in Uganda and the territory rarely figured in State Department papers. When serious riots broke out in 1949, the London embassy and the consulate in Nairobi did produce reports.

The report from London contained the customary discussion of the riots' alleged ringleader and his possible connections to communists. It went on to speculate that the British had learned their lesson from events in the Gold Coast and elsewhere and were cracking down harder on the Uganda disturbances. The Nairobi consulate reported that police forces in Uganda were inadequate to deal with widespread unrest. The riots reflected conflict within the kingdom of Buganda, the largest native administration within Uganda. The consulate wondered whether dissatisfaction would focus on the British, who had sided with the ruler of Buganda, the kabaka. The consulate also noted that Uganda lacked educated Africans who were prepared to play a positive role in the country's affairs.[12]

The 1949 riots arose from two overlapping tensions, one between Buganda and the rest of the colony and one within Buganda. Buganda's leaders signed an agreement in 1900 creating a British protectorate. Buganda's inhabitants, from the kabaka and his council, the lukiko, to the farmers in the countryside, considered that the 1900 agreement gave Buganda a special status, separate from the rest of Uganda. If Buganda's political status changed, it should be an independent entity, they believed. Steps that looked likely to submerge Buganda within East Africa or within Uganda provoked unhappiness in Buganda. The kabaka's government opposed creation of the East Africa High Commission for this reason. Similarly, many in Buganda resisted including representatives of Buganda in the Uganda legislative council. Many in Buganda also thought that the kabaka and his officials had taken advantage of British rule to increase their power and wealth. Buganda's farmers nursed grievances about land ownership and were unhappy about procedures for the processing and sale of cotton for export. They thought the lukiko failed to represent their interests.

Serious unrest had erupted in Uganda in 1945. After the British squelched both the 1945 and 1949 troubles, their conclusions were the same. The riots were the work of a few troublemakers. In 1949, the culprits were the Bataka party, an organization that arose in the Buganda countryside after the 1945 troubles, and Semakula Mulumba, a Buganda resident in London. Besides beefing up the police and advising the kabaka's government to do the same, the British decided that political reforms would avoid future clashes. They arranged for members of the lukiko to be elected, albeit through indirect elections: first, thirty-one of the eighty-nine members; then thirty-nine; and finally, in 1950, forty members. The British also increased African membership in the legislative council. In 1950, the council contained thirty-two members, half of whom were unofficials: eight Africans, four Europeans, and four Asians. Because the lukiko continued to oppose naming Buganda representatives to the council, the British had to rely on the kabaka to nominate representatives over the lukiko's objections.

Federation in Central Africa

The relationship among the three British possessions in Central Africa, Nyasaland, Northern Rhodesia, and Southern Rhodesia, remained the principal political issue in the region during the Truman administration. European settlers favored closer ties among the three territories. The Labour government considered the idea. It found the prospect of accelerated economic development attractive, but was wary of the vociferous African opposition. Churchill's Conservative regime dismissed African concerns. It moved to join the territories in the Federation of Rhodesia and Nyasaland (also referred to as the Central African Federation).

Fusing Northern and Southern Rhodesia into a single state, referred to as "amalgamation," had been the goal of European settlers in the two territories. They anticipated that combining the two territories would spur economic growth. Northern Rhodesia's copper mines were a prime consideration. Amalgamation might also serve to bolster European rule, particularly in Northern Rhodesia. Europeans were a tiny minority in both territories: twenty thousand in a population of about 1.6 million in Northern Rhodesia and eighty thousand in about the same size population in Southern Rhodesia. Europeans in Nyasaland were scarcer: about two thousand in a population of over two million.

A major barrier to close ties among the three Central African territories was their different constitutional statuses. Southern Rhodesia had gained internal self-government in the early 1920s and its constitution and electoral rules put control in European hands. Voting was based on a common roll, but the imposition of educational and financial qualifications barred all but a handful of Africans from voting. Africans were second-class citizens in Southern Rhodesia, subject to legal discrimination in many areas of life. On the other hand, Northern Rhodesia and Nyasaland were British protectorates, subject to Colonial Office rule. On several occasions, the British government had announced that African interests would remain paramount in Northern Rhodesia and Nyasaland.

In 1949, Sir Godfrey Huggins, long-time prime minister of Southern Rhodesia (later Lord Malvern), and Roy Welensky (later Sir Roy Welensky), leader of the Europeans in the Northern Rhodesia legislative council, convened a meeting at Victoria Falls to discuss closer ties among the three territories. The conference was private and involved only European representatives. Welensky persuaded the group to drop amalgamation in favor of federation, leaving the status of the territories intact while subjecting them to a federal government. Under Welensky's proposals, electoral rules would ensure European control of the federal legislature. The federal government would control most important matters. In a gesture to African sensibilities, the topics thought most important to Africans, agriculture, education, and native administration, would remain territorial responsibilities.

From a London perspective, combining the three Central African territories offered advantages. It created a larger economic base and more attractive conditions for outside investment. British business and mining interests favored closer ties among the territories. The Labour government viewed the Nationalist regime in South Africa with its apartheid policies as a menace. A federated Central Africa would be able, and more likely, to resist South African blandishments, Labour leaders thought. Nyasaland was a poor territory, requiring substantial subsidies from London. Including it in the federation might shift these costs to the two Rhodesias. Most British officials and politicians imagined that the Europeans were a permanent part of Central and East Africa. Forging a working relationship with them seemed a step forward, just as creating alliances with educated Africans in West Africa made sense.

Federation received a mixed reception in London. As in the case of East Africa, closer ties among the Central African territories had been a part of government policy for some time. The three governors met regularly to discuss matters of common concern. The British had created an inter-territorial conference and then the Central African Council as a formal coordinating mechanism, comparable to the East African High Commission. In the late 1940s, officials in the Commonwealth Relations Office, responsible for oversight of Southern Rhodesia, favored closer ties. Most Colonial Office officials remained unenthusiastic. The critical exception was Andrew Cohen. He became convinced that federation would benefit all three territories. Creech Jones was open to the idea at first. After a tour of Central Africa, however, he concluded that African opposition ruled it out. Confronted with African opposition, he said that the British government would not implement federation without first consulting with the people involved. Creech Jones reported to the cabinet that everywhere Africans rejected the Victoria Falls proposals. He went on to list his personal objections, including a retreat from African representation and allowing Southern Rhodesia majority control of the proposed federal government. The Attlee government then rejected the federation proposals.[13]

The failure of the Victoria Falls proposals proved temporary. Huggins and Welensky intensified their campaign for federation. Griffiths replaced Creech Jones at the Colonial Office and Cohen persuaded Griffiths to assemble a committee of civil servants from Britain and Central Africa to consider the feasibility of federation. The committee acknowledged African concerns about federation, but concluded that sufficient safeguards could be erected to protect African interests and, perhaps, overcome African objections. Citing the need to counteract South African influence, the committee recommended federation. Griffiths and his counterpart at the Commonwealth Relations Office, Patrick Gordon Walker, embarked on a tour of Central Africa to gauge public feelings. Like Creech Jones, they encountered opposition from Africans. At the end of the tour, they convened another conference at Victoria Falls, this time including European and African representatives. Griffiths and Gordon Walker resisted many of Huggins's and Welensky's ideas. Word of Attlee's decision to call a general election caused Griffiths and Gordon Walker to bring the conference to a halt. Over African objections, they persuaded it to issue a press release accepting federation in principle. Lyttelton, colonial secretary in the incoming Churchill administration, quickly announced complete support for federation. In a series of conferences in London during 1952 and 1953, negotiators from the British government and the three Central African governments devised a complicated federal structure. In the process, they eliminated or weakened many of the safeguards proposed by the civil servants' committee. On August 1, 1953, the federation went into effect.

While the British and Central Africa's Europeans were fashioning the federation, Central Africa's African population continued to resist it. They held protest meetings, submitted petitions, and sought allies in Britain. The protests included educated Africans and chiefs. African representatives to the several London conferences boycotted the proceedings almost to a man. As Africans agitated against federation, African political organizations, especially the Nyasaland African Congress and the Northern Rhodesia African National Congress, gained greater prominence, even if they remained small and weak. New African political leaders emerged, particularly Harry Nkumbula in Northern Rhodesia. Hastings Banda, a physician trained in the United States and Britain and resident in Britain and then the Gold Coast, spoke for Nyasaland's Africans in London. He served as an influential, if distant, adviser to the protest movement.

Lyttelton and the Conservative government did not take African opposition seriously. Shortly after taking office, Lyttelton told the cabinet that African opposition was so strong because the Labour government had not provided firm guidance and allowed federation's opponents to misrepresent the proposals. He offered hope that the Conservative administration would win over African opinion by taking a firmer position. When Henry Hopkinson, minister of state in the Colonial Office, toured Central Africa, he encountered the same opposition from chiefs and politicians, but he refused to accept that the protestors spoke for the African population. He told the press that the claims that Africans opposed federation were untrue. African opinion on the subject hardly existed, Hopkinson said.

Even when the governor of Nyasaland warned the Colonial Office that Nyasaland's African population was unlikely to change its mind about federation, neither Lyttelton nor Cohen were deterred.[14]

Federation needed approval by the Southern Rhodesian electorate. Its proponents were, in fact, more worried about European opinion there than African opinion. While the Labour government was in power, some Europeans in Southern Rhodesia worried that it might implement political reforms in Northern Rhodesia and Nyasaland that would lead to African states similar to the Gold Coast. Building on this fear, a senior Rhodesian official observed that federation was perhaps not the best way to limit South Africa's influence in Central Africa. A larger political role for Africans in the northern territories would lead to discontent among Southern Rhodesia's Africans, and African discontent would provoke European resistance and conflict within Southern Rhodesia. Forced to choose, Southern Rhodesian Europeans would leave the federation and seek South Africa's support, he predicted. Nevertheless, reassured that the federation's mechanisms favored European control and offered significant economic benefits, 62 percent of Southern Rhodesia's voters voted for federation. Fewer than four hundred of the forty thousand voters participating were Africans.[15]

Ambivalence

State Department staff disagreed about the wisdom of federation. A 1950 paper prepared in the Johannesburg embassy argued in favor of federation. It took the position that only "white supremacy" in Central Africa could ensure economic development and protection from communist inroads. The alternative, "black equality," was not feasible since the "ignorant natives only recently emerged from savagery and still living in primitive tribal conditions" could not manage economic development. Creech Jones and "many misguided and also false idealists, not to mention fellow travelers and downright communists," advocated "black equality," the report claimed. Two years later, the consul general in Salisbury took a different tack. He wrote that imposing a European-controlled federation on the native populations would create fertile ground for communist activity. He mourned the absence of a strong leader capable of producing a fair and workable political alignment between black and white. Anything short of that would be only a stopgap until the majority overthrew European predominance. He criticized local European leaders for approaching race relations in a "timid and camouflaged manner designed to perpetuate the traditional British attitude of superiority."[16]

State Department documents regarding Central Africa featured both sensitivity to Africans' situations and criticism of them and their leaders. In 1949, the London embassy observed that the key question regarding the Victoria Falls proposals was whether they would yield a fair deal for Africans should Britain relax its control. A 1952 dispatch from the Salisbury consulate reported, approvingly, British intent to advance Africans to the point that they could participate in local and central government. Dispatches from Salisbury also repeated negative appraisals of the African population and African politicians. One report recounted that a government official discounted African complaints about federation because many African leaders were "self-seeking embryonic politicians" who coveted positions in a future African state. African opposition to federation was a case of the "blind leading the blind." Another dispatch reported that one "student of African affairs" thought that the typical educated African had the education of an eleven- or twelve-year-old European. One could only imagine what would happen if Africans had control, the dispatch warned.[17]

African efforts to bring the federation issue before the United Nations and British resistance to such efforts forced the State Department to take a position. The department sidestepped the question of the U.N.'s competence to consider the issue. It disagreed with the British contentions that federation was a constitutional issue or a matter of domestic jurisdiction outside the United Nations authority. Nevertheless, it took refuge in a British assertion that federation might not necessarily happen. The U.S. delegates argued that the General Assembly should not consider hypothetical issues. The department acknowledged federation's possible economic benefits, but urged that nothing be done without considering the wishes of the inhabitants. The State Department paper pronounced that implementing federation over African objections would damage Britain's reputation for wisdom and justice and would jeopardize the West's friendship with Africans.[18]

The U.S. efforts to distance itself from federation did not go unnoticed. During September 1952 talks regarding colonial issues, the Colonial Office's Sir John Martin objected to the wording of the State Department paper. He laid out the case for federation, pointing to the prospect of rapid economic development and the potential for blocking South African expansion. Martin discounted African objections. Most Africans did not understand the issues and Britain had no way to determine what the Africans wanted. Britain had African interests at heart, but it could not wait for African opinion to become clearer.[19]

State Department officials accepted Martin's objections with good grace. John Hickerson, assistant secretary for United Nations Affairs, acknowledged that the wording was "unnecessarily stiff." The United States was not delivering a lecture, Hickerson said, but was interested in the federation question. Martin's explanation had been "most helpful," Hickerson added.[20]

Nyasaland

The Colonial Office imagined that the future of the Central African territories was as a multi-racial partnership. In revising constitutional arrangements in Nyasaland and Northern Rhodesia, the office struggled to create such arrangements, however. In 1946, the office approved an unofficial majority in the Nyasaland legislative council, provided the new members were Africans and Indians. The office was willing to nominate African members. Governor Colby, on the other hand, warned that no Africans were sufficiently sophisticated to stand up to the European members. Colby also worried that if the office created an unofficial majority but insisted on safeguards for African interests, the European population might take offense and replace the European members with less cooperative members, who might then provoke anti–European sentiments within the African population. The office's official guidance conceded that the revised constitution needed to specify the division of seats by race. It urged that everything be done to persuade all members to view issues in light of Nyasaland's best interests, and not the interests of their own community's. The office thought that adding educated Africans to both territories' legislative council would spur progress. Yet it worried that African members might form a "race of politicians apart."[21]

Nyasaland's European population was so small that the Colonial Office ruled out electing European members to the legislative council. The office put Nyasaland in the same category as Tanganyika and Uganda, territories where nominating only European members made sense.[22]

The European population in Northern Rhodesia was larger, intent on gaining political control, and played a large role in government. As of 1945, the Northern Rhodesia legislative council included nine officials, and thirteen unofficial members. Eight were elected and five appointed. All were Europeans. Four appointed members were responsible for representing African interests. Satisfying the Europeans posed challenges for the Colonial Office. In 1948, a member responsible for African interests proposed granting Northern Rhodesia control of its internal affairs. African opinion was outraged. The Colonial Office was loath to accept the proposal. If the office accepted the proposal, it would want to safeguard African interests. Welensky opined that the European members would accept one African member but appointing two might provoke serious opposition. The office worried that if it rejected the proposal, it might find itself at loggerheads with the unofficial majority and be unable to conduct business.[23]

The office eventually rejected the proposal. It reaffirmed its partnership policy and arranged for two Africans to be named to the council. The European members were not pleased. When Creech Jones visited Northern Rhodesia a year later, Welensky confronted him, charging that the British intended to eliminate all European settlement in Northern Rhodesia.[24]

Some U.S. officials had doubts about the future of "partnership" in Central Africa. W. Stratton Anderson, writing from the Johannesburg embassy, conceded that the British might be able to withdraw from their East and Central African colonies with a clear conscience if the European settlers adopted what he termed a "more progressive" attitude. More likely, Britain faced a hard choice. Britain was committed to granting self-government to each colony at the appropriate time. The settlers in Northern Rhodesia were unlikely to accept majority African rule. If Britain granted self-government to the settlers in Northern Rhodesia, settlers elsewhere, such as those in Kenya and Tanganyika, would want equal treatment. Anderson thought this ran counter to British traditions and would have serious repercussions in Africa and the United Nations.[25]

By the end of the Truman administration, colonial reform in Central and East Africa had not progressed far. The British had taken only tentative steps towards constitutional change. The most significant constitutional change, creation of the Federation of Rhodesia and Nyasaland, was nearly complete. Some British officials, especially Andrew Cohen, saw federation as consistent with the changes the British were making in West Africa. Both European settlers and Africans in Central Africa were more likely, however, to see federation as a barrier to African political advancement and, therefore, at variance with events in West Africa.

In West Africa, British reforms seemed to have smothered unrest. In Kenya, however, British actions over several decades stirred up sufficient unrest among the Kikuyu that the British discarded their accustomed methods of administration for a state of emergency and armed repression. Political or other reforms, therefore, did not seem imminent.

In the Truman administration, U.S. officials were peripheral to events in East and Central Africa. U.S. consuls were content to report on events and worry about future developments.

8

Egypt, Britain, the United States and the Sudan, 1946–1954: A Bargaining Chip

No U.S. officials were stationed in the Sudan until the end of the Truman administration. Nevertheless, Acheson and State Department officials in Washington, London, and Cairo sought an Anglo-Egyptian agreement and Egypt's incorporation in a strategic alliance friendly to the United States. They came to see the Sudan as a valuable bargaining chip in Anglo-Egyptian negations. As the U.S. worked to push the British and Egyptians toward an agreement, it played a critical role in moving the Sudan to the brink of independence by 1952.

Postwar Proposals

September 1945 saw Sir Hubert Huddleston, governor-general of the Sudan, lobbying Foreign Secretary Bevin for a British initiative in the Sudan. Huddleston told Bevin that the educated Sudanese were ill-equipped to govern, but would continue to push for greater political power. Huddleston conceded that the educated Sudanese would get their way in the end and the Sudanese would throw off foreign rule. If the British wanted to retain Sudanese friendship and prevent educated Sudanese from seeking Egyptian assistance, Huddleston argued, they needed to announce as soon as reasonably possible that self-government was their policy. They also needed to commit to a substantial program of economic, social, and educational development. Sudan could not afford to fund development from its own resources. Egypt, Huddleston thought, was more than willing to offer financial assistance in order to win Sudanese support. If the British did not want the Sudanese to seek Egyptian aid, they had to provide it themselves.[1]

Bevin agreed to invest £2 million in Sudanese development projects, but resisted issuing a statement about political changes. In December 1945, the Egyptian government asked for renegotiation of the Anglo-Egyptian treaties, however. In March 1946, a Sudanese delegation that included representatives of all political parties was preparing to leave for Cairo and talks with Egyptian government officials. Despite British attempts to split the delegation, the Sudanese parties settled on self-government in union with Egypt as their common aim. To preserve a unified position, they avoided the role of Egyptian king Farouk in a self-governing Sudan. In the new circumstances, the Sudan government, the British embassy in

Cairo, and the Foreign Office agreed that a public statement was needed. On March 26, 1946, Bevin told the House of Commons that Britain's only goal in the Sudan was the welfare of the Sudanese. The welfare of the Sudanese required a stable and disinterested administration. The administration had to establish the organs of self-government as the first step towards eventual independence, Bevin added. The Sudan government had to accelerate the appointment of Sudanese to higher government posts and increase the Sudanese capacity for citizenship. Looking ahead to negotiations with Egypt, Bevin promised that treaty revisions would not change the Sudan's status unless Britain consulted the Sudanese.[2]

As British officials were preparing the statement on self-government, they were debating Sudanization, the replacement of British officials by Sudanese. Faced with pressure to accelerate and expand Sudanization, Sir James Robertson, the Sudan's civil secretary, laid out the Sudan government's assumptions about the road to self-government. Robertson argued that Sudanization required at least twenty years. It would be possible to appoint Sudanese to technical or administrative positions in fields such as education, agriculture, or public works. It would not be possible to appoint Sudanese to political positions, as provincial governors or district commissioners. To keep the trust of the Sudanese population, British officials had to remain in the important political positions. Political change had to come through reform of local government and changes in the native administrations. It could not come through substituting Sudanese for Britons as provincial governors or district commissioners.[3]

Foreign Office officials in Cairo and London were not convinced. They thought Britain could not wait twenty years to place Sudanese in key political positions. If Sudanese did not hold government posts, the pressure to appoint Egyptians would be overwhelming. Sudanese appointees might be less efficient and less effective than the British officials they would replace, but they were better than Egyptians. The Sudanese delegation to Cairo broke up over Egyptian insistence on an Egyptian-Sudanese union under the Egyptian crown. Nevertheless, Sir Ronald Campbell, the British ambassador in Cairo, urged Huddleston to announce a bold plan of Sudanization. Unless the British developed a bolder plan and publicized it better, educated Sudanese were liable to throw in their lot with the Egyptians. Campbell opposed overt political changes, such as creation of a legislative council, lest they undermine the Anglo-Egyptian negotiations.[4]

Although Campbell was nominally Huddleston's superior, the governor-general ignored the ambassador's advice. Four days after meeting with Campbell, Huddleston announced plans for a conference to consider steps towards self-government. He volunteered that he expected Sudanese to govern their own country in twenty years, assisted by non–Sudanese specialists and technicians. The most Huddleston offered for Sudanization was establishment of a committee to consider the issue.

Bevin and an Anglo-Egyptian Agreement

Bevin and the Attlee government were more concerned about reaching an agreement with Egypt to replace the 1936 Anglo-Egyptian treaty and the 1899 condominium agreement than they were about preparing the Sudan for self-government. Bevin saw a British alliance with Egypt as critical to maintaining Britain's position in the eastern Mediterranean. Forging a meaningful alliance would require resolving difficult issues, however, and the Sudan was only one and not the most important. Moreover, Bevin and some Foreign Office officials harbored doubts about the Sudan's capacity to function as an independent state. They wondered whether the Sudan might not be better off tied to Egypt. Sudanese self-government seemed a distant prospect while an Egyptian alliance was an immediate concern.

Bevin worried that U.S. and world opinion might make an Anglo-Egyptian agreement more difficult to achieve. Bevin thought that the United States government expected that self-government should be part of the solution to every colonial problem. He also believed that if self-government were not a viable option, the United Nations expected some form of international trusteeship. Bevin feared that conceding Egyptian sovereignty over the Sudan might attract international opposition, since it might appear to delay or prohibit Sudanese self-government. Bevin was especially opposed to trusteeship. He professed to believe that the British and Egyptians could handle the problem themselves.[5]

Anglo-Egyptian negotiations proceeded slowly and painfully. The two sides exchanged draft treaties in May 1946, but were far from agreement by early October. The British complained that they had made concessions across the board only to meet Egyptian intransigence. On the Sudan, the Egyptians insisted on the unity of the Nile Valley, on a union of Egypt and the Sudan under the Egyptian crown. The British were willing to concede Egyptian sovereignty. Key officials believed that Britain had conceded Egyptian sovereignty in past pronouncements. Under Bevin's proposal, Egyptian sovereignty would be nominal, however. The British administration would remain in place and, in the future, the Sudanese would be free to choose their status.

To move the negotiations forward, the Egyptian prime minister, Isma'il Sidqi, traveled to London in October 1946 and met with Bevin. By October 24, the two men thought they had reached an agreement. They agreed that Egypt would retain sovereignty in the Sudan, but that the primary aims would be Sudanese welfare and preparation for Sudanese self-government. Bevin pressed Sidqi to acknowledge that the Sudanese had the right to determine their own status regardless of Egyptian sovereignty. Sidqi made approving noises, but refused to be pinned down, especially in writing. He argued that it would be many years before the Sudanese would be ready to govern themselves; therefore the issue was premature. Bevin decided that the benefits of an agreement with Egypt outweighed the risks posed by a lack of clarity about the Sudan. That both Bevin and Sidqi believed that most Sudanese favored his country and that self-government was a generation away made an unclear agreement more palatable.

Bevin was wrong. The lack of clarity about the Sudan doomed the agreement. Concessions about the Sudan were a volatile issue in Egyptian politics. When Sidqi returned to Cairo, he proclaimed that the agreement guaranteed the union of Egypt and Sudan under the Egyptian crown. He made no mention of Sudanese self-government or self-determination. Once it became clear that Sidqi's interpretation differed from Bevin's, a firestorm of criticism erupted in Cairo and London. Attlee found himself telling the Commons that the talks had been personal and exploratory. His government planned no change in the Sudan's status, the prime minister claimed. By December, Sidqi was forced to resign and his administration was followed by one less interested in an agreement with Britain.

The Sudan government viewed conceding Egyptian sovereignty as a betrayal. It did its best to dissuade Bevin and the Foreign Office from doing so. Once Sidqi made his announcement, Huddleston and Robertson were furious. Huddleston traveled to London to meet with Attlee. Huddleston demanded a public statement that the Bevin-Sidqi agreement did not foreclose ultimate Sudanese independence. He talked about resigning and insisted that he would not return to Khartoum without an appropriate public statement.

Attlee conceded that he had not realized that no Egyptian troops had been stationed in the Sudan since 1924 or that a significant number of Sudanese opposed union with Egypt. A flurry of meetings and anxious communications followed, including a London visit by 'Abd al-Rahman, the most prominent Sudanese opponent of union with Egypt. In the end, all Attlee was willing to provide Huddleston was assurance that the British understood the agreement to allow ultimate Sudanese self-determination.

The Bevin-Sidqi negotiations reinforced the Sudan government's efforts to go its own way. During a November 1946 meeting, Robertson told Sidqi that he was a British citizen but had nothing to do with the British government. Robertson professed surprise that Sidqi and others could not understand that although he was a British subject, he was a loyal servant of the Sudan government, willing to oppose the British government. In December, Huddleston made known his intention not to renew the contract of Sudan's chief judge, an Egyptian. Huddleston claimed that a qualified Sudanese was available. Bevin was concerned that the chief judge position might be a bargaining chip in negotiations with Egypt. He wrote to Huddleston asking him to withhold any statement until Bevin had an opportunity to review the matter. Huddleston replied that Bevin's request was unprecedented. The 1936 Anglo-Egyptian Treaty gave the governor-general full authority to appoint Sudan government officials. Huddleston added that he was pushing ahead with Sudanization as he had been instructed. Bevin could only remind Huddleston that the two nations responsible for the Sudan, Britain and Egypt were in the midst of negotiations. They might agree to recommend to the governor-general that he renew the contract.

Sidqi's assertion that Egypt was sovereign in the Sudan sparked serious unrest in Sudan. The Umma Party sent a protest to London. It announced that it would boycott the Advisory Council for the Northern Sudan and the committees reviewing possible steps towards self-government. Several thousand Umma supporters marched through Omdurman and presented a protest to British officials. Two days later, the Ashiqqa Party, which favored union with Egypt, obtained permission to stage its own demonstration. Clashes between supporters of the two parties followed. Ashiqqa militants attacked the offices of two pro-Umma newspapers. To restore order, the British rushed troops from Khartoum to Omdurman and flew a brigade of reinforcements from Palestine to Khartoum.

Huddleston had warned London officials that violence would follow concessions to the Egyptians. Nevertheless, senior officials in the Sudan government believed that they still had the support of vast majority of Sudanese. They worried about the politically minded young men in the capital. Yet they thought other Sudanese recognized that anarchy and chaos would prevail without the British officials. Robertson told the provincial governors that rural Sudanese preferred the British to any of the obvious alternatives — the Egyptians, 'Abd al-Rahman, or the educated Sudanese.[6]

Huddleston's Reforms

In early 1947, the Administrative Conference, the committee chartered by Huddleston to consider steps towards self-government, issued its reports. The reports described a cautious reform program. The conference included British officials and carefully selected Sudanese, mostly native administration officials and Sudanese allied with the Umma Party. Once the Ashiqqa Party realized it would have less representation in the conference than native administration officials, it boycotted the proceedings. The conference recommended establishment of a legislative assembly and an executive council. The legislative assembly was to include representatives from throughout the Sudan, including the largely non–Muslim South for the first time. A few members from urban areas were to be elected directly. Most were to be selected by provincial councils where native administration officials predominated. At least half the council was to be Sudanese representatives. The rest would be British officials. Under the proposals, the governor-general retained considerable power. He retained the power to veto executive council decisions, to issue ordinances, and to determine the subjects about which the assembly could legislate.

In August 1947, Sir Robert Howe, a former Foreign Office official appointed to replace Huddleston as governor-general, submitted the proposals to the British and Egyptian governments. The Egyptians were willing to accept movement towards self-government so long as it did not prejudice final resolution of the Sudan's status, but offered several criticisms, including the absence of any meaningful Egyptian role. British and Egyptian representatives spent nearly a year trying to resolve the Egyptians' complaints and reach agreement. In June 1948, the British government gave up. It authorized the Sudan government to implement the reforms.

As the Sudan government implemented the reforms, the divisions among the Sudanese political parties re-emerged. The Ashiqqa Party, the party of young educated Sudanese and the party most favorably disposed towards Egypt, boycotted the elections and won no seats in the assembly. Demonstrations by Ashiqqa supporters in Omdurman turned violent in November 1948 during the elections, and again in December, when the assembly convened. Hundreds were hurt and ten were killed. As troops restored order, the government arrested Isma'il al-Azhari, the Ashiqqa leader.

Sudan in the United Nations

In early 1947, the Egyptian government broke off negotiations with Britain and announced that it would take the Sudan issue to the United Nations. When the issue came before the Security Council, Egypt argued that it had inherited the Ottoman Empire's claims to the Sudan and that it was sovereign in the Sudan under international law. Britain countered with the argument that the welfare of the Sudanese and their right to self-determination should be paramount. The Egyptian representatives argued that Egypt would protect Sudanese interests. There was no need to consider a Sudanese right of self-determination. The Sudanese political parties attempted to form a joint delegation to the United Nations, but failed. All they could agree on was that the British should leave the Sudan. Both the Umma and Ashiqqa parties sent delegations, the former supporting the British position, the latter the Egyptian. The Security Council could not unravel the mess. The best it could do was to pass a motion urging Egypt and Britain to negotiate a settlement.[7]

Both the Egyptians and the British tried to enlist U.S. assistance in keeping the dispute out of the United Nations. Foreign Office officials suggested that the United States inform King Farouk that Egypt had a weak case and that it would not receive U.S. support. The State Department's initial reaction was negative, since the United States did not know what sort of case Egypt would present. Acheson was concerned that intervening on Britain's behalf would stir nationalist feelings in Egypt and discourage other countries from bringing their disputes to the United Nations.[8]

In the Security Council, the United States agreed that Egypt and Britain should reach an agreement on their own. The U.S. representative professed that Egypt and Britain ought to be friends. If they pursued negotiations conscientiously, they would reach an agreement. The United States opposed an Australian proposal that the Security Council mandate consultation with the Sudanese about the future of the Sudan.[9]

Before Egypt took the issue to the United Nations, State Department officials in Washington prepared a policy paper on the Sudan that was broadly supportive of the British position. According to the paper, the status of the Sudan ought to be resolved through Anglo-Egyptian negotiations. The United States supported slow, steady movement toward Sudanese self-government, and perhaps independence. Since incorporation of the Sudan into Egypt would inhibit development toward self-government, the United States did not support union between Egypt and the Sudan. The policy paper described reasons why the Sudan remained far from ready for self-government. Educated Sudanese represented a tiny fraction of the population. Few Sudanese, even in the more developed North, took an interest in, or understood, political issues. No political group commanded broad support. Even some of the Sudanese who openly criticized British rule recognized that the Sudan profited from British protection.[10]

The State Department perceived in the Sudan's lack of readiness for self-government an opportunity to satisfy Egyptian concerns. Since Sudanese independence was at least twenty years away, a proposed Anglo-Egyptian agreement need not refer to preparation for self-government or a Sudanese right of self-determination, references that Egypt opposed. The agreement could be less precise, referring only to evolution in accordance with the United Nations charter. The State Department concluded that Egypt was more concerned about issues like control of the Nile's waters than it was about control of the Sudan itself. An Anglo-Egyptian-Sudanese commission might find some middle ground. Egypt might settle for a larger role in administration of the Sudan and increased investment opportunities in the Sudan.[11]

When the United States shared its thoughts with the Foreign Office, the response was negative. The head of the Foreign Office's Egyptian division said that it was too late to introduce Egyptian officials into the Sudan. Sudanization was well underway and it would take Egyptians a long time to match the Sudan government's understanding of Sudanese issues. Britain had proposed establishment of a joint commission to consider Sudanese issues, but the Egyptians had rejected it.[12]

A Lull: 1948–1950

From December 1948, when the legislative assembly took office, until late 1950, the Sudan government appeared to have the situation under control. It had achieved one of its principal goals, excluding the Egyptians from any significant role in the Sudan. The legislative assembly and executive council were in place. The assembly was under the control of the Sudan government's local allies, the Umma Party and native administration officials. The exclusion of the Ashiqqa Party and its principal supporters, 'Ali al-Mirghani and the khatmiyya brotherhood, from the legislative assembly suited the Sudan government's immediate political aims and offered an excuse for slowing the pace of political change. How could the Sudan government take steps towards self-government while the Sudanese remained so much at odds with one another?

Despite 'Abd-ah-Rahman and the Umma Party's willingness to cooperate with the

Sudan government, they were unhappy with the slow pace of political change. An end to the Anglo-Egyptian condominium and Sudanese independence remained Umma's avowed goals. Umma leaders were dismayed that the Sudan government joined British officials in dismissing Umma's proposals during the Security Council presentations. They worried about the Sudan government's increased attention to Sudan's southern areas, largely non–Muslim and, in terms of education, far behind the North. The Sudan government appeared to be considering treating the South as a special case, perhaps to be detached from the Sudan. Whatever the South's ultimate fate, the differences between North and South offered the British an excuse for slowing the pace of political change. Umma leaders also worried aloud that Britain and the United States might be willing to sacrifice the Sudan in order to forge an alliance with Egypt. When the United Nations announced plans to grant Italy's former African colonies, Libya and Somaliland, independence on a definite schedule (Libya in 1952 and Somaliland in 1960), the Umma leaders redoubled their pleas for Sudanese independence.[13]

Umma's insistence on independence worried British officials. To the extent that independence was a means for Umma to demonstrate its anti–Egyptian credentials and to separate itself from its Ashiqqa rivals, it posed no threat to the British. What if Umma meant independence from Britain as well? How could Britain satisfy its closest Sudanese allies without sacrificing control of the Sudan? If Umma was serious about independence, might it cut a deal with the Egyptians behind Britain's back? Despite the political rivalries that characterized the Sudan, particularly between 'Abd-ah-Rahman and 'Ali al-Mirghani and their followers, the British sensed that the current coalitions were unstable. Might the educated Sudanese put their differences aside long enough to combine against the British?[14]

Perhaps the Sudan government's reforms were too cautious, its foot-dragging too successful. Senior officials in the Sudan concluded that the legislative assembly and executive council had accomplished little. They had little to do and did not do it well. The native administration officials struggled to understand complicated legislation and the two bodies fell well short of what educated Sudanese wanted. To British officials, they appeared to undermine the government's credibility in the countryside and among native administration officials. To rural notables, the new bodies seemed unnecessary. For all the talk of reforming the native administrations, little change had taken place. Robertson came to believe that the pace of political change was critical. It should not be so fast as to produce maladministration, nor so slow as to provoke disturbances and civil disorder. As appealing as it had been to pack the legislative assembly with government supporters, Robertson decided that further steps towards self-government were needed. Such steps required bringing 'Ali al-Mirghani's followers into the legislative bodies.

Robertson's Reforms

In 1950, Robertson and Howe pushed through modest political changes. To address Umma's desire for greater self-government, they added a fourth Sudanese to the executive council, creating a Sudanese majority. They made changes to electoral procedures intended to guarantee Ashiqqa's and the khatmiyya's participation in the next legislative assembly elections. Robertson wanted to appoint a khatmiyya member to the new executive council position, but none would serve.[15]

Bolder proposals were available, but the Sudan government rejected them. A senior official in the Sudan government put forward a plan for limited self-government. An elected assembly and Sudanese cabinet would be responsible for all matters except defense and foreign affairs. After ten years, an international commission would decide whether the Sudan was ready for full self-government. Howe thought the plan too complicated and premature. The Egyptian government proposed replacing the governor-general with a Sudanese appointee and creating a fully representative legislative assembly. Sir Ralph Stevenson, the new British ambassador to Egypt, thought that the proposals were well beyond Sudanese capabilities. Finding a suitable Sudanese appointee acceptable to all major parties would be impossible.[16]

Working for an Anglo-Egyptian Agreement

An Anglo-Egyptian agreement remained vital, the State Department thought. For the Egyptians, the most pressing issue was the continued presence of British troops in Egypt. While aware of Egyptian sensibilities, Acheson and the State Department believed it was essential that the British be able to maintain military facilities in Egypt and to re-occupy them in time of crisis. A continued British military presence in the eastern Mediterranean also supported the U.S. strategic aims. An Anglo-Egyptian agreement could pave the way for Egypt's inclusion in a proposed Middle East Defense Organization, another prop for U.S. interests in the area.

Beginning in mid–1950, U.S. officials became concerned about prospects for an agreement and dubious about British bargaining tactics. In May 1950, Acheson's instructions to Jefferson Caffrey, the U.S. ambassador in Cairo, were to inform the Egyptian government that the United States wanted an agreement and that the United States supported Britain. The U.S. believed that Britain had strategic interests in the Suez Canal and needed access to military facilities there in a crisis. By November, Caffrey communicated to Washington that a new policy toward Egypt was needed. The British were unlikely to develop one by themselves. The United States had to take a role, even if it were independent of the British. In April 1951, George McGhee advised the Foreign Office that an impasse with Egypt was dangerous. The British needed to be as flexible as possible and must not adopt any irrevocable positions. In May, McGhee told Pentagon officials that British resistance to nationalism in the eastern Mediterranean was foolhardy. It turned U.S. support for Britain into a liability, a liability perhaps greater than whatever military value Britain represented.[17]

The Sudan's status remained an obstacle to an Anglo-Egyptian agreement. Egyptian officials insisted that Egypt was sovereign in the Sudan and that the Sudan should be united with Egypt under the Egyptian crown. The British countered that Sudanese interests were paramount. The Sudan was on a path to self-government and self-determination. The British maintained that they had promised the Sudanese that they would not agree to any change in the Sudan's status without first consulting them. According to the British, proclaiming Farouk "King of the Sudan" would provoke serious violence in the Sudan.

The initial U.S. contribution was to suggest that negotiations about a defense arrangement be separated from those about the Sudan. When the suggestion went unheeded, United States officials persuaded themselves that the key to breaking the stalemate was publicly acknowledging King Farouk as Sudan's sovereign, as "King of Sudan" or some comparable title. Acheson and his subordinates persisted in the belief that such a proclamation would save sufficient Egyptian face so that the Egyptian government could negotiate a defense agreement with Britain. It did not matter that all parties might recognize that a proclamation had no impact on the situation in the Sudan. Despite rebuffs from Britain, State Department officials pushed the idea, arguing that as long as there was any hope, the idea was worth pursuing. By July 1951, the State Department was advising Acheson that it would be sufficient that the United States, and not Britain, accept Farouk as the Sudan's symbolic sovereign.[18]

From 1950 through July 1952, the status of the Sudan figured prominently in U.S. dealings with Britain. For Caffrey and his British counterpart in Cairo, Stevenson, an Anglo-Egyptian agreement was the foremost item of business. They expended hours discussing and devising schemes to produce one. At one point, the State Department and the Foreign Office had them develop a joint evaluation of the situation. Acheson became personally involved. The Sudan was on the agenda when Churchill and Eden came to Washington in January 1952 and at several meetings between Acheson and Eden. In March 1952, Acheson overrode the objections of Walter Gifford, the United States ambassador to Britain, and sent Eden a strongly worded, personal message conveying his concerns about the lack of progress toward an agreement. It urged Eden to accept the U.S. proposal regarding Farouk's title.[19]

Along with the notion of Farouk as "King of the Sudan," the U.S. floated other suggestions. It proposed a referendum in the Sudan about its status, a "neutral" governor-general, and a joint British-Sudanese-Egyptian commission to oversee administration of the Sudan. The United States proffered such ideas as proposals Britain should make to the Egyptians. When British officials balked or reworked the ideas into a form U.S. officials thought the Egyptians would not accept, the U.S. response was to back away, reverting to having no official position on the Sudan. U.S. officials thought the United States retained credibility in Egypt and with the Egyptian government. As eager as U.S. officials were for an agreement, they were unwilling to risk the American standing by associating themselves with a flawed British proposal or offering a questionable scheme to the Egyptians themselves.[20]

A defense agreement for the eastern Mediterranean was one of Acheson's higher priorities. As an agreement appeared less likely and the State Department became frustrated with what it perceived as British rigidity and Egyptian ineptitude, the tone of its external and internal communications became waspish. The mood in Washington deteriorated when the absence of an agreement undermined stability in Egypt and threatened to undermine King Farouk's regime. The presence of British troops remained a serious provocation to Egyptian sensibilities. In January 1952, riots broke out in Cairo. British lives were lost and British property destroyed. British reprisals made the situation worse. U.S. officials feared Egyptian expectations were so high that no Egyptian regime could survive without resolving Egypt's relationship with Britain, the status of the Suez Canal and the military facilities associated with it, and the Sudan.[21]

Despite the importance of an Anglo-Egyptian agreement in State Department thinking, some officials harbored doubts about the department's chosen approach. Within the State Department, the Office of Near Eastern, South Asian, and African Affairs headed by George McGhee and then by Henry Byroade, had lead responsibility for the Sudan issue. It prepared analyses and recommendations for Acheson. Given an opportunity, their colleagues in the Office of European Affairs voiced their dissent. In April 1952, staff in the Office of European Affairs reviewed a draft message from Acheson to Eden. The U.S. position was almost complete capitulation to the Egyptian demands, the staff said, the demands of the wildest and most dangerous elements in Egypt. The staff wondered whether the British seemed to be yielding to U.S. suggestions only because they realized that they could not proceed without United States support. Was the United States ready, the staff asked, to pick up the pieces once British fears proved justified?[22]

More Anglo-Egyptian Negotiations

Like Acheson, Bevin had visions of a defense arrangement for southern and western Asia, a pact that included Egypt. Bevin was willing to attempt negotiations with the Egyptians. Ill health forced Bevin to resign in March 1951, however. His successor in the Labour government, Herbert Morrison, was less open to concessions to the Egyptians. He was less concerned about the fate of the Sudan than he was about maintaining British prestige. When the Conservatives under Churchill took power in October 1951 and Eden became foreign secretary, the barriers to an agreement increased. To Churchill, a diminished British role in Egypt and the Sudan was distasteful, but he took little interest in the details. When provoked, he looked to military solutions. His response to the Cairo riots was more British troops. His first priority was securing U.S. support for British positions around the eastern Mediterranean. When he met with Truman in January 1952, he suggested sending United States troops to Egypt to reinforce British forces in Egypt. When Truman ignored the idea, Churchill included it in his speech to a joint session of Congress. Acheson had to explain to an agitated Egyptian ambassador that the idea had not originated in the U.S. administration. Nevertheless, for the most part, Churchill deferred to Eden's views about the region.[23]

Though willing to negotiate with the Egyptians and to consider U.S. proposals, Eden proved unyielding on the Sudan. He refused to take the path Bevin had chosen. He refused to accept Egyptian sovereignty, even if only symbolically. He believed that doing so would invite attacks from members of Parliament opposed to concessions to the Egyptians and members opposed to abandoning the Sudan and the Sudanese. Eden cited British promises to consult the Sudanese before agreeing to any changes in the Sudan's status. He talked about not feeding the Sudanese to the Egyptians. U.S. officials found him maddeningly reluctant to initiate consultations with the Sudanese. When pressed, Eden admitted that the Sudan government had been "naughty," in attempting to undermine Anglo-Egyptian negotiations. Nevertheless, he was willing to repeat its dire warnings that proclaiming Farouk "King of Sudan" would provoke a wholesale revolt in the Sudan. Regardless of Eden's willingness to discuss the issues with the United States, he was more concerned about standing up to the Egyptians and maintaining British prestige than he was in promoting Acheson's Middle East Defense Organization.[24]

Eden assigned the United States some responsibility for the failure to resolve the dispute with Egypt over the Sudan. In July 1952, as successive Egyptian governments failed to reach agreement with Britain and fell from power, the Foreign Office sent a message to the State Department asking that the United States inform King Farouk that his insistence on Egyptian sovereignty would lead to disaster. The British asked that the United States work to install an Egyptian government that would accept the terms the British were willing to offer. The alternative was, the Foreign Office wrote, maintenance of the British position at whatever cost and by force if necessary. Acheson recognized and angrily rejected the implication that the United States was responsible for the Egyptian situation.[25]

The Egyptian government was also concerned about the failure to reach an agreement. It worried that the British were stalling so that events in the Sudan could progress to the point that Egypt could not exercise sovereignty. The Egyptians feared that the Sudanese would have moved so far towards self-government that they would not accept union with Egypt. To forestall the possibility, the Egyptian government attempted to outbid the British. In November 1950, it announced its intention to abrogate its 1936 treaty with Britain and the 1899 condominium agreement.

A Vote for Independence

The Umma Party was concerned that Anglo-Egyptian negotiations would produce British concessions and lead to Egyptian sovereignty. In December 1950, it proposed a motion in the legislative assembly calling for Sudanese independence by the end of 1951. After two days of debate, the Umma Party carried the motion by a one-vote margin over the opposition of the native administration officials and others in the assembly.

Robertson professed to be pleased by the outcome. The narrow margin of victory demonstrated that Umma lacked a working majority. It therefore allowed the governor-general to ignore the motion. The disagreement between Umma and the Sudan government also demonstrated that the two were not tied irrevocably together. It opened the way for broadening the government's support to include 'Ali al-Mirghani and his khatmiyya supporters.

If Robertson was happy with the outcome, he was alone. British opposition to independence upset the Umma Party. The party concluded that the native administration officials and other British appointees to the assembly were more hindrance than help. During 1950, Umma officials viewed with distrust thinly disguised British attempts to organize native administration officials and others into a new political party, the Socialist Republican Party. Umma saw the new party as a move to undermine its support in the countryside. The native administration officials and the Sudan government's other allies in the countryside worried about a rush to self-government and resented Umma's tactics in seeking a majority. The Egyptians were angry that Howe had allowed the debate without consulting them in accordance with the Anglo-Egyptian agreements. The Foreign Office was miffed that Howe had not consulted it.

The assembly's vote prompted Howe and Robertson to consider more steps towards self-government. Taking advantage of another measure passed by the assembly, Howe moved to convene a commission to consider changes to the legislative assembly ordinance. Hard bargaining with the Sudanese political parties produced a mandate to look beyond amending the legislative assembly ordinance. A commission included one native administration official, one representative of the southern Sudan, and fifteen educated northerners. The northerners included members of the Umma Party and of the National Front, a group favoring union with Egypt but competing with the Ashiqqa Party. The constitutional amendment commission met from April to June. It made considerable progress but adjourned without completing its work.

Egyptian Abrogation

In October 1951, the Egyptian government carried out its announced plan and propelled the Sudan further toward a changed status. The Egyptian government announced that it had abrogated the 1936 treaty and the condominium agreement. It produced an outline for a new Sudanese constitution. Under the constitution, the Sudan would have control of its internal affairs, but the king of Egypt would be responsible for defense and foreign affairs.

The Sudanese political parties and the members of the constitutional amendment commission welcomed the Egyptian announcement. They concluded that it meant the end of the condominium and, ultimately, of British rule. Without Egyptian adherence, the condominium agreement was dead. Without the agreement, the legal basis for the current Sudan government was gone. Although abrogation brought the Sudanese parties closer together, they disagreed about the immediate next steps. The Umma Party called for immediate independence. The party sent representatives to a United Nations meeting in Paris who joined with the Egyptian foreign minister to issue a statement that called for a plebiscite in the Sudan and withdrawal of foreign troops. It also criticized British officials and their motives. The National Front's members of the commission, on the other hand, called for the United Nations to take over administration of the Sudan until it was ready for self-government. Disagreements caused five members of the commission to resign in November 1951.

The Sudanese most closely allied to the Sudan government did not welcome abrogation. In the wake of the Egyptian announcement, a group of native administration officials and southerners held a press conference and announced their support for the Sudan government until the country was ready for self-government. The other Sudanese political parties perceived the conference as a British puppet show.

Abrogation of the condominium agreement sent the Sudan government into a fury. Like the Sudanese, Robertson and Howe focused first on the legal basis for a continued British role. They considered declaring a British protectorate or turning the Sudan into a United Nations trusteeship. The Foreign Office had serious misgivings about involving the United Nations. Robertson concluded that the Sudan government had to move faster toward self-government, regardless of the legal niceties. The government took the work the constitutional amendment commission had completed and reshaped it into a new constitution. After securing London's approval over the objections of Stevenson in Cairo, the government presented the package to the Sudanese legislative assembly in April 1952. Some wondered whether the Sudan government had, not for the first time, timed the announcement to disrupt the ongoing Anglo-Egyptian negotiations.[26]

The Sudan government's sense of urgency did not translate into sweeping reforms. The new constitution left considerable power in the hands of the Sudan government, in part at the expense of Britain and Egypt. Consistent with the constitutional amendment commission's recommendations, the proposed constitution purported to establish Sudanese self-government. It called for a cabinet form of government, a bicameral legislature, and an independent judiciary. British officials would remain as advisers to key ministries. One minister would have responsibility for the southern Sudan. Other features differed from the commission's recommendations. The legislature's lower house and sixty percent of the upper house would be filled through indirect elections. The governor general would appoint the other 40 percent of the upper house. The government assumed that indirect elections would favor native administration officials and other pro-government elements. Under the constitution, the governor general also could veto legislation regarding the public service and the southern Sudan and he could declare a constitutional emergency. Long at odds with the Sudan government, Stevenson told Caffrey that the proposed constitution was autocratic. In Stevenson's view, it made the governor general the "King of the Sudan," and eliminated any role for the British or Egyptian governments.[27]

In May 1952, the Egyptian government invited 'Abd-ah-Rahman and the Umma Party to Cairo to discuss the Egyptian proposals for the Sudan. The Sudan government encouraged 'Abd-ah-Rahman to participate. What it thought the talks would accomplish is not clear. Eden and the Foreign Office doubted that 'Abd-ah-Rahman would accept Egyptian sovereignty and they portrayed the negotiations to U.S. officials as a promising development. In the most optimistic case, they might be a way around the stalemate with the Egyptians. Eden and the Foreign Office also suggested that other Sudanese groups meet with the Egyptians. 'Abd-ah-Rahman and the Egyptians agreed on most points, but sovereignty proved an insuperable barrier. The Sudanese returned to Khartoum in June without an agreement. Nevertheless, the meetings demonstrated to the Egyptians that 'Abd-ah-Rahman, while opposed to Egyptian sovereignty, was not averse to acting independently of the Sudan government.[28]

A Coup in Egypt

Beginning in July 1952, events in Egypt propelled the Sudan still closer to a changed status. Frustrated by the inability of King Farouk's various governments to resolve the disagreement with Britain, a group of Egyptian army officers, the Free Officers, seized power and sent Farouk into exile. General Mohammed Neguib became prime minister and president of the republic. Neguib was half-Sudanese, had lived in the Sudan, and attended secondary school there along with prominent Sudanese politicians. In August, Neguib announced that Egypt was willing to separate the issue of the Sudan's future from negotiations about an Anglo-Egyptian defense agreement and the status of the Suez Canal. In October, Neguib went further, declaring that Egypt would accept immediate Sudanese self-government, followed, after a suitable transition period, by self-determination. Neguib and the Free Officers were nearly as interested as Farouk and his allies had been to unite Egypt and the Sudan. Nonetheless, they calculated that removing the British from the Sudan and resolving the disputes over the Suez Canal were worth risking a Sudanese vote for independence rather than union with Egypt. The Egyptians proceeded to negotiate agreements with all the Sudanese political parties. Having come out in favor of Sudanese self-government, the British government had little room for maneuver. Despite the objections of the Sudan government, the British and Egyptian governments signed an agreement in February 1953 committing themselves to Sudanese self-government and, in three years, Sudanese self-determination.

The terms of the Anglo-Egyptian agreement were based on the Sudan government's self-government proposals, but the Egyptian government negotiated amendments with the Sudanese political parties that curtailed the Sudan government's power and influence. A five-man international commission was to advise the governor general. Another international commission would supervise elections to the assembly that would determine Sudan's future. Still another commission would review all government positions held by non–Sudanese with an eye to accelerating Sudanization of all key positions. The Egyptians were intent that British officials in the Sudan not be positioned to sway the Sudanese against union with Egypt.

The Sudanese political parties welcomed the new Egyptian stance. Now that the role of the Egyptian monarch was no longer an issue, the Sudanese politicians who had adopted a pro–Egyptian position were free to favor both Egypt and self-government. The Free

Officers and the Ashiqqa Party discovered considerable common ground and Neguib was instrumental in regrouping the pro-Egyptian elements into a new party, the National Unionist Party. The London government encouraged 'Abd-ah-Rahman and the Umma Party to reach an agreement with Neguib, perhaps believing that 'Abd-ah-Rahman would never accept union with Egypt. Worried that the Sudan government was working against him and recognizing that a deal with the Egyptians would rid him of the British, 'Abd-ah-Rahman traveled from London to Cairo and signed an agreement. The Socialist Republican Party was the last holdout, but even it could not resist the prospect of self-determination.

Howe, Robertson, and the Sudan government resisted an agreement with the Egyptians. Senior officials in the Sudan clung to the notions that the Sudanese could not govern without British advisers and that the responsible Sudanese wanted British officials to remain. The status of the southern Sudan and its vulnerability to exploitation by northerners became the Sudan government's favorite rationale for rejecting the Egyptian proposals.

An Anglo-Egyptian Agreement

Churchill had balked when the Sudan government proposed a specific date for self-government and he was upset by the terms of the proposed agreement with Egypt. In a cabinet meeting on February 13, 1953, he claimed that the agreement would not command a majority of the Conservative members of Parliament. The Anglo-Egyptian negotiations were as rancorous as ever, but Eden recognized that the Egyptians were accepting his own proposals for Sudanese self-government and self-determination. To assuage Churchill's concerns, the cabinet delayed its decision for four hours while Eden briefed Conservative members of Parliament. Once Eden could report that the parliamentary party understood that the agreement was the best alternative open to the government, the cabinet voted to accept the agreement.[29]

The Colonial Office was an unhappy bystander to the Anglo-Egyptian negotiations and preparations for self-government in the Sudan. In December 1951, the Colonial Office fussed that a statement drafted by the Foreign Office was too specific regarding self-government. The Colonial Office had been carefully imprecise, not defining self-government as independence within the commonwealth or something less than that. During 1952, Colonial Office officials told their Foreign Office counterparts that proposals for the Sudan would cause problems because they were different from what had been promised to the Gold Coast and Nigeria. The Colonial Office objected to excluding British officials from the proposed Sudanese cabinet. It also criticized the Egyptian notion that British officials had to leave the Sudan before the Sudanese chose between independence and union with Egypt. Such proposals would put ideas into the heads of nationalists elsewhere and gave the impression that Britain was ready to liquidate its overseas dependencies.[30]

Approval in Washington

U.S. officials welcomed the change of government in Egypt. U.S. officials in Cairo were aware that army officers were plotting a coup. The State Department was prepared to work with the Free Officers when and if they seized control. As the coup unfolded, Farouk telephoned the United States embassy and pleaded for Caffrey's assistance, to no avail.[31]

An agreement between the new Egyptian government and the British government remained a high United States priority. U.S. officials in Cairo met with Gamel Abdel Nasser and other representatives of the Free Officers to discuss the Sudan issue. Caffrey worried that the Free Officers lacked the patience to negotiate an agreement. He feared that they might revert to the nationalistic posturing that had characterized Farouk's regime. When Anglo-Egyptian negotiations seemed about to break down, the State Department instructed the London embassy to communicate its concerns to the Foreign Office. The department said the British needed to do everything in the their power to reach an agreement. Another opportunity to settle the Sudan issue and pave the way to agreement on other issues might not come again. Furthermore, the British could not expect an agreement that satisfied all their demands. Given that an overall Anglo-Egyptian agreement offered so many benefits, concessions to the Egyptians were warranted, the department advised. When the Foreign Office asked if the United States would participate in the proposed Sudanese electoral commission, the State Department responded positively.[32]

In the last two weeks of January 1953, Acheson and the State Department pushed the British and the Egyptians towards an agreement. Acheson authorized Caffrey in Cairo to hint that the United States would be more likely to supply Egypt with arms if an agreement regarding the Sudan were signed. The State Department had the London embassy warn the Foreign Office that the United States might negotiate its own defense agreement with Egypt if no Anglo-Egyptian agreement was forthcoming.[33]

Dwight Eisenhower was inaugurated as president on January 20, 1953, and John Foster Dulles took Acheson's place as secretary of state. Nevertheless, U.S. policy regarding the Sudan agreement was unchanged. On February 4, Dulles met with Eden and other senior British leaders in London. Dulles voiced concern about the arms to be supplied to the Egyptians and the speed with which they would be delivered. He assured Eden, however, that he would instruct Caffrey to tell the Egyptians that arms sales were dependent on a Sudan agreement.[34]

U.S. Officials in the Sudan

To the extent that U.S. officials focused on the Sudan itself, they anticipated that the Sudan would become an independent state. Nevertheless, until February 1952, few if any State Department representatives had visited the Sudan. While the Sudan figured prominently in U.S. dealings with Egypt and Britain, the U.S. representatives nearest to Khartoum were in Cairo, twelve hundred miles away. While the United States was prodding the British to reach an agreement with Farouk, it used its ignorance of Sudanese conditions as an excuse for not becoming more involved. The conventional wisdom in the Cairo embassy was that most Sudanese favored independence from both Britain and Egypt, but did not agree about how to achieve it. When Wells Stabler, a senior State Department official, visited the Sudan in February 1952, he brought back a similar analysis. The Sudanese wanted to run their own country, but were undecided about accepting some sort union with Egypt.[35]

Although U.S. officials viewed British administration of the Sudan favorably, they grew to distrust the Sudan government. Stabler reported that the British had moved the Sudan well along the path to self-government. Nonetheless, Caffrey repeated the criticisms of the Sudan government offered by Stevenson, his British counterpart in Cairo. By 1952, the State Department thought the Sudan government was undermining an Anglo-Egyptian agreement. It suggested to the Foreign Office that it remind Khartoum of the need for an Anglo-Egyptian defense arrangement. By the end of 1952, State Department staff were stationed permanently in Khartoum. They reported that Robertson and other senior British officials in the Sudan government thought that the Sudan was still a generation away from self-government. British officials intended their self-government proposals to ensure their continued control, behind the scenes. State Department officials reported that top British officials in the Sudan blamed the United States for dragging the Sudan into its strategic plans. Senior members of the Khartoum government thought that the U.S. was willing to give the Sudan to Egypt in exchange for an Anglo-Egyptian defense agreement.[36]

State Department officials took to refuting many of the Sudan government's assertions. Burdette, the U.S. representative in Khartoum, agreed that Sudanization would reduce governmental efficiency. Counter to the Sudan government's claims, however, Burdette doubted that it would cause the government to collapse. When the Sudan government raised the backward state of the southern Sudan as a reason to reject the Egyptian self-government proposals, Burdette toured parts of the south. He reported that British officials in the south feared the coming of self-government. On the other hand, southerners seemed more receptive. Burdette doubted that failing to grant the south a separate status within the Sudan would pose a threat to public security.[37]

Just as the Truman administration ended, the Sudan stood poised for independence. To the extent that the Sudan's political advancement resulted from external sources, it owed little to the notion of colonial reform developed in the Colonial Office or, for that matter, to the U.S. stance of support for granting colonies their independence. Instead, it had everything to do with Britain's and the U.S. interests in the eastern Mediterranean and their perceived need for an alliance with Egypt. Moreover, it was more than a little ironic that Dean Acheson, at best a skeptic about independent African states, played a key role in moving the Sudan towards independence.

9

The Eisenhower Administration and British Africa, 1953–1960: At Arm's Length

Early in the Eisenhower administration, Secretary of State John Foster Dulles announced that he favored a more vigorous, more independent U.S. stance regarding British Africa. The Eisenhower administration devoted more time and attention to colonial Africa than had the Truman administration. During the Eisenhower administration, the United States issued a series of pronouncements about U.S. policy toward colonial Africa. Nevertheless, the fundamental U.S. policy remained unchanged — a search for the middle ground between the colonial powers and their critics and opponents. Some State Department officials found the basic U.S. stance unsatisfactory, but repeated efforts to devise something better failed.

Neither Eisenhower nor Dulles was interested in open collaboration with Great Britain regarding colonial issues. Over-identification with Britain would harm the United States in the court of world opinion, they thought. Eisenhower and Dulles believed that the African colonies would become independent in the end. When the colonies achieved independence, U.S. leaders wanted them to view the United States as a friend. Open support for British colonial policies would make friendly relations with independent African states that much less likely.

Nevertheless, the United States and Great Britain remained close allies. Their leaders and officials discussed colonial Africa and sought common understandings. The British still imagined that they could recruit American support for their colonial efforts. U.S. officials thought that their advice could help the British manage the colonies' transition to independence.

Eisenhower and Great Britain

Dwight Eisenhower was wary of overt Anglo-American collaboration, including about colonial issues. When he met with Churchill in New York shortly after the 1952 election, he warned Churchill about the dangers of their two nations seeming to collude with each other. Doing so would create jealousies and suspicions and undermine their long-term goals, the new president said. Eisenhower thought that a special relationship between Britain and the United States could not be acknowledged publicly. It would be enough if the two countries agreed informally on broad objectives and purposes and followed their own methods for achieving them. When Eisenhower and Churchill met in Bermuda in December 1953, Churchill campaigned for a united front on colonial issues. Eisenhower demurred. He argued that each colonial situation should be considered on its merits. Britain and the United States might play different roles, depending on the circumstances. A publicly proclaimed, consolidated position was not necessary.[1]

Eisenhower's attitude stemmed in part from a dislike of the personal diplomacy practiced by Franklin Roosevelt. He told Churchill that he was happy to carry on a personal correspondence. Official agreements between Britain and United States had to flow through the proper channels, however. Eisenhower said he wanted to be sure that proper records were kept. Agreements should also receive the approvals that the British and American forms of government required. Eisenhower observed that it may have seemed that Churchill and Roosevelt managed the world's affairs together from on high. He knew from personal experience, however, that the two wartime leaders had left others to solve nasty local problems.[2]

Domestic politics also dictated that Eisenhower avoid the appearance of a cozy relationship with Britain. Republicans hammered the Truman administration about Acheson's allegedly close ties to British officials and his alleged willingness to protect British interests. Eisenhower needed, therefore, to create some distance between his approach and that of his predecessor.

Eisenhower thought that Churchill was living in the past. Churchill was charming and interesting as ever, but showed the effects of passing years, Eisenhower wrote in his diary. Eisenhower wished that Churchill would relinquish leadership to a younger generation. Churchill was trying to relive the Second World War, in Eisenhower's view. Churchill, Eisenhower wrote, wanted the United States to treat Britain differently from other nations. Churchill had developed an almost childlike faith that answers were to be found in British-American partnership.[3]

Eisenhower was committed to an Anglo-American alliance, but he was also willing to use U.S. wealth and power to bring Churchill and Britain into line with U.S. policy. Despite Eisenhower's reluctance, Churchill was eager to orchestrate a summit meeting including Britain, Russia and the United States in 1953. Churchill suggested that he would go to Moscow alone if Eisenhower continued to oppose the idea. Eisenhower replied that Churchill was welcome to do so, but it would jeopardize U.S. military and financial aid to Britain.[4]

Eisenhower and Nationalism

Eisenhower was also opposed to open Anglo-American cooperation regarding colonial issues because he thought that nationalism would overtake the European colonial empires. Eisenhower perceived nationalism as an irresistible, but dangerous, force. In a 1954 private letter, he referred to the "intensity and force of the spirit of nationalism that is gripping all the peoples of the world today." When Secretary of the Treasury George Humphrey suggested that the United States support the colonial powers because they could improve living conditions faster than independent governments, Eisenhower retorted: "It is my personal conviction that almost any one of the newborn states of the world would rather embrace communism or any other form of dictatorship than to acknowledge the political domination of another government, even though that brought to each citizen a far higher standard of living." Eisenhower compared the impact of the breakup of the European colonial empires to the waves caused by a large stone tossed into a pond. Elsewhere, Eisenhower described it as a torrent over-running everything in its path, including the best interests of those concerned. He told Churchill that any attempt to maintain the European empires by force would produce only resentment, unrest, and conflict. The spirit of nationalism had become rampant and often uncontrollable in the world, Eisenhower said.[5]

Eisenhower attributed his views about nationalism to his service in the Philippines in the late 1930s. Under the terms of the Tydings-McDuffie Act, Douglas MacArthur was detailed from the U.S. Army to the Philippines to organize a Philippines army. Eisenhower accompanied him as an aide and chief of staff. Eisenhower's fundamental attitude toward the Philippines was arrogant. When MacArthur decided to accept appointment as a field marshal in the Philippines army, Eisenhower objected. He told MacArthur that being a four-star general in the United States Army was a proud thing. "Why in the hell do you want a banana country giving you a field marshal-ship?" Eisenhower asked. Eisenhower also found his time in the Philippines trying. MacArthur was a difficult boss and Filipino politics hampered efforts to build the Filipino armed forces. Nevertheless, Eisenhower came away impressed by the Filipinos' determination to govern their own country.[6]

Like Roosevelt and Truman, Eisenhower believed that the United States had strategic interests around the globe. In his 1953 inaugural address, he argued that there was no free nation too humble to be forgotten and that nationalism in Asia or Africa was a concern to the United States. Like his immediate predecessors, Eisenhower put the United States on the side of the nationalists, at least rhetorically. In 1956, he told an audience at Baylor University that the United States had nothing to fear from nationalism itself. The U.S. had helped small nations gain their independence. It would continue to welcome the independence of other nations who became peaceful members of the world community.[7]

Witnessing the movement of colonies to independence put the U.S. in a difficult situation, in Eisenhower's view. The European colonial powers were American allies. Since the U.S. felt compelled to support nationalists as well, Eisenhower worried that the United States could find itself hated by both the colonies and their mother countries. Eisenhower believed that cooperation and mutual restraint could permit the U.S. and its European allies to survive and prosper despite the rise of nationalism. Privately, he expressed frustration with the failure of Britain and the other colonial powers to move more forcefully to transform their empires. He thought that they put their selfish and parochial interests above their long-term interests and those of the U.S.[8]

Early in his first term, Eisenhower had a plan to harness nationalism to American interests. In July 1954, Eisenhower described his scheme in a private letter to Churchill. Britain and the United States, Eisenhower wrote, were publicly committed to self-government. They could not renege on their commitment, but they realized that many colonies were not ready for self-government. Colonialism was finished, nevertheless. Britain and the United States could not halt nationalism. If they tried to dam up it up, it would burst the barriers like a mighty river and create havoc. If Britain and the U.S. were intelligent enough, however, they could make constructive use of nationalism's energy to their own advantage, particularly in their competition with Russia. Eisenhower suggested that Churchill make, as one of his last acts as prime minister, a speech proposing a joint Anglo-American initiative. The U.S. could not raise the issue, Eisenhower said, without seeming to criticize Britain. Instead, Churchill should propose expanding education in the colonies and creating voluntary economic ties between the colonies and the colonial powers. In the interests of balance, he should also describe the responsibilities that self-government brought: for law and order, the administration of justice, and the provision of public services. Most important, Churchill should commit Britain to having its colonies ready for self-government within a specified period, perhaps twenty-five years, and to offering its colonies the right of self-determination within that period. Eisenhower reassured Churchill that none of its colonies would choose independence if Britain did as he proposed. They would, Eisenhower predicted, "cling more tightly to the mother country and become a more valuable part thereof."[9]

John Foster Dulles

Eisenhower's secretary of state, John Foster Dulles, belonged to the main stream of American foreign policy in the 1940s and early 1950s. Dulles served as an adviser to senior Republican politicians Thomas E. Dewey and Senator Arthur Vandenberg. He was also part of the U.S. delegation at the United Nations conference in San Francisco and served as U.S. delegate at subsequent U.N. meetings. As a consultant to the Department of State during the Truman administration, he played a key role in negotiating a peace treaty with Japan. During Dulles's service at the U.N., he was comfortable with the Truman administration's approach to the issues posed by European colonies.

When Dulles became secretary of state, his contribution to colonial issues was a stated preference for a larger, independent, and more energetic role for the United States in shaping a new world order. After Roosevelt and Churchill issued the Atlantic Charter, Dulles characterized it as a "tentative and incomplete statement." It reflected the "old sovereignty system" and was reminiscent of the Treaty of Versailles, without any of the "liberalizing international institutions." It was likely to create an Anglo-Saxon hegemony whose self-interest would be bound to the maintenance of the status quo. During World War II, Dulles traveled to London and met with Eden and Lord Cranborne, the colonial secretary. While Dulles favored Anglo-American collaboration after the war and publicly praised Britain's colonial accomplishments, he dismissed proposals for collaboration in the colonial field. He told his British colleagues that the American public would see such collaboration as participation in imperialism and exploitation, and would oppose it. Within the U.S. delegation to the United Nations, Dulles was eager for the United States to compete with Russia for the allegiance of the anti-colonial members. He warned against becoming identified with the colonial powers. In 1948, Dulles told a friend in the context of disputes about Palestine that the United States could not rely on the British because all their estimates and prophecies had been wrong. While the U.S. had to work with Britain, America had always to be in the lead. Early in Dulles's tenure, he told a congressional committee that the colonial powers were old, tired, worn out. They were almost willing to buy peace in order to have a few years more of rest. The world would be saved only if it got out of the United States what was lacking in the rest of the world.[10]

One of Dulles's first acts as secretary of state was to tour the countries around the eastern Mediterranean. When Dulles returned to Washington, he laid out an expanded role for the United States in the region. Dulles reported that Britain could no longer defend the area on behalf of the Western powers. He thought that Britain's standing in the area was bound to decline regardless of what the United States did. Dulles recognized Britain's interests, but opposed overt cooperation with Britain. The American association with British and French imperialistic policies was a millstone. Because newly independent states were wary of the colonial powers, Dulles proposed that the U.S. undertake efforts on its own to steer nationalist regimes towards the United States and the NATO alliance. The U.S. should be able to do so without worsening relations with Britain.[11]

Regarding colonies generally and African colonies in particular, Dulles saw the United States performing a difficult balancing act. "Walking a tightrope" was a favorite image. Maintaining the U.S. alliance with Britain and the other colonial powers was of the utmost importance. Reaching an agreement with the colonial powers would be a good thing. Failing an agreement, the U.S. could not risk the alliance by pushing its allies too hard to change their colonial policies. European rule probably benefited the colonies, Dulles told British officials. On the other hand, the long-standing U.S. policy was to favor independence. Sticking with a pro-independence stance would help the United States gain the friendship of colonial peoples. Misguided colonial policies, ones that provoked armed resistance as in Indochina endangered U.S. interests. The United States needed to disassociate itself from them.[12]

Churchill and Eden

Even after Britain had granted India and its other principal Asian colonies independence, Winston Churchill remained enamored of the British empire. When Eisenhower suggested that Churchill end his political career by announcing Britain's commitment to granting its colonies self-government, Churchill declined. He wrote to Eisenhower that he thought Britain could be proud of its accomplishments in its colonies, particularly India. Churchill assured Eisenhower that Eisenhower's thoughts about moving the colonies towards self-government were consistent with Britain's current policies. Churchill admitted that he remained a laggard on the subject. He was skeptical about "universal suffrage for Hottentots even if refined by proportional representation." After all, the Britain and the United States had "slowly and painfully" forged their democracies and they were far from perfect.[13]

Just as Churchill had tried to draw Truman into a "special relationship," he attempted to recreate with Eisenhower the sort of arrangement between Britain and the United States that had characterized the early years of World War II. Churchill told Eisenhower that the English-speaking world was the world's hope. Cooperation between Britain and the United States could become the foundation of all effective policy. Churchill told Eisenhower that he abhorred the notion that Britain and its commonwealth were just one among many foreign nations from the U.S. perspective.[14]

As Churchill's foreign secretary and as prime minister, Anthony Eden sought to carve out an independent role for Britain in world affairs. Eden understood that Britain needed U.S. support, but looked for opportunities for Britain to go its own way. He thought that an increasingly complex world would create chances for a country of the second rank, like Britain, to act independently. Regarding Egypt and western Asia, Eden wanted United States support, but he was not convinced that a common front with the United States was necessary. At the 1954 Geneva negotiations, regarding Indochina in particular, Eden worked hard to construct a settlement that met British and French interests, but not necessarily those of the United States.[15]

Playing second fiddle to the United States did not please either Churchill or Eden. Churchill did not like being treated as if Britain were just another part of a crowd, he told Eden. Eden took to complaining that the U.S. was trying to run the world and to make former colonial territories economically and politically dependent upon itself. Dulles's preference for an independent and energetic approach to colonial issues and ill-disguised sense of moral superiority did not endear him to British leaders. Churchill thought that Dulles was not smart. He once said that Dulles was the only bull he knew that carried his china shop around with him. Eden often referred to Dulles as "that terrible man."[16]

British Officials and the United States

British officials, in the Foreign Office, the Washington embassy, and the Colonial Office, shared their political bosses' anxieties about the United States and its policies toward the colonies. Recognizing that Britain was a second-class power with first-class colonial responsibilities, British officials were aware that U.S. power and wealth could be critical to the colonies' future. British officials scrutinized official statements and press reports for clues about U.S. thinking. They speculated about the U.S. officials responsible for what seemed to be anti–British or anti-colonial tendencies. They imagined ways to enlist American power in preserving Britain's colonial interests. Given the ambiguity embedded in U.S. policy on colonialism, British reactions could appear schizophrenic, eager to see signs of United States support and fearful, even bitter, about signs of U.S. independence.

Given the potential importance of American backing, British reports about U.S. policy and attitudes easily took on a Pollyanna air. Many British officials wanted to believe that the United States supported British colonial interests. The Eisenhower administration, a 1954 report contended, was becoming more sympathetic to Britain's colonial policies. U.S. officials were beginning to understand that premature self-government would lead to political instability and raise the risk of communist infiltration. A 1956 report conceded that public opinion in the United States tended to be anti-colonial. The report also maintained, however, that the State Department was more realistic about the dangers of premature independence and supported British policies. While Democratic foreign policy experts might be pushing pro-nationalist views, senior State Department officials remained wary of nationalist movements, another 1956 report contended. Older administration figures might be hostile to British interests but their younger, more junior colleagues were more open to British views, stated another.[17]

Involving the United States in Africa seemed both inviting and dangerous to British officials. The Eisenhower administration's anti-communism appeared to offer an opportunity to secure United States support for Britain's colonial policies. If Britain could frame colonial discussions in terms of repelling communism in the colonies, United States support might be forthcoming. Britain might be able to stimulate U.S. interest in Africa while fending off American interference in British interests. Once invited to participate, could the United States be dissuaded from exerting its considerable power to Britain's disadvantage? Other British officials were skeptical, preferring to shield the African colonies from U.S. activity.[18]

Some British officials thought the United States was trying to undermine the European empires. The more common complaint was that the United States was being two-faced. The British ambassador to the United Nations, Sir Gladwyn Jebb, complained about the foolishness of the United States providing financial aid to Uganda while encouraging what he considered anarchy in East Africa by clinging to outmoded policies in the U.N. Sir Harold Caccia, a British ambassador to the U.S., reported to London in 1958 that Dulles and others were suffering from a "chronic American phobia," fear of being seen alone with the British. The United States, Caccia wrote, wanted a secret liaison with Britain. It was "scared stiff" that Britain would ask for marriage bells.[19]

British officials, in their darker moments, suspected key U.S. officials of anti–British views. Herbert Hoover, Jr., a special adviser to Dulles and under secretary of state, was thought to be anti–British. Various organizations within the State and Defense departments were suspected of anti–British tendencies. Dulles was a lightning rod for apprehension among lesser British officials as much as he was for Churchill and Eden. His willingness for the United States to chart its own course regarding Egypt and western Asia raised a red flag for British officials. They worried that Dulles was ready to sacrifice British colonial interests around the globe in the interests of competing with Russia.[20]

British anxieties made them hard to please. U.S. and British officials met regularly to discuss colonial issues. British officials also attended meetings where organizations within the State Department developed a common position on colonial issues. Nevertheless, British complaints about the American failure to consult properly were common. Foreign Office officials feared that U.S. officials were not thinking through and resolving Anglo-American disagreements.[21]

Anglo-American Pronouncements

In terms of general principles, the United States and Britain could cooperate. Twice in Eisenhower's first term they issued a joint statement trumpeting adherence to the Atlantic Charter and to self-determination. Apparently, such statements did not violate Eisenhower's strictures regarding collusion between Britain and the United States. In June 1954, Eisenhower and Churchill ended a meeting in Washington by issuing a statement dubbed the "Potomac Charter." It announced that Britain and the United States upheld the principle of self-determination. They would secure independence for all countries that desired and could sustain an independent existence. After a similar meeting in early 1956, Eisenhower and Eden, now prime minister, issued a longer statement, most of which focused on Russia and the dangers of communism. The so-called "Declaration of Washington" also proclaimed British and American adherence to the Atlantic Charter and the United Nations charter. The declaration repeated the familiar language about favoring self-government and independence for all countries that desired and could sustain an independent existence.[22]

Creating even such broad pronouncements did not come easily. In late 1953, Eisenhower shared with Churchill a draft speech intended for presentation to the United Nations. Churchill took the time to persuade Eisenhower to delete a reference to an "obsolete colonial mold" which was now over or being broken. In 1954, the original U.S. draft of the Potomac Charter, which Churchill attributed to Dulles, referred to the "right" of self-determination. Churchill felt compelled to insist that the wording be changed to the "principle" of self-determination.[23]

Unlike the Atlantic Charter, the Potomac Charter and the Declaration of Washington remained just press releases. Since they announced business as usual regarding Anglo-American attitudes towards the colonies, they attracted little or no attention. Neither the State Department nor the Foreign Office conceded them much importance in the colonial sphere.

Suez and Its Aftermath

In October 1956, British, French and Israeli troops invaded Egypt in order to wrest control of the Suez Canal from the Egyptian government headed by Gamel Abdel Nasser. Despite being allies of the United States, Britain, France, and Israel launched the invasion without warning the U.S. Eisenhower and his government reacted quickly to impose a ceasefire and to force the invaders to withdraw their troops. The U.S. government took the issue to the U.N. Security Council and, when Britain and France blocked action there, to the General Assembly. The United States moved elements of its Mediterranean fleet close to the Egyptian coast and stood aside while Saudi Arabia halted oil shipments to Britain. When international investors began to sell their sterling holdings, the U.S. took no action to support the British currency.

Eden's government acted because it convinced itself that Egyptian control of the Suez Canal threatened its vital interests. Britain's agreement with Egypt over the Sudan led to an agreement in October 1954 regarding the Suez Canal and the associated British military installations. Britain agreed to withdraw its troops within two years. Despite the agreement, relations between Egypt and Britain deteriorated. In 1955, Britain negotiated a military alliance with Iraq, Turkey, Pakistan, and Iran, dubbed the Central Treaty Organization or Baghdad Pact. Feeling threatened, Egypt arranged to buy arms from Czechoslovakia and other Eastern European countries and sought to strengthen its ties to Saudi Arabia. When Britain and the United States withdrew promised financial support for construction of the Aswan dam, Nasser retaliated by nationalizing the Suez Canal. Oil shipments to Britain passed through the canal and Eden thought that Britain could not risk leaving it in Egyptian hands. Eden and his closest advisers came to believe that Nasser represented a threat to Britain's interests throughout the region and to British international prestige. In August 1956, Lord Home encouraged Eden in his anti–Nasser sentiments by saying that he believed that Britain was finished if "the Middle East goes and Russia and India and China rule from Africa to the Pacific." Eden became convinced that political leaders in the African colonies would not take Britain seriously if it allowed Nasser to retain control of the canal.[24]

Nasser worried Dulles and Eisenhower as well. The arms deal with Czechoslovakia, Egypt's recognition of the communist regime in China, and concerns about the competence of Nasser's government prompted the United States to back out of the Aswan dam agreement. Nevertheless, Dulles remained committed to pursuing an independent American approach to the eastern Mediterranean. While remaining supportive of British interests, Dulles looked for ways to enhance U.S. standing and to avoid over-identification with the British. Between July and October 1956, while Eden plotted with France and Israel to attack Egypt, Dulles and the State Department conducted a series of conferences and produced several proposals intended to defuse tensions over the canal.

For Eisenhower, Britain's attack on Egypt raised fundamental principles. In 1950, Britain, France, and the United States pledged to protect any nation around the eastern Mediterranean from aggression. When it appeared that Israel alone had attacked Egypt, Eisenhower thought that the United States had to honor its pledge. He was upset that Britain and France thought they could maneuver the U.S. into a position where it would not honor its commitments. Eisenhower thought that Britain had double-crossed the U.S. and that Eden had deceived him. Eisenhower told Dulles that he did not see much value in an unworthy and unreliable ally.[25]

Dulles put the Suez situation in the context of colonialism. The invasion was "the straight old-fashioned variety of colonialism of the most obvious sort," Dulles told the National Security Council. For many years, the United States had been walking a tightrope, trying to maintain its ties to the colonial powers while seeking the friendship of the newly independent states that had "escaped from colonialism." The U.S. had to show some leadership, Dulles urged. Otherwise, Russia would, and the United States would appear tied forever to British and French colonial policies. Then American survival would be tied to the fate of colonialism. France and Britain were finished. They had acted against both principle and their best interests, Dulles argued. The United States needed to put its own resolution before the United Nations before the Russians introduced a harsher measure. If the U.S. were forced to oppose a Russian measure, it would appear to the world to be siding with Britain and France. It was tragic that the U.S. felt compelled to abandon its closest long-term allies, Dulles lamented. Otherwise, the United States would seem to favor using force to reassert colonial control over the less developed nations.[26]

By late 1956, Britain's financial situation showed real improvement, particularly over the dark days of 1947 and 1951. As the world economy expanded in the wake of the Korean War, Britain was able to increase its exports and accumulate surpluses in its balance of payments. Britain's finances improved enough in the early 1950s that British policymakers were willing to shift British financial policy toward the multilateral arrangements preferred by the United States. In 1954, the Conservative Party discarded any attachment it retained to the notion of imperial preference, converting the commonwealth into some sort of trading bloc. British officials saw that half the world's trade was still conducted in sterling and the Treasury imagined that sterling's international role could be enhanced further. The Treasury loosened controls on the sterling balances held in London and inched towards full convertibility of sterling.[27]

Britain's financial reserves in 1956 were insufficient, however, to withstand the run on sterling that took place after the Suez invasion. As chancellor of the exchequer, Macmillan was forced to seek financial assistance from the United States. He discovered that the U.S. would help only if Britain agreed to halt the invasion and withdraw its troops. Confronted with U.S. financial dominance, Britain was forced to yield.

Eden's government attacked Egypt even though it was aware of Britain's financial frailty, especially compared with the robust finances of the U.S. In June 1956, officials from the Treasury, the Foreign Office, and the Ministry of Defense produced a paper entitled "The Future of the United Kingdom in World Affairs," which laid out Britain's situation. The paper counseled the cabinet that Britain could not play a major or dominant role in world affairs based on its material strength alone. Britain would be competing with countries with larger populations, greater wealth, or greater control of essential food or raw materials, especially oil. The paper suggested various remedies, including reductions in military expenditures and greater orientation toward Europe. The paper compared Britain's situation with that of the United States in vivid and concrete terms, pointing out that Britain owed the United States $140 million each year through 2000 to repay the 1946 loan. The paper argued that the $140 million was significant in terms of Britain's balance of payments. It was, however, trivial in the context of American finances. The paper estimated that it represented one third of one percent of U.S. receipts from income tax.[28]

When Eden's calculation that the United States would stand aside while Britain and its allies seized the Suez Canal proved mistaken, the repercussions were considerable. The British government, including Macmillan, who had supported the invasion, concluded that it could not continue in the face of open U.S. opposition. In January 1957, Eden resigned as prime minister and Macmillan took his place. A leading general observed that Britain's military capabilities were of little value unless British domestic opinion and international opinion were aligned. International opinion included the United States. As the editors of *The Economist* wrote, it was now indisputable that the British must play a junior role in any Anglo-American alliance. The British were not Americans nor could they be.[29]

America's superior wealth and power dictated that it had the larger say in any Anglo-American arrangements. Credibility was a factor as well. Sir Harold Caccia thought that the Eisenhower administration and U.S. public opinion would not be swayed in the long term by sentiment. The United States was impressed by results. Britain would have a harder time gaining United States support because Britain's attack on Egypt had failed to achieve its aims.[30]

Some have suggested that Eden's resignation and Macmillan's, rather than R.A. Butler's, elevation to Number 10 were part of the U.S. price for restoring normal relations with Britain. The evidence for an active American role is questionable. The suggestion demonstrates, however, the changed nature of the relationship between London and Washington at the beginning of Eisenhower's second term. No one would have imagined that the United States government had a hand in Attlee, Churchill, or Eden becoming prime minister. That Eisenhower preferred Macmillan and that Eisenhower's preference mattered in Britain seems within the realm of possibility, on the other hand.[31]

When Caccia met with Dulles on Christmas Eve 1956, they sounded like a couple mending their relationship after one of them had strayed. When Caccia complained that relations between Britain and the United States were not better, Dulles replied that Britain could not expect that everything would suddenly be as before. Britain had deceived the U.S. and it would take some time for the U.S. to regain confidence in Britain. Eisenhower and Dulles did not want Britain and the United States to be estranged, but Britain would have to wait for time to heal the wounds. When Caccia referred to growing sentiment in Britain that the United States was not sufficiently sympathetic to Britain's situation, Dulles retorted that the administration could have shared with the press the fact that Eisenhower had warned Eden that using force would backfire. The administration had not done so, Dulles, said, because it did not want to appear to be attacking the Eden government.[32]

Eisenhower and Macmillan

In the wake of Suez, the Eisenhower and Macmillan governments invested considerable time and energy in trying to cooperate, on colonial and other issues. Cooperation was now easier. The U.S. was the senior partner. Macmillan was no less focused on Britain's vital interests than Eden, but he discarded Eden's prickly search for independence in favor of a more affable, compliant approach. Cooperation seemed more imperative. The launch of the Sputnik satellite in October 1957 revealed Russia's increased capabilities. The Khrushchev regime had also made plain its intention to compete with the Western powers for the friendship of nations around the globe.

Renewed cooperation went far enough to produce significant changes regarding atomic weapons and missile technology. The Eisenhower administration persuaded Congress to revise the McMahon Act to facilitate sharing nuclear technology with Britain. The Eisenhower administration agreed to share key elements of the U.S. missile program with Britain. Gaining access to American technology allowed Britain to acquire nuclear weapons and the means to deliver them without incurring most of the research and development costs. It also allowed Macmillan's government to postpone decisions about reducing Britain's military expenditures, including those tied to its colonial possessions.

Nonetheless, not everything went smoothly in Anglo-American relations. Macmillan lobbied Eisenhower hard to agree to a four-power summit meeting involving the United

States, Britain, France, and Russia. When Eisenhower was willing to allow the Paris summit meeting to collapse in the wake of revelations about U-2 flights over Russia, Macmillan was devastated. He thought he had played his hand badly and was worse off than before. His private secretary reported that the Paris summit meeting convinced Macmillan that Britain now counted for nothing. Macmillan told the queen, "We have fallen from the summit into a deep crevasse."[33]

By the end of 1960, Macmillan was pessimistic about Britain's situation. Britain, Macmillan thought, no longer had the economic or political power to take the leading role. It was beset with problems. Its economy was fragile. Converting its empire into a commonwealth was difficult and Britain's relationship with continental Europe was uncertain. The U.S. attitude towards Britain varied, Macmillan thought. Sometimes the United States treated Britain as an ally in a special and unique category. At other times, the United States treated Britain as just another country.[34]

Close cooperation was more important to British leaders and officials than it was to their U.S. counterparts. After Suez, key cabinet members believed that Britain should not launch important foreign policy initiatives without consulting the United States. The cabinet concluded that Britain could not hope for the same relationship it had had with the United States during World War II, but it could aspire to be treated as an equal. Nevertheless, as one report stated, an Anglo-American partnership was not a "law of nature." The Macmillan government devoted considerable thought to how it could maintain U.S. trust. Being a reliable ally against communism was high on the list, along with maintaining a healthy economy, offering scientific and technical expertise, and maintaining a reputation for political expertise in the world outside Europe. Recognizing the U.S. desire to appear supportive of nationalist movements, British officials worried that a British failure to deal effectively with such movements in East and Central Africa would drive Britain and the United States apart.[35]

One of the first steps towards closer ties between Britain and the United States was a bilateral meeting in Bermuda in March 1957. Preparations for the meeting were detailed and elaborate, more so than for earlier meetings between Eisenhower and British leaders. Before the meeting, teams of British and U.S. officials prepared papers on a wide range of subjects. The meeting covered three days during which Eisenhower, Macmillan and their staffs worked through an extensive agenda, including a paper on combating communist influences in Africa.

Before the Bermuda conference, Lord Perth, minister of state in the Colonial Office, laid out the office's views for Macmillan. Perth argued that what he characterized as the U.S. misinterpretation of British colonial policy was a major obstacle to a proper understanding between Britain and the United States. He thought that it colored U.S. attitudes on key issues, including Suez. The United States was not hostile to Britain's colonial policy. It assumed, however, that the colonial relationship was inherently wrong. The U.S. position on colonial issues was "everlasting compromise." Perth contended that compromise undermined both British and U.S. interests, particularly in the United Nations. U.S. officials understood that the United States would have to assume greater economic and strategic commitments if Britain withdrew prematurely from its African colonies. Nevertheless, U.S. officials persisted in seeking compromises, admitting only that they faced a painful dilemma. The U.S. should discard the idea that colonialism was wrong, Perth told Macmillan. Faced with a disagreement between Britain and the anti-colonial powers, the United States should consult with Britain and be guided by British views. If the U.S. thought that Britain was doing a good job in the colonies, it should say so publicly.[36]

Macmillan declined to add colonialism to the agenda for the Bermuda meeting. He told Perth that the United Nations was already on the agenda. Adding colonialism to the list of topics would put British representatives in a defensive posture. Macmillan did not want to warn Eisenhower in advance that he wanted to discuss colonial policy, but he assured Perth that he would do so if the opportunity arose.[37]

The materials prepared by the State Department for Eisenhower and Dulles took the position that disagreements between Britain and the United States over Britain's colonies were limited. The State Department's background paper conceded that a too-hasty British withdrawal from its African colonies would not serve U.S. interests. Nevertheless, the State Department counseled against a blanket endorsement of British policy, anticipating that the British would seek U.S. support for its policies, portraying them as the best means to combat communist influence in Africa. The department advised that the United States might comment favorably on British policy in specific circumstances, such as it had done regarding Britain's grant of independence to the Gold Coast. Word of a blanket endorsement might become public, however, with negative consequences for the United States. The anti-colonial powers would think the U.S. was conspiring against them. The other colonial powers would also resent the U.S. involvement in what they considered their responsibilities.[38]

In preparing for the Bermuda conference, British and U.S. officials agreed on a paper drafted in London entitled "Means of Combatting Communist Influence in Tropical Africa." For the most part, the paper covered familiar ground. The best way to combat communist influence, the paper stated, was moving colonies to self-government or independence as rapidly as possible and in such a way that they would retain their ties with the Western powers. The United Kingdom, the paper reported, believed that its current policies were a sincere attempt to achieve this goal. Circumstances differed, the paper warned, and progress toward self-government could not be uniform. Striking the right balance was difficult. Progress toward self-government should be neither too fast nor too slow. Britain and the United States should continue to consult informally about colonial issues, the paper recommended. The paper's new elements were the emphasis on alleged communist plans to dominate tropical Africa and the framing of Anglo-American cooperation regarding the African colonies as an anti–Soviet measure.[39]

Although records of the conference indicate that the British and U.S. officials agreed on the paper, the State Department representatives communicated to their British counterparts that the U.S. was not offering a blanket endorsement of British policies in Africa. Alan Lennox-Boyd, the colonial secretary, described the conference's proceedings to the governors of the African colonies. He reported that the State Department maintained that moving colonies towards self-government was only part of British colonial policy. United States support for preparing colonies for political change did not equate, the department made clear, to support for everything Britain was doing in Africa.[40]

At the Bermuda conference, Dulles tried to reassure Selwyn Lloyd, Macmillan's foreign secretary, about the U.S. intentions in Africa. The United States did not intend to exert pressure that would lead to premature independence, Dulles said. If the British thought the United States was doing so, Dulles wanted to be informed. Dulles told Lloyd that he understood that granting independence was an important step, because it could be followed by an attempted communist takeover. Groups in the United States might press for immediate independence and, in doing so, embarrass Britain or the other colonial powers, Dulles warned. Nevertheless, the U.S. government could not control such groups or prevent them from acting, he added.[41]

At the conference, Eisenhower shared with Macmillan his notion that some colonies might not choose independence. Eisenhower spoke at length about the possibility of getting colonial peoples to accept autonomy within the old colonial framework. He cited Puerto Rico as an example. He argued that the colonial powers could convince colonies to settle for autonomy if they offered sufficient incentives and communicated that the colonies retained the right to choose their status.[42]

Anglo-American Meetings

During Eisenhower's second term, formal consultations between British and U.S. officials regarding colonial issues, and African issues in particular, expanded. Officials from the two countries continued to meet each year to prepare for the upcoming United Nations session. Beginning in 1959, the State Department also met regularly with British officials to discuss developments in Africa. The talks were at a high level — an assistant secretary on the U.S. side and an assistant undersecretary on the British side. Africa was also on the agenda in October 1958 when Dulles met with Lloyd at the U.S. airbase at Brize Norton, England. They agreed that their two countries should take a joint look at Africa and that they should hold talks with other colonial powers — France, and perhaps Belgium and Portugal. In April 1959, British, French, and U.S. officials discussed African issues, among others, at a six-day meeting in Washington.[43]

British officials took suggestions from U.S. officials seriously. The Dulles-Lloyd conversation at Brize Norton prompted Macmillan to task a high level interdepartmental committee with preparing a survey of Africa over the next ten years. In June 1958, Dulles shared with Macmillan his concerns about introducing democratic institutions into "backward" countries. A committee of British officials subsequently considered the issue and prepared a report for the Foreign Office.[44]

Both U.S. and British officials considered their interactions regarding colonial Africa in the second Eisenhower term satisfactory. British officials worried that the United States might push Britain to accelerate political changes in the colonies. An official in Britain's Washington embassy told Lloyd that close cooperation between the United States and Britain might create in the U.S. a reluctance to "jog the elbow" of those making the decisions. It might also generate anxiety to see more vigorous action and "an itch" to take a hand in the process. U.S. officials were concerned that Britain might expect the United States to increase its financial aid to African colonies. Nevertheless, State Department staff in the London embassy thought that Britain and the United States disagreed on few colonial issues. Foreign Office staff thought likewise. The United States had come to respect British colonial policies and to collaborate increasingly with Britain, stated a 1959 British analysis.[45]

The increasingly warm relations between Britain and the United States regarding colonial policies during the second Eisenhower administration reflected a fundamental change in British policy. In October 1959, Macmillan named Iain Macleod to replace Lennox-Boyd as colonial secretary. The pace of political change in the African colonies then quickened. U.S. officials recognized that Macleod had shifted British policy much closer to the traditional U.S. stance. Disagreement was possible, especially about the timing for political changes and about developments in individual colonies, but the two countries were much closer on the fundamentals.

Consultations were also friendlier after 1957 because they increasingly involved sharing information rather than discussing or debating policy. After Macleod signaled that the pace of political change would accelerate, the nature of policy making changed. The focus shifted from the general to the specific. The important policy decisions applied to individual colonies, not to colonies generally. British officials in London and in the colonies struggled to manage change in the context of each colony's politics. Given the diverse and ad hoc nature of the process, British officials in London were usually unable to describe to their U.S. counterparts their plans for each colony. Instead, they shared their appreciation of the political situation. Consultations consisted of British officials briefing their U.S. counterparts about the current situation in each colony, not discussions about the broad sweep of British colonial policy.[46]

The paper "Africa: the Next Ten Years" that originated with Dulles's 1958 conversation with Lloyd at Brize Norton exemplified the situation. The paper was intended to spark a discussion by Britain and the United States about fundamental policies. Once U.S. and British officials saw the document, however, they concluded that it was a fine intelligence report, but left something to be desired as a statement of policy. The British explained that policy was in such flux in many colonies that they could not lay out clear policy recommendations. U.S. officials anticipated that the same would be true of any future talks.[47]

State Department

As political change gained momentum in Africa during the Eisenhower administration, the State Department devoted increasing attention and resources to the continent. As of June 1952, the department had 111 Foreign Service officers of all types stationed in Africa, excluding Algeria and Egypt. By June 1960, the number had more than doubled to 271. The increase was more notable because the department's staffing decreased by nearly 19 percent over the 1950s, from 16,319 in 1950 to 13,294 in 1960. In 1956, the department shifted responsibility for South Africa and Madagascar from the Bureau of European Affairs to the Bureau of Near Eastern, South Asian, and African Affairs. Later in 1956, it created the post of deputy assistant secretary for African affairs. In 1957, the Eisenhower administration sent Congress a proposal to establish a Bureau of African Affairs headed by an assistant secretary. Without waiting for congressional approval, the department carved out a semiautonomous area of African affairs within the Bureau of Near Eastern, South Asian, and African Affairs. The department transferred thirty-nine positions and appropriate funds to the new area and added twenty-two new positions. When the Bureau of African Affairs gained responsibility for the Sudan in 1960, it was responsible for the entire continent, except for Algeria and Egypt.[48]

In the frugal atmosphere of the Eisenhower administration, allocating more people and money to African issues was a struggle. In 1955, a senior department official worried that opening new posts in Africa and adding more staff would mean curtailing activities elsewhere unless the department could wrest new money from Congress. The Congress was slow to act on State's request for an assistant secretary for African affairs. The House Committee on Foreign Affairs sat on the proposal for nearly a year and the full House failed to pass the necessary legislation the first time it came up for a vote. When the State Department inquired about the bill, a consultant to the Foreign Affairs Committee explained that the leadership feared that the bill would create an opportunity for members to snipe at the department. The committee was also concerned that the department had created a new position, deputy under secretary for administration. The committee thought that the department should shift the existing assistant secretary for administration position to African Affairs, rather than creating a new assistant secretary position.[49]

Despite the new status and resources, the Bureau of African Affairs remained the new kid on the block, and not a robust kid. African appointments carried less prestige and status within the department than appointments in Europe and elsewhere. In 1957, the department had more Foreign Service officers in West Germany than in all of Africa. Moreover, the bureau's leadership had limited experience in Africa. Joseph Satterthwaite, the first assistant secretary, had served in Syria and in the Office of Near Eastern Affairs before being named ambassador to Ceylon and then Burma.[50]

U.S. Policy

In November 1953, Dulles included a passage in his speech to the Congress of Industrial Organizations explaining the Eisenhower administration's policy towards dependent territories. Dulles contended that the administration was pushing for self-government more than it appeared on the surface. If the administration showed restraint, it was because it feared that independence would lead a colony to a captivity under communist control, worse than its current dependence. The United States had good reason, Dulles said, to side with the colonial powers. Nevertheless, it had not forgotten that it was the first colony to win its independence. The United States remained convinced that "the orderly transition from colonial to self-governing status should be carried resolutely to a completion."[51]

A few weeks earlier, the assistant secretary of state for Near East, South Asian and African affairs, Henry Byroade, devoted an entire speech to the same themes. Byroade proclaimed that the United States believed in the eventual self-determination of all peoples and that the evolutionary development toward self-determination should proceed with a minimum delay. Much blood and treasure would be saved if the Western nations hastened, rather than hampered, the process. Self-determination did not necessarily mean national independence, however. Territories could choose to unite themselves with their former colonial rulers. Nevertheless, colonialism was on its way out. The only question was what would replace it. Byroade also warned that independence could come too soon. The withdrawal of foreign control could create a power vacuum, an invitation to internal disorder and external aggression. Newly independent countries had to be strong enough, like India, Pakistan, and Ceylon, to resist Soviet imperialism. Independence alone would not cure all the colonies' problems. The colonies needed governments that would represent their interests, protect liberties, and promote economic and social progress. The United States, Byroade went on, could not disregard the colonial powers' interests without endangering its own security. The colonial powers had legitimate economic interests in their colonies. An evolutionary approach to self-determination would preserve such interests while providing the colonies with economic opportunities and benefits.[52]

Dulles's and Byroade's assumption that independence was in the distant future was consistent with the Eisenhower administration's analysis of nationalism in Africa. Early in the Eisenhower administration, the consensus within the U.S. intelligence community was that colonial rule in Africa would last at least another decade, despite increased nationalist activity. A 1953 National Intelligence Estimate and an earlier State Department report predicted that the Gold Coast would move towards self-government, as would Nigeria's Eastern and Western regions. These changes plus similar changes in the Sudan and Italian Somaliland would stimulate demands for self-government elsewhere. Despite the creation of the Central African Federation, friction between Africans and European settlers in East and Central Africa was likely, the reports predicted. The European settlers seemed unlikely to make the adjustments needed to meet African demands. The State Department paper maintained that the British were likely to accept settler dominance in Central Africa. Colonial governments lacked the means to satisfy African political and economic demands, but they had sufficient resources to maintain control for another ten years and to stifle large-scale revolutionary violence.[53]

State Department officials treated the Dulles and Byroade speeches as definitive statements of administration policy. When France and Belgium complained to Washington about statements by U.S. representatives in the Trusteeship Council, Edward Gerig, one of the representatives, explained to officials in Washington that the U.S. delegation was adhering to the line taken by Dulles and Byroade. Gerig wrote that members of the delegation kept copies of the speeches "constantly at our elbow" and measured their statements and questions against these "basic documents." Their statements had reflected Dulles's and Byroade's guidance, Gerig maintained. The United States favored self-determination, which might or might not mean independence. It worried about the dangers posed by premature independence. The U.S. wanted the colonial powers to move their dependent territories towards self-determination so that colonial issues would not divide the colonial powers from the other members of the "free world." Progress toward self-determination must be fast enough to satisfy the legitimate demands of local peoples but not so fast as to expose them to communist infiltration or aggression.[54]

Dulles's involvement in enunciating U.S. policy on colonial issues marked a change from Acheson's indifference. Nevertheless, Dulles's basic policies resembled earlier U.S. positions. Cordell Hull stressed that dependent territories should gain independence only when they were ready for it. George McGhee talked about the need for orderly development towards independence. Dulles's formulation retained the ambiguity of earlier U.S. pronouncements. Insisting on orderly and evolutionary development towards self-determination and warning of the dangers posed by premature independence while trumpeting the U.S. commitment to self-determination left a great deal to the listener's imagination.

Dulles's and Byroade's speeches made it hard to know what the U.S. intended to do regarding specific colonial issues. Byroade acknowledged as much in his presentation. He was speaking about French North Africa, but his words applied to all dependent territories. Byroade admitted that the United States faced a dilemma regarding the French colonies. He argued that the situation called for a middle-of-the-road policy that would permit U.S. officials to determine the country's position on practical issues as they arose. Gerig included a similar thought in his reply to the State Department. Regardless of the status of the Dulles and Byroade speeches as basic policy documents, Gerig suggested that the U.S. representatives at the United Nations meet with the relevant assistant secretaries and other officers to discuss tactics at the U.N.[55]

The next public statement of U.S. policy seemed less receptive to change than Dulles's or Byroade's. When George Allen, Byroade's successor as assistant secretary, addressed the American Academy of Political and Social Sciences in April 1956, he stated that application of the American traditional opposition to colonialism to Africa required "patient understanding" and "a high sense of responsibility." While the United States remained sympathetic to the colonies' desire for independence, Allen said that no one could doubt the benefits that colonial rule had brought to Africa. Allen was wary of nationalism. He said that the U.S. would encourage those elements of nationalism that contributed to genuine independence and stability. It would also attempt to curb those that were purely negative, anarchic, and disruptive. Allen also emphasized the need to preserve economic ties between the colonial powers and their colonies. The colonial powers should avoid precipitate grants of independence that would create power vacuums, he warned.[56]

Looking for a Better Policy

As in the Truman administration, the sense that the U.S. policy towards Africa and towards colonies was lacking prompted the State Department to embark on several policy-writing enterprises. The State Department cast its net widely, involving organizations within the department, as well as outside experts and State Department staff in the field. None of the efforts was successful in articulating more persuasive and cohesive policies or in gaining high-level approval.

In 1955, the Office of African Affairs produced a long memorandum on U.S. policy towards Africa south of the Sahara. The paper was intended for a planned conference of the principal State Department officials in Africa. The conference was eventually cancelled for lack of funds. The memorandum started with the familiar proposition that the U.S. found itself caught between its European allies and African nationalists. It went on to describe the Western orientation of nearly all African territories and America's current, limited stake in Africa: access to raw materials, military links with Liberia and Ethiopia, possible supply routes in a time of crisis. More than protecting such interests, the United States should aim to keep unfriendly powers out of Africa and to ensure that Africa evolve in a manner friendly to the U.S. Over the next decade, the colonial powers were likely to remain dominant, but pressure for change would mount, the memorandum predicted. African nationalism would increase. It would be emotional, exaggerated, and xenophobic. The memorandum anticipated that the United States would have to favor its European allies over any African group if forced to choose, and talked about shedding outworn notions about Africa and bringing order to policies that were adopted in "a fit of absent-mindedness." Nevertheless, all the memorandum offered was a "more independent" policy, a rejection of a "me too" attitude toward the colonial powers. This was not to be a revolutionary new policy, the paper said. It was to be an acceleration of what had been begun and creation of policy where none had existed. The principal concrete proposal was a slow, steady increase in the number of consulates and State Department staff in Africa.[57]

The Office of African Affairs' memorandum received a cool reception. Richard Jones, the consul in Monrovia, distinguished between anti-colonialism, which he thought was a negative force, and nationalism, a positive force. He suggested that the United States needed to appear more sympathetic to nationalism and to the colonial powers' stated commitment to African development if it wanted African states to favor the United States. Robert McGregor, consul in Leopoldville, thought that nationalism in Central Africa was superficial and ephemeral. Yet he warned that the United States would find itself without a policy that would appeal to Africans if it continued to tie itself to the colonial powers. Secretary Dulles read the paper and authorized further detailed studies, but he also characterized it as so general that it did not warrant his approval. Dulles's special assistant interpreted this to mean that Dulles did not want to be pinned down.[58]

In 1956, a paper entitled "A Reconsideration of U.S. Policy Toward Colonialism" emerged from the State Department's Policy Planning Staff. It was produced by a working group with members drawn from across the department. Much of the paper covered old ground. The paper argued that nationalist movements would achieve self-determination despite the colonial powers' resistance. Many dependent territories would choose to become independent states, the paper predicted. It recommended that the United States seek to facilitate orderly and peaceful movement towards self-determination while minimizing self-determination's adverse consequences for the colonial powers. The paper also recommended that the U.S. hold a high-level meeting with Britain to discuss the new policy. Once the United States had consulted with its allies, the president or the secretary of state should make a major address explaining the new policy. The paper recommended that the U.S. establish closer contacts with dependent peoples, especially leaders of bona fide nationalist movements. The paper defined bona fide nationalist movements as significant non-communist movements with growing local support highly likely to create a government tolerable to local peoples. If necessary, the U.S. should use covert means to develop ties with nationalist leaders. The United States should also alter its positions in the United Nations to allow a larger role for the U.N. in colonial disputes.[59]

The "Reconsideration" paper received an even cooler reception than the Office of African Affairs' paper. The Bureau of European Affairs participated in the working group, but refused to approve the paper's final version. The paper went forward to the secretary's office, accompanied by the Office of European Affairs' dissenting views. The European office argued that only results mattered. Nationalist movements would only be satisfied with independence. Expressions of sympathy and friendships would not buy the United States much. The U.S. would have to offer all-out support for nationalist aspirations. Short of offering nationalists military aid, the U.S. could employ only diplomatic means to promote self-determination. Given all the other issues where the United States wanted European cooperation, pursuing an independent approach to colonialism was not likely to succeed. The European office warned that the U.S. would be better off trying to bring the European powers along. The United States was not likely to gain anything in Asia or Africa that would make a policy shift worthwhile, the Bureau of European Affairs concluded.[60]

In the end, the paper appears not to have reached Dulles. After drafting a transmittal note, staff in Dulles's office changed their mind. They concluded that the paper was too complicated for the secretary to read and sent it back for revisions. Later, word came back from the Office of the Secretary that the paper had not gone forward. The Suez crisis and other difficulties made one of its principal recommendations, a high-level meeting with British officials, impractical.[61]

Dulles may not have been as troubled by the middle-of-the-road character of U.S. policy as were many of his subordinates. Or he was more adept at making lemonade from a lemon, at least rhetorically. In October 1956, Dulles told a press conference that the United States had a special role in the long-term shift from colonialism to independence. The U.S. sought to see that the process proceeded in a constructive, evolutionary way and neither halted nor took a violent revolutionary turn. Dulles said that the United States was unlikely to identify completely with either the colonial powers or the countries striving to become independent.[62]

At the same time that the State Department convened the working group to reconsider policies towards colonialism, Dulles had it establish a non-governmental group. The advisory group was to consider the problems that colonialism and colonial issues posed for the United

States and the policies that the U.S. had developed to deal with such problems. Dean Rusk, president of the Rockefeller Foundation, headed the group. The group suffered from the same sort of disagreement as the State Department experienced. One view, espoused by Rusk and others, was that the United States should do more to favor nationalists. The opposing view was that doing so would involve the U.S. in misguidedly supporting timetables for independence.[63]

Some State Department officers in Africa shared Dulles's avowed preference for a more energetic approach to Africa. Consuls stationed in Africa anticipated that political change might come to the African colonies sooner than many imagined. They pointed to increased Russian interest in anti-colonial and nationalist movements and to increased activity by African and Asian countries not aligned with either the United States or Russia. The conference of non-aligned nations at Bandung, Indonesia, in 1955 was the most obvious manifestation of such activity. Consuls in Nairobi and Leopoldville argued that the U.S. should continue to support the colonial powers and their efforts to move their colonies towards self-government. The United States also needed to take the initiative. If it did not, it might lose the allegiance of African peoples when they gained greater political powers. Edmund Dorz, the U.S. consul in Nairobi, recommended that the United States increase its presence in Africa and reach out to African leaders. He proposed opening more consulates and expanding U.S. information, education, and foreign assistance programs. Robert McGregor, in Leopoldville, wanted the United States to support nationalism more openly. At the same time, McGregor was skeptical about the prospects for African colonies. He thought that a federation of African colonies would be more viable than independent states. He proposed that the United States convene a conference of colonial powers to coordinate economic and political developments.[64]

Nixon and Africa

Vice President Richard Nixon took an interest in U.S. policy towards colonial Africa. Some time in late 1953 or early 1954, he asked that the National Security Council consider what problems in Africa, if any, the United States should address. In 1956, the State Department prepared a paper and an intelligence assessment for him outlining the problems associated with U.S. policy towards Africa.

In 1954, Nixon's interest elicited stock, perfunctory replies. The Department of Defense, the Central Intelligence Agency, the Foreign Operations Administration (responsible for U.S. foreign aid programs), and the Department of State said that an orderly and evolutionary transition from colonial rule in Africa to self-government was in U.S. interests. Defense noted that U.S. ability to influence events in Africa was limited. The CIA counseled minimizing differences with European allies over colonial policies. The State Department recommended avoiding extremes — supporting premature independence or "inexcusable procrastination" by the colonial powers. The National Security Council subsequently discarded the notion of a policy paper on Africa and concentrated its attention on unfolding events in the French North African colonies.[65]

The package assembled by the State Department for Nixon in 1956[66] described an Africa undergoing massive change. It predicted that the Gold Coast and Nigeria would soon become independent. Other British colonies — Uganda, Sierra Leone, and the Central African Federation — were on the same track. As nationalist movements sought to displace colonial governments, outbreaks of violence were likely, the paper warned. Among the British colonies, Kenya seemed the most likely location. Britain was the only colonial power committed to guiding its colonies to independence. It hoped to keep its former colonies within the commonwealth, the paper said.

African political movements were the principal driving force in the State Department's analysis. Nationalist movements were becoming strong enough to challenge the colonial governments. Colonial governments could point to nationalist leaders' weaknesses and failures. Whatever the failings of nationalist leaders, however, they tapped into local peoples' profound dissatisfaction with the colonial situation and determination to change it. The Mau Mau uprising in Kenya, the State Department's paper argued, demonstrated what happened when discontent found an outlet other than nationalism. Sheer desperation could propel Africans into any political movement — communist, totalitarian, or messianic — which promised land, status, and power through the violent overthrow of the existing order.

The State Department thought that Britain faced a dilemma in its East and Central African colonies. The European settler minorities sought to remain in control even as the colonies achieved their independence. Britain felt compelled to preserve the settlers' position until the African majority was willing to share political power on an equitable basis. Britain was unwilling, however, to entrust the African majority's fate to the settlers. Britain saw multiracial governments as the solution. The State Department doubted that such governments would represent both African and European interests. It thought the best the British could do was to press for legal safeguards for African rights and delay self-government for Kenya and the Federation of Rhodesia and Nyasaland.

In colonies where nationalist movements seemed destined to gain political power, the U.S. role should be that of a friendly bystander, the State Department recommended. The United States needed to expand its influence to ensure that the newly independent states remained friendly. In most of East and Central Africa, the State Department thought that Britain would grant independence to governments under European settler control. The State Department recommended that the United States encourage Britain's efforts to assemble coalitions of moderate Africans and Europeans to rule these colonies.

Responding to Events

Once the Gold Coast achieved its independence in 1957, U.S. policy towards Britain's African colonies began to change. The Sudan became independent before the Gold Coast, but U.S. officials considered Sudanese issues within the context of Egypt and the eastern Mediterranean. Once the British granted the Gold Coast its independence and Nkrumah began preaching independence for other colonies, U.S. leaders and officials concluded that African nationalism had achieved sufficient strength that the British colonies in Africa would gain their independence in the near future. The colonies would become independent regardless of their political stability, their capacity to govern themselves, or their economic viability. Since the newly independent states were likely to be poor and weak, U.S. policymakers feared that they would be ripe targets for Russian or Chinese blandishments. They concluded that the United States needed to increase its presence in Africa and prepare to compete with its rivals for the alliance of the newly independent states.

Vice President Nixon represented the United States at Ghana's independence ceremony, visiting several other countries on his trip. When Nixon returned to Washington, he recommended to Eisenhower that the U.S. increase its presence in Africa's independent states. In addition to Ghana, Nixon discussed Liberia, Egypt, Ethiopia, Libya, and Sudan. Nixon proposed that the Department of Defense and the International Cooperation Administration, the principal U.S. foreign aid organization, make African states a higher priority. The State Department should assign more and better qualified staff to its African posts. The United States should, Nixon wrote, extend moderate amounts of technical and economic assistance to newly independent states in Africa.[67]

Nixon's visit to Ghana demonstrated that, as much as the United States wanted to concentrate on the independent African states, it had to contend with the British. When it became known that Nixon would attend the Ghanaian independence celebration, the Foreign Office voiced concerns about the tone the vice president would adopt. The Foreign Office was afraid that Nixon would indulge in anti-colonial rhetoric. The Foreign Office warned such talk might stimulate calls for independence elsewhere in Africa, and serve Russian aims. The Foreign Office recommended that Nixon portray Ghana's independence as a testimonial to the wisdom and beneficence of British colonial policy. Nixon included kind words about the British in his Accra remarks and British officials interpreted them as support for their policies.[68]

In early 1958, Julius Holmes, Dulles's special assistant, returned from a ten-week tour of Africa with thoughts similar to Nixon's.[69] Holmes's immediate recommendations were for a multilateral aid program for Africa and enhanced Foreign Service staffing. Holmes proposed that the United States adopt a more active approach. Events were moving fast in Africa, he wrote. The U.S. needed to plan, anticipate problems, and avoid the need to carry out expensive and inefficient rescue operations.

Nevertheless, Holmes was pessimistic about Africa's future. The movement toward independence was strong and accelerating, he warned. A few thoughtful African leaders realized that there was too much haste and too little preparation, but were in no position to stem the tide. They were often captives of their own actions, declarations, and ambitions, Homes wrote. The reigning sentiment, according to Holmes, was: "Better the ragged shirt of independence than the warm blanket of colonial protection." All the dependent territories would achieve independence. Before they created political, economic, and social systems that met their needs and preserved democracy and individual liberty, however, African states were likely to suffer through a long period of uncertainty, bad management, retrogression, and conflict, Holmes conceded.

Nationalist movements were in the hands of moderates, Holmes told Dulles. The United States and the colonial powers needed to gain the confidence of such nationalist leaders so that they could counsel moderation and patience. African peoples expected nationalist leaders to produce economic and social improvement. The United States and the colonial powers could support nationalist leaders by providing aid and promoting private investment.

Russia and its allies were positioned to claim the allegiance of newly independent African states, Holmes warned. Holmes saw the U.S. playing a key role in preserving Africa for Europe. The United States needed to work with its allies, especially those with African colonies, to blunt the Russian threat. The United States needed to get its allies to understand its African objectives and to trust its motives.

Holmes was not the first to describe nationalist leaders as moderates or advocate a policy of supporting moderates. The term appeared frequently in U.S. and British documents regarding Africa. It appeared so often and in so many contexts as to be almost meaningless.

It seemed to mean leaders thought to be friendly or open to negotiation. African leaders thought to be extremists at one point could become moderates and vice versa. "Moderate" appeared to mean non-communist, but usually in the sense of not friendly with Russia or China, not in any ideological sense. A 1958 State Department paper offered a more rigorous definition. It suggested that the department was at least as concerned about stability in Africa as it was on competing with the Russians and their ideology. The paper described several categories of African political groups, distinguished by their attitudes towards change: traditionalist, conservative modernist, and radical modernist. The paper argued that any group could split into moderate and extreme factions. Moderate groups favored moderate tactics. Extreme groups favored drastic, violent tactics. The paper argued that the more the colonial power resisted the independence struggle the larger the role an extreme faction played in the nationalist movement and the more drastic the tactics adopted by the movement.[70]

With African colonies on the path to independence, Africa assumed new importance within the U.S. foreign policy apparatus. National Security Council staff coordinated the development of several high-level policy documents. The council discussed and Eisenhower approved them. Eisenhower and his closest advisers discussed policy towards Africa. The intelligence community forecasted developments in the region in National Intelligence Estimates.

The focus was on U.S. relations with the newly independent states. The National Security Council was concerned about increasing Russian and Chinese involvement in Africa, for example, Russian trade with Ghana. It discussed reactions to Russian initiatives. It debated whether the United States should be content that African states remain neutral in any competition between Russia and the United States. Eisenhower and his advisers concluded that financial and technical assistance should be an important part of U.S. efforts to woo the new African states. They debated how much aid was appropriate and how the U.S. should coordinate its aid efforts with the programs conducted by the former colonial powers. After the outbreak of disorder in the former Belgian Congo, U.S. officials considered the possibility of United States intervention in Africa and the circumstances under which it might be needed.

U.S. policymakers assumed that independence was imminent and left U.S. policy regarding the process leading to independence unchanged. The first National Security Council report on Africa, NSC 5719/1, adopted by the council and approved by Eisenhower in August 1957, included the same language about gaining independence that appeared in earlier documents. The report said that the United States favored the principle of self-determination, as long as the process was orderly and people seeking independence were ready to discharge the responsibilities it involved. The paper retained a reference to self-government as an alternative to independence and mentioned the dangers of premature independence. The report stated that U.S. policy was to support the colonial powers' policies and actions that led to independence and to avoid identification with policies or actions that were stagnant or repressive. The United States, the paper said, would support nationalist movements that looked likely to succeed. It would use public statements by U.S. officials, visits by prominent U.S. officials to Africa, visits by influential Africans to the United States, and general public and private sympathy for colonial peoples' desire for greater self-government.[71]

The general mood of Eisenhower and his top advisers was more resignation than enthusiasm about the prospect of more independent African states. In 1958, when the National

Security Council considered revisions to NSC 5719/1, Eisenhower wondered whether the United States could not focus on education and development and leave the colonial powers to prepare the colonies for independence. He acknowledged several officials' concerns about offending the colonial powers. Nevertheless, he said that he would like the United States to be on the side of the natives for once, rather than slow down independence. Regardless of the risks of jeopardizing relations with the colonial powers by supporting the right to independence, the United States, Eisenhower concluded, had to go along with the trend toward independence.[72]

For all Eisenhower's misgivings, recognizing that independence was near at hand represented a shift in U.S. thinking. As late as October 1956, Dulles told a press conference that the process of moving from colonialism to independence might last for another fifty years.[73]

As events unfolded in Africa, particularly in the Congo, the mood in Washington grew darker. At a January 1960 National Security Council meeting, Eisenhower agreed with an assessment that none of the African colonies about to become independent was capable of governing itself. He said that allowing colonies to become independent before carrying out economic development was putting the cart before the horse. Nixon observed that it was naïve to think that independent African states would be democratic. Some of the peoples of Africa had been out of the trees for only fifty years, he said. Eisenhower and Secretary of the Treasury Robert Anderson agreed that the United States might be better off trying to deal with strong men in Africa. The U.S. might take the same approach it had followed in the Philippines where a United States army officer, Edward Lansdale, operated as President Magsaysay's chief adviser. In July 1960, after conditions in the Congo worsened, Eisenhower told Secretary of State Christian Herter, who had replaced the terminally ill Dulles in April 1959, that he hoped the Congo situation made other African colonies rethink their desire for independence.[74]

As U.S. policymakers accepted the inevitability of independence, their public statements changed. During 1957, speeches by Dulles and senior State Department officials stressed the dangers of premature independence while proclaiming United States support for self-determination. In October 1958, Joseph Satterthwaite, the new assistant secretary for African affairs, left out any references to premature independence when he gave a major speech on U.S. policy. Dulles included the old formula in a November 1958 speech, but coupled it with a warmer tone towards independence. Dulles said that the United States had encouraged the movement towards independence and rejoiced in it. In April 1960, Satterthwaite proclaimed that peoples acquired independence, whether they were ready or not, on their own timetable. In October, Satterthwaite said that the United States welcomed every step by colonial powers that promoted readiness for self-government.[75]

Throughout the Eisenhower administration, the United States sought the middle ground regarding British Africa, a way to support Britain and remain on friendly terms with African nationalists. The U.S. was willing to risk a serious breach with its British ally over the Suez invasion to preserve its anti-colonial credentials. At the same time, the U.S. stuck to familiar positions even as the pace of political change in Africa accelerated. Eventually, the emergence of independent African states prompted the United States to anticipate a new era in which it would compete with others, particularly Russia and China, for the friendship of independent African states.

Colonialism in the United Nations During the Eisenhower Years, 1953–1960: Still in the Middle

Throughout Eisenhower's administration, colonial issues remained a prominent and contentious part of the United Nations agenda. The time and attention paid to colonialism and its fruits by the U.N. probably increased over the course of the 1950s. The admission of additional newly independent states, particularly after 1955, contributed to the trend. During the Eisenhower administration, the United States clung to a middle-of-the-road policy, trying to stay on friendly terms with both the colonial and anti-colonial nations in the U.N. In most instances, the United States was willing to risk upsetting its British allies in the process. The principal exception came at the end of the Eisenhower regime when the U.S. voted against an anti-colonial measure with broad support.

The colonial issues that the United Nations considered in the Eisenhower years included both the familiar and the novel. Many dealt with dependent territories generally. Some of the most contentious concerned individual territories, particularly France's possessions in North Africa. What information should the United Nations collect about dependent territories? Who should review such information? What recommendations should the U.N. make after reviewing such information? Did nations have a right to determine their own political status? Should such a right be included in a U.N. declaration on human rights? Should representatives of colonial peoples be included in the colonial powers' delegations to the United Nations? Should U.N. bodies hear oral petitions from representatives of colonial peoples? Should the colonial powers be required to set timetables for bringing their colonies to self-government or independence? Were Tunisia, Morocco and Algeria entitled to independence?

The divisions within the United Nations over colonial issues remained unchanged from the Truman years. The states that administered dependent territories, especially Britain, France, and Belgium, resisted any U.N. role. They saw it as interference in their internal affairs. Most other United Nations members were opposed to colonialism. For countries like Egypt, India and the Philippines, anti-colonialism was important. They generated proposals designed to use the U.N. as a lever to break up the European colonial empires. Russia and its closest allies attempted to curry favor with the anti-colonial nations and embarrass the colonial powers by introducing their own anti-colonial measures. Intent on holding together a broad anti–Russian coalition, the United States inhabited a middle ground between the colonial powers and their adversaries.

A Middle-of-the-Road Policy

The United States sought compromises intended to avoid a break between its European allies and the bulk of the U.N. membership while bolstering its own proclaimed support for self-determination. In 1955, Asian countries proposed that the Special Committee on Information be made permanent and that representatives of colonial peoples be part of the committee. The colonial powers were opposed. The United States proposed instead that the committee's life be extended for another three years. The administering powers should be invited to include representatives of colonial peoples in their delegations, the U.S. argued. The United States opposed, unsuccessfully, including the right of self-determination in the U.N. declaration of human rights. The U.S. thought it had regained lost ground by persuading the United Nations to begin a program of reports on human rights, over the objections of the colonial powers. When Britain threatened to walk out of the Special Committee on Information in 1955 if the committee were allowed to make recommendations on problems that occurred in several territories, the United States worked to have the offending resolution withdrawn. Before votes on contentious anti-colonial measures, U.S. representatives often spoke in favor of whatever general principle was at the heart of the resolution, but abstained on the vote.[1]

The United States was more comfortable with statements of general principles than with resolutions aimed at individual territories. It was one thing to support a general principle to be implemented in the future. It was another to join in public efforts to force a U.S. ally to loosen its hold on a colony. Efforts by the anti-colonial powers to push France to free its North African possessions, in particular, put the U.S. delegations in a bind. The U.S. position was that the United Nations had little to offer in the dispute between France and its colonies. France was capable of dealing with the problem. The best forum for resolving the issue was private negotiations between France and her colonies, the U.S. contended. The anti-colonial states persisted, however. In 1953, for the first time, the U.S. found itself voting to keep an issue, the status of Morocco, off the Security Council's agenda. The U.S. made the narrow argument that the Moroccan situation was not a threat to international peace and security. The United States abstained or voted against every U.N. resolution between 1955 and 1960 aimed at mediating the conflict between France and the Algerian nationalists.[2]

The State Department explained the U.S. voting record in the United Nations by maintaining that the U.S. sought constructive solutions and judged each issue on its merits. In 1959, after a Ghanaian representative to the United Nations criticized the U.S. role within the U.N., the State Department provided the embassy in Accra and the U.S. delegation in New York with a defense of the U.S. record. The U.S. opposed the colonial powers on several issues, the department asserted, including the participation of colonial peoples in the Trusteeship Council and the establishment of intermediate target dates leading to self-government. On other issues, the transmission of information about dependent territories and the establishment of final target dates, the United States opposed resolutions proposed by non-administering countries. In the General Assembly, administering and non-administering countries adopted extreme positions, the department claimed. The U.S. sought to play a moderating role. Sometimes, it voted with the administering powers. Sometimes, it sided with their critics. When the General Assembly established committees over U.S. objections, the United States volunteered to serve on the committees in order, the State Department wrote, to make a constructive contribution. The U.S. made every effort to support the recommendations of U.N. visiting missions to trust territories and other fact-finding groups. Such small and carefully chosen bodies could collect facts and make recommendations regarding difficult technical issues.[3]

Ill Ease at the State Department

State Department officials, particularly the staff responsible for U.N. issues, were unhappy with the U.S. record. While it might be described as middle-of-the-road or balanced, it seemed uncertain and erratic to some officials. Agreeing with one side and then the other was untidy. It was potentially ineffective, some State Department officials thought. The United States could not expect to win popularity contests with its usual stance on colonial issues in the U.N., they argued. In attempting to please everyone, the U.S. risked pleasing no one, the argument went. Moreover, resolving every colonial issue in the United Nations on its merits generated contention within the department, usually between the staff most directly involved with the U.N. and those responsible for dealing with the colonial powers. State Department officials involved with the U.N. argued that the United States should move towards the positions advocated by the anti-colonial states. If the task were assembling a majority within the U.N., linking the U.S. to the handful of colonial powers was a handicap. State Department staff in the Bureau of European Affairs expressed similar concerns about the country's apparent vacillation between pro-colonial and anti-colonial positions in the United Nations. Their solution was, however, for the United States to guide and channel and, where necessary, resist the efforts of the anti-colonial majority, without alienating the majority and without abandoning U.S. adherence to self-determination and self-government.[4]

The several attempts to write a U.S. policy on Africa were, in part, attempts to devise a different policy regarding colonial issues in the United Nations. During the Eisenhower administration, the State Department carried out similar exercises focused on the United Nations. The results were the same, nonetheless. Dramatically different recommendations were not forthcoming. A 1956 paper recommended that the U.S. consult more thoroughly with other nations before U.N. sessions. The United States should revert to its former practice of agreeing to allow the U.N. to discuss almost any colonial issue, even issues that were likely to elicit a U.S. vote in opposition to a U.N. majority. The United States should favor establishment of intermediate target dates. The State Department papers did not produce dramatic changes in U.S. behavior in the United Nations, however. At the end of the Eisenhower administration, State Department portrayals of the U.S. record in the United Nations sounded similar to such portrayals from the beginning of the administration. A State Department assessment of the 1960 Trusteeship Council session portrayed the United States as the most liberal of the administering powers and as exerting a liberalizing influence on other administering powers. Nevertheless, the assessment continued, the United States voted with the other administering states on most controversial issues because their positions were more in line with U.S. objectives.[5]

Lodge and Sears

Criticism of the U.S. stance on colonial issues in the United Nations during the Eisenhower administration was not confined to career staff in the State Department. Two key political appointees, Henry Cabot Lodge, Jr., the U.S. ambassador to the United Nations, and Mason Sears, the U.S. representative to the Trusteeship Council, grew dissatisfied with U.S. policy and pressed for changes.

Lodge was an influential figure within the Republican Party. In 1936, Lodge was elected to the U.S. Senate from Massachusetts, the only successful Republican senatorial candidate that year. He won re-election in 1942 and, after resigning to serve in the army, again in 1946. Lodge was a leader among moderate Republicans, uncomfortable with Robert Taft heading the Republican ticket in 1952. He played an important role in recruiting Eisenhower as the Republican candidate for president and served as Eisenhower's campaign manager. Lodge lost a close re-election contest to John F. Kennedy in 1952. Eisenhower rewarded Lodge by naming him ambassador to the United Nations and raising the position to cabinet rank. Cabinet rank allowed Lodge to communicate directly with Eisenhower without going through the State Department.

Lodge viewed the United Nations as an arena in which the U.S. competed with Russia for the allegiance of other countries. Lodge began his tenure at the United Nations believing that it had not been created as a debating society on colonialism. He came to believe, however, that the United States had to alter its policies regarding colonialism if it were to compete with Russia. Most of the world was non-white, Lodge told Eisenhower's cabinet, and, emotionally, found itself on the Russian side because the U.S. so often supported the colonial powers. On at least two occasions, Lodge proposed significant changes in U.S. policy intended to attract the support of the non-colonial or anti-colonial nations.[6]

In 1956, Lodge wrote to Eisenhower and Dulles that the United States was losing the support of young people around the globe because of its apparent sympathy for the colonial powers. The U.S. needed to become more anti-colonial. Lodge argued that the European empires could not last. Moreover, the colonial powers had no alternative but to ally themselves with the U.S. Lodge suggested that Eisenhower recommend to Congress that it set a timetable for granting U.S. possessions self-government. He proposed that the United States introduce a resolution in the U.N. calling on the colonial powers to establish similar timetables within the next ten years.[7]

In 1959, Lodge addressed a similar plea to Dulles. Lodge pointed to the accelerating growth of nationalism in Africa. Africans had seized the initiative from the colonial powers, Lodge argued. If the U.S. was to win the nationalists' goodwill, it needed to do more. Lodge proposed that the United States reach out to nationalist leaders; bring more influential Africans to the United States; and appoint a special representative to call upon on African leaders to make the U.S. case.[8]

Lodge was no more successful than his career subordinates in shifting U.S. policies. In 1956, Dulles told Lodge that he and Eisenhower had often discussed a change in the public position on colonialism. Nevertheless, Dulles thought that the time was not ripe. Apparently, Dulles replied without consulting with Eisenhower. A few days after Lodge received Dulles's answer, Eisenhower wrote back to say that he would give the idea serious consideration. He would discuss it with Dulles at the first opportunity. In 1959, the notion of a special representative to Africa gained no support among State Department officials on the continent. The consul in Nairobi thought that a special representative would have to make public statements to be effective. Public statements would be disruptive, however, and the administering powers would object to U.S. interference. Open United States support for accelerated movement towards independence would undermine moderate African groups in colonies like Tanganyika and Kenya and upset the colonies' precarious stability. The State Department put Lodge's proposal aside.[9]

Mason Sears, the U.S. representative to the Trusteeship Council, was not content to lobby for changes behind the scenes. Sears was related to Lodge by marriage and served as his campaign manager. Lodge picked Sears for the Trusteeship Council because of his political skills. Colonial issues required a politically astute mind to protect U.S. interests, Lodge thought. Sears concluded that U.S. policies toward colonialism were flawed. He too suggested changes to policy and was, in fact, the source for Lodge's 1958 proposals. Sears used his seat on the Trusteeship Council to issue a series of public statements supportive of political change in Africa.[10]

Sears, in his memoirs, described frustration with the State Department's inability to discard its fears about offending the country's European allies. Sears told Lodge that agreeing to the colonial powers' pleas and reversing traditional support for self-determination would not win the United States any friends. Sears thought that Dulles was right in seeking a more independent approach to colonial issues. Nevertheless, Sears judged that the State Department and successive assistant secretaries could not turn Dulles's insight into meaningful and effective policies. In major public pronouncements, State Department officials felt compelled to hedge the U.S. commitment to self-determination with so many caveats and concerns that the commitment became meaningless. Sears placed much of the blame on the Bureau of European Affairs. It opposed, Sears contended, any U.S. support for African nationalists.[11]

Confronted with the State Department's inability or unwillingness to devise different policies, Sears decided that staking out a public position supportive of nationalism was the solution. He told a State Department official that the United States needed to issue a constant stream of statements that would be a catalyst in the colonial situation. The U.S. should make sure its position was known and understood and the Trusteeship Council was the right forum for doing so. "The right man in the right place at the right time" could get the United States out of the hole it had dug for itself, Sears claimed. In Sears's time on the Trusteeship Council, he took almost every opportunity to portray U.S. policy as supportive of African nationalism.[12]

Sears's outspoken approach disturbed career State Department officials. Robert McGregor, consul in Leopoldville, thought that Sears was sincere in his desire to push U.S. policy toward self-determination, but McGregor also thought that Sears was bitter about British attempts to discredit him. Sears was naïve in believing that British public opinion favored Colonial Office policies, MacGregor thought. John Barrow, the consul in Nairobi, was less kind. Barrow objected to Sears's habit of describing U.S. policy in bold terms and omitting the many caveats and qualifications the State Department had developed. Barrow contended that Sears's approach antagonized local British officials who were trying to move Africans towards genuine self-government. It raised false hopes among Africans. It was difficult to explain why Sears's statements in the Trusteeship Council seemed to differ from official U.S. policy, Barrow wrote.[13]

Similar concerns emerged higher up the State Department chain of command. In 1955, David Key, assistant secretary for international organization affairs, reported to Deputy Undersecretary Robert Murphy about a meeting with Sears. According to Key, Sears believed that the United States should make friends with Africans even if it meant irritating the colonial powers. Key explained to Sears that the department wanted to make friends with Africans without, however, alienating the country's European allies. It was admittedly a difficult task, requiring the greatest tact and diplomacy. Key reported that he had pointed out to Sears that U.S. policy on colonial issues often represented a compromise among the state, interior, and defense departments. Policies the cabinet departments could agree to reflected what was practical, safe, right, and diplomatically expedient.[14]

British officials objected to Sears and his speeches. In his memoirs, Sears recounted with considerable glee an episode in the Trusteeship Council. Sir Andrew Cohen, the British representative, repeatedly nudged his shoulder in an attempt to get Sears to cut short a speech. Sears finally asked Cohen to stop so that he could complete his statement. The British were upset when, as a member of a 1954 U.N. visiting mission to Tanganyika, Sears voted with the members from India and El Salvador to recommend a timetable for self-government. Roger Makins, Britain's ambassador in Washington, met with Dulles to complain. Dulles admitted that he thought Sears was naïve. He later directed that Sears make a clarifying statement to reassure the British.[15]

For the Colonial Office, Sears remained a dangerous nuisance. A British representative at the U.N. told a colleague in London that he could make predictions about improved U.S. conduct only with great diffidence "since the unaccountable Mason Sears was very much in evidence and while he is about the place nobody can tell what is going to happen next." Colonial Secretary Alan Lennox-Boyd thought that outside support emboldened African nationalists. Outside support usually meant support in the United States, and in and around the United Nations. If the United States wanted to promote orderly advance in the colonies, it had to consider the consequences of its actions and speeches. Sears's positions on Tanganyika and his speeches in the Trusteeship Council, Lennox-Boyd complained, disturbed a situation previously characterized by racial harmony and well-balanced political progress.[16]

Nonetheless, Sears's activities did not alter U.S. positions on key colonial issues. The United States opposed every resolution in the General Assembly proposed by the Trusteeship Council between 1957 and 1959 that recommended steps leading to independence for trust territories. Sears remained the U.S. representative in the Trusteeship Council, however. He continued to speak out in favor of nationalism. Sears's statements and speeches were a convenient way for the United States to signal its commitment to self-determination without compromising important policies. In tolerating Sears's behavior as a loose cannon, the Eisenhower administration was following a pattern set by Roosevelt when he had Wendell Willkie tour the world and make speeches attacking colonialism.[17]

United States–Great Britain Exchanges

Throughout the Eisenhower administration, State Department and Foreign Office officials met each year to discuss the colonial issues anticipated in the upcoming United Nations session. Neither country changed its fundamental approach and, for the most part, the two sides talked past each other. The disagreements about colonial issues remained unresolved. In 1950, the department identified thirty issues as involving significant differences between Britain and the United States. In 1955, a State Department official noted that colonialism was one of a handful where important differences remained.[18]

U.S. officials explained to their British counterparts that they could not support many British positions in the United Nations. The United States believed that nationalism would prevail. While the U.S. was not interested in supplanting any of the colonial powers, it would not join in suppressing or discouraging bona fide nationalist movements. The colonial world had become the principal battleground in the competition between Russia and the United States and the U.S. had to adopt policies that would appeal to colonial peoples. On some issues, distancing the country from the British position was necessary to gain the friendship of anti-colonial countries, U.S. officials argued. U.S. officials advised their British counterparts that more flexibility and moderation might help Britain's cause in the United Nations. It might motivate the anti-colonial members to soften their criticisms. The British ought to work harder to explain to the U.N. their successes in moving colonies towards self-government.[19]

British officials questioned the value of allowing the U.N. to consider colonial issues. Regarding the Special Committee on Information, Britain had tried to cooperate by including educational and economic experts in its delegation, they claimed. Most U.N. members were not interested in the wellbeing of colonial peoples, the British insisted. They were more interested in having the United Nations supervise all dependent territories, even if it meant interfering in Britain's internal affairs and endangering the colonies' progress toward self-government. British officials advised their U.S. colleagues that it was a mistake to create the impression that the United States was interested in Africa only to exclude the Russians. The U.S. needed to demonstrate real concern for Africans as Africans and for the advantages of close relationships between the U.S. and African countries. Trying to outbid the Russians would weaken the colonial powers' position, decrease the chances of installing stable regimes in Africa, and increase the chances of communist subversion, British officials complained.[20]

The ambiguity at the heart of U.S. policy toward Britain's African colonies made it difficult for State Department officials to take a firm line with their British counterparts and reduced the value of their annual meetings. According to a Colonial Office account of the 1955 meetings in Washington, Edward Gerig began his presentation with the assertion that people in the United States reacted negatively to situations where one people ruled another. A British official interjected that he thought many in the U.S. favored the sentiments included in Henry Byroade's 1953 speech. The U.S. would not give the colonial powers a blank check, but would not support colonial agitations without examining the facts, Byroade had said. The United States and Britain, the official continued, did not disagree on principles, only on timing. Gerig had to concede that an orderly transition to self-government figured prominently in official U.S. statements, and in U.S. public opinion.[21]

The inability to cooperate meaningfully with Britain on colonial issues annoyed U.S. officials. They bemoaned their repeated failures to persuade the British to make more of what the U.S. considered accomplishments in the colonies. They lamented that, when criticized, Britain and the other administering powers adopted positions that were more rigid. State Department officials thought it unfortunate that Britain and the United States often voted differently on colonial issues. U.S. officials blamed the anti-colonial states for introducing bitterness and suspicion into colonial debates. At the same time, they accused the colonial powers of being so accustomed to resisting perceived interference that they opposed U.N. resolutions consistent with their own colonial policies.[22]

British officials thought that U.S. positions were more realistic than they had been immediately after World War II. They thought that the United States tacitly supported British colonial policies and they acknowledged that Britain would be much worse off if the U.S. withdrew this tacit support. Nonetheless, British officials resented U.N. involvement in colonial issues. A senior Foreign Office official told Eden that abolishing the Trusteeship Council would do nothing but good for the British colonies. British officials thought the U.S. unwillingness to join in the British struggle to fend off United Nations interference was illogical and hypocritical. The U.S. admitted that many U.N. debates over colonial issues were pointless. Why would it not agree to block discussion of political developments in individual territories or recommendations about individual territories? British officials charged the State Department with wishful thinking at the expense of others. They doubted that the State Department could draw closer to Britain on essential colonial issues and emphasize in the United Nations a certain aloofness from the colonial powers.[23]

Timetables for Independence

Timetables for independence were the U.N. issue most relevant to the fate of Britain's African colonies. The critical target date was for the granting of self-government or independence, but the issue encompassed other intermediate target dates. Such target dates could involve the establishment of a common voting roll, the introduction of direct elections, or the delegation of increased powers to regional or local governments. The timetable issue exemplified U.S. efforts to position itself between the colonial powers and their critics in the United Nations. It provided evidence that the British objected to such efforts even when the United States offered assurances that it was engaging in tactical maneuvers, not altering its basic policies.

As early as 1952, India, the Philippines, and other countries proposed resolutions in the General Assembly calling for timetables. The 1953 resolution adopted by the assembly called upon the colonial powers to indicate in their annual reports to the Trusteeship Council how soon they expected their trust territories to gain self-government or independence. In 1953, the assembly reaffirmed the resolution and added a provision calling upon administering countries to provide information about the success of their efforts to move trust territories toward self-government. In 1955 and 1956, the assembly considered and approved similar resolutions. In 1956, the Trusteeship Council adopted the recommendations of its visiting mission to Tanganyika. The recommendations included the establishment of intermediate target dates.[24]

The U.S. did not vote for any of the timetable resolutions. It abstained on the first two and voted against the others. During the debate on the 1956 resolution, however, Edward Gerig announced that the United States supported the establishment of intermediate target dates, for the achievement of economic, social, and educational goals and goals related to political advancement. Such goals, Gerig said, could promote an atmosphere of understanding and confidence in which the trust territories could move rapidly and harmoniously ahead. Gerig praised British achievements in the colonies. He also reaffirmed U.S. opposition to long-range dates for independence. Long-range dates were too rigid, he said. They could not achieve anything that intermediate dates could not.[25]

The new U.S. position reflected the pressure from Lodge, Sears, and career staff for greater accommodation of the anti-colonial states' views. As U.S. officials explained to their British counterparts, the United States needed to adopt policies that would gain the sympathies of colonial peoples. It was better, the U.S. thought, to act too soon rather than too late. Differences between the United States and Britain on such issues were good, U.S. officials claimed. They demonstrated a flexibility of approach and independence of thought on the part of the United States. U.S. interests, and British and French interests, were not served by the country's appearing to be an out-and-out defender of the colonial system. After the British protested United States support for intermediate target dates, Dulles attempted to soothe them with the assurance that the country's immediate aims were to undercut more radical proposals and to channel the debate about timetables into a rational and manageable form.[26]

Dulles's explanation did not appease British officials. Sir Alan Burns, one of Britain's representatives at the United Nations, argued that timed political development was unthinkable because it would be absolute guesswork and had no any factual or physical basis. Lord Perth characterized intermediate timetables as a rigid and unrealistic doctrine. He told Macmillan that such compromises could only undermine the administering powers' authority. London's instructions to its U.N. delegation were that it should oppose timetables of any kind in public or private talks with the United States. The lesson, London wrote, was that the British would have to "watch the Americans as closely as ever" and indicate clearly that Britain opposed compromise solutions of such colonial issues.[27]

If Dulles and the State Department expected that embracing intermediate target dates would change the debate at the United Nations, they were disappointed. In 1957, 1958, and 1959, the General Assembly debated and passed resolutions instructing states administering trust territories to set final target dates. The United States voted against all the resolutions.[28]

U.N. Resolution 1514

At the end of the Eisenhower administration, a U.N. resolution on colonialism exposed, in a painful way, the difficulties of the country's middle-of-the-road approach to colonialism. In September 1960, Russia introduced a resolution in the General Assembly that called for immediate independence for all colonial territories. The resolution failed to gain even a simple majority. Nevertheless, forty-three African and Asian nations introduced their own resolution, intended to separate the colonial issue from the rivalry between Russia and the United States. The State Department, especially the delegation to the United Nations, recommended that the U.S. vote for the resolution. Secretary of State Herter was inclined to agree, although reluctantly. Eisenhower went along, but when Macmillan wrote him a letter in protest, he instructed the State Department to have the United States abstain. The General Assembly passed the resolution eighty-nine to zero, with nine abstentions (the United States, Australia, Great Britain, the Dominican Republic, France, Portugal, Spain and South Africa). The U.S. delegation to the General Assembly was appalled. One member stood and joined in the cheers when the General Assembly passed the resolution. Another charged that the United States was allowing Russia and its allies to champion the cause of colonial peoples.[29]

The resolution introduced by the African and Asian nations, the "Declaration on the Granting of Independence to Colonial Countries and Peoples" (U.N. Resolution 1514), was hortatory only. It stated the sense of the General Assembly, without mandating any actions by its members. The declaration proclaimed the necessity of ending colonialism. It said that colonialism was contrary to the United Nations charter and an impediment to world peace and cooperation. All peoples had the right to self-determination, the declaration stated. They had the right to determine their political status and pursue their economic, social, and educational development. Armed action or repressive measures directed against dependent peoples should cease, the declaration stated. Immediate steps should be taken to transfer power in all dependent territories to their inhabitants.

Most of the State Department was willing to have the U.S. vote for the resolution. It was so broadly worded that it was compatible with U.S. attacks on what it characterized as communist or Soviet colonialism, some staff thought. The resolution was sure to pass, moreover. A U.S. abstention would serve no purpose, they argued. A vote in favor might, however, gain favor with the General Assembly majority. The United States proposed amendments to the resolution. Nevertheless, it accepted the sponsors' position that they would have to consider Russian amendments if they entertained the proposed changes of the U.S. Doing so might make the resolution worse from a U.S. perspective. To appease the colonial powers, the American delegation planned to employ its familiar tactic of criticizing any objectionable language in the resolution before voting for it.[30]

Staff in the Bureau of European Affairs was opposed to the resolution. It was intrinsically bad, one staffer wrote. It embodied principles the United States had opposed and ignored principles the U.S. had espoused. It assumed that only the desire for independence was relevant, not a territory's capacity to maintain it. It set independence as the only goal, regardless of the unsuitability of many areas for independence and the charter's language about self-government, the Bureau of European Affairs claimed. The United States needed to disabuse the Asian and African countries of the notion that they could steamroller the United Nations whenever they chose to. The U.S. should make it plain, the staffer concluded, that it was not prepared to support absurdities simply because the absurdities were widely proclaimed.[31]

After Herter briefed Eisenhower about the impending vote, Eisenhower was willing to accept the State Department's recommendation. Herter explained the disagreements within the State Department. He reported that the British were very much opposed and said he could understand why Eisenhower might favor an abstention. In part because the resolution was hortatory, Herter recommended a vote in favor. Eisenhower replied that the U.S. might as well go along with the resolution. He insisted, however, that the delegation make clear various American objections to the resolution's wording.[32]

Herter had discussed the impending vote with Ambassador Caccia and revealed the misgivings about the resolution. Caccia informed London, observing that this was a subject on which the U.S. was traditionally governed by emotion rather than common sense. Macmillan wrote to Eisenhower pleading for a U.S. abstention. Macmillan argued that criticizing the resolution but voting for it would gain the U.S. little credit. The U.S. failure to stand with Britain would discourage the British officials. They were working hard to promote peaceful development in the colonies and to keep communism out. Britain and the United States ought, Macmillan wrote, to disassociate themselves from a resolution that had no connection with reality.[33]

Macmillan won Eisenhower over. Eisenhower told Herter that the U.S. had to yield to the views of its strongest ally. Eisenhower instructed Herter to have the delegation explain its reasons for abstention.[34]

Eisenhower's decision stands in contrast to his earlier position that the U.S. should distance itself from Britain and its colonial policies. Macmillan's Britain was tied more closely to the United States than had been Churchill's or Eden's. Perhaps Eisenhower though he owed Macmillan something. In December 1960, Eisenhower was a lame duck president. Perhaps Eisenhower's short-term status emboldened him to take a potentially unpopular position. Independence had come more quickly in Africa than Eisenhower had originally imagined. Independent Africa had been nearly as unsettled as some critics of independence had predicted. Perhaps supporting independence seemed a riskier strategy than before. The resolution had no teeth. The U.S. was always going to speak against it, even if voting for it. Perhaps Macmillan's argument that criticism plus an abstention was little different from criticism plus an affirmative vote was persuasive.

Despite U.S. opposition to Resolution 1514, the Eisenhower administration was usually at odds with the British government over colonial issues. The administration sought understandings with the British and was sensitive to British interests. British and U.S. officials met frequently to discuss colonial matters. Nevertheless, during the Eisenhower years, the United States stayed in the middle of the road, unwilling to offer its British ally open and consistent support. To the extent that the British hoped and expected that the United States would shield it from anti-colonial attacks and thwart pressure in the United Nations for political change in Africa, they were disappointed.

Colonial Policy Under the Conservatives, 1952–1959: Foot Dragging

The late 1940s were a busy time for colonial policymakers in London. The Attlee government and civil servants in the Colonial Office energetically and enthusiastically considered new approaches to colonial policy in Africa. The early and middle 1950s, in contrast, were a quiet time. Civil servants continued to produce analyses and reviews, but the Churchill and Eden governments viewed earlier commitments to self-determination with regret. They were unwilling to reverse official policy, but looked wistfully for a cheap and painless alternative. Unsuccessful, they were left with a policy of delay.

When Harold Macmillan became prime minister in 1957 after the Suez debacle, the British government began to re-think its approach to the African colonies. Macmillan came to office seemingly convinced that independence was inevitable; others within his government also sensed a need for change. Macmillan quickly ordered civil servants to reassess the current policies; their report opened the door to significant changes. Macmillan retained Eden's Colonial Secretary, Alan Lennox-Boyd, but by mid–1959 it was clear that Macmillan intended to play a larger role in colonial policy and that business as usual as practiced by the Colonial Office was much less likely.

Churchill and Eden

After 1952, colonial policy remained a low priority for the Churchill and Eden governments. Churchill and Eden were content to leave most colonial matters to their colonial secretaries, Oliver Lyttelton, and, after July 1954, Alan Lennox-Boyd. The full cabinet discussed colonial policy only occasionally. Despite a series of colonial crises, Eden did not establish a cabinet standing committee on colonial affairs until October 1955.

The cabinet's attitude towards the colonies continued to be that Britain had started a process that it could not stop when it announced self-government as the ultimate goal for the colonies. In 1953, Lord Swinton, commonwealth relations secretary, addressed the issue of commonwealth membership for newly independent colonies. He told the cabinet that he assumed that the colonies would continue their process toward independence, even if they were not fitted for independence or capable of shouldering the responsibilities that came with commonwealth status. Swinton recommended that the Colonial Office continue to offer judicious and carefully timed political concessions to the colonies while avoiding the appearance of weakly yielding to extremist pressure. If colonial politicians were offered sufficient control over internal affairs and were allowed to participate in commonwealth meetings about issues that affected their interests, they would be less eager to assume the responsibilities and privileges of independence, Swinton claimed.[1]

When the Churchill and Eden governments took up colonial issues, they demonstrated discomfort with the speed of political change in the colonies and with the prospect of granting all colonies their independence. They explored means to halt political change in some colonies before they reached independence without openly reversing official government policy. The cabinet revisited the notion of limited self-government and looked for ways to redefine the final stage of political change in order to leave more power in Britain's hands. Through 1957, the British government sought means to retard the pace of political change within colonies. It also resurrected the idea that colonies had to pass certain economic and political tests before gaining independence.

Commonwealth Membership and Limited Self-Government

In 1953, the cabinet faced the prospect that an independent Gold Coast would expect to become a full member of the commonwealth and that at least South Africa would raise objections. Lord Salisbury, lord president of the council (who, as Viscount Cranborne, had been colonial secretary in the wartime Churchill cabinet), was opposed to admitting the remaining colonies to the commonwealth. He told the cabinet that none of the territories being discussed was fit for independence. They were small countries inhabited by primitive peoples not mentally equipped to handle defense or foreign policy. They were not ready to be full members of the commonwealth. Allowing them to join the commonwealth would destroy the organization, Salisbury maintained. Salisbury's views defined one end of the spectrum of opinion within the cabinet, but he was not alone in worrying about the direction and pace of government policy.[2]

The cabinet's response was to return to the notion of limited self-government as the end for political change in the colonies. Swinton suggested a lesser form of commonwealth membership, for territories that controlled their internal affairs, but not external affairs or defense. Lyttelton favored the idea. He told a committee chaired by Swinton that moderate nationalists would not object, because they were most interested in controlling domestic matters. Lyttelton resisted calling Nkrumah prime minister, including him in commonwealth prime ministers meetings, or allowing Gold Coast ministers to participate in discussions of defense issues.[3]

Nevertheless, the report Swinton submitted to the cabinet was not optimistic about substituting self-government for independence. It stated that three African colonies, the Gold Coast, Nigeria, and the Federation of Rhodesia and Nyasaland, were certain to attain full independence within the next five years. The result of political development in four others, Kenya, Tanganyika, Uganda, and Sierra Leone, was uncertain. Along with twenty or so other small territories, Gambia was unlikely to become independent. Swinton's report maintained that the only safe assumption was that anything short of full commonwealth membership would be unacceptable for the colonies appeared headed for independence. The British government should not raise the issue, however. It should arrange it so that, when the issue arose, it was under circumstances likely to produce an agreement between Britain and its colony.[4]

Persuaded by Charles Arden-Clarke, the governor of the Gold Coast, Swinton recommended in 1954 that colonies become full members of the commonwealth when they became independent. Several cabinet members thought it unfortunate that the policy of assisting dependent peoples to attain self-government had proceeded so far and so fast, but Swinton warned against attempting to delay unduly the pace of political change. He contended that no British political party could afford charges that it had reneged on a promise of independence. Nationalist leaders who had been promised independence expected independence in their political lifetimes. Artificial delays would undercut responsible nationalists and ensure that anti–British leaders were in charge when a colony became independent. Swinton maintained that the British government could control the pace of change only to a limited degree. The strength of nationalist feeling and the development of political consciousness in a colony would determine the speed of development.[5]

The next year, Lennox-Boyd returned to the topic of limited self-government. He recommended to the cabinet that Britain steer the smaller dependent territories towards a constitutional status somewhere between independence and dependency. Under Lennox-Boyd's proposal, "island states" or "city states" would control their internal affairs, but not external affairs or defense. Zanzibar, Sierra Leone, Gambia, and the three high commission territories (Bechuanaland, Swaziland, and Basutoland) fell into one or other of these categories. Nevertheless, Lennox-Boyd added Kenya, Tanganyika, and Uganda to the list of African colonies that could aspire to full independence. Lennox-Boyd also thought Britain needed to clarify its plans so that colonial leaders did not develop unrealistic expectations and accuse Britain of a breach of faith in the heat of a crisis.[6]

In 1955, the cabinet decided to describe the intended end of political development as "full self-government" rather than "independence." After the fact, Colonial Office officials pointed out that "self-government" meant something less than "independence" in United Nations parlance. It was unlikely, they argued, that the Gold Coast would be happy celebrating "full self-government day." The officials conceded that self-government was a useful phrase because it could be said to include independence, but did not necessarily mean independence. Promising self-government was not the same as promising independence, however. The officials noted, correctly, that changing government terminology about political change would be nearly impossible and would not alter basic policy.[7]

In the midst of the discussions, a senior civil servant, Sir Charles Jeffries, reminded the cabinet that it had other options. Jeffries warned against focusing on the colonies' lack of readiness for independence. The Gold Coast was no more ready for independence than a teenage daughter was ready to have her own house key, Jeffries asserted. The colonies might not be much more prepared in five or ten years. The cabinet needed to choose the approach most likely to prepare the colonies for greater responsibility. The current approach of doling out small doses of responsibility and trying to keep one step ahead of demand might work. Nevertheless, nationalist politicians were apt to concentrate on securing the next constitutional concession rather than building up their capacity to govern. Rival groups might be more likely to work together if they had to bear responsibility for governing. It might make more sense for the cabinet to skip the intervening stages and hand the colonies full responsibility for government.[8]

When an opportunity arose for the cabinet to publicize an intention not to grant independence to certain territories, it backed away, however. Amidst preparations for the 1956 meeting of commonwealth prime ministers, a cabinet committee decided that announcing that some territories would not become independent would do more harm than good. It was an entirely negative message, the committee concluded. It would disappoint leaders in the colonies and would provide fodder for anti-colonialist propaganda. A territory responsible for its internal affairs, but not external affairs or defense, was little different from a territory in the last stage before independence. Announcing that such status was a possible end state would not amount to a major departure in policy and would not be worthwhile, the committee advised.[9]

In 1955, Lennox-Boyd brought the cabinet more proposals intended to slow the pace of political change within colonies. Lennox-Boyd told the cabinet that Africans had come to equate universal adult suffrage with democracy. Yet it posed great dangers for developing polities. It could, Lennox-Boyd argued, prejudice a colony's future by giving power to demagogues adept at handling uneducated masses. Universal suffrage put European and Asian minorities at risk, he claimed. "Backward tribes" could be exploited by the more advanced. The illiterate peasant would be exploited by the townsman, the real intelligentsia by the "half-educated demagogue." Lennox-Boyd offered what he termed "qualitative democracy" as an alternative. Lennox-Boyd persuaded the cabinet that the best approach was to allow greater weight to certain voters, based on property, educational, or other criteria, as elected members replaced appointed members in legislative councils in East and Central Africa.[10]

Under Lennox-Boyd, the Colonial Office put renewed emphasis on the criteria a territory had to satisfy in order to attain self-government and independence. A Colonial Office memorandum prepared for the 1956 commonwealth prime ministers conference returned to language used by Creech Jones. It stated that a colony could not become self-governing until it could ensure its people a fair standard of living and freedom from aggression from any quarter. The Colonial Office elaborated on the same themes in a draft speech prepared for Lennox-Boyd to deliver at the 1956 West Indies constitutional conference. Independence meant more than Britain relinquishing power, the draft said. It meant that a territory had to have sufficient financial and economic resources to that its people could lead a decent life without external subsidies. The territory had to be able to finance its own administration, be recognized as financially sound, and be able to raise money on its own credit. A territory aspiring to be independent had to be able to assume responsible for its own defense and its international relations.[11]

For all the committee meetings and reports, neither the Churchill nor the Eden governments devised a different approach to colonial policy. Particularly while Lennox-Boyd was colonial secretary, they were left with what amounted to foot dragging. Renouncing the oft-stated commitment to self-government was unthinkable, but the pace toward self-government need not be rapid. The colonies would be ready to manage their own affairs, but that might not be for some time. Political change should be delayed so that economic and social development could take place. When Eden established a cabinet committee on colonial affairs, he was concerned that colonial crises were catching ministers and their departments unawares. He charged the committee with helping the cabinet control constitutional development in the colonies. In discussing possible commonwealth status, Swinton included the hope that the pace of political change under the Conservatives would be slower than under their Labour predecessors.[12]

Grappling with Britain's Strategic Dilemma

While the Churchill and Eden governments were agonizing over colonial policy, they were also wrestling with Britain's fundamental challenge, the mismatch between its imperial responsibilities and ambitions and its financial and economic resources. Senior British politicians and officials recognized that Britain could not afford the military expenditures thought necessary to garrison its imperial possessions, protect its interests around the globe, maintain its prestige, and satisfy the obligations that came with its alliance with the United States. They recognized that Britain's financial situation was not sustainable. An imperial Britain could not remain dependent on U.S. financial aid and on the sterling balances belonging to the colonies but held in London, in effect forced loans from the colonies to Britain.

Military Expenditures

In 1954, Britain spent 60 percent more on defense than it had in 1947. That year, defense spending equaled 9.1 percent of Britain's gross domestic product, compared to 8.4 percent in 1947. In 1954, Britain's military forces numbered 957,000, significantly down from the three million under arms in 1947, but close to the 1,066,000 in the armed forces in 1949.[13]

The money and men devoted to defense posed problems for the Churchill and Eden governments. Until 1946, Britain rarely conscripted men into the military during peacetime. The Attlee government felt compelled to retain conscription at the end of World War II and to increase the required period of service from twelve to eighteen months in 1947, and to twenty-four months in 1950. Conscription was unpopular with the British public, and with military officials. Conscription was a cheap means to secure foot soldiers. Nevertheless, military officials complained that it was inadequate to train and retain the skilled soldiers needed to operate complex weapons and equipment. Moreover, the perceived need for new, sophisticated weapons threatened to drive defense spending still higher. At the beginning of the Eden administration, the Treasury anticipated that defense spending would increase by another £500 million, or roughly a third, by 1959–60. The Treasury warned that Britain's economy could not sustain such spending.[14]

The Conservative governments' response to the problem was twofold: attempt to restrain overall defense spending and focus on nuclear weapons. Despite criticizing the Attlee government for failing to increase military spending sufficiently, the Conservatives under Churchill cut back on the rearmament plans drafted by their Labour predecessors. The Churchill and Eden governments struggled to impose additional economies on the armed forces. They concluded that they could not afford to arm British forces with both nuclear and conventional weapons. The Churchill and Eden governments eventually decided that Britain required nuclear weapons to be considered a global power. In addition, nuclear weapons were the more cost-efficient approach to military power. They determined to continue investing in nuclear arms, while cutting back on conventional forces.[15]

The shift in defense policy had long-term implications for the colonies. Removing garrisons from the colonies was not immediately imperative. The dependent territories represented a small part of Britain's military effort in the mid–1950s. In 1954, nearly all the British army's divisions were overseas, ten and a half divisions out of a total of eleven and a third. Nevertheless, fewer than four were in colonial possessions, two in Malaya and portions of two others in Hong Kong and Kenya. Maintaining order in dependent territories, even combating insurgents as in Malaya and Kenya, involved the kinds of weapons and equipment used in World War II. In the mid–1950s, Britain had ample stocks of such arms. Nevertheless, at some point, Britain would need defense savings wherever it could find them. Moreover, British officials realized that colonial responsibilities could cost far more. The conflicts in Malaya and Kenya demonstrated that the colonies represented potential claims on Britain's military resources. Maintaining order in the colony could require the rapid infusion of substantial troops and equipment. Eventually, controlling military expenditures would require re-thinking colonial policy.[16]

Economic and Financial Issues

During the Churchill and Eden administrations, Britain's economic and financial situation changed, including its links to the African colonies. Britain's economic situation improved in the 1950s, starting with the global boom that accompanied the Korean War. By the time of the Suez crisis, however, Britain's financial status was still not strong enough to protect the value of the pound without U.S. assistance. The economic potential posed by the colonies appeared diminished. The ambitious development plans favored by the Attlee government were no longer credible. British investors were beginning to look to developed economies, especially that of the United States, rather than to the colonies. The African colonies' exports and imports increased roughly fivefold between 1946 and 1955. In 1955, the African colonies' imports outstripped exports for the first time since 1949 and would do so for five of the next six years.[17]

During the early and mid–1950s, official thinking about Britain's economic and financial future shifted. The notion of Britain as the center of a self-contained trade and finance area lost favor. By the early 1950s, the Conservative Party had discarded any attachment to imperial preference. Officials in London began to favor moves toward multilateral trade and toward a convertible currency. Britain was unable to resist pressure from Kuwait and other holders of sterling to allow increased convertibility. The Suez financial debacle provided more impetus to align Britain's financial strategy with U.S. preferences.[18]

Changes in London's economic thinking also had implications for the colonies for the long term. Rather than the source of dollar earnings or important raw materials, the colonies were apt to be perceived in official circles as financial burdens. In the short term, Britain could not afford to allow the colonies to withdraw the sterling balances held in London. During the 1950s, British officials fretted a great deal about the issue. Nevertheless, the colonies' sterling balances were incompatible in the long term with sterling's proposed role as a reliable international currency. For sterling to function as an important currency Britain would need to maintain substantial sterling reserves. Since the colonies' sterling balances constituted claims against sterling, Britain needed to manage their gradual reduction. The import controls and other economic practices in the colonies that had generated the sterling balances were also incompatible with a world economy defined by multilateral trade.[19]

Macmillan

Harold Macmillan was a complicated and changeable politician. He often relied on his instincts rather than the advice of civil servants or political colleagues. Macmillan thought Conrad Adenauer a false and cantankerous old man and, therefore, undid much of the work his government undertook to improve Anglo-German relations in the late 1950s. In the face of impending calamity, Macmillan was capable of rapidly changing course. During the

Suez crisis, he moved from strident advocacy of military action against Egypt to emollient courting of the United States. Macmillan had a knack for the apt phrase and for catchy rhetoric, words that he did not always follow with action. Macmillan avoided clear-cut, far-reaching decisions. He was more comfortable feeling his way along, testing the political wind at each stage. In a world of uncertainties and conflicting arguments, it was a bold man who would reach a final conclusion, Macmillan observed.[20]

Crises promote change. The Suez crisis demonstrated Britain's weaknesses and called into question the wisdom of much of postwar British policy. Macmillan's flexible, some might say shifty and opportunistic, cast of mind fit Britain's circumstances in the late 1950s. Macmillan recast Britain's relationship with the United States, accepting a subordinate role more readily than his predecessors. He ordered major reductions in defense spending, something the Churchill and Eden administrations had talked about, but shied away from. As part of the defense overhaul, his administration ended conscription. Over several years, he also coaxed his cabinet into rethinking Britain's relationship with Europe and applying for membership in the European Economic Community.[21]

During the Macmillan administration, political change proceeded so quickly and unrest surfaced so readily in Africa that the continent seemed to be in a state of perpetual crisis. Perhaps to the surprise of Britain and the United States, Nkrumah and Ghana emerged as loud and persistent advocates for independence across Africa. A 1957 Pan African conference in Accra attracted a host of nationalist leaders and reinforced their efforts to overturn colonial regimes. In 1958, President De Gaulle offered the French colonies a choice between independence and association with France. A year later, De Gaulle shocked many by offering Algeria self-determination. In 1960, most former French colonies entered the United Nations as independent states. In 1959, the Belgians announced plans to grant the Congo its independence. A year later Congolese independence was followed by unrest, the virtual breakdown of the Congolese state, and intervention by the United Nations.

The ongoing crisis in Africa prompted the Macmillan administration to review and revise its colonial policies. Developments in French and Belgian Africa suggested that the traditional colonial regime was no match for nationalism. The old methods were no longer sufficient to maintain European control of African colonies. British leaders had come to believe that Britain set the standard in colonial reform. They took pride in Britain's efforts in the Gold Coast and Nigeria. Now Britain risked being left behind, a standard bearer for an outdated regime, accompanied only by the Portuguese, the Spanish, and the South Africans. If Britain wanted to retain the friendship of its colonies and former colonies, it could not be seen in public with such company.[22]

Before Macmillan became prime minister, he did not have fixed views about the African colonies. In the 1940s, he was critical of European settlers in Kenya and Rhodesia, predicting that they would come into conflict with the African population over land issues. As foreign secretary in 1955, he acknowledged that working towards self-government for the colonies was government policy, but commented, "Surely we ought not to make a fetish of this." The following year, as chancellor of the exchequer, he questioned the decision to grant the Gold Coast its independence since an independent Ghana might withdraw its sterling balances, and he resisted continuing financial aid to the Gold Coast after its independence. When the Eden administration was reviewing the discrepancy between its imperial ambitions and its financial resources, however, Macmillan said he was willing to consider shedding some colonial burdens.[23]

As Macmillan became prime minister, African nationalism was on his mind. In July

1957, he gave a speech in Bedford usually remembered for Macmillan's quip that Britain "never had it so good." In the same speech, Macmillan warned his listeners that nationalism had become a tidal wave sweeping from Asia to Africa. It was now the swiftest and most powerful political force loose in the world, he said. It could be led, but not driven back.[24]

Balances of Advantage

Within three weeks of becoming prime minister, Macmillan asked the Colonial Office to assess the "balances of advantage" of Britain's losing or keeping each colonial territory. Macmillan said he assumed that Britain had vital interests in some colonies, but that it could allow constitutional change to proceed in others, even if the newly-independent colony were likely to leave the commonwealth.[25]

Macmillan's request made Lennox-Boyd uneasy. He feared a premature withdrawal from the empire. He reminded Macmillan of Britain's responsibilities to colonial peoples and warned against forsaking Britain's friends. If Britain handed power to governments that could not govern well, the repercussions would be significant for both Britain and the former colonies. Whereas Macmillan distinguished between colonies that became independent within the commonwealth and those that left the commonwealth, Lennox-Boyd attempted to bring the prime minister back to the Colonial Office's preferred distinction between colonies that attained independence within the commonwealth and those that gained control only of their internal affairs.[26]

The final report that Sir Norman Brook, the cabinet secretary, forwarded to the Cabinet Colonial Policy Committee was consistent with colonial policy under Churchill and Eden in important aspects. It presumed that the government did not intend to depart from the past policy of moving colonies toward the "greatest practicable measure of self-government" nor weaken the past policy by erecting artificial barriers to political change. It acknowledged Britain's responsibilities to colonial peoples, particularly in territories inhabited by more than one race or tribe. It warned against a premature withdrawal of British authority. It foresaw that Nigeria would become independent by 1960 or 1961 and the Federation of Rhodesia and Nyasaland some time after 1960. It imagined that most of the other African colonies would achieve self-government within ten years.[27]

In other aspects, the report moved away from notions cherished by Lennox-Boyd and the Colonial Office. The idea that colonies should not attain independence until they were viable in economic, social, and political spheres disappeared. Only readiness in the political sphere received mention. Britain's civilizing mission also received scant attention. The Colonial Office's treasured distinction between self-government and independence survived as a formality. As the report was being prepared, the Colonial Office had proposed expanded economic aid to the colonies. The final report ignored the proposal.[28]

More than half the report dealt with economic matters. The Treasury had a strong hand in shaping the final version. The report's key conclusion dealt with the colonies' economic value. The report concluded that the colonies could be of financial and economic value to Britain. The decision to grant a colony its independence would not determine whether Britain would realize the economic or financial value, however. The determining factor would be the colony's economic and financial policies before and after independence. Britain was free to make decisions about independence on political grounds. It need not fear losing the opportunities for trade and investment that the colonies offered. Managing the transition to independence was important, but granting independence would not deprive Britain of the colonies' economic value.

The conclusion was consistent with the Treasury's strategic thinking. Having dispensed with the notion of the sterling area as a self-contained trading area, the Treasury envisioned sterling as an international currency second only to the dollar. In the future imagined by the Treasury, colonies played a minor role. Establishing sterling's international role required the liquidation, albeit gradual, of the colonies' sterling balances and dismantlement of their economic and trade controls. The Treasury anticipated that trade and investment would focus on the developed world, on the United States and Europe. As prices for primary products continued to decline from their peaks in the early 1950s, colonies seemed less likely sources of profit.

The 1957 "profit and loss" report evidenced that official thinking outside the Colonial Office was changing. It also evidenced that the Colonial Office could not necessarily impose its views once colonial issues rose above the Colonial Office and other ministers became involved. Nevertheless, the report did not signal a change in colonial policy. Lennox-Boyd remained at the Colonial Office. He chose to interpret the report as supporting his views.[29]

New Flexibility

In 1958, senior civil servants completed a review of the government's fundamental policies. Like the "profit and loss" report, the review appeared to reaffirm longstanding policies, but hinted at the possibility for change. The review conceded that Britain could no longer operate from a position of overwhelming strength. It no longer had the power to impose its will. Nevertheless, the officials thought that Britain could have a substantial influence on world affairs through its remaining resources and its position in the commonwealth and in Europe. Relinquishing nuclear weapons and discarding overseas commitments to become like the Netherlands or Sweden were unacceptable. Britain was reducing its overseas commitments as fast as was prudent, but a wholesale retreat from empire would be unsafe, the review argued. Britain needed, the officials wrote, greater flexibility in overseas policy. Britain must be ready to improvise, to adapt to changing circumstances, and to take advantage of fleeting opportunities. "We shall not maintain our influence, if we appear to be clinging obstinately to the shadow of our old imperial power after its substance is gone," the review concluded.[30]

In April 1959, Lennox-Boyd submitted a memorandum to the Cabinet Colonial Policy Committee. He proposed continuation of the Colonial Office's past policies. Lennox-Boyd had met with the governors of the East African colonies in January to discuss and coordinate policies and his memorandum focused on Tanganyika and Uganda. Lennox-Boyd identified two British interests in East Africa: preservation of friendly relations with the region's territories and retention of various defense assets, in particular, the right to station a reserve force in Kenya. Lennox-Boyd offered the committee three options for preserving Britain's interests: rapid withdrawal, consolidation of British rule, and step-by-step constitutional progress. According to the colonial secretary, the first option would create a dangerous political vacuum, since newly independent governments would be incapable of governing effectively. The second option would require the use of force, would alienate world opinion, and would alienate the local populations. When Britain did withdraw, the independent governments would be hostile to British interests. The third option, a middle-of-the-road approach, was the best option, according to Lennox-Boyd. He told the committee that con-stitutional changes were likely in Tanganyika and Uganda within a year. Thereafter, he pro-posed that the British continue a policy of delay. He recommended that they attempt to draw out the process so that the colonies would not gain full control of their internal affairs for another ten years. Once the colonies achieved full internal self-government, Lennox-Boyd thought that prior experience demonstrated that full independence would soon fol-low.[31]

Lennox-Boyd thought the other East African colonies needed different treatment. He was on record that Britain intended to retain control of Kenya for the near future and he recommended no change to his policy. He warned the committee, however, that refusing to contemplate a different future for Kenya would be more difficult once neighboring terri-tories gained more control of their affairs. Lennox-Boyd characterized Zanzibar as an excep-tional case because of its small size and the Sultan of Zanzibar's claims to territory on the mainland administered as part of Kenya.

The cabinet committee accepted Lennox-Boyd's recommendations, but signaled that Lennox-Boyd and the Colonial Office were no longer free to pursue business as usual. Mac-millan had assumed chair of the committee in November 1958. Lennox-Boyd's presentation of multiple options demonstrated that the colonial secretary was no longer the key decision maker. Lyttelton usually offered the cabinet a single option and pronounced that the gov-ernment had no choice but to accept it. In summing up the meeting, Macmillan expressed doubts about Britain's need for a defense presence in East Africa and about insisting on democratic governments for newly independent colonies. He told Lennox-Boyd to bring a draft of the governor of Tanganyika's proposed announcement back to the committee for review.[32]

Two months after Lennox-Boyd presented his East African policies, a committee of civil servants produced a report envisioning Africa in the next ten years. The report's analysis followed the familiar lines laid out by the colonial secretary. Britain needed to follow a middle way, slowly relinquishing political control to local populations. Delay was essential to ensuring stable, effective governments. Satisfying both the African majorities and Euro-pean settlers would be difficult. So would coordinating constitutional change in colonies with different political conditions. Nevertheless, Britain needed to succeed so that it retained the friendship of independent African states and blocked South African expansion north-ward. A multi-racial Federation of Rhodesia and Nyasaland would serve as a buffer between the Union of South Africa and the independent African states. Smaller colonies like Zanzibar and Sierra Leone probably should not be independent. Britain should retain control of their foreign relations and defense.[33]

As civil servants churned out papers, doubts about the wisdom of contemporary policies began to surface within the Macmillan administration. Iain Macleod, minister of labor and national service, forwarded Macmillan a memorandum in May 1959. The memorandum was the work of David Stirling, chair of the African Capricorn Society, a group advocating an Africa free of racial discrimination. Stirling criticized British policy in Kenya, calling it a retreat towards independence conducted in the despondent spirit of a rear guard action. Stirling advocated a more positive approach, more responsive to African nationalists. In a cover note, Macleod reminded Macmillan of an earlier conversation in which Macmillan had indicated interest in changing colonial policies. Macmillan told a colleague in July that he was not interested in a hasty shift in policy, but that it was time to start thinking about the future. Philip de Zulueta, Macmillan's private secretary, described the civil servants'

June 1959 report as permeated by the unimaginative spirit of colonial administration in decadence. It would result in the wrong policies being adopted or no policy at all, he warned.[34]

By mid–1959, the British government had cleared the way to a new colonial policy. It had all but discarded the notions that colonies must meet certain criteria before gaining self-government and that self-government meant something less than full independence. All that remained was a hope that self-government could be delayed. Over the course of the 1950s, the British government had also come to see that whatever economic, financial, and strategic rationales may have existed for African colonies were no longer persuasive.

12

Anglo-American
Sponsored Development:
A Road Not Taken

The notion of economic and social development, steps taken to increase economic activity and improve living standards in the colonies, was part of British thinking about their African colonies, particularly after 1938 or so. Sometimes, the British saw development as a component of political change, preparation for colonial peoples to assume a greater share of political power. The British also saw development as a criterion for political change. Colonies would have to achieve a certain level of development before they could make political progress. Some times, development was seen as an alternative to political change. Perhaps colonial peoples would trade higher wages and better public facilities for political power. Throughout, British officials considered the possibility of enlisting the United States in development. Perhaps Britain could spend U.S. wealth to improve its African colonies.

MacDonald and the Colonial Development and Welfare Act

While the British government was brainstorming about political changes in the colonies during the Second World War, it was also taking concrete steps towards economic and social change. Again, the impetus for change preceded the war. In 1935 and 1937, riots in Britain's West Indian colonies resulted in 39 deaths and 175 injuries. The British concluded that poor economic and social conditions were at the root of the unrest. MacDonald, as colonial secretary, organized a royal commission headed by Lord Moyne to investigate and make recommendations. Armed with the commission's findings, MacDonald then proposed a program of investment in economic development and social welfare projects in the colonies, a significant break with past policy. Britain's traditional approach had been to avoid subsidies from London and to require each colony to be financially self-sufficient. In 1940, the government proposed and Parliament passed the Colonial Development and Welfare Act. The Act called for spending up to £50 million over ten years on development and welfare projects along with £5 million on research.[1]

The act had wide support within the Churchill government. MacDonald argued that the wretched conditions revealed in the West Indies demanded remedies. Reform would strengthen Britain's claim to keep the colonies. When the war was over, the Colonial Development and Welfare Act would allow Britain to defend its record of colonial stewardship,

MacDonald asserted. Lord Cranborne thought the colonies needed to be more effective, especially in economic and social spheres. The Foreign Office urged a revised colonial policy that commanded American respect. Lord Hailey remarked: "I sometimes wish that we could place our hands on our hearts a little less and set them to explore our pockets a little more." Colonial Secretary Stanley pleaded with the Treasury in 1944 to make funds available for the act. He described it as an opportunity which might not occur again to set the colonial empire on lines of development that would secure its loyalty to Britain. If Britain were to justify its position as a colonial power, it needed to promote economic development and social improvement.[2]

It was not certain that Britain would possess the financial resources to develop the colonies after the war. Junior officials in the Colonial Office and the Foreign Office toyed with a more ambitious notion, using U.S. resources to develop and maintain the British empire. A.A. Dudley in the Foreign Office thought that Britain was short of capital to promote economic development in the colonies. It should encourage U.S. investment there. In the Colonial Office, Andrew Cohen foresaw similar possibilities for encouraging U.S. involvement in colonial development and for using U.S. economic aid to develop the colonies.[3]

British officials disagreed about the relationship between economic and social development and political changes. Some saw political and other changes proceeding in parallel. Others, notably Hailey, thought that the colonies would not be ready for political change without economic growth and improved social conditions. Development must precede political advances, he argued. If colonial peoples accepted this proposition, development might become a painless way to delay political change. Still others suggested that ordinary Africans might prefer economic and social programs to constitutional changes. Lord Swinton, resident minister in West Africa, argued that political change might not be necessary if Britain focused on the things that mattered to ordinary Africans: jobs, schools, farming, health and the like. The Colonial Office worried that the poor social and economic conditions in the colonies would promote agitation after the war. Africans would want rapid improvements in both political and economic spheres, before any development scheme could take hold. Sir Arthur Dawe, a senior Colonial Office official, was skeptical about buying off Africans with development programs. He wrote: "Improved health services and education will not be accepted by these people as a substitute for the freedom to develop according to their own political consciousness. The problem before the British government, therefore, is to find a method by which these inexorable African forces can be reconciled with future British interests."[4]

Britain's colonies were not necessarily ready for a larger development effort. Sierra Leone's director of education was invited in 1941 to submit a program of education development with Colonial Development and Welfare Act funds. The best he could do was to provide, two years later, a patchwork request for more rapid development along existing lines. The Colonial Office advisory committee reviewing the proposals thought that the colony needed something more substantial.

Development Under Attlee

The most intense interest in African development within the Attlee government had little to do with self-government. In 1947, Bevin was at the center of a flurry of activity aimed at using the African colonies as the means to restore British economic health and secure its independence from the United States. Bevin became convinced that Britain in cooperation with France and other colonial powers could dramatically and quickly expand African production of minerals and foodstuffs. African products could meet British domestic needs, especially for vegetable oils. They could be exported to the United States, earn dollars, and help solve Britain's balance of payments problems. At Bevin's urging, the Attlee government wrote papers, convened committees, and concocted schemes during 1947 and 1948 to increase African production.

Bevin and others recognized that development aimed at increasing African production might seem inconsistent with a professed interest in African well being, but were undeterred, nonetheless. Bevin warned that Britain needed to present its development plans carefully in order to avoid charges of exploitation. Otherwise, Britain would face bitter but baseless criticism in the United Nations. Bevin reminded his readers that the possibilities for misrepresentation in the U.N. were almost endless. A senior civil servant, Sir Norman Brook, made the same point. He counseled ministers that critics could characterize the plans as imperialistic, as exploiting native peoples to support the British standard of living.[5]

For all the civil servants' time and paper consumed, Bevin's notion produced remarkably little. The Attlee government established two new government corporations, the Colonial Development Corporation and the Overseas Food Corporation, responsible for encouraging production of food and minerals in the colonies. The preferred approach was a kind of industrial agriculture, reliant on machinery and skilled European staff. The two corporations funded various projects. The largest and most prominent was the Tanganyika groundnut scheme, funded by the Overseas Food Corporation. By 1951, the Tanganyika project had failed, costing the British government £36 million. The Colonial Development Corporation lost money each year through 1955 and abandoned many of its projects. By the standards of Britain's African colonies, the sums involved were not trivial. The money lost on the groundnut project exceeded the Tanganyika government's total expenditure between 1946 and 1950.[6]

Colonial Development and Welfare Act

Attlee's government also continued and expanded the development program begun by the wartime coalition under the authority of the Colonial Development and Welfare Act. The first Colonial Development and Welfare Act, enacted in 1940, permitted expenditure of £5 million a year for ten years plus £500,000 per year on research. In 1944, Oliver Stanley wrested from the Treasury authority for £120 million through 1955–56. In 1950, Attlee's government increased the amount available under the act to £140 million. The Attlee government had each colony draw up a ten-year development plan and allocated the available funds. The plans were to cover all spending on development: the funds made available under the act, a colony's own funds, and funds borrowed from other sources.[7]

The funds provided through the act were in stark contrast to the British parsimony before the war. Nevertheless, the total funds available overstate the size and economic impact of the program. Particularly during the war, the funds made available fell short of the authorized amounts and actual expenditures lagged behind allocations. Only £2 million was made available between July 1940 and October 1942. Increases in the cost of goods and services during and after the war meant that the £12 million per year authorized in 1944 represented an increase of only 65 percent in buying power over the £5 million per year authorized in 1940. The Colonial Office had contemplated tripling the amount originally authorized. Moreover, many colonial governments were slow to embrace the notion of development. Their plans were shopping lists, not strategies for increasing economic activity and boosting standards of living. Most colonies lacked the economic and social data needed for a development plan, not to mention workable theories for promoting economic growth. Development projects, both those planned and those funded, focused more on social development, that is, schools, housing, health facilities, and water supply and sanitation, than on economic development.[8]

Moreover, the funds moving from London to the colonies for development were more than matched by funds moving in the opposite direction. When the war ended, the London government held about £600 million belonging to the colonies, including about £215 million belonging to the African colonies. The funds derived from several sources: the colonies' trade surpluses (the excess of exports over imports), their financial surpluses (the excess of government revenues over expenditures), various government reserves, and deposits in colonial savings banks. In the postwar financial settlement, U.S. officials wanted Britain to cancel the colonies' sterling balances, but backed off, settling for Britain's commitment to make the pound convertible in 1947. British officials realized that the colonial balances supported the pound. The colonies' ability to earn dollars through sales of minerals and agricultural products helped offset Britain's, and the entire sterling area's, trade deficit with the United States. Through 1951, the value of colonial exports grew rapidly, more because of increased prices than of increased production. Furthermore, the British maintained measures implemented during the war: restricting colonial imports, buying colonial products in bulk at less than market prices, and controlling colonial exports, particularly cocoa from the Gold Coast, through marketing boards. Doing so allowed the British government to maximize the colonies' contribution to lowering its trade deficit. The value of dollar imports to African colonies fell by 46 percent between 1947 and 1950. For all these reasons, the colonies generated a dollar surplus of $1.83 billion between 1946 and 1951. African colonies, almost entirely the West African colonies, generated about 30 percent of the total. Rather than funding additional development projects, more of the money earned by the colonies ended up in London. By 1951, the colonial sterling balances had grown to £852 million. The East African colonies' balances stood at £217 million, compared with £100 million in 1946.[9]

Marshall Plan

British officials and politicians compared U.S. wealth and British poverty and wondered whether Britain could not enlist U.S. resources in developing the African colonies. A 1947 paper prepared in the Colonial Office offered the option of "tapping American resources" to accelerate the pace of development. In 1952, when Chancellor of the Exchequer Butler surveyed Britain's precarious financial state, he pointed out that Britain was spending £200 million a year on the colonies. In 1938, the sum had been only £16 million. In reply, Eden suggested that encouraging larger U.S. investments in the colonial empire would be one way to reduce the colonial burden on British finances.[10]

Some officials in Washington held parallel views. A 1947 State Department report noted, with some skepticism, British plans to develop the colonies through the Colonial Development and Welfare Act. The report observed that the funds involved, while considerable, were still too small for the task. Expenditures on social welfare would have little immediate economic impact and population pressures would frustrate efforts to raise the standard of living. A 1948 CIA report offered U.S. loans and investments as a means to forestall political revolutions inimical to U.S. interests. The report anticipated that the European empires were breaking up. It would be prudent, therefore, for the United States to heed nationalists' needs, even in the colonies of Central Africa. The State Department's attempts to construct a U.S. policy for Africa emphasized the role of U.S. aid. In 1950, George McGhee reported to Acheson that an advisory panel of outside experts recommended accelerating development as the basic objective of U.S. policy in Africa. The panel believed that U.S. aid programs combined with a bold statement of U.S. policy on colonialism could achieve the country's goals. By emphasizing aid, the United States could combat misrepresentations of its intentions regarding the colonial world, gain new support in the United Nations, and secure a powerful weapon in its competition with Russia.[11]

Marshall Plan aid was available for colonial areas. As of June 1951, over $560 million in Marshall Plan funds had been allocated to European colonies, at least $300 million to colonies in Africa. In 1950, the Marshall Plan program added a special reserve fund of $20 million targeted at economic development projects in dependent areas. Administrators assumed that most of the $20 million would go to African projects. Relatively little Marshall Plan money found its way to Britain's African colonies, however. Through mid–1951, Britain spent $98 million in Marshall Plan funds in dependent areas. Most went to Malaya, where British forces were combating an insurgency. France spent over $250 million in its Marshall Plan funds in its African colonies in the same period.[12]

Aid to dependent areas in Africa proved a peripheral element in the Marshall Plan. The principal goal was bolstering European economies. Africa figured in the plan to the extent that it could contribute to European recovery. U.S. officials came to approve the arrangement whereby Britain's African colonies earned dollars by selling minerals and agricultural products to the United States. The arrangement arose without U.S. aid. In addition, the Marshall Plan was to be short-term and U.S. officials thought it was not well suited to the long-term development needs of the African colonies. Furthermore, Marshall Plan aid to Britain ceased at the end of 1950, two years sooner than planned. A marked improvement in Britain's balance of payments convinced officials that Britain's economy had regained its health. Marshall Plan administrators recognized that the aid they could provide to Britain's African colonies would be marginal, aimed at key projects within extensive development plans.[13]

The colonial powers, particularly Britain, resisted overt U.S. involvement in their colonial development efforts. In 1950, a Marshall Plan official stationed in Paris told his State Department counterparts that he had spent eighteen months soothing European fears about U.S. aid to their colonies. Officials in colonial governments did not understand the kinds of aid the Marshall Plan could provide, the official said. In 1951, the U.S. consul in Salisbury reported that senior members of the Southern Rhodesian government suspected that U.S. aid signaled American designs on Central Africa. From the Marshall Plan's inception, both Bevin and the Colonial Office perceived dangers in allowing the United States to take credit for, much less control, African development projects. British leaders were content to accept Marshall Plan aid, including aid that ended up in the African colonies, while limiting the direct involvement of the U.S. Without the Marshall Plan and other financial assistance from the United States, the British could not have afforded to promote development in Africa. The British were careful, however, not to advertise the link between their development programs and U.S. financial support or to allow the United States any role beyond providing money.[14]

For U.S. officials, cooperation with Britain was more important than African economic development. They had little incentive to risk a clash with the British by insisting on a larger role in African development projects. Officials in Washington insisted that the British government in London approve all requests for aid to British possessions in Africa. Even when Kwame Nkrumah, as leader of the Gold Coast's dominant political party, appealed to U.S. officials for technical and other aid, the State Department deferred to London's wishes.[15]

Point Four

The group of eleven experts on Africa that met at the State Department in February 1950[16] focused on a program of economic development in cooperation with the colonial powers. The main thrust of the panel's recommendations was that the United States seek to work with the European colonial powers to foster development in the African colonies. The panel thought that the U.S. could use monies appropriated for the Marshall Plan and administered by the Economic Cooperation Administration, as well as funds to be appropriated for Truman's proposed program of technical assistance, Point Four.[17]

McGhee's advisory panel was optimistic about U.S. aid to Africa in part because Truman had announced a new aid program in his 1949 inaugural address. The program came to be styled "Point Four" because it was the fourth point in Truman's speech. Truman pointed out that more than half of the world's population was living in poverty and was a target for leftist revolutionaries. Truman proposed that the United States launch a new program intended to share the benefits of its scientific and industrial progress with underdeveloped areas. Truman contrasted the new program, built on the concept of democratic fair dealing, with the old imperialism, characterized by exploitation of colonial areas for foreign profit. Point Four was to have two components: one to encourage foreign investment in dependent areas and one to fund small-scale, long-term, technical assistance projects.[18]

Point Four was a White House creation and lacked support in the State Department. White House staff planned that Truman use his inaugural speech to improve America's image outside Europe. Truman's special assistant Clark Clifford and his staff reworked ideas that had circulated within the State Department but failed to gain Acheson's approval. From them they created the Point Four notion and inserted it in Truman's speech. The speech caught Acheson by surprise, but he managed to get the State Department assigned responsibility for fleshing out the proposal. The department struggled to write a coherent program, however. Its experts were hard pressed to give concrete expression to Truman's vision. A proposal considered worthy to send to Congress did not emerge until June 1949. Once the department completed its work, Acheson proved a lackluster advocate. He preferred programs that relied more heavily on private capital and doubted that Point Four would help the United States compete with Russia.[19]

In addition, Congress was not interested. In a highly partisan environment, Republicans perceived Point Four as Truman's program and attacked it. Senator Robert Taft called it a "global WPA." Private businesses professed little interest in the program's investment provisions, further undermining congressional support.

Point Four was also caught in a tidal shift in U.S. thinking about foreign aid. The Truman administration lost confidence that economic aid could solve Western Europe's problems. Its revised view of the country's global role, captured in National Security Council Document 68, required massive rearmament by the United States and its allies. The outbreak of the Korean War intensified the commitment to military preparedness. In the new thinking, foreign aid was a short-term measure intended to contain Russian expansionism. Truman and his advisers also recognized that Congress was more willing to approve military assistance than economic aid. Truman proposed, and Congress approved, a substantial new program of military aid. The Marshall Plan was wound up. Point Four moved from the State Department to the new Mutual Security Administration.[20]

A scaled-down version of Point Four eventually emerged. Congress passed the Point Four authorizing legislation in May 1950. In September 1950, it appropriated $26.9 million for 1951, a tiny amount compared with the Marshall Plan's $2 billion annual appropriation. Larger appropriations followed, $147.9 million for 1952 and $155.6 million for 1953. The perception in Washington remained, however, that Point Four remained little more than a slogan concocted by the Truman administration.[21]

Development Under the Conservatives

The Churchill government's financial policies had immediate implications for the colonies. In 1954, Lennox-Boyd proposed that grants under the Colonial Development and Welfare Act total £150 million in the period 1955–60. The grants were to be funded by £115 million in new money and £35 million carried over from funds made available earlier but unspent. Butler, the chancellor of the exchequer, resisted the proposal. He argued that the Colonial Office had not sufficiently explored the colonies' ability to fund their own development or the willingness of the United States to make funds available. In the end, Lennox-Boyd had to settle for £80 million in grants.[22]

Lennox-Boyd's request echoed the modest recommendations of a government working party on colonial development and welfare. The working party pointed out that the colonies had funded half their development needs since 1950, rather than the one-third envisioned by the Attlee government. Favorable economic conditions since the Korean War allowed the colonies to invest more than originally planned in development projects, but economic conditions were unlikely to be as good in the rest of the decade. Colonial governments would be hard pressed to maintain the same level of spending. Nevertheless, the working party took a conservative approach. It assumed that the colonies would contribute half the necessary funding. It argued that the London government had to provide £150 million just to maintain the current pace of development.[23]

Eisenhower and Aid

During Eisenhower's first term, political support for U.S. foreign aid was low. Eisenhower came to office determined to reverse the Truman administration's approach to foreign aid. The Eisenhower administration was skeptical of aid to United States allies and opposed broad, long-term aid programs. Administration leaders believed that private investment was a more effective means of stimulating economic development. To the extent that the administration favored aid, its preference was for short-term, low cost programs targeted on areas vulnerable to Russian or Chinese pressure. Eisenhower's 1954 budget request for the Mutual

Security Agency was for $5.5 billion, $2.1 billion lower than Truman's budget request for the same period. Congress was even less enamored of foreign aid. Conservative Republicans attacked the mutual security program as a global giveaway program that did not protect U.S. interests. Critics pointed to India and Indochina as two locations where mutual security expenditures had not worked. The Eisenhower administration had to work hard, therefore, to get foreign aid appropriations through Congress.[24]

During Eisenhower's second term, sentiment in Washington shifted in favor of foreign aid. Policymakers in the administration and in the Congress came to see foreign aid as a means of competing with Russia and its allies for the allegiance of less-developed nations. In 1954, Russia began to offer technical assistance, financial credits, and trade to developing countries. Later, the Khrushchev government made plain its intention to woo the poorer nations. U.S. leaders did not take Russian initiatives seriously at first and remained committed to private investment. Confidence in the United States government's ability to administer aid programs was also low. Starting in 1955, however, high-level committees sponsored by the administration or the Congress recommended expanded expenditures for foreign aid. If further evidence were needed, anti–U.S. demonstrations during Vice President Nixon's tour of Latin America in 1958 and the emergence of the Castro regime in Cuba in 1960 convinced U.S. leaders that changes were in order.[25]

In Africa, the critical events prompting increased support for U.S. foreign assistance were the growing number of independent states and the breakdown of law and order in the Congo. Eisenhower concluded that the emergence of new nations raised critical problems of economic development. Eisenhower included in his foreign aid request for fiscal year 1961 a $20 million program of special assistance for Africa. He told the Congress that U.S. aid as well as aid from other countries would have to increase if Africa were to grow economically.[26]

While Washington was reconsidering its foreign aid policies, almost no U.S. foreign assistance went to Britain's African colonies. Throughout Eisenhower's administration, technical assistance to poor countries under the Point Four program, the most likely form of aid for British Africa, remained insignificant. In 1959, expenditures for technical assistance totaled $129 million, less than 5 percent of the foreign aid budget. From 1945 to 1958, the United States dispatched $65 billion in aid to foreign countries. Only about $8.5 million went to British Africa, including $6.6 million to British East Africa. Independent countries in Africa (Egypt, Tunisia, Ethiopia, Liberia, Libya, and Morocco) received about $295 million. In the same period, the United States lent $20 billion to foreign countries. The only British African colony to receive a loan was the Federation of Rhodesia and Nyasaland. The United States lent the federation $60 million to promote copper production.[27]

State Department officials in Washington were skeptical about aid to African colonies. In 1953, a staffer argued that the colonial powers were reluctant to allow U.S. technical assistance projects in their possessions. He also thought that the U.S. aid organization's plans were overly ambitious and unrealistic. When the Foreign Operations Administration (successor to the Mutual Security Agency) wanted to send an official to Salisbury to facilitate investments by United States firms in Rhodesian enterprises, other officials were opposed. They argued that the United States government should not be involved in private transactions. Intervention by a United States official was bound to raise false expectations in the Rhodesian government.[28]

The Foreign Operations Administration was not uniformly in favor of U.S. aid to British African colonies. In 1955, the State Department's best judgment was that the Gold Coast would be independent within a few years and that the departure of British civil servants would tax the new country's capacity to govern itself. When the Office of African Affairs raised the possibility of offering substantial technical assistance to the Gold Coast, the Foreign Operations Administration's response was frosty and parsimonious. Providing aid to the Gold Coast would set a bad example, the administration claimed. Every country on the verge of independence would expect U.S. aid. In addition, U.S. aid would only accelerate political change artificially. It would motivate the Gold Coast to dismiss British civil servants sooner rather than later. U.S. policy had been to wait for official requests from London. Doing otherwise would set a pattern that the United States would regret.[29]

The department was willing to reconsider the policy of letting the Colonial Office screen aid requests, but the policy remained unchanged. In 1955, the department instructed the London embassy to raise the issue of informal aid requests with the Colonial Office. Two years earlier, the Colonial Office opposed the U.S. considering requests from the Gold Coast government. The department thought attitudes in London might have changed and a joint U.S.–Great Britain aid program might be possible. London's position remained unchanged, however, and U.S. policy continued to require Colonial Office approval for all aid requests from British colonies. In 1955, the consul general in Lagos argued that the United States needed to disassociate itself from British colonialism. Having U.S. aid programs work with the Nigerian government would be a good first step. The department replied that the orderly transfer of power from the British to Africans remained U.S. policy. Seeking to work with the Nigerians would undermine British rule and disrupt American relations with Britain.[30]

When technical assistance projects won approval, implementation proved slow and uncertain. The Kenya government and U.S. aid officials were interested in promoting U.S. aid to Kenya. Ernest Vasey, the Kenyan minister of finance and development, visited Washington in January 1955 to drum up support for technical assistance and development projects in Kenya. Vasey made a good impression. In May, the International Cooperation Administration (successor to the Foreign Operations Administration) approved an $800,000 technical assistance grant to the Royal Technical College in Kenya plus funds for several prominent Kenyans and Kenyan students to visit the United States. The International Cooperation Administration struggled to carry out the projects, however. In 1957, the consul general in Nairobi warned a senior Kenyan official interested in securing aid that delays in starting the earlier projects had generated substantial disillusionment in Kenya.[31]

In 1956, the International Cooperation Administration's new leadership turned even further against aid to colonies. When John Hollister, a former Republican congressman, became director, he attempted to stop new funding for technical assistance in African or Caribbean colonies. He told Dulles that the projects did not serve U.S. interests. The colonial powers should be responsible for developing their own territories. Hollister reminded Dulles that Congress remained unhappy about the size of the technical assistance program. He recommended that U.S. aid be limited to territories that would be independent within three years.[32]

Hollister's proposals generated opposition within the department, but technical assistance programs in African colonies were cut back. Hollister's opponents argued that reducing aid would compare badly with Russian initiatives. They contended that limiting aid to territories on the verge of independence was rigid and unworkable. George Allen, assistant secretary for Near Eastern, African and South Asian affairs, argued for a modest aid program in African and Caribbean territories. If the United States provided no aid, nationalists would look elsewhere for assistance, Allen said. U.S. aid would promote evolution rather than revolution in Africa. Herbert Hoover, Jr., the undersecretary of state, resolved the dispute. He agreed to end aid to French, Belgian, and Portuguese colonies, but insisted that the 1957 budget request include new funds for technical assistance to the Federation of Rhodesia and Nyasaland. Hoover cited U.S. interest in the federation's mineral resources and its interest in supporting what Hoover termed the federation's "moderate approach to racial and other policies."[33]

The State Department in Washington warned the U.S. consul in Salisbury against promoting U.S. aid projects. Leo Cyr, director of the Office of African Affairs, wrote that funding for aid projects was uncertain. Recruiting technicians for projects took so long that British officials in London were more skeptical about U.S. aid than they had been. Cyr told Salisbury that British officials had requested that the United States not promote or initiate aid projects. It should wait for colonial governments to request aid. U.S. officials in London and Washington concurred with the British request.[34]

New Interest from Macmillan

Macmillan's government was more open to U.S. aid than its predecessors. In March 1957, Lord Perth, minister of state in the Colonial Office, told U.S. officials in London that Britain welcomed U.S. aid. Britain had long recognized that it lacked sufficient resources to develop the African colonies, he said. Perth offered to share information about British development efforts so that the United States could develop well-coordinated programs for the African colonies. In 1958, Perth complained to Joseph Satterthwaite that the United States was not promptly processing the colonies' applications for loans.[35]

Britain's newly found interest in U.S. aid worried State Department officials. The briefing materials the department prepared for Eisenhower's meeting with Macmillan in Bermuda warned the president that the British might ask for more aid. The materials recommended that Eisenhower indicate a willingness to discuss aid, but the president should warn the British that the amounts were bound to be modest, given congressional opposition. The president should also warn the prime minister that the United States considered such aid as supplemental to British efforts, only a demonstration of U.S. sympathy for British efforts. In 1960, U.S. officials in London worried that aid for African colonies might disrupt Anglo-American relations. One official recommended that the best way to avoid a British request for massive economic assistance was to recognize the limits under which the British were operating in Africa.[36]

U.S. officials were concerned in part because they wanted to direct aid to colonies about to become independent. In 1957, Eisenhower requested and the Congress approved a development loan fund. It was intended to provide long-term loans to development projects that were economically sound, but could not secure loans from other sources. The Kenya government applied for several loans. Officials within the State Department recommended approval. The department told the consul in Nairobi, however, that colonies like Nigeria, that were about to become independent, would be the first priority, since loan funds were limited. The department would not process applications from colonies like Kenya. The department advised that the consul should tell anyone who asked that all colonies were eligible for loans. He should not share information about the department's decision not to process some applications.[37]

The Nairobi consulate was left to fuss. In 1959, Charles Withers, the consul general, complained to Washington that the United States needed to prime the pump. Withers thought that British officials in Kenya were convinced that they knew how to deal with the colony's problems. Withers had little confidence in their capability, however. For reasons of "prejudice, pride, ignorance or otherwise," Kenyan officials, Withers wrote, were wary of U.S. aid. They were content to ask for a few technicians from time to time. Only if the United States provided significantly more aid would the Kenya government understand what could be accomplished. Withers's immediate suggestion was a four-fold increase in education grants provided to Kenyans wanting to study in the United States.[38]

Although the Federation of Rhodesia and Nyasaland received more U.S. assistance than other British African colonies, the State Department was lukewarm towards expanded aid in the late 1950s. Between 1945 and 1958, the United States lent the federation roughly $60 million, more funds than any other British colony in Africa. The International Bank for Reconstruction and Development, in which the U.S. played a major role, lent the federation and its constituent territories an additional $122 million. Most was to help construct the Kariba dam and associated hydroelectric facilities. In the late 1950s, the State Department professed interest in targeting financial aid to the federation on projects that would benefit Africans. Nonetheless, a 1958 inquiry from the Salisbury consulate regarding loans from the development loan fund prompted a less-than-enthusiastic reply from Washington. The department told Salisbury that the federation could apply for loans from the fund. The projects needed to contribute to economic development, and be economically sound and technically feasible. Moreover, the fund would make loans only when the recipient could not obtain financing elsewhere. Washington declined to give the federation's requests high priority because funds were scarce. It appeared the federation could obtain financing from other sources.[39]

The idea of an Anglo-American effort to develop Britain's African colonies came to nothing. British leaders and officials were willing to take financial aid, but they were afraid to allow the United States any overt role in development programs. Various U.S. officials were interested in participating in development programs in African colonies, but neither the Truman nor the Eisenhower administrations were willing and able to invest significant funds in any such effort. Not until independent African states seemed a certainty did the Eisenhower administration opt for an expanded aid program.

13

West Africa and the Sudan, 1953–1960: Final Steps

By the beginning of 1953, three British African colonies, the Gold Coast, Nigeria, and the Sudan, had experienced significant political change. Elections had put African nationalists in office and African politicians controlled considerable areas of public policy. Further political change, and, in fact, self-government, seemed likely. It remained to be seen how fast it would come.

Renewed Nationalist Pressure in the Gold Coast

In early 1953, the British faced renewed pressure from Nkrumah and the CPP for further advances toward full self-government. Nkrumah wanted to appoint African ministers to the portfolios held by British officials, notably finance and justice. He also wanted the British to commit themselves to granting the Gold Coast self-government sooner rather than later.

Many British officials and politicians believed that political change in the Gold Coast had been too fast and too extensive. A senior British official in Accra described a crisis-ridden atmosphere in which he felt like a "man laying down track in front of an oncoming express train." In 1951, Lennox-Boyd, the second-ranking politician in the Colonial Office, lamented that changes in local government had not preceded what he described as virtual self-government at the center.[1]

Some British officials were tempted to believe that Gold Coast nationalists would settle for the appearance of political change. Lyttelton had a hard time taking the new African government seriously. He referred to the Gold Coast constitution as a "stucco façade" and African ministers as "nominal" ministers. He wanted to deny Gold Coast ministers access to sensitive information such as political intelligence reports. An official in London thought that the question was not what the British should concede to Nkrumah. It was, instead, how they should present their proposals in order to convince Nkrumah that he had achieved self-government while ultimate control remained in British hands.[2]

British officials were tempted by the notion that moderate nationalists would emerge to displace Nkrumah. A Colonial Office official imagined that moderates from the CPP and from opposition parties would unite to support the British if Britain took a firm line regard-

202

ing Nkrumah's demands. Prominent chiefs might also align themselves with a new moderate grouping. The official was encouraged by the thought that some Gold Coast political leaders realized how dependent the territory was on British cooperation.[3]

The British eventually concluded that they had few cards to play. British officials in London and Accra acknowledged that few Africans in the Gold Coast were likely to openly oppose self-government. Instead, rival political groups were likely to outbid each other in demands for faster advance. If the British and the Gold Coast nationalists reached an impasse, Britain could use force, withdraw its officials, or impose sanctions on the Gold Coast. None of the options guaranteed success, however. All would endanger dealings with nationalists in other colonies, particularly Nigeria, where African leaders followed developments in the Gold Coast closely. Officials realized that the Churchill government would have a hard time justifying drastic measures to Parliament or to world opinion when the dispute appeared to involve only the timing of steps already agreed to.[4]

Lyttelton appeared to take a firm line, but conceded the CPP most of what it was seeking. For talks with Nkrumah, Lyttelton devised a list of non-negotiable items, intended to leave ultimate control in British hands. Lyttelton wanted a non-political attorney general and British control of external affairs, defense, and the police. Nevertheless, Lyttelton told the cabinet that further political change in the Gold Coast was inevitable. Limited self-government was preferable to full self-government, he argued. Churchill and the cabinet offered Lyttelton their full backing. If the Gold Coast nationalists insisted on taking control of defense or external affairs, the cabinet decided, they should be warned that the Gold Coast would not be allowed to remain in the commonwealth. Such warnings proved unnecessary. Nkrumah and the CPP were willing to accept less than full control of the Gold Coast's internal affairs in the short term. Nkrumah and some other CPP leaders accepted that the Gold Coast needed additional time to prepare for independence.[5]

The agreement the Colonial Office reached with Nkrumah included a declaration by Britain. Britain announced that it was ready to grant the Gold Coast full self-government within the commonwealth once the necessary administrative and constitutional arrangements were complete. When Lyttelton presented the cabinet with the proposals, he was explicit that the proposals did not commit Britain to a timetable. He told his cabinet colleagues, however, that rejecting the proposals would hasten demands for independence. A senior official observed that everyone concerned thought that the Lyttelton proposals constituted "theoretically over hasty political advance." Nevertheless, the sense in London after the 1954 revisions to the Gold Coast constitution was that independence for the Gold Coast was imminent. One official commented that the pace of change seemed headlong. He conceded, nevertheless, that it was difficult to apply the brakes once Britain had started on the path to self-government. Another thought the negotiations with the CPP involved only the "shape and size of the article to be thrown to the wolves before they overtake the political sledge carrying full self-government, if not full commonwealth status."[6]

The only ploy left to the British was to delay the process. Arden-Clarke, an official hoped, could spin out the next stage of constitutional change for eighteen months or so. Three or four years might elapse before the Gold Coast was ready for full commonwealth membership. It would take that long for the Gold Coast to develop a defense establishment, station representatives in a few foreign capitals, and appoint Africans to key civil service positions. Arden-Clarke asked Nkrumah to guarantee that the revised constitution would last three or four years. All Nkrumah would concede was that it would take time to work out all the details.[7]

An Opportunity for Delay

Beginning with the 1954 elections, events in the Gold Coast provided Britain with an opportunity to delay independence. Opposition parties with strong regional or local roots increased their representation in the legislature. Political groups based in the Ashanti region and the Northern Territories capitalized on regional loyalties by demanding a federal constitution. The Gold Coast government controlled the price paid for cocoa, the principal export crop. Farmers in the cocoa-producing areas, in central and southern Gold Coast, demanded that the price be increased to reflect the higher prices paid on the international market. When the government failed to act, disturbances broke out in Kumasi, the Ashanti capital, and elsewhere. Furthermore, the CPP was in turmoil. Elements of both the leadership and the rank and file pressed for faster progress toward independence.[8]

Control of the army and police gave the British leverage. Lennox-Boyd was unhappy about the prospect of granting independence to the Gold Coast. Nkrumah and the CPP government needed to resolve the unrest in Ashanti and settle their differences with the proponents of a federal constitution, he thought. Moreover, he was sympathetic with the claims of Nkrumah's regional opponents. Lennox-Boyd and the British government were persuaded, however, that Nkrumah and his party represented the best hope for a stable, independent Gold Coast friendly to Britain. British officials concluded that undue delay posed real dangers inside the Gold Coast and in Britain's relations with other nationalist parties. The British continued to work with Nkrumah and the CPP to bring the Gold Coast to independence and friendly relations with Britain. When Nkrumah's government could not come to terms with its opponents, the British dispatched a constitutional expert, Sir Frederick Bourne, to study means of devolving greater power to the regions. The National Liberation Movement, the principal opposition group, rejected Bourne's recommendations. Nkrumah's attempts to reach an understanding with the movement and the government's other critics also failed. In response, Lennox-Boyd insisted on another general election. Lennox-Boyd said he wanted evidence that the Gold Coast people desired immediate independence and accepted the current constitution.[9]

Lennox-Boyd and Nkrumah spent nearly a year, from mid–1955 to mid–1956, haggling over the need for an election. Nkrumah and the CPP were reluctant to fight another election, even one that amounted to a plebiscite on independence. They warned Lennox-Boyd that an election might provoke unrest. A failure to secure independence in 1956 would cost the CPP its credibility. They insisted that they and their federalist opponents agreed that the Gold Coast should be independent. Lennox-Boyd remained firm, probably intent on using a CPP election victory as a shield against criticisms that he had ignored the Gold Coast opposition or that he had recommended independence too soon. Lennox-Boyd was optimistic about Nkrumah's ability to secure a majority for independence in a newly elected legislature.[10]

Gold Coast Independence

Lennox-Boyd talked about the need for a reasonable majority in the new legislature, a majority of perhaps ten or twenty. The CPP won a majority of forty, gaining seventy-two seats to their opponents' thirty-two. In September 1956, the British cabinet approved Lennox-Boyd's proposal that the Gold Coast gain full self-government as of March 1, 1957. In the intervening months, Lennox-Boyd brokered an agreement between Nkrumah and the opposition regarding the constitutional details. The opposition knew it had to strike the best deal it could. It may have even thought it could outwit Nkrumah. Certain that independence was won, the CPP could afford to yield on what it considered minor issues.[11]

1953 Crisis in Nigeria

In early 1953, the Colonial Office told the governor of Nigeria, Sir John Macpherson, of Lyttelton's plans for further political change in the Gold Coast. Macpherson returned to his complaints that events in the Gold Coast were undoing his good work in Nigeria. Macpherson argued that the Nigerian political parties would be content to work within their new constitution but for British concessions to the CPP. The two southern political parties were adamant that political changes in Nigeria should keep pace with those in the Gold Coast. Southern agitation was, in turn, unsettling political leaders in the northern region, worried that their region would lose out in an independent Nigeria. Macpherson warned London that it faced a choice between resisting Gold Coast demands for change or doing the same in Nigeria. If Lyttelton went ahead with his plans for the Gold Coast, the British would have to apply sanctions to southern Nigeria to forestall similar changes in Nigeria, Macpherson warned. If they conceded further change to the southerners, they would have to do the same to northern Nigeria to force it to accept the changes. Macpherson argued that he and the other British officials were keeping Nigeria together. If the British gave in to southern demands, the North would insist on leaving Nigeria. The country would disintegrate.[12]

Colonial Office officials tried to calm Macpherson. A senior official, Sir Thomas Lloyd, wrote to Macpherson, without sharing the letter with Lyttelton or other ministers. Lloyd reminded Macpherson that the British government had pledged to grant self-government to the colonies. The Gold Coast was already well down the path to self-government. Ministers, Lloyd wrote, would be unlikely to risk offending Parliament and world opinion by using force in a dispute that appeared to be about timing.[13]

Macpherson soon had his own crisis to deal with and, therefore, little time to worry about the Gold Coast. A member of the Action Group, Anthony Enahoro, introduced a measure in the Nigerian legislature calling for independence in 1956. Northern representatives proposed an alternative measure calling for independence as soon as practicable. In the council of ministers, a majority composed of the four northern ministers and the six British officials voted to bar ministers from participating in the legislature's debate on the independence resolution. The four Action Group ministers representing the Western Region resigned in protest. In the legislature's March 1953 session, northern votes defeated the Enahoro resolution. Representatives from the East and West then walked out when the legislature took up the North's alternative motion. Crowds in Lagos booed northern representatives. Newspapers in southern Nigeria attacked both British officials and northern politicians. Papers controlled by the Action Group talked of a Mau Mau–like rising in Nigeria and the party threatened a nationwide campaign of civil disobedience. The Action Group announced plans to hold a rally in Kano, the largest northern city, but British officials banned the rally. In mid–May, four days of fighting between northerners and southerners in Kano left thirty-six dead and 241 injured. On June 2, Coronation Day, riots broke out in Lagos. Finally, the northern regional assembly and house of chiefs adopted a program that amounted to call for the dissolution of Nigeria.[14]

The Colonial Office blamed Macpherson for some of the troubles in Nigeria. It cast doubts on any connection with developments in the Gold Coast. The Colonial Office thought Macpherson had been naïve to think that the Action Group would accept defeat on the independence motion. Attempting to bar ministers from supporting the motion in the legislature had been unwise. Lyttelton assured the cabinet that the unrest in Nigeria stemmed from internal issues, in particular the friction among the regions. Moving ahead with constitutional changes in the Gold Coast would not worsen the Nigerian situation, Lyttelton said.[15]

Lyttelton Constitution

Lyttelton also told the cabinet that Nigeria needed a new constitution. The Colonial Office decided that the Macpherson constitution was cumbersome and unwieldy. It highlighted as key problems the limitations on ministers' powers and the distribution of authority between the central government and the regions. Lyttelton proposed to shift power from the center to the regions and give central ministers greater authority over their ministries. The new constitution would also incorporate safeguards to reassure the North. To satisfy nationalist politicians in the East and West, the constitution would provide a further shift of power from the British to Nigerians.[16]

As the British began negotiations with the Nigerian nationalists about a new constitution, a junior Colonial Office official identified three options for the British negotiators: refusing Nigeria self-government in 1956, continuing to concede incremental amounts of self-government over a longer period, and offering the regions self-government immediately. The official argued that the first option was feasible, but not acceptable to British or world opinion. The second would only prolong the agony without changing the result. If, however, the British offered Awolowo and Azikiwe immediate self-government for their regions, the British would regain the initiative and put the nationalist leaders in a bind. If the nationalists rejected immediate self-government, the British could follow their own timetable. If the nationalists chose self-government, the official thought that they would fail to govern effectively. The British could then reassert control within eighteen months and do so with wide public support in Nigeria.[17]

Macpherson agreed with the official's recommendation. Senior Colonial Office officials and some of Macpherson's key subordinates opposed it, however. They argued that no Nigerian politician could reject an offer of self-government and expect to retain popular support. More important, the British could reclaim control after granting a region self-government only if they stipulated from the start that they reserved the power to do so. Nigerian leaders were unlikely to accept such an arrangement as real self-government. If the British moved to reclaim control, Nigerian politicians would charge that whatever reasons the British offered were false and unfounded.[18]

As in the case of the Gold Coast, Lyttelton's rhetoric sounded tough. He insisted that the British retain control of the police, the judiciary, and the civil service. Explaining his position to Macpherson, Lyttelton said that the Nigerians needed to understand that if the governor did not control the police, the British would leave Nigeria immediately. The Nigerians would have to deal with whatever mess they found themselves in. The British staff would leave, and foreign investors would follow them. If Nigerians balked at Lyttelton's conditions or insisted that he set a date for self-government, he would end the discussion.[19]

Again, Lyttelton ended up conceding most of what the nationalists wanted. The constitution worked out at conferences in London in the summer of 1953 and in Lagos in early 1954 followed the pattern Lyttelton described to the cabinet. It moved powers to the regions from the center and gave central ministers a larger role in their ministries. It replaced British officials with Nigerian ministers in the eastern and western regions. It provided direct elections for the legislatures in the two southern regions. Despite long-standing opposition to timetables, Lyttelton agreed that the government would convene another conference after three years to review the constitution. The British pledged to grant self-government beginning in 1956 to any region that requested it.[20]

Favoring the North

Conceding the possibility of regional self-government bought off the southern politicians. It also served to reassure the northerners by giving them an effective veto over Nigerian self-government. Nigeria would not gain self-government until and unless the North chose self-government for itself. The agreement probably seemed to Lyttelton and his officials an effective brake on political change. Moreover, the British saw northern politicians as cooperative and conservative. Describing the London conference to the cabinet, Lyttelton complimented Abubakar Tafewa Balewa, one of the northern leaders, while calling Azikiwe and Awolowo unreliable and characterizing their relationship as an unholy alliance. Northerners, Lyttelton told the cabinet, were dignified, courteous, and conservative. British officials continued to play a larger role in the northern regional government than they did in the other regions. Relations between British officials and prominent northerners were cordial, in contrast to the estrangement between southern politicians and the British.[21]

Over the next several years, the British bent over backwards to keep northern leaders happy. Despite substantial and obvious ethnic diversity within the North, a government commission recommended against carving another region out of the North. The British did not push local government reforms in the North, while changes in local government proceeded rapidly in the south. Until 1957, the North kept its own electoral law. Women could not vote in the North and elections were still indirect in most instances.[22]

Azikiwe and the NCNC

Azikiwe and the NCNC remained the British nemesis. The Action Group under Awolowo was nearly as aggressive and outspoken, but British officials thought they could work with the westerners. In the 1954 elections, the NCNC reclaimed control of the eastern region from a breakaway faction. To the surprise of many, it also won a majority in the western assembly. The NCNC was intent on spurring economic development in the East without British participation. Eastern leaders visited Europe and the United States in search of foreign investment and the eastern regional government established several government corporations. The NCNC attempted to control civil service appointments and proposed local government reforms that would remove British officials from key positions. NCNC leaders and newspapers controlled by the NCNC launched personal attacks on British officials, attacks that were deeply resented. In 1955, the NCNC proposed a budget for the East that eliminated supplemental payments to British officials holding senior civil service positions. If the budget had been enacted, it would have paved the way for appointing Nigerians to the more than sixty senior positions. In 1956, infighting within the NCNC produced the revelation that the eastern regional government had invested funds in a bank owned by Azikiwe. Furthermore, the bank had cooperated with the regional government in a series of questionable transactions.[23]

Conditions in the East provided a test for the notion that the British should grant self-government only if a territory could manage its affairs in an orderly fashion. In 1955, Lennox-Boyd and officials in London considered withdrawing or suspending the offer to grant the East self-government in 1956, given the behavior of the eastern regional government. Lennox-Boyd anticipated that orderly government would soon break down in the East. He thought that drastic measures were needed. Nevertheless, officials in London and Nigeria dissuaded him from acting. Postponing self-government in the East would generate unrest, officials said. Britain lacked the police and troops to restore order, they warned. Postponing self-government might make conditions worse and would be difficult to explain to the outside world. Conditions might be bad and many Nigerians might recognize that they were bad, but no Nigerian was about to openly oppose self-government. Lennox-Boyd summoned Azikiwe to London in November 1956 and lectured him on the need for honest government and on the folly of attacking British officials in public. In early 1957, a commission dispatched by the Colonial Office to the eastern region issued a report highly critical of Azikiwe. It stated that his actions fell short of the expectations of honest, reasonable people. Some British officials hoped that the report would cause Azikiwe to resign. Instead, he called new elections. He and his party were returned with an increased majority.[24]

1957 Constitutional Conference

Beginning in spring 1956, British officials reviewed their options for the upcoming constitutional conference promised by Lyttelton. They were pessimistic about Nigeria's prospects as an independent nation. Sir James Robertson had come from the Sudan to replace Macpherson as governor of Nigeria in 1955. He thought Nigeria would have to rely on outside assistance to run its government for a considerable period. Surely, it was a mockery of independence, Robertson told the Colonial Office, if a country needed outside resources to run its government machine. Regions were apt to secede from an independent Nigeria, a Colonial Office briefing paper warned. Corruption was rampant, it went on. Governmental chaos or regional dictatorships were real possibilities.[25]

The prevailing view was that Britain should attempt to delay Nigerian independence as long as possible. Robertson advised that Lennox-Boyd stress to Nigerian leaders the dangers posed by independence. He should refuse to commit to a definite date for independence or for the next round of constitutional review and revision. Colonial Office staff proposed that the British arrange two stages of constitutional change. They should retain a large enough role in the central government, perhaps several British officials as ministers, to justify another constitutional conference in three or four years' time. At that conference, the British could commit to independence in another three or four years.[26]

Nevertheless, some officials recognized that delay could be risky and difficult. Sir John Rankine, governor of the western region, counseled that a strategy of delay needed to be qualified by a commitment to retaining Nigerian goodwill. Rankine repeated the dictum that it was better to yield concessions with good grace than be forced to concede. The Colonial Office briefing paper noted that delaying self-government at the federal level would be hard to justify once all three regions chose self-government. If the British used the fear of ethnic conflict to justify delay, they would be open to charges of divide and rule.[27]

The constitutional conference originally scheduled for September 1956 was delayed while the investigation of alleged corruption in the eastern region proceeded. Before the conference could resume in May 1957 and after the Gold Coast gained its independence, the Nigerian house of representatives surprised the British by voting to demand independence in 1959. This time the northern representatives supported the demand. The Action Group now controlled the western region and the independence resolution had the support of all three major political parties and all three regions. The North's decision surprised the British. A year earlier, the British had learned that the northern region planned to ask for self-government in 1959. Nevertheless, Sir Bryan Sharwood-Smith, the governor of the northern region, had assured Robertson that the North remained opposed to independence in the near future. If Nigeria became independent sooner than northern leaders thought wise, they would consider secession, Sharwood-Smith wrote. As late as 1958, senior British officials in Nigeria struggled to accept that the northern leaders were unwilling to oppose independence and were willing to take their chances in an independent Nigeria.[28]

Colonial Office staff advised that the northerners were unlikely to renege on their commitment to independence, however. Regardless of Nigeria's apparent lack of readiness for independence, the civil servants argued, the best way for Britain to keep Nigeria friendly was to grant independence soon. Lennox-Boyd and his cabinet colleagues were reluctant to agree. Lennox-Boyd conceded that refusing independence in the face of a unanimous demand from the Nigerian political parties would be dangerous. Britain would be risking Nigerian goodwill. Nevertheless, he flirted with the idea that the northerners would slow the process. Lord Home (Sir Alec Douglas-Home), the commonwealth relations secretary, opposed independence in 1959. Nigeria should not gain its independence before the Federation of Rhodesia and Nyasaland did, Home maintained. The federation's status was due for review in 1960. Home proposed that Nigerian regions govern themselves on an experimental basis for five years. A commission could then review their status. The Cabinet Colonial Policy Committee decided that Lennox-Boyd should avoid committing to independence in 1959. He should persuade the Nigerians to accept a commitment to further consultations about the constitution.[29]

During the 1957 conference, Lennox-Boyd, like Lyttelton before him, gave in to Nigerian demands. He agreed that if a newly elected Nigerian Federal parliament in 1960 requested independence within the year, Britain would consider the request with sympathy and would be prepared to fix a date for independence. When Lennox-Boyd brought the issue back to the cabinet in September 1958, he professed considerable misgivings. He said that he doubted that it would be right to relinquish control of Nigeria if the British government had a free hand. He saw irreconcilable differences within the country and the prospect of a northern secession. Nevertheless, Lennox-Boyd proposed a clear commitment to Nigerian independence in 1960. After careful thought, Lennox-Boyd told the cabinet, he had concluded that Britain gained nothing by delaying further. Britain needed to retain Nigerian goodwill. President de Gaulle had recently offered the French colonies in African independence. Britain could not afford to lag behind the French. Refusing independence would produce only a temporary delay, Lennox-Boyd admitted. It would unite the Nigerian politicians against the British. Robertson and the governors of the two southern regions recommended independence. Lennox-Boyd, reluctantly, agreed.[30]

Bystanders

U.S. officials in Accra and Lagos were bystanders to political events in West Africa. The State Department liked to think of the United States as a friendly bystander in West Africa. U.S. officials were more likely to be friendly to British officials, however, than to African nationalists in the 1950s. U.S. consuls in West Africa identified more closely with British civil servants than they did with African nationalists. U.S. officials remained skeptical about African politicians and self-government and professed serious doubts about the future of the Gold Coast or Nigeria as independent states.

Reports from Accra portrayed local conditions in a negative light. Local government reforms were not going well, the consuls reported. British officials did not trust African politicians and doubted their ability to govern an independent country. The CPP was likely to disintegrate once independence was certain. Corruption was endemic in the Gold Coast, consular reports maintained. Offering gifts was a part of almost every business or government transaction. Arden-Clarke was well suited to guide the Gold Coast to independence, consuls reported. Yet his ethnocentric and narrow views blinded him to the need to import technical assistance from countries other than Britain.[31]

In September 1953, William Cole, the consul-general in Accra, filed a particularly unflattering report on the CPP. The party, Cole wrote, was monolithic in the style of communist parties. It was left wing. Its appeal centered on improving the lot of the common man. It expected to do so through monolithic control of the state and social apparatus and through provision of state services to the greatest number possible. It was not tied to Russia, however. It was a homegrown nationalistic party, with an ideology more akin to fascism than communism. Still, it was a party of revolt, intent on overthrowing the power of the chiefs. It was an anti-traditional party. According to Cole, its supporters were teachers, clerks, farmers, and ill-paid employees of all kinds. Its supporters resembled the disgruntled lower middle classes that supported Hitler or Mussolini.[32]

Reports from Lagos were similar. Robert Ross, the consul general in Lagos in 1953, focused on instability in the eastern region, on corruption, and on what he characterized as the absence of responsible and able political leaders. He wrote that the Nigerian regions were not ready to govern themselves. Independence for Nigeria would bring social and economic retrogression and bitter struggles for political power, he maintained. Nigerians were not clear about the meaning of self-government. In the western region, they held no animosity towards the British. Westerners thought that things had never been better. Nevertheless, everyone supported the nationalist parties and expected conditions to be better when Nigeria was independent. Ross acknowledged the ideal of national self-determination, but contended that no nation existed in Nigeria.[33]

The Lagos consulate focused on the contrast between the abilities of British officials and the ambition of Nigerian politicians. British officials were keeping Nigeria together. They were doing the hard work of administration, while Nigerian politicians jockeyed for position. It was only British officials and the police who prevented a breakdown in law and order, the consulate argued. If Nigerian politicians had been more reasonable and cooperative, the Macpherson constitution could have been made to work.[34]

By April 1955, the consulate in Accra concluded that the Gold Coast was on a sure path to independence. Donald Lamm, the consul-general, discounted the possibility of the National Liberation Movement displacing the Congress People's Party. The British, Lamm reported, were definitely and openly on the CPP's side. The British were not about to change their minds. The British wanted to get out of the Gold Coast as soon as they could. They might do so even in the midst of bloodshed, as they had done in India. The unrest in Ashanti and any constitutional questions were Nkrumah's to solve.[35]

The consulate in Lagos was slower to anticipate Nigerian independence. Despite nationalist agitation, it thought that British gradualism would prevail. It remained focused on northern reluctance to remain within an independent Nigeria, even after northern politicians supported the 1957 independence resolution. Edward McLaughlin, the consul general in late 1955, told Washington that nothing startling was likely to emerge from the upcoming constitutional conference. The offer of regional self-government in 1956 had taken the steam out of the nationalists, he wrote. It would be five or ten years before they made a serious push for independence. As late as December 1957, Ralph Hunt, the consul general, told Washington that Awolowo privately wanted independence postponed to at least 1962. Northern leaders were continuing to prepare secretly for secession, he claimed.[36]

The somber reports from Accra and Lagos were in sharp contrast to Mason Sears's cheery report about his 1954 African tour. Sears reported that West Africa was no longer a colonial region. There was no economic or racial exploitation. Economic development and progressive political advancement were the order of the day. The "seeds of self-sustaining freedom are almost certainly beginning to bear fruit," Sears reported.[37]

Mason Sears met with Nkrumah and found him a friendly, earnest, and astute man. Nkrumah understood the responsibilities that came with independence, Sears wrote. According to Sears, the Gold Coast was essentially self-governing despite British control of defense and external affairs. The Gold Coast could, Sears understood, declare its independence, and apply for membership in the commonwealth at any time. Sears had good words for the British as well. They deserved great credit, he wrote, for the way they were assisting the people of the Gold Coast assume the responsibilities of nationhood.

Sears was non-committal about Nigeria. Maintaining Nigeria's unity was the major issue. Key leaders like Awolowo were concerned about it. The British were determined not to permit Nigerian self-government until all three regions had agreed.

Awolowo and Azikiwe visited the United States in the middle 1950s. Their encounters with senior State Department officials suggest that Washington was not ready to embrace Nigerian nationalism in the flesh. The briefing materials prepared for Azikiwe's visit in 1954 included discussion of his newspapers' alleged adherence to the communist line. The conclusion was that Azikiwe was friendly to the United States although he allowed his papers to print anti–American articles. At a luncheon for Azikiwe, Assistant Secretary of State Byroade noted U.S. support for self-government, but mentioned the dangers of premature independence. Byroade praised the British for moving Nigeria towards self-government, regardless of the serious problems facing the colony. When Azikiwe returned in 1955, a meeting with Assistant Secretary of State George Allen went less well. Allen was confused about Azikiwe's position in the Nigerian government. He thought Azikiwe was the prime minister. Allen was also unaware that Azikiwe had lived in the United States. When Awolowo met with Allen in 1956, Allen praised Britain's work in Africa and warned Awolowo that the problems of independence would surpass whatever problems the nationalists currently faced.[38]

Sierra Leone

Official U.S. contact with Sierra Leone during the Eisenhower administration consisted of occasional visits by officials stationed at Monrovia, Liberia. Reports to Washington indicated that self-government for Sierra Leone was inevitable despite the absence of a strong nationalist movement. In January 1957, Thomas Simons, charge d'affaires in Monrovia, wrote that the British could not restrain the pressure for self-government. They lacked the will to do so. According to Simons, morale among British officials in Sierra Leone was low. They felt that the local people did not appreciate their efforts and that the United Nations subjected British colonial policies to unfair criticism. British officials believed that Britain was draining its resources to develop the colonies and reaped only ill will and criticism. The same year, Richard Jones from the Monrovia consulate reported that almost no African he spoke with in Sierra Leone favored the early departure of the British or Sierra Leonean self-government. Nonetheless, the Gold Coast's independence had spurred both envy and interest in political change. Sierra Leone had been a British colony longer than the Gold Coast. According to Jones, Sierra Leone would gain self-government because local politicians wanted to claim their place in history and the British wanted to leave as quickly as possible.[39]

The Sierra Leone People's Party, led by Milton Margai, was the territory's principal nationalist party. The party was perceived as moderate. It was thought likely to cooperate with the British and to respect British investments in diamond mines and British strategic concerns about access to Freetown harbor. In 1958, some of the party's militant elements left to form the People's National Party and agitate for rapid political change. U.S. officials then sensed a quickening of the political pace in Sierra Leone. They began to predict that independence would come sooner rather than later. The British would move quickly, they said, to shore up the position of Milton Margai and the Sierra Leone People's Party. In November 1958, Washington told the Monrovia consulate to station an official in Freetown to oversee developments in Sierra Leone and Guinea, its newly independent neighbor.[40]

In the late 1950s, attitudes in Washington shifted from concern about Sierra Leone's future to satisfaction that an independent Sierra Leone was likely to be friendly to the United States. In late 1957, State Department staff were concerned that Sierra Leone was not ready for independence. Independence in 1961 or 1962 might produce chaos and jeopardize the stability of West Africa, they predicted. They worried that the split in the Sierra Leone People's Party might undercut the party's ability to govern. U.S. officials came to appreciate, however, that both parties in Sierra Leone were willing to work with the British. By late 1960, the official U.S. view was that Sierra Leone was moving to independence with moderation. Absent was the fire-eating nationalistic demagoguery that developed elsewhere. Sierra Leone was likely to retain the kind of government the British had installed, officials believed. Sierra Leone would not borrow from its neighbors, notably Guinea. At the time, Washington thought the former French colony was flirting with Russia and its allies. Sierra Leone's leaders were, instead, well disposed towards the United States. American missionaries had been active in the territory and many prominent Sierra Leoneans had attended schools staffed by American teachers.[41]

British Choices in the Sudan

Despite the February 1953 agreement with Egypt over the Sudan, Churchill and his closest advisers remained unreconciled to the prospect of an independent Sudan. Churchill imagined that forceful action in the Sudan would repair the damage to British prestige he thought the agreement with Egypt caused. He and Selwyn Lloyd, second ranking minister in the Foreign Office, offered 'Abd al-Rahman full support if he would repudiate the agreement the Sudanese political parties had negotiated with the Egyptians. Churchill's aides grumbled that the Sudan agreement was another step in a policy of scuttle, which they thought would cost Britain her African colonies.[42]

On the other hand, Eden identified a prosperous, stable, and self-governing Sudan with Britain's interests. He told the governor-general that Britain had little or no strategic or economic interests in the Sudan. Britain had an interest in ensuring that the Sudan did not become a center for communism or for unrest and subversion. Reconciling northern and southern Sudan was important so that unrest in the south did not affect the neighboring British colonies. According to Eden, Britain's tasks were now to make the 1953 agreement work, help the Sudan progress toward self-determination, and ensure that blame attached to the Egyptians if anything went wrong.[43]

In the Sudan, Robertson probably spoke for his colleagues in the political service when he said that the Sudan agreement meant no real and lasting good for the Sudanese or British interests. Robertson told the provincial governors that Britain faced a hard choice: unrest and war in Egypt in the near future or civil war and administrative chaos in the Sudan later. He worried that he had failed the Sudanese by encouraging opposition to 'Abd al-Rahman and the Umma Party. More to the point, he blamed shortsighted Sudanese politicians, Egypt, the Foreign Office, and the United States. Robertson told his colleagues that the United States was intent on an agreement and the British government was unlikely to withstand the pressure.[44]

British and Egyptian officials saw that the situation in the Sudan had changed dramatically. Before the overthrow of King Farouk, Egyptian insistence on sovereignty over the Sudan had guaranteed the British support from significant elements of the Sudanese population. 'Abd al-Rahman, the Umma Party, and anyone with links to the Mahdist cause were likely to prefer the British to the Egyptians. By renouncing sovereignty, the Free Officers detached the Umma Party from the British. They created an opportunity for the Sudanese political parties to strengthen their claim to self-determination by reaching an agreement with the Egyptians. A Sudan-Egypt agreement, in turn, pushed the British toward their own agreement with Egypt.

In the new circumstances, the upcoming elections to the new Sudanese parliament appeared the most likely means for Egypt and Britain to bolster their standing in the Sudan. Both nations deployed money and influence to help the parties they believed most amenable to friendly ties: the National Unionist Party for the Egyptians and the Umma Party for the British. The British negotiated an agreement with the Umma Party. The British offered cooperation in return for promises from the Umma Party. The party was to support Sudanese independence rather than union with Egypt. It was to forge an alliance with the Socialist Republican Party and permit British officials to remain in southern Sudan after independence if southern representatives requested their retention. In an attempt to deny the National Unionist Party support in the south, the British also sponsored a new party, the Southern Party.[45]

1953 Elections

In the November 1953 elections, the National Unionist Party won a clear victory. It won fifty-one of ninety-seven seats in the house of representatives and twenty-two of the thirty elected seats in the senate. The Umma Party won only twenty-two seats in the house of representatives and three elected senate seats. The Southern Party took ten house seats, the Socialist Republicans three seats, and independents won the remaining ten seats.

Nevertheless, the meaning of the election results was not clear. Had the Sudanese voted for union with Egypt? Had they voted against British rule by favoring the politician and party who had most consistently opposed the British? Or had they voted for the National Unionists out of fear of 'Abd al-Rahman and his ambitions?

The British interpreted the results as something less than a final defeat. They attempted to curry favor with the National Unionists. Eden instructed Howe to reach out to them. He should support elements of the ruling party willing to move away from the Egyptians. At the same time, Howe should encourage 'Abd al-Rahman to organize an effective opposition party. Yet he should also warn him that the British felt obligated to work with the elected government, if only to block an Egyptian takeover. British officials feared Sudanization, the substitution of Sudanese for British officials. It would reduce the effectiveness of the Sudan's administration and lead to violence and disorder, they worried. Nonetheless, they recognized that Sudanese political leaders all favored more rapid Sudanization. Sudanese leaders would interpret British reluctance to appoint Sudanese to key positions as a sign of British unwillingness to relinquish control. The British had already committed to Sudanization within three years. To remove an area of contention with the new government, the British decided not to oppose faster change. The British were also concerned about conditions in the southern Sudan, about the possibility of conflict between southerners and northerners. Nevertheless, the thinking was that the British should downplay such concerns lest Sudanese think the British were trying to prolong their rule.[46]

The National Unionist leader, Ismail al-Azhari, offered the British reassurance. In mid–February 1954, he told a senior British official that no sensible person would overthrow one master just to replace him with another. Most Sudanese saw an alliance with Egypt as the surest way of ridding themselves of the British. The Sudanese did not want to subject themselves to the Egyptians.[47]

The British were not without resources. Howe was an able diplomat. Despite al-Azhari's long record of opposition, Howe forged a working relationship with the Sudanese prime minister. Al-Azhari was open to working with Howe and the British. He needed support wherever he could find it. The National Unionist Party was an uneasy coalition. 'Ali al-Marghani and his khatmiyya supporters probably had a stronger voice than did al-Azhari. At least twice in 1954 and 1955, dissension within the party nearly drove al-Azhari from office. 'Ali al-Mirghani's fear of 'Abd al-Rahman played a large role in saving al-Azhari on both occasions.[48]

Riots in Khartoum

The tensions within the Sudan resurfaced in March 1954. On March 1, 1954, General Neguib arrived in Khartoum for the reconvening of the Sudanese parliament. The Egyptian leader's arrival sparked fighting between Umma supporters and followers of the National Unionist Party. Twenty civilians and ten police were killed, including the British police commandant. The British had only one, under-strength battalion in Khartoum. The British cabinet considered dispatching two additional battalions and a fighter/bomber squadron. In the end, the British pressured 'Abd al-Rahman to have his followers leave the city and forced al-Azhari to declare a state of emergency.[49]

The Khartoum riots propelled British officials and Sudanese politicians further toward Sudanese independence. The police's inept performance reminded the British that their ability to maintain law and order was limited. British officials had considered ways to bolster their position, including introducing more troops and arresting the Sudanese cabinet. Such notions now seemed fanciful. Violence in the streets raised worries in the Sudanese cabinet about the Egyptians and the Umma supporters. National Unionist leaders decided that accelerated Sudanization was the correct response. With support from the Foreign Office and the State Department, but not from Howe, al-Azhari's government contrived a Sudanization committee that followed the government's lead. The committee recommended that all British police and military officers be gone by the end of summer 1954. All members of the Sudan political service would leave by July 1955.[50]

In the end, the British were willing to place their bets on a National Unionist government. When Umma Party leaders asked the British to repudiate the agreement with Egypt in June 1954, the British turned them down. The Egyptians could not withstand Sudanese nationalism, the British explained. Tearing up the agreement would turn the Sudanese against the British and the Umma Party. The governor-general observed that the National Unionists were probably nationalist before they were unionist. They might not discard an Egyptian connection until they were felt secure from 'Abd al-Rahman and the Umma. In any case, they were unlikely to cede their newly won power to the Egyptians.[51]

By the fall of 1954, the Egyptians signaled that a Sudanese union with Egypt no longer seemed attractive. The Sudanese government was weak, Egyptian officials told the British. The country was bedeviled by tension between the two main political parties and between the north and south. Violence and bloodshed were on the horizon. Sudanization was making the situation worse everywhere. The only possible link between Sudan and Egypt would be a loose union. British officials reported that the Egyptians had come to understand how much money union with the Sudan would cost them.[52]

End Game

In summer 1955, the Sudan again lurched towards independence. Most British members of the Sudan political service left the Sudan by November 1954. Howe had resigned. His replacement was Sir Alexander Knox Helm, an experienced diplomat, but viewed by many as a placeholder. Al-Azhari's government was hanging on. Without Egyptian support or consistent support from southern representatives, its future appeared to depend on an understanding with the Umma Party. When disturbances broke out in the southern Sudan, the British and al-Azhari agreed that the sooner independence came the better. The British realized that while they continued to rule the Sudan, they lacked the means to govern it. "Authority without power" was their concern. They convinced themselves that the sooner the Sudan was independent the sooner a Sudanese government could turn its full attention to revolving differences with the south.[53]

After nearly six months of working through the technicalities, the Sudan gained its independence. The 1953 agreement called for elections to a constituent assembly before the constituent assembly could ask that Sudan become independent. In summer 1955, the Sudanese proposed that a plebiscite be substituted for elections to an assembly. The British and Egyptians were agreeable. By October, the government in London decided that it would be sufficient for the Sudanese parliament to ask for independence. To make the point clearer, the Foreign Office announced that Knox Helm would resign for personal reasons before Christmas 1955 and that the British did not plan to appoint a successor. On December 15, 1955, al-Azhari introduced a motion for Sudanese independence. By December 22, both houses approved the measure and the Sudan became independent on January 1, 1956.[54]

Support for Independence

Dulles and the State Department were pleased with the February 1953 Sudan agreement. In the months immediately following the agreement, they were intent that its provisions be implemented. Dulles sent a congratulatory note to Eden and Mahmoud Fawzi, the Egyptian foreign minister. Dulles also had the London embassy pass along his personal thanks to Eden. Throughout spring 1953, the State Department urged that the elections mandated by the agreement take place sooner rather than later. When it appeared that the onset of the rainy season in the southern Sudan would require postponement until the fall, the State Department suggested that only the elections in two southern provinces be delayed, a suggestion that was ignored. When the Egyptians complained to Caffrey about the uncooperative attitude of the Sudan political service, Caffrey relayed the complaints to his British counterpart in Cairo. The British representative assured Caffrey that the London government was taking steps to address the problem. Later Caffrey admonished Egyptian leaders for exaggerating British misdeeds in the Sudan.[55]

Nevertheless, a defense agreement between Britain and Egypt was a higher priority for the United States than the future of the Sudan. The State Department viewed Sudanese issues in terms of their impact on Anglo-Egyptian negotiations. In December 1953, the Foreign Office asked the State Department to dissuade General Neguib from visiting the Sudan. The office claimed that a triumphal journey by Neguib to Khartoum would upset Churchill and Conservative backbenchers. It would also jeopardize the Foreign Office's negotiations with Egypt. The State Department replied that Neguib would ignore a suggestion from Washington. The best way to ensure an agreement with Egypt, Washington told the London embassy, was to accelerate the negotiations. An agreement should be in place before the opening of the Sudanese parliament. When the State Department debated the merits of a United States statement about the 1953 elections, a principal consideration was the statement's impact on the Anglo-Egyptian negotiations.[56]

Still, after the 1953 Sudan agreement, the United States remained committed to the emergence of an independent Sudan. In August 1955, the State Department had U.S. representatives in Khartoum advise Sudanese leaders to vote for independence, rather than union with Egypt. The United States would not send aid to the Sudan if parliament chose union with Egypt, the Department's instructions said.[57]

A consistent policy did not prevent friction within the State Department. In December 1953, Caffrey's report about the Sudanese elections lamented the British failure to retain its hold on the Sudan. Caffrey observed that the British would not have lost out had they followed American advice. The State Department office responsible for Anglo-American relations felt compelled to reply. It could not locate any relevant advice the United States had offered Britain about the Sudan. The British would probably retort that it was following U.S. advice when it negotiated an agreement with Egypt and arranged early elections in the Sudan. When the State Department drafted a statement congratulating Britain and Egypt on arranging the Sudanese elections, the Bureau of European Affairs refused to approve the draft. It contended that any statement would irritate public opinion in Britain and complicate negotiations about an Anglo-Egyptian defense agreement.[58]

In the Sudan, relations between the U.S. representative and the Sudan Political Service were testy. In 1953, the Sudan government issued permission for appointment of a U.S. liaison officer, the first official United States presence in the Sudan. Joseph Sweeney, the first liaison officer, was given to sharp criticism of the Sudan political service. The British officials did not appreciate Sweeney's outspokenness. The Sudan government sought to have Sweeney recalled. It invested time and energy in looking for evidence of malfeasance on Sweeney's part.[59]

In retrospect, it is clear that the Gold Coast, Nigeria, and the Sudan were securely on the road to independence several years before the fact. At the time, divisions among nationalists seemed to threaten continued political change. The British appeared to hold some important cards. Nevertheless, the nationalists were agreed at least that the British should leave. British leaders talked a good game, but, in all cases, decided that discretion was the better part of valor. Further delays would only alienate nationalist leaders.

East Africa, 1953–1959:
Political Transformations

In 1953, a rural insurgency continued in Kenya, but most of East Africa seemed quiet. Unlike in West Africa, African nationalists were not much in evidence. Africans played only small roles in colonial government. By 1959, Tanganyika, however, seemed headed for self-government under an African majority government. Despite the absence of strong, united nationalist parties, both Uganda and Zanzibar had seen significant constitutional changes. Even in Kenya, the African nationalists had grown in strength and forced political reforms.

In 1953, U.S. officials in East Africa remained bystanders. As in West Africa, they worried about British capacity to manage a transition to self-government and about the African capacity to govern itself. By 1959, however, U.S. officials had become players in local affairs, particularly in Tanganyika, Kenya, and Uganda. They conferred with and counseled nationalist leaders. They lobbied for particular political changes and sought to identify Africans who would be influential once self-government came.

Quelling Unrest in Kenya

With a state of emergency in place, the Kenya government moved to crush the uprising in the Kikuyu areas in early 1953. Operations began slowly because the Kenya police were ill-prepared for combating widespread violence. By summer 1953, however, the London government dispatched senior police and military officials to the territory and flooded the restive areas with British troops. At the height of the emergency, Britain deployed twelve infantry battalions (roughly thirteen thousand troops), armor and artillery units, and a Royal Air Force bomber squadron in addition to twenty thousand police and twenty-five thousand home guards recruited from among Kikuyu loyal to the government. The government resettled rural Kikuyu in fortified villages, expelled nearly all Kikuyu from Nairobi, and detained thousands of suspected insurgents. The detention camps held seventy thousand Africans at their peak. At least 150,000 Africans were detained at one time or another. Furthermore, the government imposed stringent laws and established special courts to enforce them. Over three thousand Africans were tried for capital offenses and nearly eleven hundred were hanged. Suppressing the uprising cost roughly £60 million, most borne by the Kenyan budget.[1]

In military terms, the British effort was successful. After two years of intense military and police activity from summer 1953 to summer 1955, active resistance was reduced to isolated bands in the forests. By December 1955, the army and police abandoned routine patrols and large-scale operations. In November 1956, the army withdrew from security operations, leaving the Kenya police in charge.[2]

As the British moved to crush the uprising, U.S. officials remained critical of their performance and skeptical of Kenya's future. The London embassy portrayed the Colonial Office as groping for a solution in the absence of the dynamic and imaginative leadership of Sir Andrew Cohen, named governor of Uganda in 1952. From Nairobi, Consul General Edmund J. Dorsz reported that the British would quell the rebellion, but he doubted the effectiveness of British intelligence efforts. He continued to question whether Africans were capable of organizing such prolonged resistance. The British reported no sign that Kenya's Indian community was assisting the dissidents, but Dorsz had his doubts. Dorsz also thought that the unrest arose from economic and social problems. A long-term solution required accelerated economic, social, and political development. On the political front, Dorsz imagined a middle approach, somewhere between what happened in the Gold Coast and South Africa. Dorsz doubted, however, whether Kenya had sufficient resources to carry out the necessary development or whether the European settlers would allow such development to proceed. In Washington, the State Department's Office of Intelligence and Research produced an analysis of the rebellion in June 1953. It and the office's August 1953 survey of conditions in Africa echoed Dorsz's thinking. The fighting in Kenya was the result of poor economic and social conditions, they said. Once the British dealt with the unrest, they would face renewed nationalist agitation. A lack of resources and of enlightened leadership in African and European communities was likely to produce a long and bitter struggle for power in Kenya, they predicted.[3]

Kenya's European settlers saw the uprising as an opportunity to strengthen their hold on the colony. They agitated for tough measures against insurgents and demanded a say in directing military and police operations. A settler leader, Michael Blundell, became a member of a three-man war council. Nevertheless, the settlers' ambitions encountered stern resistance from British military and political officials.

The senior military and police officials assigned to Kenya were often at odds with the settlers. Some of the officers sent from Britain developed low opinions of the colony, its administration, and its European population. General Erskine, British army commander after June 1953, said of the settlers, "I hate the guts of them all; they are all middle class sluts." Particularly in the uprising's early days, the British struggled to sort out who was in charge: the military, the police, or provincial and district officials. The settlers' insistence on a larger role for themselves made a bad situation worse. British suppression of the unrest in the Kikuyu territory was brutal. The army and police units composed of settlers were especially ill disciplined and indiscriminate and the British professionals often found them more trouble than they were worth. The professional soldiers and police concluded that the situation in Kenya demanded more than military measures. They warned that political and social changes were needed as well, a message the settlers were not ready to hear.[4]

Lyttelton and the London government worried that Baring and the Kenya administration were going overboard to suppress the uprising. Lyttelton warned Baring that the British were in danger of losing the game, despite whatever military success they might have. General Sir Gerald Templer gained a reputation as a counterinsurgency expert in Malaya. Nevertheless, he was appalled by Baring's proposal to deny appeal rights to Kenyans convicted of crimes associated with the unrest.[5]

In addition, Lyttelton was not comfortable with the settlers. When he visited Kenya in 1954, he confronted Blundell. Did he want to end the emergency or exact revenge? Lyttelton told the settlers that sixty thousand Europeans (a little more than 1 percent of the population) could not expect to exclude the Africans from political power. The settlers complained about British rule, but were not shy about asking for British help when they had provoked a rebellion, Lyttelton complained. Force was a not a long-term solution, he said. The settlers needed to accept political reforms. Their safety could not depend on British troops and they needed to build a multi-racial society. Lyttelton threatened that if the settlers did not accept political changes, the British would impose a military governor with complete powers.[6]

Lyttelton had Churchill's support, despite the prime minister's willingness to employ force. When Blundell met with Churchill in December 1954, Churchill pressed the Kenyan settler to find a negotiated settlement. Churchill admitted that he did not think black people were as capable or efficient as white people. Yet he said the Kikuyu resistance demonstrated that they were people of considerable ability and "steel." The Kenya government needed to negotiate from strength, but it needed to negotiate. It was a terrible situation when Britain risked its reputation by using the power of a modern nation against savages, the prime minister observed. He added that they were savages armed with ideas and, therefore, much more difficult to deal with.[7]

Lyttelton Constitution

Lyttelton and Baring devised a new Kenyan constitution intended to draw all elements of the population — Europeans, Asians, and Africans — into government, with Europeans retaining the largest role. Baring thought it necessary to placate the settlers by giving them greater political power before expanding African participation in government. The executive council became a council of ministers, and ministers gained greater powers. The council included six new unofficial members, three Europeans, two Asians and an African. Civil servants and Europeans retained the most important portfolios. The African member was to be the minister for community development, responsible for social and welfare programs focused on the African population. The legislative council gained eight appointed African members, but the European seats equaled those held by Asians and Africans. Since the settlers were not ready to allow Africans to vote, the most Lyttelton would concede was a promise of direct elections for the African seats in a few years. Lyttelton and Baring thought that the new constitution could buy them time. It was not scheduled for revision until 1960.[8]

In political terms, the Lyttelton constitution was a partial success. Among the settlers, Blundell and his followers joined the government. They formed the United Country Party and proclaimed their support for a multi-racial society. Hard-line settlers opposed the concessions to Asians and Africans, however, and formed an opposition party, the Federal Independence Party. Settler fears limited Baring's choices for the African minister and the African seats in the legislative council. Only the most cooperative Africans were acceptable. Prominent Africans were reluctant to join the government, however. Baring's choice as minister of community development hesitated for a month. He felt compelled to tour his home province before accepting the post. Most politically conscious Africans remained unconvinced of British commitment to a society where non–Europeans would have any real power.[9]

Economic and Social Reforms

British officials in Nairobi and London recognized that political reform was not enough. They needed to correct the social and economic problems that underlay the unrest in the Kikuyu areas. In 1954, the Kenya government announced a plan to redress the most pressing land issues afflicting the Kikuyu areas. The plan proposed to provide Africans with farms large enough to provide a family with food and generate a cash income. The government also removed its restrictions on the crops Africans could grow. Africans could now grow coffee, tea, and other potentially profitable crops. The same year, a government commission recommended equal pay for equal work in the civil service, opening the door to eventual replacement of British officials by Kenyans. To address urban problems, a government committee proposed minimum wages for African families in urban areas. To promote collective bargaining, the government encouraged the formation of employers' organizations. It sought to replace combative trade unions with more cooperative labor organizations.[10]

Throughout the 1950s and early 1960s, social and economic issues remained on the British agenda in Kenya. As the Kenya administration struggled to control political changes, it attempted to carry out economic and social reforms, particularly land reform. Initially the London government made £5 million available for agricultural reforms, a considerable sum for the times but less than Baring had requested and less than 10 percent of the amount spent to suppress the uprising. At first, London refused to provide additional funds for African education. By the end of the 1950s, however, London was providing Kenya with about £10 million a year for all purposes. In 1955, a royal commission proposed removal of restrictions on non–European ownership of land in the so-called "white highlands." Settler objections blocked immediate implementation, but eventually the government accepted the commission's recommendations. In the last stage of political change in Kenya, the Macmillan government made several million pounds available to a Kenyan land settlement and development board. The board was to lend the money to Africans seeking to purchase land.[11]

A Larger U.S. Role?

In December 1954, Consul General Dorsz dispatched to Washington a plea for a more active U.S. presence in East Africa. Dorsz accepted that U.S. policy in East Africa should be to support the British as long as doing so did not endanger the U.S. relationship with local populations. Relations with the East African governments were good, Dorsz reported. Cooperation and understanding were excellent. Nevertheless, the United States risked losing long-term influence in the area by supporting the British, Dorz argued. British power was on the wane. The U.S. needed to start making itself known to the local peoples. When the British left and the Africans held political power, the United States should be positioned to promote stability in the region and keep it aligned with the West. Dorz recommended that the U.S. open a consulate in Uganda, increase the Nairobi consulate's staff, expand the United States Information Service's efforts, and provide more development aid.[12]

Washington counseled caution and tact and turned down the requests for increased staff and expenditures. It warned against generalizations about the future of individual colonial territories or about possible U.S. policies towards them. The department pointed out that the United States remained committed to the U.N. charter, but needed to remain flexible about future courses of action in East Africa. Keeping a low profile was important. U.S.

policy was to work with and through the British. Creating the impression that the United States would determine the area's future or that it sought to create a shadow government would be mistakes, the department warned. U.S. officials needed to promote their objectives and present their point of view. They also needed to proceed with tact and care. If they encountered British opposition or non-cooperation, they should consult Washington.[13]

In December 1955, the Nairobi consulate assured Washington that it was remaining neutral in Kenyan politics. It was friendly, it said, to Europeans, Africans, and Asians, but had not committed itself to any of their policies or positions. The situation was too fluid for the United States to pick sides. The consulate added that multi-racial government faced many obstacles. The U.S. would be better positioned if it avoided identification with the British strategy. Over the next several years, the consulate increasingly assumed that the African nationalists would prevail in Kenya and focused its efforts on cultivating future African leaders. After the 1957 legislative council elections, the consulate told Washington it would step up its efforts to forge relationships with the new African members. One tool available to the consulate was the foreign leader grants, which paid for visits to the United States by potential foreign leaders. In May 1957, the consulate reported that senior officials were working to identify suitable candidates for the program despite British suspicion of the consulate's motives.[14]

Kenyan Nationalists and Tom Mboya

Beginning in 1955, the Kenya administration moved tentatively to widen African participation in government. In mid–1955, it permitted the formation of new political parties at the district level. Countrywide political organizations and all political organizations in the Central province, the Kikuyu heartland, remained banned, nevertheless. In 1956, the government announced elections for the African seats in the legislative council. The franchise was limited. Age, property, education, and occupation qualifications applied. African voters in Kikuyu areas needed a loyalty certificate from a local British official.

The imprisonment of Kenyatta and the Kenya African Union leaders created a power vacuum among the Kenyans opposed to British rule. As the British opened the electoral process to Africans, new nationalist leaders emerged. Prominent among them was Tom Mboya, a young Luo from western Kenya. In Nairobi, Mboya pursued a brand of trade unionism less militant and more acceptable to British labor officials than that favored by the unions associated with the Kenya African Union. Mboya rose to the leadership of an umbrella group, the Kenya Federation of Labor. At first, he used the federation as a platform for nationalist agitation. As political parties were legalized and elections scheduled, Mboya moved into the political arena. Before the 1957 elections, he became president of a political organization called the Nairobi Peoples' Convention Party.[15]

Mboya was adept at convincing people that he was a man they could work with. He forged working relationships with the British officials responsible for regulating Kenyan labor unions. Mboya also gained the trust of key leaders of the British Trade Union Congress (TUC) and influential members of the Labour Party. When the Kenya administration attempted to curtail the Kenya Federation of Labor's quasi-political activities, TUC and Labour leaders intervened to forge a compromise. Lennox-Boyd was impressed with Mboya. In 1956, he told Baring that Mboya was young enough to be open to influence. With the right direction, Mboya could play a great part in helping Africans in Kenya. Lennox-Boyd suggested that Baring find someone to keep an eye on Mboya and become his "guide, counselor, and possibly a friend." When Mboya took militant positions, sympathetic European observers were apt to conclude that these were only temporary, tactical choices.[16]

Baring was not among Mboya's admirers, however. In 1957, Baring wrote to his wife that while Mboya might someday be brought around, he was currently sinister and evil. Later Baring wrote home that he intended to fight Mboya. He was, Baring said, intensely arrogant, a lapsed Roman Catholic with the morals of a monkey.[17]

Yet the Kenya government was unwilling to exclude Mboya from the electoral process. Candidates in the 1957 elections for the African legislative council seats had to satisfy educational or income requirements. Mboya did not qualify. The government then enacted legislation that opened a loophole that benefited Mboya and almost no one else. Later the Kenya government prosecuted Mboya and others for public statements attacking Africans more willing to cooperate with the government. The court case became an opportunity for the Kenyan nationalists to rally support and raise funds. Mboya and his colleagues were acquitted of conspiracy but convicted of defamation. Nonetheless, the judge imposed only fines, explaining that imprisonment would bar Mboya from participation in the legislative council. In 1959, the police searched Mboya's home, arrested thirty-four members of his political party, and proscribed the party's newspaper. Despite Mboya's prominence, or perhaps because of it, the authorities did not proscribe the party or arrest Mboya.[18]

Mboya benefited from direct and indirect support from sources in the United States. Beginning early in his career as a labor organizer, Mboya received support and advice from the International Confederation of Free Trade Unions (ICFTU). The American Federation of Labor helped engineer the confederation's creation in 1949 as an alternative to the World Federation of Trade Unions, amidst fears that the World Federation was falling under communist control. During the 1950s, the ICFTU received financial support from both U.S. trade unions and from the Central Intelligence Agency. In 1956, Mboya visited the United States with the assistance of the American Committee on Africa (ACOA), a group founded in 1953 to support non-violent opposition to colonial regimes in Africa. While in the United States, Mboya obtained a $35,000 contribution from the AFL-CIO to build a Kenya labor center. Mboya had asked the ICFTU for the money but had been turned down. When Mboya visited the United States in 1959, he raised money for both relief and political work in southern Africa and for educating young Kenyans at universities in the United States. With the cooperation of George Houser, executive director of the American Committee on Africa, and others, Mboya created the African-American Students Foundation to provide higher education in North America for African students.[19]

U.S. officials in Kenya were favorably inclined towards Mboya. Robert Stephens, the cultural affairs officer at the United States Information Service in Nairobi, accompanied Mboya and William Scheinman, an American businessman, on an extended tour of Kenya in 1957. Scheinman later became the first president of the African-American Students Foundation and Stephens served on the panel that screened applications from African students. The consulate reported regularly to Washington on Mboya's activities, often in a favorable vein.[20]

The State Department was alert to the possible emergence of a Kenyan leader comparable to Nkrumah in the Gold Coast. It was not sure, however, that Mboya would fill the role. In late 1957, the State Department's position was that it supported orderly, progressive, and properly timed development of Kenya toward self-government. While the State Department was aware of the "controversial and promising" Mboya, the situation in Kenya was too fluid for the United States to be committed to specific solutions. In 1960, U.S. officials asked their British counterparts about Kenyatta's possible future role in Kenya. They noted that Mboya seemed unpopular with the other Kenyan leaders. Nonetheless, no other Kenyan leader, with the possible exception of Kenyatta, seemed capable of becoming the undisputed leader of Kenyan nationalism, the department thought.[21]

The State Department was not sure that Vice President Nixon should meet with Mboya when the Kenyan visited Washington in 1959. Assistant Secretary Satterthwaite listed the pros and cons for William Macomber, the assistant secretary for congressional relations. On the positive side, a meeting between the vice president and Mboya would gain goodwill among nationalist leaders. Mboya was the president of the All-African Peoples Conference. A meeting would repair some of the damage done by a tardy message to the conference's meeting in December 1958. It would appease Congressman Charles Diggs, Democrat of Michigan, a frequent critic of the Eisenhower administration's African policies. On the other hand, a meeting with Mboya might be perceived as an endorsement of a violent and racist movement and might upset the British. Agreeing to a meeting might reflect well on Mboya's hosts, the American Committee on Africa and George Houser, whose positions did not always coincide with U.S. policies. The United States could not be sure that Mboya would become the most important Kenyan politician. It had not extended the same courtesy to other African leaders, notably Julius Nyerere, under similar circumstances.[22]

The Eisenhower administration decided the positives outweighed the negatives. Nixon met with Mboya. The Kenyan also visited with State Department officials, Adlai Stevenson, Senator Hubert Humphrey, and members of the Senate Foreign Relations Committee's Subcommittee on African Affairs.[23]

1957 Elections

Britain's multi-racial strategy for Kenya required cultivation of political leaders, European and African, willing to cooperate and commanding support in their communities. On the European side, the British favored Blundell and his followers whenever they could. On the African side, the government tried to shape electoral politics to favor the Africans it thought most likely to prove cooperative. Besides the restrictions on African political organizations and elaborate qualifications for African candidates, the British imposed what they called "qualitative" democracy. Voters had to meet educational and other qualifications. A voter could also receive up to two additional votes depending on his income, education, or occupation. British officials saw favoring the educated, the relatively well-off, and government employees as a necessary alternative to a "one-man, one-vote" system. "Quantitative democracy" they considered surrender to African nationalism and an invitation to chaos. In Nairobi, qualitative democracy in 1957 meant that fewer than twenty-five hundred of more than a hundred thousand Africans could vote. Together, the eligible African voters could cast roughly forty-eight hundred votes.[24]

Keeping the state of emergency in place was also part of the British electoral strategy. After the army withdrew in 1956, the Kenya administration made no move to discard the laws and regulations imposed to fight the uprising. Baring realized that the government would have to lift the emergency at some point, but his administration was in no hurry. It was intent instead on devising permanent internal security laws. The Kenya administration's proposals proved sufficiently draconian that officials in London worried that they would violate the European Convention on Human Rights or the International Labor Organization's Forced Labor Convention. Retaining the emergency also facilitated keeping Kenyatta and other potential political leaders under wraps. As the Kenya administration slowly emptied the detention camps, Baring was less worried about releasing former fighters than he was about unleashing the "politicals." As early as 1954, he had imagined keeping a dozen or so key leaders behind bars forever.[25]

The government's multi-racial strategy suffered a setback in the 1956 elections for the European seats in the legislative council. The hard line Federal Independence Party won eight seats, and Blundell's United Country Party only six. Group Captain Briggs, the Federal Independent leader, accepted a ministry. The two European parties merged in early 1957.[26]

More damaging to the government's plans were the 1957 elections for the African seats. Six of the eight Africans appointed to the legislative council in 1954 lost their seats. Among those defeated was Eliud Mathu, the most prominent African member of the council and an outspoken critic of the uprising. Ethnic rivalries explained some of the results. Mathu was a Kikuyu, but most of the Kikuyu in his constituency were ineligible to vote. The larger explanation was that cooperation with the government discredited the appointed members even among the narrow African electorate created by the Lyttelton constitution. Among the electoral winners were Mboya and Oginga Odinga, another Luo.[27]

The Nairobi consulate thought the 1957 elections marked a watershed in Kenyan politics. In reports to Washington, the consulate noted the election's orderly nature and the high percentage of registered voters who participated. According to the consulate, the election demonstrated the growth of political consciousness throughout the colony. The results represented a vote of no confidence in the Lyttelton constitution. The consulate predicted that the new legislative council members would be responsible and moderate, but insistent on faster progress toward self-government. The Kenya government would be hard pressed to withstand their pressure for political concessions. The consulate thought that economic and social conditions for Africans in Kenya had improved. More civil service jobs were open to Africans. More businesses were willing to bargain with African trade unions. Nevertheless, most Africans remained poor and subject to onerous restrictions of various kinds. The consulate predicted that economic and social dissatisfaction would fuel demands for political changes.[28]

The consulate warned Washington that reaching out to African leaders aroused suspicions within the Kenya government and among the European population. Whatever tact and discretion the U.S. officials in Kenya may have exhibited, they were soon perceived as both interested and influential in Kenyan affairs. In February 1957, a European farmer told a consulate official that many Europeans believed that the United States was trying to push the Europeans out of Kenya and convert it to an African state. In November 1957, newspapers reported that a United States Information Service officer met Mboya and other African leaders at the Nairobi airport when the Kenyans returned from London. Rumors sprang up that the Kenya government planned to ask the officer to leave. Confronted by consulate officials, the relevant Kenyan minister denied any intent to expel a United States official. In April 1958, a European member of the legislative council voiced concerns about the U.S. Information Service activities. He tabled a question inquiring whether the government had rules barring consulate staffs from intervening in local politics. In December 1960, another European member attacked U.S. policies towards Kenya and referred to Assistant Secretary Satterthwaite as "sinister."[29]

Lennox-Boyd Constitution

Between the 1957 elections and mid–1959, the Kenyan nationalists, with Odinga and Mboya in the lead, used their positions in the legislative council to agitate for an African majority government. Having evicted Mathu and the more compliant Africans from office, the nationalists could demonstrate that the government had little or no African support. They denounced the Lyttelton constitution. They refused to accept ministerial posts and demanded fifteen additional African seats. In response, Lennox-Boyd imposed a new constitution in late 1957. The new constitution added six elected African seats and created twelve special seats, four from each community, elected by the council. The British saw the special seats as a way to bring less militant Africans into the council. The enlarged African contingent in the council rejected the new constitution, however. They attacked the Africans willing to stand for the special seats as collaborators and traitors. Believing that the British had rejected demands for further political change, the nationalists initiated a boycott of the legislative council in late 1958. They demanded that Britain clarify its long-term goal for Kenya and convene a conference to discuss a new constitution.[30]

While giving ground, Lennox-Boyd continued to search for ways to slow the pace of change and establish a multi-racial government in Kenya. The British recognized that creating a multi-racial arrangement would not be easy. In 1957, a committee of civil servants wrote that the task was to manipulate European fears, Asian timidity, and African impatience to create a delicate and changing balance, while allowing "no member of the team to run off the field." Besides creating the twelve special seats, the 1958 constitution forbade further constitutional changes for ten years. It created a second African minister and provided that both African ministers could be selected from the four Africans elected to the special seats, not from the fourteen elected African members. The constitution did away with qualitative democracy and created a single voting roll. Yet it left open the possibility of voter qualifications high enough to limit severely the number of African voters. In early 1959, as agitation for a constitutional conference grew, Blundell was instrumental in creating a new political group. The New Kenya Group consisted of most of the council's Europeans plus all twelve special members. When Lennox-Boyd acceded to demands for a constitutional conference, he tried to communicate that he was responding to the New Kenya Group's request, not Mboya's demands.[31]

Doubts

Charles Withers, the consul general in Nairobi, welcomed the Lennox-Boyd constitution. He conceded that Lennox-Boyd had imposed the new constitution. Nevertheless, all communities in Kenya had participated in the negotiations, he wrote. All would get something out of the new arrangements. Withers detected considerable elements of common consent. He thought the new constitution could produce stability for ten years if all parties acted in good faith. If that were the case, it would be a milestone in the growth of benevolent British colonialism.[32]

By mid–1958, Withers was less confident about Kenya's prospects. He reported an increase in crime and general unrest. He attributed it to unemployment and other socio-economic factors, rather than nationalism. Nevertheless, nationalist agitation was on the increase as well. Mboya and other African politicians were demanding independence. Withers thought that Kenya was far from ready for self-government. Perhaps Mboya was playing to the crowd and would settle for much less than independence. Yet his demands were likely to enflame the general population. Withers told Washington that he agreed with the British officials who feared that African leaders would be unable to rein in their followers.[33]

Reports prepared by the Office of Intelligence and Research in late 1958 and early 1959 were pessimistic. The British had decided to hold the line for the moment, the reports said. The British did not believe that Africans could be trusted with more political power. They imagined Kenya as the site for a major military base. In the face of escalating demands from African politicians, the British might make concessions, but resistance from the European community and the plans for a continued British military presence would make concessions less likely. The British were handicapped by their lack of effective allies among African leaders, the reports observed. The more militant African politicians were likely to press for concessions. If frustrated, they would turn to strikes, boycotts, and other forms of mass actions, the reports predicted. The reports concluded that repressive measures by the government would favor the extremists among the African leaders and induce them to turn to outside sources for support.[34]

U.S. officials in Kenya briefly embraced the New Kenya Group as a way forward. In April 1959, the consul general urged Washington to provide support to the group. The group offered the prospect of moderation and stability, the consul general wrote. British officials predicted that several African members of the legislative council would join the group. The consul general also thought that it would gain bi-partisan support in Britain. Washington responded that it welcomed establishment of Blundell's group and would consider the consulate's request. Less than two weeks later, the consul general sent another telegram to Washington asking that the State Department and the Central Intelligence Agency help two New Kenya Group members arrange a lecture tour in the United States. The consul general added that he was trying to stop another New Kenya Group member from joining the tour because his personality was apt to put off potential supporters. By late May, however, the U.S. officials in Nairobi had lost faith in Blundell's group. The consul general praised the group's policies, but conceded that its chances of surviving in its present form and with its present leadership were remote.[35]

Constitutional Conference

In April 1959, Lennox-Boyd agreed to hold a constitutional conference before the next Kenyan elections scheduled for 1960. He did not view the concession as critical. In the negotiations with the Kenyan leaders, Lennox-Boyd took a firm line. He did not mention elections on a one man, one vote basis and refused to commit himself to ending the emergency. He rejected any suggestion that Kenyatta might be released. In January 1959, the colonial secretary met with the governors of Kenya, Tanganyika and Uganda at Chequers, the British prime minister's country residence. The British leaders agreed that pressure for political change was mounting across East Africa. Their efforts to craft multi-racial solutions were not faring well. Using force was not a realistic option. Nevertheless, they agreed that Tanganyika might not attain independence until 1970 and Uganda shortly thereafter. Kenya would not do so until at least 1975. When Lennox-Boyd described his plans for Kenya to the cabinet and to the House of Commons in April 1959, his position remained unchanged. He said that he did not see any prospect in the near future of the British government relinquishing control in Kenya. He went on to describe his expectations for a new Kenyan constitution, including retention of a multi-racial executive.[36]

Lennox-Boyd and the British accepted that they faced serious challenges in Kenya. The Kenyan nationalists were afflicted by ethnic and personal rivalries, but remained united in their demands for a larger African role in the Kenyan government. Through Mboya, they had an effective spokesman and important links to British and American supporters. Lennox-Boyd told the cabinet that he expected Mboya to pursue a war of nerves in order to drive the European settlers out. British security officials thought the nationalists capable of active resistance to British rule, including strikes, boycotts, and general civil disobedience. They worried that such actions would lead to attacks on non–African lives and property. Beginning in late 1957, officials detected in rural Kikuyu areas the kind of organizing and sporadic violence that preceded the 1953-54 uprising. They remained confident that continuation of the emergency regulations plus the various development efforts would prevent large-scale violence. Nevertheless, one senior official warned that past experience dictated that the government be prepared for unpleasant surprises.[37]

Skepticism

By late 1959, the State Department had concluded that the British attempt to establish a multi-racial regime in Kenya would fail. In a briefing prepared for Senator Mike Mansfield, Democrat of Montana, in December 1959, the department said that U.S. policies regarding Kenya were based on the assumption that Kenya would become independent in six to nine years under an African-dominated government. In the meantime, the department told Mansfield, the United States was working to keep Kenya aligned with the West, supporting Britain as it attempted to manage the transition to independence. The U.S. was, the department claimed, supplementing British development efforts with projects targeted on Kenya's African population.[38]

Now the consulate was more worried about recalcitrant colonial officials than about militant nationalists. The consulate thought that ultra-conservative colonial administrators elsewhere had stalled reforms long enough that African leaders had turned against the colonial power. It was concerned that colonial officers in Kenya were capable of doing the same. They might push the nationalists to choose methods other than moderation and cooperation.[39]

Tanganyika: Twining Constitution

After several years of studies and committees, Tanganyika acquired a new constitution in 1955. Edward Twining, the governor since 1949, appointed thirty unofficial members to the legislative council, ten Africans, ten Asians, and ten Europeans. Tanganyika's eight provinces, the city of Dar es Salaam, and the colony's business interests were each represented by a member of the three communities. Eight government officials became ministers and six unofficial members, four Africans, an Asian, and a European, became assistant ministers. Sufficient unofficial members associated themselves with the government so that it retained a majority in the legislative council.

Among the Africans appointed to the council was Julius Nyerere, president of Tanganyika's principal political party, the Tanganyika African National Union (TANU). Nyerere earned degrees from Makerere College in Uganda and the University of Edinburgh and taught in secondary schools in Tanganyika. After returning from Scotland in 1952, he was elected president of the Tanganyika African Association, a quasi-political organization dominated by government employees and teachers. In 1954, Nyerere was instrumental in converting the Tanganyika African Association into TANU, a political party, and setting TANU's goal as preparing Tanganyika for self-government. TANU accepted only Africans as members, but under Nyerere's leadership its tone was moderate and its approach gradual. Nyerere was intent on expanding TANU's reach throughout Tanganyika, while maintaining firm control from his headquarters in Dar es Salaam. In 1955, Nyerere remained focused on securing an African majority government. Heeding advice against accepting a government office before his party gained a majority, he refused Twining's offer of an assistant minister's position.[40]

Rural Reforms

Twining was a colonial administrator of the old school, more interested in the rural development and the native administrations than in constitutional changes. Under Twining, the Tanganyika administration was intent on improving agricultural practices. The government's chosen instrument was the native administration. It pushed the native administrations to adopt and enforce regulations intended to eliminate harmful farming and herding techniques. Whatever the impact of the government's intervention in the countryside on Tanganyikan agriculture, it had long-term political consequences. It irritated the rural population, alienated it from the native administrations and the chiefs appointed by the British, and put it at odds with the British administration.

In 1954, Twining visited the town of Mwanza, in an area troubled by the new agricultural rules. When a deputation of local farmers presented their grievances, Twining lost his temper. He refused to meet a delegation from the Tanganyika African Association and denounced them to an assembly of chiefs. He told the chiefs that the association represented uneducated, ignorant people who were trying to undermine the chiefs. The local people subsequently appealed to the Colonial Office. In the meantime, the chiefs moved to silence the dissidents.[41]

TANU remained ambivalent toward the local protests. Protest leaders often became TANU activists, but the TANU leadership did not endorse or encourage resistance to agricultural development schemes. Nyerere and his closest associates worried about potentially violent protests that they might not be able to control. They were also likely to agree with British officials about the need for improved practices in the countryside.

In the early 1950s, Twining embarked on local government reforms, with no more success than he had had in the agricultural arena. Twining set out to establish county councils, encompassing several districts, and below them district councils, intended to replace the native administration councils. The county councils were to be multi-racial, with equal African, Asian, and European representation. They were to control significant funding and manage important local government functions. If the goal was to increase local, particularly African, involvement in local government decisions, the first county council was a failure. British officials continued to control decisions and African representatives lost interest. The chiefs continued to dominate the native administration councils. Young, educated Africans were forced to look to TANU as the means to increase their political voice.

1954 Visiting Mission

As a trust territory, Tanganyika hosted a United Nations visiting mission every three years. The 1954 visiting mission's report was a rock tossed into a stagnant pond. The report, released in early 1955, envisioned Tanganyika as a self-governing African state. It foresaw self-government within twenty years and recommended the establishment of intermediate target dates for political, social, and economic development. The report was favorable to TANU, describing it as a national movement. The official British response was that the multi-racial constitution was not intended to be permanent, but would last for some time. It opposed any sort of timetable and cast doubt on the feasibility of self-government in twenty years. The report, the British argued, had overestimated both the local peoples' capacity for development and the level of advancement reached. In Dar es Salaam, Twining claimed that Tanganyika's Africans had neither a national organization, nor an articulate spokesperson.[42]

The TANU leadership identified the Trusteeship Council's consideration of the visiting mission's report as an opportunity to establish its credibility. It sent Nyerere to New York in March 1955 to address the council. The TANU president told the council that his party, the government, and the United Nations were intent on moving Tanganyika to independence. While Tanganyika had important immigrant populations, it was, Nyerere insisted, an African country. Nyerere's speech was considered a success. When he returned home, membership in TANU grew rapidly.

Much to British relief, the Trusteeship Council's reaction to the visiting mission's report was lukewarm. The council called only for an early and progressive increase in African representation in the legislative council and for self-government or independence as soon as possible. Nevertheless, the British worked hard behind the scenes to limit the damage. They persuaded the U.S. government to require Nyerere to leave the United States within twenty-four hours of his presentation to the United Nations. It asked that he be restricted to an eight-block radius of the U.N. building while he was in New York. The U.S. representative on the Trusteeship Council, Mason Sears, was a member of the visiting mission and the British blamed him for much of its unsavory contents. British representatives complained to the State Department about Sears's involvement. Sears had his critics within the State Department. British officials received sympathetic words from their United States counterparts, but there was no change in Sears's status. While in Dar es Salaam, Sears had stayed with the U.S. consul, Robert McKinnon. When the State Department reassigned McKinnon to Washington, the Tanganyika government circulated the story that his departure was the result of Foreign Office's complaints to the State Department.[43]

Combating TANU

Like other colonial governments, the Tanganyika government tried to use law and regulation to inhibit nationalist organizations. In 1953, the administration forbade government employees from participating in political organizations, including the Tanganyika African Association. Since many educated Africans worked for the government, in government departments or in the schools, the measure seemed designed to deprive a nationalist organization of its most likely members. The following year, the government enacted a societies ordinance. The ordinance required every branch of any society to register with the government. It established strict requirements for registration, and mandated that any society obtain police permission before collecting subscriptions or holding public meetings. In 1955, the Tanganyika administration enacted the Incitement of Violence Act, which made inter-communal attacks equivalent to sedition. TANU feared that a clause in the act could be interpreted as outlawing advocacy of an African state in Tanganyika.[44]

Confronted with a growing TANU, Twining created a potential counterweight, a multi-racial political party, the United Tanganyika Party. Twining convinced the legislative council's European and Asian members and about half the African members to organize themselves into the new party in early 1956. He told them their goal should not be to defeat TANU, which was beyond their abilities, but to force Nyerere into a political deal. The United Tanganyika Party received funding from British companies operating in Tanganyika and employed a former Conservative Party official as its executive director. The British made no secret of their preference for the United Tanganyika Party. When the Trusteeship Council took up the issue of Tanganyika's future in 1957, the British representative lavished praise on the party, contrasting its multi-racial approach to TANU's Africans-only policy.[45]

Initially, the Dar es Salaam consulate thought that the UTP could play a useful role in Tanganyika, but soon discarded the idea. In February 1956, Consul Robert McKinnon told Washington that the UTP might attract support from Tanganyika's chiefs and from the more enlightened Africans. The chiefs felt threatened by TANU. If UTP came out strongly against racial discrimination, educated Africans might also join its ranks. A strong UTP posed dangers, McKinnon added. It might strengthen the hand of militants within TANU against Nyerere's moderate leadership. By April, however, McKinnon judged the UTP a mistake. TANU had managed to label it as a government party. It was not enough to espouse a worthy cause like inter-racialism. A political party needed to appeal to the population's self interests, something UTP was unlikely to do, McKinnon added.[46]

Twining attempted to add the chiefs to an anti-nationalist coalition. He interpreted the ban on government employees' involvement in political organizations as not applying to chiefs and several prominent chiefs joined the United Tanganyika Party. In 1957, he summoned the chiefs to Tanganyika's first conference of chiefs. He told the chiefs that Britain intended to remain in Tanganyika for a long time. Twining offered the prospect that a properly organized chiefs' organization might evolve into a second legislative chamber. He said he expected them to meet regularly to discuss issues of common interest. In Tanganyika, chiefs had limited powers. The trend in Britain's African colonies was to check any inclination towards autocracy by requiring chiefs to consult a native administration council. Nevertheless, the Tanganyika administration granted chiefs the power in 1957 to enact rules on their own regarding any native administration activity, regardless of the existence of a council.[47]

The Colonial Office viewed Nyerere as someone it could work with, potentially a "moderate and sensible chap" whose friendship was worth seeking. The Tanganyika administration thought otherwise. They thought they could assemble a viable unofficial majority without the TANU leader. In early 1957, the administration attempted to silence Nyerere. After a particularly militant speech, the government charged him with criminal libel and banned him from public speaking.[48]

The effort to stifle Nyerere failed and Twining then attempted to co-opt the TANU leader. In July 1957, Twining lifted the speaking ban. The government would have needed to use force to enforce the ban, he concluded. A United Nations visiting mission was scheduled to arrive in August. Twining appointed Nyerere to the legislative council and offered him a ministerial position. Nyerere refused the post and soon resigned from the legislative council.[49]

1957 Visiting Mission

The 1957 United Nations visiting mission followed the same path as its 1954 predecessor. The mission recommended setting a date for independence, a date much sooner than twenty years in the future. Sears was again a member of the mission and advocated its recommendations before the Trusteeship Council. While Sears was in Tanganyika, he met with Nyerere to discuss how the United States could help promote political progress in Tanganyika. Sears later claimed that the British had bugged the meeting, held at the U.S. consul's residence. Sir Andrew Cohen, now the British representative to the council, spoke against the mission's report. Nyerere presented TANU's view. Much to Britain's surprise, other Africans with close links to the Tanganyika government supported Nyerere.[50]

By 1958, Twining's anti-nationalist strategy was unraveling. The government's rules and regulations were burdensome, but TANU continued to recruit new members and extend its influence. Nyerere later said that Twining's open but ineffective opposition to TANU provided the party with an unpopular opponent without hindering party activists. TANU headquarters worried that disorder would delay independence. To an extent, it used the government's regulatory scheme as an opportunity to impose discipline on its branches. The United Tanganyika Party was poorly led and struggled to construct a credible party platform. In September 1957, it attempted to steal TANU's thunder. It came out for establishing a target date for independence, conceding Africans the largest share of legislative seats, and moving towards universal suffrage. By the end of 1957, however, the party was in debt and unable to pay its professional staff. Moreover, many chiefs had come to doubt Britain's ability to remain in control. They were looking to forge links with TANU. In 1958, a prominent chief decided to run for a legislative council seat with TANU support. In June, the chiefs' convention endorsed his decision.[51]

At the same time, TANU was demonstrating its strength. The government's agricultural reforms continued to spark disorder in the countryside, particularly in the Lake Province. The disorder troubled Nyerere and the TANU leadership. They appointed a new TANU district secretary in the most troubled district. The TANU official cooperated with the local British administration to calm the unrest and to dismantle the multi-racial local government the Twining administration had imposed. An all–African district council was subsequently elected and the obnoxious agricultural regulations repealed.[52]

1958/59 Elections

The 1958/59 elections to the legislative council doomed Twining's anti-nationalist strategy. Under Twining's multi-racial constitution, each voter cast a vote for three candidates, an African, an Asian and a European. Since the European and Asian populations were tiny, Twining was counting on rigorous voter qualifications to limit the number of African voters. The original qualifications were so high that even the appointed members of the legislative council and the United Tanganyika Party objected. Their protests forced the government to lower the qualifications. As a result, a large majority of the eligible voters were Africans. In 1957, Twining tried to persuade Lennox-Boyd to change the voting arrangements. Lennox-Boyd was trying to sell multi-racial government to Kenyan politicians, however, and he told Twining it was too late for changes. TANU objected to the constitution's multi-racial features and to the revised voter qualifications, strict compared to other British colonies. Most TANU members wanted the party to boycott the elections. Nyerere, however, persuaded the party to participate in the elections. The original plan was to contest only the African seats, but the party eventually decided to support candidates for all seats. Candidates nominated or supported by TANU won twenty-eight of the thirty seats.[53]

Before the elections, the British in London and Tanganyika accepted that constitutional change and a larger African role in government were inevitable in the near future. Midway through 1956, Twining discarded his notion that constitutional change could be postponed until 1967 or 1970. He decided that it might be possible to change the constitution after the 1958 elections so African representation equaled that of Asians and Europeans combined. The Colonial Office was uncomfortable with discarding racial parity so soon, but was willing to accept Twining's judgment. Neither Twining nor the Colonial Office equated faster constitutional change with yielding to Nyerere and TANU. They remained convinced that they could assemble a coalition of Asians, Europeans, and what they termed "responsible" Africans.[54]

Sir Richard Turnbull

Sir Richard Turnbull, who replaced Twining as governor in July 1958, introduced a more conciliatory tone into Tanganyika's politics. He met with Nyerere and assured him that "multi-racialism" was not meant to be permanent. Turnbull told the legislative council that the British recognized that Africans would always predominate in Tanganyika and parity among the races was a temporary measure. He attempted to reassure the chiefs that the government and TANU agreed on many issues, including self-government as the ultimate goal, and disagreed only about timing. Nevertheless, until the first round of legislative council elections in October 1958, Turnbull remained committed to the timetable Twining had discussed with the Colonial Office. It included another round of elections in 1964 followed by the introduction of a minority of elected members into the executive council.[55]

When the three East African governors met with Lennox-Boyd at Chequers in January 1959, they agreed on a similar schedule, responsible self-government for Tanganyika in 1963-4 and independence in 1970. Nevertheless, Turnbull became convinced that he was working from a position of weakness. Turnbull told the Colonial Office that he would face a united opposition when the new legislative council convened. He had thought that some Europeans and some chiefs would coalesce into an opposition, but he concluded that TANU had beguiled or intimidated everyone into agreement. TANU was intent on an unofficial majority in the legislative council. If TANU did not get what it wanted and began a program of direct action across the colony, the Tanganyika police lacked the men and equipment to quell it, Turnbull predicted. Turnbull argued that TANU had the support of nearly all Africans in Tanganyika. Turnbull served in Kenya before coming to Tanganyika. He warned that the British in Tanganyika would not be able to recruit police or auxiliaries from the local population as they had done in Kenya.[56]

The causes of Britain's weakness in Tanganyika extended beyond the territory itself, Turnbull explained. If violence broke out, it would be coordinated with and assisted by nationalist groups in other British colonies. Egypt and Russia would encourage the nationalists. The United States would sympathize with them. The Labour Party would raise the issue in Parliament. Turnbull warned that U.S. officials were encouraging the idea that it was better to be poor and independent than to be poor and dependent on the British Treasury. Moreover, subsidies from the Treasury were likely to be skimpy. Aid from elsewhere, the United States or Russia, might be substantial, or so the Tanganyika nationalists thought. The legislative council's membership was exactly the sort of government Britain had said it wanted for Tanganyika, representatives of all races united in their commitment to common political goals. Britain would struggle to explain to the world community why it was unwilling to cooperate with such a coalition, Turnbull counseled.[57]

Turnbull was pessimistic about British ability to retain control in Tanganyika partly because he had witnessed the erosion of the government's moral authority. In August 1958, Turnbull traveled to Geita, in one of the most restive areas. He did not intend to hold any public meetings. When he learned that a crowd had gathered on the town's sports field in anticipation of his visit, however, he insisted on going to the field. Turnbull left his police escort behind and was accompanied by only two British officials. When the governor arrived at the field, the speaker who was addressing the crowd told everyone to ignore the visitors. When people started to get to their feet in deference to the governor, the speaker asked them to sit down. When the crowd remained seated, Turnbull and his officials left.[58]

In the short term, Turnbull thought he could count on Nyerere's cooperation. After Nyerere spoke publicly about the possibility of self-government in 1959, the idea spread throughout Tanganyika. Nyerere was now doing his best to lower expectations. Turnbull thought Nyerere and the more responsible TANU leaders would cooperate while proposals for further constitutional change were being developed. Nyerere was willing to serve as a minister. Nevertheless, he would probably resign, Turnbull warned, if the British refused TANU's demands. He might walk out of the legislative council and take most of the members with him. Otherwise, Nyerere would risk attacks from TANU's more militant members and possible removal as TANU's leader.[59]

Turnbull's assessment of Nyerere was correct. In March 1959, Turnbull and Nyerere reached an agreement that allowed both to save face and paved the way for constitutional change. TANU wanted the governor to announce a date for responsible government when the new legislative council convened on March 17, but Turnbull was not empowered to set a date. After lengthy and tense negotiations, Turnbull offered TANU five ministries, three for Africans, and one each for an Asian and a European. He proposed to establish two committees to recommend further electoral and constitutional changes. Nyerere accepted the offer and persuaded the TANU representatives to accept it as a temporary measure. Nevertheless, to Turnbull's disappointment, Nyerere declined to become a minister. The committees eventually recommended that all taxpayers vote in the next election along with all women who were literate or owned houses. Legislators would be elected from fifty single-member constituencies. Eleven special seats would be reserved for Asians and ten for Europeans. In October, Turnbull announced that the next elections would take place in September 1960. On Lennox-Boyd's instructions, he declined to set a date for responsible government.[60]

As the political changes unfolded in Tanganyika, Turnbull did not anticipate that the territory would become what he termed an "African" state. Nor did he think that the changes he had agreed to were anything more than the least of all possible evils. Turnbull told Sir Frederick Crawford, the governor of Uganda, that he was struggling to preserve Tanganyika as a partnership state, not the sort of African state Uganda was destined to become. Supporting Nyerere now was the best way to cement a real partnership among the races in Tanganyika and preserve British influence, Turnbull believed. If the British did not work with Nyerere now, more militant leaders would take his place. Postponing political change would only embitter the African population. Turnbull thought that constitutional changes would lead to deterioration of administration and government services, but he also thought that delaying political changes for twenty years would not avoid the same deterioration.[61]

Worries in London

Politicians and officials in London were less committed to rapid change in Tanganyika. In April, Lennox-Boyd told the Cabinet Colonial Policy Committee that he intended that the next constitutional change in Tanganyika would not occur until 1969. Full internal self-government would occur later. Nevertheless, Lennox-Boyd warned the committee that Tanganyika lacked the police and other resources to confront TANU. Concessions might be needed. In May, Lennox-Boyd's deputy, Julian Amery, raised the alarm that Turnbull appeared to be abandoning the understanding reached at Chequers. In June, civil servants warned that Tanganyika would not be ready for an elected majority in the legislature by 1965, much less 1960 or 1961. An elected majority would not be the last change demanded by TANU, they claimed. Delaying the change for four years might not, however, be worth risking disorder. Nevertheless, the governor ought to assess the possibility of pre-empting widespread resistance by detaining TANU leaders throughout the territory.[62]

John Macpherson, former governor of Nigeria and now a senior Colonial Office official, added a note of caution. He told his colleagues that it was easy to draft a telegram in London directing a governor to provoke a showdown. Once the writer was finished, he could return to a safe home and the only reason he might be awakened during the night was to draft another telegram. When Lyttelton had suggested to Macpherson that they break off talks with the Nigerians in 1953 and govern with the aid of troops, Macpherson told Lyttelton that it would be easy enough for six months or so. You could not govern with machine guns forever, he added. Eventually you would have to negotiate and it would be with the same African leaders.[63]

Mixed Feelings

British officials remained sensitive to real or imagined pressure from U.S. officials, particularly Mason Sears, regarding Tanganyika. In February 1959, British officials in both Dar es Salaam and London complained about a speech Sears made in the Trusteeship Council. Turnbull told the consul that the speech was irresponsible and did nothing to promote Anglo-American cooperation. A Tanganyika official told the London embassy that he was relieved that Sears said he expected to see the British officials in the same debate next year. At least Sears did not expect Tanganyika to be independent before then, the official concluded. In April 1960, Lord Perth called in the U.S. ambassador, John Hay Whitney, to complain about alleged statements by Sears about independence for Tanganyika in a matter of weeks. A flurry of telegrams produced a denial by Sears. Washington observed that Tanganyika officials were probably nervous about what Sears might say. Sears told Washington that he thought that the British were unrealistic in believing they could postpone independence much beyond mid–1961.[64]

U.S. officials in Tanganyika identified Nyerere as a politician worth watching and supporting. According to the Dar es Salaam consulate's reports, he seemed reasonable and moderate, willing to accept gradual progress towards self-government. He was politically astute, able to negotiate with British officials and to restrain TANU's militant members. Moreover, he recognized the importance of conciliating Tanganyika's European and Asian communities. During the 1950s, the consulate produced a stream of reports extolling Nyerere's abilities and virtues. They expressed the hope that he retain control of TANU. Consulate officials talked to Nyerere and TANU leaders on a regular basis. In 1955, amidst British complaints about a U.N. visiting mission, Washington advised the Dar es Salaam consulate to remain circumspect in its conversations with Nyerere and others. They should avoid the appearance that they were offering TANU political advice.[65]

The consulate's analysis of the visiting mission report, signed by the vice-consul, was far from flattering, however. William Edmondson told Washington that the report was poorly written, extremely undiplomatic, and unconcerned with practical politics. The authors seemed intent on discrediting the Tanganyika government and appealing to world opinion. Edmondson thought timetables were of questionable value and the mission's notion of self-government within a generation was impractical. The Africans in Tanganyika were not likely to be able to maintain a stable government in twenty-five years. A goal of fifty years would be more realistic. Edmondson wrote that the mission should have deferred to African leaders and supported only the changes they proposed. He predicted that the British were likely to accept any reasonable proposals without any prodding from the United Nations.[66]

In mid–1958, the Dar es Salaam consulate remained convinced that self-government for Tanganyika was inevitable. Nyerere was the only African leader of any importance and TANU faced no serious rivals, U.S. officials thought. Nevertheless, the consul in 1957 and 1958, Robert Ware, was far more pessimistic about Tanganyika than most U.S. officials in Tanganyika during the 1950s. In March 1957, Ware compared Nyerere's speech at the United Nations to speeches made by "a sorry succession of dictators, demagogues, and evil persons." Ware claimed that Nyerere cloaked a few truths in a fog of half-truths and distortions and consciously avoided mention of the Tanganyika government's many accomplishments. While admitting he had no real evidence, Ware repeatedly suggested that Nyerere might have communist connections. Nevertheless, Ware believed that the "free world" should help Tanganyika achieve self-government as soon as practicable, lest a frustrated nationalism turn to radicalism. Ware thought that Tanganyika would not be ready for self-government in the near future. Tanganyika's African leaders were semi-literate at best and had not the slightest understanding of government. While Nyerere and TANU had the support of most politically engaged Africans, Ware thought they were a small fraction of the population. They had gained influence only because no credible rivals had emerged. The chiefs and the United Tanganyika Party had proved inept or self-interested, he claimed.[67]

As of mid–1959, the State Department remained content with Tanganyika's status. William Duggan, the consul in Dar es Salaam, told a conference of State Department officials that Tanganyika was the one country in the region that did not face a crisis. The British had a sound program for the colony and an independent Tanganyika would have a stable administrative framework. A year earlier, after Turnbull replaced Twining, Duggan told Washington that Tanganyika would certainly become an independent African state, as early as 1962, but no later than 1965.[68]

U.S. officials were comfortable with developments in Tanganyika, but worried about British perceptions of the U.S. role. A National Intelligence Estimate described TANU as a strong political movement. Presumably, strength in this context referred to the party's capability for maintaining order in the territory. Fred Hadsel, first secretary in London, worried that the British thought that U.S. activity in the Trusteeship Council had forced the pace of political change in Tanganyika. Hadsel anticipated that the British resentment towards the United States would occasionally surface. He predicted that the British would expect the U.S. to assume some responsibility for the territory's economic welfare.[69]

Uganda: Cohen's Reforms

After Oliver Lyttelton appointed Sir Andrew Cohen governor of Uganda in 1952, Cohen implemented the reforms he and other civil servants in the Colonial Office had debated for nearly a decade. Cohen initiated economic and land reforms intended to address the grievances that sparked the 1945 and 1949 disorders. He ordered a study of local administration. The study's aims were to give local governments greater powers, make them more efficient, and introduce a greater element of democracy. Cohen also offered constitutional changes. He proposed that the number of African members in the legislative council be increased to fourteen, three from Buganda and eleven selected from districts outside Buganda. The African members would be elected indirectly, by district councils or by an electoral college in the case of Buganda. Nevertheless, Cohen wanted to co-opt the African members into the government, rather than create an embryonic opposition. He referred to the African members as "representative" members rather than "unofficial" members. Besides official members and seven European and Asian members nominated by the governor, the council would include cross bench members. They were bound to support the government on important issues but were otherwise free to speak and vote as they pleased.[70]

Consistent with Colonial Office thinking, Cohen's reforms put the government one step ahead of any Uganda nationalists. A nationalist political party, the Uganda National Congress, emerged in March 1952. It brought together trade union leaders, politically engaged students from Makerere College, and leaders of farmers' organizations linked to the 1949 unrest. Nevertheless, while Cohen launched his reforms, the Uganda National Congress remained a small organization with limited political influence.

Cohen's program for Uganda was consistent with Colonial Office thinking in that it saw the colony's future as a unitary state. While Cohen sought to upgrade local governments, he imagined a strong role for the legislative council and the central government. Some of the local governments Cohen envisaged were derived from Uganda's kingdoms, pre-colonial African states that the British had preserved. Nevertheless, Cohen intended that the remnants of the kingdoms would be subordinate to a Ugandan government. He did not envisage Uganda's future as a federation of entities, the largest of which were descendents of the pre-colonial states.

The heads of Uganda's kingdoms, Ankole, Toro, Bunyoro, and the largest, Buganda, were the most likely losers in Cohen's reforms. Responsibility and power would shift from them to the legislative council and to district or local councils. The introduction of democratic and parliamentary practices in local governments would limit their power. Nevertheless, Cohen persuaded the kabaka of Buganda, Mutesa II, to agree to the reforms. The kabaka was relatively young, twenty-nine years old in 1953. He had been educated in Britain and served as an officer in the Grenadier Guards. He had a reputation of being a playboy, but had intervened in 1945 and 1949 on the side of the British to halt unrest in Buganda.

1953 Crisis

In June 1953, newspapers reported that Lyttelton, speaking at a dinner in London, hinted that the British might create an East African federation. Civil servants in the Colonial Office thought Lyttelton's refusal to heed their advice about the speech had led to a serious blunder. When the kabaka raised concerns, Lyttelton wrote to him saying that the newspaper had misquoted him. Lyttelton claimed that the Colonial Office's policy regarding a federation remained unchanged. The damage was done, however. The mention of an East African federation stirred fears in Buganda of European domination. Many feared that British plans for economic development would lead to a larger role for Europeans in Uganda and repeal of prohibitions on the sale of land to Europeans. Moreover, the kabaka's close relationship with the British had distanced him from the rural population, which harbored economic grievances, and from Buganda's subordinate chiefs, who feared that the local government reforms would undermine their positions. Opposition to inclusion within the Uganda government remained strong in Buganda. In October, the Buganda legislature, the lukiko, voted against selecting Buganda representatives to the legislative council. The kabaka apparently decided that he could no longer ignore the discontent and the anti–British sentiments festering in the kingdom. To preserve his political support, he needed to identify himself more closely with Buganda. In November 1953, he sent Lyttelton a letter containing three requests: an assurance that the British would not create an East African federation, transfer of responsibility for Buganda from the Colonial Office to the Foreign Office, and independence for Buganda on a definite timetable.[71]

The kabaka's letter sparked a crisis. In a series of meetings, Cohen assured the kabaka that federation was not in the offing. He refused to consider ending Colonial Office responsibility for Buganda, or independence for Buganda separate from Uganda. The kabaka argued that he was acting as a constitutional monarch, representing positions taken by the lukiko. Cohen pointed out that the original agreement between Buganda and Britain required the kabaka to accept formal advice from the British. Nevertheless, the kabaka refused. He said that, if he had to choose between the Uganda government and his own people, he would choose his people. He would not present to the lukiko the statement the British had prepared for him.[72]

To the Colonial Office, Cohen couched the problem in terms of nationalist politics. The danger was that the kabaka's demand for Buganda independence would give the Uganda National Congress the issue it was looking for. Cohen thought his reforms had deprived the congress of meaningful economic or land issues. The kabaka and Ignatius Musazi, the Uganda National Congress leader, were building an alliance, Cohen reported. Cohen said he felt bad deposing an African ruler over the issue of independence and he regretted risking disturbances when the situation in Kenya was acute. Nevertheless, Cohen's advice was that the British nip the situation in the bud by removing the kabaka from office.[73]

Later, Lyttelton blamed Cohen for failing to defuse the situation in Buganda. At the time, the colonial secretary took a hard line. He relayed to the cabinet Cohen's assessment that riots would break out if the kabaka voiced his demands in public. Lyttelton claimed that the riots would be more serious than those in 1945 and 1949 because the British would no longer have the kabaka's cooperation. He added his own view that the kabaka was a weakling who had lost face with his people. The kabaka, Lyttelton claimed, was trying to redeem the situation by adopting an extreme nationalist position.[74]

The kabaka's subsequent deposition and deportation led to a debate in the House of Commons. In the course of the debate, Lyttelton said that Uganda's future was as an African state with adequate safeguards for the rights of minorities. To the Colonial Office, Lyttelton's statement did not mean an end to pursuing a multi-racial approach in Uganda. The Colonial Office proposed to Cohen that Uganda would gain self-government only when no racial fears existed and when Uganda's population accepted that all inhabitants should be treated the same regardless of race. Cohen disagreed. He argued that Uganda would be the same as other colonies. Britain would yield control when the political pressure was so strong that it would be foolish to resist. Cohen anticipated that Uganda would follow the Gold Coast's path to self-government. The only difference would be that the British would insist that minority rights be written into the Uganda constitution.[75]

1954 Reforms

Cohen pushed ahead with his reforms and attempted to bring Buganda into the process. He imported Sir Keith Hancock, a British constitutional expert, to consult with Buganda representatives about constitutional changes. From the consultations with Hancock and subsequent consideration by a committee assembled by the lukiko emerged proposals to reform Buganda's government. They called for changing the responsibilities and authority of ministers and the process for appointing subordinate chiefs. The committee also called for direct elections to the lukiko. Cohen implemented local government reforms outside Buganda, giving districts an opportunity to create elected district councils. Cohen also proposed to expand the Uganda legislative council to sixty members, including thirty Africans, and to create five unofficial ministers, including three Africans. The lukiko agreed to use an electoral college to select Buganda's representatives to the legislative council and to use direct elections starting in 1957. Cohen agreed that no further constitutional changes would occur until 1961.[76]

Despite the agreement with Cohen, a majority in the lukiko and probably a majority of the Buganda population remained unreconciled to the prospect of being subsumed into Uganda. A condition of Buganda's acceptance of the 1954 reforms was that the British reinstate the kabaka. When the kabaka returned in November 1955, he allied himself with the lukiko majority. He removed subordinate chiefs who had accepted his deposition and favored those who had opposed it. The Buganda leadership set about separating themselves from Uganda and Ugandan politics. Despite the earlier agreement, the lukiko refused to hold direct elections for the Buganda seats in the legislative council. Uganda National Congress members won seats in the lukiko and supported the majority position. Nevertheless, the lukiko told the Uganda government that it, and not any political party, spoke for Buganda.[77]

Uganda Nationalists

The Uganda National Congress proved a weak and fragile party. Squabbles, resignations, and splits marked its history. Like many nationalist parties, the congress included ambitious, energetic activists who competed for power and influence. The congress also faced serious ideological divisions. Most of its early membership came from Buganda. It had some success in elections to the lukiko. Yet it was difficult to reconcile Uganda nationalism with loyalty to Buganda. The congress leadership quarreled about how it could establish its nationalist credentials without alienating the mass of the population in Buganda. In 1958, the congress advocated direct elections in Buganda, in opposition to the position taken by the lukiko. The congress, however, favored a federal structure for Uganda and proposed that the Buganda government have considerable autonomy. Congress leaders disagreed about the organization's links outside Uganda, particularly when they appeared to signal adherence to a militant version of nationalism. Several congress leaders attended the 1958 Pan African Conference held in Accra. Other congress members opened an office in Cairo in 1958 and began broadcasting programs over Radio Cairo. The Cairo office received support from a group funded by the People's Republic of China called the Afro-Asian Solidarity Movement. A group associated with Ignatius Musazi, one of the party's founders, opposed both the Cairo office and the resolutions adopted at the Accra conference. A party conference in January expelled Musazi and his followers from the party.[78]

Buganda politics also developed a religious dimension. The Buganda leadership was overwhelmingly Protestant. In particular, the kabaka's regime was identified with the Anglican Church. Many positions within the Buganda government were reserved for Protestants. Adherents of the Catholic Church were the largest religious group within the kingdom, however. In 1956, the Democratic Party emerged as an advocate for Catholic interests within Buganda in opposition to both the Uganda National Congress and the lukiko majority. The party also opposed independence for Buganda. Under the leadership of Benedicto Kiwanuka, the party widened its focus to include all of Uganda, although the bulk of its membership was in Buganda. The party's overall tone was moderate. It considered rapid Africanization of the Uganda civil service more important than Ugandan independence, and was content with gradual movement towards independence. In addition, the party was openly anti-communist. It attacked the Uganda National Congress as a communist front.[79]

Through mid–1959, political change in Uganda followed the pattern set out by the British. The British expected Uganda to move by stages to internal self-government by about 1965 and to independence about 1970. The next major step would be direct elections throughout the country in 1961 followed by a greater measure of self-government. In 1958, Sir Frederick Crawford, Cohen's successor as governor, committed to establishing a committee to study and recommend constitutional changes as of 1961. As early as 1957, African members of the legislative council introduced motions calling for self-government and agitated for greater measures of self-government. They pushed, successfully, for direct elections to the legislative council throughout Uganda in 1958, and not just in Buganda. Nevertheless, the nationalists were comfortable with the rate of political change. They were in no position to force a faster pace. The political parties remained small, weak, and loosely organized. The 1958 elections to the legislative council returned one independent, one Democratic Party member and the rest nominally associated with the Uganda National Congress. After the election, seven legislative council members, all from outside Buganda, established a new party, the Uganda Peoples Union, leaving the congress with only three members. At the same time, the legislative council remained unrepresentative of the country as a whole. The lukiko blocked Buganda's participation in the elections and the five Buganda seats remained vacant.[80]

In 1959, the Colonial Office considered the situation in Uganda complex and threatening. The Uganda nationalists were part of the problem, but because of their weakness, not their strength. The nationalist parties' internal weaknesses and the tension between the parties and the lukiko majority and similar groups in the other kingdoms prevented the nationalists from posing any threat to British rule. The Colonial Office thought the nationalists were incapable of taking on many responsibilities of government. They were not apt candidates, in the office's view, for inducing Buganda to participate in Ugandan politics or for resolving the friction between Buganda and the rest of Uganda. The Buganda leadership's insistence on a separate status for the kingdom irritated the rest of the country, as well as the British. British officials were undecided about how to deal with Buganda. To the dismay of the Ugandan nationalists, Lennox-Boyd announced in April 1959 that he was willing to hold separate constitutional discussions with the kingdom's leaders, but it was not clear that the colonial secretary meant to discard the notion of a unified Uganda. Furthermore, Buganda contained a disproportionate share of the educated population. Leaders from outside Buganda feared that the kingdom could dominate an independent Uganda, even though it represented only about a third of the population. Finally, the British were concerned about the reappearance of rural unrest in Buganda. A group calling itself the Uganda National Movement was engaged in a campaign of intimidation, violence, and destruction of property aimed at real or imagined enemies of Buganda, including members of the Democratic Party. The movement was avowedly in favor of the kabaka, but was as much at odds with the Buganda government as it was with the central government.[81]

A New Consul in Kampala

Through 1957, the occasional reports about Uganda filed by the Nairobi consulate painted a familiar picture. Sir Andrew Cohen was a reforming governor, handicapped in part by the conservatism of other British officials, they said. As long as Uganda's economy continued to flourish, widespread unrest was unlikely. Any downturn could provoke political problems. The appeal and influence of nationalist parties was growing surprisingly fast. Uganda might attain self-government as soon as 1961 or as late as 1972, the Nairobi consulate claimed.[82]

In 1957, the United States opened a consulate in Kampala. The flow of information to Washington increased and the United States became a player within Uganda politics. The new consul, Peter Hooper, proved energetic and willing to promote his own ideas about Uganda's future.

Hooper concluded that Crawford and the Uganda government were mishandling the situation. According to Hooper, Crawford was attempting to restrain Uganda nationalism, rather than trying to manage it as Cohen had done. Crawford clung too long to Cohen's promise that no constitutional changes would take place until 1961 and Crawford's proposed timetables for political change were unrealistically slow. Hooper thought that Uganda's future depended on the emergence of effective political parties and he criticized Crawford's disregard for them. Lower level British officials were more intent on maintaining British control and were too ready to impose repressive measures, Hooper worried. Hooper thought that the British lacked the financial resources to prepare Uganda for self-government. He observed that a multi-racial approach made little sense in Uganda. The British were slow to discard it for fear of undermining their efforts in Kenya and Tanganyika.[83]

Hooper portrayed the Uganda nationalists as intent on change and potentially unified in their demands. In September 1957, Hooper told Washington that the nationalists' objections to repressive legislation introduced by the British demonstrated that African political demands were more explosive and unanimous than generally assumed. In April 1959, he thought the 1958 elections showed that Ugandans were more politically interested than expected and he detected a quickening in the pace of political activity. He also looked for an African force to unify the nationalists. In October, he thought that British willingness to make political concessions would bring the nationalist parties together.[84]

In March 1959, as Ugandan politicians and British officials struggled to resolve Buganda's place within Uganda, Hooper became enamored of a proposal prepared by African leaders in Uganda's other kingdoms. An African leader from Toro gave Hooper a copy of the draft constitution he planned to present to a meeting of the so-called "kings" in April 1959. The proposal called for a federal Uganda organized around the kingdoms, including Buganda. The proposed constitution would preserve the power and influence of the kingdoms' leaders. Hooper thought that Ugandans mistrusted the legislative council and British plans to use the council to unify the country were likely to fail. He suspected British officials of seeking to keep Uganda divided and saw their public support of a unified Uganda as a diversion. He imagined that a federal approach built around the kings' proposal would be more likely to succeed.[85]

Hooper's other favorite solution to Uganda's problems was more financial aid from the United States. In November 1958, the Uganda National Congress approached Hooper about arranging U.S. financial support for an office in New York. Hooper warned Washington that the party might turn to Cairo or Moscow if the United States did not offer aid. Recognizing that the British might object to official United States support, Hooper suggested that the State Department approach the American Committee on Africa. Hooper also used the foreign leader grant program to send several Ugandan leaders to the United States, including A.K. Maynaja, a founding member of the Uganda National Congress. In July 1959, Hooper tried to use the program to fund a visit by the kabaka to the United States. The State Department turned down Hooper's request. Nevertheless, the department solicited support, unsuccessfully, from the African-American Institute, another organization involved in providing aid to Africa. Hooper also promoted proposals to build schools and roads in Uganda. After the Uganda National Movement began agitating about trade and economic issues, Hooper proposed dispatching an American business expert to Kampala to work with groups of Uganda traders.[86]

Zanzibar

Politics in Zanzibar during the 1950s resembled those in Uganda more than those in Tanganyika or the Gold Coast. Nationalist political parties were small and divided. Like Uganda, Zanzibar lacked a single, countrywide party and dominant nationalist leader like Nkrumah and the CPP, or Nyerere and the TANU. The political parties' energy derived as much from social, ethnic, or regional differences as from opposition to British rule. Partly as a result, constitutional changes owed as much or more to British initiatives than to nationalist agitation. As in Uganda, outside influences were beginning to make themselves felt in Zanzibar's nationalist politics by the end of the 1950s.

Divisions with Zanzibar

Zanzibar exhibited significant ethnic, social, and regional differences. In 1948, Zanzibar had a population of roughly 265,000. Seventeen percent identified themselves as Arab. The sultans of Zanzibar were, in fact, originally from Oman. Arabs predominated in the government and in local governments throughout the islands. About half the owners of large clove plantations and about a third of the owners of smaller clove plantations were Arabs. Zanzibar had few government schools and most offered only elementary education. Fewer than 2 percent of the population had more than five years of education. Those that did were most likely to be Arabs. After the British opened civil service positions to Zanzibaris in 1947, most successful candidates were Arabs. Another 6 percent of the population identified themselves as Asian. They were mostly clerks and shopkeepers from the Indian subcontinent. They were frequently well-to-do, but were politically quiescent.[87]

The remainder of the population, about two hundred thousand, was identified as African. Some, particularly those living on Zanzibar's second island, Pemba, considered themselves the islands' original inhabitants and identified themselves as Shirazis. About fifty thousand Africans were migrant workers from the mainland. The rest were descendants of slaves brought to the islands or of migrant workers who had come to work on the clove plantations. The Shirazis tended to support Arab rule. Some were substantial landowners. Otherwise, Africans were farmers and agricultural workers. They were most likely to think of themselves as outsiders or on society's bottom rungs.

By the late 1940s, each community in Zanzibar, Arab, African, Shirazi, and Indian, had its own association. Each association was dominated by a small elite and sought to protect its group's interests. The African Association and the Shirazi Association were at odds over the seat in the legislative council reserved for an African. Until 1956, the seat usually went to the head of the Shirazi Association. In the early 1940s and early 1950s, the Arab Association, supported by the Shirazi Association, resisted British attempts to treat Indians as Zanzibaris.

Nationalist Politics

By 1953, the Arab Association evolved towards being a nationalist pressure group and came into conflict with the British authorities. After anti–British articles appeared in an Arab Association publication, the British arrested all but one member of the Arab Association's executive council and charged them with sedition. The Arab Association leaders were found guilty and heavily fined. In June 1954, the Arab Association presented the resident, the senior British official, with demands for universal adult suffrage, elections on a common electoral roll, an unofficial majority in the legislative council, and establishment of government ministers. Sir John Rankine, the resident, thought he had already gained the agreement of all legislative council members for more limited constitutional changes. The Arab Association repudiated the agreement, however, and launched a boycott of the legislative council. Some Arabs were prepared to use violence to enforce the boycott. In November 1955, an Arab Association member returned to the legislative council, but was assassinated a week later.

The Arab Association's boycott only delayed Rankine's changes. Rankine proposed to expand the executive council to include three unofficial members, an African, an Asian, and an Arab. He would also expand the legislative council to twenty-five members, including twelve unofficial members, six nominated and six elected. In the face of the Arab Association's boycott, Rankine held off any constitutional changes temporarily. In late 1955, however, he decided to proceed without the Arab Association's agreement. In October 1955, he announced that Zanzibar would move by appropriate steps to self-government. In 1956, the government enacted the appropriate legislation and scheduled the first legislative council elections for 1957. In response, the Arab Association ended its boycott.[88]

The prospect of elections and eventual self-government sparked the creation of political parties. In December 1955, Ali Mushin Barwani and Abdurrahman Muhammad Babu founded the Zanzibar National Party as a territory-wide party committed to independence, a rapid increase in the number of Zanzibaris in the civil service, and establishment of a constitutional monarchy under the Sultan. Arabs predominated within the party's leadership. It had the support of the Arab Association and appeared pro-Arab. Nevertheless, the party sought African support and opposed the communal representation embedded within Rankine's constitution. Given the Arab population's larger share of educated Zanzibaris, however, African leaders worried that the Zanzibar National Party would take advantage of rapid political change to reinforce Arab dominance in Zanzibar. African leaders favored retention of communal representation in the short term. As the elections approached, they established their own political party, the Afro-Shirazi Union. Like the Zanzibar National Party, the Afro-Shirazi Union campaigned on an independence platform, but it was willing to accept gradual steps under British guidance.[89]

The electorate for the 1957 elections was small, forty thousand, or 13 percent of the population. The qualifications for voting seemed to favor the Arabs and the Zanzibar National Party. Voting was limited to literate males who were subjects of the sultan and who were at least twenty-five years old or had an annual income of £75. Nevertheless, the results reflected Zanzibar's ethnic and social makeup. The Afro-Shirazi Union gained 60 percent of the vote and won five seats. The Zanzibar National Party gained 22 percent and no seats. Other parties won 17 percent and one seat. All successful candidates had been endorsed by or were members of communal organizations.[90]

Beginning in 1956, nationalist politics in Zanzibar felt the influence of outside parties, nationalists elsewhere in Africa and countries further afield. Nyerere visited Zanzibar several times in 1956 in a vain effort to persuade the African and Shirazi Associations to combine. The Afro-Shirazi Union initially planned to boycott the elections, but Nyerere persuaded them to participate. In 1958, the two Zanzibar parties attended a meeting of the Pan African Freedom Movement of East Central and Southern Africa (PAFMECSA), a group initiated by Nyerere. A PAFMECSA delegation later visited Zanzibar, criticized the Afro-Shirazi Union for favoring gradual steps towards independence, and recommended that the two Zanzibar parties form a united front. Even after the two parties formed the Freedom Committee, Nyerere complained that they were letting communal animosities interfere with the struggle for independence. By the late 1950s, both Egypt and the People's Republic of China sponsored radio broadcasts to East Africa, including Zanzibar. China also made scholarships at Peking University available to Zanzibar students. Abdurrahman Muhammad Babu, the Zanzibar National Party's number two leader, visited China several times and was thought to have close ties with the Chinese.[91]

Based on occasional visits to Zanzibar, the Dar es Salaam consulate formed a pessimistic view of Zanzibar politics. British officials had allowed the situation to drift, the consulate claimed. Senior British officials were indolent, inept, and unwilling to encourage social and economic development. The British were smart enough to realize that Zanzibar's Africans needed time to catch up with the Arabs' educational and other attainments. Yet the British entertained the fanciful notion that Arabs and Africans would work together. Consulate officials believed that early independence would bring Arab domination and African resentment. The two communities would be "at each other's throats," the consulate predicted.[92]

During the 1950s, the four East African territories nearly caught up with the West African colonies in terms of African participation in government and in progress toward self-government. The British continued to seek opportunities for delay, but constitutional changes remained about the only card they could play. In the background, U.S. officials became more involved, counseling British officials and nationalist leaders and looking for the African leaders most likely to lead independent African states.

Central Africa, 1953–1959:
Hopes Unfulfilled

As the Eisenhower administration began, the Churchill government was putting the finishing touches to the Federation of Rhodesia and Nyasaland. From London's perspective, the federation represented another version of colonial reform, providing economic and financial benefits to the three Central African colonies and strengthening British rule by solidifying ties between the London government and the European settlers. Churchill's ministers chose to ignore African opposition to federation, but the most significant unresolved question was whether Central Africa's European leaders could secure sufficient African support to preempt the emergence of nationalist leaders and political parties.

London's Views

During the federation's first five years, the government department in London responsible for the federation and for Southern Rhodesia, the Commonwealth Relations Office, remained optimistic about the federation's future. The office conceded that Africans needed to be persuaded of the federation's benefits. The federal government also needed to forge better relationships with the governments of the three constituent territories. Nevertheless, the office foresaw the emergence by 1971 of a prosperous and strong member of the commonwealth, linked politically and economically to Britain. The office interpreted the absence of unrest in Southern Rhodesia as evidence that a multiracial partnership was possible. To allow the federation time to develop political arrangements that could attract African support, the office warned against the political tactics British governors were using in other colonies. Statements of precise long-term objectives were to be avoided. Piecemeal political concessions, such as adding African members to the legislative councils, were suspect.[1]

Officials in the Colonial Office, which oversaw Northern Rhodesia and Nyasaland, were less sanguine. They also harbored reservations about political concessions to Africans in Nyasaland or Northern Rhodesia, but they thought that conditions in the two northern territories were worsening. Africans remained unconvinced that federation was in their best interests, officials worried. Colonial Office officials anticipated that the Gold Coast's and Nigeria's progress toward self-government would intensify African opposition to the federation. It would swell the ranks of the African political parties. European demands that the federation become independent would stir up the African population.[2]

The Colonial Office was short of credible solutions, however. It toyed with the idea

246

that detaching Nyasaland, with its overwhelmingly African population, from the federation would make partnership more likely, but discarded it because the result could be perceived in Britain as handing Southern Rhodesia control of Northern Rhodesia and its copper mines. On the other hand, political changes in Nyasaland might persuade Africans that the territory would attain self-government within the federation. Officials questioned Nyasaland's readiness for an increased African role in government, however. They also worried about the impact changes in Nyasaland would have on African expectations elsewhere in the federation. At the federation level, officials thought a gesture was needed that would convince Africans that the offer of multiracial partnership was real, that they would be able to participate fully in the federation's affairs. The best the office could imagine, nonetheless, was electoral arrangements that would preserve European control but allow some educated Africans to vote.[3]

Relations between the Colonial Office and the British governors of Northern Rhodesia and Nyasaland were testy. Yet the governors' views resembled those of their colleagues in London. The governor of Nyasaland until 1955, Sir Geoffrey Colby, thought the Colonial Office neither understood nor cared about the colony. He told his successor, Sir Robert Armitage, that the heaviest cross a colonial governor had to bear was the "conglomeration of smart alecks" at the Colonial Office. Nevertheless, both Colby and Sir Arthur Benson, the governor of Northern Rhodesia from 1954 to 1958, advised the federation government that it needed to woo African leaders. Colby emphasized opening up civil service jobs to qualified Africans and giving Africans a greater say in government. The governors approached political change gingerly in their own territories. Colby and Armitage envisioned Nyasaland as a self-governing African state within the federation, but only in the distant future. In 1956, Armitage thought Nyasaland would not be self-governing for another twenty-five years. In 1955, Benson advocated strengthening Northern Rhodesia's native administrations as a way to avoid nationalist agitation and slow the pace of political change. In 1953, the Colonial Office and Benson revised Northern Rhodesia's constitution. They rejected the European settlers' demands for a majority in the legislative council. Nevertheless, they increased African representation only slightly, from two to four members in a twenty-six-member council. European members were elected, but the governor nominated the African members. Africans could not vote. In 1955, Armitage enlarged the Nyasaland council to twenty-three members, including six Europeans elected directly and five Africans elected by the colony's three provincial councils.[4]

Welensky and Home

Through 1958, the initiative lay not with officials in London or with the British governors, but with the federation's European leadership, the federation's prime minister from 1953 to 1956, Sir Godfrey Huggins, and his successor, Sir Roy Welensky. Neither Huggins nor Welensky were motivated to make federation more attractive to Africans. Welensky proved more amenable to allowing Africans participate in government than many other Europeans, particularly those in Southern Rhodesia. In the middle and late 1950s, however, Welensky was intent on convincing European voters than he would hold the line against African political advance. He told European audiences that he opposed social equality. Africans would never be capable of holding European jobs, he said. Welensky proclaimed that he would not hand the federation over to the "backward mass" of Africans. Under Huggins and Welensky, racial segregation remained in place within the federation, in public facilities, in stores, in transportation, and in the civil service. Highly visible decisions suggested that the federation was to serve the needs of Southern Rhodesia and its European population. The federation capital was in Salisbury, the Southern Rhodesian capital. The federation's largest development project, the Kariba dam and hydroelectric facility, appeared to serve Southern Rhodesia's interests.[5]

Huggins and Welensky's highest priority was securing the federation's independence as a European dominated state. Beginning in 1956, the federation's leaders sought to persuade the British government, in particular Lord Home, the commonwealth relations secretary, that the federation should gain dominion status. Huggins and Welensky dispatched letters and traveled several times to London seeking to win Home over. They argued that federation should receive the same treatment as the Gold Coast and that independence was implicit in the agreement that created the federation.

Home was inclined to give Welensky and Huggins what they wanted, but he and the British cabinet recognized that the federation had to win over some Africans first. Home and Lennox-Boyd accepted that Britain had pledged not to make major constitutional changes in the federation without consulting with the African populations. The federation constitution was scheduled for a review as soon as 1960. If the federation, with help from the governments of Northern Rhodesia and Nyasaland, could persuade enough Africans of the federation's benefits by 1960, the path to independence might be open. In April 1957, Home and Welensky issued a communiqué that described significant concessions to the federation, but stopped short of independence. The British government relinquished its right to legislate for the federation without the federation's consent. The federal assembly could be enlarged and the federation gained a larger role in its external affairs. Territories could not secede from the federation and the federation could not amalgamate territories into a unitary state. The federal review conference would take place in 1960, the earliest possible date under the terms of the federation constitution. It would consider constitutional advance for the federation that could lead to independence.[6]

The European settlers with Welensky in the lead moved to cement their control while conceding an African presence on the electoral rolls and in the legislatures. The first federal assembly was elected based on the franchises existing in the three territories. No Africans could vote in Nyasaland. Few could vote in Northern Rhodesia. Southern Rhodesia featured a single electoral roll, but educational and income requirements barred nearly all Africans. Welensky submitted legislation that would enlarge the federal assembly, increase the number of African elected members in the federal assembly, and allow more Africans to vote in federal elections. Nevertheless, the African share of assembly seats would decline. Moreover, African candidates would be dependent on European votes and income and educational qualifications would still bar most Africans from voting. The Southern Rhodesian government introduced legislation that would similarly alter the franchise and ensure European control of the legislature.[7]

If Welensky's reforms were intended to demonstrate good faith and concern for African rights, they were a conspicuous failure. Under the federal constitution, the African Affairs Board was responsible for protecting African rights and was empowered to scrutinize federal legislation and refer discriminatory measures to London. The board deemed Welensky's legislation discriminatory and recommended that the British government throw it out. Based on earlier understandings with Welensky, however, the London government declined to do so. Subsequently, the head of the African Affairs Board resigned and the board lost whatever credibility it had as a defense against discrimination. Governor Benson was appalled. Privately he accused Home of utter cynicism and a lack of regard for the federation, Africa, and Britain's future role in Africa.[8]

Nevertheless, Benson did not object to limiting access to the ballot. Under the new constitution he proposed for Northern Rhodesia, more Africans would be able to vote, but a complicated array of educational and income qualifications, multiple electoral rolls, and special constituencies would limit their impact. Benson's proposals were still too generous for Welensky. Among other things, Welensky thought they would allow nationalists too much influence.[9]

Welensky's heated complaints to London about the Benson constitution brought home to the British government the difficulties it faced in Central Africa. Welensky was proving a difficult interlocutor. He was slow to compromise but quick to launch charges of bad faith. He readily issued threats about declaring independence and London was ill-equipped to counter them. Officials in London realized that they had no plans and few resources to deal with a unilateral declaration of independence by the federation government. Since officials thought that they could not rely on British troops to suppress a European coup in Central Africa, military intervention seemed not to be an option. British officials also struggled to rationalize denying Northern Rhodesia and Nyasaland majority rule when they were granting it to other African colonies. They would be hard pressed to justify it in the court of world opinion. Britain had promised to consult the African populations before changing the federation's constitution, but it had signaled a willingness to consider independence under European control in the near future. Granting the two northern territories self-government within the federation might allow the British to honor all their pledges, but self-government for the northern territories was a long-term proposition. Welensky did not seem prepared to wait. Home thought that the federation could only proceed to independence in the near term under European leadership. According to Home, Britain needed to convince Welensky to accept wider African participation in government and educated Africans to settle for less than majority rule.[10]

Nationalist Opposition

By November 1958, when Home shared his views with the cabinet, the prospects for attracting sufficient African support for the federation to guarantee its survival were probably nil. Most politically aware Africans in Northern Rhodesia and Nyasaland had never been reconciled to the federation. They viewed it as an element of European domination and a barrier on the path to self-government. In 1953, the federation's creation had sparked scattered outbursts of violence in the northern territories. Nevertheless, the African opposition lacked the means to mount an effective campaign. By 1958, however, a nationalist party was opposing the federation and British rule in each of the federation's territories. The nationalist parties were cooperating with each other and were receiving encouragement from nationalists outside the federation.

In Northern Rhodesia, the Zambia African National Congress led by Kenneth Kaunda was organizing a boycott of the first elections under the Benson constitution, scheduled for March 1959. Since 1953, the African National Congress, the original Northern Rhodesian nationalist party, had established branches throughout Northern Rhodesia, organized anti-discrimination campaigns, and supported African trade unions. It advocated democracy on a "one man, one vote" basis. The ANC'S original leader, Harry Nkumbula, proved overly controlling and insufficiently militant for many members, however, and alienated the party's most militant members by arguing for participation in the March elections. As a result, Kaunda and others walked out and formed a rival party.

In Nyasaland, Hastings Banda, the head of the African National Congress, was touring the territory, denouncing British rule and calling for secession from the federation. In 1956, ANC members won four of the five African seats in the legislative council and, thereafter, used the council as a platform to advocate their views. Besides pushing for a larger African voice in government, the congress resisted attempts to shift responsibility for regulating European-run farms to the federal government. As in Northern Rhodesia, younger, more militant members played a larger role in the party as time went on. While practicing medicine in Britain and the Gold Coast, Banda advised and assisted congress leaders and organized their attempts to block creation of the federation in 1952 and 1953. Congress leaders pleaded with Banda to return to Nyasaland. When he arrived in August 1958, he was named congress president and began speaking against the federation.

In Southern Rhodesia, the political atmosphere was less heated, but a recently reconstituted African National Congress was active. In September 1957, the Salisbury-based City Youth League, which had organized a bus boycott the year before, joined with African trade unionists to revive the African National Congress. A trade union leader, Joshua Nkomo, became president. The party's manifesto attacked the distribution of land within Southern Rhodesia and called for majority rule.

By late 1958, the nationalist parties within the federation had forged an alliance and had gained support from outside the federation. In December 1958, Banda, Kaunda, Nkumbula, Nkomo, and other nationalists from the federation attended the All African Peoples Conference in Accra, a meeting of nationalists from across the continent organized by Nkrumah. Nkumbula remained intent on cultivating an image of moderation and remained the odd man out. Yet when the nationalist parties drafted an agreement to oppose the federation, even he joined in. Kaunda remained in Ghana for a month. When he returned to Northern Rhodesia, he claimed that the Ghanaian government had promised his party financial and other support. Both Kaunda's and Banda's speeches displayed a more militant tone after the Accra conference.[11]

State of Emergency

As nationalist activity increased in late 1958 and early 1959, the governments of the three territories decided to put the nationalist leadership out of action. In Northern Rhodesia, Benson was concerned that Kaunda's boycott would undermine the credibility of the March elections. The Southern Rhodesian government was accountable to European voters and was apt to view almost any African nationalist activity as a threat to the established order and to its continued electoral success. The government had been threatening to ban the African National Congress since its revival in 1957. In Nyasaland, clashes between the police and demonstrators and other violent incidents had accompanied the ANC's organizing efforts. Governor Armitage was concerned about maintaining public order. He had been anticipating a showdown with the congress since mid–1958. The three governments were supported, and perhaps encouraged, by both the British government in London and the federation government in Salisbury.

During February and March 1959, the governments acted in quick succession. Welensky, Armitage, and Benson met with Sir Edgar Whitehead, the prime minister of Southern Rhodesia, and other senior officials. The federal government moved troops into Nyasaland. The Southern Rhodesia government declared a state of emergency, banned the African National Congress and detained five hundred of its leaders, but not Nkomo, who was out of the country. The Nyasaland government detained thirteen hundred congress members, including Banda and other leaders. The Northern Rhodesian government detained Kaunda and his principal colleagues and banned the Zambia African National Congress. In Northern Rhodesia and Nyasaland, the government also set out to harass and hinder any nationalist leaders who remained at large, but Nkumbula and the African National Congress were free to participate in the elections.[12]

In the two northern territories, the governments did not intend to retain control through armed force. The day before Armitage declared the state of emergency, a reporter asked him whether the British could hold Nyasaland against the wishes of three million Africans. Armitage replied that he doubted it. The government's logic resembled that of the Gold Coast government when it arrested Nkrumah and of the Kenya government when it detained Kenyatta. The nationalist leaders were extremists, intent on violence. British leaders thought that detaining them would slow their organizing, discourage violence, and create an opportunity for moderate African leaders to take control.

As in the case of Kenyatta, British leaders justified the arrests with lurid accusations. Lennox-Boyd told the House of Commons that the Nyasaland nationalists were planning a massacre. They intended to murder Europeans, Asians, and moderate African leaders. Julian Amery, minister of state in the Colonial Office, compared the Nyasaland leaders to Mau Mau in Kenya. In a radio address, Governor Benson claimed that the Zambia African National Congress had joined with the other nationalist parties in planning a violent revolution. They were prepared to kill anyone who resisted them. He went on to compare the congress to Murder Inc. A small group of killers was trying to intimidate the great mass of law-abiding people, he said.[13]

The arrests and detentions took place swiftly and smoothly. British officials had been preparing to arrest nationalist leaders for some time. Since at least 1954, the Nyasaland government had maintained a list of Africans it would arrest in case of trouble. Banda and other African leaders anticipated that the governments would act. They did not resist when the police apprehended them.

The aftermath of the arrests was anything but smooth, particularly in Nyasaland. Kaunda was committed to non-violence and his party was small and struggling. On the other hand, Banda was given to extreme rhetoric. The African National Congress in Nyasaland had the political field to itself and enjoyed wide support. Nyasaland had already seen considerable unrest. Beginning on the afternoon of the arrests, Africans across Nyasaland resisted. For nearly two weeks, they blocked roads, burned huts, attacked police, and attempted to free detainees. By the time the police and troops regained control, they had killed fifty Africans.

Qualified Support

Through 1956, the U.S. consuls in Salisbury approved of the federation. John Hoover told Washington in 1953 that British policy in Central Africa was moderate and beneficent.

In an atmosphere of racial harmony, the African population was being brought along the road toward education, health and general well being. In 1954, Lloyd Steere called the federation a bold and imaginative action to use Southern Rhodesia as an anchor to prevent Northern Rhodesia and Nyasaland from going the way of the Gold Coast or Kenya. Eighteen months later, Steere described the federation as a land of law and order, stability, and progress. The country, he wrote, was fortunate to have a substantial group of able, experienced leaders and civil servants.[14]

Opinion in Washington was less optimistic. A December 1953 National Intelligence Estimate characterized British Central Africa as the greatest threat to western interests in tropical Africa. Economic expansion, European immigration, and the emergence of an African urban class had complicated political development and aggravated tensions. Britain was yielding to pressure from European settlers. The settlers were unlikely, however, to take sufficient action to convince Africans of their good intentions. Most Africans might seem reconciled to federation, but a hard core of dissidents would continue to agitate. Violent conflicts between Europeans and Africans were likely within the next decade, the report predicted.[15]

The consuls on the spot were critical of the African population and skeptical about reports of their resistance to federation. Hoover thought that no more than five hundred or so of Southern Rhodesia's African population were intellectually alert. No more than half of those understood federation, he estimated. He thought that Africans would force the Europeans out and revert to barbarism if they gained control of the federation. Hoover characterized the reaction of most Africans to federation as the vast apathy of primitive conservatism. He attributed the unrest in Nyasaland that accompanied the federation's creation to political agitators. He complained about exaggerated and misleading reports in the press. Over the next three years, Hoover's successors downplayed the significance of unrest within the federation. Steere assured Washington that any new country experienced stresses and strains and that the federation was not coming apart at the seams.[16]

While recognizing that government actions often fell short of African aspirations, U.S. officials continued to stress the positive. Southern Rhodesia's prime minister from 1953 until early 1958, Sir Garfield Todd, introduced stringent security measures aimed at limiting African political activity as well as land and economic reforms aimed at addressing African grievances. The Salisbury consulate focused on the reform measures. It described Todd as one of the few Rhodesian leaders interested in gaining African goodwill. Steere thought that the Southern Rhodesian voting system that applied the same educational and income qualifications to all potential voters had considerable African support, although few Africans could vote. U.S. officials contrasted Todd's approach with the federation government's persistent reluctance to dismantle discrimination against Africans. After Welensky introduced his federal electoral legislation, Steere identified its limitations in African eyes and predicted that it would gain little African support. Nevertheless, he told Washington that Welensky's bills were a sincere attempt to provide African political advance. After Joshua Nkomo described the drawbacks the African National Congress saw in new rules promulgated by the Southern Rhodesian government for native councils, Steere told Washington that the rules were a sincere attempt by the government to inculcate political and financial responsibility among Africans.[17]

As nationalist agitation emerged, however, the consuls became concerned. They looked for moderate African leaders, willing to operate within the federation. As early as September 1954, Steere thought that the African members of the federal assembly had discredited themselves with their supporters among the European population. Steere thought more moderate and responsible African leadership was needed. Steere was surprised and concerned in the summer of 1956 when African members of the federal assembly and the Nyasaland legislative council were outspoken in their criticism of the federation and demanded the right to secede. Steere labeled the speeches as outbursts of racialism. He worried that they would undermine the federation's policy of multiracial partnership. Later, he characterized the Nyasaland African National Congress's strategy as injecting racial issues into every possible situation in order to consolidate African sentiment against white rule. Steere harbored hope that the Southern Rhodesia African National Congress would prove more moderate than its two northern counterparts. His preference was for African political leaders in southern Rhodesia to join the Constitution Party, a fledgling multiracial party. In 1958, Vice Consul David Gottlieb expressed the hope that new electoral procedures in Nyasaland and Northern Rhodesia would cause many Africans to leave the nationalist parties and participate in federal elections.[18]

After Banda returned to Nyasaland to campaign against federation, the Salisbury consulate saw him as an extremist, aiming to displace and discomfit moderate African leaders. In January 1959, Consul General Joseph Palmer told Washington that Banda was intent on moving towards extremism and on brushing moderate African leaders aside. Banda had eclipsed Wellington Chirwa, one of Nyasaland's African representatives in the federal assembly, and had made life uncomfortable for other moderates in the Nyasaland nationalist movement. Palmer saw Banda having a similar impact in Southern Rhodesia, putting moderates on the defensive and giving hope to the more militant.[19]

As tensions rose, the U.S. consuls became less optimistic about the federation's future. Steere saw danger in the preference of the federal and Southern Rhodesian governments for what he called "firm" handling of conflicts between Africans and Europeans. In October 1958, Consul General Curtis Strong thought that the government was unlikely to restore order to the northern portions of Northern Rhodesia. The local population, Strong wrote, did not understand the issues involved in federation, but had been convinced by the African National Congress to oppose it. The British administration was worried and likely to react quickly and ruthlessly to any lawless behavior. Strong thought that the Southern Rhodesian government might be able to attract African support. Yet it needed to advertise any reforms to the European voters as hardheaded realism and not any sort of liberalism. Strong doubted that the governments in the two northern territories could move fast enough to satisfy the politically aware Africans.[20]

The men in the field remained more upbeat than their counterparts in Washington. In April 1958, the State Department's Office of Intelligence and Research produced a report that predicted a "stormy future" for the federation. The analysts in Washington portrayed a British government caught between militant nationalists and recalcitrant settlers. The concept of partnership had proven hollow and no real power sharing seemed likely. The European-dominated governments were intent on maintaining control in the short term and on securing independence in the longer term. African opposition to federation had hardened and widened, the report stated. African extremists held the upper hand in the two northern territories and they might be poised to seize control of the nationalist party in Southern Rhodesia as well. Furthermore, the constitutional review scheduled for 1960 would confront British leaders with a difficult choice. The report predicted that Britain would grant the federation independence under settler control. Nevertheless, it predicted that the Africans' numerical superiority would eventually yield African control of the federation.

The report doubted that the transition from European to African control would be peaceful.[21]

In December 1958, the Office of Intelligence and Research produced a similar analysis of the most recent election in Southern Rhodesia. In the election, the moderate European party, the United Federal Party led by Whitehead, won seventeen seats to the hard-line Dominion Party's thirteen seats. The more liberal United Rhodesia Party led by former prime minister Sir Garfield Todd won no seats. The United Federal Party was more popular with the British government and proclaimed a commitment to moderation and gradualism. The report concluded, however, that both Europeans and Africans thought the party's platform was a cloak for inaction. The United Federal Party included Africans and several Africans had been elected to the legislative council on the party's ticket. Nevertheless, the report thought the party unlikely to reduce opposition to federation in the northern territories or to reverse the steady deterioration of relations between Europeans and Africans in Southern Rhodesia.[22]

Through 1958, the thinking within the State Department was that the United States should hope that the federation proved a success while not identifying itself closely with it. State Department staff thought that federation leaders were unlikely to make sufficient changes to win African support. Programs funded by the United States might make a difference. Nevertheless, the federation was unlikely to approve any such effort or heed U.S. advice. The best the United States could do was to stand aside and hope for the best. The U.S. should avoid obvious ties to the federation government or even the government's European critics since either would alienate African leaders.[23]

By 1959, the European settlers and British officials in Central Africa had failed to gain meaningful African support. European leaders were more interested in solidifying European control and demonstrating their toughness to their European constituents. British governors were little more comfortable with political change. Faced with growing and persistent nationalist agitation, both European politicians and British officials saw the police and the military as the solution.

U.S. officials in Central Africa saw the federation as a positive development and discounted African complaints. When nationalism persisted, U.S. officials worried about the federation's future. By 1959, the U.S. stance was to stand back and hope for the best.

16

British Colonial Policy, 1959–1960: Macleod Accelerates the Pace

In October 1959, the Conservatives led by Harold Macmillan won their third successive general election victory. In the midst of an economic boom, British voters kept the Conservatives in power with a majority of a hundred seats, an increase of twenty over the previous government's. In Macmillan's new government, Iain Macleod, formerly minister of labor and national service, replaced Alan Lennox-Boyd as colonial secretary. Macleod's roughly two years as colonial secretary marked a break with Lennox-Boyd's approach and propelled the remaining British colonies in Africa towards independence. Replacing Lennox-Boyd with Macleod was consistent with Macmillan's growing doubts about the viability of Lennox-Boyd's policy of delay. Nevertheless, Macleod moved faster and farther than Macmillan initially intended.

Multiple Crises

In the months leading up to the October 1959 election, external events suggested that the European empires in Africa were at risk. African nationalists met in Accra at the All Africa People's Conference. Some observers in East Africa thought that the U.S. reaction to the conference signaled support for African nationalism. The United Nations held an economic conference in Addis Abba at which Secretary General Dag Hammarskjold seemed to indicate that economic and political change had to proceed together. De Gaulle informed Macmillan that France intended to allow its African colonies to become independent. In January, the Belgian government announced that elections would take place in the Congo as the first step towards independence.[1]

In summer 1959, the Macmillan government's policies in Nyasaland came under fire in Britain. The Nyasaland government's declaration of a state of emergency provoked questions and criticism in Parliament. The Macmillan government felt compelled to appoint an independent commission, headed by a high court judge, Sir Patrick Devlin, to investigate. The Devlin Commission's report refuted Labour's allegations that Welensky had unduly influenced the Nyasaland government to act and acknowledged that Nyasaland officials had no choice but to act in the tumultuous conditions of early March 1959. Nevertheless, the report expressed skepticism about Lennox-Boyd's charges of a nationalist murder plot and charged that the government had used unnecessary and illegal force in rounding up nationalists. In a telling phrase, the report characterized Nyasaland as a police state. Despite the government's attempts to steer the commission away from the issue of the federation, the report also asserted that opposition to the federation was nearly universal in Nyasaland. The government recognized that the report was damaging. It hurriedly produced a companion report, signed by Governor Armitage, that attempted to uphold the government's position.[2]

The government suffered another blow when word leaked out that guards had killed eleven prisoners and injured at least sixty others at the Hola detention camp in Kenya and that the Kenyan government had attempted to cover up the incident. In the ensuing Commons debate, the worst damage to the government came from a speech by the independent-minded Conservative member, Enoch Powell. In a scathing denunciation of government policy, Powell argued that the government must uphold basic British values. It could not hold itself to African standards in Africa, and Asian standards in Asia, and British standards only at home. In Africa, Powell said, Britain needed to follow the highest standards in terms of accepting responsibility.[3]

Macmillan and other Conservatives saw serious political risk in colonial crises. In May, Macleod wrote to Macmillan that Africa was the Conservative Party's weakest area for middle voters. It was the only policy area where the Conservatives were subject to serious criticism. For Macmillan, the risks were at least as much within the Conservative Party. Beginning with the Suez incident, a group of backbench members thought Macmillan's approach insufficiently imperial. In 1957, Lord Salisbury resigned from the government over Macmillan's decision to release the Cypriot leader, Archbishop Makarios, from detention. In 1959, Salisbury remained available as a focal point for Conservative opposition to political change in Africa. Macmillan told Lord Swinton that the first priority was keeping the party together and likened his situation to someone trying to keep five balls in the air at the same time.[4]

Colonial policy was a domestic political issue in 1959 partly because the Labour Party had shifted away from a bipartisan colonial policy and toward support for majority rule. During the middle 1950s, the Movement for Colonial Freedom, headed by Fenner Brockway, replaced the Fabian Colonial Bureau as the leading Labour colonial pressure group. The movement distinguished itself from the bureau by advocating the establishment of target dates for each stage towards independence. Creech Jones, a long time member of the bureau, considered target dates anathema. The movement went on to advocate rapid progress toward independence. After Hugh Gaitskell became party leader in 1955, Labour pledged to grant independence only when a constitution based on one-man, one-vote was functioning. The party put aside any insistence on economic development or establishment of democratic foundations before independence. As the Sudan and the Gold Coast gained their independence, key Labour members saw Britain competing with Russia and China for the loyalty of colonial peoples by dismantling the remaining colonies. Labour leaders, notably Barbara Castle, developed links with African nationalists, and raised colonial issues in the House.[5]

Macmillan Shifts Course

Amidst the controversies and tumult of 1959, Macmillan concluded that the current colonial policies were not longer tenable. After the Nyasaland government declared the state of emergency, Macmillan wrote in his diary that it now appeared that the federation, while beneficial economically, was politically unacceptable to Africans. In May 1959, Macmillan told the Kenyan leader Michael Blundell that he saw Britain caught between the European settlers and the African nationalists. If the government were not careful, the future might bring a Boston tea party by the settlers or an explosion among the Africans.[6]

Macmillan, in his memoirs, attributed his change of mind to a 1958 conversation with Sir James Robertson, governor-general of Nigeria. When Macmillan asked Robertson whether the Nigerians were ready for self-government, Robertson replied that they were not. When Macmillan asked when the British should grant Nigeria self-government, Robertson replied: "As soon as possible." Robertson explained that if Nigerian political leaders were likely to spend the next twenty years learning how to govern, he would favor delaying self-government until then. Nevertheless, if self-government did not come soon, the nationalist leaders were likely to spend the next twenty years rebelling against the government. Rather than fighting the nationalists, the British ought to grant self-government immediately, Robertson advised.[7]

In a 1962 conversation with Welensky, Macmillan offered an explanation that rested more on British weakness. Macmillan told Welensky that Britain could have held on to Cyprus if it were willing to use the tactics employed by the Germans during the Second World War, hanging and shooting people wholesale. It was a mistake to believe that a country could maintain control through force, Macmillan contended. The French had a million men under arms, yet they could not avoid a humiliating defeat in Algeria.[8]

In thinking that Britain needed to alter its colonial policy in late 1959, Macmillan was following, not leading, opinion in British official, political, and business spheres. Colonial Office officials believed that progress toward independence would continue to be rapid. Their colleagues in the Commonwealth Relations Office, less inclined towards political change in the colonies, believed that political pressures, both foreign and domestic, were such that Britain would have to concede independence sooner rather than later. Lord Home, the commonwealth relations secretary, harbored doubts about granting African colonies their independence, but he conceded that Britain needed to focus on winning the friendship of the newly independent African states. The Labour Party was inclined towards political change in Africa. The newly elected Conservative majority in parliament was thought to be more open to political change than its predecessor. Business and mining interests, important players in Central Africa, showed signs of anticipating a shift to African majority governments. Sir Ronald Prain, chairman of a major mining company, the Rhodesian Selection Trust, communicated to the Macmillan government his view that business interests would seek accommodations with African leaders like Kaunda and Banda. Prain thought that the European settlers had to offer concessions to moderate African leaders so that leaders more prone to violence could not seize control of the nationalist movements.[9]

In addition, Macmillan did not hold either British officials or settler leaders in Central Africa in high regard. When Macmillan visited Nyasaland in early 1960, he had a heated argument with Governor Armitage. Later Macmillan wrote that he found the Nyasaland administration both tired and too ready to resort to repression. Macmillan also harbored prejudices against the European settlers in Africa. In his view, they were the rag-tag sweepings of Europe, with an unhealthy admixture of decayed British aristocrats. Senior British officials admired Welensky's political and administrative abilities. To Macmillan, he was just an emotional Lithuanian Jew. Macmillan came to believe that dealing with the settlers was far more difficult than dealing with the African nationalists. In December 1959, he wrote that Africans were not the problem in Africa; Europeans were.[10]

In 1959 and 1960, Macmillan was open to change, but had not decided to install African majority governments in East and Central Africa. Macmillan thought that the future lay with the kind of coalition Michael Blundell was attempting to create in Kenya, open-minded settlers allied with moderate African leaders. He told Blundell that the British would have time to use economic development to woo the African masses if such coalitions emerged. Macmillan acknowledged that African majority governments were inevitable, but hoped to postpone them. He thought that the Central African territories were not ready for self-government. He preferred "qualitative democracy" involving significant educational and other qualifications for voting to "quantitative democracy" with its "one man, one vote" arrangements.[11]

Despite concerns about colonial policy, Macmillan did not force Lennox-Boyd out of the Colonial Office. Lennox-Boyd's wife was an heir to the Guinness brewing fortune and Lennox-Boyd was in line to become the company's managing director. As early as November 1958, Lennox-Boyd had decided to give up his parliamentary seat before the next general election in order to take up the post at Guinness. Nonetheless, Macmillan asked Lennox-Boyd to stay and to postpone any announcement about his political plans. During 1959, as the Kenyan and Nyasaland crises embarrassed the Macmillan government, Lennox-Boyd offered his resignation more than once, but Macmillan refused the offers. Lennox-Boyd then decided to contest the 1959 elections, believing that doing otherwise would give comfort to his critics.[12]

Macmillan did not intend everything that Macleod accomplished. Macmillan did not give Macleod specific instructions. Macleod recalled that he had not discussed colonial policy in any depth with either Macmillan or his deputy, R.A. Butler, before becoming colonial secretary. Macleod assumed that Macmillan had an instinctive sympathy for what Macleod intended to do and that he had the backing of Macmillan and Butler. Macleod thought that Macmillan wanted more rapid change than Lennox-Boyd had approved. Macleod also claimed that Macmillan was ready for a rapid move toward independence. Nevertheless, Macleod admitted that the speed with which he acted startled Macmillan. Macleod thought that Macmillan often wanted the best of both worlds, effective change without upsetting anyone in East or Central Africa. Macleod professed to believe that you could not make an omelet without breaking eggs. You could not be effective in Central or East Africa and remain friends with everyone, Macleod said.[13]

Macmillan's famous "wind of change" speech was consistent with his acceptance that change in Africa was inevitable and his reluctance to commit Britain to specific political changes. In late 1959, Macmillan decided to embark on a two-month tour of Africa. A high point was to be a major address to the South African parliament. Macmillan wanted to recapture the moral high ground for British policy in the face of criticism at home. On February 3, 1960, Macmillan delivered a lecture to the South African legislators. He warned them that African nationalism was a powerful force. A "wind of change" was blowing through the continent. The West, Macmillan said, had come to terms with African nationalism and the South Africans needed to do the same. If South Africa did not change, the communists were likely to benefit. By publicly acknowledging the potential strength of African national-ism, Macmillan broke new ground for a British government. Yet nowhere in the speech did he commit his government to do anything. In a similar speech in Salisbury, he said that the British government would not remove its protection for Northern Rhodesia or Nyasaland unless and until the people of the two territories wished to join an independent federation. Settler leaders perceived Macmillan's statement as a new commitment, but British govern-ments had been saying the same thing since the late 1940s.[14]

Accelerating the Pace

After leaving office, Macleod stressed the continuity between his policies and those of his predecessors, reaching back to Creech Jones and to Joseph Chamberlain, a late nineteenth century colonial secretary. In 1967, Macleod told an interviewer that British colonial policy had always sought to bring colonies to independence at the right time. If you read speeches about the transition to independence, Macleod claimed, you could not readily determine which colonial secretary had given them. It could have been Creech Jones as easily as Lennox-Boyd.

Much as Macleod described his impact as merely quickening the pace of change, he accepted that this constituted a break with the past. Macleod did not openly criticize Lennox-Boyd, but the essence of Lennox-Boyd's approach was delay, drawing out the process of handing over power as long as possible. Macleod agreed with Lennox-Boyd that the African colonies were not ready for independence, any more than India had been in 1947. Like Attlee and his Labour colleagues, however, Macleod thought that no colonial power, not even Britain, could halt the movement towards independence, a view Lennox-Boyd might not have questioned. In 1959, however, Macleod thought delaying independence in Africa risked serious bloodshed. Moving quickly to address the nationalists' demands posed risks, but moving slowly posed greater risks. Macleod set out not to change Britain's commitment to moving its African colonies to self-government and independence, but, in his phrase, to "telescope" events contemplated under current policies.[15]

Macleod thought that Britain had set a precedent in West Africa. Having conceded independence to the major West African colonies, Nigeria and the Gold Coast, Britain could not refuse to do the same elsewhere, even if European settlers were present. The West African precedent related to expectations among nationalists in other colonies as well as among the British electorate and the world community. The European settlers had their supporters in Britain. Otherwise, hardly anyone was likely to accept that the outcome in Kenya or Northern Rhodesia should be different than in the Gold Coast.

Like Macmillan's, Macleod's analysis rested in part on his sense of British weakness. Britain could not treat East and Central Africa differently because Britain lacked the resources to impose its will by force in Africa. The Macmillan government planned to end conscription in 1960. It would then be unable to expand the armed forces quickly and cheaply to combat an African rebellion. Even if Britain could assemble the necessary troops, the costs of fighting a long African war were beyond Britain's means. Quelling the Kenyan uprising had consumed more than £60 million.

For both Macleod and Macmillan, the French predicament in Algeria offered lessons about violent encounters with nationalists. Colonial conflicts could be costly in men and material. Even with conscription, France seemed unable to find sufficient troops to crush the Algerian revolt. When colonial conflicts involved European settlers, they could be brutal. Atrocities on both sides were likely. Harsh methods employed by colonial forces could become embarrassments to the metropolitan government, at home and abroad. The Algerian conflict also suggested that a colonial power was unlikely to defeat a nationalist movement in the late 1950s.

Moreover, the Franco-Algerian war highlighted the pivotal position of the United States in a colonial conflict. Macmillan and Macleod were aware that the United States provided France with military assistance in Algeria, but pushed successive French governments to reach an understanding with the rebels. The U.S. persisted in agitating for a settlement even when doing so threatened to undermine the Fourth Republic. Dulles did not believe that the French could defeat the rebels. Eisenhower feared that openly siding with the French would damage the Americans' anti-colonial credentials. Both worried that the Algerian nationalists would turn to Russia for assistance and put Western control of the Mediterranean at risk. Anticipating a French defeat, the U.S. government cultivated covert links to the rebels. When Macleod and Macmillan talked about avoiding another Algeria in East or Central Africa, they did not refer to the U.S. role. Yet they almost certainly included in their fears the prospect of finding themselves in the same position as the French government, waging war in Africa against the wishes of their primary benefactor.[16]

Macleod did not see himself managing a retreat. The Macmillan government was not embarking on a series of Dunkirks, gallant, prolonged, bitter rearguard actions. Macleod saw himself putting aside stagnant and wishful thinking. In his view, he was striving to convert the empire into a family, an arrangement that satisfied nationalist ambitions and served British interests. Macleod thought that by designing constitutions properly, the Macmillan government could steer nationalists into moderate policies. Moderate meant cooperative and malleable more than anything else.[17]

Accelerating the transition to independence became a personal crusade for Macleod. Personal involvement by the colonial secretary was not new. Colonial secretaries had traveled to the African colonies since the Second World War. Lyttelton and Lennox-Boyd negotiated with nationalist leaders and, in 1957, Lennox-Boyd intervened to impose a new constitution on Kenya. Nevertheless, when Macleod took over the Colonial Office, the way was open for a new colonial secretary to play a large role. As of late 1959, a vacuum existed at the highest level of British colonial government in Africa. Several African governors were new to the job or seemed destined to depart in the near future. Moreover, Macleod took personal involvement to a higher level. He allegedly told a friend that he intended to take a radical line in winding up the British empire in Africa and to be, in fact, the last colonial secretary. Before becoming colonial secretary, Macleod had never set foot in Africa, and began his tenure with a lengthy tour of East and Central Africa. On his return, he shared his personal observations and recommendations with Macmillan. Macleod maintained good relations with the senior civil servants in the Colonial Office, but his policy recommendations seemed his own. In the Macleod era, specific policy recommendations were at the heart of the office's efforts. Under Macleod, the Colonial Office's focus shifted from writing the general policy reviews and papers to devising political settlements and constitutions for individual colonies. Furthermore, Macleod took the lead in negotiating political arrangements in the African colonies. He met with nationalist and settler leaders. He chaired and played a key role in the many constitutional conferences that the Macmillan government convened.[18]

Because Macleod was deeply involved in policy deliberations, negotiations, and meetings, his personality and style colored the Macmillan government's dealings with the colonies, especially the government's interactions with European settlers and colonial administrators. Whereas Lennox-Boyd had maintained cordial relations with administrators and settler leaders, acrimony and ill will marked Macleod's tenure. Colonial governors perceived Macleod as an obnoxious back seat driver. Prominent settlers found him difficult to converse with or to trust. Once convinced of a policy's worth, Macleod was direct and determined, bullying even. When he visited Nyasaland and met with the senior British officials, he asked no questions but announced how the Nyasaland government was to proceed. Macleod could also be sly, subtle, and secretive. Dealings with Macleod left colonial administrators and settler leaders complaining about a lack of honesty and openness.

The contrast in styles between Lennox-Boyd and Macleod reflected in part their personal histories. Lennox-Boyd benefited from the right connections throughout his career. His marriage made him wealthy. He could be firm, but his manner was relaxed, that of a confident aristocrat. He impressed his subordinates as less focused and less intellectual than Lyttelton, his immediate predecessor. On the other hand, Macleod came from a family of limited means and built a career on his wits. Before and after military service in the Second World War, he earned his living as a professional bridge player. Early in his political career, he worked in the Conservative Research Department, a common starting point for brainy political aspirants. Elected to Parliament in 1950, he was spotted by Churchill as a potential political star and made minister of health in 1952.[19]

In part, Macleod did not get along with many of the Europeans in Africa because he shared with Macmillan a low opinion of their abilities. Macleod suspected that many British officials were stale and unimaginative and, therefore, ineffective. Macleod's view of the settler politicians was lower still. After the European-dominated United Federal Party in Nyasaland tried to block a speech by Hastings Banda, Macleod wrote to Macmillan of the "bottomless stupidity" of all the party's members. He predicted that they would prove too stubborn for all the Macmillan government's efforts.[20]

Macleod brought a moral tone to colonial policy that was absent under Lennox-Boyd. The Hola camp incident upset Macleod and he was part of the cabinet minority that argued that the government should communicate that it did not condone maltreatment of prisoners. Macleod and Lord Hailsham argued for prosecuting the British officials responsible or forcing the resignation of their superiors. When Macleod met privately with Lennox-Boyd after replacing him as colonial secretary, the contrast in the two men's approaches became evident. Lennox-Boyd shared with Macleod the details of other incidents in Kenya that involved mistreatment of prisoners or other crimes by British officials that Lennox-Boyd and Governor Baring had covered up. When Macleod expressed shock and disapproval, Lennox-Boyd's reply was to wish Macleod good luck applying "the canons of the cloister to tribal Africa."[21]

Sierra Leone

Macleod quickly recommended independence for Sierra Leone. Colonial Office thinking had been that the colony would become self-governing in the early 1960s. Nationalist forces were not strong or forceful, but Sir Milton Margai and his Sierra Leone People's Party seemed the sort of cooperative nationalists the British should support. Moreover, the Colonial Office doubted whether it could retard political change in Sierra Leone when virtually every other colony in West Africa, British and French, was moving towards independence. In March 1960, Macleod proposed to the Cabinet Colonial Policy Committee that Britain offer Sierra Leone independence in 1961, provided a satisfactory defense agreement between Britain and Sierra Leone was in place. The British wanted to retain access to Freetown harbor, in particular. Otherwise, Sierra Leone was of marginal importance to Britain. Macleod conceded that Sierra Leone would need British financial aid after independence, but no more than it was already receiving in development aid from Britain. Finally, conceding independence would bolster Britain's image. The cabinet accepted Macleod's recommendation. Sierra Leone became independent on April 27, 1961.[22]

Gambia

British officials did not know what to do about the Gambia, a tiny colony, twenty miles wide at its widest point and 180 miles long on both banks of the Gambia River. In 1957, a committee of officials termed it "a happy backwater." Yet they anticipated that its inhabitants would seek political change as their West African neighbors were. The colony did not seem viable as an independent nation. Withdrawing British control would be irresponsible, some officials thought. Perhaps some form of internal self-government would be possible. In 1959, another committee thought that maintaining the British connection was the right answer. The committee acknowledged that association with Senegal, which bordered the Gambia on three sides, would become increasingly probable.[23]

Macleod had no ready answer. His initial thought was that the Gambia should be federated with Sierra Leone. Once he realized that the two colonies were three hundred miles apart and that Sierra Leone was too poor to take on more responsibilities, he discarded the idea. Nevertheless, Macleod and the cabinet assumed that constitutional changes would proceed in the Gambia along the pattern set by the Gold Coast and Nigeria. In January 1961, they anticipated granting the Gambia self-government in 1962, but decided that association with Senegal was the correct future for the colony. Reluctant to put pressure on the Gambian leaders, however, the cabinet decided that Britain would indicate only that it would not stand in the way of some form of association, provided it was the wish of the Gambian people.[24]

Senegal and the Gambia formed a joint commission to study areas of possible cooperation in the early 1960s. Nevertheless, the Gambian political parties focused on achieving self-government and then independence. Association with Senegal was not popular with the Gambia. It raised concerns about language and legal differences, and fears of outside domination, particularly among Gambian chiefs. The Gambian leaders ignored British concerns about viability and the colony followed the familiar path to self-government in 1962 and independence in 1965.

Tanganyika

Macleod accepted Turnbull's analysis of Tanganyika. The British lacked the resources, especially in the Tanganyika police, to resist TANU's demands. If TANU launched a resistance campaign and the British attempted to quash it, they risked failure as well as worldwide criticism. Macleod dismissed worries about the impact political changes in Tanganyika might have on the other East African colonies and cited Nyerere's public statements to that effect. Macleod anticipated that the British could persuade Nyerere and TANU to focus their energies on managing the government and promoting economic and social development.

Initially, Macleod believed that the British could postpone independence for Tanganyika until 1968. He anticipated two further rounds of constitutional changes, each new constitution to last four years, the normal life of a legislative council. He predicted that the Tanganyikan nationalists would press for a faster pace but told the cabinet's Colonial Policy Committee that they would have every justification to dig in their heels. Macleod thought that TANU's entrance into government would allow latent jealousies and personal ambitions to surface. The British might be able to exploit any splits within TANU to justify delaying independence.[25]

The Colonial Policy Committee accepted Macleod's recommendations for an elected legislative council, with most seats open to candidates of any race. The committee worried that widening the franchise in Tanganyika would lead to increased demands for similar changes in Nyasaland and Northern Rhodesia and thought that the British could not accede to such demands. Nevertheless, the committee conceded that conditions in Tanganyika differed from those in Central Africa. The committee thought that all interested parties in Tanganyika agreed on the proposed constitutional changes and believed that the British could count on Nyerere to guide peaceful development on multiracial lines.[26]

Macleod's visit to Tanganyika reinforced his positive mood. He told Macmillan that the demonstrators demanding early independence when he arrived in Dar es Salaam were focused more on Nyerere than on the British. Any African politician who cooperated with the British had to expect abuse from extremists, he said. Nevertheless, Nyerere could ride out the storm, Macleod predicted. Nyerere's ideas about the final changes on the new constitution were so close to Macleod's proposals that a constitutional conference would not be needed before the next elections. London and Nairobi could merely exchange dispatches, Macleod announced.[27]

Nyerere and TANU were committed to a faster schedule than Macleod's, however, and by summer 1960, the British shortened the timetable to independence. The London government warned Turnbull against making a public announcement, but said it was contemplating independence as soon as 1962. The thinking in London was now that delaying independence would not make Tanganyika significantly better prepared to manage its own affairs. It would, however, expose Britain to external criticism, in the United Nations and elsewhere. Moreover, Nyerere was proving exceptionally cooperative. He understood the need to retain British officials after independence and to attract Western investors and expertise. Expecting him to continue to rein in TANU's militants was unrealistic and risky, officials advised. Given the changes that had taken place in Africa since the cabinet committee's decision in November 1959, delaying Tanganyikan independence beyond 1962 was impractical.[28]

In the second half of 1960, Tanganyika took major steps towards independence. In September, elections took place under the new constitution. TANU won all but one seat. Turnbull named Nyerere chief minister and appointed a cabinet of nine elected ministers.

Kenya

In November 1959, Macleod told Macmillan and the cabinet's Colonial Policy Committee that the way to more peaceful conditions in Kenya was now open. He argued that the prospect of the constitutional conference promised by Lennox-Boyd scheduled for January 1960, and the emergence of new political parties marked a transformation of Kenyan politics. He recommended that Sir Patrick Renison, the new governor of Kenya, announce the end of the state of emergency when the Kenya legislative council next met on November 10. Lennox-Boyd and the Kenya government planned to end the state of emergency after enacting new security legislation. Lennox-Boyd had, however, been reluctant to introduce any such legislation before the British general election. Renison and his staff were still working out the details. Macleod agreed that stronger security legislation was needed, but decided that signaling a fundamental change in the Kenyan situation by ending the emergency was more important. Macleod intended to keep the alleged hard-core leaders of the uprising, including Kenyatta, in prison for the indefinite future, whether or not new legislation was in place.[29]

In quickening the pace of political change in Kenya, Macleod was heeding advice from both politicians and officials. In October 1959, Spencer Summers, a Conservative member of Parliament, told Macleod that rapid constitutional change in favor of Africans was needed if the British expected to win the support of moderate Africans. Conditions were changing too fast for the kind of multi-racial approach promoted by Michael Blundell. Attitudes among most other European settlers had hardened to the point that reconciliation between them and African politicians was impossible. The British should stop courting them, the advice went. The second ranking civil servant in the Colonial Office, Sir John Martin, agreed that rapid change was needed in Kenya. He told Macleod that they needed to move extremely fast. They had to accept that the Africans were calling the tune if they wanted to avoid the breakdown of law and order that had occurred in the Congo.[30]

During 1959, the political landscape in Kenya underwent important changes. Among the Europeans, the United Party remained committed to the status quo. Blundell's New Kenya Group, viewed as the government's preferred party, sought a multi-racial solution. In July, elected members of the legislative council met to form a rival multi-racial party, the Kenya National Party. Mboya refused to sign the party's policy statement, arguing that the party needed to make more specific demands. Mboya said that it needed to strengthen its hand at the upcoming constitutional conference and to distinguish itself from the New Kenya Group's vague positions. Mboya joined with Odinga and others to form a rival party, the Kenya Independence Movement. The new party was open only to Africans and cast itself as more militantly nationalist than the Kenya National Party. Mboya's party advocated independence in 1961. The Kenya National Party proposed 1968. The Kenya Independence Movement demanded Kenyatta's release from detention and immediate changes in Kenya's land laws. In addition to policy differences, the split within the nationalists reflected rival personal ambitions and ethnic rivalries. The Kenya Independence Movement looked like a Kikuyu and Luo party. The Kenya National Party seemed to represent most of the other Kenyan ethnicities.

Constitutional Conference

Macleod thought that he could exploit the divisions within the Kenyan nationalists during the constitutional conference. Acting on the advice of Julius Nyerere, Mboya was intent on creating a united African delegation, however. At first, he was reluctant to make concessions to the Kenya National Party, thinking that the Africans within the rival party would recognize their mistake and join his organization. In the end, the two parties agreed to create a united front, with Ronald Ngala from the Kenya National Party at its head. The Kenya National Party's African leaders then discarded the party's multi-racial notions and expelled its Asian and European members.[31]

The Kenya constitutional conference in early 1960 proved a triumph for Macleod. At the start of the conference, his goal was to get moderate Africans and the Blundell group to agree on a new constitution that would allow all communities in Kenya to participate in government. He anticipated that the new constitution could lead to a moderate, multi-racial government in Kenya. Blundell and Ngala, one of the more cooperative Africans, were instrumental in assembling a majority for the final proposals. Macleod undercut opposition from the more militant Africans by threatening to withdraw the proposals. He warned that, if there were no agreement, they would have to wait perhaps a year for constitutional changes until the government could assemble a commission of inquiry and dispatch it to Kenya. The constitution that emerged from the conference fell short of the nationalists' initial demands. Africans would hold the majority in both the legislative council and the council of ministers, but legislative seats would be reserved for Asians and Europeans. The government would nominate some members. Ministers would not be responsible to the legislature; the governor would continue to name them. The constitution made no provision for a chief minister.[32]

Macleod also defused efforts to introduce the issue of Kenyatta and the uprising into the conference. African representatives asked that Kenyatta attend the conference. Renison was able to reply that the meeting was limited to legislative council members and that Kenyatta could not attend even if he were freed. Odinga proposed that Peter Koinage, an old associate of Kenyatta who had left Kenya at the beginning of the uprising, serve as an adviser to the African delegation. Some British officials considered Koinage one of the uprising's authors. Odinga's proposal seemed a provocation intended to establish his militant credentials. When the British resisted including Koinage, the African delegation agreed to accept an additional entry pass that they could assign to anyone. The holder of the pass could enter the conference site, Lancaster House, but not the conference room.[33]

Proposing a Kenyan adviser served Odinga's purposes by highlighting the difference between Mboya's United States connections and his own Kenyan focus. Mboya used his connections to secure the services of Thurgood Marshall, the NAACP lawyer, as adviser to the African delegation, and Mboya's American support was apparent throughout the conference. While most African representatives stayed in a Bloomsbury bed and breakfast, Mboya stayed in a hotel with his key supporters from the American Committee on Africa.[34]

To pave the way for an agreement, Macleod began the conference with a critical concession. Macleod told the conference members that they must realize that majority rule would come to Kenya. Africans represented an overwhelming majority of the population. His listeners, particularly his African listeners, recognized that Macleod's pronouncement meant that the nationalist movement had turned a corner. All that remained was negotiating the transition to majority rule and independence. The final conference report documented Macleod's concession. It stated that Kenya would become independent. The report added several conditions for independence, including the participation of all communities in the government and safeguards for minority rights. None seemed likely to bar continued movement towards majority rule. Macleod retained the initiative throughout the conference and the new constitution met few of the nationalists' demands. Nevertheless, Ngala felt confident enough to proclaim when he returned to Nairobi that the conference had broken European domination of Kenya.[35]

Macleod may have felt comfortable conceding eventual independence because he believed that Kenya's transition to independence might be protracted. He thought that the British had time to construct an arrangement in Kenya to their liking. Before the conference, he complained to Macmillan about an article in *The Economist* contending that the Kenyan settlers must accept the kind of settlement proposed for Tanganyika. Presumably, Macleod was referring to both the nature of the Tanganyika constitution and the pace of political change. Macleod thought *The Economist* was exhibiting "weak thinking." Kenya was emerging from a seven-year reign of terror, he told the prime minister. The Kenyan political parties were not united as they were in Tanganyika. The European and Asian presence in Kenya was much larger and more powerful than in Tanganyika.[36]

Some European representatives came away from the constitutional conference with similar ideas. They thought the transition to independence might last as long as ten years. Blundell's group continued to promote multi-racial arrangements. Eventually, it transformed itself into the New Kenya Party. Most in Kenya saw the constitutional conference as the beginning of rapid progress toward independence, however. African expectations rose, strikes broke out, and unrest emerged in the countryside. Many Europeans feared the worst and business activity declined. Morale among British officials sank, because the end of their regime seemed imminent and because London was now making all the important decisions.

Mboya remained intent on forcing the pace. When he returned from the conference, he announced that he would not accept office under the transitional scheme that was to precede enactment of the new constitution. He denounced the new constitution and predicted that it would not last four years, the normal life of a legislative council. He and the other leaders of the Kenya Independence Movement formed a new party, the Kenya African National Union. They positioned the party as the successor to the banned Kenya African Union. They acknowledged Kenyatta as the leader of the nationalist movement and demanded his release.

Divisions continued to bedevil the Kenya nationalists. A rival party, the Kenya African Democratic Union, emerged in June. The split had several origins. The new party included many of the less militant leaders who had been part of the Kenya National Party. They were willing to work with Blundell, the New Kenya Party, and business interests in Kenya and Britain. The new party also featured representatives of Kenya's many small ethnic groups, fearful of domination by the two largest groups, the Kikuyu and the Luo.

Misgivings

The U.S. consul in Nairobi, Charles Withers, did not consider the 1960 constitutional conference a success. The conference did little to relieve tension in Kenya, he reported. The African nationalists thought they had obtained too little. The hard-line Europeans in the United Party thought they had conceded too much. In the consulate's view, the New Kenya Party and the Asians were caught in the middle. More cooperation was needed, but the Blundell group and the nationalists had different ideas about the future. Someone would have to make concessions, Withers predicted. The consulate thought that the Africans would not. They would demand more and at a more rapid pace. Withers thought it would not be a happy time for Kenya.[37]

The London embassy worried that the British would attempt to draw the United States into the Kenyan situation, with unfortunate consequences for the U.S. The first secretary in London, Fred Hadsel, told Washington that Britain would mount an economic program designed to attract all the communities in Kenya as it struggled to manage the transition in Kenya. Hadsel thought that the British would look to the United States for help in paying for an expanded development program. Hadsel also worried that anti–U.S. sentiments would bloom in Kenya, even among British officials. He predicted that the open support by private American groups for Mboya would be an irritant.[38]

In the last months of 1960, the Nairobi consulate remained concerned about the situation in Kenya. The consulate portrayed militant nationalists as potential communists. While assuring Washington that Odinga was unlikely to "make much hay for the communist cause" in Kenya, the consulate reported that the key factor would be the position taken by the "Moscow-trained" Kenyatta when he was released, but the consulate reported that it had too little information to predict Kenyatta's position. The consulate deplored the nationalists' resort to violence and to physical intimidation of their opponents. The consulate saw intimidation as rooted in tribal practices. It thought it hardly surprising that the Kenya African National Union had resorted to strong-arm tactics since its main strength was among the Kikuyu, the principal participants in the uprising. After the government warned African politicians against making reckless statements, the consulate thought the advice would be no more effective than earlier attempts to promote calm.[39]

Uganda

In 1959 and 1960, the course of African nationalism in Uganda resembled that in the other East African colonies. Demands for political change became louder. During 1959, a committee of legislative council members chaired by J.V. Wild, a British official, deliberated about the political arrangements for the period after the 1961 elections. Published in December 1959, the Wild committee report called for universal adult suffrage and rapid progress toward responsible government with an elected chief minister. At the same time, the nationalists tried to be better organized. After splits within the Uganda National Congress, leading nationalists attempted to form a united front. Elements of the congress merged with the Uganda People's Union to form the Uganda People's Congress. Benedicto Kiwanuka, leader of the Democratic Party, participated in the unity discussions, but withdrew. Kiwanuka's version of unity had the other nationalists joining the Democratic Party. Potential national leaders in addition to Kiwanuka also emerged. The principal organizer behind the Uganda People's Congress, Milton Obote, became Kiwanuka's principal rival. Obote belonged to one of the many small ethnic groups outside Uganda's kingdoms. He attended Makerere College and worked in Kenya before returning to his home district to contest the 1958 legislative council election.[40]

Uganda also experienced rural unrest. In spring 1959, the Uganda National Movement announced a boycott of all rural shops not owned by Africans. The movement later extended the boycott to all shops not owned by Africans. For nearly eight months, the boycott had considerable success, but sparked violent incidents. In June, police opened fire on a mob in a town outside Kampala. Nine police and seven demonstrators were seriously hurt. In July, seven Africans were killed in a clash between African proponents and opponents of the boycott. The Uganda government moved to quash the boycott. It banned the Uganda National Movement and several successor organizations and forbade large public meetings. It arrested and deported key leaders. Finally, it prevailed upon the kabaka and his government to oppose the boycott. By September 1959, conditions were more peaceful, but intimidation and violence did not end until the middle of 1960.[41]

Unlike the Kenyan and Tanganyikan nationalists, the Ugandan nationalists encountered significant resistance from traditional African leaders. The leaders of Uganda's kingdoms, notably the kabaka and the Buganda government, resisted Uganda's movement towards self-government as a unified state. The Buganda government refused to cooperate with the Wild committee and rejected its recommendations. The Buganda government also tried to ban political parties in the kingdom. Buganda leaders negotiated with their counterparts from the other kingdoms to devise a federal structure that would preserve the kingdoms as separate political entities. For much of 1960, the Buganda government agitated with no success for an autonomous status within a federal Uganda with its own armed forces, courts, and police. Frustrated, the Buganda legislature passed a resolution on December 30, 1960, declaring Buganda independent as of January 1, 1961.[42]

The rural elements represented by the Uganda National Movement did not support the Ugandan nationalists. The movement was centered in Buganda and had links to the earlier economic agitation and unrest in the 1940s. The farmers involved identified with Buganda, but opposed economic measures imposed by the Buganda government and the Uganda government. The movement's organizers considered various political and economic goals. They settled on Bugandan independence, opposition to the Wild committee's recommendations, and elimination of non–African firms from the Uganda economy as their immediate targets.[43]

When Macleod visited Uganda in December 1959, he characterized the political situation as "utterly confused." Macleod thought the political parties were weak and splintered. He also told Macmillan that he would be confident about the future were it not for the kabaka. The kabaka, Macleod reported, was both weak and obstinate. He was "running" his ministers and not acting like a constitutional monarch. The kabaka had refused to allow Buganda to participate in the legislative council until the kingdom received virtual self-government. Macleod thought that the situation had deteriorated to the same point it had reached when Lyttelton deported the kabaka.[44]

Macleod recommended constitutional change in Uganda. He decided that the Wild committee's report should be published immediately, if only because its contents were sure to be leaked to the press. Macleod doubted that the government should adopt all the committee's recommendations, particularly those related to the appointment of responsible ministers. Nevertheless, he thought that the government could offer important changes to the nationalists.[45]

When the Cabinet Colonial Policy Committee considered Macleod's recommendations in February 1960, it hesitated to approve an expanded franchise. The committee worried that establishing a wide franchise on a common voter roll would undermine efforts to implement restricted franchises and multiple voter rolls in the Federation of Rhodesia and Nyasaland. At the same time, the committee was reluctant to reject the Wild committee's recommendations regarding both ministers and voting rights. It decided that the Uganda government should announce its sympathy for a wider franchise. Nevertheless, it should delay a final decision until the summer, when arrangements for voting in the Federation of Rhodesia and Nyasaland were likely to be complete.[46]

By May, Macleod was less confident about the situation in Uganda and more inclined to seek an understanding with the kabaka and the other African traditional rulers. Macleod told Macmillan that the struggle between the political parties and the kingdoms continued since no national leader had emerged. The situation was explosive, according to Macleod. The only bright spot for the government was the absence of a European population. It meant that Uganda did not attract the press attention that Kenya and the federation did. Macleod's goal was to maintain a balance between the nationalists and the traditionalists and not sacrifice either's support. He proposed to continue with preparations for colony-wide elections in early 1961. In addition, he planned to empanel a commission to study the relationships between the kingdoms and the rest of the colony.[47]

The nationalists persisted in their demands for more rapid progress toward independence. When Obote led a Uganda People's Congress delegation to London in June 1960, he proclaimed that the Ugandan people wanted immediate independence under a strong government. Obote said that his party was prepared to uphold the dignity of the traditional rulers. The majority within Uganda wanted a responsible African government immediately, he claimed. They wanted universal adult suffrage and appointment of an African chief minister.[48]

Macleod tried to satisfy the nationalists and the Buganda government, but with little success. After the meetings in London, the Uganda government announced that it was postponing voter registration in Buganda and delaying the relationships commission because of objections from the Buganda government. The nationalists were upset when Macleod invited the kabaka and his advisers to London for talks. Nevertheless in September Macleod concluded that Buganda's objections to voter registration were unreasonable. The Uganda government should proceed to register voters throughout the colony, he decided. The Buganda government's response was to order its subjects not to cooperate with the government's efforts.[49]

Discretion

In January 1960, Consul General Peter Hooper described the U.S. roles in Uganda as including using aid to fill gaps in the country's preparations for self-government, encouraging Uganda leaders to support the United States, and providing discreet support to African aspirations for early independence. Hooper's efforts collided, however, with the State Department's understanding of discretion. Hooper was convinced that the British should hold a constitutional conference before proceeding with further political changes. Governor Crawford was out of the country. Hooper considered the acting governor opposed to African demands and was reluctant to raise the issue with him. Hooper asked Washington to have the London embassy raise the matter with the Colonial Office. The embassy opposed offering the British advice, however. The department agreed. The embassy's view was that the British resented advice from the sidelines, where they thought the United States was and should stay. Washington told Hooper that he should continue his conversations with Ugandan politicians and British officials. The department said it was reluctant to lay down hard and fast rules. Nevertheless, its preference was that U.S. officials become involved in local politics only on an informal and personal basis. U.S. officials should not offer formal advice to colonial governments in Uganda or anywhere in British Africa, it reminded Hooper.[50]

Hooper was not easily deterred. Hooper explained to Washington that he had intended that the London embassy inform the Colonial Office that the kabaka and others wanted further negotiations before the British acted. If the Colonial Office asked for advice regarding the information, the embassy could provide it, as Hooper did in Uganda.[51]

Nor were Hooper or the Kampala consulate less involved in Uganda affairs. In September 1960, the consulate reported that, in the wake of reports that Buganda was threatening to secede from Uganda, a consulate official told a senior British official that secession was a "venture into fantasy." The consulate official also declared the U.S. interest in the situation. The United States was concerned about any violence and U.S. citizens in Uganda. Buganda might approach the United States and other countries for aid. The next month, Buganda officials, in fact, asked for U.S. funding for a Buganda delegation to the United States.[52]

The consulate thought that Kiwanuka was worth cultivating. In November 1959, the consulate arranged for the Democratic Party leader to visit the United States as an official guest of the government. During a two-month stay, Kiwanuka secured funding for three hundred scholarships at American colleges and universities. When he returned to Uganda, he announced that interested Ugandans should submit their applications to his office.[53]

Zanzibar

Macleod decided that Zanzibar should move further towards self-government. When the colonial secretary visited the islands in late 1959, the Zanzibar National Party pressed for early independence. Macleod told Macmillan that the colony was ready for further political change, but nothing drastic. Macleod postponed the elections scheduled for 1960 and appointed a veteran colonial official, Sir Hilary Blood, as a constitutional commissioner charged with devising Zanzibar's next constitution.

Issued in June 1960, the Blood Report called for responsible government, but not independence. The franchise was to be widened. Women would vote for the first time. Educational and property qualifications for all voters would be lowered. The legislative council would have an elected majority of twenty-two seats. The majority party in the legislative council would appoint the chief minister, but the British resident would retain important powers. Elections to the legislative council would take place in 1961. The most militant nationalists were not satisfied, however. Macleod praised the report as helpful and imaginative. The Afro-Shirazi Party saw it as a step forward. The Zanzibar National Party rejected Blood's recommendations and party members burned the report in the streets.

As the Eisenhower administration ended, the State Department in Washington was concerned about two aspects of Zanzibar politics, local opposition to a U.S. space tracking station and Chinese ties to the Zanzibar National Party. In December 1960, Olcott Deming, director of the Office of Eastern and Southern African Affairs, sent Assistant Secretary Satterthwaite a background memorandum about Zanzibar, for the use of the incoming Kennedy administration. Deming reported that local groups had learned of proposals to build a tracking station in Zanzibar for Project Mercury, the American manned spaceflight program. The United States and Britain reached an agreement about the station in October, but were trying to keep the agreement secret until after the next Zanzibar elections. The Zanzibar National Party had become the station's most vocal opponent. Deming thought it possible that the Chinese were responsible for the ZNP's position. According to Deming, the ZNP could emerge as the dominant party in an independent Zanzibar. He worried that a government sympathetic to communism would be in a position to cause mischief in Africa.[54]

Between October 1959 and December 1960, Iain Macleod moved Britain's African colonies closer to independence. Macleod put Sierra Leone and Gambia securely on the road to independence. Likewise, in Tanganyika, Macleod confirmed British support for Nyerere and shortened the timetable for independence. In Kenya, Macleod pushed through constitutional changes, but even he thought that an African majority government was still years away. The situations in Uganda and Zanzibar were unsettled, but even so Macleod ordered further steps towards self-government.

Macleod harbored hopes that the British could control the pace of political change and that they could install something other than African majority governments. Nevertheless, he was convinced that concessions to African nationalists in the form of increased political power was the best way to preserve Britain's long-term interests in Africa and acted accordingly.

In the same period, U.S. officials in Africa fidgeted on the sidelines. Particularly in

Uganda, U.S. consuls imagined larger roles for the United States in the unfolding events. They doubted Britain's ability to manage affairs and worried that British failure might alienate African nationalists from Britain and its most prominent ally, the United States. U.S. officials were not, however, wholehearted supporters of the nationalists. In most cases, they doubted the nationalists' abilities and looked for what they thought were more moderate solutions. The consuls did not get much encouragement from Washington, however. The State Department discouraged greater involvement in local affairs. It worried about upsetting the British or being expected to invest in economic development schemes.

Federation of Rhodesia
and Nyasaland, 1959–1960:
Rough Waters

By mid–1959, officials in the Macmillan government recognized that the federation government posed a dilemma. The federation offered economic and strategic benefits, but officials struggled to fulfill the British government's pledges and satisfy competing interests of African nationalists and European settlers. The British government was on record that it would not relinquish control of Nyasaland and Northern Rhodesia until the majority of their populations agreed. It had also issued pronouncements that European settlers interpreted as commitments to grant the federation its independence, perhaps after the federal constitution review scheduled for late 1960. By late 1959, African nationalists in all three territories were pressing for larger political voices. European leaders resisted, fearing that African majority governments would withdraw from the federation. A June 1959 report by a committee of officials described the challenges the government faced and the possible consequences of failing to resolve them. It offered no solution other than federal review.[1]

Macmillan attached considerable importance to the federation's future and shared his officials' worries. He warned that failure to establish a multi-racial state would endanger the territories within the federation as well as Kenya. Rather than being a source of pride and profit to the Europeans who had developed them, the African territories would become a "maelstrom of trouble into which all of us will be sucked," he fretted.[2]

Macmillan imagined that the solution to the federation's problems lay in a middle way, a combination of well-intended Europeans and moderate Africans. Africans, he wrote, could not be dominated permanently, as the South Africans were trying to do. The Africans had to have the opportunity to develop themselves and govern their own countries. The British government could not abandon the European settlers, however. It would be wrong to do so and fatal to African interests. In Macmillan's view, the British government could not use force against the European settlers should the federal government declare its independence or attempt to seize control of Northern Rhodesia.[3]

In 1959, Macmillan's solution was to appoint an independent commission to review the federation's status and produce a report for the federal review to consider. The commission was to be relatively large, twenty-six members. It was to include a broad range of members, both African and European, from Britain and the federation. Heading the commission was Lord Monckton. Monckton served in the Churchill and Eden governments and his involvement in sensitive political issues dated back to the 1936 abdication crisis.

In assembling the Monckton Commission, Macmillan encountered the same sort of apparently irreconcilable differences that bedeviled the federation, but he managed to patch over the problem, at least temporarily. Welensky and the federation government were suspicious of the proposed review. They were concerned that the commission might recommend granting Northern Rhodesia and Nyasaland the right to secede from the federation. Welensky's price for cooperating with the commission was an assurance from Macmillan that the commission's terms of reference not extend to secession. Macmillan also wanted the Labour Party to participate. Labour leaders refused, but Macmillan persuaded Sir Hartley Shawcross, a former Labour minister and British representative at the United Nations, to join the commission. Shawcross, and perhaps other members, wanted the freedom to consider all options for the federation, including the right of secession. Macmillan agreed that the commission could do so, without, however, sharing the information with Welensky.[4]

Lord Home, the commonwealth relations secretary, agreed with Macmillan about fundamental goals. Home thought that the British government needed to satisfy the Africans' legitimate political aspirations and protect the position of the European settlers. He foresaw political changes in the federation's three territories, but imagined that British control of the two northern territories would last ten to fifteen years.[5]

Home had more definite ideas than Macmillan about near term steps. Home was adamant that the British government needed to develop a plan and stick to it. He told Macmillan that Britain had reacted to colonial crises and allowed nationalist leaders to extort constitutional changes. Home thought that the federal review would bring constitutional advance in the northern territories. He also anticipated that the review would bring the end of the remaining British controls over Southern Rhodesia. After the review, the British government should establish a blueprint for moving a colony to independence, a series of mandated steps, according to Home. He warned against assigning dates to the steps, however, arguing that doing so removed the nationalists' motivation to cooperate. Home urged that the British insist that all political activity remain within the law. He proposed strengthening the federation's armed forces so that the British could crack down on any politically motivated unrest. Furthermore, he imagined a sustained effort to make the federation work and make it acceptable to both Europeans and Africans. Presumably, Home meant a program of economic and social development. Earlier, Home suggested creation of an African development fund. Home referred to a Marshall Plan for Africa and suggested that Macleod seek U.S. funding for it.[6]

Nyasaland

By the end of December 1959, Macleod had a plan for resolving the situation in Nyasaland. He concluded that the British government could not justify the state of emergency and the wholesale detention of nationalist leaders. He thought that efforts to write a new constitution for Nyasaland and to preserve the federation could not proceed under the prevailing circumstances. He, therefore, recommended that the Nyasaland government release most detainees. Macleod also thought that the British should work with Banda. Experience had demonstrated, he told Macmillan, that moderate nationalists did not emerge to replace leaders who were in jail. Macleod believed that Banda was the most moderate of all the Nyasaland leaders and had firm control of the Nyasaland nationalist movement. Macleod asked Orton Chirwa, a long-time nationalist and interim head of the Nyasaland nationalist party in Banda's absence, whether he could imagine continuing links between Nyasaland and the two Rhodesias. Chirwa said that he could not and that the only person who could compromise on the issue was Banda. Macleod recommended that the Nyasaland government improve the conditions of Banda's detention and prepare for his early release. When Banda was released, he should be free to participate in Nyasaland politics and to advocate the nationalist cause, in particular before the Monckton commission. To increase the chances that Banda took a moderate course, Macleod proposed to separate him from the "hard core" nationalists by keeping fifty or so of them in custody.[7]

Macleod's aim was to preserve the federation. He thought that the federation's and Southern Rhodesia's European leaders were blind to the African resentment against the federation, especially in the two northern territories. To allay African concerns, Macleod thought that the British needed to calm the situation by releasing the detainees and ending the states of emergency. Macleod anticipated that the Monckton commission would produce imaginative proposals for the federation's future. Combined with rapid progress toward a new Nyasaland constitution, these could mollify the moderate nationalists. At the same time, new security laws would allow long-term detention of the more militant nationalists. Finally, the British could convene a conference to review and revise the federation's constitution. They could then look forward to a period of stability during which they could convince Africans of the federation's merits.[8]

Macleod's proposals upset Governor Armitage and the Nyasaland government. Armitage and his officials recognized that the state of emergency could not continue indefinitely. They accepted that some detainees should be released to reduce tensions in the colony. Like Macleod, they anticipated the need for new security laws that would allow long-term detention. Nevertheless, they disagreed with Macleod about the number of detainees to be released and the speed with which releases were to happen. They also questioned Macleod's approach to Banda. They recognized that Banda might be part of the long-term solution, but they opposed negotiating a new constitution while Banda was in Nyasaland. They imagined a process whereby the government would negotiate a new constitution with moderate Africans and the European and Asian communities, while Banda remained in detention or in exile in London. Once the constitution was in place, Banda could be permitted to return. In particular, Armitage and his officials opposed releasing Banda before the Monckton commission visited Nyasaland. If Banda were free, more reasonable Africans would be reluctant to talk to the commission, they argued. Armitage believed that Banda's release would spark renewed violence in Nyasaland and irritate the other governments within the federation.[9]

Like the Nyasaland government, Home had a low opinion of Banda. He thought Banda could not be trusted. According to Home, Banda wanted to make the white man the servant of the black. Home thought Banda might agree to cooperate, however, if the British offered a definite plan for the near future. Home thought the British needed to communicate to Banda that they remained in control. If Banda resorted to unconstitutional methods, he would be banished for life. To destroy Banda's "apparatus of violence," the government should imprison his most militant lieutenants for at least ten years, Home recommended. With Banda in check, the government could negotiate a new constitution with the "right leaders of opinion." It could expect a settled period of ten to fifteen years during which the federation could demonstrate its worth.[10]

Welensky and Whitehead adamantly opposed Banda's release. It was illusionary to think that you could deal reasonably with Banda, they told Home. He will campaign against the federation and for Nyasaland's secession at every opportunity. His presence in Nyasaland will pose a security risk. His release will encourage others to intimidate more moderate Africans from testifying before the Monckton Commission.[11]

The European leaders were wary of the Macmillan government. Welensky disagreed with Macleod's views and resented his methods. Macleod was too ready, by Welensky's standards, to carry on negotiations or make decisions without consulting with the federation government. In January 1960, Welensky managed, through Home, to tone down a speech Macleod was preparing regarding the situation in Nyasaland. More often than not, however, neither Macleod nor Macmillan paid Welensky the deference he thought he was owed. Ignored by London, the European leaders grew suspicious that Macmillan intended to sacrifice their interests to appease Nyasaland's African nationalists.[12]

Banda's position was clear and firm. He would cooperate if he and his colleagues were released from detention. He wanted to be released in Nyasaland and nowhere else. He said he would testify before the Monckton commission and would advise his followers to do the same. He opposed violence and would negotiate about a new Nyasaland constitution. He urged the government to be bold and take risks and said he would meet the government halfway. He warned that he alone could speak for Nyasaland's nationalists. The British ought not to look for other leaders with whom they might negotiate. Banda's British lawyer, Dingel Foot, told Macmillan that the Nyasaland leader would never change his opposition to the federation.[13]

The government in London came to view its decision about Banda's fate as critical to the federation's future. Macleod thought that conceding Africans a larger say in the Nyasaland government was the way to preserve the federation. He worried that keeping Banda and the others in detention would provoke more violence. Releasing Banda in time for him to present evidence to the Monckton commission was essential to Macleod's strategy. Home pointed to the fears of African nationalism expressed by federation and Southern Rhodesian leaders. Home thought that releasing Banda before the Monckton Commission left Central Africa might push the federation or Southern Rhodesia to declare its independence. Both ministers felt strongly about the issue and Macmillan was caught in the middle. Macmillan thought releasing Banda against the wishes of the federation and Southern Rhodesia might destroy the federation. Failing to release Banda, however, would undermine the Monckton Commission's credibility and risk renewed violence in Nyasaland. It would give the impression that Macmillan and his government were in thrall to the federation and Southern Rhodesia.[14]

Macmillan decided to have Banda released shortly before the Monckton commission left Nyasaland. Home negotiated an agreement with Welensky. The Nyasaland government would release Banda, but the new Nyasaland constitution would give Africans no greater say than they had under Northern Rhodesia's constitution. Moreover, the new constitution would not go into effect until after the review of the federation's constitution. The Southern Rhodesian constitution would be revised to remove most of the controls that Britain retained. Nevertheless, none of the key players in London or Salisbury was happy with the situation. Macleod told the cabinet that the decision would "greatly increase his difficulties in carrying out his responsibilities as colonial secretary." British ministers viewed the arrangement as a compromise and the best they could do.[15]

Macleod thought that Banda would not prove an obstacle to British aims. Macleod told Macmillan that Banda was a vain and ignorant man. Once exposed to the British press and public, his appeal would decline, Macleod predicted. Banda's constitutional ideas were naïve and inadequate and the proposed constitutional conference would produce a constitution crafted by the Colonial Office. Banda out of jail was less of a menace, Macleod observed. Unless Banda could prove his leadership abilities, his authority in Nyasaland would diminish.[16]

London and Salisbury made concessions to each other. By the end of 1960, it was apparent, however, that Banda had conceded little and was on his way to gaining all that he wanted. In July, Macleod and the Nyasaland representatives negotiated a new constitution. About the constitution Banda proved as cooperative as he said he would be. The constitution offered little more than Armitage had been willing to offer. It fell well short of the one-man, one-vote franchise and ministerial system that the Malawi Congress Party, a reincarnation of the Nyasaland African National Congress, sought. The franchise was limited and non–African members remained in the legislative council. The executive council could only advise the governor; officials remained among its members. Yet during the constitutional conference, Macleod conceded that Nyasaland was destined to have an African majority government. He continued to believe that by prolonging the process leading to self-government and involving Banda and his colleagues in the affairs of government he could convince them to support the federation. Nevertheless, Macleod did not secure concessions from Banda about the federation. As Macleod and Armitage intended, the Nyasaland government enacted new security legislation. But, senior British officials in Nyasaland realized that Banda was their principal hope for maintaining order. Committed to working with Banda and the Malawi Congress Party, they became reluctant to deploy troops and the police. When violent incidents reoccurred, they asked Banda to rein in his followers. Banda did, but extracted concessions from the government, in particular the release of the last, hard-core detainees. The government orchestrated the release so that Banda could present the released prisoners in dramatic fashion to the September 1960 party congress. In the process, the government solidified Banda's position among the Nyasaland nationalists and revealed its dependence on him. Finally, the government named Banda to the executive council, solidifying his position as their chief African interlocutor.[17]

Northern Rhodesia

From the British perspective, the situation in Northern Rhodesia in mid and late 1959 was tenuous, but not as dire as in Nyasaland. Elections under the Benson constitution took place in March. The European-controlled United Federal Party won a majority of seats, but six Africans, including Harry Nkumbula of the African National Congress, were among the twenty successful candidates. Despite the Zambia African National Congress's attempted boycott, African turnout on polling day was substantial. The number of Africans qualifying to run for office or to register to vote under the constitution's complicated procedures was, however, so small that it was obvious that African influence on the overall results would be minimal. The constitution, therefore, failed in its principal purpose, demonstrating to educated Africans that they could have a real voice in government, even if Europeans continued to play the larger role. Sporadic violence in the towns and countryside remained a concern. In October 1959, a new militant nationalist party, the United National Independence Party, emerged to take the place of the banned Zambia African National Congress.

British officials in Northern Rhodesia were short of ideas, particularly about blunting the United National Independence Party's organizing efforts. After violence in the Western

Province, the government banned the party and its leaders from the province. They recognized, however, that repression was not a permanent solution and lifted the bans in November 1960. Officials considered promoting a moderate African party to compete with the nationalist party, but worried that the nationalists already had the upper hand. In any future election, they thought that any moderate Africans would join the nationalists. The best the Northern Rhodesia government could offer was a policy of delay. In April 1960, Sir Evelyn Hone, who had replaced Benson as governor, told Macleod that the government needed to announce that it would not yield to the United National Independence Party's demands in 1960. Otherwise, it would not retain the support of loyal Africans, native administration officials, government employees, and teachers. In June, Hone maintained that the government needed to make clear its determination to resist the nationalists. Yet he conceded that it was unrealistic in the Africa of 1960 to expect that the Benson constitution could continue for four years, its scheduled life. Despite good intentions, the constitution had produced a legislative council too slanted to the European point of view. Hone told the Colonial Office that constitutional talks would probably be necessary as soon as 1961.[18]

The European presence in Northern Rhodesia made it a more difficult problem than Nyasaland, and Macleod was slower to make proposals. The government released Kaunda in January 1960. Almost immediately, he assumed leadership of the United National Independence Party. In the midst of a trip to the United States and Britain, Kaunda met with Macleod in London. Macleod's position was that constitutional change was impossible in 1960, despite the nationalists' demands for self-government by the end of the year. Political changes in Northern Rhodesia had to wait for the Monckton commission's recommendations, he said. Macleod welcomed Kaunda's embrace of non-violence and urged him to persuade his colleagues to do the same. Kaunda retorted that an announcement of constitutional talks would make violence less likely. In September, Macleod announced that a constitutional conference would take place in early 1961, after the review of the federation's constitution. The timing of Macleod's announcement was a small victory for the nationalists because it preceded publication of the Monckton commission's report. By early December, Macleod concluded that the next step should be a legislative council with more African than European elected members. A combination of European elected members and government officials would hold a majority.[19]

Even announcement of constitutional talks was anathema to Welensky. After Macleod asked his opinion in May 1960, he replied that holding talks would be seen as a concession to the United National Independence Party's campaign of intimidation. He reminded Macleod that between January and May 1960, eighty-four members of the nationalist party had been convicted of 117 criminal offenses, including attempted murder, riot, assaults on the police, and public incitement to violence.[20]

Southern Rhodesia

The nationalists in Southern Rhodesia persisted, despite government repression. The government ended the state of emergency in May 1959 and gradually released most detainees. In December 1959, the nationalists organized a new party, the National Democratic Party, to replace the banned African National Congress. Party organizers were busy in the towns and cities and began to move into the countryside. Joshua Nkomo was active abroad seeking financial and other support. In October 1960, he was elected president of the new party. The party adopted a militant position, proclaiming that it would not contest the next election unless it was conducted based on "one man, one vote." Its members would not register to vote or stand for election.

The Southern Rhodesian government continued to pursue a two-pronged strategy: reform and repression. Prime Minister Whitehead believed, like his predecessor, Garfield Todd, that Africans should eventually participate in government and benefit from government programs. Whitehead also proposed expanding the legislature in a way that was likely to allow several Africans to win seats. Whitehead's government introduced legislation to reduce discrimination against Africans in hotels and in government employment and moved to expand housing and public services available to Africans in cities and towns. Furthermore, Whitehead proposed to change Southern Rhodesia's laws regarding land ownership, a volatile issue for both Africans and Europeans, in ways that he thought would benefit Africans in the end. Nevertheless, Whitehead and his supporters believed that the nationalists did not represent the bulk of Southern Rhodesia's African population and posed a threat to the territory's security. During 1959 and 1960, the Whitehead government enacted successive pieces of security legislation of increasing severity, intended to give the government the power to stifle nationalist organizing and imprison nationalist leaders. The government's proposals were sufficiently sweeping and draconian that the leaders of Southern Rhodesia's Christian churches and others objected. To address the complaints, the government made revisions. Nevertheless, the government equipped itself with powerful tools for repressing its opponents.[21]

The government moved to expand its powers in part because its first repressive measures collided with the growing nationalist activity and produced Southern Rhodesia's first significant violence in decades. In July 1960, the arrests of National Democratic Party leaders provoked strikes and riots in Salisbury and in Bulawayo. Sporadic violence persisted across the territory for months. In October, riots broke out in Salisbury and Gwelo. In restoring order in the capital, the police killed seven Africans and injured 170.[22]

Whitehead's aim was to secure independence as soon as possible. Southern Rhodesia benefited from the federation and Southern Rhodesia's long-time prime minister, Huggins, had been one of the federation's chief proponents. Yet many Europeans in Southern Rhodesia remained wary of it. Whitehead worried that Southern Rhodesia might suffer if the federation collapsed. He was also concerned that the federation might dominate Southern Rhodesia. It might be forced to make concessions to its own African nationalists if the federation survived but African nationalists won control of Nyasaland and Northern Rhodesia. Shedding what remained of British control would allow Southern Rhodesia to separate itself from the federation's fate. Moreover, Southern Rhodesian leaders believed that they would have attained full self-government had it not been for the federation's establishment. They argued that they had joined the federation with the understanding that the federation's creation would not impede their progress toward self-government. Southern Rhodesia had controlled its internal affairs since 1923 and Britain rarely exercised the legal powers it retained over the territory's affairs. Whitehead and other European leaders, therefore, felt that they should gain full control of their affairs at least as soon as Britain's other African colonies. It pained Southern Rhodesian leaders to watch as the Gold Coast and Nigeria discarded British rule while they continued to battle with the London government. The notion that Nyasaland and Northern Rhodesia might attain full self-government before Southern Rhodesia was even more repugnant.

Whitehead attempted to use the London government's interests in preserving the federation and the proposed review of the federation's constitution as levers to secure Southern Rhodesia's independence. In January 1960, he announced that Southern Rhodesia would not participate in the federal review unless three conditions were met. The British government must eliminate its remaining controls on the Southern Rhodesian government. Control of the federation must remain in "civilized" hands, by which Whitehead meant European hands. The governments of Nyasaland and Northern Rhodesia also could not be operated by African nationalists "on a nationalist basis." If the conditions were not met, Southern Rhodesia would secede from the federation, Whitehead said. Throughout 1960, Whitehead made public statements claiming that Southern Rhodesia should gain its independence before the end of the year. He might resign if it did not, he warned. To British negotiators, he contended that he would face European opposition at home and be forced to call an election if they did not accede to his demands. His political opponents, who were more impatient with continued British rule and more hostile to African ambitions, might win a majority and proceed to derail British plans.[23]

The Macmillan government resisted Whitehead's demands. It accepted that many of Whitehead's arguments had some validity. As recently as 1957, the British government seemed poised to do away with the remnants of its control over Southern Rhodesia. In the changed political circumstances of 1959 and 1960, however, the Southern Rhodesian claims were a potential embarrassment. Nevertheless, the Macmillan government was prepared to trade the vestiges of British control for constitutional safeguards for African rights in southern Rhodesia. Constitutional safeguards, however, involved complex details and their efficacy depended on the government's goodwill. Critics of colonial rule in Britain and elsewhere remained suspicious of the Salisbury regime. They were certain to criticize any deal Macmillan and Whitehead might make. African nationalists throughout Central Africa was also on record in favor of universal suffrage on a "one-man, one-vote" basis. A deal with Southern Rhodesia was likely to disrupt negotiations with the nationalists in the northern territories and derail preparations for the federal review. From London's perspective, the nationalists posed the immediate problem. Putting Whitehead off seemed the wisest approach.[24]

A lack of trust between the London and Salisbury government complicated the negotiations. Members of the Macmillan government and the Whitehead government had a great deal in common, certainly more than Macleod had with Banda or Kaunda. Yet the two governments did not trust each other. The Southern Rhodesians, like Welensky, were quick to suspect that their colleagues in London were being less than forthright. From the Southern Rhodesians' perspective, Macleod seemed intent on pandering to African nationalists. He could not be trusted, they thought. Home and Sandys, Home's successor as commonwealth relations secretary, seemed more reasonable, but proved nearly as difficult to deal with. Macmillan and his ministers, for their part, doubted Whitehead's ability and willingness to implement constitutional safeguards that could be seen to be effective.

Southern Rhodesia was no closer to independence in December 1960, on the brink of the federal review, than it had been a year earlier. Through a long series of negotiations, the two governments agreed in principle that Southern Rhodesia would become independent provided it enacted sufficient safeguards for African rights. Agreement on the details proved elusive, however. By December 1960, the British called Whitehead's bluff. They prolonged the negotiations long enough so that the best the Southern Rhodesian prime minister could manage was a commitment from Sandys to hold discussions about the Southern Rhodesian constitution in parallel with the review of the federation's constitution.[25]

Monckton Commission and Federal Review

The Monckton Commission's report, published in October 1960, proposed that the federation continue. The commission stressed the economic benefits the federation could generate. It also warned that the changes were needed if the federation were to overcome African fears and hostility. The commission charged that the federation's efforts at partnership were failures. The federation needed to eliminate discrimination against Africans quickly and firmly. It should widen African participation in government at the federal and territorial levels and broaden the franchise so that many more Africans could vote. To dispel African fears, the commission recommended shifting authority from the federal government to the territorial governments. Critically, the commission recommended that territories gain the right to secede from the federation after a trial period.[26]

If Macmillan thought that the Monckton commission would save the federation, he had to be disappointed. The degree of change advocated by the commission was a surprise. The shock factor was considerable for several reasons. The commission was nearly unanimous in supporting the key recommendations. The Macmillan government picked the commission's members and the conventional wisdom was that the members were generally conservative. The commission had ignored Africans not thought to be moderate and the principal nationalist leaders refused to appear before the commission. The Monckton report documented, however, that responsible opinion in Britain and Central Africa had shifted toward the nationalists and away from even the European settlers willing to contemplate partnership with Africans. Welensky was outraged by the report, especially by its recommendations regarding secession. Macmillan had misled him, he claimed. He charged that the future of the federation was in the hands of the nationalists, the African leaders he called extremists. For all the report's reasonableness, however, it did nothing to reduce the key nationalists' opposition to the federation.[27]

The long-awaited review of the federal constitution proved a non-event. The Macmillan government's plan was to hold constitutional conferences for Southern and Northern Rhodesia after the federal meeting. The nationalist leaders, Kaunda, Banda, and Nkomo, threatened to boycott the federal meeting unless the two territorial meetings were held first and produced African majority governments. Kaunda's party also wanted Africans to form a majority of the Northern Rhodesian delegation. The nationalist leaders wanted secession to be on the agenda and Nkomo to attend the meeting as part of the Southern Rhodesian delegation. Eventually, Macleod, Sandys, and the three nationalist leaders agreed that the nationalists would attend the federal meeting and the territorial meetings would meet concurrently with the federal meeting. Nkomo would participate as leader of the National Democratic Party's delegation. After roughly two weeks of fruitless discussions, however, the three meetings were adjourned. Sandys announced that the territorial meetings would resume in the new year: the Northern Rhodesia meeting in London, and the Southern Rhodesia meeting in Salisbury. The federal meeting would not reconvene until the two territorial meetings had shown some progress. Banda thought the nationalists had scored a victory. When he returned to Nyasaland, he proclaimed that the federation was dead. All that remained was to make the burial arrangements, he said.[28]

A Larger Role?

After the British moved to suppress the African nationalist parties and imprison their leaders in early 1959, Joseph Palmer, consul general in Salisbury, advocated a more active

U.S. policy. From February to May, Palmer dispatched messages to Washington criticizing the British actions against the nationalist parties and questioning the British justifications for them. Palmer was skeptical about Lennox-Boyd's allegations of a murder plot in Nyasaland and Benson's allusions to Murder Inc. Palmer also thought that repression would fail. Instead of stifling nationalist activity, it would push moderate leaders towards violence. The British needed to address African concerns, but Palmer doubted that federation leaders would do so. He recommended that the United States press the government in London to carry out a three-pronged program. The federation and Southern Rhodesia should end discrimination against Africans. The British should prepare to grant Nyasaland self-government within five years and the British should undertake a major development program in Nyasaland.[29]

Staff in the Office of Eastern and Southern African Affairs accepted Palmer's analysis. They believed that the federation was in serious trouble. It would be better for U.S. interests if Nyasaland and Northern Rhodesia gained self-government than if they remained within a European-controlled federation against the will of their African populations. The department was not ready to press London on the issue, however. Washington told Palmer that the British were preparing for talks with the United States about African issues in the fall, around the time of the annual talks about United Nations issues. The talks might provide an opportunity to discuss the future of the federation, the department said. The London embassy was open to the possibility, but warned that it knew little about British thinking. A British initiative was unlikely before the next British general election, thought likely in October. The embassy counseled that the United States needed to avoid being caught between the African nationalists and the federation government. It needed to decide how much, if anything, it was willing to contribute towards economic and social development within the federation. A summary of U.S. policy toward the federation prepared in September 1959 described a passive role for the United States. The U.S. should rely on Britain to encourage and support the federation as long as doing so was consistent with U.S. interests, the summary said. As long as the federation seemed likely to promote stability and prosperity, the United States should discreetly encourage it. The U.S. should not indicate approval for the current situation, but should avoid generating unrealistic African expectations of direct United States support.[30]

Regardless of the State Department's preference for a passive stance, European politicians and newspapers in Salisbury blamed the United States for the rise of African nationalism. In May 1959, for example, the Daily Mail quoted Lord Malvern (the former federation prime minister, Sir Godfrey Huggins) to the effect that the United States posed a greater danger to the free nations of Europe and their African colonies than Russia. In January 1959, Welensky attacked the anti-colonial attitudes he claimed were common in Britain and the United States. He charged that many Americans and Britons thought whites in Africa were an archaic inheritance and that anti-colonialism would solve all Africa's problems.[31]

Palmer assured Welensky that the United States government wanted the federation to succeed. At a meeting with Welensky in early February, Palmer cited Vice President Nixon's praise for British colonialism and referred Welensky to statements by State Department officials that Europeans had a role to play in Africa. Palmer told Washington that Welensky seemed to understand that the United States supported the federation.[32]

Palmer also advised Welensky that his government needed to do more for Africans so that moderate African leaders could hold their own against the extremists. Palmer argued that dramatic changes across Africa necessitated reforms within the federation. Welensky indicated that he understood the problem. He claimed that he intended to end discrimination against Africans in hotels and post offices and would appoint an African junior minister. Nevertheless, he told Palmer that the Nyasaland government had been too lenient with Banda. Palmer reported to Washington that Welensky lacked a sense of urgency and was slow to face facts. His reforms were too limited to revive African support for multiracial partnership.[33]

Despite Palmer's intervention, Welensky continued to attack American support for African nationalists and Palmer felt compelled to reply. In November 1959, Welensky told the federal assembly that he had protested to the State Department about the lavish support the American Committee on Africa offered Tom Mboya. He compared it with the meager hospitality offered by the State Department to African visitors from the federation. When Palmer met with the federal prime minister, he complained that the United States offered considerable aid to Guinea but offered little financial support to the federation. Welensky characterized the former French colony as an irresponsible regime, soft on communism. Palmer told Washington that he spent a long time explaining to Welensky the Americans' thinking about foreign aid. Welensky seemed to understand, Palmer reported. Palmer warned Washington, however, that Welensky was mercurial and unpredictable. He was likely to launch more attacks on the United States when the mood struck him.[34]

In September 1959, Palmer dispatched another gloomy assessment to Washington. Palmer wrote that African aspirations in the federation's territories were rising faster than the European responses, both in London and in Africa. Africans were turning to extremists, he reported. Africans were unrealistic about their ability to run the complex machinery of a modern state. Nationalists in Nyasaland would not wait ten years for self-government and their colleagues in Northern Rhodesia would not settle for anything less than an African majority. Both nationalist groups would demand the right to secede from the federation. Palmer predicted that the widening gap between African aspirations and European responses would lead to an "upheaval of cataclysmic proportions." Palmer thought the federation's governments should stop suppressing the nationalists and recognize the nationalist parties. The British should be prepared to grant Nyasaland self-government and Northern Rhodesia an African majority government within five years.[35]

In November, Palmer returned to his proposals for a more active U.S. role. The United States wanted the federation to succeed, but could do little to help it, he wrote. Since the odds for the federation's survival were poor, the U.S. should avoid public identification with it. It should also avoid an open break with the London government, but should push the Macmillan regime to act decisively. Palmer recommended that Washington look for an early opportunity to have full and frank discussions with the British, without informing the federation government. The United States should also prepare itself to repair the situation should the federation fail.[36]

In addition, Palmer advocated a substantial increase in U.S. aid to the federation. He suggested that the World Bank assess the federation's development potential. The United States and Britain should also review the federation's development plans and agree about the amount and type of U.S. aid. According to Palmer, the focus should be on projects that benefited Africans. The U.S. should be careful to work through the British government and should avoid direct ties to the federation, Palmer wrote. Finally, the United States should not undermine British authority or become openly linked to the federation.

Palmer emphasized that he was not advocating African advancement for its own sake. The federation's stability and development depended, he wrote, on a multiracial partnership.

African development was needed because a real partnership was not possible until African accomplishments more closely approximated those of the Europeans. United States support for African advancement was important. When the inevitable African majority took power, a friendly relationship between the United States and the African population could protect the West's interests and ensure the European minority's survival.

State Department representatives met with their British colleagues to discuss African issues in winter 1959. The British were not ready to discuss the federation in detail, however. They opted to postpone any discussion until after the Monckton commission presented its report. When informed of the British position, Palmer was unhappy. He told Washington that he saw no basis for what he considered British complacency. The nationalist parties were regrouping and moderate Africans were losing faith in the Monckton commission. Palmer thought that imagination and sustained progress were needed. Since the British seemed incapable of either, Palmer urged Washington to take the initiative.[37]

The London embassy agreed with some of Palmer's substantive proposals, but resisted putting pressure on the Macmillan government. According to the embassy, Nyasaland should be self-governing and Banda should be released from detention. The British should change their goal in Northern Rhodesia, to undercut the nationalists' more extreme demands. Economic development should be sped up. Nevertheless, intervention by the United States would be counterproductive, the embassy warned. Britain and the U.S. had the same goals for Central Africa. The British understood the situation was serious and would resent any U.S. interference, especially since it would be only advice. Britain realized that the chances for substantial financial aid from the United States were slim. As the responsible party, Britain was sure to proceed carefully, the embassy counseled. Three government departments were involved as well as several interest groups. London would focus on the details and take a less drastic outlook.[38]

In January 1960, Washington rejected Palmer's recommendations. The State Department told Palmer that it agreed that the United States should avoid undermining the British in Central Africa or becoming identified with the federation and its current policies. The United States should also continue to favor multiracial development. The department would remain alert to opportunities for discussing the federation with British representatives. Nevertheless, the British were not interested in detailed talks about the federation at present. They were waiting for the Monckton commission report and were more optimistic about the federation than Palmer. Moreover, the prospects for substantial financial aid to the federation were not bright. U.S. policy was to offer limited, technical assistance to advance its interests, but to leave development assistance to Britain and the federation government.[39]

Palmer persisted. By April, he was again urging a larger U.S. role in the federation. Palmer saw signs of new British policies and of political changes within the federation, particularly Nyasaland. He wondered whether the British might be more open to talks than they were in November. If Nyasaland were to be self-governing, accelerated economic and social development would be needed, he wrote. U.S. aid and assistance could make a difference.[40]

The London embassy now supported Palmer's ideas. The embassy reported to Washington that the Colonial Office and the Commonwealth Relations Office seemed immobilized and bereft of ideas. It agreed with Palmer's assessment that the British appeared to be taking a different political approach to the federation. Their plans for economic development were less clear, however. The United States should initiate talks with the British, support their political initiatives, and encourage them to increase their economic assistance to the federation. The embassy thought the price for offering the British unsolicited advice would be a U.S. financial contribution to economic development in the federation.[41]

Increased U.S. aid to the federation ran counter to the thinking within the Eisenhower administration. A Treasury official pointed out that any offer of aid to British dependencies would undermine the administration's efforts to persuade other governments to increase their foreign aid. The economic development program contemplated for the federation seemed within British capabilities. If, after the United States pushed Britain to expand its own development programs, it refused to do so, it would be difficult for the Eisenhower administration to justify increased U.S. aid.[42]

Palmer's advocacy of a larger U.S. role sprang from disapproval of British and federation policies rather than from support for the African nationalists. In May 1960, the Salisbury consulate filed several reports critical of the United National Independence Party in Northern Rhodesia. The party was poorly organized and prone to violence, the consulate wrote. Palmer thought Kaunda reasonable, but doubted that the Northern Rhodesian leader was tough enough to stick to democratic methods and to control his followers. In July, Palmer assured Washington that he was not wholly sympathetic to the nationalist cause. The British were right to be firm in the face of unreasonable expectations. Nevertheless, the two Rhodesias' reliance on force would lead to an explosion, sooner rather than later, the consul warned. The African nationalists were bound to win. A forceful intervention by the United States could forestall violence and protect the West's long-term interests in Central Africa.[43]

In July, Washington suggested an initiative, an informal approach to Welensky while he was in Washington. The department proposed to warn Welensky that repressing African nationalism threatened to isolate the federation. It would inhibit communicating to Africans that a multiracial partnership was required. The London embassy approved the proposal, but wanted to undertake parallel discussions with the Foreign Office. Palmer was opposed, nonetheless. Talking to Welensky would suggest that the United States thought the federation and territorial governments, not Britain, were the responsible parties. In addition, Welensky would resent the warning, Palmer claimed. It would be easier for the State Department to work with the British. Finally, Palmer thought that his talking to Welensky would be just as effective. The department backed off its proposal and indicated interest in approaching the British. At the same time, it warned Palmer against approaching Welensky. It thought plain talk to European leaders would come better from the British.[44]

Palmer remained focused on the need for rapid and substantial development in Central Africa. He welcomed British political concessions in Nyasaland and Northern Rhodesia. He warned Washington that British efforts to prepare Africans to govern themselves were inadequate. Crash as well as long-term development programs would be needed, he said. At the same time, Palmer criticized Banda's unwillingness to cooperate with the Nyasaland government's development efforts. Banda was pursuing his own narrow political ends at the expense of the Nyasaland people, Palmer thought.[45]

In fall 1960, the Southern Rhodesian government's relationship with the National Democratic Party caught the attention of State Department officials. The Salisbury consulate hoped that moderates would gain control of the party. The consulate also hoped that the Southern Rhodesian government would recognize that the party could be moderate and that its leaders were not troublesome agitators. The Intelligence and Research staff in Washington warned the secretary that bloodshed might result if the Southern Rhodesian government tried to repress the African nationalists. The reaction throughout Africa would be highly emotional, would threaten the British commonwealth, and would undermine British prestige, the staff contended. The Intelligence and Research staff anticipated that the British would attempt to broker an accommodation among the divergent interests in Southern Rhodesia. The long-term prospect was not bright, however, because the interests of the European settlers and the African majority were not compatible.[46]

A proposal developed in the Office of Eastern and Southern African Affairs incorporated the need for development and for viable African political parties. The office's paper assumed that the American goals in Central Africa were to avoid violence, promote interracial cooperation, and ensure that newly independent African states would cooperate with the United States. It argued that political parties and other institutions provided the means for Africans to attain their legitimate aspirations through peaceful and moderate methods. It criticized Southern Rhodesian policies towards African political parties. According to the paper, federation and multi-racial partnership were doomed to failure. Modifying the federation might buy some time, but Britain needed to assert itself on the side of African advancement. Britain needed to launch private talks with federation and Southern Rhodesian leaders and boost development efforts. The United States should push the British to act. It should also recognize that advice without a financial contribution was unlikely to be effective. The U.S. had to assume part of the development costs.[47]

In November 1960, U.S. and British officials again met to discuss African issues. As Palmer urged, the federation was on the agenda, but the U.S. position was less forceful than the Salisbury consulate and others recommended. U.S. officials praised British efforts to address the situation in the federation. They said that a federation was the best means to achieve political stability and economic viability. Referring to the Monckton commission report, they argued that altering the federation, and not force, was the way to secure the support of the African majority. They expressed concern about Southern Rhodesia's reliance on repressive legislation as its response to African nationalism. African self-government would require financial aid from Britain, they observed. The United States hoped that Britain would increase its aid to Central Africa. The U.S. could not, the officials said, commit to providing any aid. The department was prepared, however, to promote planning for increased U.S. assistance to the Central African territories.[48]

By December 1960, British efforts to preserve the Federation of Rhodesia and Nyasaland had foundered. The Macmillan government was at odds with the African nationalists in the three Central African territories as well as with the European settlers. Macleod's efforts to widen African participation in government had collided with the European settlers' very different notion of Central Africa's future. A moderate coalition of reasonable Europeans and cooperative Africans increasingly seemed a chimera.

U.S. officials sensed that the British were on the path to failure. Like the British, the consul in Salisbury imagined that power need not pass to the African nationalists. To secure a moderate regime, he urged a more active U.S. role, including expanded economic aid. Washington was not persuaded, however. The State Department was still content to offer advice and hope for the best.

Kennedy, Macmillan,
and Africa, 1961–1963:
A New Style

John Kennedy's style related to Africa contrasted sharply with Dwight Eisenhower's. Kennedy spoke positively about Africa and welcomed African leaders to the White House. In terms of policy toward British Africa, however, the two administrations were more alike than they were different. Kennedy dealt with an Africa composed of independent states or colonies about to be independent, whereas Eisenhower had confronted a colonial Africa for most of his tenure. Otherwise, Africa remained a low priority for the United States and the United States remained anti-colonial without necessarily being pro-independence. The United States continued to discuss African issues with its British ally, without supporting every British policy. In the United Nations, the United States continued to pursue a middle of the road policy, even at the risk of disagreement with its British ally.

Presidential Candidate

As John Kennedy sought the presidency in the late 1950s, he cultivated the image of someone interested in Africa and prepared to diverge from the policies followed by the Eisenhower administration. In 1957, he attacked Eisenhower's policy regarding Algeria and staked out a distinctive position on the Algerian conflict. He became chairman of the Senate Foreign Relations Committee's new subcommittee on Africa, but found little time for committee work. The subcommittee met only three times in the two years he was the chairman. Kennedy continued to speak on African topics. In 1959, he unveiled a proposal for an African Educational Development fund. Kennedy also met with prominent African visitors to the United States. Sekou Toure, the prime minister of Guinea, visited the United States in 1960 and expressed interest in meeting Kennedy. Kennedy sent a helicopter to fly him to Disneyland for a brief discussion. During the 1960 presidential campaign, Kennedy hammered away at the Eisenhower administration's alleged failures in Africa.[1]

In July 1957, Kennedy made a long speech[2] in the Senate attacking the Eisenhower administration's policy regarding French efforts to suppress a nationalist uprising in Algeria. Kennedy argued that the United States, as the leader of the free world, needed to address the Algerian problem. France had demonstrated that it was incapable of resolving the problem, Kennedy claimed. Failure to end the conflict would endanger French and U.S. interests, particularly in North Africa, the junior senator from Massachusetts warned.

Kennedy began his speech by pronouncing that imperialism was the single most powerful force in the world. Dealing with imperialism was the most important test for U.S. foreign policy. The country needed to confront both Soviet and Western imperialism. The judgment of the "uncommitted millions in Asia and Africa" as well as of the "hopeful lovers of freedom behind the Iron Curtain" was critically important. Kennedy told the Senate that he would follow his speech on Western imperialism in Algeria with another on Soviet imperialism in Poland.

The Eisenhower administration, Kennedy said, was pursuing a "head-in-the-sand" policy regarding Algeria and similar situations. The administration's policy consisted of "tepid encouragement and moralizations on both sides, and a cautious neutrality on all real issues." The administration merely restated "the United States' obvious dependence upon its European friends, its obvious dedication nevertheless to the principles of self-determination, and its obvious desire not to become involved." According to Kennedy, the administration's policies represented a "retreat from the principles of independence and anti-colonialism." The administration was too concerned with "diplomatic niceties, legal technicalities, or even strategic considerations." The Eisenhower government provided military aid to France and the vice president ignored the Algerian problem when he reported on his recent trip to Africa, Kennedy charged.

Algeria was an American problem, Kennedy said. France's failure to end the conflict was undermining the NATO alliance and disrupting progress towards greater unity in Europe. France's investment of men and money in the Algerian conflict was hurting a key U.S. ally. The Algerian issue had come before the United Nations, but the American unwillingness to broker a solution had undermined its leadership within the world organization. Apparent support for France was also damaging U.S. relations with Tunisia and Morocco and endangering the administration's policies in the Middle East. Failure to resolve the Algerian situation was damaging the American role as leader of the free world.

Most of Kennedy's speech addressed French and U.S. failures in Algeria, but towards the end, he discussed the challenges posed by nationalism. Kennedy said that economic and social reforms were no substitute for political independence. Because the French had been slow to offer a meaningful settlement, Algeria was now part of the irreversible movement towards African independence. Kennedy said that national self-identification could take place quickly and, when it did, repression could not extinguish it. Algerians would take heart from the success of their neighbors, Tunisia and Morocco, in gaining their independence.

The desired result, Kennedy said, was a politically independent Algeria that was economically interdependent with France. Having argued that the United States should take ownership of the Algerian problem, Kennedy had little to say about how the country could promote Algerian independence. He said that the U.S. should not impose a solution, but should "make a contribution toward breaking the vicious circle in which the Algerian controversy whirls." Kennedy added that the U.S. need not use the "cumbersome procedures" of the United Nations. He suggested NATO, the leaders of Tunisia and Morocco, or India as possible contributors to achieving the right result.

As Kennedy undoubtedly intended, his Algeria speech attracted considerable attention, particularly because it criticized a principal U.S. ally. Eisenhower and Dulles were especially critical. Dulles observed that Kennedy should concentrate on the Soviet version if he wanted to oppose colonialism. The chief foreign policy spokesmen within the Democratic Party were also negative. Adlai Stevenson thought it a terrible speech. Acheson called it a "foolish attack" on a "dispirited ally." Nearly 140 newspapers published editorials about the speech; two-thirds of them were negative. Despite the speech's concentration on U.S. responsibilities as a global power and on U.S. interests in North Africa, others came to focus on its acceptance that Algerian independence was inevitable and its implied support for the Algerian nationalists. Stevenson and Eleanor Roosevelt remained wary of Kennedy. Yet other Democrats who favored African independence such as Chester Bowles, Hubert Humphrey, and G. Mennen Williams upgraded their opinion of Kennedy, until then not known for his support of allegedly liberal causes. African nationalists, including Nkrumah, saw Kennedy's speech as a welcome change from the Eisenhower administration's cautious approach to African issues.[3]

Herve Alphand, the French ambassador to the United States, implored Dulles to repudiate Kennedy's views and block passage of the Senate resolution Kennedy had proposed. Dulles assured Alphand that the resolution would not affect the Eisenhower administration's action even if the Senate adopted it. In fact, Kennedy's speech may have served Dulles's purposes by increasing the pressure on the French to resolve the Algerian situation. It demonstrated how American opinion was turning against the French and proposed the sort of approach the Eisenhower administration had suggested to the French.[4]

During the 1960 presidential campaign, the Kennedy organization decided that it could exploit African issues. The Eisenhower administration and, therefore, Vice President Nixon, appeared vulnerable on African issues. Although Nixon had advocated greater U.S. involvement and investment in Africa within the administration, the public face of the Eisenhower policies towards Africa remained cautious and frugal. The Eisenhower administration avoided public criticism of the colonial powers and did not seek to expand foreign aid to Africa until late in its second term. Promoting greater engagement with Africa allowed Kennedy to appeal to liberal and African-American voters while still avoiding the inflammatory topic of civil rights in the United States.

Like Kennedy's Algeria speech, nearly all the candidate's references to Africa[5] focused on the U.S. role as a global power and on its rivalry with Russia. Kennedy told campaign audiences that the world was at a decision point. People in Africa, Asia, and Latin America were beginning to doubt that the future belonged to the United States. They were looking to Russia for inspiration, leadership, and assistance. Young, ambitious Africans were beginning to quote Karl Marx rather than Thomas Jefferson. The United States, said Kennedy, had the best system of government and was the most powerful country in the world. It should work with other free nations to strengthen the political and economic independence of the emerging African nations and prevent the chaos that could lead to communist expansion. Otherwise, the balance of power would tilt away from the United States and in favor of Russia.

The Eisenhower administration neglected Africa, Kennedy charged. It had not allied the U.S. with the cause of African independence. It was slow to provide African students with opportunities to study in the United States. Kennedy claimed that the administration's failure to educate Africans was responsible for the lack of Congolese with sufficient training to run an independent country and for the resultant turmoil in the former Belgian colony. The administration provided too little financial aid to African countries. It assigned fewer Foreign Service officers to all of Africa than to Germany, was slow to recognize newly independent African states, and failed to appoint ambassadors to five independent African countries. Kennedy claimed that the administration appointed ambassadors who could not speak the local language or even pronounce the head of state's name. Because of Eisenhower's neglect, countries like Guinea and Ghana were moving away from the United States and towards Russia. A pro–Russian and anti–American prime minister, Patrice Lumumba, was in charge of the Congo, Kennedy pointed out. Only Liberia and South Africa among African countries voted with the United States to keep China out of the United Nations.

In most campaign speeches, Kennedy was content to attack the Eisenhower record, without offering any alternatives. His speech to the National Council of Women in October 1960 dealt almost entirely with Africa, however, and laid out a substantial program of initiatives for Africa. Kennedy returned to the notion of increased educational aid for African students. He proposed a multi-national African educational development fund to address the continent's long-term educational needs. He also proposed expanded development assistance to African countries and a fund capable of extending long-term development loans. In all initiatives, Kennedy said, the United States should work with and through the United Nations.

Throughout the 1960 campaign, Kennedy's emphasis was on post-colonial Africa, on the United States competing with Russia for the friendship of independent African states. Nevertheless, in the National Council of Women speech, Kennedy referred to U.S. policy towards the remaining colonial territories. Kennedy said that the United States should ally itself with African nationalism, the most powerful force in the modern world. The U.S. had to side with man's right to govern himself. It was a fundamental principle. Nationalism would inevitably succeed. Nationalism was the one force strong enough to threaten the communist empire. Kennedy also argued that the U.S. needed to end discrimination at home if it hoped to win the respect of African peoples.

In the midst of the 1960 contest, the State Department and the Nixon campaign combined to create an opportunity for Kennedy to demonstrate his commitment to educating Africans. During 1960, the African-American Students Foundation, a group associated with the American Committee on Africa, raised more than $1 million to fund scholarships at U.S. universities for students from East and Central Africa. When the foundation asked the State Department to help pay for the students' airfares to the United States, the department refused. Looking for funding, the foundation contacted the members of the Senate Foreign Relations Committee, including Kennedy. Kennedy then met with Tom Mboya, who had flown from Kenya to secure the transportation funds. Kennedy offered to have the Kennedy Foundation provide $100,000 to fly two to three hundred students to the United States, provided Mboya and the foundation did not announce the source of the funds. The Nixon campaign learned of Kennedy's offer and put pressure on the State Department to make funds available. The department did so, but the foundation declined the funds, suggesting that the department use them for additional scholarships. Presumably at the prompting of the Nixon campaign, Senator Hugh Scott, Republican of Pennsylvania, announced the State Department's decision to offer the funding. On the Senate floor, he also attacked Kennedy for preempting the department's efforts. Kennedy took advantage of the opportunity to explain how his family had helped the African students when the Eisenhower administration had refused to do so.[6]

Kennedy in the White House

After becoming president, Kennedy cultivated a pro–Africa image while reaching out to the liberal elements within the Democratic Party. He appointed Stevenson the U.S. representative at the United Nations and Chester Bowles as under secretary of state, the department's number two position. Bowles was a former governor of Connecticut, congressman, and ambassador to India. In 1956, he published a book entitled *Africa's Challenge to America*. Bowles was one of the first prominent liberals to support Kennedy's bid for the presidency. Before naming a secretary of state, Kennedy nominated G. Mennen Williams to be assistant secretary of state for African affairs. Williams was a former governor of Michigan. Like Bowles, he had come out early for Kennedy. Williams had no background in Africa but was a flamboyant campaigner and a long-time civil rights advocate. Williams wanted to be secretary for health, education, and welfare. Kennedy persuaded him to take the African post in part by promising that Williams would have direct access to the president.[7]

Williams brought with him the instincts of a political campaigner. His principal contribution to the Kennedy administration was to embellish its pro–Africa image. Williams was a "big picture" person, given to dealing in broad generalities rather than in specifics. He was more interested in promoting a friendly relationship between the United States and African countries than he was in policy details. His principal recommendations were that the president continue to display an interest in Africa, that administration officials make frequent tours of Africa, and that they use their public speeches to educate the public about African issues. Regarding public relations, the administration followed Williams's advice. Kennedy met with twenty-eight African leaders in the nearly three years of his presidency. Williams also made several long African tours. In 1961, he was overseas for a total of thirteen weeks and gave thirty-three major speeches in the United States.[8]

Along the way, Williams became the Kennedy administration's Mason Sears. He was a prominent official whose pro–African public statements appealed to nationalists, appalled the colonial powers, and threatened to stray beyond administration policy. The most famous example of Williams's capacity to embarrass the administration occurred in early 1961. Before leaving for East Africa, Williams met with Kennedy. According to Williams, Kennedy and he agreed that U.S. policy amounted to wanting for Africa what the Africans wanted for themselves. When Williams repeated the phrase at a press conference in Nairobi, reporters translated it into "Africa for Africans." It acquired the implication that Europeans did not belong in Africa. Reaction in East and Central Africa, London, and Washington was immediate and negative. During the same trip, Williams warned Kenyans about the dangers of communist aggression, saying that Kenya should avoid replacing colonialism with another tyranny. The local press interpreted the comment to mean that Williams considered British rule in Africa as tyrannical. Kennedy defended Williams in public. Asked about the assistant secretary's remarks, the president pointed out that Williams had been talking about everyone who considered himself an African, regardless of skin color. In any case, whom else should Africa be for? Behind the scenes, however, Kennedy was upset. He ordered Bowles to meet with Williams. The president directed that the undersecretary insist that Williams clear all future public statement with Bowles or Dean Rusk, the secretary of state. Rusk had already cabled Williams instructing him to have his speeches cleared and to stop trying to explain his earlier remarks.[9]

Williams's remarks reverberated throughout the British government. Averell Harriman, ambassador at large in the Kennedy administration, dined with Macmillan in early March 1961. Macmillan cited Williams's comments and complained about unthinking U.S. anti-colonialism. Careless comments would make Britain's task in Africa harder and undo the careful compromises it was negotiating, Macmillan complained. Macmillan asked that officials in Washington and on tour in Africa be more understanding of British efforts. Otherwise, observers would conclude that the United States did not support British aims. Harriman replied by praising Macmillan's "wind of change" speech. He pointed out that it was blunter than anything Williams had said. Williams was enthusiastic and sincere, Harriman said. Macmillan would like him once he got to know him. Macmillan was not convinced.[10]

Williams's instinctive sympathy for nationalists and his belief that colonialism was a lost cause brought him to conflict with others within the administration. In late 1962, when Williams learned that State Department officials were refusing to meet with nationalist leaders from Portugal's colonies, he appealed to Rusk. Williams conceded that meeting with insurgent leaders posed issues, but argued that U.S. policy had been to maintain contacts with nationalists, even if the colonial authorities objected. Williams wrote that closing the door to nationalists would be to deny U.S. heritage just as the colonial empires were collapsing. Refusing to meet with nationalists would damage America's position in the free world, Williams concluded. William Tyler, the assistant secretary for European affairs, responded that the United States could not "work both sides of the street at the same time." Meetings with nationalists were insignificant in themselves, Tyler wrote. Nevertheless, nationalists and others, including the colonial powers, were apt to interpret such meetings as indications of U.S. support for nationalist movements. George McGhee, under secretary for political affairs, handled the matter because Rusk was immersed in the Cuban missile crisis. McGhee told Williams to stop advocating a review of the department's policies regarding meetings with nationalists.[11]

Within Kennedy's first year in office, it was evident that Williams belonged to an endangered minority within the administration. In November 1961, Kennedy shifted Bowles from the under secretary post to a position as the special adviser for African, Asian, and Latin American affairs with vague duties. In Bowles's place, Kennedy named George Ball, a self-proclaimed "Europeanist," as under secretary. When rumors that Kennedy had lost confidence in Bowles began to circulate, Williams and Stevenson wrote to Kennedy to defend him. Bowles told Stevenson that he and Williams would be the next to go. Some of Williams's State Department critics also interpreted Bowles's transfer as a sign that Williams was on his way out.[12]

Bowles's transfer and Stevenson and Williams's eclipse within the administration reflected the Kennedy administration's foreign policy orientation. As Kennedy said in his campaign speeches, competing with Russia was the first priority. The competition with Russia took place primarily in Europe and, to compete successfully, the U.S. needed firm alliances with the Western European powers. Africa, therefore, had to be a lower priority than Europe. The United States remained interested in securing the allegiance of independent African states. Nevertheless, cultivating friendly relations with African states had to be a lesser priority, particularly when it risked offending the European allies. To the extent that the U.S. was involved in Africa, it was largely to compete with the Russians and Chinese. The administration's sense was that the United States must oppose Russian or Chinese influence everywhere, including in Africa. The United States also had to be wary regarding nationalist movements. Nikita Khrushchev had pronounced in January 1961 that wars of national liberation were a continuation of the worldwide socialist revolution and Russia and China had both made clear their eagerness to assist nationalist movements.[13]

Kennedy's choice of Ball over Bowles demonstrated that the conflict between officials focused on European affairs and those interested in the rest of the world persisted within the State Department. It signaled, moreover, that the Europeanists retained the upper hand. Bowles thought that his advocacy of African issues upset what he termed "the Achesons" with the department, experienced officials with a "Europe first" mentality. During the Kennedy years, some such officials demonstrated that they shared the former secretary's penchant for offensive remarks. One reportedly said that the trouble with Bowles and Williams was that, when they saw a band of black baboons beating tom-toms, they saw George Washingtons. Another said that Bowles wanted U.S. diplomats to wear sarongs and make love to the natives. Ball referred to African nations as having names that seemed like typographical errors. In retirement, Rusk objected to allegations that he was indifferent to Africa. He explained, nevertheless, that the United States was always the junior partner in Africa in the Kennedy and Johnson years. European nations provided three-quarters of the foreign aid to Africa, Rusk said. That was as it should be since the European powers had little involvement in Asia or South America. This division of labor irritated some within the department, particularly ambassadors to African countries, Rusk reported. They wanted to play "Mr. Big" in every African capital. Rusk saw his job as calming them down.[14]

Key Kennedy advisers were skeptical of a large U.S. role in Africa. In May 1961, Walt Rostow, the president's deputy special assistant for national security affairs, wrote to his boss, McGeorge Bundy, that the United States had enough commitments around the globe. The U.S. should feel no compulsion to become overly involved in Africa. Moreover, the region posed only modest military and political dangers. In the best case, it might form a constructive part of the Western system. Strengthened by healthy economic growth during the 1950s, the U.S. allies could deal with the situation, Rostow predicted. The United States should meet with Britain and France to establish a common strategy and tactics. Rostow argued that the colonial powers had already used statesmanship to create a favorable situation for the West in Africa.[15]

Bowles and Williams also came into conflict with the established order within the State Department. Williams was a foreign policy neophyte. Bowles and Williams were political appointees in an organization of career civil servants. Williams replaced a career foreign service officer. Even before Kennedy took office, Bowles and Williams intervened to block the Eisenhower administration's nomination of career diplomats as ambassadors to several African countries. In addition, Kennedy's initial appointments to ambassadorial posts in Africa included younger outsiders. Furthermore, Williams was offended by the shabby furnishings and cramped office space allocated to the African Bureau when he arrived. Presumably, he took steps to improve working conditions. Bowles told Kennedy that the African Bureau's relative inexperience was an advantage. It was the most creative and flexible organization in the department, he wrote. The staff understood Kennedy's policies and was determined to carry them out, Bowles claimed. The older parts of the department probably would not have agreed.[16]

In naming young political appointees to key ambassadorships, especially William Attwood to Guinea and William Mahoney to Ghana, Kennedy broke with the Eisenhower administration's pattern. The contrast between the two administrations should not be overstated, however. Eisenhower named thirty-one ambassadors to African countries. Twenty-seven were career foreign service officers. Kennedy named thirty-two ambassadors, twenty-one of whom were career foreign service officers. Eisenhower's political appointments appear to have been rewards for prior political service or continuation of the practice of naming an African-American as ambassador to Liberia. Eight of Kennedy's political appointments also had clear ties to the Democratic Party or to prior Democratic administrations. One was a former congressman from Missouri. The other three included an oil executive and two academics. The average age of Eisenhower's appointees was fifty-three. The average age of Kennedy's was fifty.

Within six months of taking office, Kennedy grew disillusioned with the State Department. He found it slow and ineffective. He concluded that it could not present policy alternatives clearly or offer practical suggestions for use of American power. Rusk was cautious to a fault, slow to make decisions, and unwilling to deviate from what he thought was the official line. A Kennedy aide remarked that the secretary of state never stood for anything. In earlier administrations, the under secretary had been responsible for managing the department's operations. Nevertheless, Bowles struck many as arrogant. He was not detail person, and found it difficult to work with Rusk. Kennedy decided that replacing Bowles offered an easier solution to the department's ills than replacing Rusk.[17]

Issues of style, moreover, separated Bowles, Williams, and Stevenson from other key foreign policy officials and from Kennedy. The so-called liberals were wordy and idealistic in an administration that prided itself on being precise, terse, and tough-minded. In the Kennedy administration, foreign policy readily became crisis management. The president was most comfortable dealing with the issue at hand even at the risk of slighting long-term consequences or the bigger picture. Kennedy's aide, McGeorge Bundy, disliked Williams's verbosity and idealism to the point that he limited the assistant secretary's access to the president. Kennedy and his closest aides also valued hard work and attention to detail. Bowles and Stevenson were thought sloppy and lazy. The Kennedy team was serious. Williams affected polka dot bow ties and a folksy style. He arranged a square dance for African diplomats with himself as the caller.[18]

Kennedy's African Policy

The Kennedy administration assumed that Britain's African colonies would soon become independent. In April 1961, the consensus of the intelligence community was that virtually all the remaining British dependent territories would be independent within three years. The State Department's Bureau of Intelligence and Research contributed a slightly more conservative estimate. It thought that all British colonies would be independent within five years, with the possible exceptions of Gambia and the three High Commission Territories.[19]

Both analyses worried that the path to independence might not be peaceful. The consensus view was that violence was possible in Kenya and the Rhodesias, territories that had sizeable European populations. The State Department predicted that violence was more likely in Kenya if Jomo Kenyatta assumed a leadership position. It thought that the Federation of Rhodesia and Nyasaland might see sporadic but not major violence between Africans and Europeans.

The Kennedy administration remained focused on post-colonial Africa, on how it should deal with the new African states. It did not see the need to document in detail its goals regarding African independence. In the State Department's Bureau of African Affairs, African independence was now a U.S. objective. A draft paper produced in the Office of Eastern and Southern African Affairs set independence or full self-determination for all African territories within ten years as the long-term objective. Identifying the United States with African aspirations for independence was a short-term objective. Another short-term objective was to promote a gradual and non-violent transition to majority rule while protecting minority rights. If a peaceful transition to majority rule were not possible, the U.S. should seek a transfer of power in which the United States was not identified with minority rule.[20]

The African Bureau's policy paper saw the United States wielding influence in a troubled continent. The paper assumed that the U.S. could not shape African institutions, but could influence the direction of their growth. It assumed that there existed not one Africa, but several Africas. In making policy, the paper urged, the United States needed to consider the differences among African countries and regions. Since Africa would continue in turmoil for many years, stability was not a realistic objective. With well-planned outside help, a few countries might become strong points in a fluid situation. The paper assumed that the United States might be able to take advantage of the fact that Africans wanted to stay out of the Cold War. It imagined that America's revolutionary background and democratic aspirations constituted a basis for sympathy between Americans and Africans.

In April 1962, the State Department staff responsible for dealing with the United Nations produced a policy paper[21] that revealed the department's thinking about British colonial Africa. The paper was further documentation that the State Department considered that the end of Britain's African empire was at hand. The paper also demonstrated that some U.S. officials now considered themselves the senior partners in whatever arrangement the United States had with Britain in Africa. The U.S. was at least as responsible as Britain for planning the future of the African colonies, the paper claimed. The paper also showed that the same State Department officials considered questions of economic viability and governmental structure as at least as important as political independence for African territories. State Department officials now sounded like their Colonial Office counterparts of a decade earlier.

The paper produced by the Bureau of International Organizations Affairs dealt with what it called the "bits and pieces" of colonialism. Its objective was to identify political and economic relationships for the remaining non–self-governing territories in Africa that were more viable than complete independence. In doing so, the paper's aim was to limit the number of new members of the United Nations. The paper argued that not all territories should become independent. The pressure to grant them independence would be irresistible unless someone offered an alternative, it contended. The paper identified four categories of dependent territories: candidates for independence and U.N. membership, candidates for continuing ties with the administering powers, candidates for association with neighboring countries, and "genuine enigmas." Kenya, Uganda, Zanzibar, Northern Rhodesia, Southern Rhodesia, and Nyasaland were candidates for complete independence, the paper conceded. Gambia should form an association with a neighboring country, presumably Senegal. The three High Commission territories, Basutoland, Bechuanaland, and Swaziland, were enigmas. Perhaps the best solution for them would be to substitute the United Nations for the administering power. The paper was to be the means by which the United States shaped thinking and planning about colonial Africa in the U.N. The paper's authors proposed that the United States use the paper's proposals to stay ahead of the U.N. committee responsible for colonial matters. The first step should be discussions with British officials.

Reactions from other State Department organizations were lukewarm. They were ironic in the context of the longstanding tension between Africanists and Europeanists. The Bureau of African Affairs objected to the paper because it assumed that the three territories in the Federation of Rhodesia and Nyasaland would become independent. The Africanists argued that the British were working to preserve an association among the three territories. Continued association served the best interests of the United States, Britain, and the federation's inhabitants, the Africanists argued. The paper might strengthen those who opposed United States and British policy in Central Africa, the Africa Bureau worried. The Bureau of European Affairs agreed that a respectable substitute for independence was needed in some territories and that the department should raise the issue with the British. The Europeanists pointed out that the desire for political independence was nearly universal, however. It was not affected by considerations of economic viability. If the United States attempted to promote a substitute for independence, it would be taking on a complex and hazardous task, the Europeanists warned. It would leave itself open to charges of neo-colonialism.[22]

In the Kennedy and Johnson eras, administration figures publicly proclaimed U.S. support for self-determination, but, like those in the Eisenhower administration, also tried to stay in the middle of the road. Williams said that foreign policy was based on certain principles, including self-determination. Self-determination was a universally recognized principle. All people had the right to determine their form of government. To another audience, Williams referred to the "continuing tide of self-determination" that had U.S. sympathy and support. About the Congo, Stevenson said that the first aim was to end outside imperial control. Williams praised the British for encouraging African advancement in Central Africa, for promoting political education, and for helping the territories evolve towards democratic self-government. Jonathan Bingham, a U.S. representative at the United Nations, lauded the British and French for attempting to resolve the "difficult problem" of applying self-determination to territories that included both European and African populations. Williams acknowledged that groups in Central Africa disagreed about the pace of political change. No group had set its face against history, Williams claimed. Everyone was working towards self-government and an inter-racial society. Bingham and Williams both counseled patience. The Congo demonstrated, Bingham said, that building an independent nation took time. Independence could come too soon. Williams said that deliberate and expeditious preparation for self-government was essential to African advancement.[23]

Britain in the Kennedy Era

By 1961, civil servants in London saw Africa's weakness as its defining characteristic and its major importance. A paper produced by the Foreign Office, the Colonial Office, and the Commonwealth Relations Office pronounced that Africa south of the Sahara was less important than its geographic area might suggest. Its population was a third of India's and a fourth of China's. Africa exported almost no manufactured goods and only 4 percent of the world's raw materials. Some of Africa's exports such as diamonds and copper were valuable, but not nearly as valuable to Britain as the Middle East's oil. Africa's economic activity was unlikely to increase in the near future. Africa had some strategic importance to Britain, but nothing like Europe or the Middle East. What made Africa important to Britain in the early 1960s was, however, that its countries were weak and open to outside influences. Unlike Asia or South America, Africa had not taken sides in the struggle between the West and the East. Nevertheless, losing Africa would be less damaging to the Western alliance than losing France or Germany, the civil servants' paper concluded. Britain and its allies could lose influence in Africa without a major upheaval; it could lose out through neglect and indifference. The civil servants recommended that Britain remain involved in Africa. Despite Africa's limited value, a concerted effort to save the continent for the West was essential.[24]

In the last three years of the Macmillan government, which coincided with the Kennedy administration, colonial policy making was more likely to involve cabinet debates about individual colonies than it was wide-ranging policy papers. By appointing Macleod as colonial secretary, Macmillan irretrievably tilted British colonial policy towards rapid constitutional change and independence. The remaining decisions involved the timing of political change in individual colonies. As the cabinet's focus narrowed to the colonies with significant numbers of European settlers, Kenya and the Federation of Rhodesia and Nyasaland, disagreement within the cabinet was more common. The initial tension was often between Macleod as colonial secretary and Duncan Sandys as commonwealth relations secretary. According to one commentator, their relationship was as cold and bleak and silent as that between the Matterhorn and Mont Blanc. Both were stubborn and strong-willed. During these years, Macleod threatened to resign more than once. Macleod was far more open to political change and to partnerships with African nationalists than was Sandys. In part, the tension also reflected the two men's responsibilities. Macleod was responsible for most of the African colonies, including two within the federation, Nyasaland, and Northern Rhodesia. For these, independence under African majority rule was the likely result of government policy. Sandys was responsible for the federation and for Southern Rhodesia. Until the late 1950s, independence under a European controlled government seemed the likely outcome of British policy. Whether and how British policy towards the federation and Southern Rhodesia would change in an environment friendlier to African nationalism were among the most controversial issues facing the Macmillan government.

Disagreements between the two ministers posed political threats to the Macmillan government. Sandys and Macleod had their supporters within the cabinet. In the midst of disputes about the future of Northern Rhodesia, Macmillan feared that ministers might resign regardless of the final decision. He also thought that the government's supporters in Parliament were split on African issues. Macmillan was particularly concerned that some within the Parliament were far more opposed to Macleod than Sandys. One center of opposition to Macleod's policies was the Watching Committee, organized by Lord Salisbury. Among its members were former ministers and governors, including Lord Boyd (Alan Lennox-Boyd), Lord Milverton (Sir Arthur Richards), and Lord Twining (Sir Edward Twining). Salisbury was the first patron of the Monday Club, an organization founded by ten Conservative members of Parliament to oppose Macmillan's African policies. "Monday" referred to "Black Monday," the day Macmillan gave his "wind of change" speech.[25]

In general, Macmillan accepted Macleod's approach because it made political sense. In early 1962, Macmillan explained to Sir Roy Welensky that the whole point of democratic government lay in deciding how fast to yield to public opinion. A government could not turn the tide. The French had tried in Algeria and failed. The British could have held Cyprus if they had been willing to be brutal, but British troops would probably have resisted carrying out the necessary measures. You could not, Macmillan said, solve political problems by simple exercise of power.[26]

Nevertheless, Macmillan was intent on keeping his government together, even at the cost of replacing Macleod. Macleod could be difficult. Colleagues could find him arrogant and overbearing. Over time, he became a lightning rod for Conservative attacks on the government's colonial policies. After Macleod announced new constitutional arrangements for Northern Rhodesia in February 1962, ninety-seven Conservative members of Parliament supported a motion urging the colonial secretary to go slow in Africa. In the House of Lords, Salisbury attacked Macleod and his policies. Macleod was brilliant, Salisbury said, but also "too clever by half." Referring to Macleod's past as a bridge player, Salisbury argued that it might be acceptable for a card player to outwit his opponents, but it was not acceptable for the colonial secretary to treat the European settlers as his opponents and try to outwit them. In September, the government's Conservative critics were again upset. Macleod had announced that the government would consider reopening talks on the Northern Rhodesian constitution if the African nationalists would cooperate in restoring law and order. In October, Macmillan sensed the need for a change on colonial and other issues and reshuffled his cabinet. Macleod became the government's leader in the House of Commons. Reginald Maudling, another rising star in the Conservative party, replaced him as colonial secretary.[27]

Appointing Maudling did not solve Macmillan's problems within the cabinet, however. The policy disputes went beyond personalities. Macmillan thought Maudling capable, if lazy and vain. He proved more amiable than Macleod, but just as determined to move the African colonies towards independence. Macmillan soon complained that Maudling was "more black than the blacks" and more difficult and intransigent than his predecessor. Maudling, too, could threaten to resign.[28]

In March and July 1962, Macmillan tried to reorganize his way out of difficulty. To end conflicts between Maudling and Sandys, Macmillan created a new organization, the Central Africa Office, responsible for the federation and its constituent territories. To gain favor with African nationalists and European settlers, Macmillan put R.A. Butler, the senior member of the cabinet, in charge. Butler had a reputation for impartiality. He appeared sympathetic to the settlers, but held generally enlightened views. Amidst a wider cabinet reshuffle in July, Macmillan made Maudling chancellor of the exchequer. He put Sandys in charge of both the Colonial Office and the Commonwealth Relations Office. Butler became deputy prime minister and first secretary of state while retaining responsibility for Central Africa.[29]

Macmillan's improvised arrangements ended with his regime. Ill health forced Macmillan to resign in October 1963. After a controversial selection process, Lord Home became prime minister as Sir Alec Douglas-Home. In the new government, Butler, thought by some to be Macmillan's obvious successor, became foreign secretary. The Central Africa Office was abolished. Sandys retained responsibility for the Colonial Office and the Commonwealth Relations Office. Macleod led an effort to head off Home's appointment. He thought Home too old-fashioned and passive to be a prime minister. Failing to block Home's accession, Macleod refused to serve in the Douglas-Home government.

Home often differed with Macleod, arguing for slower change in Africa. Nevertheless, his accession to power did not mark a significant change in British policies. By late 1963, the government had resolved the status of most colonies. Southern Rhodesia was the most important and controversial African issue remaining on the government's agenda. In November 1963, Harold Wilson, leader of the Labour opposition, demanded in the House of Commons that the government pledge to implement a democratic constitution in Southern Rhodesia before granting the territory its independence. Douglas-Home's response was that the pledge was implicit in one of his earlier statements.[30]

Relations with Macmillan and the British

Kennedy's relationship with Macmillan and his government was friendly. The two leaders developed a warm personal relationship with Macmillan playing an avuncular role. On key occasions, Kennedy bailed out the Macmillan and Douglas-Home governments. In

1960, Eisenhower promised Macmillan access to the Skybolt missile system. The missiles were to be capable of delivering nuclear warheads and figured in Britain's efforts to remain a major power. When the Kennedy administration moved to cancel the system in 1962, Macmillan objected. Despite misgivings, Kennedy agreed to provide Britain with Polaris missiles instead. In late 1961, Macmillan faced a difficult debate in the House of Commons regarding U.N. actions in the Congo. A significant group of Conservatives opposed the U.N. efforts to squelch the secession of Katanga province. When the British government pressed Kennedy to support a cease-fire in Katanga, Kennedy agreed, over the objections of Stevenson and others. In the summer of 1963, the Security Council was considering steps to halt a nationalist rebellion in Angola and propel the Portuguese colony towards independence. Stevenson took the initiative to write a compromise resolution. Stevenson's aim was to push Portugal towards a settlement and undercut a tougher resolution promoted by the anti-colonialist group in the United Nations. After Douglas-Home asked that the United States withdraw its support for the compromise, Kennedy ordered Stevenson to abstain on the vote. Stevenson thought the abstention was as embarrassing as the U.S. abstention on the 1960 anti-colonialism measure in the General Assembly, when Eisenhower yielded to Macmillan's pleas.[31]

Other actions signaled, however, that Kennedy did not consider Britain America's equal or even an especially close partner. Kennedy dismissed Macmillan's offer to act as a broker in negotiations with Russia. Many U.S. officials hoped that canceling the Skybolt project would deprive the British of their independent nuclear force. The Kennedy administration launched the Bay of Pigs invasion of Cuba without informing or consulting Britain in advance. When Acheson criticized Britain in a 1962 speech as having lost an empire but not found a role, Kennedy authorized an official rejoinder. Special relationship was not a perfect phrase, the statement said, but no one should sneer at Anglo-American cooperation. Nevertheless, Acheson's analysis of British weakness and decline touched a nerve in Britain because it was more than plausible and it might just reflect thinking within the Kennedy administration.[32]

Kennedy administration officials met with their British counterparts to discuss colonial issues in the series of meetings in spring 1961, culminating with a meeting between Kennedy and Macmillan in April. The British laid out their plans in more detail than they had in the most recent meetings with the Eisenhower administration. Tanganyika was to become independent in 1962; Kenya in two or three years, they said. The British planned to push ahead with political changes in Uganda despite the potential for violence in Buganda. The Federation of Rhodesia and Nyasaland remained the largest challenge, in Britain's view. The British aim was to remain friendly with the African population while preserving the federation's economic value. Sir Andrew Cohen contended that Britain could have little influence on Southern Rhodesia. Preservation of the federation was the best hope for African advancement. Britain was walking a tightrope in Central Africa, Cohen said. It had to get the pace of political change just right, neither too fast nor too slow.[33]

The United Nations continued to be a bugaboo for the British. Except for Tanganyika, the United Nations did not have authority over the British colonies, the British maintained. If Nigeria had been a trust territory, the British contended, it would not have become independent so quickly or so peacefully. The U.N. could profitably discuss economic or social issues in the colonies. Discussions of political issues, however, impeded orderly transition to self-government. Britain's aim was to stave off any U.N. intervention while it settled the fate of its African colonies. When Macmillan met with Kennedy, he emphasized Britain's objections to setting target dates for dependent territories. Belgium's setting a date for Congolese independence had led to a breakdown in law and order, he claimed. Macmillan contended that there was no disagreement between the United States and Britain about the U.N.'s handling of colonial issues. Yet he went on to question the wisdom of voting with the African and Asian nations. Since Britain rarely sided with the anti-colonialists in the United Nations, Macmillan presumably was referring to American willingness to support the anti-colonialists. Foreign Secretary Home added that broad resolutions by the United Nations were harmful, but they were preferable to specific resolutions. Worse were resolutions that contained timetables. Britain needed U.S. assistance to steady matters in the United Nations, Home said.[34]

U.S. leaders and officials were unwilling to promise the British consistent support in the United Nations. In February, the U.S. position was that it understood British concerns about U.N. intervention in dependent territories, and the setting of target dates in particular. Nonetheless, U.S. officials said the United States was looking for a stance that would take into account its own dependent territories and reputation. The background papers prepared by the State Department for the Kennedy-Macmillan meeting described considerable agreement with British views. They stressed the importance of consultation between the two countries. They maintained that the United States should not support a resolution that mandated a target date for independence for all colonies. The U.S. should also not support U.N. missions to all dependent territories. Nevertheless, the papers advocated that the United States consider U.N. resolutions, including those that contained target dates, on their merits. Stevenson assured Macmillan and Home that the United States and Britain did not disagree on colonial issues. Stevenson also pointed out that the U.S. won favor with newly independent countries by favoring self-determination. Doing so could restrain extremists, he said. It was not essential that the U.S. and Britain vote together on all resolutions, especially when the resolution was extreme or of little consequence. Kennedy added that it was difficult for the United States to oppose a moderate resolution. The goodwill the country gained by supporting moderate resolutions might be ephemeral, the president conceded. Stevenson and, by extension, the United States, could not, however, dissipate their great prestige by voting against such resolutions.[35]

Over the remainder of the Kennedy administration, meetings of British and U.S. officials on colonial issues followed a pattern. The tenor of the meetings remained cordial. Officials from both countries could agree about supporting African leaders like Nyerere and the need for training more Africans for administrative and technical posts. At the same time, the British remained unhappy about U.S. votes in the United Nations. In December 1961, Home complained that the United States and others felt it necessary to support resolutions calling for rapid independence even though such resolutions would lead to a "belt of complete chaos across Africa." U.S. officials, for their part, remained uneasy about the pace of change in the British colonies and skeptical of British policies. As it became clear that Sierra Leone and the four East African colonies would gain their independence, U.S. anxieties came to focus on the Federation of Rhodesia and Nyasaland, especially on Southern Rhodesia, and on the High Commission Territories. In 1962, Harland Cleveland, assistant secretary for international organizations affairs, suggested that the U.N. might assume responsibility for the three High Commission Territories. In a December 1962 meeting in London, U.S. officials pushed the notion of offering educational opportunities to Southern Rhodesian nationalists once the government released them from detention. The British counseled caution.[36]

United Nations Issues

When the United Nations took up the question of target dates once again in 1961, the U.S. ended up supporting the British position. In April, the U.N. considered mandating the establishment of target dates for granting independence to African colonies. The measure took the form of an African amendment to a U.S. proposal regarding independence and development in Africa. The State Department and the U.S. delegation to the United Nations were unhappy when several African states proposed the amendment. The Bureau of International Organizations Affairs, however, viewed the amendment favorably. The Bureaus of European and African Affairs opposed it. Both organizations argued that the British were moving expeditiously and responsibly to move their African colonies to independence. Directing Britain to set target dates would disrupt a reasonable process. It would constitute unfair and unnecessary criticism of British policies. Both bureaus agreed that the only British colonies not on the path to independence, the High Commission territories, were not viable as independent states. The British delegation opposed the measure. To avoid being caught between the colonial and anti-colonial groups, the U.S. delegation pursued alternatives to the African proposal, settling on compromise language that would refer the question of target dates to the U.N. Fourth Committee. Washington favored the compromise language. The British refused to yield, however. Home insisted that Britain needed U.S. support on the issue. Washington instructed Stevenson to abstain on the entire resolution. Stevenson was to explain that the United States opposed blanket resolutions and believed that mandating target dates would impede progress toward independence.[37]

Later in 1961, the United States and Britain agreed to support a Nigerian proposal that directed that all dependent territories in Africa achieve independence by December 1, 1970. Staff in the Bureau of African Affairs still opposed target dates. The U.N. delegation's first thought was to postpone consideration of the measure to the next United Nations session. The British concluded that the measure was innocuous, since it applied only to Africa and did not single out specific territories. The Foreign Office saw the measure as a way to distance Britain from Portugal and its harsh repression of nationalist movements. The State Department decided that the Nigerian resolution offered an opportunity to undercut Russian attempts to exploit the colonialism issue. Moreover, the department anticipated that all dependent territories in Africa would have achieved independence or self-government by 1970.[38]

On other colonial issues, the Kennedy administration retained long-standing U.S. positions, most of which coincided with British views. During the Kennedy administration, the American view was that the United Nations could discuss individual dependent territories. The United States conceded that the U.N. had the authority to make recommendations about individual territories but the country's position was that doing so was unwise and counterproductive. Along with the other colonial powers, Britain opposed discussion of individual territories. The U.S. agreed with Britain that the United Nations should not hear petitioners from dependent territories, other than trust territories. The colonial powers need not allow U.N. committees to visit dependent territories.[39]

On substantive issues, the United Nations turned its attention away from colonialism and toward the fate of individual territories. In the case of Britain, Southern Rhodesia and the High Commission Territories drew the most attention. In dealing with both broad and specific colonial issues, the State Department's strategy and attitude remained much as it had been in the Eisenhower years. The U.S. aim was to create and maintain the broadest possible coalition, including its European allies and the more responsible African and Asian nations. The department's view was still that the United States should stay in the middle of the road. It should seek to blunt extreme proposals from the anti-colonial countries and it should reassure the colonial powers that differences on specific issues need not detract from friendly relations. The view from the middle of the road remained that nearly everyone else was unreasonable. The so-called Committee of Seventeen, later expanded to twenty-four, was responsible for implementing the 1960 United Nations Resolution on colonialism. The State Department thought the committee acted irresponsibly and provocatively. Strongly worded resolutions regarding Rhodesia and the High Commission Territories, the department complained, were likely to be counterproductive and would elicit only non-cooperation from Britain. The department toyed with the idea that a U.S. withdrawal from the committee might lead to Russia's withdrawal and produce a more productive atmosphere. At the same time, U.S. officials complained that the British needed to keep the United States better informed about its plans. More important, it should move more quickly to resolve the remaining colonial issues.[40]

In 1962, the department feared that the Committee of Seventeen would stake out a position on Zanzibar that would threaten U.S. interests. In early July, the U.N. delegation reported that the committee was about to discuss the situation in Zanzibar. The delegation thought that the Russians would push for early independence. They might also advocate an end to the emergency measures to halt the riots that followed the June 1961 elections and call for withdrawal of the U.S. satellite tracking station from Zanzibar. The delegation recommended that its first priority should be deleting references to the tracking station from any committee resolution. If the U.S. could not head off a resolution, the delegation proposed to push for a statement of minority views that would acknowledge Zanzibar's right to self-determination. The delegation warned that a committee resolution on Zanzibar would force the United States to choose between supporting Britain and retaining the confidence of the wider U.N. membership. Britain expected the United States to oppose resolutions that included recommendations regarding individual territories. The United States had promised to do so. The delegation believed that the U.S. could not persist in opposing such resolutions and expect to serve on the committee in the future.[41]

The delegation's fears proved excessive. The complexity of the Zanzibar situation provided the United States an escape. The Russians did not mention the tracking station in their statement. Committee members attempted to resolve the differences between the two principal Zanzibari political parties before drafting a final resolution, but failed to do so. Tanganyika and Ethiopia sided with the Afro-Shirazi Party, considered the "African" party. Arab countries backed the Zanzibar National Party, the alleged "Arab" party. The committee produced what U.S. officials considered an innocuous resolution.[42]

The Kennedy and Macmillan governments coexisted peacefully regarding colonial Africa. Their attitudes were compatible and their disagreements, as in the United Nations, followed familiar and acceptable patterns. In fact, the two governments' high-level policies and relationship reflected considerable continuity from the late 1950s. Nevertheless, in the Kennedy years, the principal energy in colonial policymaking no longer centered on broad statements and overarching goals in either Britain or the United States. The spotlight was now on individual territories and their transition to independence. Most decisions involved the timing of independence and considerations of territory-level politics.

19

West and East Africa, 1961–1963:
Carrying on Regardless

Once Macleod accelerated the pace of political change in colonial Africa, the British government found it hard to apply the brakes. Events in Tanganyika followed the preferred script. Timely political concessions seemed likely to produce a stable African nationalist government favorably disposed to Britain. In Kenya, Zanzibar, Uganda, and the Gambia, one or more ingredients seemed to be missing. In Uganda and Zanzibar, credible nationalist governments seemed out of reach. In Kenya, the British resisted turning power over to Kenyatta or abandoning the European settlers. Nevertheless, Macleod and his successors at the Colonial Office did not know how to slow progress toward independence.

As independence approached, the United States became more involved, looking for future allies and protecting its perceived interests. Despite the country's longstanding support for self-government, U.S. officials were often unhappy with events in British colonies. They doubted the wisdom of granting the Gambia independence and feared that Zanzibar's independence was premature. They worried about the activities of other countries in the region.

West Africa

Political change in Sierra Leone and the Gambia followed the pattern set by the Gold Coast and Nigeria. Successive constitutional changes gave Africans an increasing share of control. By the beginning of the Kennedy administration, the process in Sierra Leone was well advanced. The colony achieved its independence in April 1961 without much notice from U.S. officials in Washington or Africa. The Gambia did not attain self-government until 1965. Here, U.S. officials found themselves opposing independence.

The State Department representatives closest to the Gambia were in Dakar, in neighboring Senegal. The United States maintained a consulate and, after Senegal's independence in 1960, an embassy in Dakar. Although reporting about the Gambia was a low priority for the Dakar staff, reports from Dakar during 1961 and 1962 kept Washington informed about the situation.

Officials in the field told Washington that the Gambian nationalists wanted independence just as much as their larger neighbors. Nevertheless, British officials thought that the Gambia should form an association with Senegal. In April 1961, the Dakar embassy reported that senior British officials in Bathurst envisioned the Gambia as a province of Senegal, with international guarantees for the Gambia's existing language, schools, and legal system.

302

The embassy reported that most Gambians were not interested in merging with Senegal, however. They wanted only economic cooperation focused on currency and customs issues. The leaders of Gambia's nationalist parties were concentrating on self-government and independence. A constitutional conference in May 1961 did not take up the issue of relations with Senegal.[1]

U.S. officials also favored federation with Senegal rather than independence for Gambia. Assistant Secretary Williams thought that Gambia lacked the prerequisites for independent nationhood. Moreover, if the Gambia applied for U.N. membership, it would give more ammunition to the United Nations' domestic and foreign critics. Gambia would be one more tiny member of the world body. U.S. officials also thought that creating an independent Gambia would increase friction with Senegal, rather than decrease it. A 1962 Africa Bureau paper added the concern than an independent Gambia would separate the Casamance region from the rest of Senegal and increase separatist tendencies in the region. Furthermore, the Gambia was so poor that it would require regular infusions of financial aid from Britain and perhaps from the United States. A weak Gambia would invite meddling by Ghana and others. In 1962, the Dakar embassy assured Washington that the rival Gambian parties were downplaying relations with Senegal. Nevertheless, the embassy thought that the Gambian leaders would eventually recognize that association with Senegal and a status short of full independence was the correct course.

U.S. officials grew impatient with Britain's low-key attitude toward Gambia's future. In November 1961, Williams and his staff urged Foreign Office and Commonwealth Relations Office officials to hold a plebiscite in the Gambia to determine whether the population was willing to join Senegal. The British demurred, arguing that they would not hold a vote until they were sure of the outcome. The British response to repeated State Department inquiries about their plans was that Britain favored association with Senegal. Nonetheless, the British also argued that pressure on the Gambian leaders would be counterproductive. By the end of 1962, the Africa Bureau contemplated exerting pressure on the British. In late 1963, the issue of Gambia's future came before the United Nations. Washington directed the U.S. delegation to propose a resolution that affirmed the Gambia's right to self-determination and encouraged talks between the Gambia and Senegal about association.[2]

In the end, the Africa Bureau's worrying came to nothing. The Gambia became an independent state and member of the United Nations in 1965.

Tanganyika

As of January 1961, Tanganyika was moving rapidly towards independence. In a January 3, 1961, memorandum, Macleod characterized the conference scheduled for March in Dar es-Salaam as Tanganyika's "independence" conference. Macleod saw Tanganyika as a model of friendship, goodwill, and progress. Nyerere and TANU seemed capable of governing and opposing them seemed foolish. British officials were pleased that the Tanganyika nationalists were willing to retain key British civil servants and to have a British governor-general as head of state rather than a president. When Macleod departed for the March conference, the most important unresolved issue was the date for independence, late 1961, as Nyerere wanted, or early 1962. Macleod worried that the earlier date would send the wrong message to nationalists in Kenya and Uganda. In the end, the British decided that a few months were not worth the risks of a disagreement with Nyerere. They concluded that they were not strong enough to impose a solution and did not want to undermine Nyerere's position with his fellow nationalists. Tanganyika gained full self-government on May 15, 1961, and independence on December 9, 1961.[3]

Kenya

Sir Patrick Renison replaced Baring as governor of Kenya in October 1959, about the time Macleod replaced Lennox-Boyd as colonial secretary. In January 1961, Renison's presentation to a meeting of East African governors revealed the principal challenge the British faced in Kenya as they tried to manage the transition to independence. Renison thought that the British ought to stay in Kenya as long as they could. He hoped that consideration of an East African Federation, to include Kenya, Tanganyika, and Uganda, would buy the British some time. In Renison's view, progress toward independence ought to be slow enough so that the Africans would have sufficient time to solve the problems facing them. Renison thought that most nationalists, including Mboya, wanted to inherit a modern state with a developed economic structure and constructing one would take time. Unlike the extremists like Odinga, the moderates would cooperate with the British, Renison predicted. To secure the moderates' cooperation, however, the British would need to demonstrate that they were committed to granting Kenya independence. The logical conclusion seemed to be that the British needed to drag their feet in the manner of Lennox-Boyd while moving fast enough to retain the nationalists' confidence.

The Macmillan cabinet was inclined toward delay. Shortly after the East African governors' conference, the Cabinet Colonial Policy Committee concluded that Britain's withdrawal from Kenya could not be as fast as the Colonial Office envisioned. The committee thought that another eight to ten years of British rule was needed to train enough Africans to run the government. Leaving sooner would create another Congo, the committee thought. Britain was also considering spending considerable sums to expand its military bases in Kenya. Under the proposed plan, Kenya was to house a strategic reserve that Britain could deploy to protect its interests in the Middle East and elsewhere. A decision to proceed with the base expansion would make more sense if the cabinet knew that Britain would control Kenya for another decade.[4]

Macleod favored moving faster. He anticipated that KADU would win at least a third of the seats in the upcoming legislative council elections and that the chances of a KADU-KANU coalition government were good. He thought that Blundell and his New Kenya Party, the more cooperative Europeans, would also do well in the elections. The British, Macleod warned Macmillan, could not sustain a sound working relationship with a nationalist government, even a coalition government, if the British goal were to retain power for eight years. Kenyan nationalists could see that Tanganyika, Uganda, and Zanzibar were moving towards independence. They would think that Kenya was better prepared for independence than its East African neighbors and they would bristle at the idea that Kenya should move more slowly because 1 percent of its population was European. Moreover, the British could not keep their aims secret. Once the Kenyan nationalists learned that Britain was not prepared to yield power quickly, cooperation would break down, as it had in Cyprus under similar circumstances.[5]

Macleod argued that Home and other cabinet members who counseled delay were trying to reverse government policy. He told Macmillan that the other East African colonies were moving towards independence because of constitutional proposals generated within the colonies, not at the constitutional conferences Macleod had presided over. Macleod claimed that he had, in fact, pared back some proposals. Moreover, the cabinet had approved all of the constitutional changes. At the Kenya conference, Macleod maintained, he had ensured that Kenya would move at a slower pace than the other colonies, as slow as possible. Nevertheless, as slow as possible did not mean eight more years of British rule.[6]

Macleod remained optimistic about Britain's long-term prospects in Kenya. He asked the Ministry of Defense to continue work on the new bases in Kenya. Macleod thought that cutting back might signal that the British were about to leave and exacerbate Kenya's employment problems. Macleod added that there was a reasonable chance that British troops would remain in Kenya indefinitely, although their freedom of action might be restricted once Kenya became independent.[7]

Macleod's predictions about the Kenyan election and a coalition government proved largely correct. KADU won eleven seats while KANU won nineteen. KADU formed part of a coalition government, but with Blundell's New Kenya Party and the Kenya Indian Congress, not KANU. The coalition government was too narrow and weak to be the partner the British sought, however. It depended on the votes of members nominated by the governor for its council majority. In opposition remained KANU, winner of two-thirds of the vote and of seats in every region, and the most credible vehicle for Kenyan nationalism. KANU leaders were frustrated at being denied a leadership role. They relished the opportunity, however, to agitate against all their opponents at once, KADU, the British administration, and the most recent Kenyan constitution.[8]

KANU was a ramshackle political party. Its titular leader, James Gichuru, served because Kenyatta remained under house arrest. Control and direction from the center remained weak. The rivalry between Odinga and Mboya was only the most obvious and most important among many rivalries between ambitious politicians within the party. Regional and ethnic tensions also persisted. The British were tempted to imagine that a part of KANU, the moderates, might break away, and join KADU in a stronger coalition. KADU represented many of Kenya's smaller ethnic groups, fearful of domination by the Kikuyu and Luo who controlled KANU. The British tried to bolster KADU by favoring protection for minority rights, a federal constitution, and regional governments with considerable powers. Another way to attract more nationalists to KADU was, as Macleod pointed out to Renison in May 1961, to grant the KADU–led government rapid constitutional progress.[9]

Jomo Kenyatta

The other prize the British could offer was Kenyatta's release. In the middle 1950s, Kenyan nationalists avoided the subject of Kenyatta and his alleged role in the Kikuyu uprising. In 1958, things started to change. Odinga, followed by Mboya and others, began to refer to Kenyatta in public as a respected leader of Kenyan nationalism. Releasing Kenyatta became a nationalist demand, particularly for the most militant nationalists. At KANU's formation in 1960, its leaders signaled that they were ready to offer Kenyatta the party presidency as soon as he was free. In 1961, KANU refused to join the government as long as Kenyatta remained under house arrest.

Macleod and the Macmillan government balked at freeing the alleged architect of the

Kikuyu uprising. Freeing Kenyatta might jeopardize their support among the Conservatives most committed to the colonies. Nevertheless, government leaders ultimately recognized that freeing Kenyatta had to be part of a bargain with the nationalists. In 1959, Kenyatta finished serving his sentence, but the Kenyan government continued to hold him under house arrest. Renison proposed to refer to Kenyatta as the leader "to darkness and death," in a speech detailing the government's new security legislation. Macleod was appalled, not because he doubted Kenyatta's culpability, but because he anticipated that the British would have to negotiate with Kenyatta. Renison stood firm, threatening to resign if he could not make the speech as proposed and Macleod backed down. In April 1960, as the British contemplated releasing Hastings Banda from detention, Macleod assured Macmillan than he did not intend to release Kenyatta. Some day it might be possible to free him, perhaps to Ghana, Macleod told the prime minister. To reassure the Conservative faithful, Macleod told the House of Commons that the government would not release Kenyatta. He instructed Renison to issue a similar statement. By January 1961, agitation for Kenyatta's release was sufficient for Macleod to contemplate the possibility, however. He told Macmillan that the plan was to release Kenyatta in fifteen months or so, after a new Kenyan government and Kenyan chief minister were in place. By then, the press might have become bored with the subject. Nevertheless, important Conservatives remained opposed. Lord Swinton, a former commonwealth relations secretary, warned Home in April 1961 that Kenyatta's release would spark a revolt in Conservative ranks. Swinton added that he would be among the rebels. He said releasing Kenyatta was repugnant to decent-minded people. Macleod continued to believe that the government could delay a release. He characterized the notion of Kenyatta as chief minister as unthinkable. By summer, the pressure from Kenyan politicians and press, both European and African, was nearly irresistible. All parties and the major newspapers in Kenya called for freeing Kenyatta. The final blow was a message from Renison in July. Renison said that Kenyatta's character had not changed. He remained arrogant, dominating, and satanic. Nevertheless, if the government did not release Kenyatta, the KADU-led government would resign and Renison would be unable to form another. On August 14, the government released Kenyatta from house arrest.[10]

While trying to block Kenyatta's path to power, the British considered Mboya an acceptable alternative. Despite having bolstered moderates against the extremist Mboya, the British decided that Mboya was preferable to Kenyatta. Nevertheless, when approached by a senior British official, Mboya said that he would not join a government without Kenyatta if other Kenyan leaders would not.[11]

1962 Constitutional Conference

Kenyatta's release led to renewed demands from the nationalists, without producing a stable nationalist coalition. With Kenyatta in the chair, a meeting of the African members of the Kenyan assembly produced a list of demands: a constitutional conference in September, a coalition government, new elections, and independence in February 1962. Renison agreed to a constitutional conference, but said that February 1962 was too soon for independence if new elections were to take place. The subsequent conference proved acrimonious and broke down. KADU fastened on federalism as the best means to protect the interests of the smaller ethnic groups, but KANU refused to yield. In the course of the conference, KADU also repudiated Kenyatta's leadership and, in October, he accepted the KANU presidency.

The British worried that conflicts between nationalist parties would lead to violence and bloodshed. Concerns in Kenya were greater because the disputes among the nationalists took place against a background of unrest and economic stagnation. As nationalist pressure increased, Europeans and European-owned businesses appeared to be leaving Kenya and the economy slowed. Strikes broke out in Nairobi. Reports spread of renewed organizing among the poor and landless in the countryside. The principal organization active in the Kikuyu areas, the Kenya Land Freedom Army, opposed the government's efforts to assist wealthier African farmers. It also agitated for a more equitable division of land, to benefit the landless. The government proscribed the Kenya Land Freedom Army and sought to inhibit any links between it and the nationalist parties. At the same time, the government expanded its land settlement program to include more Africans, including some of the landless. The scheme was designed primarily, however, to transfer land from European owners to the more prosperous African farmers.

In November 1961, the British cabinet concluded that creating a constitution for an independent Kenya was the next step. Newly installed as colonial secretary, Maudling told the Colonial Policy Committee that Britain could attempt to maintain its control of Kenya by force or hold a conference to write a constitution that both KANU and KADU could accept. With Macmillan's support, Maudling argued for a new constitution leading to early independence. Deploying British troops, he said, would lead to another uprising and leave Britain worse off. It would expend great cost and effort to no effect. The lord chancellor, Lord Kilmuir, said that Kenya had two of the ingredients for successful independence: a viable economy and an independent judiciary. Perhaps, he wondered, a conference could produce the missing pieces: a workable form of parliamentary government and general stability. The cabinet was encouraged that KANU was willing to preserve the European-owned farms, the heart of the Kenyan economy. Nevertheless, the cabinet's mood was somber. Britain was unlikely to retain military bases in an independent Kenya, it concluded. The cabinet feared that the Europeans in Kenya would feel safe only if British troops or troops with British officers remained. A KANU-led government was unlikely, however, to retain British officers or officials as the TANU government in Tanganyika was prepared to do. Kenya had been slow to train African officers. If British officers left soon, the Kenya military would turn into an armed rabble, ministers worried. The cabinet thought that constitutional provisions, in the manner of the United States constitution, were the most likely protection for minority rights in Kenya. A federal constitution with substantial powers delegated to regions or Kenya's inclusion in an East African Federation might help. A ruthless and determined government might, however, simply tear up a constitution, the cabinet worried.[12]

With at least as much reluctance, the cabinet accepted that Kenyatta would become the leader of the Kenyan nationalists and of an independent Kenya. The immediate issue was allowing Kenyatta to become a member of the legislative council. Some argued that Kenyatta was an evil man who should be held responsible for the brutalities of the uprising. Kenya's Europeans would not trust any constitutional safeguards if Kenyatta were in charge, they argued. Britain should do nothing to help him become prime minister. On the other hand, Kenyatta was already head of the largest nationalist party. Other African leaders considered him the spokesman for Kenya's Africans. The conclusion was that Britain had little choice but to negotiate with the Kenyan nationalists to arrange a graceful exit.[13]

Early independence for Kenya made the cabinet nervous and it continued to look for alternatives. In December 1961, the cabinet noted that Nigeria was proposing in the United Nations a ten-year timetable for African independence. It asked Maudling to assess the risks of delaying Kenyan independence beyond 1963. In January, however, Maudling reminded the cabinet that retaining control of Kenya was impossible. The 1960 constitutional conference had made independence inevitable, he said. The best Britain could do was to head off chaos, civil war, and a relapse into tribalism. Britain could not expect that an independent Kenya would favor the West. Neutrality was the best hope. Maudling warned that any sign of British foot dragging would unite the Kenyan nationalists against Britain, stir up the extremists and their foreign supporters, and undermine Britain's basic objectives. On the eve of the constitutional conference in February, the cabinet concluded that early independence for Kenya would be dangerous in the extreme. Perhaps, independence could be delayed by as much as five years. Perhaps, ministers wondered, Kenya could operate under trusteeship while it prepared for independence.[14]

Working with Kenyatta remained repugnant for the cabinet. When Maudling visited Kenya in November 1961, he avoided having photographs taken that might suggest that he and Kenyatta were cooperating. Once the Kenyan constitutional conference began in February 1962, the cabinet accepted that a coalition government including both KANU and KADU was a key objective. It balked at including Kenyatta, however. Some in the cabinet argued that Kenyatta was untrustworthy. Helping him gain a position of responsibility would be both unprincipled and dangerous, some complained. Nevertheless, the cabinet recognized that excluding Kenyatta from a new Kenyan government would be difficult. It comforted itself that Kenyatta would have fewer opportunities to cause problems within a coalition. The cabinet returned to the notion of realignment within the Kenyan nationalists. Perhaps attempts at a grand coalition would falter, KANU would lose influence, and its moderate elements would join KADU in government.[15]

In the end, the 1962 constitutional conference produced a grand coalition and the framework for an independence constitution. KANU and KADU remained at odds. KADU continued to look for constitutional safeguards. KANU made concessions, believing that independence was the real goal and that constitutions could be changed. Kenyatta played a key role in achieving agreement. In a crucial meeting, he told the KANU delegation that they could not return to Kenya without a success.[16]

Malcolm MacDonald

After the 1962 conference, Kenya was on the path to independence. In January 1963, Sandys, Maudling's replacement as colonial secretary, named Malcolm MacDonald, the former colonial secretary, to replace Renison as governor. MacDonald was a politician sympathetic to nationalism and his task was to manage the final transition to independence. In April, the government published the new Kenya constitution, at 248 pages the most complex constitution for a British African colony. In May, elections produced a majority for KANU, eighty-three seats to KADU's forty-one. In June, Kenya became self-governing, gaining control of its internal affairs. In September, a final constitution conference took place in London. The Kenyan parties settled the issues left unresolved in 1962, including the powers of the new regions and procedures for amending the constitution. On December 12, 1963, Kenya gained its independence.

As Kenya progressed through the last eighteen months of colonial rule, British leaders still hoped that they could slow the process. During the 1962 conference, Maudling told Conservative colleagues that he thought that the period between self-government and independence should be long. Nevertheless, the suggestion had to come from the Kenyans not from the British, the colonial secretary said. When Sandys sent MacDonald to Kenya in January 1963, the hope was that independence might not come for another two years. Mac-Donald's tasks were to improve relations with the Kenyan politicians, ensure that they, not the British, were blamed for any delays, and identify the eventual winner in the struggle for power among the Kenyan leaders, Mboya or Kenyatta. In February, Sandys was thinking about a period of self-government long enough to train Africans for senior civil service positions. When Sandys and MacDonald described the situation to the U.S. consul in Nairobi in February, they spoke as if the onus were on the Kenyans to produce a workable government.[17]

Nevertheless, by June, Macdonald advised Sandys that further delay was unwise. The British still thought an East African Federation was a possibility. MacDonald told Sandys that granting Kenya independence would make federation more likely. Unrest among the smaller ethnic groups and among the landless Kikuyu also influenced MacDonald's thinking.[18]

Not a Pretty Scene

By 1961, the State Department assumed that Kenya would soon become independent, probably no later than early 1963. The British were committed to independence, according to the Nairobi consulate, and the Kenyan nationalists were intent on independence. British and Kenyan leaders both feared that delay would lead to disturbances and to economic stagnation. Kenya's neighbors, Uganda and Tanganyika, would soon be independent. U.S. officials in Nairobi believed that the British were intent on creating an East African federation. The British would try to resolve any issues in Kenya before independence, the consulate predicted, but they might "sweep some under the rug" rather than delay independence and federation unduly.[19]

U.S. officials were far from optimistic about Kenya's prospects, however. They anticipated that in-fighting between KADU and KANU would be intense. According to the Nairobi consulate, Kenya was beset by drought, flood, famine, unemployment, political frustration, fear, distrust, and economic stagnation in the capital sector. It was not a pretty scene, Nairobi told Washington. The only ray of hope was that 180-degree turns were common in Kenyan affairs. Consulate officials considered the dispute about Kenyatta's continued imprisonment particularly serious. They thought that Governor Renison would resist concessions for fear that the Kenyan nationalists would ask for more. Nevertheless, U.S. officials also worried that if KANU failed to secure Kenyatta's release, its moderate faction would lose out to extremists allied to the leaders of Kikuyu uprising.[20]

In early 1962, U.S. officials turned their attention to the composition of a Kenyan government. Like British officials, the Nairobi consulate focused on real and potential fractures within KANU. It thought that a coalition of KADU and the KANU moderates could gain popular support and provide Kenya with a stable government. Officials in the Bureau of African Affairs disagreed. They doubted that a coalition of moderates would retain support among the Kikuyu. The KANU moderates would have more influence within KANU than they would allied with KADU or isolated in opposition. Moreover, a rump KANU dominated by extremists would be dangerous. It might even be able to command a majority in a national election. One analysis included Kenyatta among the KANU moderates. Another put him in the extremist faction. Both preferred him as part of a broad KANU, including both moderates and extremists. The department in Washington felt strongly enough about keeping KANU intact that it instructed the Nairobi consulate to use its influence to keep KANU moderates within the party. The department also told the London embassy to warn the British against trying to split KANU or excluding Kenyatta from a moderate government.[21]

The Nairobi consulate replied that its ability to influence events was limited, aside from encouraging Kenyatta to cooperate with the moderates. Regardless of the consulate's modesty, the State Department now thought of itself as a player in Kenyan affairs rather than a bystander. In May 1961, the consulate fretted about the impact the announcement of the latest U.S. aid to Kenya might have on Kenyan politics and the American image. An announcement when KADU was taking control might prompt KANU to accuse the United States of conspiring with the British to install a stooge minority government. Nevertheless, the department thought that the KADU government seemed a step in the right direction. Announcing U.S. aid might persuade the Kenyan populace that the new government could be effective. Amidst preparations for the 1962 constitutional conference, the State Department thought the U.S. could play a role in drafting a new constitution. The State Department floated the idea that an American serve as an adviser to the Kenyan delegation, as Thurgood Marshall had during the 1960 conference. The department worried that it could not ask a prominent American judge or scholar to go to Kenya unless the Kenyans were prepared to use his services. It asked the consulate to consult with Kenyan leaders and British officials.[22]

Tom Mboya

The department thought that Marshall should not serve as an adviser again. His close ties with Mboya had created problems for Mboya and the United States. Odinga and other of Mboya's rivals already complained that the United States was meddling in Kenya affairs and that Mboya was beholden to the U.S. Richard Freund, the consul in Nairobi, was sufficiently concerned about Mboya's well-publicized support in the United States that he asked the State Department to intervene with the U.S. media. Freund wanted the Department to ask key editors and correspondents to downplay American support for Mboya. It would be better, Freund wrote, if U.S. aid to Kenya including aid from private organizations was not associated with a specific Kenyan leader. Freund said he was not trying to hurt Mboya, but trying to ensure that the United States was seen as impartial. In April, Assistant Secretary Williams recommended to Secretary Rusk that the White House offer Mboya no preferential treatment when he visited the United States. Williams recommended that the White House should treat Mboya the same way it treated the other African leaders — Banda, Kaunda, and Nkomo — scheduled to visit Washington.[23]

The department still considered Mboya a useful ally. In June 1961, Washington told the Nairobi consulate that it regretted that Mboya's strained relations with other Kenyan leaders meant that he could become isolated politically. The department thought that Mboya had undoubted ability and knowledge of world affairs. Moreover, he had adopted positions within Pan African labor organizations that were helpful to the United States. Washington asked that the consulate keep it informed about Mboya's fortunes in Kenyan politics. It expressed the hope that Mboya's domestic base would remain strong enough to allow him to remain active in international labor affairs. A year later, Williams laid out a bigger role for Mboya. While on an African tour, Williams told Washington that an independent Kenya needed Mboya as its leader and he claimed that the British agreed. Williams imagined that Kenyatta would serve in an Mboya government. Almost all observers thought Mboya was the best choice for Kenya's leader, Williams contended, although, Williams conceded, not everyone thought he would rise to the top. As late of November 1962, Freund was on record that the U.S. preference for a Kenyan government was a broad coalition headed by Mboya and including Kenyatta.[24]

Kenyatta and the United States

In mid–1961, the Nairobi consulate was not sure what to think or do about Kenyatta. In June 1961, it relayed reports that prominent European politicians thought Kenyatta was a man of reasonable views. Freund conceded that Kenyatta's recent statements were reassuring. He added, however, that he planned to reserve judgment whether Kenyatta would be a force for good or evil. The same month, Freund proposed that the several consuls in Nairobi visit Kenyatta as a group. Kenyatta was under house arrest, but the British were allowing visitors. Freund thought he should not visit Kenyatta on his own and worried that any visit would give Kenyatta more prominence than he deserved. The department reassured him that it had no objection to a visit if the Kenyan authorities approved.[25]

The London embassy shared Freund's concerns about a visit. It reported that the Colonial Office thought a visit would unwisely boost Kenyatta's prestige. According to the Colonial Office, the embassy reported, other Kenyan politicians spoke disparagingly of Kenyatta in private. Providing Kenyatta with more publicity would create problems for the Kenyan leaders who were cooperating with the British, the embassy warned. British officials in London conceded that they would defer to the judgment of Governor Renison. The embassy worried that a visit by the U.S. consul, even in the company of consuls from other nations, would complicate Kenya's delicate politics. The consulate should not reveal its plans until the Kenyan government had approved.[26]

Between Kenyatta's release in August and the end of the year, the consulate focused on Kenyatta, but remained dubious about his impact on Kenya. Among Kenyatta's visitors were Carl Rosberg and Thomas Franck, two scholars studying Kenyan politics. Based on a conversation with the two political scientists, the consulate concluded that Kenyatta was likely to be a front man for other Kenyan leaders or organizations. The consulate referred to the view that Kenyatta had served as a front for the leaders of the Kikuyu uprising. It worried that he might do the same for the militant Kenyan Land Freedom Army. Nevertheless, the consulate thought that Kenyatta was proving less a leader and unifier than some had hoped. He failed to resolve the differences between KADU and KANU and had increased the smaller ethnic groups' apprehensions about domination by the Kikuyu and Luo. Kenyatta's comments about preserving European enterprises in Kenya and about the possibility of an East African Federation were welcome. Nevertheless, the consulate contended that he had not revealed his thinking on fundamental political, economic, or foreign policy issues. By November, the consulate concluded that Kenyatta would be Kenya's first African prime minister. It told Washington that it still worried about an independent Kenya with Kenyatta in charge.[27]

The consulate was sufficiently convinced of Kenyatta'a future importance that it tried to explain away United States support for Mboya when Kenyatta raised the issue. During a January 1962 meeting with the consul, Kenyatta referred to American financial support for Mboya. The consul assured Kenyatta that the United States favored independent African states free of outside interference. The consul said that Mboya, to his credit, had gained the support of many in the U.S. Mboya's opponents in Kenya had used this against him, however, and alleged that the U.S. government favored Mboya. The consul contended that such allegations were unwarranted. The United States found them "distasteful." The consul reported favorably Kenyatta's wish that all aid, including scholarships to American colleges, be directed to the Kenyan government.[28]

By February, the Bureau of African Affairs thought that Kenyatta was the key to Kenyan politics. A Kenyatta-led KANU dominated by extremists might win a majority in the Kenyan elections, the bureau feared. In opposition, an extreme KANU would make life difficult for a coalition government. If Kenyatta supported the moderates within KANU, however, a reasonable, responsible, and popular government in Kenya might be possible. Kenyatta might be persuaded, the bureau thought, to settle for the trappings of power, rather than the substance, within a moderate government.[29]

The State Department eventually decided that it would be helpful if a private organization invited Kenyatta to the United States after the constitutional conference in London. In August 1961, the department heard a rumor that the American Committee on Africa planned to bring Kenyatta to the United States. At that point, the department agreed with the British that Kenyatta should not be invited. It hesitated to contact the committee, however, because doing so might generate adverse publicity and the committee was unlikely to heed the department's advice. Six months later, the department thought a well-publicized trip to the U.S. by Kenyatta might be in order, provided Kenyatta demonstrated suitably moderate views during the conference. When David Bruce, the ambassador in London, reported that Kenyatta wanted to meet him during the conference, Bruce and the department saw an opportunity to push Kenyatta towards moderation. At a meeting, Bruce could express the U.S. preference for a moderate KANU and offer a U.S. visit as an inducement. Bruce feared that unwillingness to arrange a visit for Kenyatta would signal that the United States preferred Mboya and it might drive Kenyatta to seek help elsewhere. Freund thought the department underestimated Kenyatta's sophistication and sensitivity about foreign interference. He also thought that it overestimated the ability of both Britain and the U.S. to influence the conference's outcome. He recommended that Bruce meet with Kenyatta, make the American views clear, but profess ignorance of any invitation to the United States.[30]

The proposed visit proved a false alarm. Throughout March, the department, the embassy, and the consulate traded telegrams about what Bruce should say to Kenyatta about an invitation. The department approached the African-American Institute, a group that received financial support from the Central Intelligence Agency, about scheduling a trip. Kenyatta's representatives asked that the meeting be delayed and it did not occur until March 29, when the conference was underway. At the meeting, Bruce complimented Kenyatta on his reasonableness. Kenyatta replied that KANU had come to London prepared to compromise and denied that KANU had any splits. The principal reason for the meeting, Kenyatta said, was to thank the United States for its support for Kenyan education and to express the hope that such aid would continue. Kenyatta did not mention a trip to the U.S.[31]

Bruce told Washington that Kenyatta made a favorable impression. Bruce had heard rumors the Kenyatta was senile and an alcoholic. The Kenyan leader seemed, however, in good physical and mental condition. His conversation was logical, coherent, and forceful. Bruce noted that Kenyatta drank only Coca-Cola during their meeting.[32]

After the constitutional conference and the creation of a KANU-KADU coalition, the path to independence seemed clear. Nevertheless, U.S. officials grew impatient while worrying about possible unrest. In September 1962, Freund told Washington that he was confident that the British realized that rapid progress was essential. Freund wrote that he doubted that the British could organize elections and install a new government in time for independence in 1963. The United States might have to put pressure on Britain, he warned. U.S. officials appear not to have been privy to British thinking about Kenya. In November, the Office of Eastern and Southern African Affairs speculated that the British were delaying independence to provoke another Kikuyu uprising that they could quash before handing power to the Kenyans.[33]

Uganda

In Uganda, the Democratic Party formed a government after the March 1961 legislative council elections. Before the elections, the Buganda government continued to resist direct elections to the legislative council. It wanted the Buganda assembly, the lukiko, to select Buganda's representatives. With great success, the Buganda government urged the kingdom's potential voters not to register or to vote. Eventually the kabaka realized that discouraging potential voters loyal to him would allow the Democratic Party to triumph and he sought an alliance with Obote and the Uganda People's Congress. Obote told him it was too late. On a low voter turnout in Buganda, the Democratic Party won twenty of the twenty-one Buganda seats and forty-three seats overall. The Uganda's People's Congress gained thirty-five and independents thirteen. The Democratic Party gained support from enough independents to form a majority and Kiwanuka presided over the new government as chief minister.[34]

By the end of 1961, the kabaka and the Buganda government corrected their mistake and positioned themselves to contest future elections. In June, large numbers of Buganda commoners gathered outside Kampala to protest the results of the March elections. That Kiwanuka, a Catholic commoner, now held a higher position than the Protestant kabaka, offended Bugandan sensibilities. The demonstrations continued for several days. Their slogan was "Kabaka Yekka" or "the kabaka alone." The protests represented a continuation of the rural discontent that had characterized Buganda since World War II. Buganda officials loyal to the kabaka may have offered covert encouragement in March. By November the relationship between the protest movement and the Buganda government was strong and overt. The protest movement evolved into a political party, Kabaka Yekka, headed by the kabaka's chief minister.[35]

1961 Conference

When the Uganda constitutional conference convened in London in October 1961, Macleod told the delegates that they faced a daunting task. To reach consensus, they would have to clear many hurdles and solve many riddles. Prominent among the riddles was the place of Buganda and the other kingdoms within Uganda. A commission headed by the

Earl of Munster had recommended a form of federalism for Uganda. Under the Munster proposals, Buganda would have a separate status, the other three kingdoms some separate powers. The Munster proposals did not satisfy Buganda's delegates, however. They wanted the federal arrangement to include Buganda's representatives to the national assembly. In particular, they wanted the lukiko to appoint Buganda's representatives and they wanted the lukiko to do so immediately, replacing the Democratic Party representatives with members loyal to the kabaka. The Democratic Party delegates, for their part, favored a unified Uganda and direct elections to the national assembly. Although Obote and his Uganda's People's Congress were probably unenthusiastic about a federal Uganda, Obote struck a deal with the kabaka before the conference. The Uganda People's Congress would concede many of Buganda's demands in exchange for support.[36]

After much wrangling, the conference produced a settlement that seemed to give the principal players some of what they sought. Buganda gained a major concession. The lukiko would select Buganda's representatives to the national assembly, but only after direct elections to the lukiko itself. Uganda would become independent in October 1962. Kiwanuka and the Democratic Party had campaigned for early independence in the face of opposition from Buganda and the other kingdoms. Obote argued that the constitutional conference could not adjourn without setting a date for independence. Uganda would also hold elections to the national assembly after it became self-governing in March 1962, but before it became independent in October. Assuming an electoral alliance between Kabaka Yekka and the Uganda People's Congress, the way was now open for the congress to form the first independent government and for Obote to be the first prime minister of Uganda.

Kiwanuka and the Democratic Party thought that Macleod had been hasty and less than honest in his management of the conference. When the delegates disagreed about Buganda's demands, Macleod began to meet separately with the Buganda delegation. When delegates objected, Macleod assured them that nothing would be decided behind their backs. When the conference considered how Buganda should select its representatives to the national assembly, a majority of delegates opposed indirect elections by the lukiko. Macleod said that the final decision was his and that the British government was inclined to accept Buganda's demands. Kiwanuka and his delegates then walked out of the conference. After Macleod assured Kiwanuka that nothing had been decided and that the conference would reconsider the issue, Kiwanuka agreed to return. The Democratic Party contingent was shocked, however, when Macleod later announced that he and the kabaka had reached an agreement that included indirect elections from Buganda to the national assembly. Before the conference's end, Macleod knew that Macmillan was about to announce a cabinet reshuffle that would move Macleod out of the Colonial Office. The conference's last session consisted almost entirely of a speech by Macleod. He announced that he and the kabaka had reached an agreement. He said that new elections would take place before the new constitution took effect. Bowing to Obote's persistent demands, Macleod also announced that Uganda would become independent in a year's time. Having advocated early independence, Kiwanuka could not object.[37]

Uganda People's Congress Government

Although another conference in June 1962 left some issues unresolved, Uganda moved to independence under a Uganda People's Congress government. The Buganda government urged its inhabitants to register to vote and Kabaka Yekka swept the board in the elections to the lukiko, winning sixty-three seats to the Democratic Party's three. The Uganda People's Congress declined to participate for fear of offending the Buganda government. In the April 1962 elections to the national assembly, the Congress won thirty-seven seats, the Democratic Party twenty-four, and independents nine. The lukiko selected Kabaka Yekka members to the twenty-one seats allocated to Buganda. The Congress and Kabaka Yekka combined to control the assembly and form a government with Obote as prime minister.[38]

Building Ties

U.S. activities in Uganda in the Kennedy administration focused on building ties with local leaders. Arranging visits to the United States remained an important tool. At the invitation of the State Department, Kiwanuka visited the United States after the London constitutional conference. He met with Rusk and Kennedy and made a brief speech before the United Nations Trusteeship Council. The U.S. consul in Kampala also asked Obote about visiting the United States. Obote replied that the press of business prevented him from making the trip after the London conference. As leader of the opposition, he would not have received the same treatment in Washington that Kiwanuka had. Obote promised to consider a trip to Washington after the April 1962 elections, when he would be either prime minister or leader of the opposition.[39]

Financial aid was another means for U.S. officials to court Ugandan leaders, but it was in shorter supply than plane tickets to Washington. Kiwanuka was disappointed that he failed to secure significant commitments from the International Bank for Reconstruction and Development or Agency for International Development, the latest incarnation of the U.S. aid agency. The absence of any U.S. aid also provoked criticism and controversy in Uganda. Hendrik van Oss, the U.S. consul, suggested that a high-level official in Washington issue a clarifying statement. The consul was already on record advocating more U.S. aid to Uganda. In March 1961, he argued that Uganda's being a British dependency without a date fixed for independence was no reason to restrict aid. Aid now would build good relations and avoid a pre-independence rush. Waiting until the eve of independence might suggest that the United States sought to replace the British.[40]

When the U.S. was ready to provide aid to Uganda, officials worried about how to manage the announcement. In early 1962, the London embassy suggested that it brief the Colonial Office about U.S. plans to send aid to Uganda, but the consul in Kampala disagreed. British officials in Uganda were in close touch with London, the consul maintained. The Colonial Office knew about the U.S. plans. Van Oss argued that minimizing discussions with British officials in Kampala and London would lessen the risk that U.S. aid would be caught up in negotiations about the final steps towards independence.[41]

Once the United States emerged as a possible source of aid, the consulate could not avoid becoming caught up in Uganda politics. In January 1961, the kabaka approached the consul about providing aid to Buganda. The department had decided that unity was preferable to fragmentation in African states approaching independence, the consul responded. The United States did not want to encourage Bugandan separatism and the British and Buganda should be left to resolve the issue. The consul also told the kabaka that all U.S. aid went through the Ugandan government and the Colonial Office. Since the consul thought that the kabaka would remain a force in Uganda politics after the British left, he pointed out that the kabaka could seek aid from private organizations in the United States. He added that the consulate was always interested in learning the kabaka's views on aid issues.[42]

The kabaka's inquiry sparked correspondence that revealed the complications inherent in U.S. efforts to ingratiate itself with all players in Uganda. The London embassy asked if it could tell the Colonial Office about the consulate's conversation with the kabaka. The department said that the embassy could inform the Colonial Office and the consulate could tell Governor Crawford. Van Oss objected, however. He kept Crawford informed about all his contacts, he said. He did not want Crawford and the Colonial Office comparing notes. The department assured Van Oss that it had told British officials in general terms about the kabaka's request. The London embassy added that Colonial Office was not troubled by the news. Staff there seemed aware of the kabaka's operating methods. Van Oss was still not happy. He complained to a colleague in the Bureau of African Affairs that the London embassy needed to understand that he shared the gist of all important conversations with senior British officials. Maintaining close relations with the British was important, he realized. In any case, the British intelligence network always knew what he was doing. Van Oss was especially concerned about his relations with Ugandan leaders. They would not be pleased to learn that U.S. officials shared with the Colonial Office and the Uganda government all their interactions with the Kampala consulate.[43]

Zanzibar

Elections in Zanzibar in January and June 1961 failed to produce the conditions the British thought necessary for continued progress towards self-government and independence. In the January election, no party gained a majority in the legislative council. The Afro-Shirazi Party won ten seats. The Zanzibar National Party won nine seats. The Zanzibar and Pemba Peoples Party, a breakaway faction of the Afro-Shirazi Party with strong support on Pemba Island, won three seats. Two members of the Zanzibar and Pemba Peoples Party supported the Zanzibar National Party and one the Afro-Shirazi Party, leaving the council evenly split. The two major parties agreed to form a caretaker government for six months with a British official, the civil secretary, serving as chief minister. The June elections produced a majority government, but precipitated serious riots. Before the election, the Zanzibar National Party and the Zanzibar and Pemba Peoples Party agreed not to oppose each other. The voting revealed a split electorate. Both the Zanzibar National Party and the Afro-Shirazi Party gained ten seats. The three seats won by the Zanzibar and Pemba Peoples Party allowed it to join with the Zanzibar National Party to form a government. On election day, June 1, fighting between members of the two major parties broke out in Zanzibar Town. The following day violence spread to the countryside. Bands of Africans attacked Arab traders and shopkeepers. The police restored order by June 8 after reinforcements arrived from Kenya and the Middle East. The official toll was sixty-eight killed, 381 injured and over a thousand arrested.[44]

Macleod had no easy answer for the situation in Zanzibar. Before the election, he expressed confidence that the British could deal with any problems Zanzibar might pose. During an April visit to Zanzibar, however, he told the press that he could not announce a date for independence. Citing the Congo, he warned against premature constitutional changes. In July, Macleod could offer the Cabinet Colonial Policy Committee only a description of the problem. He told them that the long-term task was establishing a stable government capable of maintaining law and order. The riots, he wrote, reflected a struggle between the extreme elements in both major parties. The Zanzibar National Party looked to Cairo, Peking, and Moscow for support, he claimed. The Afro-Shirazi Party feared Arab domination and envisioned ties to mainland Africa. An Afro-Shirazi Party government might serve British interests, Macleod thought, and it would be more amenable to an East African Federation. The African population that the Afro-Shirazi Party represented, however, lacked the skills to govern. The party would also find itself at odds with the Arab-dominated civil service and with the sultan. The Arab population that provided the leadership of the Zanzibar National Party was more capable, Macleod thought, but was too small to maintain control. It needed electoral support from Zanzibaris who identified themselves as Shirazi or African. Macleod took comfort from the thought that seeking broader support had caused the Zanzibar National Party to moderate its appeals.[45]

The British concluded that a coalition government involving the two major parties was the best next step, but the British remained undecided about how quickly Zanzibar should move towards independence. Sir George Mooring, the British resident in Zanzibar, argued that the divisions in Zanzibar society between Arabs and Africans and between large landowners and farm workers precluded a majority government. The social and ethnic divisions raised the risk that elections would produce more violence. Mooring proposed that the British promote a coalition government and not hold new elections before granting independence. Mooring contemplated delaying independence, perhaps until mid–1964. Nevertheless, he did not encourage Maudling when the colonial secretary suggested prolonging British rule indefinitely. Mooring told Maudling that the British could maintain control with a battalion of troops and increased funds for development. The resident added that Zanzibar lacked space to house the troops and reinforcements would need to be readily available. Moreover, Mooring said, a continued stay would not be a happy one. The Afro-Shirazi Party would not object to British control, but the militants in the Zanzibar National Party would.[46]

A constitutional conference in London in March and April 1962 failed to produce a coalition or agreement on steps towards independence. Before the conference, the Afro-Shirazi Party abandoned its longstanding preference for gradual political progress and came out for immediate independence. Otherwise, it disagreed with the Zanzibar National Party on the key issues. The Afro-Shirazi Party apparently believed that it could command majority support within Zanzibar. It wanted an enlarged assembly, an expanded electorate, and elections before independence. The Zanzibar National Party refused to yield. The Afro-Shirazi Party also refused the Zanzibar National Party's offer of three ministries within a coalition and veto power over cabinet decisions. Maudling agreed to lower voter qualifications and increase the size of the assembly. In addition, he attempted to make a coalition the price of further political change, but the Zanzibaris could not reach an agreement. The conference ended with an announcement that independence was still the goal, but the dates for internal self-government and independence remained unknown.[47]

After the conference, the British moved to suppress the most militant elements of the Zanzibar National Party, those with the most obvious ties to China and Russia. The Zanzibar government banned a militant organization within the party, called the Action Group of Youth's Own Union. The government alleged that the group planned to set fire to public buildings. The government also raided the homes of Muhammad Babu, the general secretary of the Zanzibar National Party, and his closest associates. Furthermore, it claimed to have found a bag containing Molotov cocktails and other explosives outside the Zanzibar Central

Post Office. In June 1962, Babu was convicted of publishing seditious materials in the party newspaper and sentenced to fifteen months in jail. In 1963, Babu and his followers broke with the party and formed the Umma Party.[48]

Sidelining the militants did not produce an agreement among the Zanzibari parties and the British quickly ran out of time. In spring 1963, Sandys traveled to Zanzibar and met with the sultan, government ministers, and party leaders. Failing to gain any agreement, he announced his own plan. His thinking was that Britain could not retain control of Zanzibar once it had granted independence to Kenya. The political pressure to grant independence would be intense and Britain would no longer have troops nearby with which to maintain order on the island. Sandys announced that progress towards independence would be resumed. Zanzibar would gain internal self-government in June and would hold elections for the assembly in July. After the elections, the British government would make a decision regarding independence. Sandys's principal condition was that law and order be maintained during the transition to independence. In the elections, the Afro-Shirazi Party won a majority of the vote, but only thirteen seats out of thirty-one. The Zanzibar and Pemba Peoples Party won all six seats from Pemba and joined with the Zanzibar National Party, the winner of twelve seats, to form a government. A brief conference in London in September produced an agreement on constitutional changes and the date for independence. On December 10, 1963, Zanzibar became independent.[49]

Protecting United States Assets

The Project Mercury tracking station remained one of the prime interests of the U.S. in Zanzibar. The Dar es Salaam consulate expressed satisfaction that the station was not an issue in the January 1961 elections. When riots broke out after the June 1961 elections, the State Department sought assurances from the Foreign Office that British forces would protect the station and its personnel. When, the same month, Washington dispatched a consul to Zanzibar, the London Embassy suggested that he stop in London to consult with British officials about the Mercury station. In February 1963, the Office of Eastern and Southern African Affairs drew up an action plan for Zanzibar. Securing the unhampered functioning of the station was one of its short-term goals and the subject of its first four action steps.[50]

Concern about the station intensified U.S. worries about other countries' influence in Zanzibar. Officials speculated whether the Zanzibar National Party's criticism of the station reflected the support the party received from China. Russian and Chinese influence in Zanzibar was among the State Department's prime worries. In 1961, the Dar es Salaam consulate believed that the Zanzibar government underestimated communist infiltration in Zanzibar. The first U.S. consul in Zanzibar, Frederick Picard, worried that Russia was cultivating the Afro-Shirazi Party. Zanzibar might become independent with both major parties under communist influence, he thought. The February 1963 action plan had reducing communist penetration in Zanzibar as its first objective, followed by establishment of a government capable of withstanding communist pressure and diminishing "racial" hatred. U.S. officials also expressed concern about possible Egyptian influence on Zanzibar's Arab population and about the Afro-Shirazi Party's links with Ghana. When the Afro-Shirazi Party opted for swift movement towards independence and commonwealth membership, U.S. officials attributed the shift to Ghanaian advice.[51]

U.S. efforts to compete with other countries for influence in Zanzibar resembled similar efforts in other British African colonies. U.S. officials tracked foreign assistance to prominent Zanzibari politicians. They believed that Muhammad Babu, the number two official in the Zanzibar National Party, received aid from China and was sympathetic to Chinese interests. They also believed that Ali Mushin, another Zanzibar National Party leader, received some financial assistance from the Chinese, but U.S. officials thought Mushin was an opportunist, willing to take money from anyone. U.S. officials cultivated personal relationships with Zanzibari leaders, provided grants for travel to the United States, and offered scholarships to Zanzibari students. Other American financial aid to Zanzibar was limited, however. It consisted mainly of $350,000 for a teacher training college. The U.S. position remained that financial aid to Zanzibar was a British responsibility.[52]

The U.S. consul's efforts to cultivate friends caused him to be identified with the opposition, the Afro-Shirazi Party and the connection embarrassed the consul. In October 1961, Picard attended a reception given by the Afro-Shirazi Party for a visiting Ghanaian dignitary. When Zanzibar National Party leaders arrived, they found Picard sitting in the front row with the Afro-Shirazi Party leaders. Picard told Washington that he felt like a new boy in town trying to court two girls and being embarrassed when the girl he likes invites the other girl to join them on the front porch. The following February, the British resident visited Picard to transmit complaints from Zanzibari ministers. The ministers had alleged that the United States was working against the Zanzibar National Party and the Zanzibar and Pemba Peoples Party. Picard disowned any intention to favor any one party. He claimed that his primary contacts were with the duly constituted government. He had, he claimed, kept the appropriate government officials informed of the consulate's activities.[53]

After the failure of the April 1962 constitutional conference, the Office of Eastern and Southern Affairs put forward a novel proposal, one that went beyond normal State Department practice in Britain's African colonies, or at least beyond what State Department officials normally committed to paper. The office thought that the conference's failure would strengthen extremists in both major parties and could lead to more violence. The British were better prepared to deal with unrest than before. Nevertheless, the office thought the United States needed to step up its efforts to counter communist infiltration. The office recommended that the consul have access to $10,000–15,000 in Central Intelligence Agency funds with which to advance U.S. interests. A CIA official would be readily detected in Zanzibar, however. A NASA employee, from the Project Mercury station, would lack the appropriate political judgment, contacts, and physical facilities. The consul, on the other hand, was an excellent and imaginative officer. As a safeguard, prior department approval could be required for all but certain specified types of expenditures. The available documents do not indicate whether the department accepted the recommendation. A marginal notation indicates that a senior official insisted that all expenditures be handled through normal channels.[54]

The failure to construct a coalition government and the continuing threat of violence caused the State Department to favor delaying Zanzibar's independence. The State Department professed confidence in Britain's ability to manage affairs in Zanzibar. Officials in Washington thought that Britain had learned from the 1961 riots and had sufficient forces in Zanzibar to maintain order by mid–1962. Like the British, U.S. officials favored a coalition government. In 1961, they preferred a combination of the Afro-Shirazi Party and the Zanzibar and Pemba People's Party. A coalition dominated by the Afro-Shirazi Party would favor an East African Federation and be more accepting of the Project Mercury station. By April 1962, however, U.S. officials thought a coalition unlikely. They still worried about violence on the islands. They thought that both Arabs and Africans had to be involved in the government if violence was to be avoided. The government of an independent Zanzibar needed to be equipped to deal with unrest. The Office of Eastern and Southern African Affairs recommended that Britain delay independence until the Zanzibar government could deal with subversion and a workable coalition was in place. Through early 1963, the department's position remained that independence should wait until Zanzibar had internal security forces capable of maintaining order and coping with communist subversion.[55]

By the end of 1963, the colonial era in British Africa, other than Central Africa, was over, despite British efforts to delay the process. Despite serious misgivings, the British government had granted its colonies independence, in fact, if not in name. U.S. officials shared many of the same worries and, in fact, opposed independence in the Gambia and Zanzibar. Nevertheless, the United States was at least as concerned that it be positioned to court the new nationalist leaders and to fend off Russian or Chinese involvement.

Central Africa, 1961–1963:
End of Federation

By 1963, most of British Central Africa was also clearly on the path to independence under African majority governments, despite the efforts of the British government. The Macmillan government, including Iain Macleod, worked hard to preserve the federation and, failing that, at least multiracial governments in Northern and Southern Rhodesia. Until close to the end, the political future in Central Africa still seemed different from that of the rest of Africa. British efforts failed, in part because of disagreements within the British government and the intransigence of the European settlers.

For long periods, the Kennedy government viewed British efforts favorably. The federation seemed worth preserving, although not at the cost of overt United States support. In Washington, multiracial governments also seemed the right choice. The Kennedy government was willing to support Britain against attempts in the United Nations to favor the African nationalists. As British efforts faltered, the United States was dismayed, but not to the point that intervention seemed the correct choice.

Nyasaland and the Federation

At the beginning of 1961, the Macmillan government remained committed to preserving the Federation of Rhodesia and Nyasaland, but faced formidable challenges. The federation's government was also committed to its survival, but Welensky, the federal prime minister, and his United Federal Party mistrusted Macmillan and his key ministers. Whitehead, the prime minister of Southern Rhodesia, and the Southern Rhodesian branch of the United Federal Party were on record supporting federation. They were, however, intent on securing Southern Rhodesia's independence. Welensky and Whitehead favored a partnership with the African population, albeit a partnership that left Europeans in control. Nevertheless, an important minority of Southern Rhodesia's European population was less interested in partnership and more interested in Southern Rhodesian independence than Whitehead and his followers. In all three territories, African nationalist parties were growing in size and confidence were agitating for an end to discrimination against Africans and for universal suffrage. More important, the African nationalists opposed the federation since they viewed it as a device for perpetuating European control.

In Nyasaland, the British tried to appease the leading nationalist, Hastings Banda, the leader of the Malawi Congress Party. In August 1961 legislative council elections, the party swept the board, winning all fifty seats open to Africans. The voter turnout for the lower electoral roll, where Africans predominated, was over ninety-five percent and the party won more than ninety-nine percent of the votes cast. Even on the upper roll, whose membership was limited by educational and property qualifications, the party won forty-three percent of the vote. The British recognized that they could not retain control of Nyasaland without the party's cooperation. They decided, moreover, that Banda was more likely to cooperate than his principal subordinates. The strategy the British adopted was to avoid a clash with Banda about the federation while offering him political concessions that would secure his credibility within the party and Nyasaland population. In the meantime, the British hoped to solve the federal problem. After the election, Sir Glyn Jones, the governor of Nyasaland, replaced two nominated members of the executive council with members of the legislative council, giving the Malawi Congress Party a majority in both legislative bodies. A conference in London in November 1961 led to the replacement of the executive council by a cabinet headed by a prime minister, Banda, and the promise of new constitution in the near future. Banda's position was further strengthened by the conviction and imprisonment for sedition of Herbert Chipembere, one of the most militant Party leaders. British officials moved against Chipembere, but with Banda's acquiescence.[1]

Despite British efforts, Banda remained implacable in his opposition to the federation. Before the elections, Jones thought that Banda and the Malawi Congress party would appreciate the federation's value to Nyasaland once they were part of the government. In August, however, Jones told Nyasaland's senior British officials that Banda's views were so strong that he would resent any attempt on their part to persuade him or the people of Nyasaland of the federation's possible benefits. Jones instructed them to remain neutral in discussions of the federation. Under Banda, the Nyasaland government adopted a policy of non-cooperation with the federation. In particular, it refused to sign an agreement regarding a long-planned hydroelectric project intended to serve Nyasaland.[2]

Throughout 1962, the Macmillan government yielded ground in the face of Banda's firm position. In February 1962, when Sandys met with Banda in Nyasaland, Banda laid out his position clearly. He was opposed to the federation. If the British wanted to preserve it, they would have to send an army to Nyasaland and throw Banda in jail. Sandys's response was that the Macmillan government would consider Nyasaland's right to secede from the federation. Agreeing to contemplate secession was an important concession. In London, officials recognized that Banda's intransigence meant the end of the federation. Within the cabinet, Home agreed that Britain should concede the right to secede. He argued, however, that Britain should insist that Nyasaland could not secede for at least two years. An orderly transfer would take that long. Perhaps, in the meantime, the Nyasaland leaders would realize the benefits of continued association. In May, Butler, now in charge of Central African affairs, persuaded the cabinet to appoint a committee of advisers to visit Nyasaland and assess the consequences of secession. Butler told Macmillan that doing otherwise risked precipitate action by Banda and the outbreak of disorder in Central Africa. In October, with the committee's report in hand, Butler concluded that the British could hold off no longer. The next Nyasaland constitutional conference was scheduled for November. Without accepting Nyasaland's right to leave the federation, the British could not expect the conference to accomplish anything. The cabinet accepted Butler's recommendation. Under pressure from Welensky and the federation government, however, it delayed a public announcement until December, after elections in Southern Rhodesia.[3]

Banda Gains the Upper Hand

The cabinet finally conceded that it lacked the means to govern Nyasaland without Banda's cooperation. By November 1962, Banda's position was that the British government had tacitly acknowledged Nyasaland's right to secession. He had agreed to delay an announcement so that the committee of advisers could produce their report. Further delay was unacceptable, he said. The cabinet thought that law and order would break down if Banda refused to participate in the Nyasaland government. The Nyasaland police could, at best, maintain order in the towns. If the federation's forces had to intervene for a substantial period, the negative impact on the federation's economy would be significant. Deploying federal troops in Nyasaland might exacerbate the situation since the Nyasaland population opposed federation. It might also undermine the credibility of British policies within the federation's European leadership. Finally, employing British troops would be difficult because the colony lacked any secure bases from which they could operate.[4]

Butler acknowledged that allowing Nyasaland to leave the federation would mean the federation's dissolution, but that Britain had no other option. He continued to offer the cabinet hope that bilateral negotiations between Britain and the federation government and the three territorial governments might produce an association among the Central African territories. By late 1962, Butler had decided that allowing the federation to fail was less important than delaying Nyasaland's independence and announcing Britain's intent to do so. Butler told the cabinet that Nyasaland would gain its independence and he suggested that they focus on mid–1964 as a likely date. Leaving the federation, Butler contended, would have serious economic, financial, and administrative consequences for Nyasaland. Until Britain understood the consequences and persuaded Banda's government to deal with them realistically, it could not honorably and responsibly allow Nyasaland to attempt to function as an independent state.[5]

Nevertheless, in October and November 1962, the cabinet was not ready to discard all hope of a Central African entity. During the cabinet's discussion, Home argued that the federation was a sound concept. It had improved living standards and administration. Dissolving the federation would prompt Southern Rhodesia to align itself with South Africa, what the federation and its multiracial partnership were intended to avoid. The British, therefore, had to preserve a political association between the two Rhodesias, he argued. On the other hand, Sandys thought a political association impossible. The two Rhodesias would disagree most vehemently about external affairs and defense, critical elements of any political association. An economic association, along the lines of the East African common services organization might be possible and beneficial, however. Home was willing to contemplate using force to preserve ties between the two Rhodesias. Sandys thought it dangerous to give Welensky any indication that Britain would do so. The cabinet's conclusion was that Britain should formulate plans for keeping the two Rhodesias together, but allow the details to be determined locally. The cabinet understood that success was not certain. British advocacy of continued association might alienate African nationalists further.[6]

Butler was able to postpone announcing Nyasaland's right to secede until after the Southern Rhodesian elections because Banda could be cooperative when his main goals were in sight. Butler and Banda agreed at a conference in November 1962 that they would not fix a date for independence until the second half of 1963. Banda indicated that his preference was March 1964. One reason Butler sought delay was that British civil servants worried that Nyasaland lacked the financial resources and educated population to function as an independent state. They wanted more time to assess the impact secession would have on Nyasaland and to organize the transition to independence. The officials eventually concluded that Nyasaland would need continued financial aid from Britain after independence. The Macmillan government did not, in fact, offer Banda a firm commitment about independence until September 1963. Butler told the cabinet once more that Banda wanted a firm date for independence. In Butler's view, Britain now had nothing to gain from further delay. After a meeting in London between Banda and British officials, the British government announced that Nyasaland would gain its independence in July 1964.[7]

Northern Rhodesia

The Northern Rhodesian constitutional conference in early 1961 was a failure. Macleod assumed that Kaunda and Welensky were the key players, even though the federal prime minister did not attend the conference. Macleod also believed that Welensky would accept parity between Africans and Europeans in the legislative council. Since Kaunda might demand more, Macleod hoped that Kaunda and Welensky would accept the appearance of an African majority: sixteen African members, fourteen European members, and five official members. Africans could claim they held a majority and the Europeans could be content that power remained in responsible hands. The two sides remained far apart, however. The situation became tense. The nationalists sought a majority in the legislative council and elections based on universal adult suffrage. The United Federal Party favored retention of the 1959 constitution and no increase in African representation. Welensky denounced Macleod's proposals, mobilized troops, and recalled the federal parliament. Rumors circulated that he was about to declare the federation independent. Kaunda warned that if Macleod did not produce acceptable proposals, Northern Rhodesia would see an African uprising that would make Mau Mau seem a child's picnic. Welensky then had the United Federal Party walk out of the talks. Macmillan negotiated with Julian Greenfield, the federal minister of law, to arrange their return. He succeeded only in alarming the African representatives that he was about to reach a settlement behind their backs. When the conference ended in mid–February without any agreement, all the Northern Rhodesian parties were unhappy. Welensky rejected Macleod's proposals and charged that the federal government had not been adequately consulted. The United Federal Party resigned from the Northern Rhodesia government in protest. The African nationalists claimed that the proposals were incomplete, since voting arrangements and the composition of the legislature remained undetermined.[8]

Macmillan's cabinet was equally at odds. Macleod wanted to push forward with his proposals and seek public acceptance from the nationalists. Home, Sandys, and Lord Kilmuir, the lord chancellor, favored further negotiations with Welensky and Whitehead. Macleod warned that any statement that Welensky and Whitehead would accept would be inconsistent with the current proposals. Whitehead, for example, wanted the upper electoral roll, subject to the highest qualifications and dominated by Europeans, to elect a majority of the legislative council. In Macleod's view, Welensky would never accept the current proposals because he had concluded that the United Federal Party could not win an election under them. Macleod argued that the danger of an African uprising in Northern Rhodesia outweighed the risk of Southern Rhodesia seceding from the federation. Sandys argued the opposite. Macleod threatened to resign, but Macmillan convinced him to remain.[9]

Disagreement within the cabinet was heated because the issue had attracted wider attention. Welensky had friends and allies within the Conservative Party. During 1960, the federal government courted other Conservative members of Parliament with guided tours of the federation. With the help of a British advertising agency, the federation argued its case in the British newspapers and in its own weekly paper. Delegations from Northern Rhodesia lobbied cabinet ministers and members of Parliament. Unlike the non-controversial decisions regarding the Gold Coast's or Nigeria's independence, the cabinet's deliberations about Northern Rhodesia and the federation appeared likely to have repercussions within the Conservative Party, Parliament, and the electorate.[10]

After the conference ended, Macleod announced a complicated voting scheme, intended to patch up the differences within the cabinet and among the Northern Rhodesian parties. Macleod proposed a legislative council that included forty-five elected members, up to six official members, and such nominated members as the governor chose to appoint, based on instructions from London. Voters on the upper electoral roll would elect fifteen members. Voters on a lower roll, subject to lesser qualifications, would elect fifteen members. Voters from both rolls would elect fifteen national members. To win a seat, candidates for the fifteen national seats would have to attract specified levels of support from both rolls. Macleod contended that his new proposals represented a middle way, consistent with the principle of non-racial politics. The presumption was that the upper roll would be largely European and the lower roll African. Macleod argued that the new arrangements would increase African representation while forcing both major parties to seek support from all segments of the population.[11]

Macleod's scheme introduced a significant element of uncertainty into the negotiations. Macleod, Sandys, and Macmillan recognized that Welensky would not accept an African majority. In early February, they agreed that future proposals for Northern Rhodesia would describe the voting procedures, not the intended outcome, even though the cabinet would have adopted the procedures to reach a particular outcome. Nonetheless, the complexity of the proposed system and the absence of meaningful data about voters or voting in Northern Rhodesia left the outcome of any electoral arrangement unclear. Interested parties were free to draw their own conclusions. Would requiring that candidates for the national seats gain 12 percent of both rolls produce a different result than requiring them to win 5 or 10 percent? Macmillan could tell Welensky that a party with a multi-racial appeal, like the United Federal Party, was likely to do well under the scheme although Macleod continued to believe that it would produce a small African majority.[12]

During the first half of 1961, Macleod could imagine that Northern Rhodesia was proceeding on the same path as the Gold Coast and Tanganyika. In Kaunda, the British had a cooperative and effective African nationalist leader. The first stage of constitutional change would not give the African nationalists everything they wanted, but it would meet the Macmillan government's needs. In particular, implementing Macleod's proposals would provide time for the British to save the federation. A Northern Rhodesian government split between Africans and Europeans might even favor preserving the federation. Macleod anticipated that the nationalists would be patient under Kaunda's firm leadership. They were likely to believe that parity between Africans and Europeans would soon evolve into an African majority. In fact, Kaunda and the older leaders within the United National Independence Party persuaded their less patient colleagues that the Macmillan cabinet was too divided to grant them all that they wanted. Moreover, the Northern Rhodesian population was weary. Kaunda and his allies argued that they needed to explore all options before launching another anti–British campaign. The United National Independence Party, therefore, participated in the talks organized by Governor Hone in Lusaka during April and May.[13]

British leaders were also negotiating with Welensky. Their talks produced an agreement to change the voting arrangements in ways thought to favor Europeans. At a commonwealth prime ministers' conference, Macmillan convinced Welensky that the British wanted to save the federation and that they did not intend to use force to impose their policies on Northern Rhodesia. Welensky left the conference believing that he had been promised an opportunity to seek agreement within Northern Rhodesia that would produce voting arrangements acceptable to his political allies. What emerged from subsequent meetings were provisions that would allow the upper electoral roll to select the fifteen national members plus allegedly significant concessions in other areas to the African nationalists. The leader of the United Federal Party in Northern Rhodesia told the press that the new rules would produce a European majority in the legislative council and deprive the African nationalists of any influence. The revised electoral arrangements did not go as far as Welensky wanted, however, to his dismay. He threatened to fly to London to confront the Macmillan government, but thought better of it. In June, the Macmillan government announced that it was altering Macleod's February proposals. The perception was that new provisions favored the Europeans and that the Macmillan government had yielded to Welensky.[14]

Kaunda and the United National Independence Party thought the British had double-crossed them. At a party conference in July, Kaunda proclaimed that the party would oppose the June proposals and would wage a non-violent campaign against the federation. The party would not stop until Africans controlled Northern Rhodesia, Kaunda announced. The campaign began with a boycott of the government-run beer halls. In August, the campaign turned violent as unrest erupted in several provinces. Africans burned schools, blocked roads, and destroyed bridges. Perhaps because of Kaunda's pleas, no Europeans other than security forces were attacked. The police and federal troops struggled to restore order. Through October, they arrested three thousand and the courts sent nearly twenty-seven hundred to jail. Over 80 percent were known members of the United National Independence Party. Twenty-seven people lost their lives.[15]

The violence forced the British to reconsider the June changes. Lord Perth, the British high commissioner in the federation, summed up the pros and cons for revisiting the voting arrangements. On the negative side, Governor Hone and other senior officials opposed further changes. Welensky would also feel betrayed if the British undid the June revisions. Making concessions would suggest that violence yielded benefits. If the changes produced an African majority, the federation would be closer to dissolution. If the British remained firm and the United National Independence Party proved not to represent the bulk of the African population, Northern Rhodesia might move forward under European control. On the positive side, all parties in Northern Rhodesia other than the United Federal Party favored revisions. Without changes, the United National Independence Party would boycott the election and the United Federal Party would win a majority. The African National Congress would then form the official opposition and extremists would seize control of the United National Independence Party. The changes being discussed, Perth believed, would not change the electoral outcome. They would end the unrest and allow peaceful constitutional change, however. They would also preserve African goodwill and perhaps persuade world opinion of British good intentions. Convincing outsiders that the June proposals did not favor the Europeans was difficult, Perth conceded. The Macmillan government came down on the positive side. After meetings in mid–September 1961, Macleod announced that the government would reconsider the June proposals provided the violence ended. Kaunda returned to Lusaka and the unrest subsided by early October.[16]

Maudling Takes Charge

In October 1961, Macmillan reshuffled his cabinet, replacing Macleod as colonial secretary with Reginald Maudling. If Macmillan's goals for the cabinet changes included healing the rifts over the federation, he was soon disappointed. Maudling initially told the cabinet that he needed to get his ideas clear. He needed to travel to Northern Rhodesia and talk to the Africans before reaching a decision. Nevertheless, Maudling added that he felt that the federation as presently constituted was a dead duck. If the British were to persuade the Northern Rhodesian nationalists to remain in the federation, an African majority in the Northern Rhodesian legislature in a good frame of mind was preferable to an African minority in a bad frame of mind. When Maudling returned to London in January 1962, he reported that an agreement on the June proposals was impossible. The subsequent disagreement within the cabinet resembled that of a year before. Maudling advocated four principles. After any changes, the United Federal Party and the United National Independence Party had to have an equal chance of winning an election. Neither should be in a position to win an overwhelming majority. The proposals should be simple, and the British must gain the acquiescence of at least the African nationalists. Maudling accepted that he was reopening topics considered settled in February 1961. Others in the cabinet retorted that they had reached a firm agreement with Welensky in February. The government was honor bound, they said, to reconsider only the points in dispute as of September 1961. Even Macleod thought Maudling was going too far. Maudling's response was that circumstances had changed. The government would be failing in its duty to the people of Northern Rhodesia if it refused to make the changes needed to avoid bloodshed and unrest.[17]

Macmillan wanted to preserve an agreement with Welensky, but an agreement with the federal prime minister proved as difficult as ever. Welensky had concluded that the United Federal Party could not win an election under the proposed constitution. He proposed, therefore, that the British not introduce a new constitution. Instead, he advocated separating Northern Rhodesia's copper-producing region from the rest and linking it with Southern Rhodesia. Nyasaland and the remaining parts of Northern Rhodesia would then be included in a looser form of federation. British officials had considered similar schemes in the past. Maudling, for his part, persisted, arguing that a new constitution that had popular support remained the first priority. If the African nationalists refused to work within the constitution, civil disobedience and rioting would result and the situation would get out of hand. According to Maudling, the constitution had to allow the nationalists a chance of winning at least a small majority. The nationalists could not be expected to participate in an electoral scheme that gave them no chance of victory.[18]

Once approved, Maudling's changes paved the way to an agreement with the Northern Rhodesian nationalists. Even Maudling's critics within the Macmillan government conceded that refusing to make changes would provoke the nationalists and would delay another new constitution for only two or three years. The most important of Maudling's changes reduced the votes needed to win a national seat. The United National Independence Party accepted the changes and secured several concessions from the British. The most significant was that a national seat would remain vacant if no candidate gained enough votes to win it. The governor could not nominate someone to fill the seat.[19]

Elections in Northern Rhodesia

In the elections, neither the United Federal Party nor the United National Independence Party gained an outright majority and the balance of power rested with the African National Congress. To an extent, the constitution worked as intended. It prevented the more militant nationalist party from gaining control and gave the European-controlled party a disproportionately large share of the seats. In the initial elections, the United National Independence Party won 60 percent of the vote; the United Federal Party, 21 percent; and the African National Congress, 17 percent. The convoluted electoral machinery gave the United Federal Party sixteen seats in the legislative council, the United National Independence Party fourteen seats, and the African National Congress seven. Eight national seats remained vacant.[20]

The African National Congress was unwilling, however, to delay an African majority government. Early in 1961, the congress had secured financial and other assistance from the Tshombe regime in the breakaway Katanga region of the neighboring Congo. Rumors circulated that Welensky intended to forge an alliance with Tshombe and link Katanga with at least the copper-producing areas of Northern Rhodesia. For the initial 1962 elections, the congress cooperated with the United Federal Party, agreeing on candidates for several seats. Nonetheless, for the second round of elections to fill the national seats, Nkumbula, the congress leader, agreed to cooperate with Kaunda and the United National Independence Party. Between the two rounds of elections, Kaunda and Nkumbula traveled to London to press for more constitutional change. Nkumbula told Butler that it was inconceivable that his party would stand in the way of African government after twenty years of struggle. After the final elections, Nkumbula overcame opposition within his own party by posing the question in stark terms. Who wanted African government now? The two parties agreed to form a coalition government and to share ministries equally.[21]

The nationalists used their electoral strength to force more changes. Their coalition remained uneasy. Party militants clashed violently in the second half of 1963. Rumors circulated about an alternative coalition of the congress and the United Federal Party. Kaunda and Nkumbula remained focused, however, on securing a new constitution as a further step towards independence. When the two leaders met with Butler in March 1963 to discuss alternative means of linking the Central African territories, they demanded the right to secede from the federation. They said that they wanted independence for Northern Rhodesia within a year of the federation's dissolution. They were dealing with a British government pressed by the pace of events in Central Africa and by the political controversies they generated. In August 1963, an official in London explained to Governor Hone that the situation was such that Butler felt compelled to make decisions about a new constitution on his own, without the benefit of a constitutional conference. In September, Butler told the cabinet that he had reached an agreement with the Northern Rhodesian nationalists. Elections would take place in January 1964 under a new constitution. All adults would vote to fill seventy-five seats in a new assembly. Ten seats would be reserved for Europeans. The new constitution would include a bill of rights and provisions for referring potentially discriminatory legislation to the high court in London. Under the constitution, Northern Rhodesia would govern its internal affairs.[22]

Northern Rhodesia then moved swiftly to independence under the United National Independence Party. In January 1964, Kaunda's party won fifty-five of the sixty-five seats elected by the ordinary electoral roll. The party's share of the vote was 70 percent. It would have been higher had not some of its candidates run unopposed. Kaunda became prime minister. In May 1964, the British and Northern Rhodesian governments agreed on an independence constitution and, in October 1964, Northern Rhodesia became independent as Zambia.[23]

Staying on the Sidelines

U.S. attention to events in Northern Rhodesia and Nyasaland during the Kennedy administration was limited. U.S. officials considered the federation's fate the key issue and the status of the three constituent territories was of secondary importance. U.S. officials anticipated that the federation might not survive. Nevertheless, they favored some form of association among the three Central African territories and anticipated its emergence. They favored wider African participation in government, but did not assume that Northern Rhodesia and Nyasaland would become independent African states. The country's basic stance was that the federation was a British concern. It was willing to support British efforts from the sidelines, but not become part of the game.

Into early 1962, U.S. officials in Central Africa favored a multi-racial government in Northern Rhodesia. In September 1961, Consul General Emmerson worried that the latest round of constitutional changes would alienate the Europeans in Northern Rhodesia and inhibit the creation of a multi-racial state. In February 1962, a United States official stationed in Lusaka reported that both Africans and Europeans were growing disillusioned with multi-racial solutions. Attempts at cooperation had gone unrewarded and the gap between the races was growing. Nevertheless, he reported that the U.S. reputation among Northern Rhodesian nationalists had never been higher. He anticipated that the United States might be able to use its prestige to bring racial and political groups together.[24]

U.S. officials viewed Maudling's initial proposals as a step forward. Washington characterized the proposals as promoting peaceful evolution, but not at the pace favored by Kaunda. That both Kaunda and Welensky were critical of the proposed changes but were unwilling to oppose them was a favorable development, U.S. officials reported. Alternative proposals would spark extra-legal opposition and complicate efforts to create a stable representative government. Washington told the Salisbury consulate that failure to resolve the immediate issues in Northern Rhodesia would complicate the federation situation. It would pose the risk of strikes, violence, and deployment of federal troops.[25]

The State Department was willing to intervene to support Maudling's proposals. It instructed the Salisbury consulate to tell Kaunda that the United States was pleased that he had accepted the new arrangements, at least conditionally. The consulate should urge him to participate in the upcoming elections. Washington thought that the United National Independence Party was undecided about the new constitution. Washington hoped that making U.S. views clear to Kaunda might strengthen his hand in dealing with the party's extremists.[26]

Kaunda and Banda were among Kennedy's visitors at the White House. Kennedy told Banda that the United States took great interest in African affairs. Visits from distinguished African leaders increased the country's knowledge of the current situation, the president said. Kennedy also assured Banda that he could count on his continuing interest in Nyasaland and that the United States recognized Nyasaland's need for educational and other assistance. Banda responded that he would bring a shopping list on his next visit.[27]

Personal contacts did not necessarily win U.S. or presidential support. In August 1961, after the United National Independence Party's campaign against the latest constitutional proposals for Northern Rhodesia turned violent and elicited strong responses from the police and other security forces, Kaunda cabled Kennedy. The Northern Rhodesian leader asked the president to intervene with Macmillan and to bring the matter to the attention of the United Nations. The Salisbury consulate advised against a reply from Kennedy. Williams favored a reply from the president, but only a non-committal response as a sign of courtesy. Williams also recommended discreet consultations with British officials and with Kaunda. The response drafted by the State Department stated only that the president regretted the loss of life in Northern Rhodesia and that he hoped that law and order would be restored in a way that was advantageous to all concerned.[28]

U.S. officials were no more open to suggestions from federation or British officials to become involved. In November 1961, Governor Hone of Northern Rhodesia suggested that U.S. officials might serve as a bridge between African nationalists and the lower echelons of the Northern Rhodesian government. The head of the federation's intelligence service suggested that the United States might arrange a private meeting between Banda and Welensky. U.S. officials ignored both suggestions.[29]

Regardless of the U.S. desire to maintain a low profile, its willingness to provide financial aid to Nyasaland drew it into the mix. British officials welcomed U.S. aid. They realized that Nyasaland would need all the help that it could get. They also feared that U.S. aid would strengthen Banda's resolve to have Nyasaland secede from the federation. Banda might advertise U.S. aid as support for his goals, they worried. Even if the United States denied any intent to promote the federation's breakup, outsiders might not be persuaded. In August 1962, Governor Jones of Nyasaland complained to the U.S. consul about U.S. aid officials' interactions with Nyasaland's African ministers. Jones fussed that Banda and his African ministers' dealings with U.S. officials made them less willing to cooperate with the British officials. The consul told Washington that his officials tried to maintain the correct relationships with African ministers and British civil servants. It was not easy, however. The consul assured the State Department that, in the British-Malawi-U.S. triangle, his officials would continue to be as wise as serpents and as harmless as doves.[30]

Southern Rhodesia's Constitutional Conference

The Southern Rhodesian constitutional conference seemed a success. With Sandys representing Britain, the parties negotiated an agreement by early February 1961. The agreement traded removal of most of Britain's remaining powers for constitutional safeguards for African rights. Sandys agreed to reduce Britain's role in Southern Rhodesia, but could not cede the British Parliament's power to legislate for Southern Rhodesia. As long as Southern Rhodesia remained a British dependency, Parliament would retain that power, Sandys contended. A Parliament could not bind future Parliaments. To mollify European leaders, Sandys could also point to the longstanding convention that Britain would not legislate for Southern Rhodesia without the Southern Rhodesian government's consent. The new constitution featured a declaration of rights. In addition, a constitutional council was empowered to identify and report bills that discriminated against minority rights. The council could not, however, review legislation already in place and the legislature need not accept its recommendations. Amending the constitution required a two-thirds vote in the legislature. Furthermore, amending key sections of the constitution required approval by the British government or approval in referenda of Southern Rhodesia's four racial groups (Europeans, Africans, Asians, and coloreds). As in Northern Rhodesia, voting would involve two voter rolls: the upper roll dominated by Europeans and the lower roll by Africans. The constitution called for sixty-five seats in the legislature, including fifteen elected by voters on the lower roll.[31]

Both Sir Edgar Whitehead's United Federal Party and Joshua Nkomo's National Democratic Party made concessions on their way to the agreement. At first, Whitehead thought he could secure constitutional changes without a conference. Once a conference seemed the easiest path towards independence, he opposed including any African representatives. Having then conceded a role for the National Democratic Party, he tried unsuccessfully to select the National Democratic Party leaders who could attend. Finally, the agreement did not give Whitehead the clear path to independence that he sought. For their part, the African nationalists opposed allowing Whitehead to chair the conference. They also refused to participate unless the Southern Rhodesian government released all political detainees. Eventually, they conceded both points. The constitution's voting and representation arrangements fell short of the nationalists' aims. They began the conference advocating universal suffrage and majority rule, but they seemed to settle for something less.[32]

Some European politicians in Southern Rhodesia opposed the new constitution. The Dominion Party advocated Southern Rhodesian secession from the federation and independence. It disassociated itself from the conference report and announced its intention to urge Rhodesian voters to reject the new constitution when the government held the necessary referendum. Ian Smith, a United Federal Party representative in the federal assembly, also opposed the conference report because it did not stipulate that Southern Rhodesia would become independent if the federation went out of existence.[33]

Despite announcing an agreement, Nkomo and the other National Democratic Party representatives at the conference backed away from the new constitution once its provisions became public. National Democratic Party leaders not at the conference denounced the proposed voting arrangements. Kaunda and Banda were also critical of Nkomo's willingness to cooperate with Whitehead. The federation's intelligence organization thought that the Ghanaian government threatened to cut off its financial aid to the National Democratic Party if it stuck to the agreement. Nkomo told the press that Sandys had misinterpreted the National Democratic Party's position. The party would continue to fight for "one man, one vote," Nkomo claimed. Nkomo stressed that Southern Rhodesia remained a British dependency and he said that he looked to Britain to exercise its authority over the government.[34]

The African nationalists proceeded to array themselves against the Whitehead government and the new constitution. In March, a National Democratic Party congress demanded changes in the proposed constitution, revision of Southern Rhodesia's land laws, release of all political detainees, and relaxation of restrictions on political meetings in rural areas. When the constitutional conference reconvened in May, Nkomo and the National Democratic Party delegation attended the initial meeting, but walked out. The party organized a boycott of the government's referendum on the new constitution. It held its own vote, in which all Africans over twenty-one could participate. The boycott was successful; only four thousand Africans registered to vote in the referendum. The party's referendum overwhelmingly rejected the new constitution. In October, the party congress voted to reject the new constitution and to boycott the next general election.[35]

Whitehead's government continued on its chosen course. After the constitutional conference, Whitehead told voters that Southern Rhodesia could follow one of three paths. It could attempt to maintain European supremacy by force. It could introduce African majority rule, which Whitehead warned, would end in bloody civil war. Instead, Whitehead argued that it should remain determined to have both races work together in a common political framework and to develop the county to everyone's benefit. Whitehead touted Southern Rhodesia's enlarged powers under the new constitution and portrayed the new constitution as only a small step short of independence. The overwhelmingly European Southern Rhodesian electorate accepted Whitehead's version of partnership. In a July referendum, the voters approved the constitution by an almost two to one ratio (41,949 for; 21,846 against).[36]

The Whitehead government continued its two-pronged approach to the African population. It courted moderates by encouraging eligible Africans to register to vote, eliminating discriminatory practices, and proposing changes to the land laws. The government tried to build stronger ties with the chiefs, convening a national council of chiefs for the first time. At the same time, it tried to suppress the nationalists. It enacted more security legislation, banned political meetings, and deployed police and troops to deal with the unrest that persisted in the towns. In December 1961, it banned the National Democratic Party and prohibited its leaders from addressing public meetings for four months. In September 1962, it banned a successor organization, the Zimbabwe African Peoples Union (ZAPU), arrested two hundred of its leaders, and confined them for three months.

December 1962 Elections

Whitehead's policies towards Africans failed. The National Democratic Party began with non-violent methods. It encouraged Africans to remove shoes and ties at public meetings. It organized a fast on the anniversary of the European conquest. Partly out of frustration, partly out of ill discipline, and partly out of a strategic choice, nationalists turned to violent methods. They burned schools and government facilities as well as the homes of chiefs and other Africans thought to support the government. They disrupted the government's agricultural and conservation projects and encouraged Africans to ignore or disobey government orders. The police struggled to cope with the unrest. Banning nationalist parties and their leaders proved ineffective, but the government avoided harsher measures lest it create martyrs. The police's task was harder because the nationalists had ready access to support and safe havens in nearby African countries. By the end of 1962, unrest persisted and the nationalists were as strong as ever. Moderate African backing for the government failed to materialize. The chiefs opposed interference in their affairs by either the government or the nationalists. On the eve of the December 1962 general election, roughly fifty-five hundred Africans were eligible to vote on the upper roll, but only about a third of them had registered to vote. More than fifty thousand Africans were eligible to register on the lower roll, but less than 20 percent did so. In the election itself, the United Federal Party offered more than a dozen African candidates. Nevertheless, nearly 80 percent of the registered African voters failed to cast ballots.[37]

A failed African policy was only one burden Whitehead and the United Federal Party had to bear as it contested the December 1962 election. The government's inability to squelch the unrest and its commitment to curb discrimination and reform the land laws worried European voters. Although Whitehead was intent on claiming Southern Rhodesian independence, the party was identified with the federation which now appeared doomed and which seemed to pose the risk of African rule. The Macmillan government continued to profess its determination to preserve a form of association. Nevertheless, by the time Southern Rhodesian voters went to the polls, African nationalists, hostile to the federation, controlled the governments of Nyasaland and Northern Rhodesia. When Welensky held a federal election in March 1962, only the United Federal Party offered candidates. The party swept the field, winning fifty-four of fifty-seven seats. Nonetheless, the vote totals demonstrated that only the diehards thought the federation had a future. In thirty-nine contests, the United Federal Party candidate ran unopposed. In the rest, less than half the registered voters cast ballots.[38]

In the December 1962 election, the United Federal Party met defeat. It won twenty-nine seats, fifteen elected by upper roll voters, and fourteen elected by lower roll voters. Fourteen of the successful United Federal Party candidates were Africans. A new party, the Rhodesian Front, won thirty-five seats, all elected by upper roll voters. It formed a government with Winston Field as prime minister. The front was a broad coalition, encompassing those unhappy with the United Federal Party for whatever reason. Unlike the United Federal Party, a top-down organization controlled from Salisbury, the Rhodesian Front depended on grassroots groups throughout Southern Rhodesia for members and financial support.[39]

Rhodesian Front Government

Other than repudiating Whitehead's policies and resisting the nationalists, the new Southern Rhodesian government's philosophy was unclear. Field told the press that the front did not propose South African style apartheid. It did not intend to force the races to live together or apart. Field conceded living apart was the most likely outcome, however. The Field government released the Africans held in detention and announced that it would use the courts to deal with law and order issues. If the releases were intended to court the nationalists, they failed. Nkomo said the struggle for majority rule would continue. In February 1963, the government introduced more security legislation. A mandatory death sentence was now the penalty for crimes involving fire, explosives, or gasoline. The government also put in place further restrictions on political activity outside Southern Rhodesia and on the activities of ex-officials of banned organizations. It banned political meetings on Sundays, the day favored by nationalist organizations.[40]

Since at least the Monckton commission's report in 1959, various politicians and officials in London had anticipated the federation's demise. With each concession to the African nationalists, someone within the government was likely to predict that this step would doom the federation. The Rhodesian Front's electoral victory produced a similar prophecy. Lord Alport, the British high commissioner in Salisbury, told Butler that the front's indifference to the federation made a Central African association impossible. On December 19, 1962, Butler made public the Macmillan government's decision to allow Nyasaland to secede. The sense that the federation could not survive was now widespread. Nevertheless, the Macmillan government was not ready to give up. At a minimum, Butler hoped to avoid blame for killing the federation by maneuvering the territories into asking for its dissolution. Butler proposed further talks with the federation and the two Rhodesias to explore the possibility of a revised association. In a series of bilateral talks, Butler could not even get agreement to hold a conference. The Northern Rhodesian nationalists would not agree to talks without recognition of their right to secede. The federation refused to participate without a promise that the conference would produce a political link between the two Rhodesias. Neither territory was likely to concede such a link. All Butler got for his efforts was a British concession that Northern Rhodesia could secede from the federation and a Southern Rhodesian demand that it gain its independence when the federation ended.[41]

While the Macmillan government was focused on preserving the federation, it took Southern Rhodesia's cooperation for granted. It worried that the Salisbury government might declare itself independent, but assumed that the Southern Rhodesians were as interested as it was in maintaining economic links among the Central African territories. Once Britain conceded Nyasaland and Northern Rhodesia the right to secede and eventual independence, however, the Macmillan government found itself at odds with the Field government. The Southern Rhodesians wanted their independence when the federation disappeared or no later than the other Central African territories. The Macmillan government thought Field's policies were embarrassingly reactionary and repressive. At least Whitehead talked of racial partnership and moved towards reducing discrimination. Conceding independence to a Southern Rhodesia ruled by the Rhodesian Front would produce protests in Britain and the United Nations. Both old and new members of the commonwealth were sure to object. Macmillan's government was split on the issue. Butler and others were willing to concede independence. Britain told its critics in the United Nations that it lacked the power to intervene in Southern Rhodesia. If such were the case, Butler thought, it would be best to let the colony go. Otherwise, Britain would find itself held responsible for embarrassing policies it could not alter. Macleod and others opposed independence for Southern Rhodesia until a more representative government was in place.[42]

More Delay

The British government had run out of ideas or, at least ideas that could command a majority of its members. Southern Rhodesia's status represented a major issue at home and abroad and the government was aware of the issue's importance. Nevertheless, the best it could do, under Macmillan and, after October 1963, Sir Alex Douglas-Home (the former Lord Home) was to play for time. In March 1963, the Macmillan cabinet concluded that it should defer a decision on Southern Rhodesian as long as possible. In April, it reaffirmed the same conclusion, choosing to delay as long as possible a decision about the terms under which it would grant Southern Rhodesia independence. The government rationalized delay on the ground that it could not allow negotiations about Southern Rhodesia's status to interfere with the federation's orderly termination. Distribution of the federation's liabilities and assets, especially its military forces, and other similar issues, in fact, required a full-scale conference at Victoria Falls in summer 1963. Additional staff work continued through the end of December, when the federation went out of existence. Subsequently, the Southern Rhodesians suspected that Douglas-Home was trying to avoid having Southern Rhodesia become an issue in the next British general election, thought to be likely in October 1964. Whatever the rationale, the government had reverted to Lennox-Boyd's policy of foot-dragging, putting off controversial decisions in hopes that something better would come along.[43]

The London and Salisbury governments proceeded to talk past each other through the end of 1963. In meetings and correspondence, Douglas-Home, Butler, and Sandys failed to find common ground with Field and Ian Smith, his finance minister. The Southern Rhodesians contended that they were entitled to independence. They had governed themselves for forty years. They had agreed to the federation with the understanding that its fate would not delay their independence and they had negotiated a constitution with the British government. They saw no reason why Southern Rhodesia should not be independent under the constitution. The Field government also argued that it had pledged not to alter the constitution without the electorate's approval, either in a referendum or a general election. Southern Rhodesia was entitled to the same treatment as the other Central African territories, they contended. Theirs was a prosperous and self-reliant country, loyal to Britain in two world wars. In response, the British argued that Southern Rhodesia needed to follow the same process as other colonies. It needed to discuss with Britain the terms under which it would obtain independence. Although the British were loath to specify terms, their most consistent suggestion was amendment of the 1961 constitution. The British contended that the 1961 constitution was intended only as a way station to independence. Amendments should eliminate discrimination and provide a larger role for Africans in the government, if not majority rule. Ministers warned that Britain could not agree to a settlement unacceptable to the commonwealth and the international community.[44]

The exchanges between London and Salisbury were painful, especially for the British ministers. Decisions in London produced accusations of deceit and betrayal from Salisbury. Welensky charged British negotiators with lying and breaking promises. When Butler announced that Nyasaland could secede, federation and Southern Rhodesia leaders complained that he was breaking Britain's promise not to change the federation without the agreement of the other governments. Field initially refused to attend the conference called to organize the federation's dissolution unless Britain promised Southern Rhodesia independence. He ultimately went to the conference, but claimed later that he did so only because Butler had promised him independence. That former ministers sitting in the House of Lords, including Lyttelton and Lennox-Boyd, supported the Southern Rhodesians' charges added to the government's discomfort. Butler and other ministers denied charges of dishonesty or bad faith. Both sides published documents to bolster their cases. Douglas-Home conceded privately that Southern Rhodesia was, in some sense, entitled to independence. British ministers also acknowledged that, had the African nationalists participated in the December 1962 elections, they might have won several seats. Under the 1961 constitution, they might win a majority in as little as five years, British officials believed. Moreover, Douglas-Home and others in London had to be aware that, as late as 1957, they had appeared committed to an independent federation under European control.[45]

The British government behaved as if the key to resolving Southern Rhodesia's status was reaching an agreement with the Southern Rhodesian government. In contrast to British tactics in other colonies, the Macmillan and Home governments showed little interest in seeking an understanding with the African nationalists, although Nkomo and others met with British ministers. Despite European accusations of betrayal, ministers like Butler and Sandys did not reach out to the nationalists to form the sort of alliance British officials had with Nkrumah or Nyerere.

The British did not forge a partnership with the Southern Rhodesian nationalists in large part because Nkomo and the Zimbabwe African People's Union were not as effective or credible as their counterparts in other colonies. In addition, the Southern Rhodesian government was a more determined, more ruthless, and better-equipped opponent than other British colonial regimes. The Southern Rhodesian government did not suffer the loss of confidence and resolve that overtook other colonial administrations. British colonial servants could go home to England. Most European settlers in Southern Rhodesia could not. Confronted with a strong adversary, the Southern Rhodesian nationalists struggled to devise an effective strategy and tactics. Should they discard their largely non-violent methods once it was clear that their path to majority rule would be longer and more difficult than in Northern Rhodesia? The Southern Rhodesian nationalists also suffered the personal and ethnic rivalries that afflicted other nationalist movements. Nkomo had wide support among Africans in Southern Rhodesia. Yet he gained a reputation among his fellow militants as an amiable, but soft leader, likely to be traveling abroad while they faced detention and trial. In July 1963, the tensions came to a head. Members of the party's executive committee attempted to oust Nkomo. He countered by trying to expel them from the party. In August, the rebels, with Ndabaningi Sithole and Robert Mugabe in the lead, formed a rival party, the Zimbabwe African National Union (ZANU).[46]

The availability of foreign assistance facilitated and deepened the split. Nkomo established a government in exile in an independent Tanzania. ZANU inherited it and made Dar es-Salaam its headquarters. ZAPU established itself in Lusaka, in the newly independent Zambia. Russia assisted ZAPU. China, its new rival, may have encouraged the split; it eventually adopted the ZANU as its protégé.[47]

Hoping for the Best

During 1961 and early 1962, a new U.S. consul general in Salisbury, John Emmerson, adopted a more circumspect approach than his predecessor, Joseph Palmer. In many areas, Emmerson echoed Palmer's views. Emmerson doubted that the federation could continue. He thought that a Central African association made sense, but anticipated that African majorities would come to power in all three territories. He anticipated that change would proceed most slowly in Southern Rhodesia and violence might accompany it. Emmerson thought little of the major players in Central Africa. The European settlers were shortsighted, he told Washington. No federation was possible with Welensky in charge. Emmerson also warned Washington that the Southern Rhodesian government's repression of African political parties was unwise. Denying Africans a political voice would drive them to adopt extra-legal methods. Nevertheless, Emmerson thought that the prospect of Africans taking charge in Southern Rhodesia was appalling. Nkomo and his cohorts were incompetent, ill equipped to assume positions of responsibility. The nationalists might oppose the 1961 Southern Rhodesian constitution, but Emmerson considered it a substantial advance for Africans. His vision of the future resembled that of the Whitehead government, a non-racial society that encouraged African advancement without driving out the Europeans. Unlike Palmer, Emmerson told Washington that he saw little opportunity for U.S. action in the federation. Emmerson believed that the Macmillan government was pursuing an astute and enlightened approach in Central Africa. The new constitutions in the two Rhodesias and the elections in all three territories served U.S. interests, he thought. He recommended that the United States support British policies and maintain the closest possible contact with Britain regarding the federation.[48]

In Washington, views of the federation's future remained pessimistic. A National Intelligence Estimate issued in April 1961 predicted that the federation would break up within two years. In Southern Rhodesia, it predicted, the Europeans would retain control and move towards a closer association with South Africa. Staff in the Bureau of African Affairs applauded British attempts to establish a Central African association that could gain European and African support. Nevertheless, they thought British chances for success were slim and were getting slimmer. They advised that the British needed to consider what they would do when the federation collapsed.[49]

By February 1962, Emmerson's appraisal was less positive, because of what he considered nationalist ineptitude and intransigence. Emmerson told Washington that the Whitehead government was making a sincere effort to increase African participation in government. The new constitution was a reasonably liberal document. The nationalists had reneged on their acceptance of the constitution, however. They were discouraging Africans from registering to vote. The nationalists had no real quarrel with the constitution, only with its franchise arrangements, Emmerson contended. They wanted immediate parity between Africans and Europeans in the legislature. The voting rules would produce an African majority in ten or fifteen years, but the nationalists were unwilling to wait. The nationalists were resorting to extra-constitutional methods to wring further concessions from the government. They were unlikely to succeed in the short run, however. The Europeans were too strong and too willing to use force.[50]

Assistant Secretary Williams shared Emmerson's positive appraisal of British policy in Central Africa. After a trip through Central Africa in late summer 1961, Williams reported that the federation was committed to a policy of partnership, of measured transition to self-government and independence. Williams described the federation's policy as consistent with both British and U.S. policies. Williams acknowledged that getting all parties in Central Africa to cooperate was difficult, but he thought the British governors were on the right track. On the other hand, the European leaders, especially Welensky and the United Federal Party, underestimated the seriousness of the situation. Williams recommended that the United States provide financial aid to speed African education and development. The U.S. should urge the federation to move faster to satisfy African demands. Williams also thought that promoting peace in the Congo would ease the situation in Central Africa.[51]

The Bureau of African Affairs policy recommendations in early 1962 were consistent with Williams's and Emmerson's assessments. The bureau recommended that the immediate U.S. goal should be to foster continued peaceful progress toward increased African participation in government. The United States should seek a transfer of power to Africans in a way that would promote non-racial societies and adherence to the United Nations charter. The bureau argued that further progress was dependent on continuation of the middle of the road policies of the Whitehead government. Britain held primary responsibility for Central Africa. Its goals were similar to those of the United States. The U.S. should coordinate its policies with the British. British power and authority were limited, however, by concessions made to the Southern Rhodesian government and by opposition from segments of the Conservative Party. British success was not guaranteed, moreover. If the federation failed, Southern Rhodesia might declare itself independent, reverse pro–African policies, and align itself with Portugal and South Africa. The Africans might resist with violence and calls for United Nations intervention might emerge. The bureau believed that the United States was on friendly terms with African nationalist leaders. It recommended that the U.S. use the ties to promote orderly change.[52]

When Kennedy asked Williams for an assessment of the Rhodesian situation in May

1962, the assistant secretary took the same line. He told the president that the political situation within the federation was tense. It could produce violence and bloodshed. The potential for real trouble was greatest in Southern Rhodesia, Williams predicted, although the British were working to expand African participation in government. The U.S. should continue to support the British efforts, while encouraging faster political change. African nationalists feared that the British would stand by while Welensky used force to block African advancement. Williams thought such fears exaggerated. Yet he shared the nationalists' concern that the 1961 constitution would mark the end, rather than the beginning, of political change in Southern Rhodesia. Williams warned Kennedy that reactionary Europeans might take power if Whitehead seemed too liberal to Southern Rhodesian voters. A hard line Southern Rhodesian government might then provoke a confrontation between Africans and Europeans similar to that in Algeria.[53]

Southern Rhodesia in the United Nations

Williams told Kennedy that the work of the United Nations Committee of Seventeen might persuade Britain and the federation that it was later than they thought. It might also reassure African nationalists that the world had not forgotten them. Williams recommended, however, that the U.S. oppose any committee resolution on the federation and the Rhodesias. Russia and others were pushing resolutions calling on Britain to abrogate the 1961 constitution and grant early independence to both Rhodesias. Williams warned that an immoderate resolution would make Britain's task in Central Africa more difficult. It would push Welensky to more extreme positions, and reduce Britain's willingness to cooperate with the U.N.[54]

Beginning in February 1962, several U.N. bodies, including the General Assembly, the Trusteeship Council, and the Committee of Seventeen, passed resolutions regarding Southern Rhodesia. The initial General Assembly resolution called for an investigation of Southern Rhodesia's constitutional status. Was Southern Rhodesia self-governing? If not, was Britain responsible for providing information to the United Nations regarding its status? Through October 1962, the U.N. took up a series of related resolutions that sought to escalate the pressure on Britain. Resolutions defined Southern Rhodesia as not self-governing and called upon Britain to convene a constitutional conference to replace the 1961 constitution. They also called for the release of political prisoners and an end to restrictions on nationalist political parties. The Southern Rhodesian resolutions had the support of most African and Asian countries and they passed with large majorities.[55]

The Macmillan government resisted the U.N. resolutions. British representatives tried various arguments, with little success. They contended that Southern Rhodesian affairs fell outside the U.N.'s authority. They argued that Britain lacked the authority or the means to intervene in Southern Rhodesia. They also argued that the federation could refuse to provide information to Britain. When the General Assembly adopted a resolution regarding Southern Rhodesia in June 1962, Sir Patrick Dean, the chief British representative, walked out of the assembly meeting. The Macmillan government's position reflected Britain's long-standing opposition to United Nations involvement in British colonies. The Macmillan government had tactical aims as well. It wanted to avoid irritating Welensky and federation leaders and to allow Whitehead and his government more time to solidify their position.

British representatives at the United Nations found themselves frustrated, however. In June 1962, Dean reported complete failure to Home. He could not keep Southern Rhodesia off the General Assembly agenda. U.N. members were convinced that the 1961 constitution would create a new South Africa. They thought that the British, with their history of granting independence to colonies, could do the same in Southern Rhodesia. It did not help, Dean added, that Welensky was unpopular among United Nations members, only somewhat less popular than South Africa and the Portuguese colonies. To the government's embarrassment, Sir Hugh Foot (former chief secretary in Nigeria and governor of Jamaica and Cyprus) resigned as Britain's representative at the United Nations in October 1962. Foot announced that he opposed only the government's policy in Central Africa. He said that he was resigning because he had promised Nkomo he would do so if the Macmillan government did not intervene in Southern Rhodesia. Before Foot resigned, he told U.S. officials that he hoped the United States would put pressure on Britain to alter its approach to Southern Rhodesia.[56]

The U.S. supported British efforts to resist U.N. involvement in Central Africa. Kennedy told Adlai Stevenson, the chief U.S. representative at the United Nations, that the United States should cooperate with the British on the issue. State Department officials believed that the president's instructions stemmed from his meeting with Macmillan in 1962. Then the president had told the prime minister that the United States did not intend to criticize British colonial policies or increase the difficulties involved in granting colonies their independence. The State Department also believed it important to resist United Nations intervention in any colony where the administering authority was attempting to adhere to its responsibilities under the U.N. charter. The department believed that Britain was trying to do the right thing in Central Africa, whereas Portugal was ignoring the U.N. charter in its African colonies. The department's basic position was that Southern Rhodesia was effectively self-governing. Holding Britain responsible would be pointless and unwise, therefore. The department also believed that the Southern Rhodesia government, under Whitehead, was making a sincere effort to build a multi-racial society. United Nations intervention would hinder Whitehead's efforts, disrupt political change within the federation, and complicate the U.S. relations with all parties in Central Africa.[57]

While supporting the British, the State Department maneuvered to preserve U.S. influence within the United Nations. The department did not want the United States to become isolated in a small minority or to be seen as uncritically supporting the British. It also wanted to avoid the impression that the United Nations and the United States were fundamentally at odds. U.S. representatives therefore preferred to work behind the scenes, leaving the British to argue publicly against various resolutions. When defeat seemed inevitable, the United States pressed the British to avoid a vote or to accept compromise wording. Faced with certain defeat on an unacceptable resolution, State Department officials debated the relative merits of abstentions and negative votes. Before major votes, U.S. officials often asked their British counterparts how much support Britain wanted, and whether a U.S. abstention would be sufficient. The U.S. was reluctant to vote against a resolution if the British had not made a forceful case against it.[58]

Disagreements with the State Department

Support for Britain in the United Nations on Central African issues sparked friction within the Kennedy government. The State Department and the U.S. delegation at the United Nations debated strategy and tactics. Within the State Department, the Bureau of

African Affairs and the Bureau of International Organizations Affairs were most likely to hesitate about supporting the British. In May 1962, the two bureaus opposed United States support for Britain over a Committee of Seventeen report regarding Northern Rhodesia. They lost out to a combination of the White House, the U.S. delegation at the United Nations, Secretary Rusk, and Under Secretary for Political Affairs George McGhee.[59]

Over the course of 1962, the U.S. delegation to the U.N. lost confidence in British policies in Central Africa and in its actions at the United Nations. The U.S. delegation favored low-key support for the British on Central Africa: abstentions rather than negative votes, lobbying in the corridors rather than speeches in the General Assembly. In some instances, the British did not expect complete United States support. Nevertheless, as the United Nations debates continued, Stevenson and other members of the delegation became uneasy with the quality of British arguments and presentations. The delegation reported to Washington that British representatives seemed ambivalent, indecisive, and half-hearted. They acted as if they knew they were stuck with a weak case. The delegation began to suspect that the Macmillan government had no real Central Africa policy. They feared that the Macmillan regime was divided and immobile, reduced to hoping for the best. In particular, the delegation worried that the British were prepared to wash their hands of the issue. By June 1962, Stevenson was arguing that the Africans did not believe Whitehead when he advertised the 1961 constitution as a major advance for them. Stevenson recommended that Washington push London to sidetrack the 1961 constitution and find some alternative more acceptable to the nationalists.[60]

Williams also grew to doubt the wisdom of supporting the British. In October 1962, he complained to Rusk that support for Britain over Central Africa was undermining the U.S. influence with African and Asian nations in the U.N. The immediate issue was the Whitehead government's banning of ZAPU. Williams told Rusk that if the U.S. remained passive, the majority of countries in the United Nations would conclude that the U.S. had abandoned its past positions on colonial issues. The U.S. should prod the British government to use its influence with the Whitehead government, Williams recommended. Whitehead should reach an agreement with ZAPU, rescind the ban on its leaders, and agree that a unanimous vote by the fifteen African members of the legislature could block any constitutional amendments. Williams thought that Whitehead should announce that Britain would retain sovereignty until a Southern Rhodesian government had the support of a majority of the population.[61]

Williams's doubts about the British policy stemmed in part from his meetings during 1962 with senior British officials. Williams met with Sir David Ormsby-Gore, the British ambassador to the United States, in March 1962. Williams cited African nationalists' worries that they would lose their rights once the 1961 constitution was in place. Williams said that he hoped the British would retain their powers over Southern Rhodesia and protect African rights. Ormsby-Gore replied that the British powers were only theoretical. The British government had never exercised them. The ambassador went on to share his optimistic appraisal of the federation's future. In July, Williams met with Sandys and Butler. Sandys argued that the United States should support Britain on Central Africa more or less on faith. Britain had supported the U.S. on various issues even when Britain did not agree with the U.S. position, he argued. The United States should return the favor. Butler was more amicable. Nevertheless, he resisted Williams's argument that the new constitution fell short of what the nationalists could reasonably be expected to accept. Butler countered that Whitehead could not survive politically if he offered more concessions to the nationalists. Butler argued that Britain lacked the means to change the situation. Williams did not accept Butler's arguments. He left the meeting unconvinced that the British had exhausted their legal and moral authority regarding the Southern Rhodesian situation.[62]

Williams's interactions with federation officials were likewise unlikely to stir hopes of a peaceful outcome. In September 1961, Williams told Richard Wetmore, the federation's representative in Washington, that many people misunderstood Africa south of the Congo. They thought the nationalists were communists. Wetmore retorted that the nationalists were anarchists. According to Wetmore, the danger was that they could fan the uncontrolled enthusiasm of the African masses. According to Wetmore, Welensky understood that strength and fairness were the keys to dealing with Africans and to overcoming the nationalists. During the 1959 Nyasaland disturbances, the government lacked the strength to handle the situation, Wetmore contended. In May 1962, Wetmore told Williams that United States was overly pro–African. It paid too much attention to Nkomo and Kaunda. Wetmore contended, moreover, that Kaunda was a charlatan. If the United States parted company with Britain and supported African demands, he said, it would encourage intransigence among Africans and provoke a hostile reaction from Europeans. In September 1962, O.B. Bennett, Wetmore's successor, tried to convince Williams that Russia was behind the unrest in Central Africa. Bennett claimed that concessions to the nationalists were pointless. The nationalists would settle, he claimed, for nothing less than immediate, full control of Southern Rhodesia.[63]

Looking for Alternatives

By late summer 1962, the State Department anticipated that Britain would face intensified criticism in the upcoming General Assembly session. During the session that ended in June, Britain had argued, with United States support, that United Nations demands for further constitutional change in Southern Rhodesia were premature. British representatives contended that Britain needed more time to work with the Southern Rhodesian government. Since the session's end, Britain had secured no political concessions from the Whitehead government, however. In fact, Whitehead had indicated that his government planned more stringent security measures aimed at the African nationalists. The department therefore thought that the new session would produce more attacks on British policy and harshly worded resolutions. The department worried that supporting the British position would be difficult.[64]

The department looked for alternatives. It instructed the London embassy to ask the Foreign Office, and perhaps the Colonial Office, whether they had identified new policies that might head off criticism in the United Nations. The department asked the Salisbury consulate about the ingredients for a deal between the Whitehead government and the nationalists: the concessions Whitehead could make and the concessions Nkomo and the nationalists would accept. The consulate was also to assess Whitehead's prospects for maintaining political control.[65]

The department got nothing for its troubles. The reply from London was that the British government was concerned about the Whitehead government's new security measures, but was unwilling to block them. The Macmillan government also thought that British intervention would cause Whitehead to lose his legislative majority. Salisbury reported that the nationalists wanted enough legislative seats to enable them to block constitutional amendments. The Whitehead government was willing to concede more seats, but not as many as the nationalists wanted. The consulate thought that the voters would reject White-head if he allowed the nationalists the power to stop constitutional changes. Whitehead intended to continue dismantling discriminatory laws, but was under strong pressure to repress ZAPU and curb any violence, the consulate reported. Whitehead seemed to believe that he could split the nationalists and negotiate a deal with the more moderate leaders, but the consulate considered Whitehead's hopes unrealistic.[66]

Avoiding Britain's Burden

The United States was willing to risk only limited involvement in Central African issues. In May 1962, the Salisbury consulate reported proudly that it had responded favorably to a ZAPU representative's request for help in arranging a meeting between Butler and Nkomo. The U.N. delegation discussed with British representatives the wisdom of asking other nations to put pressure on Nkomo. Nevertheless, Washington warned the Salisbury consulate in September 1962 against trying to mediate between the nationalists and the Southern Rhodesian government. The British were responsible for Central Africa, the depart-ment wrote. The U.S. did not want to assume any part of Britain's burden. Attempts at mediation would raise unrealistic expectations, would probably fail, and would discredit the United States in Africans' eyes. When Kennedy met with Foreign Secretary Home in September 1962, the State Department's advice to the president was to disavow any intent to tell Britain what to do about Central Africa. Kennedy should stress that the U.S. needed to know British plans. The president should remind Home that defending Britain in the United Nations was becoming more difficult, but reaffirm that the United States would do everything possible to avoid embarrassing the British.[67]

The Kennedy-Home meeting resembled Williams's earlier meetings with British offi-cials. Stevenson suggested to Home that British announce that they intended to retain sov-ereignty in Southern Rhodesia until the colony had a government acceptable to the majority of the population. Home told Kennedy that Britain could do nothing until after the Southern Rhodesian elections, then scheduled for March 1963. Doing anything before the election would make Whitehead's situation more difficult. After the election, Whitehead would broaden the franchise and Britain would implement a five-year development plan. By the end of five years, Britain could be rid of Southern Rhodesia. After the meeting, the State Department suggested that Whitehead guarantee that the legislature would not amend the constitution without the unanimous support of the African members, or trade lifting the ban on ZAPU for a ZAPU pledge of non-violence. If Southern Rhodesia was headed in the right direction, the department suggested, the U.S. could use its influence with moderate leaders in Africa to buy the British more time. Home rejected the suggestions, arguing that any action before the elections would undermine Whitehead. As long as the federation existed, Britain could not consider Southern Rhodesia's independence.[68]

In October, the U.N. General Assembly approved by eighty-one votes to two a reso-lution that called for suspending the Southern Rhodesian constitution and for organizing a constitutional convention. The United States abstained. Having failed to alter British policies and avert another defeat in the U.N., the State Department hung its hopes on Whitehead's re-election. The Salisbury consulate was hardly optimistic. It doubted that the Whitehead government could deal with unrest in the towns and countryside. The consulate was also convinced that Whitehead realized that he had to negotiate with Nkomo. It predicted that, once re-elected, Whitehead would release Nkomo from detention and start talks with him. When Whitehead met with Williams in November, the prime minister made a good impression. Williams was impressed by Whitehead's apparent sincerity and political astuteness. The assistant secretary told Whitehead that the Southern Rhodesian government's policies were sound, but implementation was too slow. Whitehead assured Williams that things were better than they seemed at a distance. He had kept in contact with nationalist leaders. No deal was possible now, he said, partly because Nkomo had lost control of his followers. Once the nationalists realized that they could not block the new constitution, however, they would want to negotiate. Under the new constitution, the African majority would control the government within fifteen years, perhaps sooner, Whitehead claimed. Williams subsequently sent Whitehead his best wishes in the upcoming election.

During talks on African issues in December, U.S. officials told their British counterparts that the United States was pleased that Whitehead had not rejected the idea that the U.N. secretary general could play a role in Southern Rhodesia. The U.S. expected Whitehead to make a gesture along this line after the election. Provided Whitehead won re-election and released many of the ZAPU leaders, U.S. officials indicated that the United States was prepared to fund training programs designed to prepare Africans for government positions. The U.S. understood British inhibitions regarding Central Africa, officials said. When Whitehead won, the United States hoped Britain could play a larger role. The stakes were high enough that both Britain and the U.S. ought to take a reasonable gamble, they argued.[69]

Links to Nationalists

The briefing papers prepared in Washington for the December 1962 talks argued that the United States should assure the nationalists that it sympathized with their aspirations. Such assurances would serve the interests of Britain, the Whitehead government, and the African nationalists, the papers argued. U.S. officials had, in fact, been meeting with Southern Rhodesian nationalist leaders for some time. In September 1961, the Salisbury consulate told Washington that it had established an easy and mutually respectful friendship with three nationalist leaders, T.G. Silundika, Ndabaningi Sithole, and Robert Mugabe. The consulate's aim, it told Washington, was to promote a dialogue between Africans and Europeans.[70]

At a meeting with the three nationalists in September 1961, consulate officials counseled patience, non-violence, and support for the new constitution. They argued that the Southern Rhodesian government was fundamentally different from the South African government. The British government would never agree to a constitution that seemed liberal, but worked against African interests. The Europeans in Southern Rhodesia might reverse course, if the federation failed and they confronted a recalcitrant nationalist movement. Consulate officials contended that Tunisia was a better model for nationalist movements than Algeria. The Tunisians had worked with a constitutional framework and gained their independence, while the Algerians had chosen violence and achieved nothing. Consulate officials suggested that the nationalists seek funding from private organizations in the United States. They added that such organizations might expect the nationalists to work within a constitutional framework. The U.S. officials advised that that nationalist leadership should decide whether to contest elections, rather than leaving the decision to a party congress. Party meetings were often thoughtlessly extreme, officials observed.[71]

State Department officials worked to blunt the nationalists' objections to United States support for Britain in the United Nations. In March 1962, the ZAPU executive council voted to boycott all Americans, official or unofficial. The Salisbury consulate blamed extremists for the anti–U.S. sentiments. With the possible exception of Mugabe and Silundika, the ZAPU leadership understood the U.S. position, the consulate claimed. During the U.N. sessions, U.S. officials met with Nkomo and other ZAPU leaders in New York and attempted to explain U.S. actions. The United States was sympathetic with ZAPU's goals, but public criticism of Britain would accomplish nothing, U.S. officials argued. Some U.N. resolutions were unrealistic and asked Britain to do the impossible. ZAPU should not judge the United States by a single vote in the U.N., U.S. officials pleaded.[72]

Talking to ZAPU did not stop the State Department from worrying about European sentiments in Central Africa. European opinion had troubled U.S. consuls for some time. A common view among the settlers was that the United States was pushing Britain into a hasty withdrawal from its African colonies, John Emmerson reported. He contended that every reference in Washington to freedom, self-determination, or majority rule raised a red flag for the Europeans in Central Africa. Such references provoked angry letters to the newspapers, denouncing the United States. Welensky was also apt to lash out at the U.S. Kaunda and Banda's visits to the White House were a particular irritant to the federal prime minister. After the Salisbury consulate reported criticism from both Africans and Europeans of U.S. votes in the United Nations in March 1962, the State Department pointed out that the consulate was responsible for explaining U.S. policy. The United States supported advancement of democratic principles, peaceful change, and adherence to the U.N. charter, the department wrote. Recent votes in the United Nations did not reflect a change in U.S. policy, it said. The United States was trying to moderate the extreme views found in the Committee of Seventeen, whether or not Africans or Europeans understood what it was trying to do. Overly detailed explanations might not be helpful, however. When the consulate seemed ready to publicize speeches made by U.S. representatives to the United Nations, the department directed that any such press releases be reviewed in Washington before release.[73]

Whitehead's Defeat

Whitehead's electoral defeat at the hands of Winston Field and the Rhodesian Front disappointed and dismayed the United States. The State Department concluded that the election results would harm long-term U.S. and British interests. Heated debates would resume in the United Nations. Since the anti-colonial coalition of African and Asian nations commanded a majority within the international organization, resolutions critical of Britain and calling for more drastic actions were inevitable. Chester Bowles predicted that the installation of a Rhodesian Front government would lead to violence between Africans and Europeans unless Britain intervened. After another trip to the Congo and Central Africa, Williams warned Rusk that Southern Rhodesia was the new African time bomb. If the nationalists were not offered some hope for their aspirations and brought into a constitutional dialogue, a major flare-up would occur.[74]

The immediate U.S. reaction was to communicate its concerns to London. The State Department asked for both a British assessment of the situation and an indication of how Britain planned to deal with it. Thereafter, U.S. attitudes contained equal measures of sympathy for Britain's awkward situation and impatience with British failures to act. Harlan

Cleveland, assistant secretary for international organizations affairs, told his British counterpart that it was a pity that Britain, with its fine record in the colonial arena, was now coupled with Portugal in U.N. debates. Williams sent encouraging messages to Butler, complimenting Britain on the wisdom and courage it showed in dealing with the federation's demise. Confronted with repeated assertions that Britain lacked the legal authority to act, Williams also suggested that it might have to circumvent constitutional niceties and take unprecedented actions. In Washington, Williams pressed his staff to devise means to induce Britain to be more forceful. A March 1963 State Department report concluded that working with the British was difficult because Britain had no overall policy for Africa. Britain had dealt well with most of its African colonies, but now faced the hard cases, the report said. Britain was now acting solely from the exigencies of the moment.[75]

One reason U.S. policy was uncertain was that disagreements persisted within the State Department, with officials involved with Africa and the United Nations arrayed against those involved with Britain. In March 1963, Williams referred to a stalemate within the department regarding the U.S. role in Central Africa. He went on to write that he understood Britain's problems. Nevertheless, he believed that the United States could not stand by while the Southern Rhodesian situation deteriorated to the detriment of both Britain and the United States. In September, the Bureau of European Affairs registered its dissent with a proposal authored by the Bureau of African Affairs and the Bureau of International Organizations Affairs. William R. Tyler, the assistant secretary for European and Canadian affairs, argued against pushing Britain to take some public action to satisfy what he termed unreasonable demands by African countries in the United Nations. Instead, the United States should respect Britain's sound judgment, follow its lead, and provide it continuing support.[76]

At least once, Williams's penchant for speaking freely caused him to take a public position beyond what the department was ready to approve. In October 1963, while traveling in Nigeria, Williams stated that the United States would help Britain and the African states bordering Southern Rhodesia apply economic sanctions should Southern Rhodesia declare independence. The acting secretary wired Williams that the department was still investigating the steps the U.S. could take regarding economic sanctions. Until the department had finished examining its options, the telegram admonished, U.S. officials should refrain from public statements about sanctions that might seem to promise more than the United States could, or would, deliver.[77]

The United States offered Britain suggestions, but with little effect. ZAPU leaders proposed that U Thant, U.N. secretary general, might be able to engineer a settlement. In spring 1963, the State Department pushed the British to accept the idea. Even if the secretary general or his representative could not broker a solution, his involvement might put off additional hostile resolutions in the General Assembly, the department contended. Since the idea had originated with ZAPU, backing it might gain the United States influence with the nationalists. The State Department pressed the Foreign Office for a positive response to the secretary general's offer to help. Stevenson lobbied Foreign Office officials. Nonetheless, the eventual British response was that Field was open to the secretary general visiting Southern Rhodesia, but only in a private capacity.[78]

The basic British response to U.S. concerns was that it could do little. Public opinion in Britain would not tolerate any British effort to oust the Field government. Suspending the 1961 constitution, as the General Assembly advocated, was impossible because Britain was in no position to force the Field government to act, British officials argued. Moving against the Southern Rhodesian regime would drive the Field government into closer ties with South Africa. Foreign Office officials said that Britain favored an African majority government, but its only means to promote one was to seek influence with Field behind the scenes.[79]

U.S. officials were so eager to see evidence of change in official British attitudes that they saw change where none was intended. After Home and Sandys made statements in the House of Commons in November 1963, the U.S. United Nations delegation concluded that the Home government was taking a new tack on Southern Rhodesia. It was putting, the delegation thought, new emphasis on majority rule coupled with protection for minority rights. The delegation warned Washington that a more vigorous policy in London might lead to a unilateral declaration of independence in Salisbury. Nevertheless, the delegation proposed that the United States indicate its support for a more forceful policy and offer its assistance. The delegation suggested that the U.S. might offer to tell the Field government, or even announce publicly, that it would not recognize a unilateral declaration of independence.[80]

Still a British Problem

In October 1963, the Salisbury consulate offered an ambitious plan for resolving the Southern Rhodesian situation. The consulate began with the assertion that if and when Africans used violence to gain power in Southern Rhodesia, the resulting economic dislocation and the European flight would leave the territory weak and disorganized. The consulate proposed that the United States draft a settlement. A key element would be international guarantees for majority rule and minority rights. The U.S. should seek British support and arrange negotiations between Southern Rhodesia's African and European leaders. The consulate wrote that the United States could offset what it characterized as the impertinence of the proposed approach by offering financial aid for education, agriculture, and rural development.[81]

Despite Salisbury's proposal, thinking in Washington remained less ambitious. A March 1963 State Department report suggested, with only limited confidence, that the U.S. try to get Britain to think more broadly about African issues, and to understand the wider implications for U.S. and British interests. Financial aid to Southern Rhodesia as an inducement for European cooperation remained on the agenda. The United States could also offer to help restrain debates within the United Nations. Nevertheless, the State Department's position remained that Southern Rhodesia was a British problem. The U.S. did not have a solution. State Department papers talked about encouraging a compromise, keeping the lines of communication open, maintaining a dialogue, and preserving a possible role as a mediator.[82]

The State Department's stance was clear to British officials. An official in Britain's Washington embassy told London that Williams admitted that he had no solutions to offer. That was not the U.S. role, Williams would argue. According to the Washington embassy, the State Department and Williams saw Central Africa as a British responsibility and, based on Britain's record in Africa, they expected Britain to discharge its responsibility successfully. In the embassy's view, the State Department saw its role as being occasionally a burr under the British saddle, but more usually a helpful but silent partner.[83]

Consistent with the State Department's thinking, the United States was willing to support the efforts of any credible third party. In addition to the U.N. secretary general, the State Department viewed favorably New Zealand's suggestion of a commonwealth commission. When a subcommittee of the Committee of Seventeen traveled to London to meet with British officials, U.S. officials held out hope that the subcommittee would appreciate Britain's situation and soften U.N. resolutions. The State Department also thought that the African leaders the United States had befriended, Banda, Kaunda, and Nyerere, could help. Nyerere was, in fact, active behind the scenes. He counseled ZAPU to be patient and suggested an East and Central African common services organization as a partial replacement for the federation. The State Department communicated its appreciation to Nyerere. It indicated that it hoped that he could do more, perhaps meeting with Field or breaking the deadlock between the Field government and the nationalists.[84]

U.S. officials met with representatives from the federation and from Southern Rhodesia, although the meetings produced little. In June 1963, Williams and federation officials disagreed about the reason for lessened unrest. Williams attributed the improvement to Nyerere's efforts to restrain ZAPU. The federation officials thought Southern Rhodesia's heightened security measures were the cause. Both parties agreed that a peaceful solution was the ultimate aim. The federation representatives suggested that the United States could broker a dialogue. Williams said that the United States would be glad to do so, as long as both sides were willing to give and take. When Williams asked what Field was willing to offer the nationalists, the reply was only a meeting with Nkomo. At the end of the meeting, Williams repeated his advice that talks would be possible only when Nkomo had reason to believe that they would produce something of value. In September, Harlan Cleveland counseled John Howman, the Southern Rhodesian minister of internal affairs, that the international community would not accept in 1963 what it might have accepted in 1953. Too much had changed in Africa, Cleveland warned. Howman responded that Southern Rhodesia, unlike the United States, did not consider many of the changes beneficial. Handing Southern Rhodesia over to the African majority would destroy what the Europeans had built up, he said. In October, Kennedy met with Welensky. Welensky responded to Kennedy's inquiry about the Southern Rhodesian issue by asking for U.S. help in pushing the British to make concrete proposals. The British had to take the lead, Welensky argued. Kennedy's response was not recorded. Most of the conversation dealt in general terms with change in Africa. Kennedy told Welensky that African nationalism was so strong that one could only try to moderate and influence it. Many of the problems in Africa were pragmatic rather than moral, the president added.[85]

U.S. officials were also in contact with nationalist leaders, with little apparent effect. Williams advised Sithole that rapid constitutional change and violence were not the only two alternatives. Through careful negotiations, ZAPU could reach its goals. ZAPU should not start a long struggle for majority rule when other means were available, Williams advised. Confronted with complaints about U.S. votes in the United Nations, U.S. officials said that they could not always support ZAPU. In some cases, a different vote in the U.N. would put the U.S. on one side or the other, and might deprive it of an opportunity to influence events in the future. When Sithole pressed for U.S. pressure on Britain, U.S. officials said that they favored majority rule, but Southern Rhodesia was a British problem. They contended that a dialogue between the nationalists and the Southern Rhodesian government would be the best way to solve the problem.[86]

The split in the nationalist ranks created complications for the United States, if only because Nkomo charged that U.S. officials supported his opponents. The Salisbury consulate considered Nkomo ill-suited as a nationalist leader. He was inclined towards evolutionary change, as evidenced by his initial agreement to the 1961 constitution, the consulate claimed. Neither the Southern Rhodesian Africans nor ZAPU's African allies were prepared to accept gradual change. Nkomo, however, was not strong enough to resist their pressure for rapid political change or to confront the Southern Rhodesian government to secure such change, the consulate reported. Nkomo had instead led ZAPU in making just enough trouble to discredit the Whitehead government and put Field in power. The State Department was tempted to see Sithole as more determined and organized than Nkomo and less likely to resort to violence. The department thought that a weakened nationalist movement was unfortunate just as the federation was collapsing. Consulate officials in Salisbury told Nkomo that the United States favored a united nationalist party. The embassy in Dar-es-Salaam remained in contact with all Southern Rhodesian exiles, not just Nkomo's critics, they said. Nkomo contended that Irving Brown, on behalf of the AFL-CIO and the International Confederation of Free Trade Unions, had helped the ZAPU rebels. Consulate officials conceded that Brown was a U.S. citizen, but they claimed that they were unaware of any such assistance. In any case, they said, they could not control Brown's activities.[87]

One More U.N. Resolution

Despite the State Department's efforts, the U.S. position regarding Central Africa remained unchanged as of the fall of 1963. As Britain dismantled the federation and set Nyasaland and Northern Rhodesia, but not Southern Rhodesia, on the road to independence, the anti-colonial coalition in the United Nations renewed its criticism of Britain. The transfer of federation armed forces, particularly its airplanes, to Southern Rhodesia, became a flash point. The anti-colonial countries drafted a Security Council resolution calling on Britain to block the transfer. Britain turned to the United States for help in defeating the measure.

After a vigorous debate within the State Department, Rusk decided to support the British. The anti-colonial countries managed to put the resolution on the Security Council agenda, over British objections. Cleveland and Williams submitted a joint memorandum arguing against all-out opposition to the resolution. Even with U.S. help, Britain was unlikely to convince enough countries to abstain, they argued. Britain would be forced to veto it, something Britain had never done. Britain should, instead, develop an alternative resolution that urged Britain to do its best and requested the secretary general to continue to use his good offices. Even if the alternative failed, it might help convince more countries to abstain. If Britain wanted to secure more abstentions, it would have to promise privately that it would not grant independence to Southern Rhodesia without due regard for the majority's wishes. Britain would have to make a public statement discreet enough not to upset the Field government. On behalf of the Bureau of European Affairs, Tyler countered that the United States should follow Britain's lead and offer complete support. Tyler wrote that the British were unwilling to yield. Rusk decided that the U.S. would support the British position by trying to persuade more countries to abstain. U.S. officials were not to say that Britain would not grant independence to a minority Southern Rhodesian government. They should say only that the United States thought that it would not. Rusk acted on the understanding that Britain would try to persuade commonwealth countries to oppose the admission of the People's Republic of China to the United Nations.[88]

The British delegation opposed the resolution. The vote was thirteen for and one (Britain) against. Only the United States and France abstained. Afterwards, Rusk asked Ormsby-Gore whether the British resented the U.S. decision to abstain rather than joining with the British to veto the measure. Rusk said that he was sorry that the United States had not lined up more abstainers despite some hard work. Ormsby-Gore said Britain was most grateful for the American assistance.[89]

At the end of 1963, one colonial conundrum remained, Southern Rhodesia. Both Britain and the United States wanted a government in Salisbury that featured enough African participation so that the world community would accept granting independence. Ian Smith's Rhodesian Front government, however, did not intend to allow Africans a meaningful political role and neither Britain nor the United States knew how to make him do it.

Johnson and British Colonial Africa, 1963–1968: No Rescue

Africa's place in U.S. foreign policy during the first years of the Johnson administration remained much as it had been in the Kennedy administration. Although G. Mennen Williams had argued against Johnson's selection as the vice presidential candidate in 1960, he remained assistant secretary for African affairs and retained personal access to the new president for a time. Despite some grumbling, Johnson continued to meet with prominent African leaders. Rusk remained secretary of state and Ball his under secretary. Both remained unconvinced that the United States should play a major role in Africa. Johnson's attention was elsewhere, on domestic programs and the war in Vietnam. Intent on keeping African issues off his desk, Johnson appointed Averell Harriman ambassador at large with responsibility for African affairs in April 1964. Johnson contended that he did not intend to diminish Williams's status, but many observers concluded otherwise. The administration remained sensitive to Russian and Chinese activities in Africa. The Congo absorbed considerable U.S. time and attention because of Russia's involvement. When a group with ties to China overthrew the Zanzibar government a month after independence, Johnson saw the prospect of "another Cuba." During the 1964 presidential campaign, Johnson called for a massive effort to uplift the less-developed nations. When Williams tried to convert Johnson's rhetoric into a substantial foreign aid program for Africa, however, his proposals received a chilly reception within the administration. In the competition for dollars, aid to Africa came a distant third to domestic programs and the conflict in Southeast Asia. Robert Komer, on the National Security Council staff, told Johnson that Williams thought that American money could solve all of Africa's problems. Africa was, however, so primitive that foreign aid would do little good.[1]

The principal remaining issue in British colonial Africa was Southern Rhodesia. Here too, the Johnson administration continued Kennedy's policies. State Department officials floated ideas for a larger U.S. role, but Rusk and others were content to cheer the British on from the sidelines.

Douglas-Home

The Douglas-Home government started out sounding as if it intended to take a hard line on the Southern Rhodesia issue. Shortly after becoming prime minister, Douglas-Home responded to a question from Harold Wilson, leader of the Labour opposition, to the effect that his government believed in majority rule and protection for minority rights. Later, Douglas-Home said that this statement meant his government would not concede independence to Southern Rhodesia before majority rule. Douglas-Home's commonwealth relations secretary, Duncan Sandys, told the Southern Rhodesian government that Britain could not grant independence since the Southern Rhodesian franchise was far more restrictive than in any other territory that had gained its independence from Britain.[2]

Nevertheless, the measures considered by Douglas-Home and his ministers fell far short of an insistence on majority rule. In February 1964, Butler recommended proposals he had raised earlier with the Southern Rhodesian government: an end to discrimination, lowered voting qualifications, and sufficient African seats in the legislature to block constitutional amendments. Sandys warned against pushing for faster movement towards majority rule. Douglas-Home raised the possibility of allowing Africans in an independent Southern Rhodesia to appeal to the privy council regarding discriminatory measures. Douglas-Home also toyed with offering Southern Rhodesia substantial financial support for secondary education if Southern Rhodesia would put off demands for independence.[3]

Douglas-Home and his ministers doubted that any of their proposals could bridge the gap between the African nationalists and the Rhodesian Front regime. They also doubted that they would satisfy the nationalists' supporters among the members of the commonwealth and the United Nations. Instead of resolving Southern Rhodesia's status, Douglas-Home's goal became postponing a crisis, particularly a declaration of independence by the Southern Rhodesian government. In February 1964, Douglas-Home told Butler and Sandys that the goal was to avoid a formal break between Britain and Southern Rhodesia. They needed to persuade the Southern Rhodesian government that Britain was taking a positive approach. By summer, the aim was to put the issue off until after the commonwealth prime ministers' meeting in July. In the summer, the goal became postponing the issue until after the British general elections scheduled for October. The Douglas-Home government's goal for negotiations with the Southern Rhodesians in September 1964 was to ensure that the meetings ended with an agreement that further talks were necessary.[4]

Within the Macmillan government, Home had been a skeptic about rapid movement towards majority rule and independence, often disagreeing with Macleod. Army mutinies in the newly independent Uganda, Tanzania, and Kenya, and the overthrow of the Zanzibar government within a month of independence, all in early 1964, revived his doubts. In March, he told the Nigerian prime minister, Abubakar Tafawa Balewa, that the events in East Africa demonstrated the problems created by premature independence. Giving all literates the vote was a mistake, Douglas-Home said. Pressing Southern Rhodesia to move faster toward majority rule would be wrong.[5]

Negotiations between Douglas-Home and Field in January 1964 failed to produce an agreement. Field appeared eager for a deal. He told Douglas-Home that the uncertainty about Southern Rhodesia's status was inhibiting investment in the territory and motivating Europeans to leave. As long as a link remained between Southern Rhodesia and Britain, Africans would appeal to Britain for redress rather than dealing in good faith with the Southern Rhodesian government. Field offered to end discrimination immediately and reform the land laws within four years. He offered changes in voting qualifications, but not enough for the British. Field made it clear that his government was not interested in handing over power to the African majority, only in increasing African participation in government.[6]

Field's failure to secure independence led to his replacement as prime minister in April by Ian Smith, his minister of finance. Smith took a harder line than Field. Under Smith, the Rhodesian Front government increased its repression of the African nationalists. It banned both ZANU and ZAPU and detained many of their leaders. Smith blamed communists for the unrest in Southern Rhodesia and throughout Africa. He foresaw no prospect for rapid African political advancement. He was mistrustful of the British government and intent on securing Southern Rhodesian independence. He was fond of arguing that Southern Rhodesian independence had been promised in return for acceptance of the 1961 constitution. He contended that the 1961 constitution brought with it an understanding that Southern Rhodesia would become independent if the federation should be dissolved.[7]

Meetings between Douglas-Home and Smith in September produced little beyond a joint communiqué. Smith repeated his claims that Southern Rhodesia was owed its independence. Douglas-Home and Sandys countered that independence required some demonstration that the majority of the Southern Rhodesian population desired it. Smith offered a referendum of European voters and a meeting of Southern Rhodesia's African chiefs as the means to gauge popular opinion. Smith argued that the African nationalists had forfeited their right to be consulted by refusing to participate in Southern Rhodesian elections. Douglas-Home and Sandys declined to accept a meeting of the chiefs as an adequate measure of African opinion.[8]

Back home in Southern Rhodesia, Smith and the Rhodesian Front put a positive face on the talks. They fostered the notion that the communiqué meant that the Douglas-Home government would grant independence under the 1961 constitution if the Southern Rhodesian government could demonstrate majority support for the constitution and independence. In doing so, Smith deprived his opposition of its best issues. The opposition had reorganized itself into the Rhodesia Party, with Welensky as leader and Whitehead his deputy. The party was prepared to exploit what it thought were widespread European concerns about a unilateral declaration of independence. The opposition also seemed more inclined to seek an agreement with African leaders. The British high commissioner in Southern Rhodesia contemplated an alliance between the Rhodesia Party and moderate Africans, perhaps even some nationalists. Instead, Smith could now argue that, rather than acting alone, he was negotiating with the British. Rather than amendments to the 1961 constitution, what was needed was a credible means to gauge African opinion. Whitehead and Welensky felt compelled to pledge their cooperation with the government. Welensky needed a seat in the legislature to function as party leader. In two by-elections, he and another Rhodesia Party candidate lost badly to their Rhodesian Front opponents.[9]

Wilson

In opposition, Harold Wilson and the Labour Party sounded as if they would not grant independence to Southern Rhodesia until a majority African government was in control. Labour opposed the 1961 constitution, twice voting in the Commons against it. After becoming party leader, Wilson said that a Labour government would amend the constitution to allow the people of Southern Rhodesia to control their own destinies. During the campaign leading to the October 1964 elections, Wilson repeated the same claim in a letter addressed to a Southern Rhodesian African leader and published in a Salisbury newspaper. Wilson wrote that the Labour Party was totally opposed to granting independence as long as a white minority controlled the government. Labour had urged, Wilson added, negotiations with all parties to achieve a peaceful transition to African majority rule.[10]

Within weeks of gaining office, the Wilson government publicly warned the Southern Rhodesian government of the consequences of a declaration of independence. Smith had refused to meet with Arthur Bottomley, the new commonwealth relations secretary, while Bottomley was on his way to Zambia's independence celebration. Smith had also declined Wilson's invitation for further talks. Attempting to deter rash action by the Southern Rhodesian government, the Wilson regime pointed out that a declaration of independence would leave Southern Rhodesia isolated. A declaration would be an open act of defiance and rebellion. If Southern Rhodesia declared its independence, Britain would sever relations with those responsible. Southern Rhodesia would lose its financial and trade relations with Britain. The Southern Rhodesian economy would suffer, the Wilson government warned. Few other nations, particularly members of the commonwealth, would recognize an independent Southern Rhodesia and some might even recognize a government-in-exile.[11]

Over the next year, from October 1964 to November 1965, Wilson and his ministers attempted to negotiate a settlement with the Southern Rhodesian government. The proposals they offered resembled those developed by the Macmillan and Douglas-Home governments, however. Wilson was not about to impose a settlement on Southern Rhodesia, certainly not by force. In January 1965, Bottomley conceded that the Wilson government would abide by the convention that the British government would not intervene in Southern Rhodesian affairs except with the agreement of the Southern Rhodesian government. In March, Wilson wrote to Smith that Britain would not impose majority rule or allow anyone to come to power without first serving a political apprenticeship. Wilson distilled his government's position into five principles: unimpeded progress to majority rule; no retrogressive amendments to the constitution; immediate improvement in the Africans' political status; progress toward ending racial discrimination; and independence on a basis acceptable to the people of Rhodesia as a whole. None of the principles went beyond positions taken by Conservative governments. The Wilson government rehearsed the specific measures considered by the Douglas-Home and Macmillan administrations: changes in voting qualifications, increased African seats in the legislature, and reform of the land laws. At one point or another, Wilson suggested recourse to a high-level commonwealth delegation, a referendum of all Rhodesian taxpayers, and establishment of a royal commission to recommend a settlement.[12]

Despite having Sir Hugh Foot (Lord Caradon) as its representative at the United Nations, the Wilson government clung to old positions in the international forum. In May 1965, the Security Council considered a resolution noting the serious implications of holding elections in Southern Rhodesia under a constitution unacceptable to the majority of the population. The British delegation opposed the resolution. Caradon argued that Britain could not intervene in Southern Rhodesia's internal affairs because the territory had been self-governing for many years.[13]

For the Wilson government, delay once more became the goal. The Labour government doubted that a settlement with Smith was possible. It dismissed the notion of using British troops to unseat the Smith regime and announced its decision not to do so. The Wilson government also felt hemmed in by both domestic and international political pressure. Labour held only a slim majority in the Commons. Neither imposing a settlement, particularly through force, nor conceding independence was acceptable to important segments of the British public. Most nations in the commonwealth and the United Nations favored independence under majority rule. Yet they seemed to offer Britain little meaningful assistance in achieving it. As early as November 1964, Bottomley saw the problem as avoiding either handing the problem to the United Nations or allowing immediate independence under the 1961 constitution. His solution was persuading Smith to change voting qualifications and allow the nationalists to participate in elections. When such ideas encountered Southern Rhodesian resistance, the government's aims became stringing out negotiations as long as possible and convincing the Smith regime not to declare independence.[14]

Despite Wilson's public pronouncements before coming to power, he was not an enthusiastic supporter of majority rule in Southern Rhodesia. Before becoming prime minister, his involvement in African issues had been slight. In March 1964, Douglas-Home sought, through an intermediary, Wilson's support for offering Southern Rhodesia substantial financial assistance for secondary education and administrative training in return for delaying independence. Wilson expressed regrets about his earlier commitment to altering the Southern Rhodesian constitution. He said he wished he had been aware of the proposals Douglas-Home was considering and promised to think about Douglas-Home's ideas. He warned, however, that the best he would be able to offer was a promise that Labour had no commitment. He would not be able to push his party any further.[15]

Barriers to an Agreement

The nationalists remained committed to rapid progress toward majority rule. They wanted constitutional changes and voting based on "one man, one vote." If the Southern Rhodesian government would not yield, they wanted the British to intervene. The Wilson government had little sympathy for such ideas. After meeting with ZAPU and ZANU representatives, the British high commissioner reported to London that both nationalist groups needed shock treatment. They were, he wrote, caught up in a self-constructed web of constitutional boycott, internecine rivalry, and delusion about the political realities of Britain's position. They needed to understand that Britain was not about to intervene militarily. It would not call a constitutional conference to which no one could or would come. In late October 1965, Wilson told the press and the House of Commons that anyone who expected a thunderbolt in the form of the Royal Air Force hurtling from the sky to destroy their enemies was deluded. Such delusions wasted valuable time and energy.[16]

The greatest obstacle, however, to a negotiated settlement was the intransigence of Smith and his followers. One Rhodesian Front member told a visiting British minister that the Front had won power based on certain principles. The party was willing to negotiate, but it would never retreat from its basic positions, he said. Labour's pronouncements on majority rule made Smith reluctant to engage in talks. Yet British and Southern Rhodesian representatives, including Wilson and Smith, talked on many occasions through most of 1965. Despite Wilson's willingness to make concessions and retreat from majority rule, the talks produced nothing. Wilson observed in mid–October 1965 that it was as if the two sides were living in different worlds, almost different centuries. Disagreement on each of Wilson's five principles was virtually absolute. Smith and the Rhodesian Front were intent on independence on their terms and nothing else.[17]

By late 1965, the front had firm control of Southern Rhodesia and its government. It used its extensive security legislation to repress the nationalists and their political parties. In October 1964, the government staged a conference of chiefs, securing the chiefs' unanimous support for independence in return for promises to expand their authority. In November, Southern Rhodesian voters were asked whether they supported independence under the current constitution, although not necessarily through a unilateral declaration of independence. Non-European voters boycotted the referendum and turnout was only sixty-two percent. Fifty-six percent of those voting favored independence. The government displayed a willingness to move against even European opposition, restricting the former prime minister, Garfield Todd. Furthermore, the Rhodesia Party's by-election defeats demoralized the opposition. Welensky and Whitehead retired from politics. When the government held legislative elections in May 1965, the Rhodesian Front eliminated its European electoral opponents. The front won all fifty seats elected by the A roll. It faced opposition in only twenty-eight contests. What opposition remained consisted of the Africans, including ten Rhodesia Party candidates, who won fourteen of the fifteen seats elected by the B roll.[18]

October and early November 1965 witnessed a flurry of activity in Salisbury. Wilson and a large British party flew in for talks with nationalist leaders and with Smith and his government. On October 30, Wilson left without an agreement. Six days later, the Southern Rhodesian government declared a state of emergency. On November 11, in a lunchtime radio broadcast, Ian Smith announced that Southern Rhodesia had declared itself an independent state.

Relying on the British

From the beginning of the Johnson administration through October 1964, when the Wilson government took power in Britain, the Salisbury consulate advocated an active U.S. approach to Southern Rhodesia. The consulate told Washington that things were getting worse. Europeans and Africans were moving further apart and the possibility of violence was growing. The British had become passive, given over to wishful thinking, the consulate advised. Trying to maintain the status quo underestimated the nationalists and their access to external assistance. The United States and Britain needed to develop a plan, a joint diplomatic initiative with other countries interested in a peaceful transition, like Zambia. The consulate was dubious about the steps favored in Washington, consulting with the British, keeping commonwealth members informed, and warning the Southern Rhodesian government. The consulate's view was that warnings only irritated the Rhodesian Front government. In September 1964, the consulate suggested that Washington advise the Douglas-Home government to spell out for Smith the consequences of a declaration of independence.[19]

In February 1964, Williams provided Harriman, his new boss at the State Department, with an assessment and recommendations regarding Southern Rhodesia. Williams painted a depressing picture. The Rhodesian Front government comprised inept, inexperienced politicians, capable of irrational conclusions and actions. For their part, the African nationalists were divided. Neither faction was willing to compromise for fear of being labeled a sellout. The British had no real policy and U.S. policy had been to follow the British lead. Now the United States needed to consider involving members of the commonwealth or seeking its own solution. Williams's recommendations were minimal: consult the British, warn Southern Rhodesia again, and push the British to make public a satisfactory policy statement.[20]

Papers prepared in the Bureau of African Affairs and sent to Williams in the following months went further. In May, bureau staff suggested a package of economic and educational aid as an inducement for a compromise in Southern Rhodesia. In July, the staff proposed that the United States stop following the British and act as a catalyst. The staff thought the U.S. could mobilize sympathetic commonwealth and African nations to devise a solution.

The staff recommended that the U.S. should not recognize an independent Southern Rhodesia. It should also support any constructive measures proposed in the United Nations, provided Britain did not actively oppose them. The U.S. should provide covert support to the nationalists with the goal of unifying them, but it should not recognize any government in exile.[21]

The notion of using financial aid as a lever in Southern Rhodesia cropped up in London and Washington as well. The British imagined that they could use U.S. dollars to fund a major initiative in secondary education. Nevertheless, U.S. financial aid to Southern Rhodesia declined after 1962. It fell from $312 million to $202 million in 1964. The United States suspended all aid in June 1964.[22]

At the end of 1963, Rusk remained content to rely on British reassurances. When Rusk met with Sandys in London, the commonwealth relations secretary predicted that Southern Rhodesia would not proclaim its independence. It had nothing to gain by doing so, he said. Sandys assured Rusk that his recent speech in Parliament stated plainly that Britain would not grant independence as long as the current voting arrangements remained in place. If the United States wanted a more precise statement, the British might be able to produce one. Rusk thought that other African nations had moderated their positions regarding Southern Rhodesia. Sandys agreed, but added that Britain needed U.S. help in the United Nations. When the department described the meeting to the Salisbury consulate, it commented that a solution was desirable but the status quo was the best that could be expected.[23]

The department declined to pursue the active approach advocated by Salisbury. The department told Salisbury that it needed better information before it could authorize action. All it had were press speculations about the recent talks between Field and Douglas-Home. It did not know whether the British had persuaded other commonwealth members to help. It did not know whether the nationalists intended to establish a government in exile. Pending better information, the consulate was not to initiate discussions. It was also not to respond to press inquiries regarding a United States response to a unilateral declaration of independence.[24]

More Worries

Smith's ascension to power in April disturbed the department, but it did little more than share its worries. A message from the department to the U.S. posts in Africa observed that Smith's appointment as prime minister increased the chances of a unilateral declaration of independence. It decreased the chances of successful negotiations between the British and the Southern Rhodesian government. The message added that the United States could exert little influence in Southern Rhodesian affairs. Nevertheless, national interests and policy objectives in Southern Africa might be adversely affected. Given that the United States could do little and Britain insisted it could not exert effective pressure, the department added cryptically, it was seriously considering "developing United States assets" among those in Southern Rhodesia who opposed the government's independence policy. The department may have been referring to Welensky. During the summer of 1964, officials saw him as the best hope for a solution. They were aware that he was planning an electoral alliance with Whitehead and had discussed a timetable for African majority rule with Sithole.[25]

By August, the department was worried that it did not know Britain's plans. Department officials were concerned that they could not develop contingency plans without knowing more about British thinking. Washington told the London embassy that staff hoped that the British had compiled plans for all conceivable contingencies. Otherwise, the United States would face another situation like the Zanzibar revolution, where it had to wait for the British to sort out what they would do. Department officials asked the British embassy in Washington for information. They were told to approach the Foreign Office at a senior level. The Foreign Office would understand the African and international implications better than the Commonwealth Relations Office.[26]

The department's concerns reached a peak in September when it concluded that Smith intended to declare independence if he did not get concessions from Douglas-Home. The department instructed David Bruce, the U.S. ambassador in London, to communicate with the British government as the highest appropriate level. Bruce was to convey American concerns about a declaration of independence. Since an independent Southern Rhodesia would become an issue before the Security Council, the United States wanted to avoid a declaration of independence. It would not recognize an independent Southern Rhodesia. Bruce was to ask what else the United States could to do to assist.[27]

The Douglas-Home government acknowledged the concerns, but thought them premature. The London embassy reported that the Douglas-Home government hoped that its conversations with Smith would deter a declaration of independence. After the meetings, it would be in a better position to determine its policy and to identify how the United States could assist.[28]

U.S. officials remained just as ignorant and worried after the Douglas-Home-Smith meetings. In October, the London embassy reported that attempts to get specific responses from Commonwealth Relations Office staff had been unsuccessful. The embassy concluded that the British had made no decisions regarding possible courses of action and had done no contingency planning.[29]

A Supporting Role

Through the first year of the Wilson government, the United States responded positively to its requests for help averting a declaration of independence. In October 1964, Patrick Gordon Walker, Wilson's foreign secretary, asked Rusk to issue a statement supporting Wilson's warning to Smith regarding the consequences of a declaration of independence. The secretary complied. The U.S. statement praised Wilson's message and offered hopes that the British and Southern Rhodesian governments would continue to talk and find a satisfactory solution. In May 1965, Stevenson told the Security Council that the United States would not recognize a unilateral declaration of independence by Southern Rhodesia. In June, Williams announced that the United States was ending all arms shipments to Southern Rhodesia. In Salisbury, the U.S. consul declined an invitation to attend the conference of chiefs summoned to approve independence.[30]

In the United Nations, the U.S. sought a middle way. Representatives pronounced that the United States supported independence under majority rule and opposed independence under minority rule. The U.S. refused to support resolutions that were critical of the British or that required action by the United Nations. Instead, the United States lobbied for weaker, compromise measures. When confronted with a tough measure, the U.S. usually abstained, explaining that it sympathized with the resolution's intent. State Department officials characterized their goals as keeping the debates' temperature down and advocating communication with all factions in Southern Rhodesia.[31]

The department saw Britain as responsible for Southern Rhodesia and the U.S. as playing a supporting role. When a staff report regarding contingency planning for a unilateral declaration of independence reached Under Secretary George Ball, he sent it back for revisions. His instructions were that the United States should not get out in front of Britain. The plan should contain public actions in the period after a unilateral declaration of independence and private actions aimed at the Southern Rhodesian government before a declaration. When Stevenson announced that the U.S. would not recognize an independent Southern Rhodesia, he emphasized that Britain and Southern Rhodesia were responsible jointly for resolving the issue.[32]

Calls for Action

The Salisbury consulate warned against following a British lead. The consulate argued that avoiding a declaration of independence should not be the primary goal of the U.S. The basic objective should be helping moderate Africans resist pressure from radicals and from the communist bloc to adopt violent tactics. The U.S. should take a more active role, striving for increased western and moderate African influence over events even if doing so increased the risk of a declaration of independence. The consulate imagined that the United States could stimulate a U.N. resolution that Britain could accept. The resolution would threaten sanctions in order to move the Southern Rhodesian government toward a settlement. The consulate reported that many nationalist leaders now favored a declaration of independence. The nationalists believed that a declaration would generate international pressure so that Britain would act on their behalf. The consulate's current instructions were to remain passive. Once Britain had been prodded into articulating an effective policy, the consulate hoped it would be free to engage with the Southern Rhodesian government and others.[33]

Robert Komer, on the National Security Council staff, also advocated that the United States become more active. In April 1965, he suggested to Williams that Harriman travel to Salisbury to warn Smith against declaring independence. Komer thought that the U.S. position on Southern Rhodesia was winning it no friends in Africa and failing to deter Smith from declaring independence. A scolding from Harriman might cool the Smith government's ardor for independence. In June, Komer wrote to Johnson that the U.S. stance on Southern Rhodesia and other issues in the southern third of Africa was more likely to determine the U.S. influence in the region than any aid program, no matter how big. Komer argued that the United States needed to stay slightly ahead of the issue rather than allow itself to be dragged toward the inevitable.[34]

In September 1965, with the Wilson-Smith talks in London on the horizon, a chorus of voices within the Johnson administration urged more U.S. action. Komer and Ulrich Haynes from the National Security Council staff returned to the idea of sending Harriman to Salisbury. Williams listed eight possible actions for Ball. The most important were an official statement warning of the consequences of a unilateral declaration and a direct approach to Smith. Wayne Fredericks, Williams's deputy, weighed in with similar suggestions. The Salisbury consulate recommended high-level officials communicate U.S. concerns to Smith while he was in London.[35]

Holding Back

When Rusk met with Cledwyn Hughes, minister of state in the Foreign Office, on September 20, the secretary seemed most concerned that Britain considered the United

States and Britain in agreement on Southern Rhodesia. He sought and got assurance from Hughes that they were. On September 29, the department sent Salisbury a message to be delivered orally to Smith. The message reminded Smith that the United States supported Britain's efforts to reach a settlement acceptable to the Southern Rhodesian population as a whole. The U.S. did not intend to deviate from its strong support for the British government then or if a unilateral declaration of independence occurred. The message warned Smith that it would be a grievous error to assume that the United States would condone any unilateral action by the Southern Rhodesia. At the suggestion of British officials, Consul McClelland added that the U.S. hoped that Smith's talks with Wilson succeeded.[36]

The same day, acting Secretary Ball sent the London embassy a message indicating that United States support for Britain was limited. The London embassy had suggested that now was the time to say whether United States support for Britain was in any sense qualified. The British were counting on firm United States support and cooperation regardless of what they decided to do about Southern Rhodesia, the embassy wrote. Ball replied that the embassy should tell the Wilson government that United States support was qualified. It could not make up for the export earnings, estimated at £200 million, that Britain would lose if it cut economic ties with Southern Rhodesia. Whatever help the United States could provide regarding tobacco or sugar imports would require further study, as would a complete U.S. embargo of Southern Rhodesia. United States support over Southern Rhodesia did not equate with a blank check for support in other areas, Ball reminded the embassy. Ball also wanted better information about British plans. Finally, he admonished the embassy to avoid allowing the British to use the limitations on United States support as an excuse for inaction, especially when talking to the other members of the Commonwealth.[37]

The State Department remained firm on the assistance the United States would offer Britain should Southern Rhodesia declare its independence. In an October 11 meeting with Michael Stewart, now the foreign secretary, Rusk, Ball, and Secretary of Defense Robert McNamara stressed that the administration could provide only limited economic help without congressional approval. The administration could offer Britain medium term credits for buying tobacco, but it would need congressional approval for almost any other help regarding Rhodesian exports or imports. After the Wilson administration indicated disappointment with the Johnson administration's stance, Ball reiterated the administration's position for the London embassy. The United States could not afford to give Britain another £200 million or more to protect the pound. The U.S. was providing heavy support for the pound, Ball wrote. The United States had balance of payments problems of its own.[38]

In any case, U.S. intelligence community advised that economic sanctions would not be effective against Southern Rhodesia. A Special National Intelligence Estimate dated October 13, 1965, stated that economic sanctions would not dislodge the Rhodesian Front government for at least several years. The U.S. lacked sufficient political leverage on the parties concerned to have a decisive influence. The U.S. could refuse to recognize an independent Rhodesia and it could join with Britain in imposing economic sanctions. Nevertheless, U.S. trade with Rhodesia was one-sixth Britain's. American private investment in Southern Rhodesia amounted to only $56 million. Cutting off trade and investment would not have a significant impact on Southern Rhodesia. At the same time, joining in sanctions would not earn the United States much credit in Africa. Even if the U.S. assisted with economic sanctions, Africans would still assign the U.S. some responsibility for allowing Southern Rhodesia to become independent under the Rhodesian Front government.[39]

U.S. officials stayed in contact with nationalist leaders in exile and, despite resistance from the Southern Rhodesian government, in Southern Rhodesia. Nevertheless, the U.S. intelligence community had little confidence in the nationalists. They were badly divided and bickering among themselves. Both ZANU and ZAPU were badly organized and ineffective, according to the intelligence community. Most leaders were in detention or in exile. Neither organization had gained the firm support of Rhodesia's urban workers. The government's security measures were effective enough to limit the nationalists to minor violence and sabotage.[40]

Last Exchanges

Wilson asked Johnson to communicate to Smith directly the U.S. position on independence. The president sent personal messages to both Wilson and Smith before their talks. He had the U.S. embassy in London tell Smith that the United States opposed any solution unacceptable to the majority of the Rhodesian population. Nevertheless, the State Department resisted taking a public position. Many of the officials who had urged more action earlier wanted the U.S. to release the message Johnson had sent to Smith. Ball disagreed. He believed that a declaration of independence was inevitable. The United States had done enough, he thought. Further U.S. involvement would complicate its relations with Portugal, a NATO ally. Rusk agreed with Ball. He communicated to Williams that the United States would make no public statements until and unless Southern Rhodesia declared its independence. Rusk argued that a public statement was likely to push Smith towards independence.[41]

Wilson coaxed Johnson to intervene again. On October 22, Rusk communicated to Wilson that the United States would not make a public announcement. Wilson was free to convey the president's views to Smith. Wilson responded that a message conveyed through the U.S. representatives in Salisbury would be more effective. Wilson claimed that the Rhodesians did not understand the U.S. position. They needed to hear it directly from U.S. officials. Johnson had Ross McClelland, the U.S. consul in Salisbury, tell Smith that a declaration of independence would be a tragic mistake. The United States had supported Britain throughout the crisis. McClelland was to tell Smith that the U.S. would continue to do so if Southern Rhodesia declared its independence.[42]

Johnson's message had little or no effect. Smith told McClelland that he appreciated that an extremely busy man like Johnson would take the time to communicate personally with him. He appreciated the courteous and reasonable tone that characterized U.S. messages and the emphasis on the importance of negotiation. Smith added, however, that a small country like Southern Rhodesia did not take kindly to threats that served no good purpose. Smith said that he was following the path of negotiation and would continue on it as long as any hope of a peaceful settlement remained.[43]

Bechuanaland, Basutoland, and Swaziland

Other than Southern Rhodesia, the British possessions in Africa whose status remained unsettled during the Johnson administration were three territories in Southern Africa: Bechuanaland, Basutoland, and Swaziland. All were small. In 1960, each had a population of less than one million. Basutoland and Swaziland were small in land area: Basutoland with less than twelve thousand square miles and Swaziland with less than seven thousand square miles. Britain extended protection to all three during the nineteenth century scramble for Africa. Basutoland and Swaziland were African states when they sought British protection. Bechuanaland included several ethnic groups. The three territories fell within the responsibilities of the British high commissioner (ambassador) to South Africa and were, therefore, referred to as the "High Commission territories."

Nationalism and political change emerged in the territories in the late 1950s. Each spawned one or more nationalist parties, led by educated Africans. The nationalist parties were small, poorly organized, and vulnerable to splits. Yet they seemed to represent the future. They received aid and advice from outside groups, from political parties in South Africa and elsewhere. The nationalists also found themselves opposed by traditional African rulers. British rule had preserved much of the pre-colonial political apparatus. Basutoland and Swaziland, in particular, featured paramount chiefs who retained political power and influence. All three territories included subordinate chiefs who benefited from the status quo and were skeptical of the nationalists and of political change. Finally, European settlers were a factor, particularly in Swaziland.

By 1964, the British had put the three territories on the path to independence. South Africa had had designs on the territories for many years. South African territory surrounded Swaziland on three sides and Basutoland on four. British policymakers recognized the logic of turning the territories over to South Africa, but they also realized that South Africa's apartheid policies made a transfer politically impossible. British officials thought that the territories' small populations and, in the case of Basutoland and Swaziland, diminutive size made them unlikely candidates for independence. The British considered other outcomes, internal self-government combined with continued British protection, for example. None of the alternatives proved persuasive, however. In the early 1960s, the British were left to hammer out a series of new constitutions, each moving the territory toward self-government and independence. The British had to work with reluctant chiefs and quarreling nationalists. In Swaziland, Sandys imposed a new constitution in 1963 after the Swazi factions could not reach an agreement. The chiefly element remained strong. Chiefs and their followers organized their own political parties in each territory. The new constitutions included a house of chiefs as a second legislative chamber and the paramount chief as the head of state.

Before the end of the Johnson administration, all three territories became independent. Bechuanaland gained its independence as Botswana in September 1966. Basutoland became independent as Lesotho in the following October. Swaziland became independent in September 1968.

Doubts

Some U.S. officials wished that the High Commission territories could become showpieces for non-racialism, counter examples to South Africa's apartheid policies. One official in the Pretoria embassy suggested that Swaziland might demonstrate to South Africans that the "problem of racial adjustment" was soluble. More often than not, however, U.S. officials worried about the territories' future. They were too small, too poor, and too weak compared to South Africa to survive as independent states. South Africa's potential grip on the territories was strong. Many men from Swaziland and Basutoland migrated to South Africa to work on farms or in the mines. The territories needed more time to prepare for independence, U.S. officials thought. Perhaps they would need British protection as long as the apartheid regime remained in South Africa. One official in the African bureau suggested that the United States try to convince the anti-colonial nations in the United Nations and the political parties in the territories to go slowly. Prolonging the British presence while granting the territories self-government would protect the territories from internal and external forces. U.S. officials worried that the British were pushing political change because they wanted to be rid of the territories or because they wanted to leave power in the hands of the chiefs.[44]

In July 1964, William Witt, the first secretary at the Pretoria embassy, filed a particularly negative report about Basutoland. He observed that the British were only conducting a holding operation while waiting for independence. The British wanted to leave as soon as possible, Witt wrote. They were hoping that the authorities could maintain law and order until the British could respond to a demand for Basutoland's independence. Witt considered British financial aid to Basutoland insufficient to cure the territory's economic problems. It would not convince its leaders that they should remain friendly with Britain and the United States.[45]

Expanded aid to the territories had no support among State Department officials. Joseph Satterthwaite, the U.S. ambassador in South Africa, reported numerous inquiries from the territories about U.S. aid. He argued against substantial U.S. aid, however. The prospect of U.S. aid would encourage the nationalists to be more demanding in their negotiations with the British. It would undermine the notion that Southern Africa was a British responsibility, Satterthwaite argued. The United States should, instead, encourage Britain to increase its aid to the area. Even officials who were willing to consider financial assistance to political parties in the territories thought U.S. foreign aid should be nominal. Officials contended that the territories were a British responsibility, although they had done little so far to assist development. U.S. officials feared that the British would be very happy to have the United States step in.[46]

U.S. officials also worried about links between the political parties in the territories and outside groups. State Department officials suspected that the British government was providing financial and other support to some parties. They thought that South African groups were bolstering the more conservative parties. The major concern, however, was support from communist groups, either from Russia or China or from communist elements within South Africa's African National Congress. The American working assumption was that struggling nationalist parties would take help wherever they could get it. One long-term concern was that Swaziland could become a sanctuary and staging area for South African nationalists with communist links.[47]

Staff in the Africa Bureau considered trying to counter the outside influences. In February 1964, Ulric Haynes proposed that the United States give money to the Swaziland Democratic Party and to Basutoland's Maremu Tlou Freedom Party. Haynes argued that the parties faced opponents with outside support, South Africa in the case of Swaziland and China in the case of Basutoland. Haynes considered the Swaziland party the best hope for responsible government. In his view, the Basutoland party was the best means to slow the pace of political change. In May, Haynes and other bureau staff met with officials from the Central Intelligence Agency. The meeting concluded, nevertheless, that no covert U.S. aid should be disbursed in Basutoland. It is not clear what the group decided about Swaziland. The situation in Basutoland was complicated, the group concluded. U.S. intervention would probably not help. Before acting, the United States needed more information about British efforts to stem communist infiltration and maintain political stability.[48]

British colonial Africa effectively ceased to exist in November 1965 when Southern Rhodesia declared its independence. To the end, the relationship between Britain and the United States remained complex. The United States wanted Britain to succeed, but worried that it might not. The U.S. offered advice, but little other concrete assistance. While willing to accept a European government in Salisbury, albeit one committed to reforms, the United States maintained ties to the government's African opponents.

U.S. involvement in the High Commission territories falls largely into a post-colonial category. The U.S. worried about the territories' future as independent states and hoped that independence would be delayed. Nevertheless, the main United States concern was identifying and supporting African nationalists likely to come to power and willing to favor the United States and not Russia or China.

Conclusions

U.S. policies defined the atmosphere in which the British government sought to manage its African colonies and, as a result, played a significant role in the demise of Britain's African empire. Beginning with Franklin Roosevelt and the Atlantic Charter, the United States was on record advocating self-government or independence for most colonies. Successive U.S. administrations maintained an anti-colonial stance even as they were unenthusiastic about independent African states. U.S. policies and attitudes were important because Britain was a close ally of the United States and dependent on financial and military support after the Second World War. Beginning with Winston Churchill, British leaders felt compelled to announce their commitment to eventual self-government in order to stay in step with their special ally. In reviewing options for dealing with African colonies, British leaders knew that the United States was unlikely to approve the wholesale use of soldiers or police to repress nationalist movements. The U.S. also proved unwilling to provide substantial financial aid to British colonies. Colonial matters fell within the purview of the United Nations in part because of U.S. efforts. The world organization generated persistent criticism of British colonial policies as well as attempts to undermine British rule. British leaders were sensitive to such criticism. Nevertheless, the United States, Britain's closest ally, was unwilling to help Britain cut off the debate.

During and after the Second World War, the U.S. gained the upper hand in its relationship with Britain. The United States made itself the senior partner in the "special relationship" and took advantage of Britain's wartime need for financial and other aid. It captured domination of the world's financial system and engineered Britain's continued dependence on American financial support. The United States also refashioned the world trading system to suit its own interests, partly at the expense of Britain. Having collaborated with Britain in developing atomic weapons during the war, the U.S. sought to monopolize nuclear weapons once peace arrived.

In the Atlantic Charter, the Roosevelt administration established opposition to colonial empires as a fundamental U.S. policy. Subsequent U.S. administrations were less enthusiastic about anti-colonialism, but none reversed Roosevelt's policy. In part, the continuity in U.S. policy reflected inertia. In part, it represented recognition of U.S. ideas and interests. American leaders and officials believed that history was on the side of nationalism. Independent nation states would replace the European colonial empires. U.S. leaders believed that the United States could prosper in a world of nation states as well or better than it could in a world dominated by colonial empires. The predominant view was that the United States ought not to do anything to accelerate changes in the colonial empires, lest it contribute to unrest and upset European allies. Nevertheless, the prevailing view in official circles was that the United States should also do nothing to perpetuate the colonial empires. Instead, it should position itself to gain the friendship of the post-colonial states.

Beginning with the Atlantic Charter, the U.S. counseled and prodded British leaders to adopt a pro-nationalist, pro-independence attitude. Roosevelt thought that Churchill's attachment to the British empire was old-fashioned. Eisenhower urged Churchill to commit Britain publicly to grant its colonies independence. U.S. officials at the United Nations repeatedly warned their British colleagues against what they considered mindless resistance to anti-colonial resolutions. State Department officials advised that Britain's colonial record was admirable. British speeches and papers should make more of it and Britain should attempt to soften anti-colonial resolutions rather than opposing them.

The United States was skeptical, at best, about armed efforts to maintain or re-impose colonial rule. The U.S. did not object to British repression of the Kikuyu uprising in Kenya, but officials doubted the long-term wisdom of using force. In 1956, the Eisenhower administration went further. It used its financial strength to end the Suez invasion and force withdrawal of British, French, and Israeli troops from Egypt. Eisenhower and Dulles sent the message that the United States would not tolerate trying to use force to undo nationalist gains.

U.S. financial aid to Britain, through the Marshall Plan and other vehicles, allowed Britain to fund development programs in the African colonies, but American financial aid to British colonies never materialized. After the Second World War, the British government was able to increase its economic and social development efforts in Africa in part because it received financial aid from the United States. Some British officials thought Britain should go further and solicit funds specifically for colonial development. Some British officials saw development as preparation for self-government. Others imagined it as a rival to political change. Nevertheless, Britain did not seek substantial U.S. financial aid until the late 1950s. Moreover, aid to developing areas was not a big part of the Truman or Eisenhower administrations' programs and British colonies were not among their preferred aid recipients. By the time U.S. policy shifted in favor of development at the end of the Eisenhower administration, most British colonies were independent or close to it. As a result, the U.S. provided only a trickle of financial aid to Britain's African colonies before independence.

In the United Nations, the U.S. kept Britain at arm's length. The country's anti-colonial stance caused it to participate in giving the U.N. a role in the European colonial empires. Built into the United Nations Charter was the expectation that colonies should become self-governing or independent. In addition, the U.N. quickly became a forum for anti-colonial agitation. Within the United Nations, the U.S. goal was to create and maintain the largest possible anti–Russian coalition. It was, therefore, unwilling to align itself on colonial issues with Britain and the other European colonial powers, who, from the U.N.'s inception, represented a small minority. The majority of United Nations members did not possess colonies and many prided themselves on their opposition to colonies. As colonies became independent during the 1950s and early 1960s, the anti-colonial majority in the United Nations grew and became more vociferous. U.S. policy was to stay in the middle of the road, taking positions between the colonial powers and their critics. The United States thought it could not sacrifice the support of either group.

U.S. leaders and officials remained bystanders to most British decisions about the African colonies. Official advice was usually limited to style, rather than substance. It centered on British actions in the United Nations, not on policy choices in the colonies. Beginning in the late 1950s, U.S. officials in the field, in Uganda and Central Africa in particular, urged a more active stance. The response from Washington was usually that the country needed to practice discretion. Colonial Africa was a European concern, Washington warned.

U.S. policies and actions encouraged the African nationalists, nonetheless. Pronouncements in favor of self-determination and independence, the presence of friendly U.S. officials in many colonies, and the possibility of U.S. aid and friendship after independence gave the nationalists confidence and hope. The U.S. sought to win the friendship of nationalist leaders, paying their way to the United States and inviting them to meet U.S. leaders, including the president. U.S. officials in Africa provided advice to nationalist leaders, especially Julius Nyerere and Tom Mboya. Nationalist leaders, particularly Mboya, received financial support from non-governmental organizations friendly to U.S. interests.

In total, U.S. policies and actions made it more likely that Britain would grant its colonies independence and do so sooner rather than later. Beginning with Churchill, British leaders took account of U.S. attitudes about the colonies. They hoped that they could use U.S. wealth and power to maintain British rule. Failing to gain explicit United States support for colonial rule, the British were left to worry about how their policies would appear to the United States. Knowing that the U.S. frowned on repression and was unlikely to fund widescale development, the British had to rely on their own resources, especially their stock of constitutional arrangements. Concerned about international opinion and aware that official and unofficial U.S. opinion was uneasy about colonies, British leaders were unwilling to become diehard opponents of nationalism.

Britain's situation in the 1950s contrasted sharply with its situation at the end of the nineteenth century, when it competed with other European powers to claim pieces of Africa. In the late nineteenth century, no chorus of anti-colonial states criticized British actions. No international forum for anti-colonial speeches and resolutions existed. The great powers, including the United States, at least tolerated the establishment of colonies. Most joined in the rush to seize foreign real estate. Using armed force against Africans or Asians was okay. No great power offered itself as a source of support and advice for Africans or Asians seeking to avoid European rule.

The United States did not intend to hasten the end of Britain's African colonies. The U.S. was anti-colonial without being pro-independence. A few U.S. leaders contemplated a rapid end to the colonial empires — Henry Wallace, Wendell Willkie, perhaps Mason Sears. The majority was comfortable thinking that independence, while inevitable, was in the distant future. The United States need not, should not, work to speed the process. History was on the nationalists' and the U.S. side. The United States needed only to encourage the colonial powers to manage the transition carefully. It did not need to push Britain to free its colonies. It did need to position itself to gain the friendship of newly independent states.

The U.S. policies and actions that helped prompt Britain to grant independence to its colonies stemmed, in many cases, from other motives. American predominance over Britain after the Second World War was the latest episode in a long rivalry. The country's positions on colonial issues in the U.N. were a function of the U.S. desire to assemble an anti–Russian coalition. The American lack of interest in financial aid to colonies reflected domestic politics and a fixation on Russia during the 1950s.

Of Britain's African colonies, the Sudan owed its independence most greatly to U.S. involvement. Nevertheless, United States support for Sudanese independence was a byproduct of interests in the eastern Mediterranean. The Truman administration with Dean Acheson in the lead harried the British government until it reached an agreement with Egypt that included the status of the Sudan. Acheson was most concerned about protecting U.S. interests in the eastern Mediterranean. An Anglo-Egyptian détente was part of his plan for a Middle Eastern defense pact. For the United States, the Sudan was a bargaining chip. If an independent Sudan made Anglo-Egyptian cooperation more likely, the United States favored independence. Official U.S. knowledge of or involvement in the Sudan was virtually nonexistent until Sudanese independence was a certainty.

Among the world's regions, Africa was a low priority for the United States before 1965. Other than the areas bordering on the Mediterranean, Africa offered only raw materials and possible transit routes in the case of world crisis. As long as the colonial powers arranged political change carefully, they could be trusted to manage the continent. Careful management was important lest local groups hostile to the United States gain a following and, ultimately, control. Careful management was also important to forestall efforts by Russia and China to gain footholds. Africa needed to be in friendly hands, either colonial or independent, but, in the best case, the U.S. would have to expend little or none of its own resources.

The British government sought United States support for its colonial activities, but rarely asked for or received U.S. assistance in the African colonies. Britain did not solicit U.S. financial aid for its colonies until the late 1950s. The Kennedy and Johnson administrations prided themselves on being more pro–African than their predecessors. Yet when the Wilson government asked for help in dissuading Southern Rhodesia from declaring independence, even the Johnson administration was reluctant. Johnson agreed to cajole Southern Rhodesian leaders. The State Department resisted offering financial help to Britain, however, should Southern Rhodesia break its ties to Britain. Africa was not important enough to commit U.S. resources.

The interactions between Britain and the United States over Britain's African colonies serve as a reminder that "special" can mean many things. Britain and the U.S. considered themselves close allies after the Second World War, perhaps the closest of allies. Nevertheless, their relationship was complicated. It was not the relationship of equals; the United States was always the dominant partner. Britain cared more about the relationship than did the U.S. A lack of interest in British interests was common. U.S. and British officials met frequently to discuss African issues, but often failed to agree. The British hoped for United States support, but usually accepted that it would not be forthcoming. At times, U.S. officials even tried to convince their British colleagues that disagreements were a good thing since they demonstrated to the outside world that Britain and the United States were not in collusion. If one sought a metaphor to capture the "special" relationship as it applied to African colonies, it might be a pair of high school sweethearts who repeatedly break up and get back together again. The pair may seem destined for each other, but disagreements, disappointments, hurt feelings, and harsh words were as common as cooperation.

The U.S. experience with the Philippines suggests that the U.S. preference was for independence circumscribed. When the United States advised Britain to grant political concessions and ultimately independence, it most likely had in mind an arrangement in which African states were independent but remained within a British orbit. The U.S. granted the Philippines independence out of a calculation of U.S. interests, not out of an ideological commitment to self-determination. U.S. leaders including Franklin Roosevelt considered that the costs of retaining the Philippines as a colony outweighed the benefits. Moreover, the United States designed Philippine independence so that the U.S. could preserve its economic and military interests in the islands while shedding responsibility for governing them.

State Department officials disagreed about U.S. policies towards Britain's African colonies. Some officials focused on U.S. interests in Europe. They believed that whatever interests the United States might have in Africa were trivial compared to the alliance with Britain and Western Europe. Such officials advocated support for Britain regardless of its impact on the anti-colonial nations or on African nationalists. Other officials thought Britain best placed to manage political change in Africa. They urged that the United States defer to British judgments about colonial issues. Such officials might, or might not, favor independence. Still other officials focused on the United Nations. For them, colonial issues represented an opportunity to court the majority of U.N. members. Progress toward independence for African colonies was a reasonable price to pay for the friendship of the anti-colonial nations. Other officials saw Africa as an arena for competition with Russia and China. They wanted the United States to secure the friendship of the African nationalists. They advocated United States support for political change and increased financial aid to African territories.

To some, the conflicts over U.S. policy within the State Department, the stated preference for the middle of the road and the carefully hedged pronouncements by senior officials meant the United States had no African policy. Having no policy meant, to others, having no single document that delineated U.S. policy and that, perhaps, had wide support within the State Department. The State Department expended considerable effort in the late 1940s and early 1950s trying unsuccessfully to create such a document. The Eisenhower administration produced several National Security Council documents during the late 1950s that laid out official policy regarding Africa. The National Security Council documents did not end the conflicts or simplify U.S. positions, however. To others, having no policy meant adopting a passive position, allowing others to take the lead, or giving Africa a low priority. It was not so much having no policy as having the wrong policy. They were reluctant to accept that being a bystander may not be heroic, but it was policy choice.

U.S. policies towards Britain's African colonies display more continuity than change between 1945 and 1965. The Roosevelt administration staked a claim to anti-colonialism, but made few other lasting decisions about colonial issues. The Truman and Eisenhower administrations pursued similar courses. The Truman administration paid less attention to Africa, but, as the example of the Sudan indicates, was comfortable with the prospect of independent African states. During the Eisenhower administration, conditions in Africa changed. Independence seemed imminent. U.S. policies changed as well. Preparing for independence became more important. Encouraging independence did not, however. John Kennedy brought a new style to the African policies. In Kennedy's time, African issues seemed more important and the administration cultivated a pro–African reputation. Nevertheless, U.S. policies regarding the pace of political change in Britain's African colonies remained much the same. Like the Eisenhower administration, the Kennedy administration stood back, nervously looking over Britain's shoulder.

In Africa, State Department officials displayed a learning curve. In the late 1940s and early 1950s, officials exhibited culture shock. They were put off by African conditions and were critical of Africans. As time went on, consuls seemed more comfortable and more confident. By the end of the Eisenhower administration, some consuls were champing at the bit, wanting to become more involved in local affairs. By the late 1950s, consuls advocated more active policies than Washington.

Attitudes towards Africans and African nationalists among State Department officials in Washington and in the field were likely to be critical — the disdain of the rich and powerful for the poor and weak. U.S. officials, like their British counterparts, underestimated African nationalists. They had a hard time believing that handfuls of educated Africans could nego-tiate a British withdrawal and administer an independent government. By the late 1950s, when independence seemed likely, however, U.S. officials spent less time worrying whether Africans could govern themselves and more time trying to identify those that would govern. The U.S. was most willing to support (at least verbally) those nationalist leaders they thought would succeed.

Conversely, U.S. officials in the field became more critical of the British as time went on — as the British seemed more likely to be on their way out. In the late 1940s, U.S. consuls were likely to praise British officials and methods. By the late 1950s, they were likely to worry that British officials were mismanaging the transition to independence. U.S. officials sounded like back seat drivers.

Ethnic and cultural prejudices among U.S. officials are evident. Dean Acheson is a prime example. One can assume that other U.S. officials in the 1940s, 1950s, and 1960s, like many of their contemporaries in the United States, suffered from some such prejudice. Ethnic or racial prejudice probably colored some decisions. Nonetheless, it is hard to see prejudice as a driving force in U.S. policies and actions. The focus within the State Depart-ment was on maximizing U.S. interests. Just as most U.S. officials were far from romantic about their British allies, they were hard-nosed about protecting U.S. interests in Africa, regardless of whether it meant working with and supporting people who were different from themselves.

U.S. policies and actions were only a contributing factor to the demise of Britain's African colonies. The primary reasons for the end of Britain's colonies were changes in Africa and British reactions to them. Africa in 1945 was different from Africa in 1890 or 1900. Data are sparse, but African populations probably grew significantly in the first half of the twentieth century. Certainly, by 1945, more Africans lived in cities and towns, and not in the countryside governed by native administrations. More Africans earned their livings in something other than subsistence agriculture. More Africans had Western edu-cations. More wanted Western educations for their children. They were fluent in English and familiar with European institutions like newspapers and political parties. More Africans were familiar with the material progress achieved in Europe and North America and wanted the same for themselves and their communities. More Africans were aware that, in Asia, local peoples had won their independence. An increasing number of Africans thought that they, and not foreigners, could and should govern. National independence seemed the way forward, the way to end foreign rule and achieve material prosperity.

Eisenhower believed that the nationalism, a country's desire to govern itself, was an irresistible force. Many U.S. officials agreed. They were probably right. African territories probably would have gained their independence eventually regardless of U.S. policies or even British policies. If the British had sought to maintain control and if the United States had supported the British, independence might have been postponed. The transition to independence might have been longer, bloody, and more difficult. Yet it is hard to see how the British could have overcome the demographic and other changes in Africa, defeated the nationalists, and preserved their rule.

Even before World War II, British officials recognized that the political settlement they had constructed in the African colonies had run its course. Before 1920, the British cemented their control through understandings with African leaders and establishment of local regimes styled as native administrations. The native administrations often owed something to pre-colonial regimes. They aimed to maintain control of a countryside populated by subsistence farmers. They focused on maintaining law and order and offered few public services. By the late 1930s, reliance on the native administrations was clearly insufficient, however. Too many Africans had left the countryside for cities and towns, for jobs in mines, businesses, and government departments. Too many had obtained Western educations and saw themselves and not the chiefs as the leaders of their communities and territories. Too many Africans wanted education and other services the native administration did not provide.

The sign that change was needed was unrest: strikes, boycotts, and riots, in the West Indies in the late 1930s and in Africa immediately after World War II. The British worried that they could not maintain order, especially in port cities and in towns along railway lines. Losing control was important in itself. Yet it also meant shutting down economic activity such as exporting cotton from Uganda or cocoa from the Gold Coast that postwar Britain depended on.

The initial British response focused on economic and social improvements. The thought was that more and better jobs, better pay, more schools and clinics and the like would soothe the unrest. Some officials thought that economic and social development might, by itself, solidify British rule. Others saw development as the means to prepare Africans for larger political roles in the colonies. They believed that bringing educated Africans into government would satisfy some discontented African politicians. It might deprive strikers and rioters of their most effective leaders and employ their leaderships skills and standing in the community to bolster the colonial regime, rather than undermine it.

The British improved their tools for suppressing unrest after World War II. They expanded police forces, created new intelligence organizations, and organized riot squads. In Kenya, they used police and troops to suppress an uprising among the Kikuyu. Nevertheless, the consensus among British officials was that armed force was not the answer. The superior military power that allowed Britain to defeat African armies and conquer African territories in the late nineteenth century was not well suited to the unrest of the mid–twentieth century. Dealing with unruly crowds or insurgents in the countryside was different from fighting a set piece battle against the army of a nineteenth century African state. As suppressing the Kikuyu troubles proved, employing armed force was expensive and readily produced brutality and cruelty that could be politically embarrassing. The Kikuyu troubles involved only one region within Kenya, but consumed significant resources and tied down 40,000 men. The British lacked the troops to quell a colony-wide revolt or serious troubles in more than one colony at a time. If the British needed further confirmation that armed force did not work, they could consider the French experience in Algeria.

The British were comfortable with "constitution mongering," changing colonial constitutions to make room for educated Africans. Negotiating new constitutions with colonies was a British tradition. Before British officials became enamored of native administrations, they had brought educated Africans into the governments in Nigeria and the Gold Coast. Moreover, constitutional changes were cheap and non-controversial in Britain.

When the British began to reform colonial constitutions, the aim was not to end British rule. The aim was to strengthen British rule by adding new allies, educated Africans. Once the process of change gained momentum, however, the British realized that African nationalists were not easily satisfied. More political power was the usual demand. The British discovered that political change would have to proceed faster and farther than originally conceived. Delay remained a popular option, but British leaders repeatedly concluded that further delay was not worth the risks it posed. Senior British leaders also persisted in believing that they could halt the process short of independence. For large colonies, they imagined a kind of self-government that left finance, defense, and external affairs in British hands. For smaller colonies, they imagined even more power remaining in British hands.

The Attlee government considered a larger role for the Colonial Office in managing the colonies. London, in fact, played a larger role in the African colonies after the Second World War than it did before. Nevertheless, the engine for change in the British African colonies was usually a colonial governor's interactions with key nationalist leaders, often a single nationalist leader. Colonial governors were tasked to negotiate constitutional changes that would secure nationalist agreement and prolong British rule. Since the governors had few other resources, limited police forces and paltry funds for development projects, they struggled to control the pace of political change. More political power for the nationalists was often the card they could play.

The British tried other tactics. In Central Africa, the British tried to suppress the nationalist parties, but failed. In Nigeria and other colonies, they attempted to split the nationalists and count on one group to delay independence. In nearly all cases, Africans buried their differences long enough to claim independence. The ragged shirt of independence, indeed, was preferable to the warm blanket of colonialism. In Kenya and Central Africa, the British thought that they could engineer alliances between cooperative Europeans and a nationalist faction. That did not work either.

By the late 1950s, the British faced conditions increasingly hostile to continued colonial rule. Change developed its own momentum. British officials and nationalists believed that political concessions made in one colony had to be offered to neighboring colonies. Once the Gold Coast gained independence, it joined its voice to those advocating independence across the continent. It organized meetings of nationalists and offered them support and encouragement. Nationalists in East and Central African colonies supported each other. Russia and China emerged as sources of training and assistance. The French and Belgians granted independence to their African colonies, leaving Britain in the company of Portugal and Spain as the last diehards.

The Macmillan administration, particularly Iain Macleod, recognized that foot dragging was no longer viable. The British quickened the pace of change. They granted nationalists more political power and sooner than planned. The British sought to hand power to nationalist leaders and parties that could govern an independent state effectively and remain friendly to Britain and its allies. In Zanzibar and perhaps Uganda, the British were sufficiently in a hurry that they handed power to governments unlikely to survive.

Handing power to African nationalists was not a viable strategy for Southern Rhodesia. The European controlled government was too strong and the African nationalists too weak. The Macmillan, Home, and Wilson governments failed to develop an alternative strategy. They fell back to delay and hoping that the settler government would not declare its independence. When the Smith government broke its ties to Britain in November 1965, Britain's African empire effectively ended.

Chapter Notes

NARA indicates a reference to the papers held by the National Archives and Records Administration, most at College Park, Maryland. When combined with numbers such as NARA 711.48K, or, for the period after 1963, a combination of letters and numbers, such as NARA POL 2 BAS, the terms indicate references to the State Department Central Files. *FRUS* stands for *Foreign Relations of the United States*.

Chapter 1

1. Shogan, *Backlash*, 10–11.
2. Roosevelt, *As He Saw It*, 75.
3. Roosevelt, *As He Saw It*, 86.
4. Louis, *Imperialism at Bay*, 226, 486; Roosevelt, *As He Saw It*, 115; Gardner, *Economic Aspects*, 177.
5. Roosevelt, *As He Saw It*, 114–116; Louis, *Imperialism at Bay*, 183; Kimball, *The Juggler*, 130.
6. Range, *Roosevelt's World Order*, 59; Ostrower, *The United Nations and the United States*, 13.
7. Kimball, *The Juggler*, 145; Dulles and Ridinger, "Anti-Colonial Policies," 13; Charles Taussig, Memorandum, July 13, 1944, Taussig Papers Box 47, in Louis, *Imperialism at Bay*, 357.
8. Louis, *Imperialism at Bay*, 157, 486; Kimball, *The Juggler*, 130, 145; Range, *Roosevelt's World Order*, 108; Gardner, "Vietnam," 124; Dulles and Ridinger, "Anti-Colonial Policies," 13.
9. Langer and Gleason, *Undeclared War*, 680–81; Wilson, *The First Summit*, 160.
10. Roosevelt, *As He Saw It*, 36–7, 41.
11. Roosevelt, *Complete Presidential Press Conferences*, vol. 19, 3–4; Rosenman, *Public Papers and Addresses*, 11:105ff.
12. Neal, *Dark Horse*, 231–32.
13. Neal, *Dark Horse*, 251.
14. Barnard, *Wendell Willkie*, 379.
15. Roosevelt, *Complete Presidential Press Conferences*, 20:178–9.
16. *The Times*, 11 November 1942 in Louis, *Imperialism at Bay*, 200.

17. Roosevelt, *Complete Presidential Press Conferences*, 19:156–7.
18. Rosenman, *Public Papers and Addresses*, 13:441ff.
19. Speech by Churchill in House of Commons, September 9, 1941 (Hansard Parliamentary Debates, volume 372, columns 67–9, in Porter and Stockwell, *British Imperial Policy*, 2:103–4.)
20. Speech by Churchill in House of Commons, September 9, 1941 (Hansard Parliamentary Debates, volume 372, columns 67–9, in Porter and Stockwell, *British Imperial Policy*, 2:103–4.)
21. The ambassador in the United Kingdom (Winant) to the secretary of state, November 4, 1941, in *FRUS, 1941*, 3:181–2.
22. Churchill to Roosevelt, August 9, 1942, quoted in Venkataramani, "Atlantic Charter Hoax," 20.
23. Venkataramani, "Atlantic Charter Hoax," 22; Roosevelt to Churchill, August 13, 1942, in Kimball, *Complete Correspondence*, 1:559.
24. Dallek, *Foreign Policy*, 324; Range *Roosevelt's World Order*, 112; Dulles and Ridinger, "Anti-Colonial Policies," 17.
25. Russell, *UN Charter*, 83.
26. Russell, *UN Charter*, 76; Hilderbrand, *Dumbarton Oaks*, 17.
27. Culver and Hyde, *American Dreamer*, 342–3.
28. Thorne, *Allies*, 209; Orde, *Eclipse*, 141; Louis, *Imperialism at Bay*, 198; Gardner, *Economic Aspects*, 177; Neal, *Dark Horse*, 236.
29. Thorne, *Allies*, 392; Gardner,

"Idea and Reality," 57; Renwick, *Fighting with Allies*, 121; Eisenhower to General T.T. Handy January 28, 1943, in Orde, *Eclipse*, 144.
30. Wilson, *First Summit*, 153; Gardner, *Economic Aspects*, 190; Louis, *Imperialism at Bay*, 177ff.
31. Louis, *Imperialism at Bay*, 211ff.
32. Louis, *Imperialism at Bay*, 250–52.
33. Louis, *Imperialism at Bay*, 255, 276–7; Russell, *UN Charter*, 144.
34. Louis, *Imperialism at Bay*, 361–62.
35. Woods, *Changing the Guard*, 18; Edmonds, *Setting the Mould*, 95.
36. Louis, *Imperialism at Bay*, 40; Charmley, *Churchill's Grand Alliance*, 21; Wilson, *The First Summit*, 155–58.
37. Roosevelt, *As He Saw It*, 35–37.
38. Gardner, *Economic Aspects*, 172, 279; Hearden, Architects *of Globalism*, 32.
39. Gardner, *Economic Aspects*, 262; Hearden, *Architects of Globalism*, xiii.
40. Schild, *Postwar Planning*, 91, 96.
41. Woods, *Changing the Guard*, 60–61, 325; Kimball, "Open Door," 234, 257; Gardner, *Economic Aspects*, 276.
42. Woods, *Changing the Guard*, 94–95; Freeland, *Truman Doctrine*, 28.
43. Woods, *Changing the Guard*, 212, 305; Gardner, *Economic Aspects*, 278.

44. Woods, *Changing the Guard*, 171; Herring, "Bankruptcy," 266; McKercher, *Transition*, 331.

45. Woods, *Changing the Guard*, 312, 317; Herring, "Bankruptcy," 263; Skidelsky, *Keynes*, 364; Hathaway, *Ambiguous Partnership*, 66.

46. Woods, *Changing the Guard*, 90, 313.

47. Wilson, *The First Summit*, 164, 167, 172, 174–5.

48. Louis, *Imperialism at Bay*, 184–5.

49. Hilderbrand, *Dumbarton Oaks*, 19.

50. Russell, *UN Charter*, 85–6.

51. Russell, *UN Charter*, 332, 335.

52. Russell, *UN Charter*, 336ff; Murray, *Trusteeship System*, 25; Hilderbrand, *Dumbarton Oaks*, 34–36.

53. Louis, *Imperialism at Bay*, 458.

54. Louis, *Imperialism at Bay*, 459–60; Russell, *UN Charter*, 541.

55. Sberga, "Reappraisal," 82; Pungong, "Trusteeship,"92.

56. Louis, *Imperialism at Bay*, 459–60.

57. Russell, *UN Charter*, 573, 577ff, 584.

58. Hilderbrand, *Dumbarton Oaks*, 39–40; Schild, *Postwar Planning*, 69.

59. Schild, *Postwar Planning*, 68.

60. Hilderbrand, *Dumbarton Oaks*, 51, 171; Douglas, "British Left," 148; Thorne, *Allies*, 601.

61. Churchill, Minute, March 10, 1945, PREM4/31/4, in Louis, *Imperialism at Bay*, 92; Thorne, *Allies*, 601.

62. O'Sullivan, *Sumner Welles*, chapter 6, 6.

63. Louis, *Imperialism at Bay*, 388; Villard, "American Relations with Africa," 103, 106, 108–9.

64. Office of Strategic Services, Report 1398, April 28, 1944, i-ii, 7, 11, NARA RG59, Numbered Intelligence Reports; Office of Strategic Services, "Nationalist Trends in British West Africa," Report 2279, August 30, 1944, 1, 17, 22, NARA RG59, Numbered Intelligence Reports.

65. Clymer, "Johnson," 267; Clymer, "Phillips," 28; Clymer, *Quest for Freedom*, 195; Hess, *India*, 45, 105–6; Gardner, "Idea and Reality," 61.

66. Clymer, *Quest for Freedom*, 53–54.

67. Brands, *Bound to Empire*, 91; Blitz, *Contested State*, 49; Grunder and Livezey, *Philippines and the United States*, 154, 158.

68. Blitz, *Contested State*, 48; Brands, *Bound to Empire*, 116; Grunder and Livezey, *Philippines and the United States*, 157.

69. Grunder and Livezey, *Philippines and the United States*, 195–6,

217; Blitz, *Contested State*, 62; Pomeroy, *Philippines*, 82; Friend, *Philippines*, 85.

70. Grunder and Livezey, *Philippines and the United States*, 190–1, 207.

71. Brands, *Bound to Empire*, 155; Blitz, *Contested State*, 63–64.

72. Blitz, *Contested State*, 64.

Chapter 2

1. Churchill to Eden 19 September 1943, PREM 3, 158/4, in Callahan, *Churchill*, 175.

2. Churchill, Minute, 31 December 1944, PREM 4/31/4, in Louis, *Imperialism at Bay*, 433.

3. Louis, *Imperialism at Bay*, 24, 32–33, 249; Viceroy to Secretary of State for India, January 2, 1943, CO323/1858/9057B, in Porter and Stockwell, *British Imperial Policy* 1:135; Sir R.J. Campbell, Minute, August 12, 1944, in Hathaway, *Ambiguous Partnership*, 46.

4. Thorne, *Allies*, 61; Pearce, *Turning Point*, 100; Louis, *Imperialism at Bay*, 429.

5. Skidelsky, *Fighting for Freedom*, 180; Thorne, *Allies*, 102; Sir Alexander Cadogan, Minute, April 28, 1943, FO 371/35311 U2026/G, in Louis, *Imperialism at Bay*, 246; Anthony Eden, President Roosevelt's State of the Union Message to Congress, 6 January 1945, CAB (66), in Gardner, "Idea and Reality," 49.

6. Renwick, *Fighting with Allies*, 64; Richard Law, "Consideration of Lend-Lease Aid," January 14, 1942, WP(42) 21, in Wilson, *First Summit*, 213.

7. "The Essentials of an American Policy," March 21, 1944, FO 371/38523 AN 1538/16/45, in Baylis, *Anglo-American*, 35–6; Thorne, *Allies*, 220, 222, 343, Beloff, "Commitments," 252.

8. CO323/1858/9057B and FO 371/35311, in Louis, *Imperialism at Bay*, 250;

9. Pearce, *Turning Point*, 24–25.

10. *The Times*, March 8, 1943, in Louis, *Imperialism at Bay*, 253; Stanley, Minute, August 8, 1944, CO825/42/55104, in Louis, *Imperialism at Bay*, 36.

11. Thorne, *Allies*, 2221; Joint Memorandum by Minister of Information and Minister of Economic Warfare, 15 November 1940, CAB 66/13, in Pearce, *Turning Point*, 21, 207; Hargreaves, "Sierra Leone," 77–78.

12. Lugard, Letter to *The Times*, 26 November 1942, in Louis, *Imperialism at Bay*, 200–1; Lee, "Forward

Thinking," 74; Macmillan, Minute, 1 September 1942, CO 323/1848/07322, in Pearce, *Turning Point*, 26.

13. June 24, 1942, Parliamentary Debates (Commons) (1941–42). 4th series, vol. 380, cols. 2002–20, in Porter and Stockwell, *British Imperial Policy*, 1:109.

14. Pearce, *Turning Point*, 33–35; July 13, 1943, Parliamentary Debates (Commons), 4th series, vol. 391 col. 144, in Pearce, *Turning Point*, 34.

15. Pearce, *Turning Point*, 33–35; Hailey, Note on Draft Declaration by the United Nations on National Independence, May 5, 1943, CO323/1858 9057B, in Porter and Stockwell, *British Imperial Policy*, 1:154.

16. Pearce, *Turning Point*, 27; Note of a Meeting, July 29, 1943, CO 554/132/33727, in Porter and Stockwell, *Imperial Policy*, 1:178.

17. Sanger, *MacDonald*, 145; MacDonald to Simon, October 26, 1939, CO847/21/47100/1, in Pearce, *Turning Point*, 48.

18. MacDonald, Speech at Oxford, CO847/20/47139, in Pearce, *Turning Point*, 23.

19. Sanger, *MacDonald*, 148.

20. Hargreaves, "Sierra Leone," 78.

21. Cell, *Hailey*, 241, 279.

22. Bushe, Minute November 7, 1941, CO857/17/47135, in Pearce, *Turning Point*, 47.

23. Note on Hailey's discussion with Moyne and others, March 18, 1941, CO 847/21/47100/1/1941, in Hargreaves, "Transfer of Power," 120; Hailey, *African Survey*, 529, 537–42, 1639 in Hargreaves, "Transfer of Power," 118; Cell, *Hailey*, 256.

24. Note of a Meeting held July 29, 1943, CO 554/132/33727, in Porter and Stockwell, *British Imperial Policy*, 1:178.

25. Hargreaves, "Transfer of Power," 126–7, 130; Pearce, *Turning Point*, 61.

26. Colonial Office Record of Meeting with Sir Arthur Richards, November 16, 1943, CO554/132/20 no. 16, in Lynn, *Nigeria*, 1:4.

27. Burns to Cranborne, June 30, 1942, CO554/131/4 no. 11, in Rathbone, *Ghana*, 1:12; Hargreaves, "Transfer of Power," 129; Burns to Cranborne, July 8 1942, CO554/131/4 no. 13, in Rathbone, *Ghana*, 1:14.

28. Cranborne to Burns, June 19, 1942, CO554/131/4 no. 6, in Rathbone, *Ghana*, 1:11. Wolton, *Lord Hailey*, 61.

29. O.G.R. Williams, Minute, September 3, 1942, CO554/131/4, in Rathbone, *Ghana*, 1:15.

30. Richards to Stanley, July 19,

1944, CO583/286/5 no. 1, in Lynn, *Nigeria*, 1:8; Pearce, "Nigeria," 295.

31. Cohen, Memorandum August 9, 1944, CO583/286/5 no. 4, in Lynn, *Nigeria*, 1:22; Pearce, *Turning Point*, 82.

32. Daly, *Imperial Sudan*, 155; Beshir, *Nationalism and Revolution*, 161.

33. Ibrahim Ahmed to Huddleston, April 3, 1942, FO371/31587 no. 2664, in Johnson, *Sudan*, 1:2–3; Beshir, *Nationalism and Revolution*, 161, 163.

34. Newbold, Note, September 10, 1942, FO 371/31587 no. 4388, in Johnson, *Sudan*, 1:16; Newbold, Note, September 21, 1942, FO371/31587 no. 4388, in Johnson, *Sudan*, 1:22; Newbold to Sandars November 24, 1943, FO371/35576 no.4986, in Johnson, *Sudan*, 1:35.

35. P.S. Scrivener, Minute, May 26, 1942, FO371/31587 no. 2664, in Johnson, *Sudan*, 1:9; D.S. Laskey, Minute, June 12, 1942 FO371/31587 no. 2664, in Johnson, *Sudan*, 1:11; Lampson to Cadogan, October 11, 1942, FO371/31587 no. 4388, in Johnson, *Sudan*, 1:26; Lampson to Cadogan, December 1, 1942, FO371/31587 no. 5145, in Johnson, *Sudan*, 1:29.

36. Huddleston to Lampson May 22, 1942, FO371/31587 no. 2664, in Johnson, *Sudan*, 1:1; Huddleston to Lampson, November 18, 1942 FO371/31587 no. 5145, in Johnson, *Sudan*, 1:27.

Chapter 3

1. Kennedy, *Great Powers*, 359.

2. H. Stuart Hughes, "The Second Year of the Cold War: a Memoir and Anticipation," *Commentary*, August 1969, 27–9, in Bills, *Empire and Cold War*, 209.

3. Offner, *Another Such Victory*, 18, 71, 86.

4. Bills, *Empire and Cold War*, 205; Beisner, *Acheson*, 507.

5. McLellan, *Acheson*, 115, 244; Beisner, *Acheson*, 18–19, 162; Acheson, *At the Creation*, 323.

6. McLellan, *Acheson*, 244; Beisner, *Acheson*, 43.

7. McCay, *Acheson and Empire*, 42, 52; Edmonds, *Mould*, 111.

8. Perkins, "Unequal Partners," 44; McLellan, *Acheson*, 244.

9. Beisner, *Acheson*, 174, 210–212, 512.

10. Beisner, *Acheson*, 103; Department of State, *History*.

11. Satterthwaite, Paper on United States-British Relations, February 18, 1950, NARA 611.41/2-2750.

12. Munene, *Truman*, 98; McGhee, *Envoy*, xviii–xix; McKay, *Africa in World Politics*, 289, 290.

13. Brands, *Henderson*, 128; Louis, "American Anti-colonialism," 406; Bartlett, *Special Relationship*, 58.

14. Hathaway, *Ambiguous Partnership*, 145–7, 174–5, 183–4; Herring, "Bankruptcy," 270–1, 273, 276.

15. Edmonds, *Mould*, 98–99; Gardner, *Architects*, 123; Sidelsky, *Keynes*, 401 note.

16. Offner, *Another Such Victory*, 45; Hathaway, *Ambiguous Partnership*, 147.

17. Keynes, Cabinet Memorandum, annex, August 13, 1945, CAB 129/1, CP(45) 112, in Hyam, *Labour, 1945–51*, 3:4.

18. Skidelsky, *Keynes*, 403–405.

19. Hathaway, *Ambiguous Partnership*, 189; Freeland, *Truman Doctrine*, 48; McLellan, *Acheson*, 70–71.

20. Dalton, *High Tide*, 74–75, in Hathaway, *Ambiguous Partnership*, 194.

21. Hathaway, *Ambiguous Partnership*, 148; Freeland, *Truman Doctrine*, 48; McLellan, *Acheson*, 71.

22. Hathaway, *Ambiguous Partnership*, 160; Freeland, *Truman Doctrine*, 160, 326, 329.

23. Edmonds, *Mould*, 54, 78–9; Hathaway, *Ambiguous Partnership*, 213.

24. Edmonds, *Mould*, 79.

25. Edmonds, *Mould*, 85; Hathaway, *Ambiguous Partnership*, 260–1.

26. Acheson, *At the Creation*, 317; Beisner, *Acheson*, 26; Edmonds, *Mould*, 86.

27. Kennedy, *Great Powers*, 381; Hathaway, *Ambiguous Partnership*, 302; Beisner, *Acheson*, 55–6.

28. Freeland, *Truman Doctrine*, 96.

29. Hathaway, *Ambiguous Partnership*, 303; Beisner, *Acheson*, 62.

30. Freeland, *Truman Doctrine*, 93; Hathaway, *Ambiguous Partnership*, 303–4; Edmonds, *Mould*, 159.

31. Darby, *Imperialism*, 174; Dallek, *Foreign Policy*, 511; LaFeber, "Decolonization," 27.

32. Gunder and Livesey, *Philippines*, 248; Shalom, *United States and the Philippines*, 13–4.

33. Shalom, *United States and the Philippines*, 38–9, 41; Blitz, *The Contested State*, 71.

34. Shalom, *United States and the Philippines*, 51.

35. Hess, *Emergence*, 248; Shalom, *United States and the Philippines*, 67.

36. Munene, *Truman*, 48, 64–5.

37. Department of State Policy and Information Statement, "British Colonies of West Africa," December 12, 1946, NARA 711.48K/12-1246;

Department of State, Office of Intelligence Research, Report no. 4327 (PV), "British Capabilities and Intentions," April 21, 1947, 40.

38. Munene, *Truman*, 49; Department of State, Policy and Information Statement, "British Colonies of West Africa," December 12, 1946, NARA 711.48K/12-1246.

39. George Marshall, "Address to United Nations General Assembly, September 29, 1948," 3; Dean Acheson, United States Position on Problems Confronting Fourth General Assembly," 3.

40. Department of State Policy Statement, June 11, 1948, Berlin Mission Files Lot F-169, in *FRUS 1948*, 3:1095.

41. McGhee to Hickerson, August 25, 1950, NARA RG59, 1422, George McGhee Office Files 1945–53; Franks to Foreign Office, December 22, 1949, CO537/4589 no. 24a, in Hyam, *Labour, 1945–51*, 2:457; Franks to Eden, "Anglo-American Conversations on the United Nations," October 6, 1952, FO371/101386 no.85, in Goldsworthy, *Conservative 1951–57*, 1:262.

42. Borstelmann, *Apartheid's Reluctant Uncle*, 40, 112; Franks to Foreign Office, December 22, 1949, CO 537/4589 no. 24a, in Hyam, *Labour, 1945–51*, 2:458; Morrison to Kennan, "The Problem of Joint Development of Africa by European Powers," August 4, 1948; Meeting Report, Policy Planning Staff, June 3, 1949, NARA 59, 1568, Records of the Policy Planning Staff.

43. Jester, Consul General Dakar, to Washington, February 23, 1950, NARA 611.70/2-2350 no. 54.

44. Bacon to Allen, June 14, 1950, NARA 350/6-1450.

45. Editorial notes, in *FRUS, 1952–54*, 3:1075, 1119, 1139, 1160.

46. Hickerson, Memorandum, January 19, 1950, NARA RG53, 1238 Bureau of United Nations Affairs.

47. Editorial note, in *FRUS, 1952–54*, 3:1119.

48. The papers referred to in this and succeeding paragraphs include: "United States Policy toward Colonial Areas," July 27, 1949, NARA RG59, 1456 Bureau of United Nations Affairs, SPU/DEP/P 2 Rev 1; Paper prepared by the Colonial Policy Review Sub-committee on Problems of Dependent Areas, April 26, 1950, Department of State Committee files, lot 54, D 5, Working Group on Colonial Problems, in *FRUS, 1952–54*, 3: 1076ff.

49. Hickerson to Mathews, May 13, 1952, NARA RG59, 1238, Bureau

of United Nations Affairs Papers; Editorial Note, *FRUS, 1952–54*, 3:1160.

50. Volman, *British Central Africa*, 58; Munene *Truman*, 182; Sandifer to Hickerson, May 9, 1952, NARA RG 59, 1238, Bureau of United Nations Affairs Papers.

51. Dr. Emory Ross of the Foreign Missions Conference; James A. Farrell Jr., president of the Farrell Steamship Lines; Dr. Robert G. Woolbert of the University of Denver; Dr. Derwent Whittlesey, professor of geography at Harvard University; Dr. Cornelis W. de Kiewet, acting president of Cornell University; Dr. Mark H. Watkins, professor of anthropology at Howard University; Dr. Ralph J. Bunche, director of the Department of Trusteeship for the United Nations; Dr. Channing Tobias of the Phelps-Stokes Foundation; Dr. John Morrison, professor of geography at the University of Maryland; Juan Trippe, president of American Airways; and Ogden White of the Filatures Tissages Africans.

52. McGhee, *Envoy*, 115–7, 123–4; Report prepared in the Department of State, undated, in *FRUS, 1950*, 5:1508; Conference Document no. 13, no date, NARA RG59, 1422, McGhee files 1945–53.

53. Summary of Conclusions and Recommendations, Lourenco Marques Conference, February 27 – March 2, 1950, NARA RG59 Office of West African Affairs Country Files.

54. Policy Paper prepared by the Bureau of Near Eastern, South Asian and African Affairs, April 18, 1950, in *FRUS, 1950*, 5:1524–36; Paper prepared in the Bureau of Near Eastern, South Asian and African Affairs, December 29, 1950, in *FRUS, 1951*, 5:1199–1202.

55. George C. McGhee, "United States Interests in Africa," 999ff.

56. Munene, *Truman*, 153–4.

Chapter 4

1. Russell, *United Nations Charter*, 808–9; Murray, *Trusteeship System*, 32; Schlesinger, *Act of Creation*, 233–4.

2. Louis, *Imperialism at Bay*, 534; Russell, *United Nations Charter*, 814, 817; Murray *Trusteeship System*, 38.

3. Darwin, *Britain and Decolonisation*, 42–3; Russell, *United Nations Charter*, 839; Munene, *Truman*, 54–55

4. Schlesinger, *Act of Creation*, 235.

5. El-Ayouty, *United Nations and Decolonization*, 38.

6. El-Ayouty, *United Nations and Decolonization*, 39, 73, 91, 151; *Yearbook of the United Nations 1948–49*, 133, 723.

7. *Yearbook of the United Nations, 1948–49*, 729, 758, 774–7, 851.

8. Minutes, Second Meeting of United States Group on Trusteeship, January 8, 1946, IO Files, USTC/Prel/W.P. Min. 1, 668, in *FRUS, 1946*, 1:550 Note; Alger Hiss, director of the Office of Special Political Affairs, Memorandum of Telephone Conversation, November 1, 1946, FW 501. BB/10–3146, in *FRUS*, 1946, 1:550.

9. *Yearbook of the United Nations, 1948–49*, 720–1.

10. *Yearbook of the United Nations, 1948–9*, 723, 726, 731–2, 745; Bureau of International Organizations, "Draft Position Paper on the Annual Report for Tanganyika for 1948," no date, NARA RG59, 1238, SD/T/124.

11. Douglas, *British Left*, 154–5.

12. Creech Jones, Cabinet Memorandum, January 30, 1948, CAB 129/24, CP(48) in Hyam, *Labour, 1945–51*, 2:423.

13. Creech Jones, Opening Address to Cambridge Summer Conference, August 19, 1948, CO852/1053/1 no. 18 in Hyam, *Labour 1945–51*, 2:163; Creech Jones, Cabinet Memorandum, February 7, 1949, CAB129/32/2, CP(49), 24, in Hyam, *Labour, 1945–51*, 2:438.

14. Creech Jones to Bevin, October 19, 1949, CO537/4589, annex no. 1, in *Hyam, Labour, 1945–51*, 2:445.

15. Creech Jones, Cabinet Memorandum, January 30, 1948, CAB129/24, CP(48), 36, in Hyam, *Labour, 1945–51*, 2:424; Creech Jones, Cabinet Memorandum, February 7, 1949, CAB129/32/2, CP(49) 24, in Hyam, *Labour, 1945–51*, 2:438.

16. Douglas, *British Left*, 151; El-Ayouty, *United Nations and Decolonization*, 83.

17. El-Ayouty, *United Nations and Decolonization*, 79–80; *Yearbook of the United Nations, 1948–9*, 723.

18. Benjamin Gerig, Draft Position Paper, July 29, 1947, CDA-467a, in *FRUS, 1947*, 1:283ff; United States Delegation, Working Paper, September 15, 1947, I/O Files:US/A/C.4/34, in *FRUS*, 1947, 1:290.

19. Minutes of Seventh Meeting of the United States Delegation, September 15, 1947, I/O Files 1:US/A/M(Chr)/51, in *FRUS, 1947*, 1:289; Borstelmann, *Apartheid's Reluctant Uncle*, 111–2; Minutes of the Twenty-Eighth Meeting of the United States Delegation, October 28, 1947, I/O Files: US/AM(Chr)/72, in *FRUS*, 1947, 1:305; Francis Sayre, Memoran-

dum of Conversation, I/O Files:US/A/C.4/65, in *FRUS, 1947*, 1:10.

20. D.C. Tebbit, Memorandum of Conversation, September 9, 1948, NARA 501.BE/9-848; Rusk to Gerig, September 10, 1948, NARA 501.BE/9-1049 no. 2012.

21. British Embassy to the Department of State, January 18, 1949, NARA 501.BE/1-1849, in *FRUS, 1949* 2:341–2.

22. Department of State to the British Embassy, February 17, 1949, NARA 501.BE/1-1849, in *FRUS, 1949*, 2:345–6.

23. Secretary of state to London Embassy, December 30, 1949, NARA 501.BB/12-3049, in *FRUS, 1950*, 2:434; Fletcher-Cooke, Memorandum, December 10, 1949, CO537/4589, in Hyam, *Labour, 1945–51*, 2:449; Draft Memorandum, February 14, 1949, NARA, IO/ODA Files: Lot 62D228, in *FRUS, 1949*, 2:343; Thompson, Memorandum of Conversation, April 5, 1949, NARA 501.BE/4-549, in *FRUS, 1949*, 2:348.

24. Franks to Foreign Office, December 22, 1949, CO537/4589, no. 5896, Hyam, *Labour, 1945–51*, 2:458; Secretary of State to London Embassy, December 30, 1949, NARA 501.BB/12-3049, in *FRUS, 1950*, 2:434.

25. Franks to Foreign Office, January 14, 1950 CO537/7136, Porter and Stockwell, *British Imperial Policy*, 1:322; Poynton, Minute, February 14, 1950, CO537/5698, in Hyam, *Labour, 1945–51*, 2:462; Colonial Office, "The Colonial Empire Today," May 9, 1950, CO537/5698, in Hyam, *Labour, 1945–51*, 1:359.

26. Hare to McGhee, May 9, 1950, NARA 611.41/5-950; Note of a Meeting in the Foreign Office of British and United States Officials on Major Colonial Issues, May 3, 1950, CO537/5698, in Hyam, *Labour, 1945–51*, 2:468, 473.

27. Note of a Meeting in the Foreign Office of British and United States Officials on Major Colonial Issues, May 3, 1950, CO537/5698, in Hyam, *Labour, 1945–51*, 2:468; Report on Ministerial Talks, May 9, 1950, NARA RG59, 3051, Conference Files, Min/TRI/P/23.

28. United States Delegation to Tripartite Preparatory Meetings to Secretary of State, May 5, 1950, in *FRUS, 1950*, 3:954–5; Report on Ministerial Talks, May 9, 1950, NARA RG59, 3051 B Conference Files, Min/TRI/P/23.

29. Franks to Bevin, July 13, 1950, CO537/5699, no. 102, in Hyam, *Labour, 1945–51*, 2:485; Secretary of

State to London Embassy, August 1, 1950, NARA 320/8-150, in *FRUS, 1950*, 2:471; General Introductory Note to Colonial Office Briefs, October 1951, CO936/56/6 no. 3, in Hyam, *Labour, 1945–51*, 2:496.

30. General Introductory Note to Colonial Office Briefs, October 1951, CO936/56/6, no. 3, in Hyam, *Labour, 1945–51*, 2:496.

31. *Yearbook of the United Nations, 1951*, 606, 775; *Yearbook of the United Nations, 1950*, 675; Briefing Book for Colonial Policy Discussions, June 21, 1950, NARA RG59, 1238 Bureau of United Nations Affairs; Position Paper on Resolution 334(IV), August 9, 1950, NARA RG59, 1238 Bureau of International Organizations, SD/A/AC35/12.

32. Martin, Minute, October 222, 1951 CO537/7137, in Hyam, *Labour, 1945–51*, 2:498; Hope, Minute, July 3, 1952, FO371/101383 no. 7, in Goldsworthy, *Conservative, 1951–57*, 1:259.

33. Sanders to Hickerson, December 7, 1951, NARA Office of Dependent Affairs Files, Lot 62 D223, in *FRUS, 1951*, 2:652; Bacon to Cargo, July 17, 1952, NARA 320.14/7-1752.

34. Cargo to Hickerson, June 19, 1952, NARA 350/6-1952.

35. Ross, Staff Paper, April 17, 1952, US UN Confidential 2, Hickerson-Murphy-Ley files, lot 58 D33, in *FRUS, 1952–54*, 3:3; Jessup, Memorandum for the File, April 11, 1952, NARA 611.41/4-1152.

36. United States-United Kingdom Talks on United Nations, September 24, 1952, NARA RG59, 1383 Office Files of Benjamin Gerig.

37. Bureau of United Nations Affairs, Memorandum, September 20, 1952, NARA 330.14/9-2052, in *FRUS, 1952–54*, 3:1245.

38. Martin, Informal Note on Anglo-American Discussions, CO 936/95 no. 93, October 1952, in Goldsworthy, *Conservative, 1951–57*, 1:266.

39. United States–United Kingdom Talks on United Nations, September 24, 1952, NARA RG59, 1383 Office Files of Benjamin Gerig.

40. United States–United Kingdom Talks on United Nations, September 24, 1952, NARA RG59, 1383 Office Files of Benjamin Gerig; Franks to Eden, October 6, 1952, FO371/101386 no. 85, in Goldsworthy, *Conservative, 1951–57*, 1:262; Tibbetts to Secretary of State, November 25, 1952, NARA 320.14/11-2552.

41. Franks to Eden, October 6, 1952, FO371/101386 no. 85, in

Goldsworthy, *Conservative, 1951–57*, 1:262; Lloyd to Martin, October 20, 1952, CO936/95, in Belmonte, *Reining*, 74.

42. Goldsworthy, "Critics," 8.

43. McLellan, *Acheson*, 394; Beisner, *Acheson*, 521.

44. Memorandum of Conversation, November 20, 1952, SD/A/C.4/UND/2, NARA RG59, 1238, Bureau of International Organizations; Memorandum of Conversation, November 17, 1952, SD/A/C3/UND/18. NARA RG59, 1238, Bureau of International Organizations; El-Ayouty, *United Nations and Decolonization*, 59.

45. Seldon, *Indian Summer*, 388; McLellan, *Acheson*, 390; Beisner, *Acheson*, 464; Bartlett, *Special Relationship*, 59.

Chapter 5

1. Hathaway, *Ambiguous Partnership*, 25.

2. Skidelsky, *Keynes*, 125; Darwin, *Britain and Decolonisation*, 66; Hathaway, *Ambiguous Partnership*, 25–27; Holland, "Imperial Factor," 167.

3. Ovendale, *Foreign Policy*, 7; Hathaway, *Ambiguous Partnership*, 297; Heinlein, *Government Policy*, 12–13; Darwin, *Britain and Decolonisation*, 194.

4. Attlee, Memorandum, September 1, 1945, CAB 129/1, CP (45), in Hyam, *Labour, 1945–51*, 3:207.

5. Dalton Diaries, December 20, 1946, in Pearce, *Turning Point*, 93; Dalton Diaries, February 28, 1950, in Douglas, *British Left*, 159.

6. Minister of Defence, Memorandum, October 18, 1949, annex, CAB 129/37(3), CP (49) 245 and Dalton Diaries August 8, 1947, in Heinlein, *Government Policy*, 16–17.

7. Ovendale, *Anglo-American Relations*, 61.

8. Discussion involving Foreign Office officials, March 20, 1951, FO 371/90931, in Baylis, *Anglo-American Relations*, 76–77.

9. Bradford Perkins, "Unequal Partners," 47; Edmonds, *Mould*, 26–27; Louis and Robinson, "Empire Preserved," 154–55.

10. Adamthwaite, "Eden," 243; Butler, Cabinet Memorandum, May 17, 1952, CAB129/52, in Porter and Stockwell, *British Imperial Policy*, 2:144.

11. Macmillan, Cabinet Memorandum, June 17, 1952, CAB129/52, in Porter and Stockwell, *British Imperial Policy*, 2:154.

12. Eden, Cabinet Memorandum,

June 18, 1952, CAB129/53, C(52)202, in Goldsworthy, *Conservative*, 1:11

13. Kirk-Greene, *British Colonial Governor*, 103; London to Washington, October 2, 1951, NARA 745s.11/10-251.

14. Cohen, Memorandum, April 3, 1946, CO847/35/6 no. 2, in Hyam, *Labour, 1945–51*, 1:103; Robinson, Memorandum, 1947, CO847/38/3, in Hyam, *Labour, 1945–51*, 1:154.

15. Creech Jones, Address to Cambridge Summer Conference, August 19, 1948, CO852/1053/1 no. 18, in Hyam, *Labour, 1945–51*, 1:165; Report of Colonial Office Agenda Committee on the Conference of African Governors, Appendix 2, CO847/36/1 no. 922, May 1947, in Hyam, *Labour, 1945–51*, 1:199; Robinson, Memorandum, 1947, CO847/38/3, no. 1, in Hyam, *Labour, 1945–51*, 1:155; Hyam, "Africa and the Labour Government," 130, 153; Hyam, "Trusteeship," 277.

16. Pratt, "Critical Phase," 15; Pearce, *Turning Point*, 176; Report of Colonial Office Agenda Committee on the Conference of African Governors, Appendix 2, CO847/36/1 no. 922, May 1947, in Hyam, *Labour, 1945–51*, 1:200.

17. Gater to Hall, May 22, 1946, CO847/35/6, no. 6, in Hyam, *Labour, 1945–51*, 1:110; Cartland, Memorandum, January 1946, CO847/25/7, no. 1, in Hyam, *Labour, 1945–51*, 1:98; Pearce, *Turning Point*, 147.

18. Report of the Colonial Office Agenda Committee on the Conference of African Governors, May 1947, CO847/736/1, no. 922, in Hyam, *Labour, 1945–51*, 1:206, 209.

19. Report of the Colonial Office Agenda Committee on the Conference of African Governors, May 1947, CO847/736/1, no. 922, in Hyam, *Labour, 1945–51*, 1:207.

20. Pedler, Minute, November 1, 1946, CO847/35/47234/1/1947, in Porter and Stockwell, *British Imperial Policy*, 1:264; Creech Jones, Circular Dispatch, February 25, 1947, CO847/35/6, nos. 15–24, in Hyam *Labour, 1945–51*, 1:121; Fieldhouse, "Labour Governments," 108.

21. Report of the Colonial Office Agenda Committee on the Conference of African Governors, May 1947, CO847/36/1, no. 922, in Hyam, *Labour, 1945–51*, 1:203–4; Franks to Bevin, July 13, 1950, CO537/5699, no. 102, in Hyam, *Labour, 1945–51*, 1:492.

22. Report of the Colonial Office Agenda Committee on the Conference of African Governors, May 1947, CO847/36/1, no. 922, in Hyam,

Labour, 1945–51, 1:199; McIntyre, "Small States," 251, 253.

23. Report of the Colonial Office Agenda Committee on the Conference of African Governors, May 1947, CO847/36/1, no. 922, in Hyam, *Labour, 1945–51*, 1:203; Colonial Office, International Relations Department Paper, May 1950, CO537/5698, no. 69, in Hyam, *Labour, 1945–51*, 1:335.

24. Creech Jones, Dispatch, February 25, 1947, CO847/35/6, nos. 15–24 in Hyam, *Labour, 1945–51*, 1:119–129.

25. Mitchell to Creech Jones, May 30, 1947, CO847/35/6, no. 88 in Hyam, *Labour, 1945–51*, 1:129, 131, 137.

26. Mitchell to Creech Jones, May 30, 1947, CO847/35/6, no. 88 in Hyam, *Labour, 1945–51*, 1:129, 131, 137.

27. African Governors Conference, Draft Minute 5 (Second Session), November 9, 1947, CO847/3777, no. 9, in Hyam, *Labour, 1945–51*, 1:303–306.

28. African Governors Conference, Draft Minute 5 (Second Session), November 9, 1947, CO847/3777, no. 9, in Hyam, *Labour, 1945–51*, 1:306.

29. Notes on British Colonial Policy, Colonial Office circular memorandum no. 28, March 1949, CO875/24, no. 8, in Hyam, *Labour, 1945–51*, 1:326–331.

30. Howe, *Anticolonialism*, 144; Griffiths, Address to Colonial Group of Royal Empire Society, May 1, 1951, CO96/0820/2, no. 39, in Hyam, *Labour, 1945–51*, 3:45–51.

31. Creech Jones, Dispatch, February 25, 1947, CO847/35/6, nos. 15–24 in Hyam, *Labour, 1945–51*, 1:121; Creech Jones, Memorandum, January 6, 1948, DO35/2380, no. 3 in Hyam, *Labour, 1945–51*, 2:201; Hyam, "Africa and the Labour Government,"153; Griffiths, Address to Colonial Office Summer Conference, August 20, 1951, CO879/155 African, no. 1178, in Hyam, *Labour, 1945–51*, 1:184.

32. Fieldhouse, "Labour Governments," 85, 103; Howe, *Anticolonialism*, 138, 173; Douglas, *British Left*, 146, 152, 157, 159; Pearce, "Colonial Office, 212.

33. London to Washington, September 2, 1947, NARA 880.00/9-247, no. 1987.

34. Anderson to Secretary of State, October 18, 1948, NARA 880.00/10-1848.

35. Cohen to Lloyd, October 31, 1951, CO537/6696, in Goldsworthy, *Conservative*, 2:1; Lyttelton to Churchill, November 5, 1951, CO537/

6696, no. 12, in Goldsworthy, *Conservative*, 2:2.

36. Heilein, *Government Policy*, 102; Eden, Minute, December 23, 1951, FO371/95757, no. 25, in Goldsworthy, *Conservative*, 2:2; Murphy, "Central African Federation," 65–6.

37. Heinlein, *Government Policy*, 101; Lyttelton, *Memoirs*, 337, 340; Owen, "Decolonisation and the Colonial Office," 512.

38. Strang to Lloyd, June 21, 1952, CO936/217, no. 1, in Goldsworthy, *Conservative*, 1:17.

39. Lloyd to Strang, September 9, 1952, CO936/217, no. 4/5, in Goldsworthy, *Conservative*, 1:22.

40. Strang to Lloyd, June 21, 1952, CO936/217, no. 1, in Goldsworthy, *Conservative*, 1:17.

Chapter 6

1. At this point, the British had eight battalions of African troops commanded by British officers in West Africa: four in the Gold Coast, three in Nigeria and one in Sierra Leone.

2. Alexander to Attlee, March 3, 1948, PREM 8/924, in Rathbone, *Ghana, 1941–52*, 1:62ff.

3. Scott, Memorandum March 5, 1948, CO96/795/6 no. 84, in Rathbone, *Ghana, 1941–52*, 1:61ff.

4. Bradley to Creech Jones, December 12, 1947, CO537/3559, no. 2, to Creech Jones in Rathbone, *Ghana, 1941–52*, 1:41ff.

5. Nkrumah, *Autobiography*, 76; Austin, *Politics in Ghana*, 74–75.

6. Creech Jones to Creasy, March 18, 1948, CO537/3558, no. 122, in Hyam, *Labour, 1945–1951*, 45–51.

7. Report of the Commission of Enquiry into Disturbances in the Gold Coast…1948, in Metcalfe, *Great Britain and Ghana*, 682–5.

8. Report of the Commission of Enquiry into Disturbances in the Gold Coast…1948, in Metcalfe, *Great Britain and Ghana*, 684–5.

9. Report of the Commission of Enquiry into Disturbances in the Gold Coast … 1948, in Metcalfe, *Great Britain and Ghana*, 682, 684–5.

10. Nkrumah, *Autobiography*, 85–87.

11. Cohen, Minute, June 1948, CO96/796/5, no. 4329, in Rathbone, *Ghana, 1941–52*, 1:76ff; Creech Jones to Attlee, July 19, 1948, PREM 8/924, in Rathbone, *Ghana, 1941–52*, 1:89ff.

12. Anderson to Secretary of State, August 6, 1948, NARA 848N.00/8-648, no. 1718.

13. Scott to Creech Jones, March

10, 1949, CO537/4638, no. 1, in Rathbone, *Ghana, 1941–52*, 1:118ff.

14. Hanrott, Minute, June 21, 1949, CO537/4638, in Rathbone, *Ghana, 1941–52*, 1:118ff.

15. Hanrott, Minute, March 18, 1949, CO537/4638, no. 1; Gorsuch, Minute, March 23, 1949; Creech Jones to Mangin, May 24, 1949, no. 8, in Rathbone, *Ghana, 1941–52*, 1:118ff.

16. Mangin to Creech Jones, June 9, 1949, CO537/4638, no. 19, in Rathbone, *Ghana, 1941–52*, 1:118ff.

17. Cohen, Minute, June 14, 1949, CO537/4635, in Rathbone, *Ghana, 1941–52*, 1:141ff.

18. Creech Jones, Cabinet Memorandum, October 8, 1949, PREM 8/924 CP(49), no. 199, in Rathbone, *Ghana, 1941–52*, 1:204ff.

19. Brook, Minute, October 12, 1949, PREM 8/924, in Hyam, *Labour, 1945–1951*, 3:50.

20. Cabinet Conclusions on Recommendations of Coussey Committee, October 13, 1949, CAB 128/16 CM 58 (49), in Hyam, *Labour Government, 1945–1951*, 3:51.

21. Creech Jones to Tewson, January 31, 1950, CO96/819/4, no. 11, in Rathbone, *Ghana, 1941–52*, 1:240ff; Austin, *Politics in Ghana*, 89 note; Nkrumah, *Autobiography*, 110ff.; Apter, *Ghana in Transition*, 172.

22. Arden-Clarke to family, February 3, 1950, in Rooney, *Sir Charles Arden-Clarke*, 105; Arden-Clarke to Cohen, January 28, 1950, CO96/827/13, no. 4, in Rathbone, *Ghana, 1941–52*, 1:238ff.

23. Cohen to Arden Clarke, December 23, 1950, CO96/819/4, no. 50, in Rathbone, *Ghana, 1941–52*, 1:280ff.

24. Austin, *Politics in Ghana*, 150; Nkrumah, *Autobiography*, 142.

25. Arden-Clarke to Cohen, March 5, 1951, CO537/7181, no. 3, in Rathbone, *Ghana, 1941–52*, 1:293ff; Arden-Clarke to Cohen, April 16, 1951, CO96/819/3, no. 7, in Rathbone, *Ghana, 1941–52*, 1:304ff; Arden-Clarke to Cohen, May 12, 1951, CO537/7181, no. 5, in Rathbone, *Ghana, 1941–52*, 1:322ff; Colonial Office note of meeting between Lyttelton and Arden Clarke, January 10, 1952, CO554/298, no. 11, in Rathbone, *Ghana, 1941–52*, 1:368ff.

26. Cohen, Minute, June 11, 1951, CO537/7181; Cohen, Memorandum, November 20, 1951, CO537/7181, number 17, in Hyam, *Labour, 1945–51*, 3:73, 78.

27. Cohen, Minute, June 11, 1951, CO537/7181, in Hyam, *Labour, 1945–1951*, 3:73.

28. Colonial Office Note of a Meeting with Arden-Clarke, January 9, 1952, CO554/298, no. 10; Note of a Meeting between Lyttelton and Arden-Clarke, January 10, 1952, CO 554/298 no. 11, in Rathbone, *Ghana, 1941–52*, 1:362ff, 368ff.

29. Colonial Office Note of Meeting between Lyttleton and Arden-Clarke, January 10, 1952, CO554/298, no. 11, in Rathbone, *Ghana, 1941–52*, 1:368ff

30. Gorell Barnes, Note on Lyttelton's Discussions with Gold Coast Ministers, July 7, 1952, CO554/371, no. 26, in Rathbone, *Ghana, 1941–52*, 1:377ff; Gorell Barnes, Minute, July 7, 1952, CO554/371, no. 26, in Rathbone, *Ghana, 1941–52*, 1:77ff.

31. Arden-Clarke to Gorell Barnes, September 24, 1952, CO554/371, no. 31, Rathbone, *Ghana, 1952–1957*, 1:1ff.

32. Gorell Barnes, minute, July 7, 1952, CO554.371, no. 26, in Rathbone, *Ghana, 1941–52*, 1:377.

33. Smith to Secretary of State, August 6, 1947, NARA 848N.01/8-647, no. 77; Smith to Secretary of State, September 11, 1947, NARA 848N.00/9-1147, no. 92.

34. Palmer to Smith, October 1, 1947, NARA 848B.01/8-647.

35. Smith to Secretary of State, December 19, 1947, NARA 848N.00/12-1947, no. 152.

36. Anderson to Secretary of State, March 9, 1948, NARA 848N.00/3-948, no. 618; Anderson to Secretary of State, March 10, 1948, NARA 848N.00/3-1148, no. 630; Anderson to Secretary of State, March 18, 1948, NARA 848N.00/3-1848, no. 715; Anderson to Secretary of State, June 25, 1948, NARA 848H.00BB/6-2548, no. 1427.

37. London to Secretary of State, November 23, 1948, no. 2317, NARA 848K.00B/11-2348; Anderson to Secretary of State, April 14, 1948, no. 902, NARA 848N.00/4-1448.

38. Smith to Secretary of State, March 9, 1948, NARA 848N.00/3-948, no. 27; Smith to Secretary of State, March 23, 1948, NARA 848N.00/3-2348, no. 36.

39. Smith to Secretary of State, August 11, 1948, NARA 848N.00/8-1148, no. 98.

40. "The Current Situation in British West Africa," September 29, 1950, ORE 46–40, http://www.foia.cia.

41. Bourgerie to McGhee, June 6, 1951, NARA RG 59, Office of West African Affairs Country Files.

42. McGhee, "Africa's Role," 99.

43. Bloom to Secretary of State, October 5, 1951, NARA 745K.00/10-551, no. 118; Martin to Secretary of State, March 6, 1952, NARA 745K.00/1-2152, no. 3185; Consulate Accra to Secretary of State, January 21, 1952, NARA 745K.00/3-652, no. 205; Cole to Secretary of State, January 18, 1952, NARA 745K.00/1-852, no. 176.

44. Richards to Hall Martin, August 9, 1946, CO583/277/4, no.7, in Lynn, *Nigeria*, 1:90ff; Creasey to Gater Martin, July 18, 1946, CO583/277/4, no. 5, in Lynn, *Nigeria*, 1:88ff; G. Bereford Stooke to Cohen, June 10, 1947, CO583/282/2, no. 21, in Lynn, *Nigeria*, 1:109ff.

45. Richards to Hall Martin, August 9, 1946, CO583/277/4, no. 7, in Lynn, *Nigeria*, 1:90ff.

46. Field, Memorandum, April 28, 1948, CO583/292/5, no. 28, in Lynn, *Nigeria*, 1:133.

47. Field, Memorandum, April 28, 1948, CO583/292/5, no. 28, in Lynn, *Nigeria*, 1:133; Nigeria Political Summary, March 2, 1949, CO537/4727, no. 2, in Lynn, *Nigeria*, 1:192.

48. Macpherson to Creech Jones, April 27, 1949, CO537/4631, no. 3, in Lynn, *Nigeria*, 1:197; Iwereibor, *Radical Politics*, 204.

49. Furedi, *Colonial Wars*, 253, 256; Macpherson to Creech Jones, October 10, 1948, CO583/287/4, no. 25, in Lynn, *Nigeria*, 1:159; Macpherson to Creech Jones, November 6, 1948, CO537/3557, no. 6, in Lynn, *Nigeria*, 1:164; Macpherson to Creech Jones, December 26, 1948, CO537/3557, no. 12, in Lynn, *Nigeria*, 1:170.

50. Vile, Minute, February 1950, CO537/5786, no. 9, in Lynn, *Nigeria*, 1:262; Cohen to Foot, February 23, 1950, CO537/5786, no. 20, in Lynn, *Nigeria*, 1:262; Griffiths to Macpherson, July 15, 1950, CO537/5787, no. 52, in Lynn, *Nigeria*, 1:334.

51. Furedi, "Emergencies," 99; Macpherson to Cohen, January 29, 1949, CO537/4625, no. 1, in Lynn, *Nigeria*, 1:174; Nigeria Political Summary, March 1949, CO537/4727, no. 2, in Lynn, *Nigeria*, 1:192; Macpherson to Creech Jones, April 27, 1949, CO537/4631, no. 3 in Lynn, *Nigeria*, 1:197; Cohen, Memorandum, November 20, 1951, CO537/7148, no. 17, in Hyam, *Labour, 1945–51*, 3:77; Tibbetts to Secretary of State, March 13, 1952, NARA 745H.00/3-1352.

52. Macpherson to Cohen, June 28, 1948, CO583/287/5, no. 2, in Lynn, *Nigeria*, 1:150; Macpherson to Lloyd, January 8, 1952, CO 967/173, in Lynn, *Nigeria*, 1:432.

53. Greene to Secretary of State, November 13, 1946, NARA 848L.00/11-1346; Greene to Secretary of State, January 13, 1947, NARA 848L.00/1347; Childs to Secretary of State, May 15, 1951, NARA 745H.00/5-1551; Lagos to Washington, December 31, 1952, NARA 745H.00/12-3152.

54. Greene to Secretary of State, January 13, 1947, NARA 848L.00/8-847; Lagos to Secretary of State, August 8, 1947, NARA 848L.00/8-847; Stanton to Secretary of State, October 30, 1950, NARA 745H.00/10-3050.

55. Greene to Secretary of State, February 13, 1947, NARA 848L.00/2-1347; Stanton to Secretary of State, March 17, 1951, NARA 745H.00/3-1751; Ross to Secretary of State, October 17, 1952, NARA 745H.00/10-1752.

56. Greene to Secretary of State, March 31, 1947, NARA 848L.03/3-3147; Lagos to Secretary of State, August 8, 1947, NARA 848L.00/8-847.

57. Lourenco Marques Conference, February-March 1950, Summary of Conclusions and Recommendations, NARA RG59, Office of West African Affairs Country Files; Minnigerode to Secretary of State, March 31, 1949, NARA 848L.5043/3-3149; Childs to Secretary of State, August 2, 1951, NARA 745H.00/8-251; Kuykendall to Secretary of State, September 25, 1949, NARA 848L.00B/9-2849; Lagos to Washington, June 9, 1951, NARA 745H.00/6-951.

58. Greene to Secretary of State, November 13, 1946, NARA 848L.00/11-1346; Childs to Secretary of State, May 15, 1951, NARA 745H.00/5-1551.

59. Greene to Secretary of State, March 31, 1947, NARA 848L.03/3-3147; Kuykendall to Secretary of State, July 6, 1948, NARA 848L.00/7-648; Ross to Secretary of State, June 18, 1952, 611.45H/6-1852, in *FRUS, 1952–54*, 11:272.

60. Johnson to Secretary of State, October 10, 1946, NARA 848L.00/10-1046; Ross to Secretary of State, June 18, 1952, NARA 745.03/6-1852.

61. Stanton to Secretary of State, February 8, 1951, NARA 745H.00/2-851; Childs to Secretary of State, May 14, 1951, NARA 745H.00/5-1451.

62. Lagos to Washington, June 9, 1951, NARA 745H.00/6-951; Ross to Secretary of State, October 6, 1952, NARA 745H.00/10-652.

Chapter 7

1. Note of Meeting in the Foreign Office, May 3, 1950, CO537/5698, no. 66, in Hyam, *Labour, 1945–51*, 2:475; Colonial Office In-

ternational Relations Department Paper, May 1950, CO537/5698, no. 69, in Hyam, *Labour, 1945–51*, 2:337.

2. Cabinet Conclusions on Draft Statement, November 20, 1950, CAB 128/18, CM76(500)1, in Hyam, *Labour, 1945–51*, 3:28; Griffiths, Note, December 8, 1950, PREM8/1113, CA (50)3, in Hyam, *Labour, 1945–51*, 3:34.

3. Kyle, *Independence of Kenya*, 52; Douglas-Home, *Baring*, 228; Furedi, "Colonial Wars," 163.

4. Touchette to Secretary of State, August 8, 1946, NARA 848T.00/8-846, no. 190; Dorsz to Washington, October 10, 1952, NARA 745R.00/10-1052, no. 81; Summary of Conclusions and Recommendations, Lourenco Marques Conference, February 27 — March 2, 1950, NARA RG59, Office of West African Affairs Country Files.

5. Touchette to Secretary of State, August 8, 1946, NARA 848T.00/8-846, no. 190; Ward to Washington, April 11, 1951, NARA 745R.00/4-1151, no. 276; Nairobi to Department of State, May 26, 1952, NARA 745.00/5-2652; Tibbetts to Washington, October 22, 1952, NARA 745R.00/10-2252; Dorsz to Washington, October 10, 1962, NARA 745R.00/10-1052.

6. Touchette to Secretary of State, May 7, 1947, NARA 848T.00/5-747; Nairobi to Washington, May 8, 1947, NARA 848T.00/5-847, no. 392; Neal to O'Shaughnessy, August 14, 1950, NARA 745.00I/8-1450; Groth to Secretary of State, October 28, 1949, NARA 848T.00/10-2849; Groth to Secretary of State, December 12, 1949, NARA 848T.00/12-1249.

7. Phillips to Washington, July 7, 1952, NARA 745R.00/7-752, no. 2; Dorsz to Washington, October 23, 1952, NARA 745R.00/10-2352, no. 90; Dorsz to Washington, December 5, 1952, NARA 745R.00/12-552, no. 158; Dorsz to Washington, October 10, 1952, NARA 745R.00/10-1052.

8. Munene, *Truman* 198–9.

9. Pratt, *Critical Phase*, 19, 33; Iliffe, *Tanganyika*, 481; Griffiths to Government of Tanganyika, July 25, 1951, CO537/7196, no. 18, in Hyam, *Labour, 1945–51*, 3:37.

10. Lourenco Marques Conference, Summary of Conclusions and Recommendations, February 27 — March 2, 1950, 30, 98, NARA RG59, Office of West African Affairs Country Files; Feld to Secretary of State, July 20, 1948, NARA 501.BE/7-2048; Feld to Secretary of State, September 20, 1948, NARA 501.BE/9-2048;

Feld to Secretary of State, May 20, 1949, NARA 501.BE/5-2049.

11. Draft Position Paper on the Annual Report for Tanganyika for 1948, SD/T/124, NARA RG59, 1238, Bureau of International Organizations; Munene, *Truman*, 195; Position Paper: Examination of 1951 Annual Report on Tanganyika, June 9, 1952, NARA RG59, 1238, Bureau of International Organizations.

12. Douglas to Secretary of State, May 6, 1949, NARA 848U.00/5-649; Groth to Secretary of State, August 29, 1949, NARA 848T.00/8-2949.

13. Seldon, *Indian Summer*, 360; Rotberg, *Rise of Nationalism*, 214–6; Cohen, Minute, July 16, 1948, CO 795/156/5, in Murphy, *Central Africa*, 1:82; Creech Jones, Memorandum, June 8, 1949, CAB134/56 CA(49)4, in Hyam, *Labour, 1945–51*, 3:21.

14. Ismay and Lyttelton, Joint Cabinet Memorandum, November 9, 1951, CAB129/48c(51)11 in Goldsworthy, *Conservative*, 2:282; Rotberg, *Rise of Nationalism*, 245; Baker, *Armitage*, 174.

15. Parry to Lambert, December 29, 1951, CO1015/65, no. 106, in Murphy, *Central Africa*, 1:181; Liesching, Notes, July 23, 1951, DO121/138, in Murphy, *Central Africa*, 1:167; Rotberg, *Rise of Nationalism*, 250.

16. Johannesburg to Department of State, April 11, 1950, NARA 745.00/4-1150; Sims to Washington, January 11, 1952, NARA 745C.00/1-1152; Sims to Washington, April 9, 1952, NARA 745C.00/4-952.

17. Anderson to Secretary of State, February 25, 1949, NARA 848F.01/2-2549; Hoover to Washington, October 3, 1952, NARA 745C.00/10-352; Roberts to Washington, July 25, 1951, NARA 745C.00/8-2951; Roberts to Washington, November 7, 1951, NARA 745C.00/11-1551; Gray to Washington, February 23, 1951, NARA 7450.00/2-2351.

18. Bureau of United Nations Affairs, Memorandum, September 20, 1952, NARA 330.14/9-2052, in *FRUS, 1952–54*, 3:1245.

19. Extract from Minutes of US-UK Colonial Policy Discussions, September 25, 1952, in *FRUS, 1952–54*, 11:1:311–312.

20. Extract from Minutes of US-UK Colonial Policy Discussions, September 25, 1952, in *FRUS, 1952–54*, 11:1:311–312.

21. Hall to Richards, May 4, 1946, CO525/205/44248/46, no. 29, in Hyam, *Labour, 1945–51*, 3:45; Cohen, Minute, January 8, 1946, CO525/205/44248/46, in Hyam, *Labour, 1945–51*, 3:45; Colby to Cohen, July

23, 1948, CO5525/205/44248/48, in Murphy, *Central Africa*, 1:88.

22. Cohen, Minute, March 20, 1946, CO525/205/44248/46, in Murphy, *Central Africa*, 1:17.

23. Lambert, Minute, June 24, 1948, CO795/156/5, in Murphy, *Central Africa*, 1:79; Rennie to Cohen, April 7, 1948, CO795/156/4, in Murphy, *Central Africa*, 1:74; Colonial Office Note on Discussion with Rhodesian Representative, July 5, 1946, CO795/156/45433/46, in Hyam, *Labour, 1945–51*, 3:8.

24. Creech Jones, Memorandum, June 8, 1949, CAB135/56, CA(49)4, in Hyam, *Labour, 1945–51*, 3:20.

25. Anderson to Secretary of State, March 18, 1948, NARA 848F.00/3-1848.

Chapter 8

1. Huddleston, Memorandum, September 12, 1945, FO371/45985, no. 3088, in Johnson, *Sudan*, 1:88.

2. Hanes, *Imperial Diplomacy*, 31, 33; House of Commons Debates, March 26, 1946, Vol. 421, Column 217, in Johnson, *Sudan*, 1:137.

3. Robertson, Note, February 18, 1946, FO371/53329, no. 865, in Johnson, *Sudan*, 1:124.

4. Bowker to Bevin, February 18, 1946, FO371/53329, no. 865, in Johnson, *Sudan*, 1:124; Scrivener to Bowker, March 18, 1946, FO371/53329, no. 865, in Johnson, *Sudan*, 1:135; Campbell to Huddleston, April 13, 1946, FO371/53251, no. 1634, in Johnson, *Sudan*, 1:140.

5. Bevin, Memorandum, August 29, 1946, FO371/53255, no. 3719, in Johnson, *Sudan*, 1:164.

6. Robertson to Governors, November 1, 1946, FO371/53262, in Johnson, *Sudan*, 1:225.

7. Daly, *Imperial Sudan*, 219, 229; Hanes, *Imperial Diplomacy*, 116, 120–1; Fabunmi, *Sudan in Anglo-Egyptian Relations*, 255–6.

8. Douglas to Secretary of State, March 25, 1947, NARA 741.83/3-2447; Acheson to London, March 25, 1947, NARA 741.83/3-2447; Daly, *Imperial Sudan*, 219; Hahn, *United States, Great Britain and Egypt*, 41–42.

9. *Yearbook of the United Nations, 1947–48*, 360.

10. Anglo-Egyptian Sudan Policy and Information Statement, January 13, 1947, NARA 711.48Z/1-1347.

11. Merriam to Henderson, March 28, 1947, NARA 741.83/3-2847.

12. London to Secretary of State, July 16, 1947, NARA 741.83/7-1647.

13. Howe to Strang, December 1, 1949, FO371/80358, no. 10115 in Johnson, *Sudan*, 1:379; Hanes, *Imperial Diplomacy*, 121.

14. Campbell to Wright, November 30, 1948, FO371/69195, no. 7582, in Johnson, *Sudan*, 1:340; Edmonds, Minute, March 8, 1950, FO371/80358, no. 2, in Johnson, *Sudan*, 1:384; Daly, *Imperial Sudan*, 275.

15. Daly, *Imperial Sudan*, 273–4; Edmonds, Minute, March 8, 1950, FO371/80358, no. 2, in Johnson, *Sudan*, 1:384.

16. Beshir, *Nationalism and Revolution*, 175; Stevenson to Bevin, August 25, 1950, FO371/80387, no. 13, in Johnson, *Sudan*, 1:393.

17. Acheson to Cairo, May 2, 1950, NARA 641.74/5-250; McCay, *Acheson and Empire*, 171, 173.

18. Daly, *Imperial Sudan*, 284; State to London, December 14, 1951, NARA 641.74/12-751; State to London, February 21, 1951, NARA 641.74/2-2152; Acheson to London, March 26, 1952, NARA 641.74/3-2652; Byroade to Acheson, July 14, 1952, Secretary's letters, lot 56D459, in *FRUS, 1952–54*, 9:1830.

19. Acheson to London, March 26, 1952, NARA 641.74/3-2652; London to State, March 26, 1952, NARA 641.74/3-2652.

20. Byroade to Acheson, July 21, 1952, 774.00/2-2152, in FRUS, 1952–54, 5:1838; Washington to London, May 2, 1952, NARA 745W.00/5-252; Caffrey to Washington, April 26, 1952, NARA 745W.00/4-2652; Secretary of State to Cairo, September 24, 1951, 641.74/9-2451, in *FRUS, 1951*, 5:387.

21. Caffrey to Washington, July 15, 1952, NARA 745W.00/7-1552; Daly, *Imperial Sudan*, 290.

22. Raynor to Perkins, April 1, 1952, NARA 641.74/4-1552.

23. Daly, *Imperial Sudan*, 284; Louis, *British Empire in the Middle East*, 724–5; Beisner, *Acheson*, 556; Churchill to Cherwell, November 10, 1951, PREM 11/208, in Goldsworthy, *Conservative*, 1:111.

24. Beisner, *Acheson*, 557; Carlton, *Eden*, 314–5; United States Minutes of the First United States-United Kingdom Foreign Ministers Meeting, Paris, May 26, 1952, CFM files lot M 88, in *FRUS, 1952–54*, 9:1807.

25. Byroade to Acheson, July 14, 1952, Secretary's Letters, lot 56 D459, in *FRUS, 1952–54*, 9:1830; Secretary of State to London, July 18, 1952, 745W.00/7-1752, in *FRUS, 1952–54*, 9:1835.

26. Howe to Foreign Office, Oc-

tober 17, 1951, FO371/90154, no. 55, in Johnson, *Sudan,* 2:48; Robertson, Memorandum, October 19, 1951, FO 371/90112, no. 131, in Johnson, *Sudan,* 2:51; Daly, *Imperial Sudan,* 285, 290.

27. Daly, *Imperial Sudan,* 291; Caffrey to Washington, April 8, 1952, no. 1769, NARA 745W.00/4-852.

28. Hanes, *Imperial Diplomacy,* 140; Daly, *Imperial Sudan,* 293–4; United States Minutes of the first United States-United Kingdom Ministerial Talks, June 24, 1952, Conference Files, lot 59D95, CF131, in *FRUS, 1952–54,* 9:1814.

29. Daly, *Imperial Sudan,* 255, 296, 353; Carlton, *Eden,* 325; Churchill, Minute, November 11–12, 1951, FO800/825, no. 20, in Goldsworthy, *Conservative,* 2:167; Conclusions of Cabinet Meeting, February 12, 1953, CAB 128/26 CC 9&10(53)1, in Johnson, *Sudan,* 2:211; Gilbert, *Never Despair,* 798–9.

30. Smith to Allen, December 12, 1951, FO371/90114, no. 87, in Johnson, *Sudan,* 2:75; Jeffries to Dixon, January 31, 1952, FO371/96902, no. 17, in Johnson, *Sudan,* 2:88; Morris to Allen, October 25, 1952, FO371/96911, no. 338, in Johnson, *Sudan,* 2:137; Martin to Bowker, December 16, 1952, FO371/96917, in Johnson, *Sudan,* 2:167.

31. Beisner, *Acheson,* 557; Hanes, *Imperial Diplomacy,* 142.

32. Caffrey to Washington, October 12, 1952, NARA 745W.00/10-1252; Washington to London, November 28, 1952, NARA 645W.74/11-2852; Cairo to Washington, December 13, 1952, NARA 745W.00/12-1352; Washington to London, November 17, 1952, NARA 745W.00/11-1552.

33. Acheson to Cairo, January 16, 1953, NARA 745W.00/1-1653; Washington to London, January 31, 1953, NARA 745W.00/1-1353.

34. Record of Anglo-American Meeting, February 4, 1953, FO 800/827, in Goldsworthy, *Conservative,* 1:123.

35. Patterson to Secretary of State, January 20, 1949, NARA 848Z.00/1-2049; Caffrey to Washington, November 28, 1951, NARA 745W.00/11-1251; Stabler, Report of Visit to Sudan, February 10, 1952, NARA 745W.00/1-3052; McCay, *Acheson and Empire,* 165.

36. Stabler, Report of Visit to Sudan, February 10, 1952, NARA 745W.00/1/-3052; Washington to London, April 10, 1952, NARA 641.74/4-752; Burdette to Washington, November 5, 1952, NARA 745W.00/11-552.

37. Burdette to Washington, November 5, 1952, NARA 745W.00/11-552; Daly, *Imperial Sudan,* 298.

Chapter 9

1. Renwick, *Fighting with Allies,* 186; Edmonds, *Mould,* 229; Seldon, *Indian Summer,* 391; Memorandum of Conversation, Bermuda Talks, December 4, 1953, NARA RG59 Records of the Policy Planning Staff.

2. Seldon, *Indian Summer,* 390; Callahan, *Churchill,* 261 note.

3. Seldon, *Indian Summer,* 390; Callahan, *Churchill,* 261 note.

4. Boyle, "Special Relationship," 43.

5. Griffith, "Eisenhower and the Corporate Commonwealth," 118; Kingseed, *Suez,* 27; Noer, *Williams,* 225; Darby, *Imperialism,* 184; Kresse, "Eisenhower's Policy," 129.

6. Griffith, "Eisenhower and the Corporate Commonwealth," 118; Brands, *Bound to Empire,* 168, 169.

7. Takeyh, *Eisenhower Doctrine,* 5; Kresse, "Eisenhower's Policy," 172.

8. Kresse, "Eisenhower's Policy," 176; Griffith, "Eisenhower and the Corporate Commonwealth," 117.

9. Eisenhower to Churchill, July 22, 1954, in Boyle, *Churchill-Eisenhower Correspondence,* 163–5.

10. Guhin, *Dulles,* 48, 49–50; Cohen, *Truman and Israel,* 271; Gardner, "Vietnam," 134.

11. Ovendale, *Anglo-American,* 106; Guhin, *Dulles,* 266; Takeyh, *Eisenhower Doctrine,* 10, 22, 23.

12. Nwaubani, *Decolonization,* 134; Kent, *Black Africa,* 173; Belmonte, "Reining," 28, 30, 256; Louis and Robinson, "Imperialism of Decolonization," 476.

13. Churchill to Eisenhower, August 8, 1954, in Boyle, *Churchill-Eisenhower Correspondence,* 166–7.

14. Ovendale, "Egypt and the Suez Base Agreement," 140.

15. Holland, "Imperial Factor, 173; Bartlett, *Special Relationship,* 80–81.

16. Ovendale, *Anglo-American,* 103; Bartlett, *Special Relationship,* 80–81; Kingseed, *Suez,* 12; Kent, *Imperial,* 9.

17. Colonial Office note, June 1954, CO936/317, no. 13, in Goldsworthy, *Conservative,* 1:277–8; Salt to Watson, June 11, 1956, FO371/118677, no. 24, in Goldsworthy, *Conservative,* 1:239; Colonial Office Brief, October 1956, CO936/318, no. 162A, in Goldsworthy, *Conservative,* 1:288; Baylis, *Anglo-American,* 89.

18. Salt to Watson, June 11, 1956, FO371/118677, no. 24, in Goldswor-

thy, *Conservative*, 1:239; Kent, "Reactions to Empire," 214.

19. Adamthwaite, "Eden," 249; Jebb to Eden, January 12, 1953, FO 371/107032, no. 1, in Goldsworthy, *Conservative*, 1:272; Renwick, *Fighting with Allies*, 236.

20. Seldon, *Indian Summer*, 393; Goldsworthy, "Critics," 16.

21. Belmonte, "Reining," 251; Boyle, *Special Relationship*, 36.

22. "Joint Declaration by the President and the Prime Minister of the United Kingdom," June 29, 1954, and "The Declaration of Washington: Joint Declaration by the President and the Prime Minister of the United Kingdom," February 1, 1956, in Woolley and Peters, *The American Presidency Project*, http://www.presidency.ucsb.edu; Belmonte, "Reining," 33.

23. Gilbert, *Never Despair*, 929, 1007.

24. Hennessy, *Having It So Good*, 421; Low, *Eclipse*, 211.

25. Goodpaster, Memorandum of Conference with the President, October 30, 1956, in *FRUS, 1955–57*, 16:852.

26. Gleason, Memorandum of Discussion at 302nd Meeting of the National Security Council, November 1, 1956, in *FRUS, 1955–57*, 16: 902–912.

27. Feinstein, "Golden Age, " 228; Cain and Hopkins, *British Imperialism, 1914–1990*, 280–1, 288–9.

28. "The Future of the United Kingdom in World Affairs," June 1, 1956, CAB134/1315 PR(56)3, in Goldsworthy, *Conservative*, 1:75.

29. Hennessy, *Having It So Good*, 470; Kingseed, *Suez*, 146.

30. Caccia to Lloyd, December 28, 1956, in Baylis, *Anglo-American*, 88.

31. Howard, *Butler*, 242.

32. Memorandum of Conversation, December 24, 1956, NARA RG59 Policy Planning Staff Office Files.

33. Aldous, "Macmillan," 26.

34. Ruane and Ellison, "Managing," 163.

35. Cabinet Conclusions on Political and Military Association, January 9, 1957, CAB128/30/2 CM3(57), in Hyam and Louis, *Conservative*, 1:108–9; Dean, Minute, August 4, 1959, FO371/143705, no. 58, in Hyam and Louis, *Conservative*, 1:71; Foreign Office, Note, October 6, 1959, CAB134/1935, no. 15(28), in Hyam and Louis, *Conservative*, 1:78–9; Officials Committee, Cabinet Memorandum, February 24, 1960, CAB129/100 C(60) 35, in Hyam and Louis, *Conservative*, 1:95.

36. Perth to Macmillan, February 23, 1957, PREM 11/3239 PM(57)9, in Hyam and Louis, *Conservative*, 2: 224.

37. Macmillan to Perth, February 25, 1957, PREM 11/3239 M 84/57, in Hyam and Louis, *Conservative*, 2:228.

38. Parsons to Reinhardt, March 13, 1957, and attachments, NARA 611. 41/3-1357.

39. "Means of Combating Communist Influence in Africa," March 13, 1957, BEM D-5/1a, in *FRUS, 1955–57*, 27:759–60.

40. Lennox-Boyd to African Governors, June 28, 1957, FO371/125293, no. 25, in Hyam and Louis, *Conservative*, 2:57–64.

41. Memorandum of a Conversation, March 23, 1957, in *FRUS, 1955–57*, 18:53–56.

42. Memorandum of a Conversation, March 23, 1957, NARA RG59 3051 B Conference Files.

43. Hemming, *Macmillan*, 114–5; Ovendale, "Wind of Change," 462.

44. Foreign Office Planning Report, March 8, 1960, FO371/152113, no. 3, in Hyam and Louis, *Conservative*, 2:151; Louis and Robinson, "Imperialism of Decolonization," 486.

45. Hood to Lloyd, July 10, 1958, O371/131189, no. 24, in Hyam and Louis, *Conservative*, 2:241; Hadsel to Washington, March 18, 1960, NARA 641.70/3-1860, 14; Barbour to Washington, January 11, 1960, NARA 611. 41/1-1160; Foreign Office, Note, October 6, 1959, CAB134/1935, no. 15 (28), in Hyam and Louis, *Conservative*, 1:74.

46. Minutes of Africa (Official) Committee, January 14, 1959, CAB 134/1353 AF(59), in Hyam and Louis, *Conservative*, 1:109.

47. Satterthwaite to Merchant, November 17, 1959, NARA 770.00/ 11-1759.

48. Bureau of African Affairs, Chronology, March 1, 1963, NARA RG59 Office of West African Affairs Country Files.

49. Bureau of African Affairs, Chronology, March 1, 1963, NARA RG59 Office of West African Affairs Country Files; Henderson to Dulles, August 23, 1955, NARA 611.70/7-2055; LaMont to Palmer, May 2, 1958, NARA RG59 Records of the Bureau of African Affairs, 1956–62.

50. Noer, *Cold War*, 35, 49.

51. Dulles, "Moral Imperative," 743.

52. Byroade, Speech, October 31, 1953, in *FRUS, 1952–54*, 2:55–59.

53. National Intelligence Estimates, NIE-83, December 22, 1953, in *FRUS, 1952–54*, 11(1):87; Office of

Intelligence and Research, "Conditions and Trends in Tropical Africa, August 24, 1953,

54. Gerig to Key, February 17, 1954, NARA 350/2-1754.

55. Editorial Note, *FRUS, 1952– 54*, 3:1166; Gerig to Key, February 17, 1954, NARA 350/2-1754.

56. George V. Allen, "United States Foreign Policy in Africa," 717–8.

57. Office of African Affairs, Memorandum, August 4, 1955, in *FRUS, 1955–57*, 18:21.

58. Jones to Washington, October 31, 1955, NARA 611.70/10-3155; McGregor to Washington, December 28, 1955, NARA 611.70/12-2855; Special Assistant to the Secretary to Allen, August 30, 1955, NARA 611.70/7-2055.

59. Policy Planning Staff, "A Reconsideration of United States Policy Toward Colonialism, n.d. (1956?) NARA RG59 1272 Policy Planning Staff Office Files.

60. Policy Planning Staff, "A Reconsideration of United States Policy Toward Colonialism, n.d. (1956?) NARA RG59 1272 Policy Planning Staff Office Files.

61. Bowie to Dulles (draft not sent), n.d.; Mathews to Tresize, September 14, 1956; Tresize to Mathews, October 12, 1956, NARA RG59 1272 Policy Planning Staff Office Files.

62. Excerpt from Dulles news conference, October 2, 1956, NARA RG59 1264 Office Files of Francis O. Wilcox.

63. Belmonte, "Reining," 363 note.

64. Dorz to Department of State, December 7, 1954, in *FRUS, 1952– 1954*, 11(1):379; McGregor, Memorandum, December 28, 1953, in *FRUS, 1955–57*, 18:27; McGregor to Allen, March 21, 1956, NARA RG59 Office of West African Affairs Country Files.

65. Schwartz to Bowie, March 2, 1954 and attachments, in *FRUS, 1952–54*, 11(1):97; Meriwether, "A Torrent Overrunning," 181.

66. Department of State to various posts, February 17, 1956, and attachments ("Africa: Problems of United States Policy" and Office of Intelligence and Research, "Africa: A Special Assessment," January 5, 1956), NARA 611.70/2-1756.

67. Nixon, Report to the President, April 5, 1957, in *FRUS, 1955– 57*, 18:57–66.

68. Barbour to Washington, February 20, 1957, NARA 745K.02/2-57; Belmonte, "Reining," 370.

69. Holmes to Dulles, February 6, 1958, in *FRUS, 1958–60*, 14:1–11.

70. "African Political Movements: An Assessment," Office of Intelligence and Research Report no. 7820, September 26, 1958.

71. National Security Council Report NCS 5719/1, August 23, 1957 in *FRUS, 1955–57*, 18:78–9.

72. Memorandum of Discussion, 357th Meeting of the National Security Council, August 7, 1958, in *FRUS, 1958–60*, 14:19–21.

73. Excerpt from Dulles Press Conference, October 2, 1956, NARA 320.14/10-1556.

74. Memorandum of Discussion, 432nd Meeting of the National Security Council, January 14, 1960, in *FRUS, 1958–60*, 14:74–75; Kresse, "Eisenhower," 138.

75. Dulles, "Challenge and Response," 576; Palmer, "Sub Sahara Africa," 931; McKay, *Africa in World Politics*, 342.

Chapter 10

1. El Ayouty, *United Nations and Decolonization*, 130, 32; *Yearbook of the United Nations, 1954*, 374; Belmonte, "Reining," 228.

2. Pruden, *Conditional Partners*, 179, 185; Kresse, "Eisenhower," 299.

3. Department of State to Accra and New York, October 26, 1959, NARA 611.45J/10-2659.

4. Wadsworth to Secretary of State, August 15, 1955; NARA 320.14/8.1555; Allen, Memorandum, February 19, 1954, ODA files lot 62, D225, in *FRUS, 1952–54*, 3:1339; Bloomfield to the Assistant Secretary for International Organization Affairs, February 9, 1956, in *FRUS, 1955–57*, 11:539.

5. Belmonte, "Reining," 232; Noer, *Cold War*, 36; Wilcox to Lodge, May 4, 1956, NARA RG59 Office Files of Francis O. Wilcox; Classified Report of the United States Delegation to the 26th Session of the Trusteeship Council, July 15, 1960, NARA 350/7-1560.

6. Seldon, *Indian Summer*, 395; Pruden, *Conditional Partners*, 176, 187.

7. Belmonte, "Reining," 236–7.

8. Lodge to Dulles, January 30, 1959, NARA 770.00/1-3059.

9. Nwaubani, "Decolonization," 135; Withers to Washington, April 2, 1959, NARA 770.00/4-259; Belmonte, "Reining," 238.

10. Pruden, *Conditional Partners*, 176.

11. Pruden, *Conditional Partners*, 186; Sears, *Years of High Purpose*, 71, 73, 80–82, 141.

12. Kresse, "Eisenhower," 382–3; McGregor to Cyr, January 9, 1956, NARA RG59 Office of West African Affairs Country Files; Sears to Wilcox, April 3, 1956, NARA RG59 1264, Office Files of Francis O. Wilcox.

13. McGregor to Cyr, January 9, 1956, NARA RG59 Office of West African Affairs Country Files; Barrow to Washington, June 24, 1955, NARA 745P.02/6-2455.

14. Key to Murphy, April 20, 1955, in *FRUS, 1955–57*, 28:6.

15. Hanes to Key, February 11, 1955, NARA RG 59 1264, Office Files of Francis O. Wilcox; Dulles to Lodge, February 9, 1955, in *FRUS, 1955–57*, 28:5.

16. Bourdillon to Pink, October 30, 1956, CO936/321, no. 21/22, in Goldsworthy, *Conservative*, 1:413; Lennox-Boyd to African Governors, June 28, 1957, FO371/125293, no. 25, in Hyam and Louis, *Conservative*, 2:57–64.

17. Kresse, "Eisenhower," 514; Pruden, *Conditional Partners*, 186.

18. Beale to Rayner, January 5, 1955, NARA 611.41/1-555.

19. Summary of Significant Points, United States-United Kingdom Colonial Talks, July 26–27, 1954, NARA RG 59 Office Files of Benjamin Gerig; Colonial Office Report on Talks held in Washington, October 11–12, 1956, CO 936/318, no. 176, in Goldsworthy, *Conservative*, 1:290

20. Summary of Significant Points, United States-United Kingdom Colonial Talks, July 26–27, 1954, NARA RG 59 Office Files of Benjamin Gerig; Memorandum of Conversation, April 26, 1957, NARA RG 59 457C General Records of the Office of African Affairs; Colonial Office Brief, October 1956, CO936/3 18, no. 162 A, in Goldsworthy, *Conservative*, 1:289.

21. Colonial Office Report, Washington Talks, August 23–24, 1955, CO936/317, no. 115, in Goldsworthy, *Conservative*, 1:285.

22. Gerig to Wilkins, February 1, 1956, NARA 320.1/2-156; Office of Dependent Area Affairs, Memorandum, no date, ODA Files, in *FRUS, 1953–54*, 3:1169; United States Delegation to Trusteeship Council, Classified Report, July 15, 1960, NARA 350/7-1560.

23. Note prepared in Colonial Office, June 1954, CO936/317, no. 13, Goldsworthy, *Conservative*, 1:277–8; Jebb to Eden, January 12, 1953, FO371/107032, no. 1, in Goldsworthy, *Conservative*, 1:271; Belmonte, "Reining," 73–4; Bourdillon to Pink,

October 30, 1956, CO936/321, no. 21/22, in Goldsworthy, *Conservative*, 1:413.

24. McKay, *Africa in World Politics*, 329, 332.

25. McKay, *Africa in World Politics*, 332–333.

26. Belmonte, "Reining," 243–4, 252; Colonial Office Report, Pre-General Assembly Talks, October 11–12, 1956, in Goldsworthy, *Conservative*, 1:290.

27. McKay, *Africa in World Politics*, 334; Belmonte, "Reining," 250; Perth to Macmillan, February 23, 1957, PREM 11/3239 PM (57) 9, in Hyam and Louis, *Conservative*, 2:224.

28. Kresse, "Eisenhower," 516; Belmonte, "Reining," 245.

29. Noer, *Cold War*, 59; Ostrower, *United Nations and the United States*, 94.

30. Belmonte, "Reining," 403–404.

31. Nunley to Kohler, December 7, 1960, NARA RG59 5586 Records Relating to Planning United Nations Matters.

32. Herter to Goodpaster, December 8, 1960, NARA 321.4/12-860, in *FRUS, 1958–60*, 2:454.

33. Belmonte, "Reining," 404.

34. Kresse, "Eisenhower," 519–20.

Chapter 11

1. Swinton, Cabinet Memorandum, April 8, 1953, CAB 129/60 C (53)122, in Goldsworthy, *Conservative*, 2:6.

2. Salisbury, Minute, February 16, 1953, DO35/5056, no. 6, in Goldsworthy, *Conservative*, 2:5.

3. Goldsworthy, "Aspects," 97; McIntyre, "Small States," 254.

4. Goldsworthy, "Aspects," 98–99.

5. Swinton, Cabinet Memorandum, October 11, 1954, CAB 129/71 C(54)307, in Goldsworthy, *Conservative*, 2:29; McIntyre, "Small States," 257; Goldsworthy, "Aspects," 98.

6. Lennox-Boyd, Cabinet Memorandum, September 27, 1955, CAB 129/77 CP(55)133, in Goldsworthy, *Conservative*, 2:66.

7. Goldsworthy, "Aspects," 85; Bourdillon and Poynton, Minutes, September 14, 1955, CO1032/98, in Goldsworthy, *Conservative*, 2:51.

8. Jeffries, Minute, December 16, 1955, CO1032/55, in Goldsworthy, *Conservative*, 2:68–9.

9. Brook, Note, June 18, 1956, CAB130/113 GEN 518/611, in Goldsworthy, *Conservative*, 2:73.

10. Barnes, Draft Memorandum,

October 15, 1955, CO822/929, no. 26, in Goldsworthy, *Conservative*, 2: 258.

11. Colonial Office, Memorandum, May 30, 1956, CAB134/1203 CA(0)(56)11, in Goldsworthy, *Conservative*, 2:56; Lennox-Boyd to Cabinet Policy Committee, February 1, 1956, CAB134/1202 CA(56)4, in Goldsworthy, *Conservative*, 2:53.

12. Goldsworthy, "Aspects," 84; Murphy, *Lennox-Boyd*, 102.

13. Dockrill, *Defence*, 57.

14. Dockrill, *Defence*, 36–7; 56–7.

15. Percox, *Cold War*, 64; Adamthwaite, "*Eden,*" 244; Dockrill, *Defence*, 56–7.

16. Dockrill, *Defence*, 35, 51.

17. Havinden and Meredith, *Colonialism and Development*, 236; Krozewski, "Minor Territories," 255.

18. Krozewski, "Minor Territories," 253.

19. Krozewski, "Minor Territories, 251; Krozewski, "Finance and Empire," 49, 50, 66–7.

20. Aldous, "Macmillan," 10; Heinlein, *Government Policy*, 161.

21. Cain and Hopkins, *British Imperialism, 1914–1990*, 290.

22. Horne, *Macmillan*, 177; Low, "End of the British Empire," 54.

23. Ball, *Guardsmen*, 345; Butler, *Britain and Empire*, 114; Ovendale, "Wind of Change," 459; Cabinet Conclusions, September 11, 1956, CAB 128/30/2 CM64(56)2, in Goldsworthy, *Conservative*, 2:216; Hopkins, "Audit," 238.

24. Hemming, "Macmillan," 99–100.

25. Boyce, *Decolonization*, 178.

26. Hopkins, "Audit," 240–1; Lennox-Boyd, Minute, February 15, 1957, CAB 134/1555, in Hyam and Louis, *Conservative*, 1:2.

27. Brook, Memorandum, September 6, 1957, CAB 134/1556 CPC (57)30, in Hyam and Louis, *Conservative*, 1:31–37.

28. Hopkins, "Audit," 249–257.

29. Hopkins, "Audit," 251–2.

30. Officials' Report, June 9, 1958, CAB 130/153 GEN 624/10, in Hyam and Louis, *Conservative*, 1:43–50.

31. Lennox-Boyd, Memorandum, April 10, 1959, CAB 134/1558 CPC (59)2, in Hyam and Louis, *Conservative*, 1:371.

32. Murphy, *Lennox-Boyd*, 200; Cabinet Colonial Policy Committee, Minutes, April 17, 1959, CAB 134/1558 CPC1(59), in Hyam and Louis, *Conservative*, 1:382–3.

33. Committee of Officials, Report, June 24, 1959, FO 371/137972, in Hyam and Louis, *Conservative*,

2:116; McIntyre, "Small States," 264–5.

34. Macleod to Macmillan, May 25, 1959, PREM 11/2583, in Hyam and Louis, *Conservative*, 2:160; Hemming, "Macmillan," 102; Ovendale, "Wind of Change," 467.

Chapter 12

1. Pearce, *Turning Point*, 17–19.

2. MacDonald, Memorandum, February 13, 1940, CAB67/4 WP(G) (40) 2, in Pearce, *Turning Point*, 21; Cranborne, WP(42) 249, CAB 66/25 in Thorne, *Allies*, 220; Hailey, "Some Problems Dealt with in the African Survey," 18, 194–210, in Cell, *Hailey*, 236; Stanley to Sir John Anderson, September 21, 1944, CO852/588/ 19275, in Louis and Robinson, "Liquidation of the British Empire," 39; Stanley, CAB65/144 in Wolton, *Lord Hailey*, 23.

3. A.A. Dudley, Minute, December 1, 1943, FO371/34142 in Kent, *Imperial*, 8; Louis, *Imperialism at Bay*, 105.

4. Sanger, *MacDonald* 155; Pearce, *Turning Point*, 50; Swinton, Memorandum, February 24, 1943, CO96/776/31475 and Cranborne to Stevenson August 18, 1942 CO847/ 22/47100/8/1942, in Hargreaves, "Transfer of Power," 125; Dawe, Memorandum, July 1942, CO967/ 57/46709, in Westcott, "Closer Union," 72.

5. Ovendale, *Foreign Policy*, 14; Feinstein, "Golden Age," 220.

6. Havinden and Meredith, *Colonialism and Development*, 276ff; Iliffe, *Tanganyika*, 441.

7. Havinden and Meredith, *Colonialism and Development*, 225–6, 252.

8. Havinden and Meredith, *Colonialism and Development*, 218, 227, 252.

9. Havinden and Meredith, *Colonialism and Development*, 235–7, 267, 270; Krozewski, "Minor Territories," 245.

10. Bennett, Memorandum, April 30, 1947, CO537/2057, no. 48, in Hyam, *Labour, 1945–51*, 2:419; Butler, Memorandum, May 17, 1952, CAB129/52, in Porter and Stockwell, *British Imperial Policy*, 2:144; Eden, Memorandum, June 18, 1952, CAB 129/53, C(52)202, in Goldsworthy, *Conservative*, 1:8.

11. Munene, *Truman*, 108; McGhee to Secretary, February 17, 1950, NARA 611.70/2-1750; "United States Policy toward Colonial Areas," July

27, 1949, SPU/DEP/P 2 Rev. 1, NARA RG59 Bureau of United Nations Affairs; Department of State, Office of Intelligence Research, Report no. 4327 (PV), "British Capabilities and Intentions," April 21, 1947, 40.

12. Wood, *Marshall Plan*, 56–8; Burns to Bourgerie, April 27, 1950, NARA RG59 General Records of the Office of African Affairs, 1950–56.

13. Wood, *Marshall Plan*, 41; Boyle, "Special Relationship," 38; Lourenco Marques Conference, Summary of Conclusions and Recommendations, February 27 — March 2, 1950, NARA RG59 Office of West African Affairs Country Files.

14. Kent, *British Imperial Strategy*, 143–4; Memorandum of Conversation, July 18, 1950, NARA 745P.00/7-1850; Roberts to Department of State, September 10, 1951, in *FRUS, 1951*, 5:1231.

15. Munene, *Truman*, 193–4.

16. Dr. Emory Ross of the Foreign Missions Conference; James A. Farrell Jr., president of the Farrell Steamship Lines; Dr. Robert G. Woolbert of the University of Denver; Dr. Derwent Whittlesey, professor of geography at Harvard University; Dr. Cornelis W. de Kiewet, acting president of Cornell University; Dr. Mark H. Watkins, professor of anthropology at Howard University; Dr. Ralph J. Bunche, director of the Department of Trusteeship for the United Nations; Dr. Channing Tobias of the Phelps-Stokes Foundation; Dr. John Morrison, professor of geography at the University of Maryland; Juan Trippe, president of American Airways; and Ogden White of the Filatures Tissages Africans.

17. McGhee, *Envoy*, 115–7, 123–4; Report prepared in the Department of State, undated, in *FRUS, 1950*, 5:1508; Conference Document no. 13, no date, NARA RG59 1422 McGhee Files 1945–53.

18. Borstelmann, *Apartheid's Reluctant Uncle*, 109–110.

19. Munene, *Truman*, 125–6; Beisner, *Acheson*, 212; Paterson, "Point Four," 120–1.

20. Wood, *Marshall Plan*, 64; Hagen and Ruttan, "Development Policy," 3.

21. Paterson, "Point Four," 119ff; Beisner, *Acheson*, 212.

22. Havinden and Meredith, *Colonialism and Development*, 257; Butler to Lennox-Boyd, November 17, 1954, T229/865, in Porter and Stockwell, *British Imperial Policy*, 2:348.

23. "Report of Colonial Development and Welfare Working Party,"

August 1954, T220/354, in Porter and Stockwell, *British Imperial Policy*, 2:326.

24. Pruden, *Conditional Partners*, 205; Hagen and Ruttan, "Development Policy," 4.

25. Adamson, "Foreign Aid," 56–58; Hagen and Ruttan, "Development Policy," 6–7.

26. Kaufman, *Trade and Aid*, 198–9.

27. Legislative Reference Service, *Foreign Aid*, 72–3, 110–1.

28. Longnecker to Utter, November 10, 1953, NARA RG59 1265 Office of United Nations Political and Security Affairs; Gordon to Fitzgerald, February 8, 1955, February 8, 1955, NARA RG59 1265 Office of United Nations Political and Security Affairs.

29. Dumont to Cyr, March 2, 1955, NARA 745K.5-MSP/3-255.

30. Washington to London, March 21, 1955, NARA 745K.14/3-2155; Washington to Lagos, July 3, 1955, NARA 611.45H/3-755.

31. Washington to London, January 13, 1955, NARA 745R.5-MSP/1-1355; State Department to Nairobi, May 4, 1955, NARA 611.45P/5-455; Withers to Washington, October 3, 1957, NARA 745R.5-MSP/10-357.

32. Hollister to Dulles, January 5, 1956, NARA RG59 457c General Records of the Office of African Affairs, 1950–56.

33. Hill to Dulles, January 16, 1958, NARA RG59 1265 Office of United Nations Political and Security Affairs; Allen to Secretary, December 28, 1955, NARA 745C.5-MSP/12-2855; Hoover to Hollister, February 28, 1956, NARA RG59 1265 Office of United Nations Political and Security Affairs.

34. Cyr to Steere, February 9, 1956, NARA RG59 1265 Office of United Nations Political and Security Affairs.

35. Whitney to Washington, March 14, 1957, NARA 745.5MSP/3-1457; Memorandum of Conversation, September 9, 1958, NARA 745.5MSP/9-958.

36. "Timing of Independence for Colonial Territories and United States Economic Assistance," March 20, 1957, NARA RG59 3051 B Conference Files; Barbour to Washington, January 11, 1960, NARA 611.41/1-1160; Hadsel to Washington, March 18, 1960, NARA 641.70/3-1860.

37. Dulles to Nairobi, May 1, 1958, NARA 745P.5-MSP/5-158.

38. Withers to Washington, October 29, 1959, NARA 745R.5-MSP/10-2959.

39. Herter to Salisbury, February 1958, NARA 745C.5-MSP/2-158.

Chapter 13

1. Baker, *Armitage*, 79; Murphy, *Lennox-Boyd*, 156.

2. Goldsworthy, "Aspects," 90.

3. Barnes, Minute, February 5, 1953, CO554/254, in Porter and Stockwell, *British Imperial Policy*, 2:195.

4. Arden-Clarke to Barnes, January 26, 1953, CO554/254, in Porter and Stockwell, *British Imperial Policy*, 2:190; Lloyd to Macpherson, March 25, 1953, CO554/254, in Rathbone, *Ghana*, 2:16.

5. Goldsworthy, "Aspects," 89; Lyttelton, Minute, February 9, 1953, CO554/254, in Goldsworthy, *Conservative*, 2:188–9.

6. Garner, Minute, May 12, 1953, DO35/6168, in Rathbone, *Ghana*, 2:35; Morley, Minute, May 8, 1953, DO35/6168, in Rathbone, *Ghana*, 2:35; Lloyd to Macpherson, March 5, 1953, CO554/254, in Porter and Stockwell, *British Imperial Policy*, 2:203.

7. Lloyd to Macpherson, March 5, 1953, CO554/254, in Porter and Stockwell, *British Imperial Policy*, 2:203; Colonial Office, Meeting Note, February 18, 1953, CO554/254, in Rathbone, *Ghana*, 2:7; Lyttelton, Cabinet Memorandum, September 4, 1953, CAB129/62 c(53), in Goldsworthy, *Conservative*, 2:203.

8. Austin, *Politics in Ghana*, 161–2, 245, 276.

9. Vile, Minute, July 27, 1955, CO554/805, no. 45, in Rathbone, *Ghana*, 2:138; Austin, *Politics in Ghana*, 297, 301–4; Bruce to Laithwaite, August 19, 1955, PREM 11/1367, in Rathbone, *Ghana*, 2:155; Murphy, *Lennox-Boyd*, 157.

10. Arden-Clarke to Lloyd, September 12, 1955, DO35/6170, no. 65, in Rathbone, *Ghana*, 2:170; Nkrumah to Lennox-Boyd, September 30, 1955, CO554/806, no. 112, in Rathbone, *Ghana*, 2:179; Lennox-Boyd to Cabinet Colonial Policy Committee, March 2, 1956, CAB134/1202 CA (56)9, in Rathbone, *Ghana*, 2:236; Nkrumah to Lennox-Boyd, April 20, 1956, CO554/807, no. 269A, in Rathbone, *Ghana*, 2:255.

11. Austin, *Politics in Ghana*, 356–7; Rooney, *Arden-Clarke*, 194.

12. Macpherson to Lloyd, March 16, 1953, CO554/254, no. 20, in Lynn, *Nigeria*, 1:520.

13. Lloyd to Macpherson, March 25, 1953, CO554/254, no. 29, in Goldsworthy, *Conservative*, 2:192–3.

14. Lynn, "1953 Crisis," 189, 192; Crowder, *Nigeria*, 284.

15. Lynn, "1953 Crisis," 191; Lyttelton, Cabinet Memorandum, May 13, 1953, CAB 129/61 C(53)154, in Goldsworthy, *Conservative*, 2:197.

16. Williamson, Minute, March 27, 1953, CO554/260, no. 28, in Lynn, *Nigeria*, 1:524; Lyttelton, Cabinet Memorandum, May 13, 1953, CAB 129/61 C(53) 154, in Goldsworthy, *Conservative*, 2:197.

17. Williamson, Minute, July 2, 1953, CO554/262, no. 232, in Lynn, *Nigeria*, 1:612.

18. Macpherson to Barnes, July 15, 1953, CO 554/262, no. 250, in Lynn, *Nigeria*, 1:623; Barnes, Minute, July 9, 1953, CO 554/262, no. 232, in Lynn, *Nigeria*, 1:612; Lloyd, Minute, July 11, 1953, CO 554/262, no. 232, in Lynn, *Nigeria*, 1:612.

19. Colonial Office, Note of Meeting, July 22, 1953, CO 554/262, in Lynn, *Nigeria*, 2:12; Rathbone, "Police in Ghana," 117.

20. Lynn, "1953 Crisis," 194–5.

21. Lyttelton, Cabinet Memorandum, PREM 11/1367 C(53)235, in Goldsworthy, *Conservative*, 2:199.

22. Lynn, "Nigeria in the 1950s," 154–6.

23. Lynn, Eastern Crisis," 94–100.

24. Lloyd to Pleass, July 26, 1955, CO 554/1181, no. 17, in Lynn, *Nigeria*, 2:198; Bennett, Minute, July 27, 1955, CO 554/1181, in Lynn, *Nigeria*, 2:200; Pleass to Lloyd, August 6, 1955, CO 554/1181, no. 26, in Lynn, *Nigeria*, 2:208; Robertson to Lloyd, August 7, 1955, CO 554/1181, no. 27, in Lynn, *Nigeria*, 2:211; Lynn, "Eastern Crisis," 103–105.

25. Robertson to Eastwood, June 11, 1956, CO 554/905, no. 39, in Lynn, *Nigeria*, 2:309; Colonial Office Brief, July 27, 1956, CO 554/905, no. 45, in Lynn, *Nigeria*, 2:336.

26. Robertson to Eastwood, June 11, 1956, CO 554/905, no. 39, in Lynn, *Nigeria*, 2:309; Williamson, Minute, April 5, 1957, CO 554/1583, no. 23, in Lynn, *Nigeria*, 2:391.

27. Rankine to Robertson, May 16, 1956, CO 554/905, no. 36, in Lynn, Nigeria, 2:299; Colonial Office Brief, July 27, 1956, CO 554/905, no. 45, in Lynn, *Nigeria*, 2:336.

28. Sharwood-Smith to Robertson, June 18, 1956, CO 554/871, no 13E, in Lynn, *Nigeria*, 2:315; Grey to Eastwood, July 9, 1958, CO 554/1548, no 13, in Lynn, *Nigeria*, 2:492.

29. Williamson, Minute, April 9, 1957, CO554/1583, in Lynn, *Nigeria*, 2:396; Cabinet Colonial Policy Com-

mittee, Meeting Minutes, May 13, 1957, CAB 134/1555CPC 7(57)2, in Lynn, *Nigeria*, 2:416.

30. Lennox-Boyd, Cabinet Memorandum, October 20, 1958, CAB 129/95 C(58)213, in Hyam and Louis, *Conservative*, 2:356; Cabinet Conclusions, September 11, 1958, CAB 128/32/2 CC71(58)5, in Hyam and Louis, *Conservative*, 2:353.

31. Cole to Washington, April 17, 1953, NARA 745K.00/4-1753; Cole to Washington, August 5, 1953, NARA 745K.00/8-553; Cole to Washington, November 17, 1953, NARA 745K.00/11-1753; Accra to Washington, February 3, 1954, NARA 745K.00/2-354.

32. Cole to Washington, September 28, 1953, NARA 745K.00/9-2853.

33. Ross to Washington, May 23, 1953, NARA 745H.00/5-2353.

34. Keeler to Washington, October 26, 1953, NARA 745H.00/10-2653; Lagos to Washington, February 13, 1954, NARA 745H.03/2-1354.

35. Lamm to Washington, April 29, 1955, NARA 745K.00/4-2955.

36. McLaughlin to Washington, December 2, 1955, NARA 745H.00/12-255; Hunt to Washington, December 28, 1957, NARA 745H.00/12-2857.

37. Sears to Key, June 3, 1954, ODA Files lot 62, D225 in *FRUS, 1952–54*, 3:1383.

38. Cyr to Byroade, June 11, 1954, NARA RG 59 Office of West African Affairs County Files; Belmonte, "Reining," 292–5.

39. Simons to Washington, January 23, 1957, NARA 745M.00/1-2357; Jones to Washington, May 6, 1957, NARA 745M.00/5-357; Jones to Washington, November 29, 1957, NARA 745M.00/11-2957.

40. Jones to Washington, November 28, 1958, NARA 745M.00/11-2858; Washington to Monrovia, November 5, 1958, NARA 745M.00/11-558; Reiner to Washington, October 30, 1959, NARA 745M.00/10-3059.

41. Manning, Briefing Book, no date [1957?], RG 59 1578 Records of the Bureau of African Affairs 1956–62; Division of Research and Analysis for Near East, South Asia and Africa, "African Political Movements: An Assessment, " OIR Report no. 7820, September 26, 1958; Briefing Book, Loy Henderson African Trip, October-November 1960, NARA RG 59 3105 Bureau of African Affairs Executive Director.

42. Hanes, *Imperial Diplomacy*, 165; Adamthwaite, "Eden," 249.

43. Eden to Howe, February 20, 1953 FO 371/102746, no. 269, in Johnson, *Sudan*, 2:214.

44. Woodward, *Condominium*, 124–5; Daly, *Imperial Sudan*, 301.

45. Daly, *Imperial Sudan*, 299, 357–8, 360; Bowker, Minute, July 31, 1953, FO 371/102758, no. 607, in Johnson, *Sudan*, 2:265.

46. Eden to Howe, January 1, 1954, FO 371/10760, no. 651, in Johnson, *Sudan*, 2:299; Riches to Eden, December 4, 1953, FO 371/102713, no. 36, in Johnson, *Sudan*, 2:294; Daly, *Imperial Sudan*, 361.

47. Luce, Record of Conversation, February 18, 1954, FO 371/108344, no. 2, in Johnson, *Sudan*, 2:309.

48. Robertson, *Transition*, 161; Hanes, *Imperial Diplomacy*, 160; Daly, *Imperial Sudan*, 377–8, 390.

49. Daly, *Imperial Sudan*, 368–371; Cabinet Conclusions, March 5, 1954, PREM 11/777 CC15(54)3, in Johnson, *Sudan*, 2:317.

50. Daly, *Imperial Sudan*, 369–71; Morris to Riches, May 19, 1954, FO 371/108383, no. 1, in Johnson, *Sudan*, 2:347.

51. Foreign Office Record of Meeting, June 11, 1954, FO 371/108 382, no. 6, in Johnson, *Sudan*, 2:351; Governor-General, Minute, August 13, 1954, FO 371/108324, no. 143, in Johnson, *Sudan*, 2:359.

52. Garvey to Eden, October 25, 1954, FO 371/10381, no. 14, in Johnson, *Sudan*, 2:371.

53. Luce to Bromley, December 1, 1955, FO 371/113585, no. 104, in Johnson, *Sudan*, 2:497; Daly, *Imperial Sudan*, 388.

54. Hanes, *Imperial Diplomacy*, 167; Daly, *Imperial Sudan*, 390–1.

55. Dulles to London, February 13, 1953, NARA 745W.00/2-1353; Washington to Khartoum, April 14, 1953, NARA 745W.00/4-1453; Caffrey to Washington, February 19, 1953, NARA 745W.00/2-1953; Caffrey to State, March 29, 1953, NARA 641.45W/3-2953.

56. Aldrich to Washington, December 12, 1953, NARA 745W.00/12-1253; Smith to London, December 14, 1953, NARA 745W.00/12-1453; Byroade to Secretary, no date, NARA 745W.00/7-2055.

57. Kresse, "Eisenhower," 455.

58. Caffrey to Washington, December 3, 1953, NARA 745W.00/12-553; Raynor to Hart, December 16, 1953, NARA 745W.00/12-1653; Byroade to Secretary, no date, NARA 745W.00/7-2055.

59. Daly, *Imperial Sudan*, 355.

Chapter 14

1. Berman, *Domination*, 350; Kyle, *Independence of Kenya*, 61; Anderson, *Histories of the Hanged*, 5–7.

2. Percox, "Internal Security," 93.

3. Tibbetts to Washington, January 8, 1953, NARA 756.00/1-853; Dorsz to Washington, January 2, 1953, NARA 745R.00/1-253; Dorsz to Washington, July 10, 1953, NARA 745R.00/7-1053; Office of Intelligence and Research, "The Mau Mau: An Aggressive Reaction to Frustration," Report no. 6307, June 12, 1953, iii, 1l; Office of Intelligence and Research, "Conditions and Trends in Tropical Africa," Report no. 6390, August 24, 1953, 15.

4. Gordon, *Decolonization*, 117; Furedi, "Counter-Insurgency," 145, 152; Bennett, *Kenya*, 135; Douglas-Home, *Baring*, 250.

5. Furedi, "Counter-Insurgency," 149–50.

6. Douglas-Home, *Baring*, 259; Lyttelton, *Memoirs*, 383; Kyle, *Independence of Kenya*, 63.

7. Blundell, *Love Affair*, 108.

8. Berman, *Domination*, 396; Baring to Lyttelton, October 29, 1953, CO 822/599, no. 74, in Goldsworthy, *Conservative*, 2:248.

9. Bennett, *Kenya*, 137, 145; Gordon, *Decolonization*, 128.

10. Ogot, "Decisive Years," 48–9.

11. Douglas-Home, *Baring*, 263; Low, "End of the British Empire," 57; Gordon, *Decolonization*, 117; Goldsworthy, *Mboya*, 126.

12. Dorsz to Washington, December 7, 1954, NARA 611.45P/12-754.

13. Department of State Instruction CA-7584 to Nairobi, May 4, 1955, NARA 611.45P/5-455.

14. Nairobi to Washington, December 30, 1955, NARA 745R.00/12-3055; Nairobi to Washington, March 22, 1957, NARA 745R.00/3-2257; Nairobi to Washington, May 27, 1957, NARA 745R.00/5-2757.

15. Ogot, "Decisive Years," 52; Berman, *Domination*, 390–1.

16. Furedi, *Colonial Wars*, 230; Berman, *Domination*, 391; Goldsworthy, *Mboya*, 79.

17. Douglas-Home, *Baring*, 279; Goldsworthy, *Mboya*, 78.

18. Goldsworthy, *Mboya*, 69–70, 112; Bennett, *Kenya*, 143.

19. Goldsworthy, *Mboya*, 21–2, 61–62, 118.

20. Goldsworthy, *Mboya*, 118, 120; Leach to Washington, October 29, 1957, NARA 745R.00/10-2957.

21. Manning, Briefing Book for Julius Holmes, no date, NARA RG59

Records of the Bureau of African Affairs; Talking Points for US-UK Talks on Africa, November 17–18, 1960, NARA 611.41/11-1760.

22. Satterthwaite to Macomber, March 19, 1959, NARA RG 59 3110 Office of Eastern and Southern African Affairs, 1951–65.

23. Goldsworthy, *Mboya*, 117.

24. Ogot, "Decisive Years," 54.

25. Percox, "Internal Security," 101; Furedi, "Emergencies," 97; Douglas-Home, *Baring*, 287–8.

26. Bennett, *Kenya*, 140.

27. Goldsworthy, *Mboya*, 73; Ogot, *Decisive Years*, 58; Gordon, *Decolonization*, 91.

28. Nairobi to Washington, March 22, 1957, NARA 745R.00/3-2257; Withers to Washington, September 25, 1957, NARA 745R.MSP/9-2557.

29. Dorsz to Washington, February 20, 1957, NARA 745R.00/2-2057; Leach to Washington, November 6, 1957, NARA 611.45R/9-657; Withers to Washington, April 18, 1958, NARA 745R.00/4-1858; Withers to Washington, April 3, 1960, NARA 745R.00/5-360.

30. Bennett, *Kenya*, 141–2.

31. Officials Committee, Report, September 6, 1957, CAB 134/1551 CPC(57)27, in Hyam and Louis, *Conservative*, 1:12; Darwin, "Pattern or Puzzle," 199–200; Goldsworthy, *Mboya*, 86, 114; Murphy, *Lennox-Boyd*, 226.

32. Withers to Washington, November 12, 1957, NARA 745R.00/11-1257.

33. Withers to Washington, March 12, 1958, NARA 745R.00/3-1258; Withers to Washington, April 18, 1958, NARA 745R.00/4-1858.

34. Office of Intelligence and Research, "African Political Movements: An Assessment," Report no. 7820, September 26, 1958; Office of Intelligence and Research, "Continuing Deadlock in Kenya Portends Trouble," Report no. 7963, March 3, 1959.

35. Withers to Washington, April 6, 1059, NARA 745R.00/4-659; Herter to Nairobi, April 6, 1949, NARA 745R.00/4-659; Withers to Washington, April 16, 1959, NARA 745R.00/4-1659; Nairobi to Washington, May 21, 1959, NARA 745R/5-2159.

36. Lennox-Boyd, Cabinet Memorandum, April 10, 1959, CAB 134/1558 CPC(59)2, in Hyam and Louis, *Conservative*, 1:371; Goldsworthy, *Mboya*, 113, 115–6; Murphy, *Lennox-Boyd*, 226–7.

37. Lennox-Boyd, Memorandum, April 10, 1959, CAB 134/1558 CPC(59)2, in Hyam and Louis, *Conserva-*

tive, 1:371; Percox, *Kenya*, 136, 139, 142; Percox, "Internal Security," 98.

38. Nairobi to Washington, December 23, 1959, NARA 745R.00/12-2359.

39. Nairobi to Washington, January 14, 1960, NARA 745R.00/1-1460.

40. Listowel, *Tanganyika*, 298; Iliffe, *Tanganyika*, 512, 516.

41. Iliffe, *Tanganyika*, 505.

42. *Yearbook of the United Nations*, 1955, 280–1; Listowel, *Tanganyika*, 163.

43. Listowel, *Tanganyika*, 241, 250; Belmonte, "Reining," 110, 249.

44. Iliffe, *Tanganyika*, 404, 553–4; Pratt, *Critical Phase*, 37.

45. Iliffe, *Tanganyika*, 521–2; Listowel, *Tanganyika*, 165, 295; Pratt, *Critical Phase*, 38.

46. McKinnon to Washington, February 7, 1956, NARA 778.00/2-756; McKinnon to Washington, April 24, 1956, NARA 778.00/4-2456.

47. Pratt, *Critical Phase*, 37–8; Listowel, *Tanganyika*, 300, 317.

48. Mathieson to Twining, December 28, 1956, CO 822/912, no. 30, in Goldsworthy, *Conservative*, 2:278–9; Twining to Barnes, November 12, 1956, CO 822/912, no. 26, in Goldsworthy, *Conservative*, 2:268; Iliffe, *Tanganyika*, 554.

49. Iliffe, *Tanganyika*, 554.

50. Sears, *Years of High Purpose*, 128; Listowel, *Tanganyika*, 296–7.

51. Listowel, *Tanganyika*, 166–7; Iliffe, *Tanganyika*, 561; Pratt, *Critical Phase*, 40.

52. Pratt, *Critical Phase*, 46; Iliffe, *Tanganyika*, 559.

53. Pratt, *Critical Phase*, 39; Iliffe, *Tanganyika*, 556, 560.

54. Twining to Barnes, November 12, 1956, CO 822/812, no. 26, in Goldsworthy, *Conservative*, 2:268; Mathieson and Barnes, Minutes, November 29 — December 25, 1956, CO 822/912, in Goldsworthy, *Conservative*, 2:273; Officials Committee, Report, September 6, 1957, CAB 134/1551 CPC(57)27, in Hyam and Louis, *Conservative*, 1:14–5.

55. Iliffe, *Tanganyika*, 563; Pratt, *Critical Phase*, 42, 49.

56. Turnbull to Barnes, January 13, 1959, CO 822/1448, no. 166, in Hyam and Louis, *Conservative*, 1:450ff.

57. Turnbull to Barnes, January 13, 1959, CO 822/1448, no. 166, in Hyam and Louis, *Conservative*, 1:450ff.

58. Maguire, *Toward Uhuru*, 229.

59. Turnbull to Barnes, January 13, 1959, CO 822/1448, no. 166, in Hyam and Louis, *Conservative*, 1:450ff.

60. Iliffe, *Tanganyika*, 564–5.

61. Turnbull to Crawford, July 9, 1959, CO 822/1450, no. 246, in Hyam and Louis, *Conservative*, 1:471.

62. Lennox-Boyd, Memorandum, April 10, 1959, CAB 134/1558 CPC(59)2, in Hyam and Louis, *Conservative*, 1:371; Amery, Minute, May 13, 1959, CO 822/1448, in Hyam and Louis, *Conservative*, 1:450; Webber, Minute, June 10, 1059, CO 822/1448, in Hyam and Louis, *Conservative*, 1:450.

63. Macpherson, Minute, June 15, 1959, CO 822/1448, in Hyam and Louis, *Conservative*, 1:450.

64. Duggan to Washington, February 14, 1959, NARA 320.14/2-1459; Hadsell to Washington, March 2, 1959, NARA 350/3-259; Whitney to Washington, April 14, 1960, NARA 778.00/4-1460; Huddleston to Washington, April 19, 1960, NARA 778.00/4-1960; Herter to London, April 22, 1960, NARA 778.00/4-1460; Torrance to Washington, April 23, 1960, NARA 778.00/4-2360.

65. Marvin to Washington, July 16, 1953, NARA 778.00/7-1653; Dar es Salaam to Washington, June 25, 1954, NARA 778.00/6-2554; Nairobi to Washington, December 30, 1955, NARA 745P.00/12-3055; Duggan to Washington, November 6, 1958, NARA 778.00/11-658; Duggan to Washington, December 27, 1958, NARA 778.00/12-2758; Washington to Dar es Salaam, March 1955, NARA 778.021/3-755.

66. Edmondson to Washington, January 31, 1955, NARA 778.021/1-3155.

67. Ware to Washington, March 12, 1957, NARA 778.00/3-1257; Ware to Washington, April 4, 1957, NARA 778.00/4-457; Ware to Washington, April 17, 1958, NARA 778.00/4-1758.

68. African Regional Conference, June 9–11, 1959, 20, NARA RG 59 5169 Records of Joseph C. Satterthwaite; Duggan to Washington, October 25, 1958, NARA 778.00/10-2658.

69. "The Outlook in East, Central and South Africa," National Intelligence Estimate, 76–59, October 20, 1959, in *FRUS, 1958–60*, 14:58; Hadsel to Washington, March 18, 1960, NARA 641.70/3-1860.

70. Apter, *Political Kingdom*, 266, 270–2.

71. Apter, *Political Kingdom*, 177–8, 277; Lyttelton, Memorandum, November 18, 1953, CAB 129/64 C(53)234, in Goldsworthy, *Conservative*, 2:251; London to Washington, January 5, 1954, NARA 745S.00/1-554.

72. Apter, *Political Kingdom*, 283, 285.

73. Cohen to Lyttelton, November 7, 1953, CO 822/567, in Porter and Stockwell, *British Imperial Policy*,

2:264ff; Cohen to Lloyd, July 9, 1953, CO 822/341, no. 4, in Goldsworthy, *Conservative*, 2:245.

74. Lyttelton, *Memoirs*, 402; Lyttelton, Memorandum, November 18, 1953, CAB 129/64 C(53)234, in Goldsworthy, *Conservative*, 2:251; Cabinet Discussions, November 19, 1953, CAB 128/26/2 CC68(53)7, in Goldsworthy, *Conservative*, 2:253.

75. Cohen to Lloyd, January 12, 1954, CO 822/892, no. 8, in Goldsworthy, *Conservative*, 2:254.

76. Apter, *Political Kingdom*, 291, 295–6, 299.

77. Apter, *Political Kingdom*, 333; Hancock, "Kabaka Yekka," 420; Karugire, *Uganda*, 154.

78. Apter, *Political Kingdom*, 329, 33; Ingham, *Obote*, 47; Sathyamurthy, *Political Development*, 391.

79. Ocitti, *Uganda*, 101; Apter, *Political Kingdom*, 340; Sathyamurthy, *Political Development*, 383.

80. Committee of Officials, Report, June 1959, FO 371/137972, no 24, in Hyam and Louis, *Conservative*, 1:117; Ibingira, *Forging*, 84; Apter, *Political Kingdom*, 430.

81. Lennox-Boyd, Memorandum, April 10, 1959, CAB 134/1558 CPC (59)2, in Hyam and Louis, *Conservative*, 1:71; Ocitti, *Uganda*, 104, 106.

82. Gorz to Washington, November 24, 1953, NARA 745S.00/11-2453; Nairobi to Washington, December 30, 1955, NARA 745P.00/12-3055; Barrow to Washington, January 6, 1956, NARA 745S.00/1-656.

83. Hooper to Washington, October 9, 1957, NARA 745S.00/10-957; Hooper to Washington, November 8, 1957, NARA 745S.00/11-857; Hooper to Washington, May 16, 1958, NARA 745S.00/5-1658.

84. Hooper to Washington, September 25, 1957, NARA 745S.00/90 2557; Hooper to Washington, April 27, 1959, NARA 745S.00/4-2759; Hooper to Washington, October 20, 1959, NARA 745S.00/10-2059.

85. Hooper to Washington, March 18, 1959, NARA 745S.03/3-1859.

86. Hooper to Washington, November 27, 1958, NARA 745S.00/11-2758; Hooper to Washington, March 26, 1959, NARA 745S.00/3-2659; Herter to Kampala, August 21, 1959, NARA 745S.11/8-2159; Hooper to Washington, October 26, 1959, NARA 745S.00/10-2659.

87. Lofchie, *Zanzibar*, 71, 170; Bowles, "Struggle for Independence," 81, 87; Middleton and Campbell, *Zanzibar*, 44.

88. Middleton and Campbell, *Zanzibar*, 45; Bowles, "Struggle for Independence," 101.

89. Ayany, *Zanzibar*, 48; Middleton and Campbell, *Zanzibar*, 48–9; Lofchie, *Zanzibar*, 166–7.

90. Middleton and Campbell, *Zanzibar*, 50; Ayany, *Zanzibar*, 58; Lofchie, *Zanzibar*, 178.

91. Lofchie, *Zanzibar*, 168–9, 189; Middleton and Campbell, *Zanzibar*, 59.

92. Huddleston to Washington, December 9, 1959, NARA 778.00/12-959; Duggan to Washington, January 15, 1960, NARA 745T.00/1-1560.

Chapter 15

1. Baxter, Minute, October 4, 1954, in Porter and Stockwell, *British Imperial Policy*, 2:340; Clarke to Marnham, April 15, 1954, DO 35/4633, in Porter and Stockwell, *British Imperial Policy*, 2:302; Commonwealth Relations Office, Probable Development of the Commonwealth over the Next Ten to Fifteen Years, June 1956, CO 1032/51, in Goldsworthy, *Conservative*, 1:97.

2. Bates, Minute, October 28, 1955, DO 335/4778, in Murphy, *Central Africa*, 1:285; Morgan to Barnes, June 20, 1956, CO 1015/998, in Murphy, *Central Africa*, 1:338.

3. Barnes, Minute, November 26, 1956, CO 1015/913, in Murphy, *Central Africa*, 1:351; Barnes, Minute, March 6, 1956, CO 1015/994, in Murphy, *Central Africa*, 1:311.

4. Baker, *Armitage*, 176, 181; Mulford, *Zambia*, 48–49; Benson to Colonial Office, December 6, 1955, CO 1915/1061, in Murphy, *Central Africa*, 1:293; Rotberg, *Rise of Nationalism*, 269.

5. Rotberg, *Rise of Nationalism*, 254–5, 282; Wills, *Introduction*, 327.

6. Home and Lennox-Boyd, Cabinet Memorandum, [date?] CAB 129/81 CP(56) 141, in Goldsworthy, *Conservative*, 2:299; Mulford, *Zambia*, 51.

7. Mulford, *Zambia*, 52; Barber, *Road to Rebellion*, 17.

8. Mulford, *Zambia*, 52–3; Benson to Barnes, December 30, 1957, BARN 3/8, in Murphy, *Central Africa*, 1:384.

9. Welensky, *4000 Days*, 89.

10. Home, Memorandum, November 12, 1958, CAB 129/95 C(58) 232, in Hyam and Louis, *Conservative*, 2:538; Barnes, Minute, November 14, 1958, CO 1015/1696, in Murphy, *Central Africa*, 1:429; Trend to Macmillan, November 17, 1958, PREM 11/2477, in Murphy, *Central Africa*, 1:432; Campbell, Minute, November 26, 1958, CO 1015/1598, in Murphy, *Central Africa*, 1:423.

11. Mulford, *Zambia*, 79–81.

12. Blake, *Rhodesia*, 324–5; Baker, *State of Emergency*, 6, 27.

13. Baker, *State of Emergency*, 54–6; Rotberg, *Rise of Nationalism*, 301.

14. Hoover to Washington, April 15, 1953, NARA 611.70/5-853; Steere to Utter, October 22, 1954, in *FRUS, 1952–54*, 11:344; Steere to Washington, May 22, 1956, NARA 745C.00/5-2256.

15. National Intelligence Estimate, NIE-83, December 22, 1953, FRUS, 1952–54, 11:82–3.

16. Hoover to Washington, May 8, 1953, NARA 611.70/5-853; Hoover to Washington, February 25, 1953, NARA 745C.00/2-2553; Hoover to Washington, April 15, 1953, NARA 611.70/5-853; Steere to Washington, January 6, 1955, NARA 745C.1-655.

17. Steere to Washington, March 15, 1957, NARA 745C.00/3-1557; Steere to Washington, October 7, 1957, NARA 745C.00/10-757; Salisbury to Washington, February 11, 1958, NARA 745C.00/2-1158; Steere to Washington, February 10, 1958, NARA 745C.00/2-1058.

18. Steere to Washington, September 22, 1954, NARA 745C.00/9-2254; Steere to Washington, March 18, 1957, NARA 745C.00/3-1857; Steere to Washington, August 28, 1956, NARA 745C.00/8-2856; Steere to Washington, March 7, 1958, NARA 745C.00/3-758; Gottlieb to Washington, October 10, 1958, NARA 745C.00/10-1058.

19. Palmer to Washington, January 6, 1959, NARA 745C.00/1-659; Palmer to Washington, December 22, 1958, NARA 745C.00/12-2258.

20. Steere to Washington, September 22, 1954, NARA 745C.00/9-2254; Strong to Washington, October 16, 1958, NARA 745C.00/10-1658; Strong to Washington, December 5, 1958, NARA 745C.00/12-558.

21. Office of Intelligence and Research, "The Federation of Rhodesia and Nyasaland Faces Stormy Future," OIR no. 7707, April 23, 1958.

22. Office of Intelligence and Research, "Rhodesian Election Unlikely to Reduce Racial Tension," OIR no. 7899, December 18, 1958.

23. Johnson to Palmer, August 11, 1958, NARA RG 59 Office of Eastern and Southern African Affairs, 1951–65.

Chapter 16

1. Douglas-Home, *Baring*, 285; Kyle, *Independence of Kenya*, 91.

2. Murphy, *Lennox-Boyd*, 217; Baker, *State of Emergency*, 154.

3. Murphy, *Lennox-Boyd*, 229.

4. Ovendale, "Wind of Change," 471–2; Hemming, *Macmillan*, 101–2; Ball, "Banquo's Ghost," 78–83.

5. Gupta, *Imperialism and the Labour Movement*, 361, 368, 370.

6. Murphy, *Conservative Party*, 174; Blundell, *Love Affair*, 112.

7. Macmillan, *Pointing the Way*, 118–9.

8. Welensky, *4000 Days*, 323.

9. Minutes of Meeting in Ottawa, November 26, 1959, DO 35/8804, no. 11, in Hyam and Louis, *Conservative*, 1:138; Heinlein, *Government Policy*, 239, 246; Metcalf to Home, August 29, 1959, DO 35/7620, in Murphy, *Central Africa*, 2:78.

10. Lamb, *Macmillan*, 248; Baker, *State of Emergency*, 200–201; Ball, *Guardsmen*, 346; Macmillan, Minute, December 28, 1959, PREM 11/3075, in Hyam and Louis, *Conservative*, 2:548.

11. Blundell, *Love Affair*, 112; Murphy, *Conservative Party*, 176; Shepherd, *Macleod*, 158; Ovendale, "Wind of Change," 477.

12. Murphy, *Lennox-Boyd*, 198–9, 208, 215–6; Blake, *Rhodesia*, 328.

13. Shepherd, *Macleod*, 161, 163, 199.

14. Ovendale, "Wind of Change, 474; Heinlein, *Government Policy*, 245; Barber, *Road to Rebellion*, 24; Welensky, *4000 Days*, 171.

15. Shepherd, *Macleod*, 162, 163–4; Macleod, "Trouble in Africa," *The Spectator*, January 31, 1964, in Porter and Stockwell, *British Imperial Policy*, 2:570.

16. Wall, *Algerian War*, 23–4, 115–6, 132, 167, 186–7.

17. Fisher, *Macleod*, 145, 147.

18. Shepherd, *Macleod*, 161.

19. Douglas-Home, *Baring*, 276; Welensky, *4000 Days*, 187; Baker, *State of Emergency*, 238, 243; Alport, *Sudden Assignment*, 29.

20. Lamb, *Macmillan*, 250.

21. Murphy, *Lennox-Boyd*, 210; Douglas-Home, *Baring*, 299.

22. Ovendale, "Wind of Change," 464; Officials Committee, Future Constitutional Development in the Colonies, May 1957, CAB 134/1551 CPC(57)27, in Hyam and Louis, *Conservative*, 1:4ff; Minutes of Cabinet Colonial Policy Committee, March 18, 1960, CAB 134/1559 CPC 2 (60)4, in Hyam and Louis, *Conservative*, 1:358–9.

23. Officials Committee, "Future Constitutional Development in the Colonies," May 1957, CAB 134/1551 CPC(57)5, in Hyam and Louis, *Con-

servative*, 1:11; Officials Committee, "Africa in the Next Ten Years," June 1959, FO 371/137972, in Hyam and Louis, *Conservative*, 1:114.

24. Macleod to Macmillan, May 31, 1960, PREM 11/3240 PM (60)33, in Hyam and Louis, *Conservative*, 1:178–9; Macleod, Cabinet Memo, January 12, 1961, CAB 129/104 C (61)5, in Hyam and Louis, *Conservative*, 1:363ff; Cabinet Conclusions, January 24, 1961, CAB 128/35/1 CC2 (61)6, in Hyam and Louis, *Conservative*, 1:365–6.

25. Macleod to Colonial Policy Committee, November 12, 1959, CAB 134/1558, in Hyam and Louis, *Conservative*, 1:476.

26. Colonial Policy Committee, Minutes, November 20, 1959, CAB 134/1558 CPC6(59)1, in Hyam and Louis, *Conservative*, 1:482–3.

27. Macleod to Macmillan, December 29, 1959, PREM 11/2586 PM (59)65, in Hyam and Louis, *Conservative*, 1:164.

28. Macleod to Macmillan, May 31, 1960, PREM 11/3240 PM(60)33, in Hyam and Louis, *Conservative*, 1:178–9; Monson, Minute, July 21, 1960, CO822/2299, in Hyam and Louis, *Conservative*, 1:483–4; Martin, Minute, July 22, 1960, CO 822/2299, in Hyam and Louis, *Conservative*, 1:483–4; Monson to Turnbull, August 25, 1960, CO 822/2299, in Hyam and Louis, *Conservative*, 1:488–9.

29. Cabinet Colonial Policy Committee, Minutes, November 5, 1959, CAB 134/1558 CPC(59)1, in Hyam and Louis, *Conservative*, 1:144; Percox, "Internal Security," 103–4.

30. Murphy, *Conservative Party*, 178; Kyle, *Independence of Kenya*, 120.

31. Goldsworthy, *Mboya*, 126–7.

32. Shepherd, *Macleod*, 174, 182; Bennett, *Kenya*, 149.

33. Goldsworthy, *Mboya*, 133.

34. Goldsworthy, *Mboya*, 133, 136.

35. Shepherd, *Macleod*, 176–7; Bennett, *Kenya*, 151.

36. Macleod to Macmillan, December 29, 1959, PREM 11/2586 PM (59)65, in Hyam and Louis, *Conservative*, 1:164.

37. Withers to Washington, March 3, 1960, NARA 745R.00/3-360.

38. Hadsel to Washington, March 18, 1960, MARA 641.70/3-1860.

39. Nairobi to Washington, September 8, 1960, NARA 745R.00/9-860; O'Neill to Washington, November 25, 1960, NARA 745R.00/11-2560; O'Neill to Washington, December 22, 1960, NARA 745R.00/12-2260.

40. Ingham, *Obote*, 53, 60; Ocitti, *Uganda*, 97.

41. Ghai, "Bugandan Trade Boycott," 755–758.

42. Ocitti, *Uganda*, 103, 105; Sathyamurthy, *Political Development*, 382.

43. Ghai, "Bugandan Trade Boycott," 759.

44. Macleod to Macmillan, December 29, 1959, PREM 11/2586 PM(59)65, in Hyam and Louis, *Conservative*, 1:164.

45. Macleod to Macmillan, December 29, 1959, PREM 11/2586 PM (59)65, in Hyam and Louis, *Conservative*, 1:164.

46. Cabinet Colonial Policy Committee, Minutes, February 8, 1960, CAB 134/1559 CPC1(60)1, in Hyam and Louis, *Conservative*, 1:393–5.

47. Macleod to Macmillan, May 31, 1960, PREM 11/3240 PM(60)33, in Hyam and Louis, *Conservative*, 1:178–9.

48. Ingham, *Obote*, 64.

49. Ingham, *Obote*, 65.

50. Kampala to Washington, January 12, 1960, no. 140, NARA 745S.00/1-1260; Hooper to Washington, January 12, 1960, no. G-28, NARA 745S.00/1-1260; Herter to Kampala, January 27, 1960, NARA 745S.00/1-2260; Hadsel to Washington, March 18, 1960, NARA 641.70/3-1860.

51. Hooper to Washington, January 26, 1960, NARA 745S.00/1-2660.

52. Van Oss to Washington, September 6, 1960, NARA 745S.00/9-660; Kampala to Washington, October 25, 1960, NARA 745S.00/10-2560.

53. Bade, *Kiwanuka*, 53, 57.

54. Deming to Satterthwaite, December 23, 1960, NARA 745T.00/12-2360.

Chapter 17

1. Barnes to Hone, April 27, 1959, CO 1015/2137, no. 1227 in Murphy, *Central Africa*, 2:43; Report by Committee of Officials, June 1959, FO 371/137972, no. 24, in Hyam and Louis, *Conservative*, 1:118.

2. Horne, *Macmillan*, 182–3.

3. Horne, *Macmillan*, 182–3; Bligh, Note for Record, February 10, 1961, PREM 11/3949, in Murphy, *Central Africa*, 2:196ff.

4. Murphy, *Conservative Party*, 183.

5. Home to Macmillan, December 21, 1959, DO 35/7564, no. 11E, in Hyam and Louis, *Conservative*, 2:545.

6. Home to Macmillan, December 21, 1959, DO 35/7564, no. 11E, in Hyam and Louis, *Conservative*,

2:545; Home to Macmillan, May 29, 1959, PREM 11/2787, in Murphy, *Central Africa*, 2:48.

7. Macleod to Macmillan, December 29, 1959, PREM 11/2586 PN (59) 65, in Hyam and Louis, *Conservative*, 1:164.

8. Baker, *State of Emergency*, 209; Macleod to Macmillan, December 29, 1959, PREM 11/2586 PN (59) 65, in Hyam and Louis, *Conservative*, 1:164.

9. Armitage to Morgan, March 10, 1959, CO 1015/1494 no. 144, in Murphy, *Central Africa*, 2:28; Baker, *State of Emergency*, 204, 205, 210, 221, 228.

10. Home to Macmillan, December 21, 1959, DO 35/7564 no. 11E, in Murphy, *Central Africa*, 2:98; Home to Monckton, March 22, 1960, PREM 11/3076, in Hyam and Louis, *Conservative*, 2:552.

11. Baker, *State of Emergency*, 234.

12. Baker, *State of Emergency*, 226, 234; Welensky, *4000 Days*, 165.

13. Baker, *State of Emergency*, 197, 215.

14. Baker, *State of Emergency*, 233, 236; Welensky, *4000 Days*, 197.

15. Baker, *State of Emergency*, 235; Cabinet Conclusions, February 23, 1960, CAB 128/34 CC 12(60)4, in Hyam and Louis, *Conservative*, 2:550.

16. Shepherd, *Macleod*, 203.

17. Short, *Banda*, 135–6, 141; Baker, *State of Emergency*, 241; Baker, *Glyn Jones*, 69–71, 82.

18. Mulford, *Zambia*, 153–4, 159; Hone to Macleod, April 16, 1960, CO 1015/2274, no. 11, in Murphy, *Central Africa*, 2:132; Hone to Watson, June 12, 1960, CO 1015/2274, no. 63, in Murphy, *Central Africa*, 2:143.

19. Mulford, *Zambia*, 155, 158; Macleod, Minute, May 20, 1960, CO 1015/2274, in Murphy, *Central Africa*, 2:141; Macleod to Macmillan, December 12, 1960, PREM 11/3485 PM (60)70, in Murphy, *Central Africa*, 2:183.

20. Welensky, *4000 Days*, 199.

21. Wood, *So Far*, 48, 60–1, 68; Barber, *Road to Rebellion*, 43–4, 54–5; Armitage to Morgan, March 10, 1959, CO 1015/1494, in Murphy, *Central Africa*, 2:28.

22. Barber, *Road to Rebellion*, 51; Wood, *So Far*, 44–5, 55.

23. Barber, *Road to Rebellion*, 32; Wood, *So Far*, 29, 31, 65.

24. Wood, *So Far*, 22, 31; Home to Macmillan April 6, 1960, DO 35/7559, no. 64, in Hyam and Louis, *Conservative*, 2:554–5.

25. Wood, *So Far*, 65.

26. Barber, *Road to Rebellion*, 36–38.

27. Short, *Banda*, 143; Welensky, *4000 Days*, 272.

28. Mulford, *Zambia*, 176, 179; Short, *Banda*, 145.

29. Salisbury to Washington, February 27, 1959, NARA 745C.00/2-2759; Salisbury to Washington, April 3, 1959, NARA 745C.00/4-359; Palmer to Washington, May 21, 1959, NARA 745C.00/5-2159.

30. Ferguson to Satterthwaite, August 4, 1959, NARA RG 59 3110 Office of Eastern and Southern African Affairs, 1951–1965; Washington to Salisbury, July 29, 1959, NARA 745C.00/7-2859; Whitney to Washington, July 30, 1959, NARA 745C.00/7-3059; Barbour to Washington, August 10, 1959, NARA 745C.00/8-1059; Operations Coordinating Board, Operations Plan for Federation of Rhodesia and Nyasaland, September 18, 1959, NARA RG 59 1586 State Department Participation in the Operations Coordinating Board and National Security Council.

31. Steere to Washington, May 23, 1958, NARA 745C.00/5-2358; Strong to Washington, January 30, 1959, NARA 745C.00/1-3059.

32. Palmer to Washington, February 9, 1959, NARA 745C.00/2-959.

33. Palmer to Washington, February 9, 1959, NARA 745C.00/2-959.

34. Palmer to Washington, November 12, 1959, NARA 745C.00/11-1259.

35. Palmer to Washington, September 21, 1959, NARA 745C.00/9-2159.

36. Palmer to Washington, November 6, 1959, NARA 745C.00/11-659.

37. Salisbury to Washington, December 8, 1959, NARA 770.00/12-859.

38. Whitney to Washington, January 22, 1960, NARA 745C.00/1-2260; London to Washington, February 9, 1960, NARA 745C.00/2-960.

39. Washington to Salisbury, January 29, 1960, NARA 745C.00/1-2960.

40. Palmer to Washington, April 21, 1960, NARA 745C.00/4-2160.

41. Hadsel to Washington, May 19, 1960, NARA 745C.00/5-1960; Hadsel to Washington, May 20, 1960, NARA 745C.00/5-2060; Hadsel to Washington, July 29, 1960, NARA 745C.00/7-2960.

42. Whitney to Washington, June 3, 1960, NARA 745C.00/6-360.

43. Mulcahy to Washington, May 19, 1960, NARA 745C.00/5-1960; Mulcahy to Washington, May 23, 1960, NARA 745C.00/5-2360;

Palmer to Washington, March 9, 1960, NARA 745C.00/3-960; Palmer to Washington, July 27, 1960, NARA 745C.00/7-2660.

44. Herter to Salisbury, July 25, 1960, NARA 745C.00/7-2560; Whitney to Washington, July 26, 1960, NARA 745C.00/7-2660; Salisbury to Washington, July 28, 1960, NARA 745C.00/7-2760; Dillon to Salisbury, July 29, 1960, NARA 745C.00/7-2760; Herter to Salisbury, August 1, 1960, NARA 745C.00/7-2660.

45. Palmer to Washington, September 16, 1960, NARA 745C.00/9-1660; Mulcahy to Washington, September 23, 1960, NARA 745C.00/9-2360.

46. Mulcahy to Washington, October 5, 1960, NARA 745C.00/10-560; Cumming to Secretary, October 19, 1960, NARA 745C.00/10-1960.

47. Picard to Ferguson, August 3, 1960, NARA RG 59 3110 Office of Eastern and Southern African Affairs, 1951–65.

48. Talking Points, United States — United Kingdom Talks of Africa, November 17–18, 1960, NARA 611.41/11-1760.

Chapter 18

1. Noer, *Williams*, 224.

2. Kennedy, "Imperialism — The Enemy of Freedom," July 2, 1957, www.jfklink.com/speeches/congress.

3. Mahoney, *Ordeal in Africa*, 24–25, 33.

4. Wall, *Algerian War*, 85.

5. A collection of Kennedy's campaign speeches is at www.jfklink.com/speeches.

6. Mahoney, *Ordeal in Africa*, 31–32; Senator Kennedy's Office, "The Facts on Grant to American Students Airlift," August 1960, www.jfklink.com/speeches.

7. Noer, *Cold War*, 62.

8. Noer, *Williams*, 227, 229, 242, 246.

9. Noer, *Williams*, 239–41; Noer, *Cold War*, 69.

10. Harriman to Washington, March 2, 1961, NARA 641.70/3-261.

11. Williams to Secretary, October 23, 1962, NARA 770.00/10-2362; Tyler to Secretary, October 29, 1962, NARA 770.00/10-2962; McGhee to Williams, November 5, 1962, NARA 770.00/11-562.

12. Noer, *Cold War*, 82; Noer, *Williams*, 247.

13. Noer, *Cold War*, 66.

14. Noer, *Cold War*, 82; Noer, *Williams*, 229, 247; Watts, "Problem

of Rhodesian Independence," 464–5; Newsom, *Imperial Mantle*, 161.

15. Rostow to Bundy May 13, 1961, in *FRUS, 1961–63*, 21:290.

16. Noer, *Williams*, 225–6, 230; Matongo, "Zambia," 111.

17. Noer, *Cold War*, 63, 82; Mahoney, *Ordeal in Africa*, 104–5.

18. Noer, *Cold War*, 63; Noer, *Williams*, 248.

19. "Probable Developments in Colonial Africa," National Intelligence Estimate 60/70–61, April 11, 1961, in *FRUS, 1961–63*, 21:284–5; Bureau of Intelligence and Research, Contribution to NIE 60/70-61, February 15, 1961, NARA RG59 Records of the Policy Planning Staff.

20. Draft Guidelines of United States Policy and Operations Concerning Africa, September 22, 1961, NARA RG59 3110 Office of Eastern and Southern African Affairs, 1951–65.

21. Cleveland to Tyler and others, April 12, 1962, NARA RG59 5586 Records Relating to Planning and United Nations Matters.

22. Deming to MacKnight, April 3, 1962, NARA RG59 1578 Bureau of African Affairs, 1956–62; Tyler to Cleveland, April 12, 1962, NARA RG59 5586 Records Relating to Planning and United Nations Matters.

23. Williams, "Basic United States Policy," 543; Williams, "Change and Challenge," 721; Stevenson, "United Nations," 413; Williams, "Southern Africa in Transition," 639; Bingham, "United Nations Statement," 71.

24. Policy Towards Africa South of the Sahara, Interdepartmental Paper, August 1961, DO 168/60, no.1, in Hyam and Louis, *Conservative*, 1:191–2.

25. Low, *End of British Empire*, 60.

26. Bligh, Note on Meeting between Macmillan and Welensky, March 1, 1962, PREM 11/3943, in Murphy, *Central Africa* 2:309.

27. "The Choleric Lords," *Time*, March 17, 1961; Sandbrook, *Never Had It So Good*, 298–9.

28. Sandbrook, *Never Had It So Good*, 300.

29. Wood, *So Far*, 100; Macmillan to the Queen, March 12, 1962, PREM 11/3814, in Hyam and Louis, *Conservative*, 1:331.

30. Wood, *So Far*, 184.

31. Aldous, *Macmillan*, 27; Mahoney, *Ordeal in Africa*, 118, 239–40.

32. Aldous, *Macmillan* 27; Ovendale, *Anglo-American*, 131; Edmonds, *Mould*, 239.

33. Memorandum of Conversation, United States – United Kingdom Talks, February 23, 1961, NARA 611.41/2-2361.

34. Memorandum of Conversation, United States – United Kingdom Talks, February 23, 1961, NARA 611.41/2-2361; Memorandum of Conversation, Kennedy – Macmillan Talks, April 5, 1961, NARA RG59 3051B, Conference Files.

35. Agreed Minute: Target Dates for Independence for Non-Self-governing Territories, United States – United Kingdom Talks, March 17, 1961, NARA RG59 3051B Conference Files; Memorandum of Conversation, Kennedy – Macmillan Talks, April 5, 1961, NARA RG59 3051B Conference Files.

36. Memorandum of Conversation, April 7, 1961, NARA 770.00/4-761; Draft Foreign Office Record of Discussion at Tripartite Talks between British, American, and French Representatives in Paris, December 11, 1961, FO 371/166819, no. 7, in Hyam and Louis, *Conservative*, 2:318; Bruce to Washington, December 6, 1962, NARA 770.00/12-1662; Washington to Dar es Salaam, January 14, 1963, NARA 641.70/1-1463.

37. Rusk to United States Delegation at the United Nations, March 11, 1961, NARA 770.00/2-2861; Penfield to Cleveland, March 8, 1961, NARA RG59 Records of the Bureau of African Affairs, 1956–62; Nunley to Kohler, March 18, 1961, NARA 59 5586 Records Relating to Planning and United Nations; Washington to New York, April 21, 1961, NARA 770.00/4-2161.

38. Deming to Williams, September 12, 1961, NARA RG59 1578 Bureau of African Affairs 1956–62; Stevenson to Washington, September 1, 1961, NARA 770.00/8-3161; Bruce to Washington, August 31, 1961, NARA 770.00/8-3061; New York to Washington, September 29, 1961, NARA 770.00/9-2961; Washington to New York, October 13, 1961, NARA 770.00/10-1061.

39. Problems of Non-Self-Governing Territories, no date [January 1962?], NARA RG59 1578 Bureau of African Affairs 1956–62.

40. United States Delegation at the United Nations to Washington, April 19, 1962, NARA RG59 Bureau of African Affairs 1956–62; Ball to Kennedy, August 16, 1972, NARA 59 1552 Classified Records of G. Mennen Williams; Washington to United States Delegation at the United Nations, August 13, 1963 NARA POL 10 UN.

41. New York to Washington, July 5, 1962, NARA 324.7022/7-562; Stevenson to Washington, September 10, 1962, NARA 324.7022/9-1062.

42. New York to Washington, July 18, 1962, NARA 324.7022/7-1762; Stevenson to Washington, September 10, 1962, NARA 324.7022/9-1062.

Chapter 19

1. Dakar to Washington, April 13, 1961, NARA 745N.00/4-1361; Graham to Washington, May 18, 1961, NARA 745N.00/5-1861.

2. Memorandum of Conversation, November 20, 1961, NARA 745N.00/11-2061; Rusk to Paris, March 28, 1962, NARA 745N.00/3-2862; Jones to Washington, April 27, 1962, NARA 745N.00/4-2762; Bartlett to Trimble, November 19, 1962, NARA RG59 Office of West African Affairs Country Files; Washington to New York, September 6, 1963, NARA POL 10 UN; Kaiser to Washington, April 27, 1962, NARA 745N.00/4-2762.

3. Macleod, Memorandum for Cabinet Colonial Policy Committee, January 3, 1961, CAB 134/1560 CPC (61)1, in Hyam and Louis, *Conservative*, 1:182–3; Macleod, Cabinet Memorandum, February 27, 1961, c(61)32, in Hyam and Louis, *Conservative*, 1:495; Macleod, Memorandum for Cabinet Colonial Policy Committee, April 11, 1961, CAB 134/1560 CPC (61)7, in Hyam and Louis, *Conservative*, 1:412–3.

4. Cabinet Colonial Policy Committee, Meeting Minutes, January 6, 1961, CAB 134/1560 CPC1(61)2, in Hyam and Louis, *Conservative*, 1:185–6.

5. Macleod to Cabinet Colonial Policy Committee, January 3, 1961, CAB 134/1560 CPC(61)1, in Hyam and Louis, *Conservative*, 1:182–3; Macleod to Macmillan, January 6, 1961, PREM 11/4083 M 15/61, in Hyam and Louis, *Conservative*, 1:407–8.

6. Macleod to Macmillan, January 6, 1961, PREM 11/4083 M 15/61, in Hyam and Louis, *Conservative*, 1:407–8.

7. Macleod to Watkinson, January 12, 1961, FO 371/146498, no. 20, in Hyam and Louis, *Conservative*, 1:399–402.

8. Bennett, *Kenya*, 151–2, 155; Goldsworthy, *Mboya*, 182.

9. Macleod to Renison, May 19, 1961, CO 822/2241, no. 7, in Hyam and Louis, *Conservative*, 1:519ff; Goldsworthy, *Mboya*, 182; Perth, Minute, April 13, 1961, CO 82/2235, in Hyam and Louis, *Conservative*, 1:515–6.

10. Kyle, *Independence*, 122, 132, 134; Macleod to Cabinet Colonial Policy Committee, April 11, 1961, CAB 134/1560 CPC(61)7, in Hyam and Louis, *Conservative*, 1:412–3; Macleod to Renison, May 19, 1961, CO 822/2241, no. 7, in Hyam and Louis, *Conservative*, 1:519; Lamb, *Macmillan Years*, 227.

11. Kyle, *Independence*, 130, 144.

12. Cabinet Colonial Policy Committee, Meeting Minutes, November 15, 1961, CAB 134/1560 CPC12(61), in Hyam and Louis, *Conservative*, 1:523ff; Cabinet Conclusions, November 16, 1961, CAB 128/35/2 CC 63(61)5, in Hyam and Louis, *Conservative*, 1:526ff.

13. Cabinet Conclusions, November 9, 1961, CAB 128/35/2 CC61 (61)6, in Hyam and Louis, *Conservative*, 1:522–3.

14. Cabinet Conclusions, December 19, 1961, CAB 128/35/2 CC75 (61)6, in Hyam and Louis, *Conservative*, 1:528; Maudling to Cabinet Colonial Policy Committee, January 30, 1962, CAB 134/1561 CPC(62)3, in Hyam and Louis, *Conservative*, 1:529ff.

15. Baston, *Reggie*, 166; Cabinet Conclusions, March 20, 1962, CAB 128/36/1 CC22(62)4, in Hyam and Louis, *Conservative*, 1:535ff.

16. Bennett, *Kenya*, 156; Kyle, *Independence*, 149.

17. Murphy, *Conservative Party*, 195; Kyle, *Independence*, 168; Sanger, *MacDonald*, 396; Washington to Nairobi, January 7, 1963, NARA 641.70/1-763; Freund to Washington, February 21, 1963, NARA POL 14 Kenya.

18. Kyle, *Independence*, 180; Sanger, *MacDonald*, 396.

19. Nairobi to Washington, November 14, 1961, NARA 745R.00/11-1461; Freund to Washington, June 2, 1961, NARA 745R.00/6-261.

20. Freund to Washington, July 11, 1961, NARA 745R.00/7-1161; Nairobi to Washington, November 14, 1961, NARA 745R.00/11-1461; Freund to Washington, March 15, 1961, NARA 745R.00/3-1561.

21. Chapin to Dening, January 16, 1962, NARA 745R.00/1-1662; Good to Dening, February 5, 1962, NARA RG59 3110 Office of Eastern and Southern African Affairs 1951–65; Rusk to Nairobi, January 18, 1962, NARA 745R.00/1-1862; Washington to London, March 7, 1962, NARA 745R.00/3-562.

22. Nairobi to Washington, February 22, 1962, NARA 745R.00/2-2162; Nairobi to Washington, May 1, 1961, NARA 745R.00/5-161; Rusk to Nairobi, September 12, 1961, NARA 745R.00/9-1261.

23. Freund to Washington, March 14, 1961, NARA 611.45R/3-1461; Williams to Secretary, April 12, 1961, NARA 033.7011/4-1261.

24. Washington to Nairobi, June 6, 1961, NARA 745R.00/6-261; Williams to Washington, May 13, 1962, NARA 745R.00/5-1262; Mathews to Williams, November 7, 1962, NARA RG59 3110 Office of Eastern and Southern African Affairs 1951–1965.

25. Freund to Washington, June 26, 1961, NARA 745R.00/6-2661; Freund to Washington, June 30, 1961, NARA 745R.00/6-3061; Rusk to Nairobi, July 2, 1961, NARA 745R. 00/6-3061.

26. Bruce to Washington, July 3, 1961, NARA 745R.00/7-361.

27. Nairobi to Washington, August 1, 1961, NARA 745R.00/8-161; O'Neil to Washington, September 26, 1961, NARA 745R.00/9-2661; O'Neil to Washington, October 3, 1961, NARA 745R.00/10-361; Nairobi to Washington, November 14, 1961, NARA 745R.00/11-1461.

28. Nairobi to Washington, January 5, 1962, NARA 511.703/1-562.

29. Chapin to Dening, February 5, 1962, NARA 745R.00/2-562.

30. Washington to Nairobi, August 31, 1961, NARA 745R.00/8-2561;Washington to Nairobi, February 23, 1962, NARA 745R.00/2-1262; Bruce to Washington, February 26, 1962, NARA 745R.00/2-2662; Rusk to Nairobi, February 28, 1962, NARA 745R.00/2-2762.

31. Washington to London, March 26, 1962, NARA 745R.00/3-2662; London to Washington, March 29, 1962, NARA 745R.00/3-2962.

32. London to Washington, March 29, 1962, NARA 745R.00/3-2962.

33. Nairobi to Washington, September 25, 1962, NARA 745R.00/9-2562; Mathews to Williams, November 7, 1962, NARA RG59 3110 Office of Eastern and Southern African Affairs.

34. Ocitti, *Uganda*, 109; Ingham, *Obote*, 69.

35. Sathyamurthy, *Political Development of Uganda*, 396; Ocitti, *Uganda*, 111, 117.

36. Bade, *Kiwanuka*, 83, 110; Ingham, *Obote*, 71.

37. Bade, *Kiwanuka*, 84, 85, 87; Shepherd, *Macleod*, 246; Ingham, *Obote*, 72.

38. Ocitti, *Uganda*, 118–9.

39. Bade, *Kiwanuka*, 111; Kampala to Washington, December 8, 1961, NARA 745S.00/12-861.

40. Van Oss to Washington, December 18, 1961, NARA 745S.00/12-1861; Van Oss to Washington, March 3, 1961, NARA 611.45S/3-361.

41. Van Oss to Washington, February 13, 1962, NARA 811.004S/2-1362.

42. Van Oss to Washington, January 24, 1961, NARA 745S.00/1-2461; Washington to Kampala, March 6, 1961, NARA 745S.00/2-2461; Washington to Kampala, March 9, 1961, NARA 745S.00/3-861; Van Oss to Picard, April 24, 1961, NARA RG59 3110 Office of Eastern and Southern African Affairs.

43. Washington to London, March 6, 1961, NARA 745S.00/2-2461;Van Oss to Washington, March 8, 1961, NARA 745S.00/3-861; Rusk to Kampala, March 9, 1961, NARA 745S.00/3-861; London to Washington, March 21, 1961, NARA 745S. 00/3-2161; Van Oss to Picard, April 24, 1961, NARA RG59 3110 Office of Eastern and Southern African Affairs.

44. Middletown and Campbell, *Zanzibar*, 55–57; Ayany, *Zanzibar*, 84–85; Lofchie, *Zanzibar*, 203.

45. Macleod to Cabinet Colonial Policy Committee, January 3, 1961, CAB 134/1560 CPC(61)1, in Hyam and Louis, *Conservative*, 1:182–3; Ayany, *Zanzibar*, 85; Macleod to Cabinet Colonial Policy Committee, July 25, 1961, CAB CO822/2327, no. 15, in Hyam and Louis, *Conservative*, 1:414ff.

46. Morgan, Minute, December 15, 1961, CO 822/2328 no. 213, in Hyam and Louis, *Conservative*, 1:420ff; Record of a Meeting between Maudling and Mooring, February 1, 1962, PREM 11/4600, in Hyam and Louis, *Conservative*, 1:427ff.

47. Ayany, *Zanzibar*, 93, 97–99, 101.

48. Ayany, *Zanzibar*, 102.

49. Lofchie, *Zanzibar*, 214; Ayany, *Zanzibar*, 109, 115–118.

50. King to Washington, January 18, 1961, NARA 745T.00/1-1861; Bowles to London, June 3, 1961, NARA 745T.00/6-361; Bruce to Washington, June 5, 1961, NARA 745T.00/6-561; Department of State Guideline for Policy and Operations, Zanzibar, February 1963, 14–15, NARA RG59 3110 Office of Eastern and Southern African Affairs.

51. Department of State Guideline for Policy and Operations, Zanzibar, February 1963, 13, NARA RG59 3110 Office of Eastern and Southern African Affairs; Dar es Salaam to Washington, June 5, 1961, NARA 745T. 00/6-561; Picard to Washington, October 16, 1961, NARA 745T.00/10-1661; Bruce to Washington, June 6,

1961, NARA 745T.00/6-661; Hennemeyer to Washington, August 1, 1961, NARA 745T.00/8-161.

52. Picard to Washington, July 12, 1961, NARA 611.78/7-1261; Picard to Washington, October 16, 1961, NARA 745T.00/10-1661; Picard to Washington, January 14, 1963, NARA 770.00/1-1463.

53. Picard to Washington, October 30, 1961, NARA 745T.00/10-3061; Zanzibar to Washington, February 27, 1962, NARA 750T.00/2-2762.

54. Deming to Tasca, April 11, 1962, NARA RG59 3110 Office of Eastern and Southern African Affairs 1951–65; Deming to Frederick and Tasca, April 18, 1962, and attachment, NARA 611.45T/4-1162.

55. Deming to Tasca, April 11, 1962, NARA RG59 3110 Office of Eastern and Southern African Affairs 1951–65; Deming to Frederick and Tasca, April 18, 1962, and attachment, NARA 611.45T/4-1162; O'Sheel to Halsema, February 2, 1961, NARA RG59 3110 Office of Eastern and Southern African Affairs; Deming to Fredericks, March 21, 1962, NARA 745T.00/3-2162; Department of State Guideline for Policy and Operations Zanzibar, February 1963, NARA RG59 3110 Office of Eastern and Southern African Affairs.

Chapter 20

1. Baker, *Glyn Jones*, 105; Short, *Banda*, 142, 153, 159–60.

2. Jones to Monson, May 9, 1961, CO 1015/2256, in Murphy, *Central Africa*, 2:228–9; Baker, *Glyn Jones*, 112; Short, *Banda*, 162.

3. Baker, *Jones*, 118; Cabinet Conclusions, February 26, 1962, CAB 128/36/1 CC16(62), in Hyam and Louis, *Conservative*, 2:570; Brook to Macmillan, February 13, 1962, PREM 11/3943 in Murphy, *Central Africa*, 2:305; Cabinet Conclusions, May 1, 1962, CAB 128/36/1 CC 29(62)2, in Hyam and Louis, *Conservative*, 2:574; Butler to Macmillan, April 16, 1962, PREM 11/3944, in Murphy, *Central Africa*, 2:318–9; Cabinet Conclusions, October 29, 1962, CAB 128/36/2 CC 64(62)2, in Hyam and Louis, *Conservative*, 2:579.

4. Cabinet Conclusions, November 8, 1962, CAB 128/36/2 CC 67 (62)2, in Hyam and Louis, *Conservative*, 2:582; Notes on Ministerial Meeting, February 22, 1962, PREM 11/3943, in Hyam and Louis, *Conservative*, 2:565.

5. Butler to Cabinet, October 25,

1962, CO 129/111 C(62) 167 in Hyam and Louis, *Conservative*, 2:577–8; Cabinet Conclusions, October 29, 1962, CAB 128/36/2 CC 64(62)2, in Hyam and Louis, *Conservative*, 2:579.

6. Cabinet Conclusions, October 29, 1962, CAB 128/36/2 CC 64(62)2, in Hyam and Louis, *Conservative*, 2:579; Cabinet Conclusions, November 8, 1962, CAB 128/36/2 CC 67 (62)2, in Hyam and Louis, *Conservative*, 2:582.

7. Butler to Macmillan, November 23, 1962, PREM 11/3945, in Murphy, *Central Africa*, 2:344; Watson to Jones, September 10, 1962, DO 183/58, in Murphy, *Central Africa*, 2:328ff; Central African Office, Nyasaland, Economic and Financial Situation, January 1963, DO 183/114, in Murphy, *Central Africa*, 2:352ff; Butler, Cabinet Memorandum, September 17, 1963, CAB 129/114, C(63)156, in Murphy, *Central Africa*, 2:387–9.

8. Macleod to Macmillan, December 12, 1960, PM(60)70, in Murphy, *Central Africa*, 2:183ff; Mulford, *Zambia*, 181–183, 87–188; Shepherd, *Macleod*, 221, 224.

9. Bligh, Note of a Meeting, February 17, 1961, PREM 11/3487, in Murphy, *Central Africa*, 2:202; Bligh, Note of Meeting, February 18, 1961, PREM 11/3487, in Murphy, *Central Africa*, 2:203ff.

10. Macleod to Macmillan, December 12, 1960, PM(60)70, in Murphy, *Central Africa*, 2:183f; Bligh, Note of a Meeting, February 18, 1961, PREM 11/3487, in Murphy, *Central Africa*, 2:203ff.

11. Mulford, *Zambia*, 184.

12. Bligh, Note on Discussion, February 8, 1961, PREM 11/3486, in Murphy, *Central Africa*, 2:190ff; Macmillan to Welensky, February 11, 1961, PREM 11/3486, in Murphy, *Central Africa*, 2:197ff.

13. Shepherd, *Macleod*, 205, 215, 232; Mulford, *Zambia*, 190, 192–3.

14. Alport, to Sandys, July 24, 1961, CAB 21/4625, in Murphy, *Central Africa*, 2:242ff; Mulford, *Zambia*, 184.

15. Mulford, *Zambia*, 200–201.

16. Perth, Memorandum, August 28, 1961, PREM 11/3498, in Murphy, *Central Africa*, 2:253; Mulford, *Zambia*, 200.

17. Cabinet Colonial Policy Committee, January 4, 1962, CAB 134/1561 CPC 1(62), in Murphy, *Central Africa*, 2:288ff; Maudling to Macmillan, January 12, 1962, PREM 11/3942 PM(62)3, in Murphy, *Central Africa*, 2:296; Macmillan to Macleod, January 7, 1962, PREM 11/3942, in Murphy, *Central Africa*, 2:292.

18. Cabinet Conclusions, February 26, 1962, CAB 128/36/1 CC 16(62), in Hyam and Louis, *Conservative*, 2:570ff.

19. Mulford, *Zambia*, 210, 231.

20. Mulford, *Zambia*, 286; Rotberg, *Rise of Nationalism*, 315.

21. Mulford, *Zambia*, 190, 288–289, 296, 298, 303.

22. Wills, *Introduction*, 360; Mulford, *Zambia*, 305; Watson to Hone, August 28, 1963, DO 183/63, in Murphy, *Central Africa*, 2:385ff; Butler, Cabinet Memorandum, September 17, 1963, CAB 129/114 C(63) 156, in Murphy, *Central Africa*, 2:387; Wood, *So Far*, 136, 138.

23. Mulford, *Zambia*, 314, 327.

24. Emmerson to Washington, September 19, 1961, NARA 745C.00/9-1961; Emmerson to Washington, February 13, 1962, NARA 745N.00/2-1362.

25. Washington to Salisbury, March 9, 1962, NARA 745C.00/3-662, in *FRUS, 1961–63*, 21:513–4.

26. Washington to Salisbury, March 9, 1962, NARA 745C.00/3-662, in *FRUS, 1961–63*, 21:513–4.

27. Memorandum of Conversation, May 2, 1961, Department of State, President's Memoranda of Conversation, in *FRUS, 1961–63*, 21:320–1.

28. DeRoche, *Black, White, and Chrome*, 56–58; Emmerson to Washington, August 26, 1961, NARA 745C.00/8-2661; Williams to Washington, August 30, 1961, NARA 745C.00/8-3061.

29. Shaw to Le Tocq, November 16, 1961, DO 158/43, in Murphy, *Central Africa*, 2:284; Emmerson to Washington, November 17, 1961, NARA 745C.00/11-1761.

30. Hennings to Neale, October 20, 1961, DO 158/25, in Murphy, *Central Africa*, 2:275; Shaw to Le Tocq, November 16, 1961, DO 158/43, in Murphy, *Central Africa*, 2:284; Geren to Washington, August 31, 1962, NARA 611.45C/8-3162.

31. Blake, *Rhodesia*, 333.

32. Barber, *Road to Rebellion*, 69, 70.

33. Metcalf to Sandys, February 24, 1961, DO 158/10, in Murphy, *Central Africa*, 2:209; Wood, *So Far*, 74.

34. Barber, *Road to Rebellion*, 81–2; Wood *So Far*, 74–5.

35. Barber, *Road to Rebellion*, 103, 109; Wood, *So Far*, 82, 86, 93.

36. Wood, *So Far*, 76; Barber, *Road to Rebellion*, 110.

37. Barber, *Road to Rebellion*, 126, 133, 135, 151, 163; Wood, *So Far*, 90–91.

38. Barber, *Road to Rebellion*, 124, 152–3.

39. Blake, *Rhodesia*, 343; Wood, *So Far*, 100.

40. Barber, *Road to Rebellion*, 196, 203; Wood, *So Far*, 122.

41. Alport, *Sudden Assignment*, 223; Macmillan to Butler, March 21, 1963, PREM 11/4419, in Hyam and Louis, *Conservative*, 2:591; Cabinet Conclusions, March 21, 1963, CAB 128/37 CC 17(63)5, in Hyam and Louis, *Conservative*, 2:589ff; Cabinet Conclusions, March 28, 1963, CAB 128/37 CC 19(63)2, in Hyam and Louis, *Conservative*, 2:592–3.

42. Stevens to Butler, December 18, 1962, DO 183/305, in Murphy, *Central Africa*, 2:345ff; Cabinet Conclusions, March 21, 1963, CAB 128/37 CC 17(63) 5, in Hyam and Louis, *Conservative*, 2:589ff.

43. Cabinet Conclusions, March 28, 1963, CAB 128/37 CC20(63)2, in Hyam and Louis, *Conservative*, 2:593–4; Cabinet Conclusions, April 4, 1963, CAB 128/37 CC23(63)2, in Murphy, *Central Africa*, 2:364ff; Butler, Note for Record, May 14, 1963, FO 1109/536, in Murphy, *Central Africa*, 2:373ff; Wood, *So Far*, 187.

44. Wood, *So Far*, 151, 153ff, 179; Cabinet Conclusions, April 4, 1963, CAB 128/37 CC23(63)2, in Murphy, *Central Africa*, 2:364ff; Sandys to Field, December 7, 1963, in Porter and Stockwell, *British Imperial Policy*, 2:562.

45. Blake, *Rhodesia*, 348–9; Wood, *So Far*, 125–6, 151, 159ff, 180–1; Cabinet Conclusions, April 4, 1963, CAB 128/37 CC23(63)2, in Murphy, *Central Africa*, 2:364ff.

46. Barber, *Road to Rebellion*, 198, 202; Wood, *So Far*, 170; Windrich, *Rhodesian Independence*, 23–24; Murphy, *Conservative Party*, 197.

47. Wood, *So Far*, 173.

48. Emmerson to Washington, February 16, 1961, NARA 745C.00/2-1661; Emmerson to Washington, May 19, 1961, NARA 611.45C/5-1961; Emmerson to Washington, May 31, 1961, NARA 745C.00/5-3161; Emmerson to Washington, December 21, 1961, NARA 745C.00/12-2161.

49. De Roche, *Black, White and Chrome*, 53; Deming to Penfield, February 22, 1961, NARA RG 59 Records of the Bureau of African Affairs, 1956–62.

50. Emmerson to Washington, February 1, 1962, NARA 745C.00/1-3162.

51. Williams, Report on Second Trip to Africa, August-September 1961, NARA RG59 1569 Records of Policy Planning Staff.

52. Draft Guidelines for United States Policy and Operations, Federation of Rhodesia and Nyasaland, March 19, 1962, NARA RG59 Office of Eastern and Southern African Affairs, 1951–1965; Wallner to Rusk, February 22, 1962, and attachments, NARA 745C.00/2-2262.

53. Bundy to Battle, May 7, 1962, and attachment, NARA 745C.00/5-762.

54. Bundy to Battle, May 7, 1962, and attachment, NARA 745C.00/5-762.

55. Volman, "British Central Africa," 271–2, 287–8, 288–9, 291.

56. Barber, *Road to Rebellion*, 77; Dean to Home, June 11, 1962 PREM 11/4566, in Hyam and Louis, *Conservative*, 2:352ff; Wood, *So Far*, 109–110, 118; Stevenson to Washington, January 26, 1962, NARA 745C.00/1-2662; DeRoche, *Black, White and Chrome*, 67–8.

57. Wallner to Secretary, June 9, 1962, NARA 325.45C/6-962; MacKnight to Tasca, October 8, 1962, NARA RG59 3110 Office of Eastern and Southern African Affairs, 1951–1965; Volman, "British Central Africa," 274; Washington to New York, February 5, 1962, NARA 745C.00/2-162; Rusk to New York, January 11, 1962, NARA 745C.00/1-1062; Rusk to Salisbury, January 10, 1962, NARA 745C.00/1-362.

58. Washington to New York, February 5, 1962, NARA 745C.00/2-162; Washington to New York, February 14, 1962, NARA 745C.00/1262; Wallner to Secretary, June 9, 1962, NARA 325.45C/6-962; Rusk to London, June 18, 1962, NARA 745C.00/6-1862; Washington to New York, October 10, 1962, NARA 745C.00/10-1062.

59. MacKnight to Fredericks, May 11, 1962, NARA RG59 1578 Bureau of African Affairs, 1956–1962.

60. Plimpton to Washington, March 28, 1962, NARA 745C.00/3-2762; Stevenson to Washington, March 30, 1962, NARA 324.7022/3-3062; New York to Washington, June 15, 1962, NARA 745C.00/6-1562.

61. Williams to Rusk, October 3, 1962, NARA RG59 Office of Eastern and Southern African Affairs, 1951–1965.

62. Memorandum of Conversation, March 1, 1962, NARA 745C.00/3-162; London to Washington, July 17, 1962, NARA 745C.00/7-1762; Washington to London, August 17, 1962, NARA 745C.00/8-1362.

63. Memorandum of Conversation, September 8, 1961, NARA RG 59 Classified Records of G. Mennen Williams; Memorandum of Conversation, May 3, 1962, NARA 745C.00/5-2162; Memorandum of Conversation, September 12, 1962, NARA 745C.00/9-1262.

64. Washington to London, August 17, 1962, NARA 745C.00/8-1362.

65. Washington to London, August 17, 1962, NARA 745C.00/8-1362; Washington to Salisbury, September 5, 1962, NARA 745C.00/8-1362.

66. London to Washington, August 22, 1962, NARA 745C.00/8-2262; Geren to Washington, September 13, 1962, NARA 745C.00/9-1362.

67. Salisbury to Washington, May 22, 1962, NARA 745C.00/5-2162; Stevenson to Washington, May 15, 1962, NARA 745C.00/5-1562; Washington to Salisbury, September 21, 1962, NARA 745C.00/8-3162; Ball to Kennedy, September 29, 1962, NARA 745C.00/9-2962.

68. Bundy to Brubeck, September 29, 1962, NARA 745C.00/9-2962; Memorandum of Conversation, September 30, 1962, NARA 745C.00/9-3062; Washington to London, October 5, 1962, NARA 611.41/10-562; DeRoche, *Black, White and Chrome*, 70.

69. DeRoche, *Black, White, and Chrome*, 70; Salisbury to Washington, November 5, 1962, NARA 745C.00/11-562; Emmerson to Washington, November 22, 1962, NARA 745C.00/11-2261; London to Washington, December 17, 1962, NARA 641.70/12-1762; Memorandum of Conversation, November 1, 1962, NARA 745C.00/11-162; Washington to Salisbury, November 2, 1962, NARA 745C.00/11-262; Washington to Salisbury, November 30, 1962, NARA 745C.00/11-1062.

70. Position Paper, on US-UK Talks, December 5–6, 1962, NARA RG59 3110 Office of Eastern and Southern African Affairs, 1951–1965; Emmerson to Washington, September 26, 1961, NARA 745C.00/9-2661.

71. Emmerson to Washington, September 26, 1961, NARA 745C.00/9-2661.

72. Salisbury to Washington, March 23, 1962, NARA 745C.00/3-2362; Geren to Washington, March 23, 1962, NARA 745C.00/8-762; New York to Washington, October 9, 1962, NARA 745C.00/10-962; Memorandum of Conversation, October 13, 1962, NARA 745C.00/11-262.

73. Emmerson to Washington, February 16, 1961, NARA 745C.00/2-1661; Emmerson to Washington, May 31, 1961, NARA 745C.00/5-3161;

Washington to Salisbury, March 19, 1962, NARA 745C.00/3-662; Washington to Salisbury, April 5, 1962, NARA 745C.00/3-2362.

74. Washington to New York, December 18, 1962, NARA 745C.00/12-1862; Washington to London, January 7, 1963, NARA 745C.00/1-763; Noer, *Cold War*, 189; DeRoche, *Black, White and Chrome*, 75; Volman, "British Central Africa," 292.

75. Washington to London, January 7, 1963, NARA 745C.00/1-763; Washington to London, March 20, 1963, NARA POL 19 RHOD& NYAS; Butler, "Central African Federation," 145; DeRoche, *Black, White and Chrome*, 79; Volman, "British Central Africa," 225.

76. Williams to Cleveland and Tyler, March 29, 1963, NARA POL 16 RHOD; Tyler to Rusk, September 6, 1963, NARA POL 16 RHOD& NYAS.

77. Washington to Williams, October 22, 1963, NARA POL 16 RHOD.

78. Washington to London, March 20, 1963, NARA POL 19 RHOD&NYAS; London to Washington, March 30, 1963, NARA POL 19 RHOD&NYAS.

79. Washington to London, March 20, 1963, NARA POL 19 RHOD&NYAS.

80. New York to Washington, November 19, 1963, NARA POL 19 RHOD&NYAS.

81. Pearson to Washington, October 4, 1963, NARA POL 1-2 RHOD &NYAS.

82. Volman, "British Central Africa," 225; MacKnight to Williams, May 9, 1963, NARA RG59 Bureau of African Affairs; Briefing Paper on the Federation of Rhodesia and Nyasaland, June 10, 1963, NARA RG59 5235 Bureau of African Affairs.

83. DuBoulay to Watson, March 6, 1963, DO 183/462, in Murphy, *Central Africa*, 2:359.

84. Washington to New York, July 9, 1963, NARA POL 19 RHOD& NYAS; Washington to Dar-es-Salaam, April 30, 1963, NARA POL 19 RHOD&NYAS; MacKnight to Williams, May 9, 1963, NARA RG59 5235 Bureau of African Affairs; Mulcahy to MacKnight, November 1, 1963, NARA RG59 5235 Bureau of African Affairs.

85. Memorandum of Conversation, June 3, 1963, NARA RG59 Classified Records of G. Mennen Williams; Memorandum of Conversation, September 17, 1963, NARA POL 1 RHOD&NYAS; Memorandum of Conversation, October 8,

1963, National Security Files, Countries Series, Rhodesia, Kennedy Library, in FRUS, 1961–63, 21:536–8.

86. Memorandum of Conversation, April 16, 1963, NARA RG59 1552 Classified Records of G. Mennen Williams; Memorandum of Conversation, April 12, 1963, NARA POL 19 RHOD&NYAS; Williams to Sithole, April 16, 1963, NARA POL 19 PHOD&NYAS.

87. Geren to Washington, March 27, 1963, NARA 745C.00/3-2763; Geren to Washington, July 23, 1963, NARA 745C.00/7-2363; Brubeck to Bundy, July 15, 1963, NARA POL 12 RHOD&NYAS.

88. Williams and Cleveland to Rusk, September 6, 1963, NARA POL 16 RHOD&NYAS; Tyler to Rusk, September 6, 1963, NARA POL 16 RHOD&NYAS; Memorandum of Conversation, September6, 1963, NARA POL 3 RHOD&NYAS; Volman, "British Central Africa," 300.

89. Memorandum of Conversation, September 18, 1963, NARA POL 1 RHOD&NYAS.

Chapter 21

1. Noer, *Cold War*, 273, 275, 277, 278–9, 289; Lyons, "Keeping Africa Off," 250.

2. Windrich, *Rhodesian Independence*, 22; Blake, *Rhodesia*, 355.

3. Bligh, Note for Record, February 25, 1964, PREM 11/5047, in Murphy, *Central Africa*, 2:402–3; Bligh, Note for Record, February 28, 1964, PREM 11/5047, in Murphy, *Central Africa*, 2:409ff.

4. Trend to Garner, June 1, 1964, PREM 11/5048, in Murphy, *Central Africa*, 2:426ff; Trend to Garner, August 14, 1964, DO 183/293, in Murphy, *Central Africa*, 2:455ff.

5. Bligh, Note for Record, March 19, 1964, PREM 11/5047, in Murphy, *Central Africa*, 2:414ff.

6. Bligh, Note for Record, January 27, 1964, PREM 11/5046, in Murphy, *Central Africa*, 2:399ff.

7. Johnston to Sandys, June 6, 1964, DO 183/206, in Murphy, *Central Africa*, 2:429ff; Windrich, *Rhodesian Independence*, 21.

8. Cabinet Office, Record of Meeting, September 7, 1964, PREM 11/5049, in Murphy, *Central Africa*, 2:468ff.

9. Johnston to Sandys, June 6, 1964, DO 183/206, in Murphy, *Central Africa*, 2:429ff; Johnston to Sandys, October 6, 1964, PREM 13/

85, in Murphy, *Central Africa*, 2:479ff.

10. Windrich, *Rhodesian Independence*, 29–31.

11. Windrich, *Rhodesian Independence*, 32–33.

12. Trend to Wilson, November 24, 1964, PREM 13/87, in Murphy, *Central Africa*, 2:497f; Cabinet Committee on Southern Rhodesia, Minutes, March 25, 1965, CAB 21/5513, in Murphy, *Central Africa*, 2:523ff; Windrich, *Rhodesian Independence*, 34, 44, 51.

13. Windrich, *Rhodesian Independence*, 38.

14. Windrich, *Rhodesian Independence*, 39; Trend to Wilson, November 24, 1964, PREM 13/87, in Murphy, *Central Africa*, 2:497ff; Rogers to Trend, August 27, 1965, CAB 21/5513, in Murphy, *Central Africa*, 2:530–1; Trend to Wilson, October 1, 1965, PREM 13/539, in Murphy, *Central Africa*, 2:535ff.

15. Bligh, Note for the Record, March 26, 1964, PREM 11/5047, in Murphy, *Central Africa*, 2:418–9.

16. Johnston to Bottomley, March 12, 1965, FO 371/181877, in Murphy, *Central Africa*, 2:514ff; Windrich, *Rhodesian Independence*, 49.

17. Barber, *Road to Rebellion*, 298–9; Windrich, *Rhodesian Independence*, 43.

18. Windrich, *Rhodesian Independence*, 25–6, 37, 44.

19. Pearson to Washington, December 30, 1963, NARA POL 19 RHOD&NYAS; Salisbury to Washington, April 20, 1964, NARA POL 19 RHOD-S; Pearson to Washington, September 2, 1964, NARA POL 19 RHOD-S.

20. Williams to Harriman, February 4, 1964, NARA RG59 Bureau of African Affairs.

21. MacKnight to Williams, May 1, 1964, NARA RG59 Bureau of African Affairs; MacKnight to Williams, July 9, 1964, NARA POL 19 RHOD.

22. Watts, "Problem of Rhodesian Independence," 446; Haynes to Bundy, September 13, 1965, in FRUS, 1964–68, 24:801–2.

23. Memorandum of Conversation, December 19, 1963, Secretary's Memoranda of Conversation, in FRUS, 1961–63, 21:539–40; Washington to Salisbury, December 27, 1963, NARA POL 19 RHOD& NYAS.

24. Washington to Salisbury, February 5, 1964, NARA POL 19 RHOD-S.

25. Washington to Various, April 15, 1964, NARA POL 19 RHOD-S;

Watts, "Problem of Rhodesian Independence," 447.

26. Washington to London, August 27, 1964, NARA POL 16 RHOD.

27. Washington to London, September2, 1964, NARA POL 19 RHOD-S.

28. London to Washington, September 3, 1964, NARA POL 19 RHOD-S.

29. London to Washington, October 8, 1964, NARA POL 19 RHOD-S.

30. Washington to Various, October 28, 1964, NARA POL 19 RHOD; Volman, "British Central Africa," 452; Haynes to Bundy, June 14, 1965, in FRUS, 1964–68, 24:799–800.

31. MacKnight to Williams, July 9, 1964, NARA POL 19 RHOD; Volman, "British Central Africa," 450, 451, 454–5.

32. Springsteen to Trimble, May 28, 1965, NARA POL 19 RHOD; Volman, "British Central Africa," 452.

33. McClelland to Washington, November 26, 1964, NARA POL 19 RHOD; Salisbury to London, January 5, 1965, NARA POL 19 RHOD.

34. Komer to Williams, April 28, 1965, NARA POL 16 RHOD; Volman, "British Central Africa," 443.

35. Haynes to Bundy, September 13, 1965, in FRUS, 1964–68, 24:801–2; Volman, "British Central Africa," 485–6; Fredericks, to Ball, September 28, 1965, NARA POL 19 RHOD; Salisbury to Washington, September 28, 1965, NARA POL 19 RHOD.

36. Memorandum of Conversation, September 20, 1965, NARA

POL 19 RHOD; Washington to Salisbury, September 29, 1965, NARA POL 19 RHOD; London to Washington, September 30, 1965, NARA POL 19 RHOD; McClelland to Washington, October 2, 1965, NARA POL 19 RHOD.

37. London to Washington, September 29, 1965, NARA POL 19 RHOD; Ball to London, September 29, 1965, NARA POL 16 RHOD, in FRUS, 1964–68, 24:809–10.

38. Memorandum of Conversation, October 11, 1965, NARA POL 19 RHOD-S; Washington to London, October 22, 1965, NARA POL 16 RHOD.

39. "Repercussions of a Unilateral Declaration of Independence by Southern Rhodesia," Special National Intelligence Estimate, October 13, 1965, in Central Intelligence Agency FOIA Documents, www.foia.cia.gov.

40. "Repercussions of a Unilateral Declaration of Independence by Southern Rhodesia," Special National Intelligence Estimate, October 13, 1965, in Central Intelligence Agency FOIA Documents, www.foia.cia.gov.

41. New York to Washington, October 2, 1965, NARA POL 19 RHOD, in FRUS, 1964–68, 24:813–4; Johnson to Wilson, October 5, 1965, National Security Files, Memoranda to the President, McGeorge Bundy, Vol. 15, Johnson Library, in FRUS, 1964–68, 24:817; Washington to London, October 6, 1965, NARA POL 19 RHOD, in FRUS, 1964–68, 24:819–20; DeRoche, Black, White and Chrome, 109; Volman, "British Central Africa," 490–91.

42. Washington to London, October 22, 1965, NARA POL 19 RHOD; Bundy to Johnson, October 29, 1965, National Security File, United Kingdom Memoranda and Miscellaneous, Vol. 7, Johnson Library, in FRUS, 1964–68, 24:829–30; DeRoche, Black, White and Chrome, 111.

43. Salisbury to Washington, October 30, 1965, NARA POL 19 RHOD.

44. Witt to Washington, July 16, 1964, NARA POL 2 BAS; Campbell to MacKnight, November 1, 1963, NARA RG59 5235 Bureau of African Affairs; Clack to Washington, June 4, 1963, NARA POL BECH; Bureau of African Affairs, Paper on High Commission Territories, January 20, 1964, NARA RG59 5235 Bureau of African Affairs; Satterthwaite to Washington, July 26, 1962, NARA 745D. 00/7-2662.

45. Witt to Washington, July 16, 1964, NARA POL 2 BAS.

46. Satterthwaite to Washington, November 19, 1963, NARA POL 19 BAS; Haynes to MacKnight, January 6, 1964, NARA RG59 5235 Bureau of African Affairs.

47. Witt to Washington, July 16, 1964, NARA POL 2 BAS; Witt to Washington, January 5, 1963, NARA 745F.00/1-563; Hooper to Fredericks, May 5, 1964, NARA RG59 Bureau of African Affairs.

48. Haynes to Hooper, February 17, 1964, NARA RG59 5235 Bureau of African Affairs; Hooper to Fredericks, May 5, 1964, NARA RG59 5235 Bureau of African Affairs.

Bibliography

Acheson, Dean. *Present at the Creation: My Years in the State Department.* New York: W.W. Norton, 1969.

_____. "United States Position on Problems Confronting Fourth General Assembly." *Department of State Bulletin* 21, no. 535 (October 1949): 3.

Adamson, Michael R. "The Most Important Single Aspect of Our Foreign Policy: The Eisenhower Administration, Foreign Aid and the Third World." In *The Eisenhower Administration, the Third World and the Globalization of the Cold War*, edited by Kathryn Statler and Andrew L. Johns. Lanham, MD: Rowan and Littlefield, 2006.

Adamthwaite, Anthony. "Overstretched and Overstrung: Eden, the Foreign Office and the Making of Policy, 1951–5." International Affairs 64, no. 2 (Spring 1988): 241–259.

Aldous, Richard. "A Family Affair: Macmillan and the Art of Personal Diplomacy." In *Harold Macmillan and Britain's World Role*, edited by Richard Aldous and Sabine Lee. London: Palgrave Macmillan, 1996.

Allen, George V. "United States Foreign Policy in Africa." *Department of State Bulletin* 34, no. 879 (April 30, 1956): 716–18.

Alport, Lord. *The Sudden Assignment.* London: Hodder and Stoughton, 1965.

Anderson, David. *Histories of the Hanged: The Dirty War in Kenya and the End of Empire.* New York: W.W. Norton, 2005.

Apter, David. *Ghana in Transition.* New York: Atheneum, 1963.

_____. *The Political Kingdom in Uganda: A Study in Bureaucratic Nationalism.* London: Frank Cass, 1997.

Austin, Dennis. *Politics in Ghana, 1946–60.* London: Oxford University Press, 1964.

Ayany, Samuel G. *A History of Zanzibar: A Study in Constitutional Development, 1934–1964.* Nairobi: East African Literature Bureau, 1970.

Bade, Albert. *Benedicto Kiwanuka: The Man and His Politics.* Kampala: Fountain Publishers, 1996.

Baker, Colin. *Retreat from Empire: Sir Robert Armitage in Africa and Cyprus.* London: I.B. Tauris, 1998.

_____. *Sir Glyn Jones: A Proconsul in Africa.* London: I.B. Tauris, 2000.

_____. *State of Emergency: Crisis in Central Africa, Nyasaland, 1959–60.* London: Tauris Academic Studies, 1997.

Ball, Simon. "Banquo's Ghost: Lord Salisbury, Harold Macmillan and the High Politics of Decolonization, 1957–1963." *Twentieth Century British History* 16, no. 1 (2005): 74–102.

_____. *The Guardsmen: Harold Macmillan, Three Friends, and the World They Made.* London: Harper Collins, 2004.

Barber, James. *Rhodesia: The Road to Rebellion.* London: Oxford University Press, 1967.

Barnard, Ellsworth. *Wendell Willkie: Fighter for Freedom.* Marquette: Northern Michigan University Press, 1966.

Bartlett, C.J. *The Special Relationship: A Political History of Anglo-American Relations Since 1945.* London: Longman, 1992.

Baston, Lewis. *Reggie: The Life of Reginald Maudling.* Stroud, U.K.: Sutton, 2004.

Baylis, John, ed. *Anglo-American Relations Since 1939: The Enduring Alliance.* Manchester: Manchester University Press, 1997.

Beisner, Robert L. *Dean Acheson: A Life in the Cold War.* Oxford: Oxford University Press, 2006.

Belmonte, Monica. "Reining in Revolution: The United States Response to British Decolonization in Nigeria in an Era of Civil Rights, 1953–1960," Ph.D. Diss., Georgetown University, 2003.

Beloff, Lord. "The End of the British Empire and the Assumption of World Wide Commitments by the United States." In *The Special Relationship: Anglo-American Relations Since 1945*, edited by William Roger Louis and Hedley Bull. Oxford: Clarendon Press, 1986.

Bennett, George. *Kenya: A Political History: The Colonial Period.* London: 1963.

Berman, Bruce. *Control and Crisis in Colonial Kenya: The Dialectic of Domination.* London: James Currey, 1990.

Beshir, Mohamed Omer. *Revolution and Nationalism in the Sudan.* New York: Barnes and Noble, 1974.

Bills, Scott L. *Empire and Cold War: The Roots of U.S.–Third World Antagonism, 1945–47.* New York: 1990.

Bingham, Jonathan. "Statement before United Nations General Assembly, November 22, 1961." *Department of State Bulletin* 46, no. 1176 (January 8, 1962): 69–76.

Blake, Robert. *A History of Rhodesia.* New York: Alfred A. Knopf, 1978.

Blitz, Amy. *The Contested State: American Foreign Policy and Regime Change in the Philippines.* Lanham, MD: Rowan and Littlefield, 2000.

Blundell, Michael. *A Love Affair with the Sun.* Nairobi: Kenway Publications, 1994.

Borstelmann, Thomas. *Apartheid's Reluctant Uncle: The United States and Southern Africa in the Early Cold War.* Oxford: Oxford University Press, 1993.

Bowles, B.D. "The Struggle for Independence, 1946–1963." In *Zanzibar Under Colonial Rule*, edited by Abdul Sherif and Ed Ferguson. London: James Curry, 1991.

Boyce, D. George. *Decolonisation and the British Empire, 1775–1997.* New York: St. Martin's, 1999.

Boyle, Peter, ed. *The Churchill-Eisenhower Correspondence.* Chapel Hill: University of North Carolina Press, 1990.

_____. "The Special Relationship with Washington." In *The Foreign Policy of Churchill's Peacetime Administration, 1951–55*, edited by John W. Young. Leicester: Leicester University Press, 1988.

Brands, H.W. *Inside the Cold War: Loy Henderson and the Rise of the American Empire, 1918–1961.* New York: Oxford University Press, 1991.

_____. *Bound to Empire: The United States and the Philippines.* New York: Oxford University Press, 1992.

Butler, L.J. *Britain and Empire: Adjusting to a Post Imperial World.* London: I.B. Tauris, 2002.

_____. "Britain, the United States and the Demise of the Central African Federation, 1959–1963." *Journal of Imperial and Commonwealth History* 28, no. 3 (September 2000): 131–151.

Cain, P.J., and A.G. Hopkins. *British Imperialism: Crisis and Deconstruction, 1914–1990.* London: Longman, 1993.

Callahan, Raymond A. *Churchill: Retreat from Empire.* Wilmington, DE: Scholarly Resources, 1984.

Carlton, David. *Anthony Eden: A Biography.* London: Allen Lane, 1981.

Cell, John W. *Hailey: A Study in Imperialism, 1972–1969.* Cambridge: Cambridge University Press, 1992.

Charmley, John. *Churchill's Grand Alliance.* London: Harcourt Brace, 1995.

"The Choleric Lords." *Time* (March 17, 1961).

Clymer, Kenton J. "The Education of William Phillips: Self Determination and American Policy toward India, 1942–45." *Diplomatic History* 8, no.1 (Winter 1984): 13–36.

_____. "Franklin D. Roosevelt, Louis Johnson, India and Anticolonialism: Another Look." *Pacific Historical Review* 57, no. 3 (August 1988): 261–284.

_____. *Quest for Freedom: The United States and India's Independence.* New York: Columbia University Press, 1995.

Cohen, Michael J. *Truman and Israel.* Berkeley: University of California Press, 1990.

Crowder, Michael. *A Short History of Nigeria.* New York: Frederick A. Praeger, 1966.

Culver, John, and John Hyde. *American Dreamer: A Life of Henry A. Wallace.* New York: W.W. Norton, 2000.

Dallek, Robert. *Franklin D. Roosevelt and American Foreign Policy.* New York: Oxford University Press, 1979.

Dalton, Hugh. *High Tide and After.* London: Muller, 1962.

Daly, M.W. *Imperial Sudan: the Anglo-Egyptian Condominium, 1934–1956.* Cambridge: Cambridge University Press, 1991.

Darby, Philip. *Three Faces of Imperialism: British and American Approaches to Asia and Africa, 1870–1970.* New Haven, CT: Yale University Press, 1987.

Darwin, John. "British Decolonization since 1945: A Pattern or a Puzzle?" *Journal of Imperial and Commonwealth History* 12, no. 2 (January 1984): 187–209.

_____. *Britain and Decolonisation: The Retreat from Empire in the Post-War World.* New York: St. Martin's, 1988.

Department of State, Office of the Historian. "A History of the United States Department of State, 1789–1996." http://www.state.gov/www/about_state/history/dephis.html#superpower. (Accessed August 10, 2007)

DeRoche, Andrew. *Black, White and Chrome: The United States and Zimbabwe, 1953–1998.* Trenton, NJ: Africa World Press, 2001.

Dockrill, Michael. *British Defence Since 1945.* London: Basil Blackwell, 1988.

Douglas, R.M. "An Offer They Couldn't Refuse: The British Left, Colonies and International Trusteeship, 1940–1951." In *Imperialism on Trial: International Oversight of Colonial Rule in Historical Perspective*, edited by R.M. Douglas, Michael D. Callahan, and Elizabeth Bishop. Lanham, MD: Lexington Books, 2006.

Douglas-Home, Charles. *Evelyn Baring: The Last Proconsul.* London: Collins, 1978.

Dulles, Foster R., and Gerald E. Ridinger. "The Anti-Colonial Policies of Franklin D. Roosevelt." *Political Science Quarterly* 70, 1 (1955): 1–18.

Dulles, John Foster. "Challenge and Response in United States Policy." *Department of State Bulletin* 37, no. 954 (October 7, 1957): 569–579.

_____."The Moral Imperative." *Department of State Bulletin* 29, no. 753 (November 30, 1953): 741–44.

Edmonds, R. *Setting the Mould: The United States and Britain, 1945–50.* Oxford: Oxford University Press, 1987.

El-Ayouty, Yassin. *The United Nations and Decolonization: The Role of Afro-Asia.* The Hague: Matinius Nijhoff, 1971.

Fabunmi, L.A. *The Sudan in Anglo-Egyptian Relations: A Case Study in Power Politics, 1800–1956.* Westport, CT: Greenwood Press, 1974.

Feinstein, Charles H. "The End of Empire and the Golden Age." In *Understanding Decline: Perceptions and Realities of British Economic Performance*, edited by Peter Clarke and Clive Trebilcock. Cambridge: Cambridge University Press, 1997.

Fieldhouse, D.K. "The Labour Governments and the Empire-Commonwealth, 1945–51." In *The Foreign Policy of the British Labour Governments, 1945–51*, edited by Ritchie Ovendale. Leicester: Leicester University Press, 1984.

Fisher, Nigel. *Iain Macleod.* London: Andre Deutsch, 1973.

Freeland, Robert M. *The Truman Doctrine and the Origins of McCarthyism: Foreign Policy, Domestic Politics and Internal Security, 1946–1948.* New York: Alfred A. Knopf, 1972.

Friend, Theodore. *Between Two Empires: The Ordeal of the Philippines, 1929–1946.* New Haven, CT: Yale University Press, 1965.

Furedi, Frank. *Colonial Wars and the Politics of Third World Nationalism.* London: I.B. Tauris, 1994.

_____. "Creating a Breathing Space: The Political Management of Colonial Emergencies." *Journal of Imperial and Commonwealth History* 21, no. 3 (September 1993): 89–106.

_____. "Kenya: Decolonization through Counter-Insurgency. In *Contemporary British History*, edited by Anthony Gorst, Lewis Johnson, and W. Scott Lucas. London: Pinter Publishers, 1991.

Gardner, Lloyd. *Architects of Illusion: Men and Ideas in American Foreign Policy, 1941–49.* Chicago: Quadrangle Books, 1970.

_____. "The Atlantic Charter: Idea and Reality, 1942–1945." In *The Atlantic Charter*, edited by Douglas Brinkley and David R. Facey-Crowther. New York: St. Martin's, 1994.

_____. *Economic Aspects of New Deal Diplomacy.* Madison: University of Wisconsin Press, 2000.

_____. "How We Lost Vietnam, 1950–54." In *The United States and Decolonization: Power and Free-dom*, edited by D. Ryan and V. Pungong. London: Macmillan Press, 2000.

Ghai, Dharma P. "The Bugandan Trade Boycott: A Study in Tribal, Political and Economic Nationalism." In *Protest and Power in Black Africa*, edited by Robert I. Rotberg and Ali A. Mazrui. New York: Oxford University Press, 1970.

Gilbert, Martin. *Never Despair: Winston Churchill, 1945–1965.* London: Heinemann, 1988.

Goldsworthy, David. "Britain and the International Critics of British Colonialism, 1951–56." *The Journal of Commonwealth and Comparative Politics* 29, no.1 (March 1991): 1–24.

_____, ed. *The Conservative Government and the End of Empire, 1951–57: Part I: International Relations.* London: Institute of Commonwealth Studies, 1994.

_____, ed. *The Conservative Government and the End of Empire, 1951–57: Part II: Politics and Administration.* London: Institute of Commonwealth Studies, 1994.

_____, ed. *The Conservative Government and the End of Empire, 1951–57: Part III: Economic and Social Relations.* London: Institute of Commonwealth Studies, 1994.

_____. "Keeping Change Within Bounds: Aspects of Colonial Policy During the Eden and Churchill Governments." *Journal of Imperial and Commonwealth History* 18, no. 1 (1980): 100–113.

_____. *Tom Mboya: The Man Kenya Wanted to Forget.* London: Heinemann, 1982.

Gordon, David F. *Decolonization and the State in Kenya.* Boulder, CO: Westview, 1986.

Griffith, Robert. "Dwight Eisenhower and the Corporate Commonwealth." *American Historical Review* 87, no.1 (February 1982): 87–122.

Grunder, Garel A., and William E. Livezy. *The Philippines and the United States.* Norman: University of Oklahoma Press, 1951.

Guhin, Michael A. *John Foster Dulles: A Statesman and His Times.* New York: Columbia University Pres, 1972.

Gupta, Partha Sarathai. *Imperialism and the British Labour Movement, 1914–1964.* New York: Holmes and Meier, 1975.

Hagen, James M., and Vernon W. Ruttan. "Development Policy Under Eisenhower and Kennedy." *Journal of Developing Areas* 23 (October 1988): 1–30.

Hahn, Peter L. *The United States, Great Britain and Egypt, 1945–56.* Chapel Hill: University of North Carolina Press, 1991.

Hancock, I.R. "Patriotism and Neo-Traditionalism in Buganda: the Kabaka Yekka (The King Alone) Movement, 1961–62." *Journal of African History* 11, no. 3 (1970): 419–434.

Hanes, W. Travis III. *Imperial Diplomacy in the Era of Decolonization: The Sudan and Anglo-Egyptian*

Relations, 1945–1956. Westport, CT: Greenwood Press, 1995.

Hargreaves, John D. "Assumptions, Expectations and Plans: Approaches to Decolonisation in Sierra Leone." In *Decolonisation and After: The British and French Experience*, edited by W.H. Morris-Jones and George Fischer. London: F. Cass, 1980.

_____. "Towards the Transfer of Power in British West Africa." In *The Transfer of Power in Africa: Decolonization, 1940–1960*, edited by Prosser Gifford and William Roger Louis. New Haven, CT: Yale University Press, 1982.

Hathaway, Robert M. *Ambiguous Partnership: Britain and America, 1944–1947*. New York: Columbia University Press, 1981.

Havinden, Michael, and David Meredith. *Colonialism and Development: Britain and Its Tropical Colonies: 1850–1960*. London: Routledge, 1993.

Hearden, Patrick J. *Architects of Globalism: Building a New World Order During World War II*. Fayetteville: University of Arkansas Press, 2002.

Heinlein, Frank. *British Government Policy and Decolonization, 1945–1963: Scrutinizing the Official Mind*. London: Frank Cass, 2002.

Hemming, Philip E. "Macmillan and the End of the British Empire." In *Harold Macmillan and Britain's World Role*, edited by Richard Aldous and Sabine Lee. London: Palgrave Macmillan, 1996.

Hennessy, Peter. *Having It So Good: Britain in the Fifties*. London: Penguin, 2006.

Herring, George C. "The United States and British Bankruptcy, 1944–45: Responsibilities Deferred." *Political Science Quarterly* 86, no. 2 (June 1971): 260–280.

Hess, Gary R. *American Encounters India, 1941–1947*. Baltimore: Johns Hopkins Press, 1972.

_____. *The United States' Emergence as a Southeast Asian Power*. New York: Columbia University Press, 1987.

Hilderbrand, Robert C. *Dumbarton Oaks: The Origins of the United Nations and the Search for Postwar Security*. Chapel Hill: University of North Carolina Press, 1990.

Hogan, Michael J. *A Cross of Iron: Harry S. Truman and the Origins of the National Security State, 1945–1954*. Cambridge: Cambridge University Press, 1998.

Hopkins, Anthony. "Macmillan's Audit of Empire, 1957." In *Understanding Decline: Perceptions and Reality of British Economic Performance*, edited by Peter Clarke and Clive Trebilcock. Cambridge: Cambridge University Press, 1997.

Hopley, Phil. *JFK Link*. http://www.jfklink.com/

Holland, R.F. "The Imperial Factor in British Strategies from Attlee to Macmillan, 1945–63." *Journal of Imperial and Commonwealth History* 12, 2 (January 1984): 165–86.

Horne, Alistair. *Harold Macmillan: vol. II, 1957–1986*. New York: Viking, 1989.

Howard, Anthony. *RAB: The Life of R.A. Butler*. London: Jonathan Cape, 1987.

Howe, Stephen. *Anticolonialism in British Politics: The Left and the End of Empire, 1918–1964*. Oxford: Clarendon Press, 1993.

Hyam, Ronald, "Africa and the Labour Government, 1945–1951." *Journal of Imperial and Commonwealth History* 16, 3 (May 1988): 148–172.

_____. "Bureaucracy and 'Trusteeship' in the Colonial Empire." In *The Oxford History of the British Empire*, vol. 20, *The Twentieth Century*, edited by Judith M. Brown and William Roger Louis. Oxford: Oxford University Press, 1999.

_____. ed. *The Labour Government and the End of Empire, 1945–51, Part I: High Policy and Administration*. London: HMSO, 1992.

_____. ed. *The Labour Government and the End of Empire, 1945–51, Part II: Economics and International Relations*. London: HMSO, 1992.

_____. ed. *The Labour Government and the End of Empire, 1945–51, Part III: Strategy, Politics and Constitutional Change*. London: HMSO, 1992.

Hyam, Ronald and William Roger Louis, eds. *The Conservative Government and the End of Empire, 1957–1964, Part I: High Policy, Political and Constitutional Change*. London: The Stationary Office, 2000.

_____. *The Conservative Government and the End of Empire, 1957–1964, Part II: Economics, International Relations and the Commonwealth*. London: The Stationary Office, 2000.

Ibingira, G.S.K. *The Forging of an African Nation: The Political and Constitutional Evolution of Uganda from Colonial Rule to Independence, 1894–1962*. New York: Viking Press, 1973.

Iliffe, John. *A Modern History of Tanganyika*. Cambridge: Cambridge University Press, 1979.

Ingham, Kenneth. *A History of East Africa*. New York: Frederick A. Praeger, 1967.

_____. *Obote: A Political Biography*. London: Routledge, 1994.

Iweriebor, Ehiedu E.G. *Radical Politics in Nigeria, 1945–60: The Significance of the Zikist Movement*. Zaria: Ahmadu Bello Press, 1996.

Johnson, Douglas, ed. *Sudan, Part I, 1942–1950*. London: The Stationary Office, 1998.

_____. *Sudan, Part II, 1951–56*. London: The Stationary Office, 1998.

Karugire, Samwiri R. *A Political History of Uganda*. London: Heinemann Educational Books, 1980.

Kaufman, Burton I. *Trade and Aid: Eisenhower's Foreign Economic Policy, 1953–1961*. Baltimore: Johns Hopkins University Press, 1982.

Kennedy, John F. "Imperialism — The Enemy of Freedom," July 2, 1957, http//www.jfklink.com/speeches/congress.

Kennedy, Paul. *The Rise and Fall of the Great Powers: Economic Change and Military Conflict from 1500 to 2000*. New York: Random House, 1987.

Kent, John. *British Imperial Strategy and the Origins of the Cold War, 1944–49*. Leicester: Leicester University Press, 1993.

_____. "The United States and the Decolonization of Black Africa." In *The United States and Decolonization: Power and Freedom*, edited by David Ryan and Victor Pungong. London: Macmillan Press, 2000.

_____. "United States Reactions to Empire, Colonialism and Cold War in Black Africa, 1949–1957." *Journal of Imperial and Commonwealth History* 33, no. 2 (May 2005): 195–220.

Kimball, Warren. ed. *Churchill and Roosevelt: The Complete Correspondence*. Princeton, NJ: Princeton University Press, 1984.

_____. *The Juggler: Franklin Roosevelt as Wartime Statesman*. Princeton, NJ: Princeton University Press, 1991.

_____. "Lend-Lease and the Open Door: The Temptation of British Opulence, 1937–1942." *Political Science Quarterly* 86, no. 2 (June 1971): 232–259.

Kingseed, Cole C. *Eisenhower and the Suez Crisis of 1956*. Baton Rouge: Louisiana State University Press, 1995.

Kirk-Greene, Anthony H.M. *A Biographical Dictionary of the British Colonial Governor*, vol. 1, *Africa*. Stanford, CA: Hoover Institution Press, 1980.

Kresse, Kenneth A. "Containing Nationalism and Communism on the Dark Continent: Eisenhower's Policy toward Africa, 1953–1961." Ph.D. Diss., University of Albany, 2003.

Krozewski, Gerold. "Sterling, the Minor Territories, and the End of Formal Empire." *Economic History Review* 46 (1993): 239–65.

_____. "Finance and Empire: the Dilemma Facing Great Britain in the 1950s." *International History Review* 18, no. 1 (1996): 48–70.

Kyle, Keith. *The Politics of the Independence of Kenya*. London: St. Martin's, 1999.

LaFeber, Walter. "The American View of Decolonization, 1776–1920: an Ironic Legacy." In *The United States and Decolonization: Power and Freedom*, edited by David Ryan and Victor Pungong. London: Macmillan, 2000.

Lamb, Richard. *The Macmillan Years, 1957–1963: The Emerging Truth*. London: John Murray, 1995.

Langer, William L., and S. Everett Gleason. *The Undeclared War, 1940–41*. Gloucester: Peter Smith, 1968.

Lee, J.M. "'Forward Thinking' and War: the Colonial Office during the 1940s." *Journal of Imperial and Commonwealth History* 6, no. 1 (October 1977): 64–79.

Listowel, Judith. *The Making of Tanganyika*. New York: House and Maxwell, 1965.

Lofchie, Michael F. *Zanzibar: Background to Revolution*. Princeton: Princeton University Press, 1965.

Louis, William Roger. "American Anti-colonialism and the Dissolution of the British Empire." *International Affairs* 61, no. 3 (Summer 1985): 395–420.

_____. *The British Empire in the Middle East, 1945–51: Arab Nationalism, the United States and Postwar Imperialism*. Oxford: Clarendon Press, 1984.

_____. *Imperialism at Bay: The United States and the Decolonization of the British Empire, 1941–1945*. New York: Oxford University Press, 1978.

Louis, William Roger, and Ronald Robinson. "Empire Preserv'd: How the Americans Put Anti-Communism before Anti-Imperialism." In *Decolonization: Perspectives from Now and Then*, edited by Prasenjit Duara. London: Routledge, 2004.

_____. "The Imperialism of Decolonization." *Journal of Imperial and Commonwealth History* 22, no. 3 (September 1994): 462–511.

_____. "The United States and the Liquidation of British Empire in Tropical Africa, 1941–1951." In *The Transfer of Power in Africa: Decolonization, 1940–1960*, edited by Prosser Gifford and William Roger Louis. New Haven, CT: Yale University Press, 1982.

Low, D. Anthony. *Eclipse of Empire*. Cambridge: Cambridge University Press, 1991.

_____. "The End of the British Empire in Africa." In *Decolonization and African Independence: The Transfer of Power, 1960–1980*, edited by Prosser Gifford and William Roger Louis. New Haven, CT: Yale University Press, 1988.

Lynn, Martin, "The Eastern Crisis of 1955–57, the Colonial Office and Nigerian Decolonisation." *Journal of Imperial and Commonwealth History* 30, no. 3 (September 2002): 91–109.

_____, ed. *Nigeria: Part I, Managing Political Reform, 1943–1953*. London: The Stationary Office, 2001.

_____, ed. *Nigeria: Part II, Moving to Independence, 1953–1960*. London: The Stationary Office, 2002.

_____. "Nigerian Complications: the Colonial Office, the Colonial Service and the 1953 Crisis in Nigeria." In *Administering Empire: the British Colonial Service in Retrospect*, edited by John Smith. London: University of London Press, 1999.

_____. "We Cannot Let the North Down: British Policy and Nigeria in the 1950s." In *The British Empire in the 1950s: Retreat or Revival*, edited by Martin Lynn. Basingstoke: Palgrave Macmillan, 2006.

Lyons, Terrence. "Keeping Africa off the Agenda." In *Lyndon Johnson Confronts the World: American Foreign Policy, 1963–1968*, edited by Warren I. Cohen and Nancy B. Tucker. Cambridge: Cambridge University Press, 1994.

Lyttelton, Oliver. *The Memoirs of Lord Chandos: An Unexpected View from the Summit*. New York: New American Library, 1963.

Macmillan, Harold. *Pointing the Way, 1959–1961*. New York: Harper and Row, 1972.

Maguire, G. Andrew. *Toward "Uhuru" in Tanzania: The Politics of Participation*. Cambridge: Cambridge University Press, 1969.

Maier, Charles S. "Alliance and Autonomy: European Identity and U. S. Foreign Policy Objectives in the Truman Years." In *The Truman Presidency*, edited by Michael Lacey. New York: Cambridge University Press, 1989.

Mahoney, Richard D. *JFK: Ordeal in Africa*. New York: Oxford University Press, 1983.

Marshall, George. "Address to United Nations General Assembly, September 29, 1948." Department of State Bulletin 19, no. 482 (October 1948): 432–435.

Matongo, Albert B. "United States Policy toward Zambia and Southern Africa: From Eisenhower to Reagan." Ph.D. Diss., University of Minnesota, 1999.

McCay, John T. *Acheson and Empire: the British Accent in American Foreign Policy*. Columbia: University of Missouri Press, 2001.

McGhee, George. "Africa's Role in the Free World Today," *Department of State Bulletin* 25, no. 629 (July 16, 1951), 97–101.

_____. *Envoy to the Middle World*. New York: Harper and Row, 1983.

_____. "United States Interests in Africa." *Department of State Bulletin* 22, no. 72 (June 19, 1950): 999–1003.

McIntyre, W. David. "The Admission of Small States to the Commonwealth." *Journal of Imperial and Commonwealth History* 24, no. 2 (May 1996): 244–277.

McKay, Vernon. *Africa in World Politics*. New York: Harper and Row, 1963.

McKercher, B.J.C. *Transition of Power: Britain's Loss of Global Pre-eminence to the United States, 1930–1945*. Cambridge: Cambridge University Press, 1999.

McLellan, David S. *Dean Acheson: The State Department Years*. New York: Dodd, Mead, 1976.

Metcalfe, G.E. *Great Britain and Ghana: Documents of Ghana History, 1807–1957*. London: Thomas Nelson, 1964.

Middleton, John, and Jane Campbell. *Zanzibar: Its Society and Its Politics*. London: Oxford University Press, 1965.

Mulford, David C. *Zambia: the Politics of Independence, 1957–1964*. Oxford: Oxford University Press, 1967.

Munene, Macharia. *The Truman Administration and the Decolonisation of Sub-Saharan Africa*. Nairobi: Nairobi University Press, 1995.

Murphy, Philip. *Alan Lennox-Boyd: A Biography*. London: I.B. Tauris, 1999.

_____, ed. *Central Africa, Part I, Closer Association, 1945–58*. London: The Stationary Office, 2005.

_____, ed. *Central Africa, Part II, Crisis and Dissolution, 1959–1965*. London: The Stationary Office, 2005.

_____. "Government by Blackmail: the Origins of the Central African Federation Reconsidered." In *The British Empire in the 1950s: Retreat or Revival*, edited by Martin Lynn. London: Palgrave Macmillan, 2006.

_____. *Party Politics and Decolonization: The Conservative Party and British Colonial Policy in Tropical Africa, 1951–1964*. Oxford: Oxford University Press, 1995.

Murray, James N. *The United Nations Trusteeship System*. Urbana: University of Illinois Press, 1957.

Neal, Steve. *Dark Horse: A Biography of Wendell Willkie*. Garden City, NY: Doubleday, 1984.

Newsom, David D. *The Imperial Mantle: The United States, Decolonization and the Third World*. Bloomington: University of Indiana Press, 2001.

Nkrumah, Kwame. *The Autobiography of Kwame Nkrumah*. Edinburgh: Thomas Nelson and Sons, 1957.

Noer, Thomas J. *Cold War and Black Liberation: The United States and White Rule in Africa, 1948–1968*. New York: Columbia University Press, 1985.

_____. *Soapy: A Biography of G. Mennen Williams*. Ann Arbor: University of Michigan Press, 2005.

Nwaubani, Chidiebe A. "The United States and Decolonization in West Africa, 1950–1960." Ph.D. Diss., University of Toronto, 1995.

Ocitti, Jim. *Political Evolution and Democratic Practice in Uganda, 1952–1996*. Lewiston, NY: Edwin Mellen Press, 2000.

Offner, Arnold A. *Another Such Victory: President Truman and the Cold War, 1945–1953*. Stanford, CA: Stanford University Press, 2002.

Ogot, B.A. "The Decisive Years, 1956–63." In *Decolonization and Independence in Kenya, 1940–93*, edited by B.A. Ogot and W.E. Ochieng. London: James Curry, 1995.

Orde, Anne. *The Eclipse of Great Britain: the United States and British Imperial Decline, 1895–1956*. New York: St. Martin's, 1996.

Ostrower, Gary. *The United Nations and the United States*. New York: Twayne Publishers, 1998.

O'Sullivan, Christopher, *Sumner Welles, Postwar Planning and the Quest for a New World Order*. New York: Columbia University Press, 2003 (http://www.gutenberg-e.org).

Ovendale, Ritchie. *Anglo-American Relations in the Twentieth Century*. New York: St: Martin's, 1998.

_____. "Egypt and the Suez Base Agreement." In

The Foreign Policy of Churchill's Peacetime Administration, 1951–1955, edited by John W. Young. Leicester: Leicester University Press, 1988.

_____, ed. *The Foreign Policy of the British Labour Governments, 1945–51*. Leicester: Leicester University Press, 1984.

_____. "Macmillan and the Wind of Change in Africa, 1957–60." *Historical Journal* 38, no. 2 (1995): 455–477.

Owen, Nicholas, ed. "Decolonisation and the Colonial Office." *Contemporary Record*, 6, no. 3 (Winter 1992): 497–535.

Palmer, Joseph. "The Problems and Prospects of Sub Sahara Africa: A United States Point of View." *Department of State Bulletin* 37 no. 963 (December 9, 1957): 930–32.

Paterson, Thomas G. "Foreign Aid under Wraps: The Point Four Program." *Wisconsin Magazine of History* 52, no. 2 (1972–73): 119–126.

Pearce, R.D. "The Colonial Office and Planned Decolonization in Africa." *African Affairs* 83, no. 330 (January 1984): 77–94.

_____. "The Colonial Office in 1947 and the Transfer of Power in Africa: An Addendum to John Cell." *Journal of Imperial and Commonwealth History* 10, no. 2 (January 1982): 211–215.

_____. "Governors, Nationalists and Constitutions in Nigeria, 1935–1951. *Journal of Imperial and Commonwealth History* 9, no. 3 (May 1981): 289–307.

_____. *The Turning Point in Africa: British Colonial Policy, 1938–1948*. London: Frank Cass, 1982

Percox, David A. *Britain, Kenya, and the Cold War: Imperial Defence, Colonial Security and Decolonisation*. London: I.B. Tauris, 2004.

_____. "Internal Security and Decolonization in Kenya, 1956–63." *Journal of Imperial and Commonwealth History* 29, no. 1 (January 2001): 92–116.

Perkins, Bradford. "Unequal Partners: the Truman Administration and Great Britain." In *The Special Relationship: Anglo-American Relations Since 1945*, edited by William Roger Louis and Hedley Bull. Oxford: Clarendon, 1986.

Pomeroy, William J. *The Philippines: Colonialism, Collaboration and Resistance*. New York: International Publishers, 1992.

Porter, A.N., and A.J. Stockwell, eds. *British Imperial Policy and Decolonization, 1938–1951*. Vol. 1. London: St. Martin's, 1987.

_____. *British Imperial Policy and Decolonization, 1951–1964*. Vol. 2. London: St. Martin's, 1989.

Pratt, Cranford. *The Critical Phase in Tanzania, 1945–1968: Nyerere and the Emergence of a Socialist Strategy*. Cambridge: Cambridge University Press, 1976.

Pruden, Caroline. *Conditional Partners: Eisenhower, the United Nations and the Search for a Permanent Peace*. Baton Rouge: Louisiana State University Press, 1998.

Pungong, Victor. "The United States and the International Trusteeship System." In *The United States and Decolonization: Power and Freedom*, edited by David Ryan and Victor Pungong. London: Macmillan, 2000.

Range, Willard. *Franklin D. Roosevelt's World Order*. Athens: University of Georgia Press, 1959.

Rathbone, Richard, ed. *Ghana, Part I, 1941–52*. London: Her Majesty's Stationary Office, 1992.

_____. *Ghana, Part II, 1952–57*. London: Her Majesty's Stationary Office, 1992.

_____. "Police Intelligence in Ghana in the Late 1940s and 1950s." *Journal of Imperial and Commonwealth History* 21 no. 3 (September 1993): 107–128.

Renwick, Robin. *Fighting with Allies: America and Britain in Peace and War*. Houndmills, Basingstoke, Hampshire: Macmillan, 1996.

Robertson, Sir James. *Transition in Africa: From Direct Rule to Independence*. New York: Barnes and Noble, 1974.

Rooney, David. *Sir Charles Arden-Clarke*. London: Rex Collins, 1982.

Roosevelt, Elliott. *As He Saw It*. New York: Sloan and Pearce, 1946.

Roosevelt, Franklin D. *Complete Presidential Press Conferences*. Vol. 19. New York: Da Capo, 1972.

Rosenman, Samuel I., ed. *The Public Papers and Addresses of Franklin D. Roosevelt*. Vol. 13. New York: Harper & Row, 1950.

Rotberg, Robert. I. *The Rise of Nationalism in Central Africa: The Making of Malawi and Zambia, 1873–1964*. Cambridge, MA: Harvard University Press, 1967.

Ruane, Kevin, and James Ellison, "Managing the Americans: Anthony Eden, Harold Macmillan and the Pursuit of Power by Proxy in the 1950s." *Contemporary British History* 18, no. 3 (Autumn 2004), 147–167.

Russell, Ruth B. A *History of the United Nations Charter: the Role of the United States, 1940–45*. Washington, DC: The Brookings Institution, 1976.

Sandbrook, Dominic. *Never Had It So Good: A History of Britain from Suez to the Beatles*. London: Abacus, 2005.

Sanger, Clyde. *Malcolm MacDonald: Bringing an End to Empire*. Montreal: McGill-Queen's University Press, 1995.

Sathyamurthy, T.V. *The Political Development of Uganda: 1900–1986*. Aldershot: Gower Publishing, 1986.

Sberga, John J. "The Anticolonial Policies of Franklin D. Roosevelt." *Political Science Quarterly* 101, no. 1 (1986): 65–86.

Schelesinger, Stephen C. *Act of Creation: the*

Founding of the United Nations. Boulder: West View, 2003.

Schild, Georg. *Bretton Woods and Dumbarton Oaks: American Economic and Political Postwar Planning in the Summer of 1944.* New York: St. Martin's, 1995.

Sears, Mason. *Years of High Purpose: From Trusteeship to Nationhood.* Washington, DC: University Press of America, 1980.

Seldon, Anthony. *Churchill's Indian Summer: The Conservative Government, 1951–55.* London: Hodder and Stoughton, 1981.

Shalom, Stephen R. *The United States and the Philippines: A Study of Neocolonialism.* Quezon City: New Day, 1986.

Shepherd, Robert. *Iain Macleod: A Biography.* London: Pimlico, 1995.

Shogan, Robert. *Backlash: The Killing of the New Deal.* Chicago: Ivan R. Dee, 2006.

Short, Philip. *Banda.* London: Routledge and Kegan Paul, 1974.

Skidelsky, Robert. *John Maynard Keynes: Fighting for Freedom, 1937–1946.* New York: Viking, 2000.

Stevenson, Adlai E. "The United Nations, Guardian of Peace." *Department of State Bulletin* 44, no. 1134 (March 20, 1961): 410–414.

Stockwell, A.J. "The United States and Britain's Decolonization of Malaya, 1942–57." In *The United States and Decolonization: Power and Freedom,* edited by David Ryan and Victor Pungong. London: Macmillan Press, 2000.

Takeyh, Ray A. *The Origins of the Eisenhower Doctrine: The United States, Britain and Nasser's Egypt, 1953–1957.* London: Macmillan Press, 2000.

Thorne, Christopher. *Allies of a Kind: The United States, Britain and the War Against Japan, 1941–45.* New York: Oxford University Press, 1978.

United Nations. *Yearbook of the United Nations, 1947–48.*

_____. *Yearbook of the United Nations, 1948–49.*

_____. *Yearbook of the United Nations, 1950.*

_____. *Yearbook of the United Nations, 1951.*

_____. *Yearbook of the United Nations, 1954.*

_____. *Yearbook of the United Nations, 1955.*

United States Department of State. *Foreign Relations of the United States, 1941, vol. 3: The British Commonwealth: The Near East and Africa.* Washington: Government Printing Office, 1972.

_____. *Foreign Relations of the United States, 1946, vol. 1: United Nations.* Washington: Government Printing Office, 1973.

_____. *Foreign Relations of the United States, 1947, vol. 1: General: The United Nations.* Washington: Government Printing Office, 1974.

_____. *Foreign Relations of the United States, 1948, vol. 3: Western Europe.* Washington: Government Printing Office, 1975.

_____. *Foreign Relations of the United States, 1949, vol. 2: United Nations; the Western Hemisphere.* Washington: Government Printing Office, 1975.

_____. *Foreign Relations of the United States, 1950, vol. 2: United Nations; the Western Hemisphere.* Washington: Government Printing Office, 1976.

_____. *Foreign Relations of the United States, 1950, vol. 3: Western Europe.* Washington: Government Printing Office, 1977.

_____. *Foreign Relations of the United States, 1950, vol. 5: the Near East, South Asia and Africa.* Washington: Government Printing Office, 1978.

_____. *Foreign Relations of the United States, 1951, vol. 2: United Nations; the Western Hemisphere.* Washington: Government Printing Office, 1976.

_____. *Foreign Relations of the United States, 1951, vol. 5: The Near East and Africa.* Washington: Government Printing Office, 1982.

_____. *Foreign Relations of the United States, 1952–54, vol. 3: United Nations Affairs.* Washington: Government Printing Office, 1979.

_____. *Foreign Relations of the United States, 1952–54, vol. 5: Western European Security.* Washington: Government Printing Office, 1983.

_____. *Foreign Relations of the United States, 1952–54, vol. 9: The Near and Middle East.* Washington: Government Printing Office, 1986.

_____. *Foreign Relations of the United States, 1952–54, vol. 11: Africa and South Asia.* Washington: Government Printing Office, 1983.

_____. *Foreign Relations of the United States, 1955–57, vol. 11: United Nations and General International Affairs.* Washington: Government Printing Office, 1988.

_____. *Foreign Relations of the United States, 1955–57, vol. 16: Suez Crisis.* Washington: Government Printing Office, 1990.

_____. *Foreign Relations of the United States, 1955–57, vol. 18: Africa.* Washington: Government Printing Office, 1989.

_____. *Foreign Relations of the United States, 1955–57, vol. 27: Western Europe and Canada.* Washington: Government Printing Office, 1992.

_____. *Foreign Relations of the United States, 1958–60, vol. 2: United Nations and General International Affairs.* Washington: Government Printing Office, 1991.

_____. *Foreign Relations of the United States, 1958–60, vol. 14: Africa.* Washington: Government Printing Office, 1993.

_____. *Foreign Relations of the United States, 1961–63, vol. 21: Africa.* Washington: Government Printing Office, 1996.

_____. *Foreign Relations of the United States, 1964–68, vol. 24: Africa.* Washington: Government Printing Office, 1999.

United States Library of Congress Legislative Reference Service. *U.S. Foreign Aid: Its Purpose, Scope,*

Administration and Related Information. Washington: Government Printing Office, 1959.

Venkataramani, M. "The United States, the Colonial Issue and the Atlantic Charter Hoax." *International Studies* 13, no. 1 (January–March 1974): 1–28.

Villard, Henry S. "American Relations with Africa." *Department of State Bulletin* 9, no. 217 (August 21, 1943): 103–109.

Volman, Daniel H. "United States Foreign Policy and the Decolonization of British Central Africa (Zimbabwe, Zambia and Malawi), 1945–1965." Ph.D. Diss., UCLA, 1991.

Wall, Irwin M. *France, the United States and the Algerian War.* Berkeley: University of California Press, 2001.

Watts, Carl. "The United States, Britain and the Problem of Rhodesian Independence, 1964–65." *Diplomatic History* 30, no. 3 (June 2006): 439–470.

Welensky, Sir Roy. *Welensky's 4000 Days: The Life and Death of the Federation of Rhodesia and Nyasaland.* London: Collins, 1964.

Westcott, N.J. "Closer Union and the Future of East Africa, 1939–1948: A Case Study in the Official Mind of Imperialism." *Journal of Imperial and Commonwealth History* 10, no. 1 (October 1981): 67–88.

Williams, G. Mennen. "Basic United States Policy in Africa." *Department of State Bulletin* 45, no. 1163 (October 9, 1961): 600–603.

_____. "Change and Challenge in Africa." *Department of State Bulletin* 46, no. 1192 (April 30, 1962): 719–722.

_____. "Southern Africa in Transition." *Department of State Bulletin* 45, no. 1164 (October 16, 1961): 638–642.

Wills, A.J. *An Introduction to the History of Central Africa: Zambia, Malawi, and Zimbabwe.* Oxford: Oxford University Press, 1985.

Wilson, Theodore. *The First Summit: Roosevelt and Churchill at Placentia Bay, 1941.* Lawrence: University of Kansas Press, 1991.

Windrich, Elaine. *Britain and the Politics of Rhodesian Independence.* London: Croom Helm, 1978.

Wolton, Suke. *Lord Hailey, the Colonial Office and the Politics of Race and Empire in the Second World War.* Houndmills, Basingstoke, Hampshire: Macmillan, 2000.

Wood, J.R.T. *So Far and No Further: Rhodesia's Bid for Independence During the Retreat from Empire, 1959–1965.* Victoria, BC: Trafford, 2005

Wood, Robert E. *From Marshall Plan to Debt Crisis: Foreign Aid and Development Choices in the World Economy.* Berkeley: University of California Press, 1986.

Woods, Randall B. *A Changing of the Guard: Anglo-American Relations, 1941–46.* Chapel Hill: University of North Carolina Press, 1990.

Woodward, Peter. *Condominium and Sudanese Nationalism.* London: Rex Collins, 1979.

_____. *Sudan, 1898–1989: The Unstable State.* Boulder, CO: Lynne Rienner Publishers, 1990.

Woolley, James T. and Gerhard Peters. *The American Presidency Project* (americanpresidency.org), http://www.presidency.ucsb.edu.

Index